SPLITTING HAIRS

THE HISTORY, LAW, AND FUTURE OF JEWISH LAWS
OF MODESTY AND WOMEN'S HEAD COVERING

Splitting Hairs

The History, Law, and Future of Jewish Laws of Modesty and Women's Head Covering

MICHAEL J. BROYDE

Teaneck, New Jersey

This book is a publication of
Ben Yehuda Press
Teaneck, NJ 07666
©2026 by Michael J. Broyde

No part of this book may be reproduced or utilized in any form or by any means, electronic or mechanical, including photocopying and recording, or by any information storage and retrieval system, without permission in writing from the publisher.

ISBN 978-1-953829-20-7

Set in Arno Pro by Raphaël Freeman MISTD, Renana Typesetting

26 27 28 / 10 9 8 7 6 5 4 3 2 1   260212

Library of Congress Cataloging-in-Publication Data

Names: Broyde, Michael J. author
Title: Splitting hairs : the history, law, and future of Jewish laws of modesty and women's head covering / Michael J. Broyde.
Description: Teaneck, New Jersey : Ben Yehuda Press, [2025] | Includes index. | Summary: "A comprehensive analysis of the Jewish laws regarding women's hair covering as a practice of modesty (tzniut), exploring its historical development, halakhic discourse, and sociological dimensions. It examines key rabbinic texts, including the Talmud, medieval commentaries, classical codes, and modern responsa to argue that many of the traditional norms around modesty are not as immutable as they appear"-- Provided by publisher.
Identifiers: LCCN 2025054342 | ISBN 9781953829207 trade paperback
Subjects: LCSH: Hair--Religious aspects--Judaism | Modesty--Religious aspects--Judaism | Headgear--Religious aspects--Judaism | Jewish women--Religious life | Jewish law
Classification: LCC BM729.H34 B76 2025
LC record available at https://lccn.loc.gov/2025054342

We are proud to enable the publication of this important new study by Rabbi Prof. Broyde, and do so in the confidence that it will have a profound impact on our beloved Modern Orthodox community for many years to come. In doing so we are deeply aware that this book appears at a time of great change with regard to the roles of women in learning Torah, teaching Torah, and indeed in taking Halakhic leadership. It is our belief that these changes carry with them the possibility of inestimable benefit to Orthodoxy and the Jewish people as a whole.

With that in mind, we dedicate this book to all the Orthodox women who study and teach Torah in an honest search for Truth. We do this with full confidence that their unshakeable commitment to Halakha and Orthodoxy will soon give rise to new generations of Halakhic and Hashkafic works distinguished by novel perspectives and insights, while yet reflecting the authenticity, integrity, and deep awareness of God's commanding presence that this work itself so plentifully exhibits.

Rabbi Bob Carroll and Ruthie Levi

Quotes from Rabbinic Works on Justifying Communal Practices

Let me begin with an important rule: ... All which is widely done even only in one large community of Israel is not in error since certainly it was done based on the rulings of one exceptional Sage, since it is a community of people who observe Torah and its commandments; one must find a reason why they conducted themselves this way, so they should not be considered in error, even if other communities do not engage in this practice...
– Rabbi Moshe Feinstein, *Iggerot Moshe Orach Chaim* 4:17

Because it is a commandment and an obligation to justify the practices of the community of Israel, I have therefore devoted myself to developing a permissive ruling, as we will, God willing, discuss.
– *Arukh HaShulchan* OC 345:18

All is dependent on the wisdom of heaven – this is the normative rule of Jewish law, that all is dependent on what a person sees in himself. If he needs to distance himself from his inclination more, he must do so, even such that he not look at women's colorful [garments even when they are being washed], as was stated in Avodah Zarah (20b). So too if he sees in himself that his inclination is under control and he has no erotic thoughts, he can look at and speak with a woman prohibited to him sexually and can greet a married woman.... However, one should not be lenient on these matters unless one is a greatly pious person and acutely aware of one's own desires.
– Ritva, *Kiddushin* 82a

But if all the daughters of Israel would have the practice of going out with their hair uncovered, there would be absolutely no prohibition to do so, even among married women.... And even if the opposite were to be the case, that married women would go out with their hair uncovered but unmarried women covered their hair, it would be forbidden for unmarried women [to uncover their hair] but permissible for married women... for all of [these regulations] are dependent on the practices of married women – heed this well!

– Responsa *Sefer Yehoshua*, Even HaEzer 89

Know, my child, that the prohibition of married women uncovering their hair used to be quite strong in our community by default, as it was in all the Arab lands, before the influx of the French.... Now all women go out with uncovered heads and loose hair.... Consequently, I have devoted myself to finding a justification for the current practice, for it is impossible to fathom that we can return to the status quo ante... I attempted to search through the available writings of the legal decisors, only to find stringency upon stringency and prohibition upon prohibition. I decided to seek a higher authority, to draw directly from the source – Mishna, Talmud and available commentaries: perhaps for [these women,] I would find an opening of hope through which to enter.... Many thanks to God that we have found numerous openings to this area to enter in a lawful rather than unlawful manner.

– Collected Letters [*Otzar HaMikhtavim*] of R. Yosef Messas, no. 1884

Author's Dedication

THIS VOLUME IS DEDICATED TO THE MANY WOMEN WHO HAVE made my life so happy and pleasant over these many, many years:

First, to my wife, Channah S. Broyde, Esq., without whom nothing I have accomplished would be of value. After many years of marriage, there are many more adventures to look forward to.

Second, to my daughters, Rachel Irene Broyde and Deborah Malka Broyde-Katzir, who have grown into young women whom I love so much. I look forward to watching you as wonderful adults.

Third, to my daughter-in-law, Dr. Suzanne Bodian Broyde, who has added so much joy and love to our family. You have blessed the Broyde family in so many ways.

Fourth, to my granddaughters, Ruth Margalit Broyde, Naomi Batya Broyde and Ella Weiner Broyde, who are the most recent women to add joy in my life. May you all be a blessing to us.

To my sister, Dr. Linda Broyde Haramati, who was a constant source of love growing up and still is.

To my grandmothers, now both deceased:

To my Oma, Irene Schloss Buehler, who was a refugee from Nazi Germany and who lived with us for many years as I was growing up.

To my Grandma, Deborah Last Broyde, who was a constant delight to me as a child with her magnificent stories of life.

I note as well the sadness in the passing of my mother-in-law, Pneena Sageev, whose loss more than a decade ago still pains my heart.

Most importantly to my mother, Dr. Suse Buehler Broyde, who has always served as a role model to so many for her professional accomplishments, and who is still an active biochemistry professor at NYU. Over the past many years she struggled to balance caring for my father (Rabbi Dr. Barret Broyde זצ"ל, who passed away in 2018, to our sadness) with caring for the rest of her family – and yet achieved so much professionally. I am in awe.

Additionally, as with all my recent works, I would like to add a brief dedication to the many people who offered their support when I needed it the most, many years ago. Family, colleagues and friends, and even a few strangers came to my aid and assistance. You know who you are, and you know how indebted I am to you. Thank you to each of you and please give me the opportunity to return the favor.

A Simplified Table of Contents

A DETAILED TABLE OF CONTENTS   XIII

BACKGROUND: The Intellectual History of This Work and Acknowledgments   xxv

OVERVIEW AND A ROADMAP TO THIS BOOK: Why Hair? Jewish Law, Modesty and Hair Covering   xxxi

CHAPTER 1: Exposed Hair in Biblical and Tannaitic Sources: From Where Does This Whole "Hair" Conversation Derive?   1

CHAPTER 2: Exposed Hair in Amoraic Sources: Diverse Approaches to Modesty in the Talmud   35

CHAPTER 3: Uncovered Hair in the Geonim and Rif: Three Models of Modesty in the Immediately Post-Talmudic Commentaries   91

CHAPTER 4: Uncovered Hair in the Rishonim, Model I: A Torah Prohibition and *Dat Moshe*: Modesty as an Objective Prohibition Among Some Rishonim   101

CHAPTER 5: Uncovered Hair in the Rishonim, Model II: A Subjectively Determined Custom: Embracing a Societal Conception of Modesty Among Other Rishonim   149

CHAPTER 6: *Tur, Shulchan Arukh*, Rama, and *Levush* as well as the Various Commentaries: The Primary Codes Adopt the Subjective View and the Commentaries Endorse the Objective Understanding   237

CHAPTER 7: Partial Uncovering and Hair Covering by Betrothed Women: Two Important and Relevant Debates; The Subjective School and the Objective Disagree About Some Pre-Modern Cases   293

CHAPTER 8: Uncovered Hair and Modern Jewish Law: The Objective School Dominates, but Some Modern Authorities Endorse the Subjective Approach   377

CHAPTER 9: Conclusions: Jewish Law and Modesty: Hair as a Test Case   435

AFTERWORD: A Concluding Letter [to My Daughters] About This Book   445

INDEX   455

A Detailed Table of Contents

A DETAILED TABLE OF CONTENTS   XIII

BACKGROUND: The Intellectual History of This Work and Acknowledgments   xxv

OVERVIEW AND A ROADMAP TO THIS BOOK: Why Hair? Jewish Law, Modesty and Hair Covering   xxxi
     Introduction   xxxi
     Why Hair? Part I   xxxiii
     Why Hair? Part II   xxxvi
     A Roadmap to this Book   xli

CHAPTER 1: Exposed Hair in Biblical and Tannaitic Sources: From Where Does This Whole "Hair" Conversation Derive?   1
     Part 1 – Exposed Hair as Part of a List of Improper Behaviors   1
         Divorce in the Torah   1
         Mishnah Gittin   3
         Tosefta Sotah   7
         Analysis   11
         Tosefta Ketubot   11
         Mishnah Ketubot   14
     Part 2 – Exposed Hair Generally   17
         Mishnah Bava Kamma   19
         Sifre Numbers   20
         Baraita (from Bavli Sotah)   28
     Conclusion   31

Excursus One: Hair Covering in Apocrypha Works of Susanna
and the Maccabees ... 32
    Susanna ... 32
    3 Maccabees ... 33

CHAPTER 2: Exposed Hair in Amoraic Sources: Diverse
Approaches to Modesty in the Talmud ... 35
    Introduction ... 35
    Gittin ... 36
        Jerusalem Talmud ... 36
        Babylonian Talmud ... 38
    Rumors and Improper Public Behavior ... 43
    Sotah ... 44
        Babylonian Talmud ... 44
    Implied Adultery ... 48
        Jerusalem Talmud (y. Ketubot 7:6) ... 48
        Babylonian Talmud (b. Yevamot 24b–25a) ... 50
    Ketubot ... 50
        The Husband's Behavior ... 50
        Jerusalem Talmud (y. Ketubot 7:5) ... 50
        Babylonian Talmud (b. Ketubot 71a) ... 51
        Public Weaving and Conversing with Random Men ... 52
        The "Loudmouth" ... 54
        Jerusalem Talmud (y. Ketubot 7:6) ... 54
        Babylonian Talmud (b. Ketubot 72b) ... 55
        Cursing his Parents ... 56
        Jerusalem Talmud (y. Ketubot 7:6) ... 56
        Babylonian Talmud (b. Ketubot 72b) ... 56
        Exposed Hair ... 57
        Jerusalem Talmud (y. Ketubot 7:6) ... 57
        Babylonian Talmud (b. Ketubot 72a–b) ... 58
    Modest Comportment ... 64
        b. Kiddushin (70a–b) ... 64

Mishnah – Challah	66
Jerusalem Talmud	67
Babylonian Talmud	69
Berachot versus Ketubot	76
Men Whose Passions Are Under Control	77
Taking Advantage	80
Walking and Passing	80
The Man Would "Die Without Her"	81
Which Women Cover their Hair?	84
Nedarim	84
Numbers Rabbah	85
Two Righteous Women	85
Kimchit	85
Jerusalem Talmud	85
Babylonian Talmud	86
Hair Covering – The Wife of On ben Pelet	87
Summary and Conclusion	89

CHAPTER 3: Uncovered Hair in the Geonim and Rif: Three Models of Modesty in the Immediately Post-Talmudic Commentaries   91

Introduction	91
Model 1: Follow Majority	92
Behag	92
Model 2: Following Ketubot	95
R. Yitzchak Alfasi	95
Model 3: Reconciling the Competing Text	98
R. Hai Gaon	98
Conclusion: Three Models	100

CHAPTER 4: Uncovered Hair in the Rishonim, Model 1: A Torah Prohibition and *Dat Moshe:* Modesty as an Objective Prohibition Among Some Rishonim   101

1. Rivan	102
2. Rambam (Maimonides)	105

    Mishnah Ketubot 105
    Mishneh Torah, "Hilkhot Ishut" 24:11–13 106
    Mishneh Torah – Berachot 109
  3. R. Yehonatan of Lunel 113
  4. & 5. Rid and Riaz 117
    Rid 117
    Riaz 119
  6. *Sefer Mitzvot Gadol* (Semag) 120
  7. Ramban (Nachmanides) 125
  8. Rabbi Menachem HaMeiri 127
  9. Zohar 133
  10. Aharon HaKohen 135
    A Note on the Position of the *Kol Bo* 140
  11. R. Yerucham ben Meshullam 141
  12. R. Nissim of Gerona (Ran) 144
  13. Rabbi Shimon bar Tzemach Duran 145
  Conclusion 147

CHAPTER 5: Uncovered Hair in the Rishonim, Model II: A Subjectively Determined Custom: Embracing a Societal Conception of Modesty Among Other Rishonim 149
  Introduction 149
  1. Rashi 150
    Sotah 150
    Ketubot 150
    b. Berachot 151
    Numbers 153
    Summary 153
  2. Rabbeinu Tam 154
  3. Rabbi Isaac ben Samuel the Elder of Dampierre (Ri) ... 155
  4. *Sefer Al HaKol* 155
  5. *Sefer HaIttur* 157
  6. *Sefer HaYereim* 159

7. *Sefer Chasidim*	160
8. *Sefer HaRokeach*	162
9. Rabbi Eliezer ben Yoel HaLevi (Ra'aviah)	163
b. Berachot	167
Summary	170
10. Tosafot and Tosafot HaRosh	170
11. *Sefer HaEshkol*	174
12. *Sefer HaManhig*	175
13. Ra'avad and Provencal Rishonim (*HaHaShlama, Meorot*, and *Mikhtam*)	177
Sefer HaHashlama	177
Sefer HaMeorot (b. Berachot ad loc.)	180
Sefer HaMikhtam	182
14. *Sefer Amudei Golah / Sefer Mitzvot Katan*	183
15. *Or Zarua*	186
16. R. Asher ben Yechiel (Rosh)	188
17. Rekanati	196
18. The Mordechai and the *Hagahot Maimoniyot*	199
19. The *Agudah*	201
20. Talmidei Rabbeinu Yonah	203
21. *Ohel Moed*	204
22. *Tzedah LaDerekh*	205
23. Rashba	206
Case 1: The Angry Wife Who Exposed Her Hair	206
Case 2: The Man Who Tried to Back Out of the Marriage	208
Gloss on Gittin – Answering Ra'avad's Question	210
Chiddushei HaRashba (b. Berachot 24a) – Invoking Ra'avad's Principle	211
24. *Sefer HaShulchan*	212
25. Ritva	213
26. *Terumat HaDeshen*	221
Excursus Two: The Observation of Rabbi Sinzheim as Proof to the Views Found in This Chapter	232

Conclusion 235

CHAPTER 6: *Tur, Shulchan Arukh, Rama,* and *Levush* as well as the Various Commentaries: The Primary Codes Adopt the Subjective View and the Commentaries Endorse the Objective Understanding
237

Introduction 237
Part 1 – Explaining the *Tur, Shulchan Arukh,* Rama, and *Levush* 238
    The *Tur* 238
    The *Shulchan Arukh* 242
    Levush 244
Part 2 – The Commentators on the *Tur* and *Shulchan Arukh* (Nos'ei Keilim) 247
    Model 1: Two Types of *Penuyot* 247
    Commentaries on the *Tur* 247
    Commentaries on the *Shulchan Arukh* 248
    Beit Shmuel 248
    Taz and *Chelkat Mechokek* 248
    Beit Hillel 249
    Ambiguous Elision 249
    Nachalat Tzvi 249
    Strict Elision 249
    Ba'er Heiteiv 249
    Dagul Mervavah 250
    Rosh Pinah 252
    Lenient Elision 254
    Pitchei Teshuva 254
    Arukh HaShulchan 255
  Model 2a – Braiding versus Covering (Magen Avraham) 256
    Magen Avraham 256
    Machatzit HaShekel 259
    Pri Megadim – *Eshel Avraham* 259
    Magen Gibborim 262
    Rosh Pinah – *Ikvei HaBayit* 266

A DETAILED TABLE OF CONTENTS   xxi

    Model 2b – With or Without a *Kalta* (Yaavetz)   266
    Excursus Three: On the Meaning of *Hynuma*   272
        Wedding   272
        Bride's Wedding Litter   273
        Wedding Hymns   273
        Law (*Nomos*) of Virgins   274
        The Debate in the Bavli   274
        R. Yochanan: Cover for the Sleeping Bride   274
        Surchav bar Pappa: A *Tanura* of Myrtles   276
        A Greek Word for Veil?   277
        Standard Interpretations   278
        Not a Hair Covering – Response to Yaavetz   279
        Daughters of Israel – All Girls?   281
    Excursus Four: Why Is Violating Dat *Yehudit* Prohibited and What Is *Dat Yehudit*?   283
    Conclusion: Interpreting or Arguing? Comparing the Three Models   289

CHAPTER 7: Partial Uncovering and Hair Covering by Betrothed Women: Two Important and Relevant Debates; The Subjective School and the Objective Disagree About Some Pre-Modern Cases   293
    Introduction   293
    Hair Outside the Covering (Maharam Al-Ashkar)   293
    R. Isaac HaLevi Segal   306
        Must a Betrothed Woman Cover Her Hair?   306
        Solving the Contradiction in the *Tur*   318
    Maharam Chaviv   320
    Chavot Yair   323
    Shevut Yaakov's Responsum: Must a Raped Virgin Cover Her Hair (Coiffing or Covering: What Is a *Kalta*?)   333
    Panim Meirot   344
    Responsa Sefer Yehoshua: The Betrothal of Roiza   349
    Excursus Five: The Differences of Modesty for Married and Unmarried Women   372

Conclusion	375

CHAPTER 8: Uncovered Hair and Modern Jewish Law: The Objective School Dominates, but Some Modern Authorities Endorse the Subjective Approach — 377

The Dominant Contemporary View: Hair Covering in Some Form Is Always Mandatory in Public for Married Women	377
Ben Ish Chai: The Important Authority Who Permits Married Women Not to Cover Their Hair When Modest Women Do Not	382
Framing Those Who Are Lenient In Practice	386
Why the Need for the Two Explanations?	387
Netziv	389
Rabbi Yerucham Fishel Perlow	390
Yashiv Moshe	394
Rabbi Shimon Sidon	398
The Explicit Arguments	398
Rabbi Isaac Hurewitz	398
Rabbi Efraim Zalman Slutzki	400
Rabbi Chaim Hirschenson	400
Rabbi Yosef Messas	401
Rabbi Moshe Malka	416
Rabbi Yaakov Brecher	422
Excursus Six: Details of Hair Covering: Starting When, With What, Where and How Much	423
A. Covering Hair of a Bride at the Wedding	423
B. How Much Hair Should Be Covered?	425
C. Hair Covering Not in a Public Place	427
D. The Sheitel – Covering the Hair with a Wig	429
Conclusion to This Excursus	434
Conclusion	434

CHAPTER 9: Conclusions: Jewish Law and Modesty: Hair as a Test Case — 435

A Summary of the Arguments in This Book	435

A Concluding Methodological Note 436
A Concluding Sociological Observation 440

AFTERWORD: A Concluding Letter [to My Daughters] About This Book 445

INDEX 455

BACKGROUND

The Intellectual History of This Work and Acknowledgments

THIS IS A NEW, YET OLD, BOOK. LET ME EXPLAIN. I HAVE BEEN thinking about the issues of hair covering and modesty for many decades. This book does contain new thoughts and observations, which in a sense makes it something new. However, since this volume is intended to be my capstone work on this issue, it is in this respect an old work. Or maybe a final volume, if you will, that wraps up my work in this area of Jewish law. As such, it is appropriate to reflect back on all who have contributed to and shaped my thinking, as well as those earlier works of mine that serve as antecedents to this book.

I have been thinking and writing on the topic of hair covering and halakha from the time I was a student in the *Yadin Yadin* Kollel at Yeshiva University in the late 1980s, where the two kollel directors, Rabbi Dr. J. David Bleich and Rabbi Mordechai Willig, spoke with me about this many times, many years ago. I thank them both for their contributions to my knowledge in all things Jewish – in this as well as many other topics.

I published my first thoughts on this topic in an article entitled "Tradition, Modesty and America: Married Women Covering Their Hair," (*Judaism* 40.1 (January 1991): 79–87), and I noted in that article that I was preparing a longer article on this topic. I published some more thoughts on this topic as a letter to the editor entitled "Modesty" in the *Journal of Halacha and Contemporary Society* (31 (1996), 123–26). The longer article was published almost twenty years later in *Tradition* under the title "Hair Covering and Jewish Law: Biblical and Objective (*Dat Moshe*) or Rabbinic and Subjective (*Dat Yehudit*)?" (*Tradition*: 42.3 (Fall 2009), 95–179). Shortly prior to that, I published a brief Hebrew article under the title "*Gilui se'ar beishah nesu'ah: issur torah (vedat moshe) o issur derabbanan (vedat yehudit)"* in *Tehumin* (27 (2007), 248–265), as well as an article in the volume honoring Rabbi Haskel Lookstein entitled "The Hair of a Woman is Erotic: An Explanation of the Contemporary Practice of Many Married Orthodox Women Not to Cover their Hair" in *Rav Chesed: Essays in Honor of Rabbi Dr. Haskel Lookstein*, ed. Rafael Medoff (vol. 1 (New York: Ktav, 2009), 54–117). A reply to my article, as well as my response to it, was published in "Hair Covering and Jewish Law: A Response," (*Tradition:* 43:2 (Winter 2010), 89–108). In addition, I published much on the internet on this topic, the most interesting of which is "Hair Covering By a Bride" (*Hirhurim–Torah Musings*, Sept. 13, 2011, https://www.torahmusings.com/2011/09/hair-covering-by-a-bride/).

This book represents my more collected final thoughts on this topic.

Looking back on these works, there were many individuals to thank for their previous scholarship on this topic. In a previous article, I noted:

> I wish to acknowledge an intellectual debt to previous scholarship on this topic, work which has uncovered a wealth of sources that I have utilized in my analysis. In particular, the fine manuscript by Rabbi Dr. Dov Frimer, "Grounds for Divorce Due to Immoral Behavior (Other Than Adultery) According to Jewish Law" (Heb., February 1980, unpublished Ph.D. dissertation, Hebrew University, on file with Center for Research Libraries) contains a wide array of Jewish law references that I have routinely cited. In addition, the article by Rabbi Dr. S. Carlebach, "Sources for the Prohibition of a Woman Uncovering her Hair" (Heb.), in S. Eppenstein, M. Hildesheimer, and J. Wohlgemuth, eds., *Sefer Le-David Tsevi: Festschrift on the seventieth birthday of Rabbi David Zvi Hoffman* (Ger.–Heb., Berlin: L. Lamm, 1914, h.218–247), contains much important source material.

My original article in *Tradition* bears the following dedication:

> Over the last twenty years, numerous people have read this manuscript and have commented on it in many ways. Thank you to all of them. Four of my teachers have played a great role in my intellectual development over these many years, and while they do not necessarily agree with this article's conclusions, they deserve a special note of thanks for the time they have spent teaching me and speaking with me over many years: Rabbis Moshe Bernstein, J. David Bleich, Michael Hecht, and Mordechai Willig all have invested many hours in my intellectual growth and remain role models to me in my middle age.

The dedication shown by Channah S. Broyde, my wife of twenty-five years, to me has enabled my investment in many different aspects of Torah study and halakha all these years. Without her, almost none of my work would ever have come to fruition. The words of Rabbi Akiva are certainly true: "Mine and yours are hers" (b. Ketubot 63a), and she is deserving that this article be dedicated to her – but who in his right mind dedicates a monograph whose central Talmudic text deals with grounds for faulted divorce to his beloved wife! Rather, may the Torah study contained in this work honor our beloved children: Joshua Emanuel, Aaron, Rachel Irene and Deborah Malka, all of whom should be blessed to have the virtues of their mother. As this article goes to press, my son, Aaron Broyde, commences his IDF service (along with all the other members of his year in Hesder Yeshiva Petach Tikva). Like much of my scholarship during his time in the IDF, this article is dedicated in his honor and with the prayers that he return home "safe and sound." God should watch over him and all the other Israeli soldiers.[1]

For many decades, Emory University, its Law School, and the Center for the Study of Law and Religion have served as my own little "house of study" to think about these matters and I am grateful. Without the vibrant support of my colleague and friend, Professor John Witte, Jr., the director of the Center and an esteemed scholar, none of this would have been possible. It is hard to emphasize how wonderful a home Emory Law School and its Center for the Study of Law and Religion have been. So too, Dr. David Blumenthal and his wife Ursula have been central to my academic career at Emory, and I am deeply grateful for all he has done. He should merit a joyous and well-earned retirement. My thanks as well to the Tam Institute of Jewish Studies at Emory University for their support of this work.

Over many years I have been privileged to study and teach Torah in a variety of religious settings in Atlanta, Georgia, and I thank them all for granting me these opportunities. I list them in historical order from oldest to most recent: the Atlanta Scholars Kollel; the Young Israel of Toco Hills, Atlanta; the Atlanta Torah Mitzion Kollel; the Atlanta Dayanut Institute; and the New Toco Shul. Finally, I want to thank my rabbinic colleagues

---

1. See Footnote 12 on page 442 for a discussion of the dedication to the Hebrew version of the original article.

in Atlanta who have regularly spoken to me about Torah matters: Rabbi Dr. Michael Berger, Rabbi Yehuda Boroosan, Rabbi Yossi New and Rabbi Dr. Don Seeman have all been rabbinic friends and colleagues, and I am grateful. So too, for many years I was privileged to work in the Beth Din of America and I am grateful to Rabbis Gedalia Dov Schwartz זצ״ל (who passed away as this book was in preparation), Mordechai Willig, Yona Reiss, and Shlomo Weissmann for many insights into different matters of Jewish law.

My heartfelt thanks as well to the United States Fulbright Scholars Program, which awarded me a Senior Fulbright Scholars award for an academic year and allowed me to reside in Jerusalem during that year when this manuscript was initially completed. My thanks to Stanford Law School, which provided me a home after that while this manuscript was fine tuned. I want to thank Professor Robin and Boris Feldman of Palo Alto, who hosted me so kindly during my visit at Stanford. I have taught Advanced Jewish Law at Columbia Law School these past few years and many students in my class provided insight as well.

Like any material which has been worked on for decades, countless people have edited various drafts. The longer *Tradition* article was closely worked on by Michael Ausubel, more than a decade ago for many years, and he closely compared it with a yet unpublished Hebrew manuscript. Without his work from 2000 to 2008, I doubt the article in *Tradition* would have seen the light of day. My deepest thanks to him. The *Tradition* article, many of my original sources, and the Hebrew article were reviewed and expanded upon by Dr. Zev Farber in the course of preparing this book, who also added all the material in Greek and Arabic. He expanded many sources, checked almost all of them, and greatly assisted in the process of quotation and translation. He also set up the side-by-side texts that are used in this book. I am grateful to him for his contributions. Thank you to my Emory colleague, Rabbi Dr. Don Seeman, for his help with the introduction to this work. Thank you as well to Rabbi Jonathan Ziring for reviewing this manuscript, especially his contributions to Chapter 8. Thank you to Dr. Shani Tzoref for reviewing and commenting on the final draft. Thank you to Dr. David Zeligman of Emory University for reading the whole work cover to cover one final time, to Rabbi Reuven Travis for one final round of editing, and to Gershon Klapper for his final, thorough review of sources and citations. Countless people read the various drafts or parts thereof and I am grateful to each person for their contributions. Thank you as well to the many people who commented on this work. They are literally too numerous to mention, but I am grateful to each and every person who helped me in my thinking on this matter over the many decades.

All errors remain mine alone. I welcome emails with comments and corrections. Indeed, I recognize the power of the Mishnaic statement (b. Berachot 4:2):

רבי נחוניה בן הקנה היה מתפלל בכניסתו לבית המדרש וביציאתו תפלה קצרה אמרו לו מה מקום לתפלה זו אמר להם בכניסתי אני מתפלל שלא תארע תקלה על ידי וביציאתי אני נותן הודיה על חלקי:

When Rabbi Nechunyah son of Hakanah would enter the place of study and when he would depart, he would offer a short prayer. They asked him: What place is there for this prayer? He said to them: "When entering I pray that no error should arise through my reasoning and when I leave I give thanks for my lot."

It is my fondest wish that such a prayer should be correct for me as well.

Michael J. Broyde

OVERVIEW AND A ROADMAP
TO THIS BOOK

Why Hair? Jewish Law, Modesty, and Hair Covering

THIS INTRODUCTION PLACES THE READER OF THIS WORK INTO some of the complex sociology of the traditional Jewish community and its discussions of modesty and hair covering. Unlike the rest of this book, it does not focus on the textual traditions of Jewish law, but rather on other trends in three communities: Jewish, other faiths, and secular.

Introduction

This book is an elaborate argument that nearly all of the rules related to modesty (in Hebrew: *tzniut*) that are presented as normative Jewish law (in Hebrew: *halakha*) in modern society are not necessarily correct (in the sense that Jewish law does not mandate that result) and that a correct read of the classical Jewish law sources supports the proposition that Jewish law only requires that people (particularly women) dress as modest people in their society dress. Nothing more and nothing less. There are very few immutable halakhic rules of modesty beyond that idea. The theme of this book is that this school of thought (generally called the "subjective school") is the dominant one in the classical Jewish tradition, whereas the "objective school" of modesty, which has dominated discourse in the last century, has been the minority position in Jewish law over the last two thousand years.[1]

---

1. This book uses the term *subjective* to mean dependent on the cultural norms of the time and place we are speaking about. *Objective* refers to being driven by Jewish law doctrines that stand independent of time and place. So claiming that women must cover their hair, even when modest women in one's culture generally do not,

Hence, much of this book is devoted to tracing two issues – modesty and women's hair covering – through intricacies of Jewish law and precedent spanning nearly 3,000 years, from the Bible to the present. Inevitably, it is heavy on detail and on close textual readings across a wide variety of different genres: Bible, Mishnah, Talmud, expository commentaries, and rabbinic responsa from every time and place in which Jews have lived in any significant numbers. It even extends to the latest blogs and academic journals. As such, it is easy for the reader to get lost in the textual weeds. Thus it seems important here, at the outset, to indicate how this topic might relate to some broader areas of concern. This introduction contextualizes the discussions about hair covering found in a variety of texts, in order to make the reader aware of some broader themes which are sometimes lurking just beneath the surface. This is the purpose of the two parts of this introduction, entitled "Why Hair? Part I" and "Why Hair? Part II." This is followed by a brief roadmap to this book, which will outline each chapter and allow the reader to better navigate this highly textual subject matter.

But first, as an initial matter, it is worth laying out a basic idea. This book tackles what is, on some level, the hardest issue in modesty in the Jewish tradition: hair covering. It is – as this book shows – discussed in great detail, over many centuries, in numerous texts, and in a variety of settings. What makes hair covering so fascinating is that it allows deep textual exploration of how the Jewish tradition addresses changing standards of modesty as well as different models of textual interpretation. Jews used to view uncovered hair as immodest – or even erotic – in general society[2] and it was the subject of an explicit Talmudic discussion grounded in biblical verses.[3] The clarity of the sources – or the lack thereof – and the evolving standards of society on matters of modesty is a direct and clear subtext of this work. This book focuses on how the traditional Jewish

---

places one in the objective school. The subjective school argues for a more culturally relative standard. Professor Tim Lytton of Georgia State University wisely noted to me that "in torts, for example, the reasonable man standard is called 'objective' precisely because it is relative to culture (i.e., what the person of ordinary prudence would do as determined by a jury). The term 'subjective' in Anglo-American law means relative to the personal standards or capacities of a particular individual." That is not what I mean in this book.

2. For more on this, see Eric Silverman, *A Cultural History of Jewish Dress* (Bloomsbury, 2013) in Chapters 1 and 5.
3. See Chapters 1 and 2 of this book.

community should and does address these changing standards. Indeed, the basic thrust of this book is the argument that if one defines modesty in a non-circular way (modest people are people who are committed to confining sexuality to marriage), then many, many Jewish law authorities – Talmudic, Geonic, medieval, and even modern – are inclined to rule that one needs to look at the community that seeks to confine sexuality to marriage and dress that way without a need to provide detailed and objective descriptions of rules of modesty.

Having given some parameters and rationales, let us move on to the basic question of "Why hair?"

Why Hair? Part 1

This book addresses an apparent tension between the classical Jewish tradition and modern life in Western society regarding modesty in garb and dress for women. I say "apparent" because the extensive textual analysis that makes up the core of this book shows that this tension is much less clear in the classical texts than it is in social practice. But hair? Why focus on hair? Why not focus on buttocks or arms and legs or so much more?

The answer is important. Five reasons directed my attention toward hair in particular.

First, hair has been uncovered in the Western tradition for many centuries. In the Jewish tradition (Ashkenaz and Sefard), unmarried women have not been expected to cover their hair for at least one thousand years.[4] This has created a clear impression that hair is much less sexualized than many other body parts. Yet, as we all see, there are still many societies in which even unmarried women are expected to cover their hair.[5]

Second, there is elaborate legal literature in the Jewish tradition about hair covering that is complex and nuanced and worthy of parsing. As this book shows, this discussion is ancient and detailed and comes in many different forms and formats. This allows for a more complex conversation than other areas of Jewish discourse. Texts create, modify, and help one formulate the "law" governing the Jewish practices. If this book had

---

4. See Chapter 7.
5. As one clear example, Islamic. The details of Islamic law are beyond the scope of this book. (Jewish law is complex enough!) For a simple discussion of this issue, see Jennifer Selby, "Hijab" in *The Oxford Handbook of European Islam*, Jocelyne Cesari, ed., Oxford, 2014, 701–745.

focused on other aspects of modesty in dress, the literature would be sparse and overwhelmingly modern.

Third, the question of hair covering in the Jewish tradition has developed a culturally unique accommodation: women who were interested in covering their hair without appearing overly traditional took to wearing wigs. Wigs allowed these women to adhere to the traditional mandate while still appearing secular and Western. To the best of my knowledge, no other religious tradition moved in this direction. This solidified the sense that hair was not erotic and yet emphasized that it needed to be covered. It also created an important counterintuitive narrative: One covered hair *with hair* instead of some other covering.

Fourth, a plethora of books has appeared, both in English and Hebrew, discussing modest standards of dress for women from a variety of religious and social approaches.[6] Each of these books has a very different approach to the "correct" standards; yet is mistaken, as the analysis herein will show, in its core read of the most basic sources. The simple truth is that there is no single standard that can be proven to transcend time and place. Rather, as I understand the classical Talmudic, medieval and pre-modern codes, the Jewish tradition directs dress that is modest, while steadfastly refusing to draw the type of sharp lines found in these or other modern works.

Finally, hair covering remains a subject of burning fascination among the Orthodox Jewish community and the many others who observe it. When I wrote more intensely about this on the internet, one popular blogger used to title discourse about these topics "Hair Wars,"[7] reflecting

---

6. See for example four works: Rabbi Pesach Eliyahu Falk, *Modesty: An Adornment for Life* (Feldheim, 1998), Rabbi Yehuda Henkin, *Understanding Tzniut: Modern Controversies in the Jewish Community* (Urim, 2008), Gila Manolson, *Outside/Inside: A Fresh Look at Tzniut* (2014, Kindle Edition), and Raffi Bilek (author) and Rivka Hautman (illustrator) *The Very Special Gift* (Createspace Press, 2015). (This final book presents its goal as follows: "Teaching young children about tznius has always been challenging, and all the more so in today's social and cultural climate. This book aims to help parents educate their daughters about the value and importance of Hashem's mitzvah of tznius.") So too, in 2023 Bracha Poliakoff and Rabbi Anthony Manning published *Reclaiming Dignity: A guide to Tzniut for Men and Women* (Mosaica Press) with its wonderful well done halakhic discussion essentially arguing that some aspects of modesty are subjective and communal. Since this book was written after my book was completed, references to it are sparse, though the work is excellent. *Reclaiming Dignity* hardly discusses the rishonim or classical achronim on this topic and it assumes as a starting point Chapter 9 of this present book.

7. See for example, "Hair Wars III" by Gil Student, October 21, 2010, at https://www.torahmusings.com/2010/10/hair-wars-iii-2/

the fact that when it came to areas of Jewish law that touched on three variables – fidelity to the classical sources, matters of modesty and sexuality, and the modern Jewish law and life – both the general population and even the scholarly community lost a certain amount of perspective, and discourse became loud and unpleasant.[8]

Indeed, as I was editing this book, the *New York Post* – a popular national newspaper with the fourth largest circulation of any paper in America – ran a story under the big and bold headline "Orthodox Jewish Women Slammed For Wearing 'Slutty' Wigs"[9] which told us that:

> Esther Adina Sash has received hateful online messages about her long wig, which some in her Orthodox community view as immodest. "People always say the longer it is, the sluttier it is," said Esther Adina Sash, a 30-year-old mother of two from Flatbush. Specifically, she's referring to the sheitels, or wigs, that she and other married Orthodox women wear as mandated by Jewish law, so as to not entice men who aren't their husbands. Now a heated debate is brewing over hair that some in the community view as being too sexy.

The article continued:

> "I was laughing that he would think hair length has a connection to spirituality," said Sash, who crusades for women's issues in the Jewish community and is running for district leader in the 45th Assembly District. Although, she admitted, "The wig is a very charged item." Last month, *The Voice of Lakewood*, a Jewish paper in New Jersey, banned wig makers' ads that show photos of hair, according to a memo sent to advertisers and obtained by *The Post*. It comes on the heels of a nasty dustup that took place last fall when digital fliers were anonymously e-mailed to area wig makers, reading in part: "Dear Jewish Women, how badly are you trying to look like a prostitute? How important is it for you to slap G-d in the face?!" "It was a scare tactic. 'Let's scare a bunch of people,'" said Menucha Kaminsky, a wig stylist in Brooklyn. And it seems to be working.

And then the article told us a few stories about people being blackballed from communities over these issues:

---

8. "This Orthodox Jewish wig shop in Brooklyn says covering hair doesn't mean 'you have to be ugly.'" by Alina Simone, March 25, 2019, http://tinyurl.com/y3joyq79
9. By Doree Lewak, September 9, 2018. See http://tinyurl.com/y7aa3qqp.

Another woman named Esther – a 34-year-old in New Jersey who asked that her last name be withheld for privacy reasons – felt the sting of rejection based on her coiffure a few years ago when she and her husband tried to buy a house in a Lakewood development. "I was turned away because my wig was too long," she said. "We were told that we will scare off the crowd [and] they need to sell the rest of the lots." But some young Orthodox women are increasingly more defiant of societal expectations – even though they don't wish to disobey religious convention. "I'm an Orthodox woman and I want to adhere to my traditions, but why do I have to look like I'm from 'Fiddler on the Roof'?" asked Mindy Meyer, a 28-year-old lawyer from Flatbush. "It's hotter and sexier to have long hair," she added. "I'm not trying to conform. I don't care what people think about my long wigs because, as long as I'm doing what I'm supposed to be doing, G-d is the ultimate judge."

What do these exchanges tell us? Not only that Jews who adhere to Jewish law generally seem to care deeply about this topic,[10] but also that the relationship between tradition and modesty is a fascinating topic generally, such that popular national newspapers run articles about it.

Why Hair? Part II

One of the central, recurring questions throughout this book concerns the legal meaning of a Talmudic assertion that "a woman's [uncovered] hair constitutes a form of nakedness."[11] Debates over the parameters and authority of this statement are central to this book's project. However, it is worthwhile to note in this introduction that this juxtaposition of hair and sexuality is hardly unique to Jewish law.

Some psychoanalytically oriented writers like Charles Berg and the British social anthropologist Edmund Leach argue that the hair of the human head serves as a kind of natural or universal symbol of sexuality in general, leading to a cross-cultural focus on hair management and discipline.[12] In a psychoanalytically oriented work on the personalization

---

10. Consider, for example, the number of entries in Google under the phrase "sheitels [the word for wig commonly used in the Orthodox community] for sale."
11. See Chapters 2 and 3 of this book.
12. Charles Berg, *The Unconscious Significance of Hair* (Allen and Unwin, 1951); Edmund Leach, *The Unity of Man and Other Essays* [French] (Gallimard, 1980).

of cultural symbols among Indian ascetics, Gananath Obeyesekere argues that the shaved heads of monks may represent a kind of rejection of sexuality and that matted and unkempt hair of other ascetics comes to stand for the suppression and concentration of sexual potency as a wellspring of vitality.[13] One must take, for example, the Sinhalese Hindu understanding of matted locks as a gift from the god (*sakti*), and also explore the personal history that may have lent special significance to the symbol in the (unconscious) life of the individual. The matted hair of an unkempt beggar may turn out to be merely a symptom of psychological disorder, writes Obeyesekere, but for the religious ascetic, it is a form of devotion and healing.

Obeyesekere tried to thread the needle between psychoanalytic and culturally aware accounts of hair practice, but more recent accounts by anthropologists and religion scholars have tended to emphasize the sheer diversity of local practices that weigh against any universal interpretation. Though acknowledging that hair practices are often associated with sexuality (especially in the Middle East and Mediterranean region), Christian Bromberger emphasizes that this is not by any means always the case. "[T]he same sign can have opposite meanings," writes Bromberger, "depending on cultures or contexts: a hermit's unkempt hair and beard are as much a sign of sexual abstinence as is a shaven head, and a widow's untied hair... can be a mark of grief and withdrawal from the world."[14] This is an important corrective. "A Western intellectual's long hair and beard are relatively free of erotic significance," he continues, "while in the Jewish tradition the shaving of a bride's hair marks her initiation to, not withdrawal from, sexual life."[15] Though his point is well-taken, Bromberger might be forgiven for his failure to recognize the complexity of Jewish practice to which he alludes. The fact is that the shaving of a

---

13. Gananath Obeyesekere, *Medusa's Hair: An Essay on Personal Symbols and Religious Experience* (University of Chicago Press, 1981). While largely supporting the idea that hair carries an intrinsic symbolic connection to human sexual expression, Obeyesekere's account also complicates this assertion by emphasizing the importance of individual life history and local cultural factors. Thus, while it may not be accidental that messages about sexuality and renunciation are carried by hair-related practices, those practices are also deployed in a specific local circumstance.
14. Christian Bromberger, "Hair: From the West to the Middle East through the Mediterranean," *Journal of American Folklore* 12 (482): 380.
15. Ibid.

bride's hair represents only one relatively local and contested variation on a set of practices for covering the hair of married women that includes (as we shall see) the use of hats, kerchiefs, wigs, and, in some cases, nothing at all. He may not have realized that what he calls a married woman's "initiation into sexuality" is, among other things, the complex outcome of a whole set of debates and negotiations among Jewish law authorities that might make it harder to render a simple and decisive summary of the meaning of this practice.

At the very least, it should be obvious that while the covering of a bride's hair could be interpreted as some kind of sexual initiation, it also functions simultaneously as a sign of sexual constraint or of modesty and marital privacy that are hard to disentangle. Writing in twelfth-century Egypt, Rambam posits that if a woman's uncovered hair represents nakedness then it ought to be kept covered as a matter of Jewish law no matter what the woman's marital status is. Yet, despite the apparent coherence of the argument (see Chapters 4, 5 and 6), most Jewish law authorities never accepted Rambam's position as normative. The reasons for this, and for other complex debates in this area of Jewish law, are not easily discoverable through the sociological or anthropological analysis of contemporary symbols and practice. Rather, they require detailed consideration of a longstanding textual and legal tradition whose contours have been shaped over time by the disparate and sometimes competing views of generations of scholars.

It is important for me to acknowledge therefore at the outset that this study will say very little about the lived significance of hair covering to contemporary men and women, which I leave to other writers. It purports instead to outline and make explicit the logic employed by significant Jewish law authorities over several centuries and to probe some of the implications of that logic for contemporary practice and understanding of Jewish law.

Women's hair covering was not an innovation of classical Judaism but seems to have been practiced among many or most of the Mediterranean and Near Eastern peoples among whom Jews lived.[16] Already in the

---

16. Indeed, the Talmud notes that women generally covered their hair in Talmudic times, confirming this practice as not uniquely Jewish; See Eruvin 100b. In this narrow context, see the opinion of Michael Marlowe, "Headcovering Customs of the Ancient World" at /https://www.bible-researcher.com/headcoverings3.html; "The Woman's Headcovering" at http://www.bible-researcher.com/headcovering.html

Mishnah (see Chapter 2), rabbis understood that Jews would likely need to conform to the norms of hair covering in the societies among whom they lived at least to some extent – norms, it should be noted, which differed among Arabs, Persians, and so forth. This will figure into my later argument that there is a sociological dimension to Jewish legal obligations in this area. For now, it is sufficient to note that hair covering and management have also served as important markers of communal boundaries and of the values that different societies seek to broadcast about themselves in comparison with others... Here is but one contemporary example that supports this notion:

> "In ethnic border areas of Mexico... women of Spanish origin make it a point in principle to refrain from shaving their legs in order to dissociate themselves from their naturally smooth skinned and hairless Indian counterparts."[17]

Ethnicity is not the only context in which social diversity is marked by hairstyle. In modern Turkey, devout hajjis, young Islamists, pan-Turkish nationalists, and left-wing militants each distinguish themselves through ideologically potent ways of managing male facial hair, from well-trimmed chin beards to thick, Stalin-like mustaches. The Islamic Republic of Iran, the Afghani Taliban and secularizing Turkey and Iran of an earlier period all imposed mandatory hair policies for both men and women meant to underline official state support for dominant, yet contested religious (and secular) ideologies of different kinds. "The contemporary political history of the Middle East could be written," says Bromberger, "with reports of dictatorial measures taken to standardize hair displays, the controversies engendered, and the tricks used to get around them."[18] One need only consider the perennial attempts to ban headscarves and other religious headgear in contemporary France, as just one example, to understand that the modern Middle East is not without parallel in this regard.[19]

---

17. Christian Bromberger, "Hair: From the West to the Middle East Through the Mediterranean," *Journal of American Folklore* 12 (482): 380, citing Obregon, Jimena Paz. 1989. "Il s'en faut d'un poil" in *Les figures du corps*, ed. Marie-Lise Beffa et Roberte Hamayon, pp. 145–65. Société d'Ethnographie. 164.
18. Ibid. 381.
19. Indeed, Quebec has also recently banned religious head coverings. See "She Wears a Head Scarf. Is Quebec Derailing Her Career?" *New York Times*, April 2, 2019 at https://www.nytimes.com/2019/04/02/world/canada/quebec-montreal-head-scarf-religion.html.

Let me be clear. This issue is not unique to religions outside of Judaism. Consider the recent piece by the excellent rabbinic scholar Laurie Novick, who asks, "How should we relate to perceptions about head-covering that no longer seem to apply?"[20] She observes the sociological truth:

> Many modern societies no longer associate women's head-covering with dignity or even modesty. Female dignitaries appear bareheaded at even the most formal events. In many circles, *sheitels* nearly indistinguishable from natural hair are often considered more dignified, or professional, than hats or scarves.

And then she poses the question:

> Why, then, should these Talmudic discussions resonate with us? If the Talmudic understanding of head-covering seems out of date, what does that say to us about the *mitzva*?

Although I found her particular collection of answers to be unsatisfying,[21] the formulation of the question goes to the heart of why there is such interest in the question of hair covering and Jewish law. Hair covering no longer seems to be related to actual concerns of modesty.

It is important to understand that once Jewish law conceded that

---

20. "Head-Covering 11: Rationale and Meaning" https://www.deracheha.org/head-covering-2-rationale-and-meaning/#further_reading (2019).

21. She proposes four basic answers, none of which I think respond well to the issue. Her first answer is that hair coverings are still more dignified for women: "The Queen of England still arrives at affairs in hats, and the rest of the royal family often follows suit. Even outside Jewish circles, there is a residual sense that head-covering, like a particularly elegant hat, can add to or reflect a person's dignity, whether or not it is essential to it." I think this is factually false in the modern era. Her second answer is modesty. ("A married woman was expected to adhere to high standards of modesty.") I see this as a bootstrapping argument – why hair and not face or toes or nose? Her third answer is "awe" ("a woman's head-covering can also signify awe of heaven, similar to a man's kippa"). This is completely unpersuasive as an explanation for the practice in our community, as single women do not cover their hair generally nor do married women cover their hair in prayer when men are not present. Finally, she proposes that marital status explains this issue. ("Head-covering functions as a sign of a Jewish woman's marital status.") This is undermined by the widely accepted practice of wearing a wig; why have a status that others cannot see – as well as by today's practice for most Orthodox Jewish women of wearing a wedding ring. An additional insight – communal identification – is proposed by me and addressed in the epilogue to this book and is I think correct in a way that is unrelated to the themes of this work.

single women need not cover their hair except in areas where this is the prevailing social practice, then one must further concede that hair is not intrinsically erotic and is not governed by the general prohibition to cover all erotic body parts (*guf ha-isha erva*). This explains the development in Europe of the practice of wearing a wig. It is inconceivable to imagine that a Jewish law would permit a man or a woman to cover their private parts with a picture of their private parts, since such is erotic. That hair may be covered with fake hair is an acknowledgement that hair is not erotic at all. Indeed, the transition from a society in which hair is erotic to a society where hair is not erotic is the central historical event which motivated modest Jewish women observant of Jewish law to cease covering their hair. Of course, in a society in which hair is erotic, all Jewish women must cover their hair. Consider, for example, the question posed to Rabbi Moshe Feinstein concerning whether a poor widow may go to her workplace with her hair uncovered so she can remain employed. Rabbi Feinstein permits it (because he is certain that a widow is not under any objective obligation to cover her hair); however, we certainly cannot imagine that he would likewise permit the widow to expose her thigh or breast in order to keep her job.[22]

This book focuses on that exact issue. Revealing hair is no longer perceived as immodest conduct by the secular community that American and Israeli Judaism calls home. Hence, it may well be that a detailed and extensive analysis into the sources will reveal that Jewish law does not actually require such. Indeed, this book is an elaborate argument that nearly all of the rules related to modesty are subjective and I think that halakha requires that women dress as modest people in their society dress.

A Roadmap to this Book

This book contains a prologue (which you read), an introduction (of which you are at the end), nine substantive chapters, a conclusion, and an epilogue.

The introduction explains why this work is important – indeed, why hair covering by women and general modes of dress by women within the Orthodox community has become a touchstone of community identity

---

22. *Iggerot Moshe, EH* 1:57. Let me be clear here. Rabbi Feinstein does not agree with the approach presented in this book for women who are married, because he adopts the "sotah" theory as correct, as explained in Chapters 3 and 8 in this book. Since a widow is not "sotah eligible," he adopts the subjective rule for a widow's hair.

and an important dividing line in social groups within the community that identifies with classical Jewish law. It explores the vast social changes within the traditional community in terms of the status of women, and whether – and how – this has influenced dress modes. It also explores why this issue has become so important to communal identification within the classical Orthodox community.

The purpose of the rest of this book is simple. It seeks to advance a highly textual argument that considers two critically important questions – one specific and one general.

The specific question ponders how Jewish law should regard hair covering in a society where modest women do not cover their hair. Stated simply, does Jewish law require that women cover their hair in such a setting? This book wrestles with this question over its nine substantive chapters by reading through the classical sources of Jewish law from the Bible through the Mishnah, Talmud, Codes, and onward.

The general question is more profound. In brief, to what extent are the rules of modesty found in the Jewish tradition subjective and driven by the cultural norms of the society in which Jews live? In other words, is it possible that the Jewish law tradition requires only modest dress, as subjectively determined by the cultural norms around it, and nothing more?

These are not simple questions.

The first three chapters of this work are organized chronologically and follow rabbinic taxonomies for the different historical periods in which Jewish law developed, from the earliest authorities to the most contemporary. Chapter 1 reviews the pre-Talmudic material from the Torah through the Tannaim and Mishnah, thus reviewing all the Jewish tradition on hair covering until about the year 200 CE. It reviews, translates and explains the central texts – and some not-so-central texts – from the Hebrew Bible up to the Mishnaic era.[23]

---

23. A brief note about the Hebrew text and the English translations: In general, scholarly editions of common rabbinic works are not cited by name in this book and central rabbinic texts are taken from the Bar Ilan CD (editions 23 through 27) without close examination of critical editions. When a specific text is cited that is not on the Bar Ilan CD, more detailed publication information is given unless it is a standard work of rabbinics. The English translations are nearly always unique to this work and one of the central goals has been to translate many texts into English, as that aids in clarifying understanding, even for the Hebrew speaker. The goal of this translation is to enable the English text to be read either side by side with the

Chapter 2 focuses on the Talmudic material, from the end of the Mishnah until the end of the era of the Amoraim (around the year 500 CE). It covers the Babylonian and Jerusalem Talmuds as well as all the related literature of this era. It shows the diversity of approaches regarding modesty and hair covering in the Talmud.

Chapter 3 is a smaller chapter in that it surveys the Geonim, the post-Talmudic pre-Rishonim scholars of halakha living (almost totally) in Babylonia, as well as the Rif. This chapter is more important than its length might suggest, as the basic conceptual models found in this work are already laid out by the Geonim, whose era concludes around the year 1000 CE. The three models found in this chapter constitute the basic models used for nearly a thousand years, and they remain in use to our day.

This historical emphasis ends in Chapters 4 and 5. These chapters are no longer divided historically but by approach. Chapter 4 focuses on those Rishonim who understand the obligation to cover to be an objective prohibition that does not change based on time and place. Chapter 5 focuses on those Rishonim who understand the prohibition to be subjective and acknowledge that the obligation of a married woman to cover her hair changes based on time and place. These two chapters conclude with the opinions of authorities living no later than the middle of the 15th century.

Chapter 6 has two parts. Part one focuses on the views of the *Tur*, *Shulchan Arukh*, and Rama as well as the *Levush*. This section of Chapter 6 argues that they incorporated the subjective prohibition approach. The second part is a survey of the post-*Shulchan Arukh* authorities. The section

---

Hebrew text or independently. Sometimes words are added to the English text to clarify the Hebrew text and give it context. Generally, those additions are put in brackets. Sometimes as well, Hebrew text is put in brackets to denote some textual ambiguity and those texts are also put in brackets in the English text. Furthermore, the goal of ease of use remains – as with all translations – somewhat at tension with the goal of complete accuracy. I hope the reader will be forgiving for the difficult choices made in such translations. See "A Letter of Maimonides to Samuel Ibn Tibbon," (translated by Leon D. Stitskin), *Tradition* 4:1 91–95 (1961), where Rambam discusses the translator's difficulties. I have occasionally edited the English to insert numberings for lists and the like, to aid in the translation. These texts have been selected and translated throughout the decades I have been working on this topic. Accordingly, translations are not fully consistent, and there are variations among the translations of repeated words, phrases, and passages. This is particularly the case for words whose meanings were contested by subsequent scholars.

is not completely systematic but instead focuses on the key Jewish law authorities of the last 175 (or so) years. It becomes clear in Chapter 6 that almost all of these authorities have rejected the subjective approach and instead insisted that the obligation to cover hair is objective, like the many Rishonim in Chapter 4. These two sections together summarize the primary interpretations of Jewish law regarding this topic until the onset of the 19th century.

Chapter 7 is a discussion of the two pre-modern questions about hair covering: May a woman cover less than all her hair? And, must a betrothed but unmarried woman cover her hair? Both questions are precursors to the modern question of whether married women can uncover their hair when such conduct is not immodest. The historical focus of this topical chapter ranges from the middle of the 16th century to the beginning of the 19th century.

Chapter 8 is a survey of the approaches of modern Jewish law authorities. While it briefly surveys the modern consensus that prohibits such conduct, it seeks to collect and frame all the decisors (*poskim*) who adopt the more liberal view (mostly through an analysis of how said commentaries understood Rashi). The sources found in this chapter start from the middle of the 19th century and continue to the present.

Chapter 9 contains some concluding thoughts and reexamines the central thesis of this work while reviewing the conclusions of many different parts of this book. I argue that the subjective school of thought is the better read of the classical sources of Jewish law until nearly 1850 and well past the codification of the *Shulchan Arukh*.

There is an afterword, in the form of a letter I wrote to my daughters about the Jewish law consequences of this book regarding modesty and hair covering. The afterword focuses on sexualization in modern society, the objectification of women in modern society, and the absence of reasonable standards of modesty in the contemporary secular West. In this section, I address some of these contemporary and non-textual issues. I express some hesitancy to follow the conclusions of this book fully and normatively, even as I think that this work reaches the right conclusions on matters of Jewish law. Some matters of sociology and contemporary culture are explored in this section. Some readers of first drafts of this book have suggested reading this section first, and nothing prevents the reader from turning to the conclusion and epilogue now.

I am well aware that many will note the lack of women's voices in this book about modesty and women's hair covering with chagrin. The history of high-level halakhic discourse has, for better or worse, been conducted almost exclusively by scholars who were men, and this book reflects that reality. I am hopeful that the current era will witness continued growth in high-level halakhic scholarship by women who may help to shape the future of this conversation. For more on this see the afterword.

A word about my approach to this topic: To state explicitly what will soon become obvious, I do not write here as a historian or sociologist of religion, but as a student of Jewish law (halakha), a professor in a law school who thinks about Jewish law as a legal field, and as an Orthodox rabbi and *dayan* (rabbinical court judge) who has been privileged to frequently answer a wide range of questions about the contours of Jewish law from adherents. The aim of this book is partly to make an argument about the analytic shape of Jewish law down through the ages, but also, more tentatively, to suggest possible directions for its future.

CHAPTER 1

Exposed Hair in Biblical and Tannaitic Sources: From Where Does This Whole "Hair" Conversation Derive?

CHAPTER 1 INTRODUCES US TO THE BASIC PROBLEM that this book will discuss: causes of divorce related to immodest behavior, with a focus on uncovered hair. As the introduction explains, my interest is textual, linguistic, and legal. This chapter surveys the material that discusses uncovered hair as an indication of immodest behavior from the time of the Torah to the time of the Mishnah. This chapter starts with the brief sources on divorce in the Torah and continues with the material on causes of divorce in the Mishnah and Tosefta, with a particular focus on hair covering as an improper behavior. The second half of this chapter collects all the cases in the early Rabbinic literature in which hair uncovering is mentioned or discussed, and notes how clear it is that hair covering was viewed as a sign of modest behavior in those times and places. In an addendum, we note a few places in early Jewish (but not Rabbinic) literature in which hair covering is mentioned and how it is connected to immodest behavior in these sources.

Part 1 – Exposed Hair as Part of a List of Improper Behaviors

DIVORCE IN THE TORAH

Divorce as an institution is first mentioned in Deuteronomy 24. The process is described almost as an afterthought, as part of an explication of a different law. According to this law, a couple may not remarry if the divorced wife married another man in the meantime, whether that marriage ended in divorce or widowhood:

1. If a man takes a wife and has relations with her, and if then she does not find favor in his eyes, for he found some base sexual fault[1] in her, and he writes her a divorce document and places it in her hand and sends her away from his house,

2. and she leaves his house and goes and [becomes the wife] of another man,

3. and this latter man hates her and writes her a divorce document and places it in her hand and sends her away from his house, or if the latter man, who took her as a wife, dies,

4. her former husband, who sent her away, cannot take her again to be his wife, since she has been defiled, for that is an abomination before the Lord, and you should not sully the land which the Lord your God gives to you as an inheritance.

(א) כִּי יִקַּח אִישׁ אִשָּׁה וּבְעָלָהּ וְהָיָה אִם לֹא תִמְצָא חֵן בְּעֵינָיו כִּי מָצָא בָהּ עֶרְוַת דָּבָר וְכָתַב לָהּ סֵפֶר כְּרִיתֻת וְנָתַן בְּיָדָהּ וְשִׁלְּחָהּ מִבֵּיתוֹ:

(ב) וְיָצְאָה מִבֵּיתוֹ וְהָלְכָה וְהָיְתָה לְאִישׁ אַחֵר:

(ג) וּשְׂנֵאָהּ הָאִישׁ הָאַחֲרוֹן וְכָתַב לָהּ סֵפֶר כְּרִיתֻת וְנָתַן בְּיָדָהּ וְשִׁלְּחָהּ מִבֵּיתוֹ אוֹ כִי יָמוּת הָאִישׁ הָאַחֲרוֹן אֲשֶׁר לְקָחָהּ לוֹ לְאִשָּׁה:

(ד) לֹא יוּכַל בַּעְלָהּ הָרִאשׁוֹן אֲשֶׁר שִׁלְּחָהּ לָשׁוּב לְקַחְתָּהּ לִהְיוֹת לוֹ לְאִשָּׁה אַחֲרֵי אֲשֶׁר הֻטַּמָּאָה כִּי תוֹעֵבָה הִוא לִפְנֵי ה' וְלֹא תַחֲטִיא אֶת הָאָרֶץ אֲשֶׁר ה' אֱלֹהֶיךָ נֹתֵן לְךָ נַחֲלָה:

One of the many important questions not explicitly addressed in this passage is why a couple should get divorced. Under what circumstances would it be permissible? Under what circumstances would it be advisable or even obligatory?[2] This question is taken up in the Mishnah (m. Gittin 9:10).

---

1. The exact translation of *ervat davar* is hard to capture. It can mean literally nakedness or a matter of nakedness. It often more colloquially means "something indecent" or "something offensive." I have not translated it consistently throughout the work, reflecting my sense that it has slightly different connotations when used in different sources.

2. There is a dispute whether the obligation of the husband is to divorce his wife in cases of infidelity, or whether they may stay married so long as he refrains from intimacy with her. While usually, the latter prohibition will precipitate divorce, the authorities dispute whether the husband could have the right to remain married while abstaining from intimacy, such as in a case where the husband is elderly and would not have been intimate regardless. Rabbi Yechezkel Landau (*Responsa Noda BeYehuda, Orach Chayyim* 1:35) argues that the primary obligation is for the couple to refrain from intimacy. See also *Beit Shmuel, Even HaEzer* 117:3 and *Responsa Rav Pealim, Even HaEzer* 1:1. The simplest understanding of the law is that the obligation is for the husband to divorce his wife. See the language, for example, of *Shulchan Arukh, Even HaEzer* 178:18. At any rate, if one accepts that in principle one is not

MISHNAH GITTIN

Beit Shammai says: "A man must not divorce his wife unless he found her to be at fault in sexual matters,[3] for it says: 'for he found some *base* (lit. sexual) fault in her.'" But Beit Hillel says: "Even if she burned his meal [he can divorce her], for it says: 'for he found some base *fault* in her.'" Rabbi Akiva says: "Even if he found someone more attractive than her [he can divorce her], for it says: 'If then, she does not find favor in his eyes.'"

בית שמאי אומרים: "לא יגרש אדם את אשתו אלא אם כן מצא בה דבר ערוה, שנאמר: 'כי מצא בה ערות דבר.'" ובית הלל אומרים: "אפילו הקדיחה תבשילו, שנאמר: 'כי מצא בה ערות דבר.'" רבי עקיבא אומר: "אפילו מצא אחרת נאה הימנה, שנאמר: 'והיה אם לא תמצא חן בעיניו.'"

This debate is expanded upon in the halakhic midrash compilations on Deuteronomy. The *Sifre*'s version (269) is the most expansive:

"And it will be if she does not find favor in his eyes" – from here Beit Shammai says: "A man must not divorce his wife unless he found her to be at fault in sexual [matters], for it says: 'for he found some base (lit. sexual) fault in her.'" But Beit Hillel says: "Even if she burned his meal [he can divorce her], for it says: 'some fault (lit. matter).'" Beit Hillel said to Beit Shammai: "If it says: 'some matter' why does it say 'sexual?' And if it says: 'sexual' why does it say, 'some matter?' [The answer is] if it said 'some matter' but did not say 'sexual,' I might have thought that a woman who is divorced because of 'some matter' would be permitted to remarry, but one who was divorced because of a sexual violation would not be permitted to remarry. And this should be no surprise, for if she becomes forbidden to the one who is per-

והיה אם לא תמצא חן בעיניו - מיכן היו בית שמיי אומרים: "לא יגרש אדם את אשתו אלא אם כן מצא בה ערוה, שנאמר: 'כי מצא בה ערות דבר.'" ובית הלל אומרים: "אפילו הקדיחה תבשילו, שנאמר: 'דבר.'" אמרו בית הלל לבית שמיי: "אם נאמר 'דבר' למה נאמר 'ערות' ואם נאמר 'ערות' למה נאמר 'דבר'? שאם נאמר 'דבר' ולא נאמר 'ערות' הייתי אומר היוצאה מפני דבר תהא מותרת להנשא והיוצאה מפני ערוה לא תהא מותרת להנשא. ואל תתמה אם נאסרה מן המותר לה לא תהא אסורה מן האסור לה - תלמוד לומר 'ערות... ויצאה מביתו והלכה והיתה

---

obligated to divorce an adulterous wife, in practice one would expect that if they remain married, they will be intimate. See Rabbi Ovadia Yosef's comments in *Responsa Yabia Omer, Even HaEzer* 2:2.

3. Presumably, Beit Shammai is referring to adultery here.

> mitted to her, should she not be forbidden to those who are forbidden to her?[5] [Therefore, the verse] comes to teach: 'sexual... and she leaves his house.' And if it said 'sexual' but did not say 'some matter,' I might have thought she can only be divorced for a sexual matter, but for any other matter she cannot be! [Therefore, the verse] comes to teach: 'some matter... and she leaves his house.'" Rabbi Akiva says: "Even if he found someone more attractive than her [he can divorce her], for it says: 'and it will be if she does not find favor in his eyes.'"
>
> לאיש אחר.'. ואם נאמר 'ערות' ולא נאמר 'דבר,' הייתי אומר מפני ערוה תצא מפני דבר לא תצא - תלמוד לומר 'דבר... ויצאה מביתו.'". רבי עקיבה אומר: "אפילו מצא אחרת נאה הימנה, שנאמר: 'והיה אם לא תמצא חן בעיניו.'"[4]

In this version of the argument, Beit Hillel attempts to prove its position by arguing that the superfluity of mentioning both the terms "sexual" and "some matter" demonstrates that no matter what the reason, a woman can be divorced and remarry.

The text offers no rebuttal on behalf of Beit Shammai. Nevertheless, what seems like a possible response of Beit Shammai to Beit Hillel's argument is recorded in the Jerusalem Talmud in the form of a baraita[6] (y. Gittin 9:11, y. Sotah 1:1):

> Beit Shammai says: "I only know [from the use of the term sexual] that a woman is divorced due to sexual matters alone. From where does one learn that if she goes out with her hair exposed,[7] the sides [of her clothing] in tatters or her arms exposed [that she is to be divorced?] [The verse] teaches: 'for he found in her some base matter.'"
>
> בית שמאי אומרי': "אין לי אלא היוצא משום ערוה בלבד, ומניין היוצאה וראשה פרוע צדדיה פרומין וזרועותיה חלוצות? תלמוד לומר: 'כי מצא בה ערות דבר.'"

---

4. *Midrash Tannaim l'Devarim* 24:1 has the same retelling of the three basic positions as in the Sifre, except it does not include Beit Hillel's long argument against Beit Shammai.

5. I.e., if she becomes forbidden to her husband by committing adultery, should she not become forbidden to everyone for the same reason?

6. This is suggested by the Ridbaz ad loc., commenting on y. Gitten and is referenced favorably by the *Tzitz Eliezer* 14:98.

7. As this practice is the focus of the current book, the possible meanings of this

Although from the Mishnah itself, Beit Shammai's position seems to be referring specifically to adultery; nevertheless, in the baraita, the position is expanded to include a list of other behaviors. These behaviors are all examples of immodest attire, whether exposed hair, exposed sides or exposed arms.

While this *derasha* effectively counters Beit Hillel's attack, it requires some explanation. Why would Beit Shammai allow divorce for this particular fault as opposed to any other? One may posit this baraita is working with an alternative understanding of Beit Shammai's reasoning. It would seem that the reason Beit Shammai allows divorce for adultery is not because of the enormity of the sin.[8] Rather, the key factor may be the woman's sharing of her sexuality with other men, in this case through provocative public display.

Following this baraita, what Beit Shammai seems to be saying is that provocative sexual behavior on the part of a wife is intolerable to a husband and constitutes the one valid reason for a man to divorce his wife. If this interpretation is correct, this would mean, of course, that the list is not expansive. It is not something mysterious, or even particularly significant halakhically, in her actions that make them a violation. It is the sociological reality that they are considered provocative.

Possible support for this understanding can be found in Rabbi Yehuda HaNasi's derasha recorded in the *Midrash Tannaim l'Devarim* (23:15). The glossed phrase is part of a short section discussing the rules of defecation in the desert camp of the Israelites:

(13) And there should be an appointed place outside the camp [for a privy], and you should go out to it. (14) And you should have a small shovel on your tool-belt, and when you need to 'sit' outside, you will dig with it, and then 'sit' [on that	(יג) וְיָד תִּהְיֶה לְךָ מִחוּץ לַמַּחֲנֶה וְיָצָאתָ שָׁמָּה חוּץ: (יד) וְיָתֵד תִּהְיֶה לְךָ עַל אֲזֵנֶךָ וְהָיָה בְּשִׁבְתְּךָ חוּץ וְחָפַרְתָּה בָהּ וְשַׁבְתָּ וְכִסִּיתָ אֶת צֵאָתֶךָ:

---

term will be discussed later. I will use this translation of *"rosh parua"* in general because it is both very close to the literal meaning and does not overly prejudice the reader toward any of the possible interpretations that will be discussed in later chapters.

8. A good proof for this is that Beit Shammai does not mention that it is permitted to divorce a wife who is a murderer or idolater. However, see the position of Rabbi Yishmael further on in this section, which will suggest just that about idolatry.

spot] and bury your waste. (15) For the Lord your God walks inside your camp to save you and place your enemies before you, thus your camp should be holy, and He should not see any base matter in you and turn away from you.

(טו) כִּי ה' אֱלֹהֶיךָ מִתְהַלֵּךְ בְּקֶרֶב מַחֲנֶךָ לְהַצִּילְךָ וְלָתֵת אֹיְבֶיךָ לְפָנֶיךָ וְהָיָה מַחֲנֶיךָ קָדוֹשׁ וְלֹא יִרְאֶה בְךָ עֶרְוַת דָּבָר וְשָׁב מֵאַחֲרֶיךָ: ס

The simple interpretation of "base matter" in this section is that it refers to human waste. However, two alternative interpretations of the term "base matter" are offered by Rabbi Yishmael and Rabbi Yehuda HaNasi respectively, each using a *gezera shava* (the comparison of similar words in different places in Torah) to compare the usage of this term in this passage to its use in the case of divorce in Chapter 24:

> 'And no base thing should be seen in you' – Rabbi Yishmael says: "[The term] 'base matter' is used here, and [the term] 'base matter' is used later; just like [the term] 'base matter' later refers to thinking about sexual matters and idolatry, so too does [the term] 'base matter' here refer to sexual matters and idolatry."
>
> 'ולא יראה בך ער' דבר' - ר' ישמעאל אומר: "נאמר כאן 'ערות דבר' ונאמר להלן 'ערות דבר,' מה ערות דבר שנ' להלן בהרהור ערוה וע"ז הכת' מדבר אף ערות דבר שנ' כאן בהרהור ערוה וע"ז הכת' מדבר."
>
> Rabbi says: "[The term] 'base matter' is used here, and [the term] 'base matter' is used later; just like [the term] 'base matter' later refers to something degrading, so too [the term] 'base matter' used here refers to something degrading."
>
> ר' אומ': "נאמר כאן 'ערות דבר' ונאמר להלן 'ערות דבר,' מה ערות דבר שנ' להלן משום בזיון אף ערות דבר שנ' כאן משום בזיון."

Although both Rabbi Yishmael and Rabbi Yehuda HaNasi use a *gezera shava* to interpret the passage in Chapter 23 considering the passage in Chapter 24, they have a fundamental disagreement about what the passage in Chapter 24 means. According to Rabbi Yishmael, the term "base matter" in Chapter 24 refers to a sin that the woman has committed; this is why, together with sexual impropriety, he includes idolatry – another major sin. Rabbi Yehuda HaNasi understands the term in Chapter 24 to be referring to humiliating behavior, particularly the sort of behavior that humiliates her husband, making a continued marital relationship unpalatable.

They then apply their understanding to the passage in Chapter 23. Rabbi Yehuda HaNasi is able to maintain the simple understanding of the verse, since the analogy works well: leaving feces exposed in a camp where God is said to walk is degrading to God, giving Him the right to abrogate the relationship with Israel, just like sexually provocative behavior toward other men is humiliating and intolerable to a husband, giving him the right to end the marriage in the face of it. In contrast, Rabbi Yishmael believes that the reference in Chapter 24 is to specific sins and sinful behavior. Hence, he cannot accept the simple meaning of the verse that exposure of feces allows God to abrogate His promise of protection to the Israelites. Rather, what it must mean is that the "base matter" that God sees in the camp is unrelated to the discussion of proper waste removal, but means that additionally if God sees either idolatry or sexual licentiousness in the camp, He will abandon the Israelites just like a husband abandons a wife in the face of such behavior.

What is important for our purposes is that Rabbi Yehuda HaNasi interprets the verse about a husband's finding improper behavior in a wife to be referring to the humiliation such behavior causes for him. This is in line with the interpretation of the position of Beit Shammai in the baraita suggested above,[9] and supports the understanding of Beit Shammai's list of provocative behaviors as a selection of society-specific behaviors that the reader would immediately recognize as the sort of behavior "no normal husband would put up with."

This leads to two logical correlates. First, if a wife behaves in ways that are considered unrespectable in any given society, Beit Shammai would allow divorce in such a case. Second, if a woman dresses in any of the above-mentioned ways in a society where such dress is not considered provocative, Beit Shammai would not allow divorce in such a case.

In summary, we are looking at a sociologically determined list, not one based on specific laws of modesty. Since a version of this list exists in several Tannaitic sources, we will next test the plausibility of this interpretation with reference to these sources.

TOSEFTA SOTAH

The issue of women's head covering is addressed in several places in the Tannaitic corpus. In three places it exists as part of a list of improper behaviors that place a wife in a sort of marital breach with her husband.

---

9. This does not mean, of course, that Rabbi Yehuda HaNasi decides the law in favor of Beit Shammai, only that he agrees with Beit Shammai regarding the simple meaning of the term in the verse.

The list is reminiscent of Beit Shammai's list in the baraita, although significantly expanded. I will begin with the text from Tosefta Sotah (5:9).[10]

Rabbi Meir used to say: "Just as there are attitudes towards food, so too are there attitudes towards women.	[ט] היה ר' מאיר או[מר]: "כשם שדיעות במאכל כך דיעות בנשים.
There is a type of man who, when a fly flies over his cup, leaves it and won't taste [the wine] – this is a bad fate [for] the woman, since this is a man who is intent on divorcing his wife.	א. יש לך אדם שהזבוב עובר על גבי כוסו, מניחו ואין טועמו - זה חלק רע בנשים שנתן עיניו באשתו לגרשה.
There is a type of man who, when a fly settles on the inside of his cup, throws it out and will not drink [the wine]. This is like Pappos ben Yehuda, who locked the door on his wife and left.	ב. יש לך אדם שהזבוב שוכן בתוך כוסו, זורקו ואין שותהו - כגון פפוס בן יהודה שנעל דלת בפני אשתו ויצא.
There is a type of man who, when a fly falls into his cup, he throws it out and then drinks from it – this is the character of the average man,[11] who sees his wife speaking with her neighbors or relatives and leaves her to do so.	ג. ויש לך אדם שהזבוב נופל בתוך כוסו, זורקו ושותהו - זו מדת כל אדם שראה את אשתו שמדברת עם שכיניה ועם קרובותיה ומניחה.
There is a type of man who, when a fly falls on his tray, he takes it, sucks on it, throws it away and then eats what was in [the tray] – this is the character of a wicked man, who sees his wife:	ד. יש לך אדם שהזבוב נופל בתוך תמחוי שלו, נוטלו מוצצו וזורקו ואוכל את מה שבתוכה - זו מדת אדם רשע שראה את אשתו
a. going out with her hair exposed,	א. יוצאת וראשה פרוע,
b. going out with the sides [of her clothing] in tatters,	ב. יצאת וצדדיה פרומים,
c. behaving arrogantly with her slaves,	ג. לבה גס בעבדיה,
d. behaving arrogantly with her maidservants,	ד. לבה גס בשפחותיה,

---

10. Many of these texts will be quoted again by the Talmud in its discussions of the subject, albeit in slightly different form. These variations will be discussed in the section on the Talmud.
11. Literally "every man who sees..."

e. going out to weave in the public marketplace,
f. or washing and acting playfully with random[12] men."

ה. יוצא וטווה בשוק,
ו. רוחצת ומשחקת עם כל אדם."

This source can be broken up into two main sections. The first section is Rabbi Meir's observation on the psychology of different men and their reactions to perceived impropriety or implied infidelity on the part of their wives. It is somewhat difficult to fully grasp all the nuances of Rabbi Meir's observations, since the exact meaning of each of his fly scenarios is not fully clear. Nevertheless, it appears that Rabbi Meir is suggesting that there are two types of tolerant men and two types of intolerant men. For our purposes, Rabbi Meir's two types of tolerant men are significant.

The first type of tolerant man is described as "the average man." What Rabbi Meir suggests is that at times a man will see his wife speaking with another man and feel somewhat rankled. Nevertheless, Rabbi Meir argues, most men understand that it is best to ignore this, as the wife's behavior is harmless, and such "petty jealousies" are a natural part of life.

The second type of tolerant man seems to be either totally unconcerned with marital propriety or even, as the fly analogy seems to imply, some sort of a voyeur, who derives vicarious enjoyment from his wife's inappropriate behavior. Said inappropriate behavior seems to fall into three categories. The first is provocative dress (exposed hair, scanty clothing), the second is crass behavior (acting arrogantly with subordinates), and the third is flirtatious or suggestive behavior (washing/acting playfully with other men).[13] Tolerance of this type of inappropriate behavior is considered by Rabbi Meir to be a wicked character trait, demonstrating that the husband partakes of a libertine attitude himself. Having quoted Rabbi Meir's psychological observation, the Tosefta continues with a halakhic observation:

[Such a woman] it is a mitzvah to divorce, as it says: "If a man takes a woman [as a wife] and has relations with her, and it will be if she does not find favor in his eyes, for

מצוה לגרשה, שנ[אמר]: 'כי יקח איש אשה ובעלה [והיה אם לא תמצא חן בעיניו כי מצא בה ערות דבר וכתב לה

---

12. Literally "any" or "every." For a clever read of this source, see Saul Lieberman, *Tosefta Kefeshuto* commenting on this.
13. Public weaving could be any of the three.

he found some base fault in her, and he writes her a divorce document and places it in her hand [and sends her away from his house, and she leaves him and goes and becomes the wife] of another man..." (Deut. 24:1–2) – The verse calls him "another" because he is not really similar to [the first man, since] the first man sent her away for her sin, but this one comes and joins up with her. The second man, if he has merit in the eyes of heaven will send her away from himself. If not, she will end up burying him, as it says: ["and the latter man hates her and writes her a divorce document and places it in her hand and sends her away from his house,] or if the latter man dies..." – this man is worthy of death since he brought this woman into his house.

ספר כריתת ונתן בידה ושלחה מביתו, ויצאה מעמו[14] [והלכה והיתה לאיש אחר]׳ וכת[וב] קראו "אחר" שאינו בן זוגו [של הראשון, ש]הראשון[15] הוציא מפני עבירה, זה בא ונתקל בה, השיני אם זכה לשמים מוציאה מתחת ידו אם לאו לסוף שקוברתו, שנ[אמר]: ׳ושנאה האיש האחרון וכתב לה ספר כריתת ונתן בידה ושלחה מביתו] או כי ימות האיש האחרון׳ – כדי האיש הזה למיתה שאשה זו כנס לתוך ביתו.

Invoking a midrashic interpretation of the verse in Deuteronomy, the Tosefta takes Rabbi Meir's critique of the excessively tolerant (libertine) husband a step further, turning it into a normative requirement for any husband in such a situation to divorce his wife.[16] This is reminiscent of Beit Shammai's position in the baraita reference earlier.

The derasha used to explain the basis for this ruling is an interpretation of the section in Deuteronomy 24 on divorce and remarriage referenced in the previous section. The midrash here picks up on the term "another man" and explains that what makes him "other" is not just that he happens to be a physically different person, but that he differs essentially from the first man. This is because, whereas the first husband divorced his wife because of some "base fault" he found in her, this man married her

---

14. See Deuteronomy 24:1–2. In the Masoretic Text it actually says מביתו. It would seem that our author or a later scribe was paraphrasing from memory.
15. This seems to be a necessary textual emendation, without which the sentence makes little sense. It seems as if the scribe's eye jumped from ראשון to ראשון. See the parallel texts in *Midrash Tannaim l'Devorim* (24:2) and Numbers Rabbah (*Nasso* 9), and also the later text, *Midrash Lekach Tov* to Deuteronomy (ad loc.). See footnote 23 on page x for an explanation of the brackets.
16. It is possible that this section is also part of Rabbi Meir's comment, but this is uncertain.

despite this base fault. The midrash continues this line of interpretation into the next section by saying that at this point, the "other" man has a choice. Either he can recognize his sinful ways and divorce his wife, or he will face the ultimate consequences and die as a sinner.

ANALYSIS

What we learn from this Tosefta is that while it is a good character trait for a husband to accept a certain amount of interaction between his wife and other men, it is considered an evil character trait for a husband to tolerate sexually provocative or outlandish behavior on the part of his wife and that it is actually a mitzvah for a man to divorce his wife under these circumstances.[17]

A critical question for the focus of this book is from where does this list of behaviors derive? The verse in Deuteronomy just mentions "a base fault" and there is no attempt by any midrash that I know of to derive them all from this or any other verse.[18] One could argue that there was some sort of tradition (*mesorah*) that these behaviors were forbidden, either biblically or rabbinically. However, it seems most probable to argue that the list represents behaviors that would be considered "obviously" improper in the social context in which this text was written. Indeed, I believe a further proof to this is that one of the listed behaviors above is "going to the public market to weave," which seems to be pretty specific to the social fabric of the time.

TOSEFTA KETUBOT

The same list (with some small variations) appears in a different context in Tosefta Ketubot (7:4–6):

| [4] If he makes a vow forbidding her to lend a winnow, a sieve, a grinder or an oven – she may leave and [her husband] must make the ketubah payment since he is causing her to have a bad name among her neighbors. | [ד] הדירה שלא להשאיל נפה וכברה רחים ותנור - יוציא ויתן כתובה, מפני שמשיאה שם רע בשכינותיה. |

---

17. Whether this is supposed to be understood as an actual biblical commandment or whether the *derasha* is supposed to be understood as an *asmachta* (unintentional or hinted support) for a Rabbinic commandment is hard to say.
18. The issue of exposed hair being the exception.

So too, if she makes a vow not to lend a winnow, a sieve, a grinder or an oven – she leaves without her ketubah payment since she is causing [her husband] to have a bad name in his neighborhood.

וכן היא שנדרה שלא להשאיל נפה וכבר[ה] רחיים ותנור - תצא שלא בכתובה, מפני שמשיאתו שם רע בשכונתו.

[5] If he makes a vow that she may not visit the house of a mourner or attend a celebration – she may leave and [her husband] must make the ketubah payment since tomorrow she may be left alone[19] and no living soul will feed her.[20]

[ה] הדירה שלא תלך לבית האבל או לבית המשתה יוציא ויתן כתובה שלמחר תהא מוטלת ואין כל בריא סופנה.

[6] Rabbi Meir used to say: "What lesson is derived from [the verse] 'It is better to go to a house of mourning than to go to a celebration since this is the end of all man, and a living one should take it to heart?'[21] Work so that they work for you, accompany [the body of the deceased] so that they will accompany yours, eulogize so that they will eulogize you, bury so that they bury you. This is why it says: '[it is good] to go to a house of mourning etc.'"[22]

[ו] היה ר' מאיר או[מר]: מה ת"ל 'טוב ללכת אל בית אבל מלכת אל בית משתה באשר הוא סוף כל האדם והחי יתן אל לבו'? עביד דיעבדון לך לוי דילוון לך ספוד דיספדונך קבור דיקברונך שנ': '[טוב] ללכת אל בית אבל וגו'.'"

If he makes a vow that:
a. she must allow any man to taste her cooking,
b. or that she must fill up and then pour out garbage,
c. or that she should tell random men intimate details about her life with her husband,

she may leave and [her husband] must make the ketubah payment since he has not behaved with her in accordance with *dat Moshe ve-Yisrael*.

הדירה:
א. שתהא מטעמת תבשילה לכל אדם,
ב. או שתהא ממלא ומערה לאשפות,
ג. ושתאמר לכל אדם דברים שבינו לבינה -
יוציא ויתן כתובה, מפני שלא נהג עמה כדת משה וישראל.

---

19. I.e., her husband may die or divorce her.
20. I.e., because she did not attend any of their lifecycle events and they were offended and considered her anti-social.
21. Ecclesiastes 7:2.
22. Although Rabbi Meir's statement begins the sixth halakha in the Tosefta, it is clearly attached to the previous point.

Similarly, if:
a. she goes out with her hair exposed,
b. she goes out with her clothing in tatters,
c. she behaves arrogantly with her slaves, maidservants or the neighborhood women,
d. she goes out to weave in the public marketplace,
e. she washes or is washed in the bathhouse in the company of random men,

she leaves without her ketubah payment since she has not behaved with [her husband] in accordance with *dat Moshe ve-Yisrael*.

...All the above women who violate *dat* require previous warning and can then be divorced without payment of the ketubah. If she was not warned, she can be divorced but the ketubah payment must be made.

וכן היא
א. שיוצא[ה] וראשה פרוע,
ב. יוצא ובגדיה פרומים,
ג. ולבה גס בעבדיה ובשפחותיה בשכנותיה,
ד. יוצא וטווה בשוק,
ה. רוחצת ומרחצת במרחץ עם כל אדם - תצא שלא בכתובה,
מפני שלא נהגה עמו כדת משה וישראל.

...כל אילו נשים שעברו על הדת צריכות התראה ויוצאות שלא בכתובה לא התרה בהן יוציא ויתן כתובה

What is particularly instructive about this text is the symmetry between the improper behaviors of the husband and the improper behaviors of the wife. In the first examples, in halakhot 4–5, the nature of the violation has to do with the sullying of the couple's reputation in their neighborhood, since stingy behavior makes a couple unpopular. The examples in halakha 6 have to do with humiliating one's spouse, and these are the cases that this section will focus on.[23]

According to the Tosefta, if a husband forces his wife to engage in behavior that humiliates her, this is grounds for divorce and she can demand payment of her ketubah. Similarly, if a woman engages in behavior that embarrasses her husband, he can consider that grounds for divorcing her without payment of her ketubah.[24] The Tosefta even has a term for this humiliating behavior – i.e., it is a violation of *dat Moshe ve-Yisrael*.

---

23. The types of humiliating behavior attributed to the husband are diverse and not all sexual. For example, forcing one's wife to pour things out into the trash publicly is an attempt to make her feel low.
24. It is interesting that the possibility of the husband's own behavior embarrassing his wife is not considered.

Once more, the critical question is whence these lists of behaviors arose? Yet again, the lists do not derive either from a tradition on forbidden behavior or from a derasha on a biblical verse. Rather, as I argued above, they seem to derive from an attempt to put together a list of behaviors that would be considered "obviously" improper in the social context in which the text was written. This is a crucial point since it would mean that, logically speaking, what is considered *dat Moshe ve-Yisrael* would need to be updated in each generation and social milieu.

MISHNAH KETUBOT

The primary Tannaitic source for our discussion of hair covering is Mishnah Ketubot (7:5–6). It is the parallel text to the above quoted Tosefta:

[5] If he makes a vow that she may not visit the house of a mourner or attend a celebration – she may leave and [her husband] must make the ketubah payment since he is "locking [the door] in her face."[25] However, if he claims that [the vow] is due to a "separate matter,"[26] he is permitted [to make such a vow].	[ה] המדיר את אשתו שלא תלך לבית האבל או לבית המשתה יוציא ויתן כתובה מפני שנועל בפניה. ואם היה טוען משום דבר אחר רשאי.
If he said to her [that he is making a vow] with the condition that: a. "You must tell so-and-so what you said to me or what I said to you"[27] b. or that she must fill up and then pour out garbage, she may leave and [her husband] must make the ketubah payment.	אמר לה על מנת א. שתאמרי לפלוני מה שאמרת לי או מה שאמרתי לך ב. או שתהא ממלא ומערה לאשפה יוציא ויתן כתובה.
[6] The following [category of women] may be divorced without receiving the	[ו] ואלו יוצאות שלא בכתבה: העוברת על דת משה ויהודית.

---

25. From the parallel case in the Tosefta, one can reason that the Mishnah means he is shutting the door on potential charitable supporters for her in case she falls on hard times in the future.
26. This is probably a euphemism for a suspected affair.
27. From a comparison with the parallel case in the Tosefta, one can fairly assume that the reference here is to "pillow talk," but see the next chapter for the Talmud's interpretation.

ketubah payment: One who violates *dat Moshe ve-Yehudit*.

What [violates] *dat Moshe*?   ואיזו היא דת משה?
a. Feeding [her husband] untithed food,   א. מאכילתו שאינו מעשר,
b. having intercourse with him during her menstrual period,   ב. ומשמשתו נדה,
c. not setting apart the dough offering,   ג. ולא קוצה לה חלה,
d. making vows and not fulfilling them.   ד. ונודרת ואינה מקימת.

What [violates] *dat Yehudit*?   ואיזוהי דת יהודית?
a. Going out with her hair exposed,   א. יוצאה וראשה פרוע,
b. weaving in the marketplace,   ב. וטווה בשוק,
c. conversing with random men.   ג. ומדברת עם כל אדם.
d. Abba Shaul says: "Also cursing his parents in front of his face."   ד. אבא שאול אומר: "אף המקללת יולדיו בפניו."
e. Rabbi Tarfon says: "Also, a loudmouth."   ה. רבי טרפון אומר: "אף הקולנית."

Comparing the Mishnah with the Tosefta, one notices a similar structure. There is a parallel between the rules for the husband and the rules for the wife. If the husband forces his wife to do things that humiliate her, she can leave and demand payment of her ketubah. On the other hand, if the wife behaves in such a way that humiliates the husband, he can demand a divorce and refuse payment of the ketubah.

However, there are several key differences. In the Tosefta there is one term for "breach of marriage protocol due to behavior that humiliates one's partner" and that is *dat Moshe ve-Yisrael*. The term represents only one thing, not two, and applies equally to the husband and wife. However, the Mishnah uses a different term, *dat Moshe ve-Yehudit*, and this term is used only in reference to the wife and is presented as referring to two separate things. The latter term, *dat Yehudit*, represents a variation of the standard list of behaviors which humiliate the husband referenced earlier in t. Sotah and t. Ketubot. However, the former term, *dat Moshe*, contains an original and unique list of behaviors that seem to have nothing to do with the wife humiliating the husband. Instead, the list seems to refer to activities, which the wife does or does not do, that cause her husband to sin inadvertently.

The first three cases are classic examples of a wife causing a husband to sin, by failing to do certain required rituals that he assumes she is doing as a matter of course: separating tithes and *challah* and going to the mikvah.

The fourth could be seen in a similar light, since by not canceling her vows, the husband may be partially responsible for their violation.

The Tosefta (7:6) includes a gloss on this part of the Mishnah:[28]

Rabbi Meir says: "If he knows that she makes oaths but does not keep them – he should not allow her to make oaths."	ר' מאיר אומ': "אם יודע בה שמדירה ואינה מקיימת – אל ישנה להדירה."
Rabbi Yehuda says: "If he knows that she does not take *challah* [when she makes dough] – he should take *challah* on her behalf."	ר' יהודה או': "אם היה יודע בה שאינה קוצה לה חלה – יוציא ויתקן אחריה."

Rabbi Meir and Rabbi Yehuda each dispute one of the cases, not because they think the category of *dat Moshe* is mistaken, but because they think that certain behaviors should not be considered violations of *dat Moshe*. Specifically, Rabbi Meir feels that the husband should be responsible for annulling her vows if he thinks she does not keep them, whereas Rabbi Yehuda thinks he should take *challah* himself if he thinks she is not doing it properly. Ostensibly, both agree that a woman who secretly does not tithe or go to the mikvah is in violation of *dat Moshe* and can be divorced without payment of her ketubah.

What stands out with this category is that there is no parallel case of a husband secretly causing his wife to sin based on his negligent behavior. Moreover, there is no parallel to this list in any of the previous Tannaitic sources quoted earlier. The category of *dat Yehudit*, on the other hand, is perfectly aligned with the previously referenced Tannaitic sources; it is one of three examples listing behaviors inappropriate for a Jewish wife.

Nevertheless, this version of the list is slightly different. In place of the category of "washing with random men," the Mishnah includes chatting with random men, something which seems to represent a violation of propriety of a much lower magnitude. Furthermore, instead of the usual

---

28. It is well known that certain parts of the Tosefta contain parallel material to the Mishnah, and certain parts are later glosses on the Mishnah. The above analysis distinguishes between these two layers. For discussion of current theories concerning the relationship between the Mishnah and the Tosefta, see Moshe Simon-Shoshan, *Stories of the Law: Narrative Discourse and the Construction of Authority in the Mishnah* (Oxford: Oxford University Press, 2012), 97–99 and 247; Robert Brody, *Mishnah and Tosefta Studies* (Jerusalem: Magnes Press, 2014); Paul Mandel, "The Tosefta," *The Cambridge History of Judaism* (Cambridge: Cambridge University Press, 2008), 4:316–35.

tattered clothing and verbal abuse of servants, the Mishnah includes the individual statements of Abba Shaul and Rabbi Tarfon. Abba Shaul's case is the cursing of the husband's parents, something that clearly fits into the rubric of humiliating and abusive behavior. What is unique about Abba Shaul's case is the private nature of the berating.

Rabbi Tarfon's example is, perhaps, the most surprising. A gloss attempts to explain the meaning:

| What constitutes a "loudmouth"? Any woman who speaks in her house and her neighbors can hear her. | אי זו היא קולנית? כל שמדברת בביתה ושכיניה שומעין את קולה. |

Even with this gloss, it is unclear whether Rabbi Tarfon means this term euphemistically or literally.[29] Either way, Rabbi Tarfon's view is difficult to comprehend since it seems that this behavior, although embarrassing to the husband, is unintentional.

Despite the slight differences between the Mishnah's list and the lists in the Tosefta, it would seem that *dat Yehudit* is defined as humiliating behavior and should indeed be understood as the parallel to the husband's forced humiliation of his wife. Again, there is no indication in the Mishnah that this list comes from some sort of tradition or biblical verse; rather, it seems to represent socially determined humiliating behavior.

Part 2 – Exposed Hair Generally

MISHNAH BAVA KAMMA

In certain places in Tannaitic literature, the issue of women and hair covering is discussed outside the above-mentioned list of immodest behaviors or divorce. Even so, upon examination of the sources it is clear that under discussion is a type of immodest appearance that would be considered embarrassing to a woman accustomed to modest dress.

The first source we will look at comes from the Mishnah in tractate Bava Kamma (8:6):

| One who hits his fellow must pay him a *sela*.[30] | התוקע לחבירו נותן לו סלע |

---

29. I.e., is it referring to loud moaning during intercourse or to loud mundane speech?
30. Generally, a *sela* is equal to four *zuz*, although there are exceptions depending on location and monetary system.

Rabbi Yehuda said in the name of Rabbi Yossi the Galilean: "[He must pay] a hundred [*zuz*]."

If he slaps him, he must pay him 200 *zuz*. [If he did so] with the back of his hand, [he must pay] 400 *zuz*.

- If he screamed in his ear,
- pulled on his hair,
- spit on him,
- pulled his cloak off,
- exposed the hair of a woman in public,

He must pay 400 *zuz*.

This is the general principle: Payment is evaluated based on the [victim's] honor.

Rabbi Akiva said: "Even the poorest of Israelites should be seen as if they were people of independent means that came upon hard times, for they are the children of Abraham, Isaac and Jacob.

It once happened that a man exposed the hair of a woman in public. She came before Rabbi Akiva and he required [the offender] to pay her 400 *zuz*. [The man] said to [Rabbi Akiva]: "Rabbi, give me some time." He gave [the man] time. [The man][31] waited until he saw the woman standing by the entrance to her yard and he smashed a jug which contained an *isser's* worth of oil before her. She uncovered her head and was sweeping [the oil up with her hand] and placing her hand on her head [to absorb the oil]. The man had placed witnesses before her [to testify to her behavior.] He came [again] before Rabbi Akiva and said: "Rabbi, should I pay 400 *zuz* to the likes of her?" [Rabbi Akiva] responded: "You have

רבי יהודה אומר משום רבי יוסי הגלילי: "מנה".

סטרו נתן לו מאתים זוז. לאחר ידו נתן לו ארבע מאות זוז.

- צרם באזנו
- תלש בשערו
- רקק והגיע בו רוקו
- העביר טליתו ממנו
- פרע ראש האשה בשוק - נותן ארבע מאות זוז.

זה הכלל הכל לפי כבודו.

אמר רבי עקיבא: "אפילו עניים שבישראל רואין אותם כאילו הם בני חורין שירדו מנכסיהם שהם בני אברהם יצחק ויעקב."

ומעשה באחד שפרע ראש האשה בשוק באת לפני רבי עקיבא וחייבו ליתן לה ארבע מאות זוז. אמר לו: "רבי תן לי זמן." ונתן לו זמן. שמרה עומדת על פתח חצרה ושבר את הכד בפניה ובו כאיסר שמן. גלתה את ראשה והיתה מטפחת ומנחת ידה על ראשה. העמיד עליה עדים ובא לפני רבי עקיבא. אמר לו: "רבי לזו אני נותן ארבע מאות זוז?" אמר לו: "לא אמרת כלום. החובל בעצמו אף על פי שאינו רשאי פטור, אחרים שחבלו בו חייבין. והקוצץ נטיעותיו, אף על פי שאינו

---

31. There is a small textual manuscript dispute present here. It's typical of Mishnah to switch between synonymous nouns like this within sentences, either as a

demonstrated nothing, for if one inflicts a wound upon one's self, although it is not permitted to do so, one is exempt [from a fine]. But if others wound him, they are obligated. So too, if one cuts down one's own saplings, even though it is not permitted to do so, one is exempt, but if others cut down his saplings, they are obligated."

רשאי פטור, אחרים שקצצו את נטיעותיו חייבים."

The above Mishnah characterizes the exposing or loosening of a woman's hair as an act of humiliation, comparable to spitting on a person or giving someone a backhanded slap. Rabbi Akiva takes this further, stating that even if a person does not carry him- or herself in such a way that public humiliation is an important factor, one must still treat him or her with the same dignity one would offer a well-to-do society person.

The *Sifra* (*Emor*, 20:3), commenting on Leviticus 24:19, adduces biblical support for the above ruling:

> "If a man wounds his fellow" – I only know [that this rule applies] when he causes an actual wound, how do I know it applies when he screams in his ear, pulls on his hair, spits on him, pulls his cloak off, or exposes the hair of a woman in public? This is why [the verse] teaches: "As he did, so too should be done to him."

> ואיש כי יתן מום בעמיתו – אין לי אלא בזמן שנתן בו מום, מנין צרם באוזנו, תלש בשערו, רקק והגיע בו הרוק, והעביר טליתו ממנו, ופרע ראשה של אשה בשוק? תלמוד לומר: '[כאשר] עשה כן יעשה לו.'[32]

This rule about compensation in m. Bava Kamma and in the Sifra is, in many ways, the logical converse of what appeared in the previous Tannaitic sources. If going out with exposed hair was considered immodest or provocative behavior on the part of a woman, such that her husband can claim that her behaving in such a way shames him, the converse should be true as well. In other words, if a person were to forcibly expose or uncover a woman's hair in public, this would be a way of degrading her, treating her like an immodest woman. Hence, this behavior is considered

---

stylistic motif or to reach a wider range of vocabularies, but the text of our Bavli is sometimes confused (for a very similar example, b. Bava Kamma 27a פתח בחבית וסיים בכד) as are later copyists, sometimes. (My thanks to Gershon Klapper for pointing this out.)

32. Leviticus 24:19, וְאִישׁ כִּי יִתֵּן מוּם בַּעֲמִיתוֹ כַּאֲשֶׁר עָשָׂה כֵּן יֵעָשֶׂה לּוֹ: "Anyone who injures their neighbor is to be injured in the same manner."

parallel to spitting on a man or slapping him backhanded, as these actions are intended to humiliate him and imply his lack of masculinity.

It would be extremely difficult to argue that the above halakhot can be understood as objective prohibitions unrelated to societal norms. Rather, the above list should be understood as a list of actions that were considered humiliating at the time, and an updated version of the list would apply at any given time to behaviors of equivalent severity in one's contemporary society.

SIFRE NUMBERS

A somewhat related discussion of hair-exposing can be found in the midrash halakha *Sifre* Numbers (*Nasso* 11). The derasha is a gloss on Numbers 5:18, in the section of the Torah that describes the procedure for administering the "bitter waters" to a woman accused of adultery:

And the priest will stand the woman before God and expose the woman's hair...	וְהֶעֱמִיד הַכֹּהֵן אֶת הָאִשָּׁה לִפְנֵי ה' וּפָרַע אֶת רֹאשׁ הָאִשָּׁה...

The text of the Sifre here is very complicated and the literature attempting to understand it even more so. In order to present this source as clearly as possible, we will begin with the parallel sources from the Mishnah and Tosefta. The Mishnah (m. Sotah 1:5–6) states:

If she says: "I have been made impure,"[33] she tears up her ketubah and leaves.	אם אמרה: "טמאה אני" – שוברת כתובתה ויוצאת.
But if she says: "I am pure," they bring her up to the East Gate which is at the opening of the Nicanor Gate; that is where the *sotah* women [accused of adultery] are given the drink and women who have recently given birth are declared pure and the lepers are declared pure.	ואם אמרה: "טהורה אני" – מעלין אותה לשער המזרח שעל פתח שער נקנור ששם משקין את הסוטות ומטהרין את היולדות ומטהרין את המצורעים,
The priest grasps her clothing – if it tears it tears and if it tatters it tatters – until he exposes her chest.[34] He also undoes her hair.	וכהן אוחז בבגדיה: אם נקרעו נקרעו אם נפרמו נפרמו, עד שהוא מגלה את לבה, וסותר את שערה.
Rabbi Yehuda says: "If her chest was lovely he would not expose it, and if her hair was lovely, he would not undo it."	ר' יהודה אומר: "אם היה לבה נאה לא היה מגלהו, ואם היה שערה נאה לא היה סותרו."

---

33. I.e., she admits to having had an affair.
34. Literally "heart."

If she was dressed in white, they dress her in black.	[ו] היתה מתכסה בלבנים מכסה בשחורים.
If she was wearing golden trinkets, necklaces, earrings or rings, they remove them from her in order to degrade her…	היו עליה כלי זהב וקטליאות נזמים וטבעות מעבירים ממנה כדי לנוולה…

The Tosefta (Sotah 1:7) offers a slight variation:

The priests cast lots among themselves.	כהנים מטילין ביניהן גורלות,
Whoever's lot comes up, even if it is the high priest's, goes out and stands beside the *sotah*	כל מי שעלה גורלו אפי' כהן גדול יוצא ועומד בצד סוטה
and grasps her clothing – if it tears it tears and if it becomes tatters it becomes tatters – until he exposes her chest.	ואוחז בבגדיה אם נקרעו נקרעו אם נפרמו נפרמו עד שמגלה לבה,
He also undoes her hair.	וסותר את שערה.
Rabbi Yehuda says: "If her chest was lovely he would not expose it, and if her hair was lovely he would not undo it, on account of the young priests."	ר' יהודה אומ': "אם היה לבה נאה לא היה מגלהו, ואם היה שערה נאה לא היה סותרו מפני פרחי כהונה."

The ritual described is, simply put, a ritual of humiliation. The ripping of her clothing is a sign of contempt, as is exposure of her flesh. However, this humiliation ritual comes up against another value: the avoidance of sexual display. This clash of values is the reason for the debate. Whereas the first, unnamed, source maintains that one goes ahead with the ritual regardless, Rabbi Yehuda believes that if the woman is attractive, one does not expose her, as all arousing behavior needs to be avoided.[35] The Tosefta adds that this is due to concern that the younger priests will be aroused by the display.

Whichever opinion one follows, this ritual clearly stands out as unusual, even shocking. From the above sources, one is left wondering what the source for this ritual is. Does it derive from an interpretation of biblical verses? Is it an example of oral tradition, or is it perhaps a rabbinic enactment?[36] One possible answer to these questions can be found in a baraita found in the Babylonian Talmud (Sotah 8a):[37]

---

35. It is, of course, difficult to know how one would determine this, as attractiveness is a rather subjective concept.
36. An extensive reconstruction of the relationship between the biblical and rabbinic sotah ritual is found in Ishay Rosen-Zvi, *The Mishnaic Sotah Ritual: Temple, Gender, and Midrash* (Supplements to the Journal for the Study of Judaism 160; Leiden: Brill, 2012).
37. Many commentators feel that this baraita was originally part of the Sifre, but fell

> | And he shall expose the hair of the woman – I only know about her hair, from where can I learn that her body [should be exposed]? [The verse] comes to teach you: "the woman." | ופרע את ראש האשה - אין לי אלא ראשה, גופה מנין? ת״ל: האשה; |
> |---|---|
> | If so, what does the phrase "and he shall expose her hair" teach? It teaches that the priest must unravel her hair. | אם כן, מה ת״ל ופרע את ראשה? מלמד, שהכהן סותר את שערה. |

According to this baraita, both activities recorded in the Mishnah and Tosefta derive from an understanding of the biblical verse about the priest exposing the woman's hair. The interpretive hook is the reuse of the word "the woman." The verse could have simply read: "and the priest will stand the woman before God and expose *her* hair." Why does it restate the noun "woman" instead of using the pronoun "her"? The baraita suggests that this is in order to teach that the woman should be exposed, her body as well as her hair. The baraita then asks if the priest must expose her body, why even mention the exposure of her hair, which should be obvious, as it is less extreme than the exposure of flesh? The response of the baraita is somewhat enigmatic. The answer appears to be that the priest must do more than just expose her hair, but literally undo it, ostensibly from some sort of a braid or bun.

With the above sources providing context, it is now possible to attempt to tackle the Sifre:

> | And he shall expose the hair of the woman. – "The priest turns to [stand] behind her and exposes her [hair], as a fulfillment of the obligation to expose" – *so said Rabbi Yishmael*. | "ופרע את ראש האשה - "כהן נפנה לאחוריה ופורעה כדי לקיים בה מצות פריעה" - דברי ר' ישמעאל. |
> |---|---|
> | Alternatively: this teaches that the daughters of Israel cover their heads. And although there is no explicit proof to the matter, there is an indication: "And Tamar placed ashes (*epher*) upon her head, [and the striped coat which was upon her she | ד[בר] א[חר]: לימד על בנות ישראל שהן מכסות ראשיהן, ואע״פ שאין ראייה לדבר זכר לדבר: "ותקח תמר אפר על ראשה, [וכתנת הפסים אשר עליה קרעה ותשם ידה על |

---

out due to copyist error. Thank you to Gershon Klapper who closely examined the various manuscripts for alternative text versions in the course of editing. Mostly, the author has chosen not to discuss these issues in an already long book. They are rarely part of the discourse in the later periods.

tore, and putting her hand to her head, she went to and fro wailing]" (II Samuel 13:19).

Rabbi Yehuda said: "If the place he would be revealing is lovely, he does not reveal it, and if her hair is lovely, he does not undo it."

If she was dressed in white, they dress her in black. If the black garments looked nice on her, they would remove them and dress her in unattractive ones.

If she was wearing golden trinkets, necklaces, earrings or rings – they remove them from her in order to degrade her.

Rabbi Yochanan son of Beroka says: "One should not degrade Israelite women more than is explicitly stated in the Torah. Rather 'before God he should expose the woman's hair' – he would place a linen garment between himself and the people,

the priest would [then] face her back and expose her, in order to fulfill the commandment to expose."

They said to him: "In the same way that you have not expressed concern for the honor of the Almighty, so too one need not express concern for her honor, rather all of the above-mentioned degradation is practiced upon her.

ראשה ותלך הלוך וזעק[ה]".

ר' יהודה אומר: "אם היה בית חליצתה נאה לא היה מגלהו ואם היה שערה נאה לא היה סותרו."

היתה מכוסה לבנים מכסה שחורים, היו שחורים נאים לה מפשיטן ומלבישים אותה כעורים,

היו עליה כלי זהב קטלאות ונזמים וטבעות מסלקם הימנה כדי לנוולה.

ר' יוחנן בן ברוקה אומר: "אין מנוולים בנות ישראל יותר ממה שכתוב בתורה, אלא 'לפני ה' ופרע את ראש האשה' – סדין של בוץ היה פורס בינו לבין העם,

כהן פונה לאחוריה ופורעה כדי לקיים בה מצות פריעה."

אמרו לו: "כשם שלא חסת על כבוד המקום כך אין חסין על כבודה, אלא כל הניוול הזה מנוולה."

There are numerous difficulties in this text. In order to understand it, we will start with the second half of the passage, which is more straightforward.

Like the Mishnah, the second half of the Sifre passage begins with a description of various strategies (other than nudity) used to humiliate the woman. She is dressed in black or some alternative unflattering garment and her jewelry is removed. Unlike in the Mishnah, however, a conflicting view is recorded here. Rabbi Yochanan ben Beroka argues against the above position and states that it would be improper to degrade an Israelite woman any more than is specifically commanded in the Torah.

Furthermore, he uses this principle not only to protect the woman from the donning of unflattering clothing and removal of jewelry, but he applies it to the entire ritual described above. Although he does not (and cannot) argue that the woman's hair[38] is not exposed, he argues that no one is meant to see it. He supports his point with a midrash. Rabbi Yochanan ben Beroka rereads the syntax of the passage in Numbers, placing the phrase "before God" at the beginning of the next clause instead of at the end of the previous one. The verse would read: "before God he should expose the woman's hair" – before God only, not before men. How is one supposed to expose her hair before God but not before anyone else? He explains that this would be done by spreading a sheet before her which would block the people's view. The priest would then do the ritual of uncovering her hair from behind her so as to minimize her exposure even to himself.

The Sages argue with Rabbi Yochanan ben Beroka. They maintain that there is no reason to hide her exposure from the audience any more than there is to hide her exposure from God, and that there is no reason not to add to her public shaming by removing the jewelry and fine clothes. Needless to say, they do not accept his midrashic reading of the verse.

Turning now to the first half of this passage, matters are more complex. Beginning with Rabbi Yehuda, it is clear that the Sifre is quoting the position found in the Mishnah. In fact, with the exception of one change in terminology the two quotes are identical.[39] The problem here is that Rabbi Yehuda seems to be debating a non-existent interlocutor; after all, Rabbi Yishmael only mentioned exposing her hair, not her body. By bringing up the issue of the loveliness of "the place of her exposure," Rabbi Yehuda is offering an exception to an unstated rule. Presumably, Rabbi Yehuda made his statement in response to the first position in the Mishnah, and it has simply been transferred here by the editor of the Sifre without fitting it into the new context, but the presentation remains awkward.

Regarding Rabbi Yishmael's position, matters are even more opaque. Rabbi Yishmael seems to be using the exact same phrase as Rabbi Yochanan ben Beroka, but without his derasha and its concomitant halakhic application. The reason Rabbi Yochanan ben Beroka says that the priest should

---

38. Perhaps even her body.
39. The Sifre uses "place he is revealing" instead of "heart;" both, of course, are euphemistic for chest or breasts, although the Sifre's choice is, perhaps, a touch more delicate.

step behind her and fulfill the "obligation of exposing" is because he believes that the entire act is one of humiliating the woman before God, and that people, including the priest, should not actually see her in this state. This is also why he requires a sheet to be spread between her and the audience for this ceremony. However, Rabbi Yishmael mentions neither the sheet nor the repositioning of the clause "before God." Without these, the reason the priest should go behind her is virtually inexplicable.

Finally, it is unclear what the alternative position is supposed to convey in the context of this discussion. The alternative midrash claims that the import of the statement that the priest should expose her hair is to teach the reader that Israelite women should/must cover their hair. This suggestion brings up an important exegetical question. Should we understand this position as an argument with Rabbi Yishmael? If so, does this mean that Rabbi Yishmael does not believe Israelite women should cover their hair or simply that Numbers 5:18 is not the source for the practice? Similarly, does this mean that the alternative position believes that there is no need for the priest to stand behind the woman? Furthermore, if the unnamed Tanna is interpreting a verse in Numbers, what is the point of quoting the verse in Samuel as a hint? Since when did a midrash halakha require backup from another midrash halakha?!

Trying to make sense of all this, Malbim[40] examines Rabbi Yishmael's statements and suggests that he is deriving his position from a midrashic deduction from the verse. Commenting on Numbers 5:18, Malbim suggests that Rabbi Yishmael understands the phrase "the priest will stand the woman before God" as meaning that she must be directly facing God. Therefore, the priest must stand behind her in order not to obstruct God's view, as it were. This is similar to Rabbi Yochanan ben Beroka's point, although Rabbi Yishmael does not require a sheet since he does not accept the idea that the woman is to be humiliated before God only.

Insofar as how to explain the interrelationship between the three positions, I will consider two approaches. The first approach is to suggest that the primary debate is between Rabbi Yishmael and Rabbi Yehuda. In this approach, Rabbi Yishmael claims that one must reveal/undress the sotah. One can posit that he understands the addition of the word "woman" to mean that one must expose the entire woman including her head. Rabbi Yishmael never explicitly says that he must expose only

---

40. Rabbi Meïr Leibush Michel Weiser (1809–1879, Ukraine).

her head.[41] He merely states that the priest exposes the woman in order to fulfill the commandment to expose. To this position, Rabbi Yehuda responds and says that this would only apply if she is unattractive.

Although the simple understanding of Rabbi Yehuda's reasoning is that one is exempt from stripping an attractive woman because it would excite the male audience, Malbim offers an alternative suggestion. He claims that since the intent of revealing the sotah is to humiliate her, if she is lovely then by definition showing off her attractive figure would not be humiliating. Although this explanation is clearly not the one endorsed by the Tosefta, it could be plausibly understood within this context in the Sifre as an explanation for Rabbi Yehuda's disagreement with Rabbi Yishmael.

Having established this as the basic debate, one can understand the alternative unnamed position as a secondary augmentation of the text. The editor of the Sifre is merely pointing out that there is another understanding of the reason the verse mentions the exposing of hair when we know that her body is to be exposed: to teach the reader that her hair was covered, since this is the proper attire for an Israelite woman. In this sense, the term "alternatively" functions much the same way as a modern footnote or parentheses.

A second approach is the one suggested by Rabbi David Pardo[42] in his Tosefta commentary, *Chasdei David*. He argues that the text makes no sense as is, and that a section of the original text is missing. This missing section, he argues, is none other than the above mentioned baraita quoted in the Babylonian Talmud. According to this interpretation, the first section of the Sifre would read thus:

And he shall expose the hair of the woman – "The priest turns to [stand] behind her and exposes her [hair], as a fulfillment of the obligation to expose" – so said Rabbi Yishmael.	"ופרע את ראש האשה" - כהן נפנה לאחוריה ופורעה כדי לקיים בה מצות פריעה" - דברי ר' ישמעאל.
And he shall expose the hair of the woman – I only know about her hair, from where can I learn that her body [should be exposed]? It comes to teach you: "the woman."	ופרע את ראש האשה - אין לי אלא ראשה, גופה מנין? ת"ל: האשה; אם כן, מה ת"ל ופרע את

---

41. It is worth noting that when Josephus describes this section of the Torah (*Jew. Ant.* 3:270), he writes that the kohen should "remove the veil from her head" (τῆς κεφαλῆς τὸ ἱμάτιον ἀφελών). The veil is mentioned in other Hellenistic Period Jewish sources as well; see the excursus to this chapter for more discussion.
42. 1718–1792. b. Venice; d. Jerusalem.

If so, what does the phrase "and he shall expose her hair" teach? It teaches that the priest must unravel her hair.

מלמד, שהכהן סותר את שערה.

Alternatively: this teaches that the daughters of Israel cover their heads. And although there is no explicit proof to the matter, there is an indication: "And Tamar placed ashes (*epher*) upon her head, [and the striped coat which was upon her she tore, and putting her hand to her head, she went to and fro wailing]" (II Samuel 13:19).

ד[בר] א[חר]: לימד על בנות ישראל שהן מכסות ראשיהן, ואע"פ שאין ראייה לדבר זכר לדבר: "ותקח תמר אפר על ראשה, [וכתנת הפסים אשר עליה קרעה ותשם ידה על ראשה ותלך הלוך וזעקה]."

Rabbi Yehuda said: "If the place he would be revealing is lovely, he does not reveal it, and if her hair is lovely, he does not undo it."

ר' יהודה אומר: "אם היה בית חליצתה נאה לא היה מגלהו ואם היה שערה נאה לא היה סותרו."

Although this approach is rather speculative, considering the total lack of manuscript or variant evidence, it nevertheless neatly solves some of the problems. First, it allows one to interpret Rabbi Yishmael as only referring to the uncovering of hair. His only point is to say that the priest should not be standing between the tabernacle and the woman.

In Rabbi Pardo's read, it is in fact a new derasha, with a new *sub verbo*, which first suggests that the woman's body along with her hair must be exposed. It is to this position that Rabbi Yehuda objects, stating that it only applies if the woman is unattractive. The contrast between Rabbi Yehuda's position and that of this first derasha is particularly poignant, since they both use the same, rare, term for the undoing or unraveling of the woman's hair: "סתר." Finally, the alternative view reads more smoothly in this version as well. This view states that the word "head" is not there to teach that the priest must unravel her hair, but rather to teach that women do (or should) in fact, cover their heads.

Whichever approach one takes, one difficulty that remains is trying to understand the point of the alternative view. The difficulty is twofold. First, it is unclear whether the midrash means to say that the verse teaches that women must cover their hair, i.e., an objective biblical obligation, or that women did cover their hair, i.e., a subjective societal obligation. Second, if this position means to derive a normative rule from a verse in the Torah, why does it then attempt to defend this derasha with an interpretation of a verse in Samuel? This is highly irregular for the Sifre.

I would suggest that the best way to interpret this line in the Sifre is to state that the midrash is simply positing a fact: the verse teaches that Israelite women cover their hair as a part of their general modest comportment. In other words, there is no specific requirement for a woman to do so, but since it was an entrenched part of their modest dress, the priest was commanded to remove even this covering. Since the Tanna feels that this is an unusual deduction to make from a verse, he then attempts to demonstrate its plausibility by showing that Tamar covered her hair.[43]

BARAITA (FROM BAVLI SOTAH)

In the Babylonian Talmud, a baraita is recorded that attempts to explain the reasoning behind the punishments of the sotah, including the exposure of her hair (b. Sotah 8b–9a).

Rabbi used to say: "How does one know that a person is measured by the measures he has used? For it says: "by *se'ase'ah* (measure-measure),[44] by sending out you received back" (Is. 27:8). I know this only for the *seah* measure, how do I know this principle applies to a *tirkav* and half a *tirkav*, a *kav* and half a *kav*, a *rova* and half a *rova*, *tuman* and *ukhla*?[45] The verse teaches: "for every *seon se'an* with stamping"[46] (Is. 9:4). How do I know that every penny combines to form one great debt? For it says: "One on one to find a debt" (Eccl. 7:27).[47]	היה רבי אומר: מנין שבמדה שאדם מודד בה מודדין לו? שנאמר: 'בסאסאה בשלחה תריבנה' (ישעיהו כז:ח); אין לי אלא סאה, מנין לרבות תרקב וחצי תרקב, קב וחצי קב, רובע וחצי רובע, תומן ועוכלא מנין? תלמוד לומר (ישעיהו ט:ד): 'כי כל סאון סואן ברעש.' ומנין שכל פרוטה ופרוטה מצטרפת לחשבון גדול? תלמוד לומר (קהלת ז:כז): 'אחת לאחת למצוא חשבון'.

---

43. How the verse in Samuel is meant to demonstrate this point is unclear. The Malbim suggests that the Tanna is translating the term *epher* in its less usual meaning of "cloth," as it is used in 1 Kings 20:38. The Vilna Gaon suggests in his commentary on the Tosefta that this interpretation derives from the end of the verse where Tamar puts her hand on her head.
44. Literally, the word means something like "expulsion," but Rabbi is using the fact that the word looks like the word *se'ah* (measure) doubled as the basis for his homiletic angle.
45. Smaller measures implying smaller sins.
46. Literally, this phrase means something like "for all the boots of the stamping soldiers," however, following Rabbi's derasha, the words should be understood as "miniature se'ahs," with the final *nun* understood as a diminutive. See Maharsha's *Chiddushei Aggadot* ad loc.
47. This is probably meant as an expression to convey that Ecclesiastes put together

We found the same with the *sotah*. The measure with which she measured she is measured by.

1. She stood before the entrance of her house to attract him; therefore, the kohen stands her before Nicanor Gate and shows her humiliation to all.
2. She covered her hair with beautiful ribbons; therefore, the kohen removes the covering from her hair and places it between her feet.
3. She adorned her face for him, therefore her face turns green.
4. She put on eye makeup for him, therefore her eyes bulge out.
5. She coiffed her hair for him, therefore the kohen undoes her hair.
6. She beckoned him with her finger, therefore her fingernails fall out.
7. She wore a *strophion* of netting;[48] therefore the kohen brings an Egyptian rope and ties it above her breasts.
8. She spread her thighs for him; therefore, her thigh collapses.
9. She accepted him upon her belly; therefore, her abdomen swells.
10. She fed him dainties [of the] world; therefore, she is fed animal fodder.
11. She gave him fine wine to drink in fancy cups; therefore, the kohen gives her bitter water to drink from an earthen vessel.

וכן מצינו בסוטה, שבמדה שמדדה בה מדדו לה;

א. היא עמדה על פתח ביתה ליראות לו, לפיכך כהן מעמידה על שער נקנור ומראה קלונה לכל;
ב. היא פרסה לו סודרין נאין על ראשה, לפיכך כהן נוטל כפה מעל ראשה ומניחו תחת רגליה;
ג. היא קשטה לו פניה, לפיכך פניה מוריקות;
ד. היא כחלה לו עיניה, לפיכך עיניה בולטות;
ה. היא קלעה לו את שערה, לפיכך כהן סותר את שערה;
ו. היא הראתה לו באצבע, לפיכך ציפורניה נושרות;
ז. היא חגרה לו בציצול, לפיכך כהן מביא חבל המצרי וקושר לה למעלה מדדיה;
ח. היא פשטה לו את יריכה, לפיכך יריכה נופלת;
ט. היא קיבלתו על כריסה, לפיכך בטנה צבה;
י. היא האכילתו מעדני עולם, לפיכך קרבנה מאכל בהמה;
יא. היא השקתהו יין משובח בכוסות משובחים, לפיכך כהן משקה מים המרים במקידה של חרש;

---

pieces of evidence to explain a matter, but Rabbi takes it literally as part of his derasha, making it refer to the debt one owes for cumulative sins.

48. Also called apodesmos (in Latin either *strophium* or *mamillare*); this was a belt undergarment used to accentuate the breasts.

12. She acted in secret, [therefore] "the one who "dwells in secret with the Most High" (Ps. 91:1) pays her heed, as it says: "The eye of the adulterer watches the night, saying: 'no eye will see me'" (Job 24:15).

   יב. היא עשתה בסתר, 'יושב בסתר עליון' (תהלים צא:א) שם בה פנים, שנאמר: 'ועין נואף שמרה נשף לאמר לא תשורני עין וגו'' (איוב כד:טו);

13. Another interpretation: She acted in secret, the Omnipresent made it known in public, as it says: "Hatred may be concealed with trickery, but his evil will be revealed in public" (Prov. 26:26).

   יג. דבר אחר: היא עשתה בסתר, המקום פירסמה בגלוי, שנאמר: 'תכסה שנאה במשאון תגלה רעתו בקהל (וגו')' (משלי כו:כו).

This source makes two separate references to the practice of the unfaithful woman with respect to her hair. In the first example (#2), the baraita states that the woman accentuated her hair with ribbons. In the second example (#5), the woman is said to have coiffed or done up her hair for her lover. Ostensibly, these hairstyles would have made her more attractive; otherwise the behavior would not fit into the paradigm the baraita is creating. The punishment for this behavior is the removal of the *kippah* (covering) on her head and the undoing or messing up of her hair.

The simple understanding of this source is that the author is either unaware or unconcerned with the idea that it would be immodest for a woman to go out with her hair uncovered or undone. One can deduce this from the fact that the behaviors that trouble the author of the baraita are the placing of decorative ribbons in her hair and the styling of her hair, not the exposure of her hair. In fact, the baraita does not discuss exposure at all. It either refers to the seduction (1–7, 10–12) or the act of infidelity (8–9, 13).

According to this source, what would be considered seductive behavior and dress is very context- and culture-specific. By standing outside her house, wearing eyeshadow, doing up her hair, putting in ribbons, and beckoning a young man, she has implied an interest in forbidden activity and is punished through the sotah ritual. It is possible that in the previously discussed context, i.e., public crass behavior, something less than actual interest in sin is implied, which is why the punishment is less, i.e., divorce without payment of the ketubah. Again, what we see from the early sources is that the woman's behavior is understood contextually, not with a set of objectified clothing requirements; after all, no one has suggested that eyeliner or ribbons are forbidden according to halakha.

Conclusion

In this chapter, we surveyed numerous references to hair covering and exposure of hair in the Tannaitic literature. In all of them, we found that exposed hair was considered by the Tannaim to be immodest on par with flirtation and other forms of provocative behavior.

These behaviors do not appear in lists of acceptable clothing for women or halakhic descriptions of required dress and behavior. Rather, they appear as behaviors that are assumed to be viscerally understood by the reader as outrageous. A woman who behaves or dresses in this manner has clearly humiliated her husband and lost her rights to a ketubah. So too, if one were to force a woman into one of these behaviors, by, for instance, forcibly exposing her hair in public, one would pay her a fine for the public humiliation.

The subjective nature of the list is clear from the equivalent cases quoted in the various Tannaitic sources. A woman's public quasi-exposure is compared in its level of humiliation for her husband to the humiliation she would feel if her husband forced her to speak about intimate secrets in public, or even if he forced her to sift through garbage. Sifting through garbage, of course, is not a prohibition, but it may be humiliating depending on societal norms and one's circumstances.

Similarly, the forcible exposure of a woman's hair is compared by the Mishnah to giving a man a backhanded slap. Again, a backhanded slap does not even qualify as bruising, in the technical halakhic sense, but clearly in Tannaitic society it was considered such a public shaming that one would be forced to pay double the average ketubah payment as a fine! It would seem that the Tannaim understood hair exposure as an egregiously immodest or provocative behavior in their society, which is why the fine in such a case was so large.

The only Tannaitic source which seems to imply that there may be an actual prohibition, perhaps even a biblical one, for a woman to expose her hair is from the alternative derasha in the Sifre. Nevertheless, I have shown that even in this case, the simplest and least problematic read of this source is to say that it too only means to demonstrate that the *custom* of Israelite women to cover their hair in public stems from time immemorial, since the Torah itself commands the priest to expose her hair during the sotah ritual.

In the next chapter we will look at the Amoraic sources regarding exposure of hair, and see that matters become more complicated.

Excursus One: Hair Covering in Apocrypha Works of Susanna and the Maccabees

In addition to the rabbinic sources, there are also some hints in other Jewish works from the Second Temple period that it was considered standard for women's heads to be covered.

SUSANNA

One example of this is from the story of Susanna. This is a story that appears in the Greek book of Daniel and functioned as an alternative opening to the book. In this story, an attractive and pious married woman named Susanna is aggressively propositioned by two "elders" of the community. After she turns them away, they invent a trumped-up charge of adultery against her, with the two of them acting as the witnesses. The ruse almost works until Daniel arrives on the scene, having been sent by God, and demonstrates the falsity of their claim by a shrewd interrogation of the witnesses.

For our purposes, the important part of the story is when she is brought before the court (verse 32). As there are two textual versions of this story, we will quote from both.[49]

καὶ προσέταξαν οἱ παράνομοι ἀποκαλύψαι αὐτήν ἵνα ἐμπλησθῶσι κάλλους ἐπιθυμίας αὐτῆς (Old Greek)	And the scoundrels ordered to uncover her, in order that they could be sated with her beauty.
οἱ δὲ παράνομοι ἐκέλευσαν ἀποκαλυφθῆναι αὐτήν ἦν γὰρ κατακεκαλυμμένη ὅπως ἐμπλησθῶσιν τοῦ κάλλους αὐτῆς (Theodotion)	Then the scoundrels commanded that she be uncovered, *for she was veiled*, so that they could be sated with her beauty.

From both versions of the story, it is clear that Susanna was covered in some way, and that uncovering her in the public forum of the court was both insulting to her and erotic to the male viewers. Even more interesting is the description of this covering in the small addition (or gloss) in the Theodotion text; she was veiled. Presumably this refers to a headdress of sorts that covers both the hair and, perhaps, the face.

---

49. The English translation of both versions is taken from Albert Pietersma and Benjamin G. Wright (eds.), *The New English Translation of the Septuagint* (New York: Oxford University Press, 2007), 989. For an introduction and commentary, see Matthias Henze, "The Story of Susanna and the Elders," in *Outside the Bible: Ancient Jewish Writings Related to Scripture*, ed. Louis H. Feldman, James L. Kugel, and Lawrence H. Schiffman (3 vols.; Philadelphia: JPS), 1:123–28.

3 MACCABEES

Another example can be found in what is known as the third book of Maccabees (although the name is somewhat of a misnomer since there are no Maccabees in the book.) The story is about King Ptolemy Philopater, ruler of Egypt, and his attempt to annihilate the Jews. According to the story, after defeating Antiochus of Syria, Ptolemy takes enormous offense at the refusal of the priests of the Jerusalem Temple to let him enter the Holy of Holies.

In response, upon returning to Egypt, he starts making laws in an attempt to force Jews to violate the Torah and join the cult of Dionysus. When this has only limited success, he starts rounding up Jews throughout Egypt. When even this does not seem to have a sufficient effect, he calls Hermon the elephantarch and orders him to get his elephants mad with drink and trample the Jewish neighborhoods in an attempt to kill everyone. The plan falters for one reason after another, with God's intervention. Finally, when Hermon arrives at the Jewish quarter, a pious man named Eliezer prays to God in Mosaic style, asking for help, and it is granted. Two angels appear and frighten the Egyptian-Greek army, and the elephants scatter. At this point, Ptolemy sees the error of his ways and the Jews are granted freedom and a seven-day holiday, which is observed by the Egyptian Jewish community yearly, at least up to the time the book was written down.

For us, the important reference to hair covering occurs in the section where the Jews are being gathered together for slaughter (4:6).[50]

| αἱ δὲ ἄρτι πρὸς βίου κοινωνίαν γαμικὸν ὑπεληλυθυῖαι παστὸν νεάνιδες ἀντὶ τέρψεως μεταλαβοῦσαι γόους καὶ κόνει τὴν μυροβρεχῆ πεφυρμέναι κόμην ἀκαλύπτως δὲ ἀγόμεναι θρῆνον ἀνθ' ὑμεναίων ὁμοθυμαδὸν ἐξῆρχον ὡς ἐσπαραγμέναι σκυλμοῖς ἀλλοεθνέσιν | Young women, who had just now entered the bridal chamber for the partnership of married life, soon exchanged their joy for mourning, and mingled ashes into hair still wet with unguent, and as they were led away *unveiled*, it was a dirge rather than a wedding song, they started up one and all, savaged by the barbarous cruelties of a foreign nation. |

---

50. All translations of 3 Maccabees are from: Pietersma and Wright, NETS, 523–529. For introduction and commentary, see Sara Raup Johnson, "3 Maccabees," in *Outside the Bible*, 3:2681–2707.

Again, one can see from the description of the women as having been led off "unveiled," that this was unusual and somewhat of a humiliation for them. It would further seem, at least from this text, that it was specifically married women who wore the veil, since this detail was left out of the description of the women in a different section (1:18).

αἵ τε κατάκλειστοι παρθένοι ἐν θαλάμοις σὺν ταῖς τεκούσαις ἐξώρμησαν καὶ ἀπέδωκαν κόνει τὰς κόμας πασάμεναι γόου τε καὶ στεναγμῶν ἐνεπίμπλων τὰς πλατείας	Cloistered virgins in their chambers rushed out with their mothers, sprinkled their hair with ashes, and began filling the streets with weeping and groaning.

Like the newly married women of Chapter 4, these virgins sprinkle their hair with ashes. However, there is no description of their coming out "unveiled." This could be because they were veiled, but most probably it reflects a practice where married women wore a veil and single women did not.

Finally, the fact that there was a state between veiled on the one hand and totally exposed on the other can be seen in this text as well, albeit from an unusual source. At the very beginning of the book, when the forces of Ptolemy Philopater and Antiochus are doing battle, there is a point where it appears that Ptolemy may lose. At this moment of desperation, Ptolemy's sister Arsinoe goes out to rally the troops (1:4).

γενομένης δὲ καρτερᾶς μάχης καὶ τῶν πραγμάτων μᾶλλον ἐρρωμένων τῷ Ἀντιόχῳ ἱκανῶς ἡ Ἀρσινόη ἐπιπορευσαμένη τὰς δυνάμεις παρεκάλει μετὰ οἴκτου καὶ δακρύων τοὺς πλοκάμους λελυμένη βοηθεῖν ἑαυτοῖς τε καὶ τοῖς τέκνοις καὶ γυναιξὶν θαρραλέως ἐπαγγελλομένη δώσειν νικήσασιν ἑκάστῳ δύο μνᾶς χρυσίου	A fierce battle ensued, and things began to fare considerably better for Antiochus, at which point Arsinoe *let down her hair* and began passing through the ranks, exhorting them with wailing and tears to come to the aid of both themselves, their children and their wives, boldly promising to give each of them two minas of gold should they be victorious.

Although Arsinoe is not a Jewish woman, and the reader does not know whether she is married or single, it would seem that, in general, she would not appear publicly with her hair undone; presumably it would have been coiffed or braided in some way. The status of coiffed or braided hair will receive serious attention in the next chapter.

CHAPTER 2

Exposed Hair in Amoraic Sources: Diverse Approaches to Modesty in the Talmud

THIS CHAPTER REVIEWS THE DISCUSSION OF IMMODEST behavior and exposed hair in both Talmuds. It serves as an introduction to the key Talmudic texts, provides context, and explains their interrelationship. The next few chapters focus on the normative Jewish law and aim to explain the Talmudic texts introduced here. The chapter starts with a discussion in the Jerusalem Talmud on causes of divorce and then explains the Bavli source on this same topic; then it reviews the closely related sources on rumors of impropriety and divorce in the Bavli. It is followed by the discussion in both Talmuds of conduct by the wife which indicates that adultery or other impropriety has taken place and then addresses cases of other misconduct. Finally, after reviewing all of these cases, this chapter explains sources related to hair covering directly or by implication and other related types of nudity in the Jerusalem and Babylonian Talmuds. This chapter concludes by noting that only one text in the Babylonian Talmud suggests that a woman appearing in public with uncovered hair may be a Torah prohibition.

Introduction

The issue of women's exposed hair is taken up in a number of places in both Talmuds. This chapter will present the various Talmudic discussions, focusing on how each source views the nature of the requirement. As I will try to demonstrate, there is some tension between the sources, leading to several of the complications in describing the halakhic requirements which will appear in the literature of the Rishonim.

Gittin

JERUSALEM TALMUD

As we saw in the previous chapter, one of the main contexts for the rabbinic discussion of women's exposed hair is the context of divorce for the wife's improper behavior. In this context, exposed hair was part of a list of immodest behaviors which would allow a woman to be divorced without payment of her ketubah.

This section will begin with the Jerusalem Talmud's response to the final mishnah in m. Gittin (9:11), which describes the debate between Beit Shammai and Beit Hillel regarding reasons for divorce (y. Gittin 9:11). The baraita with which the Talmud begins its discussion should be familiar, as it was already discussed in the previous chapter:

Has it not been taught: Beit Shammai says: "I only know [from the use of the term sexual] that a woman is divorced due to sexual matters alone. From where does one learn that if she goes out with her hair exposed, the sides [of her clothing] in tatters, or her arms exposed [that she is to be divorced?] [The verse] teaches: 'for he found in her some base matter.'"[1]	והא תני: בית שמאי אומרי': "אין לי אלא היוצא משום ערוה בלבד ומניין היוצאה וראשה פרוע צדדיה פרומין וזרועותיה חלוצות? תלמוד לומר: 'כי מצא בה ערות דבר.'"
How would [Beit Hillel] interpret [the phrase glossed] by Beit Shammai?[2] [The term 'base' was included] so that one would not think that a woman who is divorced due to sexual impropriety would be forbidden [to remarry] but if she were divorced for some other reason she would be permitted.[3]	מה מקיימין דבית שמאי? שלא תאמר היוצא משום ערוה אסור, משום דבר אחר מותרת.

---

1. This baraita appears in y. Sotah 1:1 as well, in a slightly different context.
2. Beit Shammai has now explained how they understand both the terms *base* and *matter*, but Beit Hillel has only explained how they understand the term *matter*. The Talmud wants to know now how they understand the term *base*.
3. This is very similar to the argument put forward in the name of Beit Hillel by the Tosefta that was discussed in the previous chapter.

Rabbi Sheyla from Kfar Temarta said: "This verse is a problem for Beit Shammai: 'her former husband, who sent her away, cannot take her again to be his wife.' How is this to be interpreted? If the intent [of the verse] is to forbid her to her former husband – she is already forbidden to him![4] Rather, the verse must be interpreted as adding another prohibition [on top of the already existing one.]"

אמ' ר' שילא דכפר תמרתא: "קרייא מקשי על דבית שמאי: 'לא יוכל בעלה הראשון אשר שלחה לשוב לקחתה.' מה אנן מקיימין? אם לאוסרה עליו – כבר היא אסורה לו! אלא כן אנן קיימין ליתן עליו בלא תעשה."

The guiding principle of this text is that in order to explain the unusual compound term "base matter" both Beit Shammai and Beit Hillel are required to learn two halakhot each, one from each term. Beit Shammai believes that divorce is only permitted in cases of sexual impropriety, which they learn from the term "base." With this as the premise, they argue that the term "matter" simply points to a slight extension of this law: a woman can also be divorced for behavior that resembles (or leads to) sexual impropriety.

Beit Hillel, on the other hand, believes that a woman can be divorced by her husband for any complaint against her no matter how trivial or unrelated to sexual impropriety. This they learn from the term "matter." Following this, they argue that the term "base" was included to show parity between base matters and other matters. This would have relevance specifically to the next part of the verse, where she remarries. Beit Hillel claims that the verse wants to point out that no matter why she was divorced, even if it was for a sexual violation, every divorced woman has the right to remarry. This point is highly reminiscent of the Sifre discussed in the previous chapter.

For the purposes of this chapter, the key point is that according to the Jerusalem Talmud, Beit Shammai has included the behaviors that resemble or lead to sexual impropriety under the rubric of "base matter" and seems to require divorce in such a case. As was argued in the previous chapter, it is difficult to assume that this list was meant either as exhaustive or as objective, especially considering the variability of the behaviors mentioned. Beit Shammai's point seems to be that behaviors suggestive

---

4. I.e., since she was unfaithful.

of adultery are reasons to allow (or require) a divorce. One would assume that the list requires updating in every society.

BABYLONIAN TALMUD

The Babylonian Talmud (b. Gittin 90a–b) takes up the same question of how Beit Shammai and Beit Hillel understand the use of both terms and will even quote the Tosefta. However, the Babylonian Talmud does not appear to quote the Jerusalem Talmud's baraita, and will answer the question on Beit Shammai's behalf very differently, by invoking a *gezera shava*, connecting this verse with the section about testimony, and claiming that the adultery requires two witnesses.[5]

Nevertheless, the same list and requirement for divorce will appear in the Babylonian Talmud's treatment of this Mishnah as well, albeit stemming from a different source and with a slightly different version:

Rav Mesharshia said to Rava: "If [a man] has his mind set upon divorcing [his wife], yet she remains with him and attends to him – what then?" [Rava replied:] "He is the referent of the verse: 'Do not plan evil against your fellow while he remains secure with your [good will].'"[6]	א״ל רב משרשיא לרבא: אם לבו לגרשה והיא יושבת תחתיו ומשמשתו, מהו? קרי עליה: ׳אל תחרש על רעך רעה והוא יושב לבטח אתך.׳
It was taught: Rabbi Meir used to say: "Just as there are attitudes towards food, so too are there attitudes towards women.	תניא: היה רבי מאיר אומר: כשם שהדעות במאכל כך דעות בנשים.
There is a type of man who, when a fly falls into his cup, throws it out but won't drink [the wine]. This was the way of Pappos ben Yehuda, who would lock the door on his wife and leave.	יש לך אדם שזבוב נופל לתוך כוסו וזורקו ואינו שותהו וזו היא מדת פפוס בן יהודה, שהיה נועל בפני אשתו ויוצא.
There is a type of man who, when a fly falls into his cup, he throws it out and then drinks from it – this is the character of the average man, who [sees his wife] speaking with her *brothers* or relatives and leaves her to do so.	ויש לך אדם שזבוב נופל לתוך כוסו וזורקו ושותהו, וזו היא מדת כל אדם, שמדברת עם אחיה וקרוביה ומניחה;

---

5. Since this understanding has no bearing on the issue of exposed hair, this chapter will not be taking up the Bavli's version of this debate and will begin in the middle of the text where the relevant subject begins to be addressed.
6. Proverbs 3:29.

EXPOSED HAIR IN AMORAIC SOURCES 39

There is a type of man who, when a fly falls on his tray, he sucks on it and eats it – this is the character of a wicked man, who sees his wife	ויש לך אדם שזבוב נופל לתוך תמחוי מוצצו ואוכלו, זו היא מדת אדם רע, שרואה את אשתו
a. going out with her hair exposed,	יוצאה וראשה פרוע,
b. weaving in the public marketplace	וטווה בשוק,
c. going out with the sides [of her clothing] in tatters,	ופרומה משני צדדיה,
d. or washing with men.	ורוחצת עם בני אדם.
Do you really mean to say with men?	עם בני אדם ס"ד?
Rather, [she washes] in the same place as the men.[7]	אלא במקום שבני אדם רוחצין.
Such [a woman] it is a mitzvah from the Torah to divorce, as it says: "for he found some base fault in her, etc., and she leaves him and goes and [becomes the wife] of another man…" – The verse calls him "another" meaning to say that he is not really similar to the first man, since [the first man] sent this evil [woman] away from his house, but this one welcomes the evil [woman] in. The second man, if he has merit will send her away, as it says, "and the latter man hates her." If not, she will bury him, as it says: "or if the latter man dies…" – this man is worthy of death, since [the first man] removed the evil [woman] from his house but this one brought the evil [woman] into his house.	זו מצוה מן התורה לגרשה, שנאמר: "כי מצא בה ערות וגו' ושלחה מביתו…והלכה והיתה לאיש אחר, הכתוב קראו אחר, לומר, שאין זה בן זוגו לראשון, זה הוציא רשעה מביתו וזה הכניס רשעה לתוך ביתו - זכה שני - שלחה, שנאמר: ושנאה האיש האחרון, ואם לאו - קוברתו, שנאמר: 'או כי ימות האיש האחרון' - כדאי הוא במיתה, שזה הוציא רשעה מביתו וזה הכניס רשעה לתוך ביתו.
'For detests divorce'[8] – Rabbi Yehuda says: "If you detest her, divorce [her]." Rabbi Yochanan says: "One who divorces is detested."	'כי שנא שלח' - ר' יהודה אומר: אם שנאתה שלח, ר' יוחנן אומר: שנאוי המשלח.
They are not really arguing; one is referring to a first marriage and one to a second marriage. For Rabbi Elazar said: "Anyone who	ולא פליגי: הא בזוג ראשון, הא בזוג שני; דאמר ר' אלעזר: כל המגרש אשתו ראשונה -

---

7. I.e., but not at the same time.
8. Malachi 2:16.

divorces his first wife, even the altar sheds tears for him, as it says: 'And further, this you do: You cover the altar of God with tears, weeping, and sighing; He refuses to acknowledge the gift [anymore] or to accept the offering of your hands. Yet you say: "Because of what?" Because God testifies between you and the wife of your youth with whom you have broken faith, though she is your companion and the wife of your covenant.'"⁹

אפילו מזבח מוריד עליו דמעות, שנאמר: וזאת שנית תעשו כסות דמעה את מזבח ה' בכי ואנקה מאין [עוד] פנות אל המנחה ולקחת רצון מידכם, ואמרתם על מה על כי ה' העיד בינך ובין אשת נעוריך אשר אתה בגדתה בה והיא חברתך ואשת בריתך.

Although the section relevant to this chapter is the Babylonian Talmud's reiteration of the Tosefta, it is worth first noting the overall context in which the Tosefta passage is brought.

The section of the Mishnah being analyzed in this part of the Talmudic text is the position of Rabbi Akiva. Rabbi Akiva believes that a man can divorce his wife without any cause relevant to her, but merely because he would like to marry someone else. The Talmud, although not disputing the technical correctness of this position, nevertheless puts great weight on the importance of remaining married and the inappropriate nature of frivolous divorce. The quote from the Tosefta is bracketed by Rava's critique of one who secretly desires to divorce his wife and the discussion of the weeping altar and the hatred God feels for one who divorces his first wife, presumably for frivolous reasons.

Considering the above, the Tosefta here stands out as a sort of compromise position. Whereas one should not mistreat or divorce one's wife for frivolous reasons, a man should divorce his wife if her behavior is improper.

Looking at the text of the Tosefta as quoted in the Babylonian Talmud, a number of differences stand out:

a. In the Tosefta, there are four types of men, whereas in the Babylonian Talmud's text there are only three. This is particularly odd since the case that is skipped is the case of the man who secretly wishes to divorce his wife, the exact case discussed by Rav Mesharshia and Rava! It is difficult to know what to make of this difference and if there is any significance to it other than textual variance.

---

9. Malachi 2:13–14.

b. The case of Pappos ben Yehuda is presented more radically in the Babylonian Talmud. In the Tosefta, the action is presented in the past simple tense, and seems to mean that he locked the door and left her, never to return. However, in the Bavli it is presented in the modal form, indicating that this is something that he would regularly do. The picture is of a man who did not trust his wife and left her locked in the house day in and day out.[10]

c. In the Tosefta, the "normal woman" would speak with *neighbors* and family, whereas in the Bavli's text it is *brothers* and family. Looking at this together with the previous example suggests that the Bavli's tradition is somewhat stricter than that of the Tosefta. In the Tosefta, normal women speak with their neighbors and bad husbands walk out on their wives for this; whereas in the Bavli, normal women speak with their brothers and bad husbands keep them locked up as prisoners in their own houses for this.

d. The list of behaviors in the Tosefta includes both provocative behavior and arrogant or insulting behavior. The Bavli mentions only the former.

e. The editors of the Talmud interrupt the quote of the Tosefta to interject that it is impossible to take the statement "washing with other men" at its word. The Talmud seems to be saying that it is one thing for a woman to act provocatively, but bathing with other men is more akin to adultery than flirtation and is so outlandish a behavior as to be unworthy of mention in a list of this nature. No matter how one understands these differences, it appears that the Babylonian Talmud's point in quoting this Tosefta is to strike a balance between the permissive positions of Rabbi Akiva and Beit Hillel and the strict position of Beit Shammai.[11]

---

10. This fits well with the Bavli's tradition that Pappos's wife was, eventually, unfaithful to him; a good example of a self-fulfilling prophecy (b. Shabbat 104b; b. Sanhedrin 67a).

11. It is worth noting that the Jerusalem Talmud quotes this Tosefta once as well (y. Sotah 1:7), and has the exact opposite approach, listing only arrogant behavior towards servants and none of the sexually provocative behaviors. For the sake of completion, the text of the Jerusalem Talmud is included below:

| Rabbi Meir used to say: Just as there are attitudes towards food and drink, so too are there attitudes amongst men. | תני בשם רבי מאיר כשם שיש דיעות במאכל ובמשתה כך יש דיעות באנשים |

The point seems to be that whereas a husband should try his hardest not to invoke the divorce option for insignificant differences or dislikes he may have formed regarding his wife, nevertheless, if his wife exhibits certain inappropriate behaviors like the ones listed by Rabbi Meir, it would be a mitzvah to divorce her.

In the Bavli, this list consists exclusively of (moderate) public displays of sexuality. As stated in Chapter 1, this position only makes sense if the list is socially determined, requiring culturally relevant adaptation in any given situation.

There is a type of man who, when a fly falls into his cup, he removes it, throws it out and then drinks from it – this is the character of the average man, who sees his wife speaking with her neighbors or relatives.	יש לך אדם זבוב נופל לתוך כוסו והוא נוטלו וזורקו ושותהו זה כשאר כל האדם שהוא רואה את אשתו מדברת עם שכיניה ועם קרוביה
Or there is a type of man who, when a fly flies over his cup, removes it and pours out [the wine] and won't taste it – this is a bad attitude for the man, since he is intent on divorcing his wife.	או יש לך אדם שפורח זבוב על גבי כוסו והוא נוטלו ושופכו ואינו טועמו זה הוא חלק רע באנשים שנתן עיניו בה לגרשה
And there is a type of man who, when a fly settles on his cup, removes it and then leaves the cup as is. This is Pappos ben Yehuda, who locked the door on his wife.	ויש לך אדם זבוב שוכן על כוסו והוא נוטלו ומניחו כמות שהוא זה פפוס בן יהודה שנעל את הדלת בפני אשתו
They said to him: "Did your fathers behave this way?!"	אמרין ליה: "נהיגין הוון אבהתך עבדין כן".
There is a type of man who, when a fly dies in his cup, he removes it, sucks on it, and drinks [the wine] – this is the character of a wicked man, who sees his wife a. behaving arrogantly with her slaves, b. behaving arrogantly with her maidservants,	יש לך אדם זבוב מת לתוך כיוסו והו' נוטלו ומוצצו ושותיהו זה הרשע שהו' רואה את אשתו א. לבה גס בעבדיה ב. ליבה גס בשפחותיה
[Such a woman] it is a mitzvah to divorce, as it says: "and she leaves him and goes and [becomes the wife] of another man..." – The verse calls him "another" because he is not really similar to the first man, since [the first man] sent away his wife for her baseness, but this one comes and falls into her trap.	והוא מצוה עליה לגרשה שנ': 'ויצאה מביתו והלכה והיתה לאיש אחר', הכתוב קראו אחר שאינו בן זוג של ראשון שהוא הוציא את אשתו משום ערוה והלה נכשל בה.
[The second man], if he has merit in the eyes of heaven, he will divorce her. If not, she will end up burying him, as it says: "or if the latter man dies..." – this man is worthy of death, since he brought this woman into his house.	אם זכה הוא לשמים הרי הוא מגרשה ואם לאו סוף שהיא קוברתו שנ': 'או כי ימות האיש האחרון' ראוי היה זה למיתה שהאשה הזאת הכניס לתוך ביתו.

Rumors and Improper Public Behavior

In the Mishnah just before that of the debate between Beit Shammai and Beit Hillel, there is a discussion of rumors about a woman's marital status and their believability. On this Mishnah, the following *sugya* (a passage from the Gemara discussing a specific issue in the Mishnah) appears (b. Gittin 89a):

Rava said: "If a rumor spreads in town that she has committed adultery, we ignore it." Why is that? People simply witnessed vulgar behavior [and assumed the worst].	אמר רבא: "יצא לה שם מזנה בעיר – אין חוששין לה." מ"ט? פריצותא בעלמא הוא דחזו לה.
This is in line with a Tannaitic position, for it was taught: Rabbi Meir said: "If she eats in the market place, if she quaffs[12] in the marketplace, or if she nurses in the marketplace – for any of these she may be divorced." Rabbi Akiva says: "Even at the point where the women gossip about her by the moonlight." Rabbi Yochanan ben Nuri responded: "If so, you have not left even one daughter of our father Abraham living with her husband! Yet the Torah said (Deut. 24:1): 'You found some base *matter* in her,' and in another place [the Torah says] (Deut. 17:6): 'Upon the testimony of two or three witnesses the *matter* should be established.' Just as in the latter case the matter must be clear, so too in the former case the matter must be clear."	כתנאי: אכלה בשוק, גירגרה בשוק, הניקה בשוק – בכולן ר"מ אומר: "תצא." ר"ע אומר: "משישאו ויתנו בה מוזרות בלבנה." אמר לו רבי יוחנן בן נורי: "א"כ, לא הנחת בת לאברהם אבינו שיושבת תחת בעלה! והתורה אמרה: כי מצא בה ערות דבר, ולהלן הוא אומר: על פי שנים עדים או על פי שלשה עדים יקום דבר, מה להלן דבר ברור, אף כאן דבר ברור."

Starting with the baraita, we see three positions. R. Meir begins with a list of public behaviors that, ostensibly, embarrass the husband, reminiscent of the Mishnah about *dat Yehudit* and the Tosefta about the four husbands referenced above. Not all of the behaviors listed are sexual. For example, public eating and drinking are not at all sexual; yet again, we are in a category of subjectively determined humiliating behavior. One would assume that in modern times, R. Meir would not argue that a woman who eats in a restaurant can be divorced without a ketubah payment.

---

12. Rashi translates "struts," understanding the term *gargar* as a reference to her throat and picturing a high-throated, arrogant walk.

Moving to R. Akiva, again he takes an expansive view of divorce. R. Akiva claims that even gossip about a woman's impropriety is enough to allow a husband to divorce her. He does not mention what examples of such impropriety would be. To this, R. Yochanan ben Nuri responds incredulously: Is every Jewish woman at risk of divorce because of gossipers? Rather, if any accusation is going to be made against a married woman, it must come with actual, courtroom admissible, evidence.

Unlike Rabbi Meir, R. Akiva and R. Yochanan ben Nuri are probably speaking about behaviors that imply infidelity, not public embarrassment. For this reason, apparently, the Talmud suggests that Rava is really saying the same thing as R. Yochanan ben Nuri. Rava claims that a rumor of infidelity should be ignored, since it is probably nothing more than extrapolation or gossip-based expansion from a lesser flirtation – Rashi suggests flirting or fondling. Why Rava would not require her husband to divorce her anyway, if he believes the rumors stem from a real, if more minor, violation of marital fidelity, the Talmud does not say.

Sotah

BABYLONIAN TALMUD

Although, from the fact that the Babylonian Talmud quotes Rabbi Meir's position without an opposing viewpoint, one might have deduced that the Bavli has decided in favor of the position that a man must divorce his wife if she behaves in the quasi-base manner described in the Tosefta; nevertheless, from the discussion in tractate Sotah (25a), this seems less clear:

The question was asked: If a woman violates *dat*, is it necessary for her to receive a warning before cancelling her *ketubah* payment or is this unnecessary? Do we say that since she is violating *dat* there is no need to warn her, or perhaps, a warning should be required since if she ceases [violating *dat*] it (i.e., her *ketubah* rights) will be returned to her?	איבעיא להו: עוברת על דת, צריכה התראה להפסידה כתובתה או אינה צריכה? מי אמרינן, כיון דעוברת על דת היא לא בעיא התראה, או דלמא תיבעי התראה, דאי הדרה בה תיהדר בה?
Come and hear: "A betrothed woman (*arusah*) and one who is awaiting a levirate union [who behaves inappropriately] does not drink [the *sotah* waters] and does not	ת"ש: ארוסה ושומרת יבם לא שותות ולא נוטלות כתובה; מישתא הוא דלא שתיא, הא קנויי מקני לה, למאי? לאו

receive a ketubah payment." She doesn't drink but her husband can still warn her [due to her inappropriate behavior]. To what purpose? Is it not to make her lose her ketubah payment? Abaye said: "No, it is to make her forbidden to her husband." Rav Pappa said: "It is to require her to drink once she is properly married, as it was taught in a baraita: 'One does not declare offense at the behavior of one's betrothed while she is only one's betrothed, but one can declare offense at the behavior of one's betrothed once she is properly married.'"

Rava said: "Come and hear: 'A widow married to the high priest, a divorcée or a *chalutza*[13] married to a regular priest, a *mamzeret*[14] or *netina*[15] married to a Jew, a Jewish woman married to a *mamzer* or *netin* – these women need not drink from the *sotah* waters and they do not receive a ketubah payment [when problems of impropriety arise].' She doesn't drink but her husband can still claim offense [at her inappropriate behavior]. To what purpose? If it were to forbid her to her husband, she is already forbidden! Rather, is it not to make her lose her ketubah payment?" Rav Yehuda of Diskarta said: "No, it is to forbid her to her lover, as we were taught in a mishnah: 'Just as she is forbidden to her husband she is also forbidden to her lover.'"

להפסידה כתובתה. אמר אביי: לא, לאוסרה עליו. רב פפא אמר: להשקותה כשהיא נשואה, כדתניא: אין מקנין לארוסה להשקותה כשהיא ארוסה, אבל מקנין לארוסה להשקותה כשהיא נשואה.

אמר רבא, ת״ש: אלמנה לכהן גדול, גרושה וחלוצה לכהן הדיוט, ממזרת ונתינה לישראל, בת ישראל לממזר ולנתין – לא שותות ולא נוטלות כתובה; מישתא הוא דלא שתיא, הא קנויי מקני להו, ולמאי? אי לאוסרן עליו, הא אסירן וקיימן! אלא לאו להפסידן כתובתן. אמר רב יהודה מדיסקרתא: לא, לאוסרה לבועל כבעל, דתנן: כשם שאסורה לבעל כך אסורה לבועל.

---

13. A woman who went through the ritual with her deceased husband's brother to remove her from the requirement of levirate marriage.
14. The female product of an adulterous or incestuous union; the male is called *mamzer*.
15. The female temple servant who is not considered fully Jewish; the male is called *netin*. For more on this category (which no longer exists) see Rambam, *Mishneh Torah, Hilkhot Issurei Biah* 12:22–24.

Rav Chanina of Sura said: "Come and hear: 'These are [the women] against whom the court may declare offense [on behalf of their husbands]: One whose husband became a deaf-mute, or became insane, or was incarcerated. And this was not said in order to allow her to drink of the *sotah* waters, but in order to disqualify her from receiving her ketubah payment.' We learn from this that she needs to have been warned – thus we learned." All of [the previous Amoraim] – why didn't they use this source? Perhaps this is a different case since she does not have the fear of her husband upon her.

א"ר חנינא מסורא: ת"ש, ואלו שבית דין מקנין להן: מי שנתחרש בעלה, או נשתטה, או שהיה חבוש בבית האסורין, ולא להשקותה אמרו אלא לפוסלה מכתובתה; ש"מ בעי התראה, ש"מ. וכולהו מאי טעמא לא אמרי מהא? דלמא שאני התם, דלית לה אימתא דבעל כלל.

The question was asked: If a woman violates *dat* and her husband wants to remain with her [anyway], may he remain with her or may he not remain with her?

איבעיא להו: עוברת על דת ורצה בעל לקיימה, מקיימה או אינו מקיימה?

Do we say that the Merciful One has made it dependent upon the attitude of the husband and in this case, he is not offended?

מי אמרינן בקפידא דבעל תלא רחמנא, והא לא קפיד,

Or perhaps since [the attitude of the average man] is [to be] offended, [this man] is [assumed to be] offended [as well]?

או דלמא כיון דקפיד - קפיד?

Come and hear [this Tannaitic source]: "These are the women to whom a warning on behalf of the jealous husband is offered by the court: One whose husband has become a deaf-mute, or insane, or is locked in a prison."

ת"ש, ואלו שבית דין מקנין להן: מי שנתחרש בעלה, או נשתטה, או שהיה חבוש בבית האסורין;

Now if one were to argue that a husband may remain with a wife [who violates *dat*] – would a court risk doing something [on the husband's behalf] that may not be in line with his wishes [namely, forcing him to divorce her]?

ואי אמרת רצה בעל לקיימה מקיימה, עבדי ב"ד מידי דדלמא לא ניחא ליה לבעל?

[Yes, since] in the average case, since she is violating *dat*, it would be according to his wishes.

סתמא דמילתא כיון דעוברת על דת היא, מינח ניחא ליה.

This section of B. Sotah poses questions about the proper treatment of a woman who violates *dat*: does she need to be warned before she loses her ketubah rights? Must her husband divorce her? The second question, which is the important one for this chapter, remains unresolved.

One ambiguity in the text that requires addressing is the meaning of the term *dat*. As was shown in the first chapter, this term can mean more than one thing. We have seen the term used in Tosefta Ketubot as *dat Moshe ve-Yisrael* and in the Mishnah as *dat Moshe ve-Yehudit*. Unlike the term in the Tosefta, the Mishnah subdivides its term into two separate categories: *dat Moshe* and *dat Yehudit*. As we saw in the first chapter, *dat Moshe ve-Yisrael* means behavior offensive to the spouse and it applies to the inappropriate behavior of either partner. *Dat Moshe* refers to actions on the part of the wife which cause the husband to sin inadvertently. *Dat Yehudit* refers to inappropriate or offensive behavior on the part of the wife.[16] To which of these three terms does the term *dat* in the above sugya refer?

For a number of reasons, it would seem that the Talmud here must be referring either to *dat Moshe ve-Yisrael* in general or to *dat Yehudit* in specific[17] (or to both, since in reference to a wife's behavior they are equivalent terms).[18]

First, the concept covered by *dat Moshe* – that she causes her husband to sin – is a very particular concern and is not discussed anywhere in rabbinic literature other than in the discussion of the Mishnah that uses it. However, the idea covered by *dat Moshe ve-Yisrael* or *dat Yehudit*, i.e., the list of inappropriate or offensive behaviors, is referenced and discussed in multiple places.

Second, Rabbi Meir's position in Tosefta Sotah, which is quoted by both Talmuds at the end of tractate Gittin, specifically discusses the *mitzvah* for a husband to divorce his wife if she behaves inappropriately or offensively. This is the exact parallel to the discussion here, albeit in this sugya the Talmud is undecided whether it is an obligation.[19]

Third, since the sugya specifically discusses the case where the husband

---

16. I.e., it is the wife's side of the *dat Moshe ve-Yisrael* category.
17. This is Rashi's position, as we will see in a later chapter.
18. It could in theory be referring to all three in a general way including *dat Moshe*, but the weight of the *sugya* is on the other two.
19. It is curious to note that the Talmud does not reference that Tosefta in the discussion. This curiosity will be noted by the Tosafot, as will be seen in a later chapter.

is locked in prison, it is not possible (at least in that case) that she has been feeding him non-kosher food or sleeping with him while in a state of impurity. However, it is possible that her public behavior could be offensive to him, even sitting in a prison.

Finally, it makes little sense to argue that the Talmud is discussing whether a woman who causes her husband to sin may remain with him. It would seem that, unless the husband believed that he could control her behavior and ensure that he was not sinning inadvertently,[20] he would have no choice but to divorce her. In other words, it is reasonable to discuss whether the act of public humiliation and offense is reason enough for halakha to require divorce; however, it is not reasonable to pose the same question with regard to the act of causing sin. Does the man really have the option to say that he agrees to keep sinning in order to stay married to his wife?!

Hence, we see from this Talmudic source that *dat Yehudit/dat Moshe ve-Yisrael* is a category which is meant to reflect behaviors that cause the husband some sort of anguish. As has been stated previously, this category only makes sense if it is reflective of the average husband's actual feelings of shame or anger. These feelings, in turn, must be dependent on social context and the list of such behaviors must vary depending on societal norms.

Implied Adultery

In a similar vein to the discussion of the Talmud about *dat Yehudit* and inappropriate behavior, the Talmud also discusses behavior that offers circumstantial evidence that the woman is being unfaithful. Since the evidence is circumstantial, but the behavior is clearly inappropriate, the rabbis decide that she may be divorced without her ketubah payment. The discussion appears in both the Jerusalem and Babylonian Talmuds.

JERUSALEM TALMUD (Y. KETUBOT 7:6)

| ...Women who violate *dat* lose their entire [ketubah payment]. Rabbi Elazar in the name of Rabbi Chaninah: "If they saw | ‏...נשים המעברות על הדת מאבדות את הכל רבי לעזר בשם רבי חנינה ראו אותה‎ |

---

20. Similar to the suggestion of Rabbi Yehuda in the Tosefta, that the husband separate his own *challah*. See Avot of Rabbi Nathan 8:8 for a discussion of the prison issues.

her putting on her undergarment while a merchant was leaving her house – this is evidence of a base matter and she leaves [without her ketubah payment]. Saliva on her bed – this is evidence of a base matter and she leaves [without her ketubah payment]. Saliva on his bed – this is evidence of a base matter and she leaves [without her ketubah payment]. His shoes in front of her bed – this is evidence of a base matter and she leaves [without her ketubah payment]. Her shoes in front of his bed – this is evidence of a base matter and she leaves [without her ketubah payment]. They both leave from a dark place together – this is evidence of a base matter, and she leaves [without her ketubah payment]. Helping each other climb out of a pit – this is evidence of a base matter and she leaves [without her ketubah payment]. Both of them beating on her thighs in the bathhouse – this is evidence of a base matter and she leaves [without her ketubah payment]." Chaninah bar Iyka in the name of Rabbi Yehuda: "In all [of the above cases], if she brought evidence to explain [her innocence], she is believed."

חוגרה בסינר רוכל יוצא מתוך ביתה כאור הדבר תצא רוק על גבי מיטתה כאור הדבר תצא רוק על גבי מטתו כאור הדבר תצא סנדלו לפני מיטתה כאור הדבר תצא סנדלה לפני מיטתו כאור הדבר תצא שניהם יוצאין ממקום אפל כאור הדבר תצא מעלין זה את זה מן הבור כאור הדבר תצא שניהם טופחות על יריכה במרחץ כאור הדבר תצא חנינה בר איקא בשם רבי יהודה וכולהן אם הביאה ראייה לדבריה נאמנת

Rav Adda bar Achuha in the name of Rav: "It happened that [a couple] came before Rabbi, and he said: 'What of it?'" They asked [Rav Adda]: "Even if they saw him placing his mouth upon hers?" He said: "Such a case occurred; they saw a man place his mouth on her mouth." The case came before R. Yossi and he said, "She should be divorced without payment." Her relatives were there, and they disputed the point saying…[21]

רב אדא בר אחוה בשם רב מעשה בא לפני רבי ומר מה בכך בעיין קומוי אפילו ראו אותו נותן פיו על פיה שלה אמר כזה באת מעשה באחד שראו אותו נותן את פיו על פיה שלה אתא עובדא קומי רבי יוסי אמר תיפוק בלא פרן והויין קריביה עררין ואמרין…

---

21. The details of the dispute of the relatives are complicated and fraught with

BABYLONIAN TALMUD (B. YEVAMOT 24B–25A)

A merchant leaving her house while the woman is putting on her undergarment, Rabbi said: "Since such is evidence of a base matter, she leaves [without payment]." Saliva above the bedding, Rabbi said: "Since such is evidence of a base matter, she leaves [without payment]." Overturned shoes under the bed, Rabbi said: "Since such is evidence of a base matter, she leaves [without payment]." Overturned shoes? Just look and see whose they are? Rather, their shoes switched places.	רוכל יוצא ואשה חוגרת בסינר, אמר רבי: הואיל ומכוער הדבר - תצא; רוק למעלה מן הכילה, אמר רבי: הואיל ומכוער הדבר - תצא; מנעלים הפוכים תחת המטה, אמר רבי: הואיל ומכוער הדבר - תצא; מנעלים הפוכים, ליחזי דמאן נינהו? אלא מקום מנעלים הפוכים.

Both of the above sources describe circumstances that make it look as if the woman is having an affair. Although *dat Yehudit* claims do not go as far as implying actual extra-marital sexual activity, the two issues are related. A husband need not put up with a marital situation which humiliates him, whether that be because his wife acts in a sexual manner in public or if her behavior implies (but does not prove) that she is actually having extra-marital relations.

Ketubot

Before discussing the specific analyses of these *sugyot* regarding exposed hair, it seems best to begin with their respective analyses of the other relevant topics in the Mishnah, in order to establish context.

THE HUSBAND'S BEHAVIOR

JERUSALEM TALMUD (Y. KETUBOT 7:5)

Commenting on the section of the Mishnah that describes the husband's inappropriate behavior towards his wife, the Jerusalem Talmud writes:

If he said to her [that he is making a vow] with the condition that: "you must tell so-and-so what you said to me" – privately,	אמ' לה: "על מנת שתאמרי לאיש פלוני מה שאמרת לי" - ביחיד,
or "what I said to you" – privately,	או "מה שאמרתי לך" - ביחיד,

---

textual problems. As the various possibilities have nothing really to do with modest behavior, I will not deal with them here.

or that she must fill up and then pour out in the garbage,	או שתהא ממלא ומערה לאשפות –
– He expels her and [her husband] must make the *ketubah* payment – Over there [in Babylon] they say: "[Filling up and pouring in the garbage] is a euphemism for *coitus interruptus*."²² The rabbis here [in Israel] say: "[It means forcing her to do] nonsense work."	יוציא ויתן כתובה – תמן אמרין: "כגון מעשה ער," ורבנין דהכא אמרין: "דברים של בטלה."

The Jerusalem Talmud first points out here that the husband is asking his wife to describe intimate conversations to a third party. This is why his request is a violation of basic dignity and grants her the right to sue for divorce with payment of her ketubah. Next, the Jerusalem Talmud discusses the ambiguity of the phrase "fill up and pour out into the garbage." Two possible interpretations are offered, each attempting to fit the phrase into the overall context of the Mishnah.

The first interpretation is that recorded in the name of the Babylonian rabbis. This interpretation assumes that the statement is really a euphemism and has a sexual connotation. According to this interpretation, the husband is requiring his wife to do something that will block her from having children, and is, perhaps, humiliating as well.²³ This interpretation maintains the sexual context of his requests, but differs insofar as the humiliation or offense is private and not public.

The second interpretation is recorded in the name of other rabbis (from Israel). They understand the phrase to mean what it says literally, as an act of pure public humiliation. Since the work she would be doing would be pointless as well as repulsive, doing it would make her look silly.

BABYLONIAN TALMUD (B. KETUBOT 72A)

If he said to her [that he is making a vow] "with the condition that: you must tell etc. – Let her tell! Rav Yehuda said in the	ואם אמר לה ע"מ שתאמרי – ותימא! אמר רב יהודה אמר שמואל: "דברים של קלון."

---

22. Lit. "the behavior of Er," who, according to the midrash, behaved this way with his wife Tamar.
23. Whether *coitus interruptus* is a technical sin or not is a separate issue, since either way it is certainly not her sin. If it were her sin, the issue here would be different, since the vow would be null automatically, since a man cannot require his wife to violate halakha.

name of Shmuel: "[He wants her to tell of] embarrassing matters."

Or that she must fill up and then pour out in the garbage – Let her do it! Rav Yehuda said in the name of Shmuel: "[He means that] she should fill up [with semen] and then scatter it." In a baraita it is taught: "[He means] that she should fill ten jugs of water and pour them out into the trash."

Shmuel's position makes sense, since this seems like a good reason for the husband to expel her and pay the ketubah. However, according to the baraita, what difference does it make to her [if she does this]? Let her do it! Rabbah bar bar Channah said in the name of Rabbi Yochanan: "Because it makes her look like an imbecile."

או שתהא ממלאה ומערה לאשפה – ותיעביד! א"ר יהודה אמר שמואל: שתמלא ונופצת. במתניתא תנא: שתמלא עשרה כדי מים ותערה לאשפה.

בשלמא לשמואל, משום הכי יוציא ויתן כתובה, אלא למתניתא, מאי נפקא לה מינה? תיעביד! אמר רבה בר בר חנה אמר רבי יוחנן: "מפני שנראית כשוטה."

Although including more details and more discussion, the Babylonian Talmud is essentially in line with the interpretations of the Jerusalem Talmud. In the first case, the husband is asking her to share embarrassing conversations, probably a reference to intimate conversations. In the second case, there is a debate about whether she is being asked to assist in making the sexual encounters with her husband non-reproductive, or whether he is asking her to behave foolishly in public.

For our purposes, it is clear from these sugyot that humiliating one's wife is a breach of marital etiquette and is grounds for divorce on the woman's side as well as grounds for collecting the ketubah payment. This suggests that the woman's breach of etiquette should have an equivalent valence, i.e., they should be acts that humiliate her husband.

PUBLIC WEAVING AND CONVERSING WITH RANDOM MEN

The Babylonian Talmud (b. Ketubot 72b) writes:[24]

Weaving in the marketplace – Rav Yehuda said in the name of Shmuel: "She exposes her arms to the men."

וטווה בשוק – אמר רב יהודה אמר שמואל: "במראה זרועותיה לבני אדם."

---

24. The Jerusalem Talmud does not discuss these cases. This work will not directly discuss the issue of red clothing. See *Rama Shulchan Arukh Yoreh Deah* 178:1 where it is classified as a subjective prohibition grounded in social norms of modesty.

Rav Chisda said in the name of Avimi: "She spins red wool before her face."

Conversing with random men – Rav Yehuda said in the name of Shmuel: "Being playful with young men."

Rabbah bar bar Channah said: "Once I was walking behind Rav Ukba. He saw a certain Arab woman sitting, casting the spindle and weaving red wool before her face. When she saw us, she stopped spinning and threw [her spindle]. She said to me: 'Young man, can you get me my spindle?' Rav Ukba referred to her [afterwards] as something."

What did he call her? Ravina said: "He called her a marketplace-weaver." The Rabbis said: "He called her an indiscriminate converser."

רב חסדא אמר אבימי: "בטווה ורד כנגד פניה."

ומדברת עם כל אדם - אמר רב יהודה אמר שמואל: "במשחקת עם בחורים."

אמר רבה בר בר חנה: "זימנא חדא הוה קאזילנא בתריה דרב עוקבא, חזיתיה להההיא ערביא דהוה יתבה קא שדיא פילכה וטווה ורד כנגד פניה, כיון דחזיתינן פסיקתיה לפילכה שדיתיה, אמרה לי: עולם, הב לי פלך, אמר בה רב עוקבא מילתא."

מאי אמר בה? רבינא אמר: "טווה בשוק אמר בה," רבנן אמרי: "מדברת עם כל אדם אמר בה."

The theme that runs through this entire sugya is that of immodest behavior.

Looking first at the case of public weaving, both positions explain the problem with the behavior as one of immodest comportment. Shmuel understands the behavior as inevitably exposing the arms, which would otherwise have been covered. Avimi understands the Mishnah to not be referring to the act of weaving in public as much as a certain type of accessory: red wool woven into the hair and hanging over the face. It would appear that this accessory was considered to be provocative.

It goes without saying that the latter interpretation only makes sense in a specific social context, as it is difficult to imagine that there is something objectively immodest about a piece of red wool hanging over a woman's face. Additionally, the first position is also best understood in a societal context. In a society where it would have been unacceptable for a woman to go out with her arms exposed, the haphazard "falling of the sleeves" that would occur to a woman engaged in weaving would be provocative precisely because her arms are otherwise not exposed.

Moving on to the case of conversing with random men, Shmuel explains that this refers to playful or flirtatious behavior. He mentions young men presumably because this would be the age group where flirtation is common. Since, as we mentioned in Chapter 1, the Mishnah's case of conversing with men seems inordinately harsh in comparison with that of the Tosefta (washing with men), Shmuel's interpretation softens this hard edge. Not all conversation is inappropriate, only suggestive conversation.

The Bavli ends this part of the sugya with a story about an immodest woman. Although this particular woman was an Arab and not a Jew, it would seem that the same social norms were supposed to apply to either. This woman functions as a sort of caricature of the above-mentioned cases. She is both weaving in public as well as weaving red wool before her face. When she sees a young man (Rabbah bar bar Channah in this case), she makes an obvious move to grab his attention by "dropping" her spindle.

That the woman was immodest is accepted by all. The only debate is what behavior stood out the most to Rav Ukva; her weaving in public, her weaving red wool over her face or her flirting with his young student. Again, this story only makes sense in a cultural context where her behavior would stand out as immodest.[25]

THE "LOUDMOUTH"

The loudmouth is another example where there is some ambiguity as to the nature of the humiliation to the husband.

JERUSALEM TALMUD (Y. KETUBOT 7:6)

Rabbi Tarfon says: "Even the loudmouth" – Who is a loudmouth? Shmuel said: "Any woman who when she speaks her neighbors hear her."	רבי טרפון אומר אף הקולנית – אי זו היא הקולנית? שמואל אמר: "כל שהיא מדברת ושכינותיה שומעות אותה."
Rav said: "Any woman whose voice bounds from bedroom to bedroom during sex."	רב אמר: "כל שקולה הולך ממיטה למיטה בשעת תשמיש."

The Jerusalem Talmud records a debate about the nature of the problem described as "loudmouth." Shmuel suggests a literal interpretation. He argues that she is simply very loud, and all the neighbors can hear her

---

25. I am referring here, of course, to the weaving. The dropping of an item as an excuse to get a desired person to grant some attention seems to be "universal language."

talk. Rav understands the term euphemistically, and assumes it means that she is loud in bed and the neighbors can hear.

What stands out about both of these cases is that this trait embarrasses the husband even though it does not reflect malice or immodesty on the part of the wife. Whether one follows Rav or Shmuel's interpretation, the bottom line is that Rabbi Tarfon allows the husband to divorce his wife without payment of her ketubah because she has a behavioral quirk that he cannot live with. The reason Rabbi Tarfon accepts this is because this particular quirk, in the society in which he lived, was so humiliating to the husband as to be impossible for a normal man to live with.

BABYLONIAN TALMUD (B. KETUBOT 72B)

Rabbi Tarfon said: "Even a loudmouth" – What is a loudmouth? Rav Yehuda said in the name of Shmuel: "One who speaks about sexual matters."	רבי טרפון אומר: אף הקולנית - מאי קולנית? אמר רב יהודה אמר שמואל: "במשמעת קולה על עסקי תשמיש".
In a baraita it states: "She speaks in one courtyard and is heard in another one." Then let it be listed among the blemishes in the Mishnah! Rather, it would appear that the first explanation is correct.	במתניתא תנא: במשמשת בחצר זו ונשמע קולה בחצר אחרת. וניתנייה גבי מומין במתניתין! אלא, מחוורתא כדשנין מעיקרא.

The Babylonian Talmud approaches this case differently. It records the position of Rav Yehuda in the name of Shmuel[26] that the loudmouth is the type of woman who speaks about sexual matters.[27] This would be an example of immodest behavior, as opposed to the Yerushalmi's interpretations (y. Ketubot 7:6), which focus on personality quirks. The Bavli quotes a baraita that suggests the same thing that Shmuel had suggested in the Yerushalmi, namely that the woman is simply loud. However, the Talmud objects to this position saying that in that case, it should have been included in the list of physical blemishes, since the trait is inadvertent.

The claim that speaking of sexual matters is inappropriate seems to be socially determined.[28]

---

26. It seems that there is some confusion about what Shmuel actually said, considering the fact that he is quoted in both Talmuds saying different things.
27. It is unclear whether it is meant that she does this privately or publicly. This is a matter of dispute among the commentators.
28. However one understands it, it *cannot* mean that she speaks about sexual

CURSING HIS PARENTS

The example of the cursing of the husband's parents is telling, since it demonstrates clearly that the operative factor in this list is offense to the husband.

JERUSALEM TALMUD (Y. KETUBOT 7:6)

Abba Shaul says: "Even one who curses his children **in front of** his parents."	אבא שאול אומר: "אף המקללת את וולדיו בפני יולדיו".

The sugya is either reinterpreting or extending Abba Shaul's original example to refer to or include the cursing of the man's children. It uses the case of doing so before his parents, but presumably it is meant to include before him as well.

BABYLONIAN TALMUD (B. KETUBOT 72B)

Abba Shaul says: "Even one who curses his parents in front of his face." – Rav Yehuda said in the name of Shmuel: "Even one who curses his parents in front of his children, and the mnemonic is 'Ephraim and Menasheh will be like Reuben and Shimon to me.'"[29]	אבא שאול אומר: "אף המקללת יולדיו בפניו" - אמר רב יהודה אמר שמואל: "במקללת יולידיו בפני מולידיו, וסימניך: 'אפרים ומנשה כראובן ושמעון יהיו לי'."
Rabbah said: "She said to him: 'Let a lion eat your grandfather' in front of his son."	אמר רבה: "דאמרה ליה ניכליה אריא לסבא באפי בריה."

The Bavli seems to be doing the same thing as the Yerushalmi, but in reverse. The case is interpreted or extended to a case where his parents are cursed in front of his children. Rabbah gives a colorful example of what this would look like.

The operant factor in both the Bavli's and the Yerushalmi's interpretations is that the behavior is not grounds for divorce and loss of ketubah because of its sinfulness, but because it is extremely offensive to her husband. Again, one would assume that this would be determined by social norms.

---

matters with other men, since that would obviously fall under the category of speaking with random men and would not be a matter of dispute.

29. Genesis 48:5.

EXPOSED HAIR

Having established context, we can now turn to the central sugya about hair covering.[30]

JERUSALEM TALMUD (Y. KETUBOT 7:6)

Her hair exposed – they stated this with regard to the courtyard, how much more so does this apply to a thoroughfare.	וראשה פרוע - לחצר אמרו, ק"ו למבוי.
Rabbi Chiyyah stated in the name of Rabbi Yochanan: "One who goes out with her hair coiffed[31] has not violated [the prohibition of going out with] her hair exposed."	ר' חייה בשם ר' יוחנן: "היוצאה בקפלטין שלה - אין בה משו[ם] ראשה פרוע."
This refers to in a courtyard,	הדא דתימ[א] לחצ[ר],
but in a thoroughfare, it would violate [the prohibition of going out] with her hair exposed.	אבל למבוי - יש בה משו[ם] יוצאה וראש[ה] פרוע.
There is a [type of] courtyard that is like a thoroughfare, and there is a [type of] thoroughfare that is like a courtyard. A courtyard that many people use as a pass-through is [considered] as a thoroughfare; a thoroughfare through which people generally do not pass is [considered] as a courtyard.	יש חצר שהוא כמבוי, ויש מבוי שהוא כחצר. חצר שהרבים בוקעין בתוכה - הרי הוא כמבוי, ומבוי שאין הרבים בוקעין בתוכו - הרי הוא כחצר.

Two important points emerge from this discussion. First, there are gradations of publicness. In between the privacy of a home and the public thoroughfare is the courtyard. The Yerushalmi begins its discussion by interpreting the Mishnah as referring even to the courtyard. According to

---

30. For an interesting discussion of these sugyot, see Chapter 4 (entitled "Inside Out and Outside In") of Cynthia M. Baker's *Rebuilding the House of Israel: Architectures of Gender in Jewish Antiquity* (Divinations: Rereading Late Ancient Religion; Stanford: Stanford University Press, 2002), 113–144.
31. I.e., not free-flowing but done up in some way. This is the simple meaning of the term. The other possible meaning of this Latin term is "with false hair." For a fuller discussion, see Elizabeth Bartman, "Hair and the Artifice of Roman Female Adornment," *American Journal of Archaeology* 105:1 (2001), 1–25. Many commentators on the Talmud, being unfamiliar with Latin and Roman customs, have translated the term based on analogy to the Bavli's term *kalta*. The meaning of that term itself is disputed as will be seen in the discussion of the Bavli.

this interpretation, even a woman who only went out into the courtyard with her hair exposed would be violating *dat Yehudit*.

Second, Rabbi Yochanan believes that there are gradations of hair exposure as well. In between the state of totally exposed, free-flowing hair and the state of totally covered hair[32] is the state of hair in *capillatus*,[33] i.e., hair done up in some way.

The Talmud attempts to line up Rabbi Yochanan's point with its previous point. According to this proposal there would be a three-tiered structure to the halakha: Inside the house the woman could have totally exposed (free-flowing) hair, in the courtyard she can have her hair uncovered but done up in some way, and in the public thoroughfare she must have her hair covered.

The sugya ends with the Talmud pointing out that there is some gray area with regard to how precisely to define courtyard and thoroughfare, and the rule of thumb should be whether many people use the area as a pass-through or public passageway.

In the context of the other examples discussed in this sugya which were analyzed in previous subsections, one would imagine that this entire discussion should also be understood as socially determined. In fact, the very distinction suggested by Rabbi Yochanan reflects the practice of Roman women; even the term he uses is a Latin one.

BABYLONIAN TALMUD (B. KETUBOT 72A–B)

This neat picture becomes complicated in the Bavli's discussion:

[Going out with] her hair exposed is a Torah prohibition! For it is written: "And he shall expose the hair of the woman" (Num. 5:18); And the school of R. Yishmael	ראשה פרוע דאורייתא היא! דכתיב: "ופרע את ראש האשה," ותנא דבי רבי ישמעאל: "אזהרה לבנות

---

32. The Yerushalmi does not state explicitly what would be considered full coverage. Following the customs of women in Graeco-Rome, full coverage would mean with a veil. See: Ramsay MacMullen, "Women in Public in the Roman Empire," *Historia: Zeitschrift für Alte Geschichte* 29:2 (1980): 208–218. This was noted in the addendum to the previous chapter as well.

33. A Latin term: *capillatus* (or possibly *capillitium*), which refers either to the custom of Roman women to curl their hair with hot irons and keep their hair in braids/curls or to the custom of wearing false hair. (The latter is the interpretation preferred by Baker in note 30 on page 57.) Either of these options would have been acceptable for Roman women when indoors or in semi-private situations. In public, all but the upper class would wear a veil.

EXPOSED HAIR IN AMORAIC SOURCES

taught: "This is a warning to the daughters of Israel not to go out with their hair exposed!"	ישראל שלא יצאו בפרוע ראש!"
[Rav Yehuda said in the name of Shmuel: "[The Mishnah refers to a woman who goes out] with a *kalta*."]³⁵	[אמר רב יהודה אמר שמואל: "בקלתה."]³⁴
As a matter of Torah law, a *kalta* would be sufficient, [while for] *dat Yehudit* even a *kalta* would be insufficient.	דאורייתא – קלתה שפיר דמי, דת יהודית – אפילו קלתה נמי אסור.
R. Assi said in the name of R. Yochanan: "[One who goes out in] *kalta* has not violated [the prohibition of going out with] her hair exposed."	אמר רבי אסי אמר רבי יוחנן: "קלתה אין בה משום פרוע ראש".
R. Zeira took issue with this: "Where [are we talking about]? If you were to say in the marketplace – this would be [a violation of] *dat Yehudit*; but if you were to suggest instead in a courtyard, if so, you have not left a single daughter of our patriarch Abraham who could live with her husband!"	הוי בה רבי זירא: "היכא? אילימא בשוק, דת יהודית היא! ואלא בחצר – אם כן, לא הנחת בת לאברהם אבינו שיושבת תחת בעלה!"
Abaye, or alternatively R. Kahana, stated: "[R. Yochanan's ruling is meant to apply to a woman who goes] from one courtyard to another by way of a thoroughfare."	אמר אביי, ואיתימא רב כהנא: "מחצר לחצר ודרך מבוי".

---

34. Although this variant is not found in any manuscript, this or something similar is the textual version of many Rishonim, such as Rif, Rosh and Rid. It is worth noting as well that three of the Vatican manuscripts read "אמר רב יהודה," "Rav Yehuda said." See *Dikdukei Soferim HaShalem* (Ketubot, vol. 2, p. 1766 n 107) for a fuller description of the textual variants.

35. This book will generally translate the term as 'braids' even as this is an incomplete and disputed translation as will be explained in other places in the book. The meaning of this term is a matter of dispute. In the context of the Yerushalmi passage and the Mishnah in Sotah about undoing the woman's hair, one would assume that it means coiffed. This, in fact, is the translation offered by Rabbi Yaakov Reischer in his *Shvut Yaakov*. However, the majority of the commentators understand the term to either mean a work basket (Rashi) or a kerchief (Rambam). (This matter is discussed at length in Chapter 7; see there for more and for citations.) Although both of these possibilities are somewhat forced and lacking historical context, the general idea of partial covering is a strong possibility, and *kalta* would then probably be best translated as "hairnet."

The sugya in the Bavli is more complicated than that of the Yerushalmi, but it can be neatly divided into two halves. The latter half of the sugya is largely parallel to the Yerushalmi sugya, so we will begin our analysis with this section.

The latter half of the sugya opens with a statement by Rabbi Yochanan that a woman going out in *kalta* is not a violation of *dat Yehudit*. Although the Yerushalmi uses the term *capillatus* instead of *kalta*, the two terms are probably synonymous. Essentially, this is the same statement of R. Yochanan recorded by the Yerushalmi, only with a different term.

As in the Yerushalmi, the Bavli continues with a discussion of what Rabbi Yochanan may have meant with this ruling. Whereas the Yerushalmi is comfortable suggesting that he must have been referring to sufficient attire for a courtyard, the Bavli is unhappy with this suggestion. The Bavli quotes Rabbi Zeira who claims that if Rabbi Yochanan was really that strict, he would effectively be claiming that all Jewish women in his time were in violation of *dat Yehudit* since, Rabbi Zeira believes, all women go out into their courtyards not in kalta.

To avoid this problem, Abaye (or Rav Kahana) suggests that there are actually three types of public appearance.[36] There is going out to the courtyard, there is using a thoroughfare for a few moments to get to the next courtyard, and there is going out to the thoroughfare. Abaye/Rav Kahana believes that Rabbi Yochanan must be referring to the middle case, the momentary use of a thoroughfare.

The first part of the sugya is novel and has no parallel in the Jerusalem Talmud. It begins by pointing out that the Mishnah in Ketubot seems to be in tension with a midrash halakha. Whereas the Mishnah, by placing exposed hair in the category of *dat Yehudit*, implies that the act is purely one of maintaining a subjective societal norm, the midrash halakha states that the Torah specifically commands women not to go out with their hair exposed.

This midrash halakha is similar to that found in the Sifre but has some important differences. First, whereas the Sifre merely states that the verse teaches about a practice women did, the baraita here states that the verse teaches about a practice women must do. Second, whereas the Sifre is discussing the practice of hair covering, the baraita in the Bavli is discussing the prohibition of fully exposed hair. Finally, whereas the

---

36. The Yerushalmi only had two: courtyard and thoroughfare.

Sifre feels the need to demonstrate that its interpretation was correct by drawing an inference from the verse in Samuel, the baraita in the Bavli feels no such need.[37] All in all, whereas the Sifre seems to be a descriptive midrash, teaching the reader what Jewish women did not do, the baraita in the Bavli seems to be a prescriptive midrash, teaching the reader what Jewish women must not do.

Considering the fact that this baraita is making a normative statement about women going out with their hair exposed being a violation of a Torah prohibition, it seems problematic, the Talmud argues, that the Mishnah would list the practice as a violation of *dat Yehudit* and leave it at that. Is there any way, the Talmud wonders, to remove this tension and understand the Mishnah and the baraita as agreeing?[38]

Rav Yehuda, quoting Shmuel, suggests a possible synthesis. He argues (like Rabbi Yochanan) that there are levels of exposure when it comes to hair. The Torah only forbids a woman from going out with her hair fully exposed; under *dat Yehudit*, even going out in kalta would be a problem. According to this suggestion, the baraita would be referring to the absolute prohibition of going out fully exposed and would in no way be forbidding a woman from going out in kalta. The Mishnah, on the other hand, would be referring to the practice of going out with her hair covered, i.e., more than just kalta.

Needless to say, this answer is a classic example of a problematically forced solution (שינויא דחיקא), since both the baraita and the Mishnah use the exact same term: "exposed hair." It is more than a little stretch to suggest that when the baraita says a woman may not go out with exposed hair, it should be understood to be permitting going out in kalta, but that when the Mishnah says that it is a violation of *dat Yehudit* for a woman to go out with her hair exposed it means that she may not go out only in kalta.

It is for this reason, perhaps, that Rabbi Yochanan seems to be presented as arguing with Shmuel. Of course, we know that Rabbi Yochanan

---

37. The Sifre has this as an unnamed position arguing with Rabbi Yishmael, whereas the baraita in the Bavli has it as the position of the school of Rabbi Yishmael itself, but this is an inconsequential difference.
38. It is, of course, possible and legitimate for a mishnah and a baraita to contradict each other, as they are both Tannaitic sources and may reflect differing views. Nevertheless, it seems to be the general practice of the Talmud to create synthesis wherever possible.

did not actually make his statement in response to Shmuel, since the Yerushalmi records his position as an independent gloss on the Mishnah. Nevertheless, from the placement and phrasing of his position in the Bavli, it would seem likely that his statement was meant to be interpreted as an alternative opinion, perhaps even a critique of Shmuel.

The simple understanding of Rabbi Yochanan in this context is that the term "exposed hair" does not refer to a woman going out in kalta. The primary halakhic import of Rabbi Yochanan's statement is to allow women in certain contexts to go out only in kalta, as was discussed earlier. However, in the context of the first part of the sugya it has a secondary import as well: it seems to neutralize Shmuel's answer. If one follows Rabbi Yochanan, one must admit that neither the baraita nor the Mishnah could be referring to women in kalta, as the term "exposed hair" never means this. Hence the baraita and the Mishnah contradict each other, and we follow the Mishnah.

As in the Yerushalmi's discussion, Rabbi Zeira simply does not believe that Rabbi Yochanan could mean that a woman could go out to a public thoroughfare with her hair essentially uncovered. On the other hand, unlike the Yerushalmi, he is unwilling to require women to go out in kalta when in a courtyard. Accepting Rabbi Zeira's two premises, the Talmud is forced to offer the very counterintuitive suggestion of Abaye/Rav Kahana: the entire import of Rabbi Yochanan's statement must be relegated only to the very specific scenario of momentary use of a thoroughfare to get to another courtyard.

As in the Yerushalmi, Rabbi Zeira's first premise (that Rabbi Yochanan cannot be permitting a woman to go out in public in uncovered hair) is independent of the baraita about the Torah prohibition of going out uncovered – a baraita that the Yerushalmi does not know. The objection is ostensibly based on a feeling about social reality. Rabbi Zeira and the Yerushalmi are essentially arguing that a woman going out in kalta/coiffed to the public thoroughfare must be a violation of *dat Yehudit* because women simply do not do this in their society! Rabbi Yochanan must have been aware of this, so he must mean something other than what he seems to be saying.

The difference between the Bavli's and the Yerushalmi's revised explanations of Rabbi Yochanan also stems from this same consideration. Whereas the Yerushalmi considers it reasonable to imagine that Rabbi Yochanan required women to have their hair done when going out into the courtyard, Rabbi Zeira considers this totally unreasonable. This debate may reflect the different societal norms in Palestine and Babylonia respectively.[39]

To summarize thus far: at first Rabbi Yochanan seemed to be suggesting that braids/kalta is always sufficient and not a violation of *dat Yehudit*. Both Talmuds respond by saying that this is empirically false, and that a woman appearing in public this way would certainly violate societal norms. Therefore, what Rabbi Yochanan must mean is that a woman going out coiffed/kalta does not violate *dat Yehudit* in certain specific situations, either in a semi-public environment (Yerushalmi) or in a momentary public appearance (Bavli).

Although this is a somewhat drastic interpretation of Rabbi Yochanan's position, one thing remains consistent: Rabbi Yochanan does not know of or believe in a distinction between partial and full exposure which is dependent on a distinction between Torah law and social norms. That was the first position in the Talmud, and was offered in an attempt to harmonize the baraita with the Mishnah. How Rabbi Yochanan would deal with the contradiction is unknown, since neither he nor the Amoraim who discuss his position ever reference it.

This fact is actually not surprising. If one keeps in mind that according to the societal norms in Talmudic times women would never appear with their hair exposed at all, and that women would only appear in public veiled, the import of the baraita is only theoretical.

However, this leaves one with a halakhic quandary. Considering the fact that the solution the Talmud offers to the contradiction between the baraita and the Mishnah is both counterintuitive and not in line with the rest of the sugya (which focuses on the position of Rabbi Yochanan), is one to understand the answer as authoritative? It is, of course, possible to accept both the solution of the Talmud as well as Rabbi Yochanan's position. Theoretically speaking there is no problem claiming that a woman going out in kalta was once, at least theoretically, totally permissible, but became a problem since modest women were accustomed not to go out this way, and at the same time accept that in the very limited situations where women still appear in kalta it would remain acceptable. However,

---

39. Since Rabbi Zeira lived in both countries at different times, this would imply that he made the statement earlier on in his life. Since the respondent (either Abaye or Rav Kahana) is also Babylonian, this would work well.

it is equally possible to argue that this was a counterintuitive suggestion offered by the Talmud as a possible resolution of the tension; in reality, the baraita and the Mishnah contradict.

If the latter interpretation is correct, it forces us to ask the question: Which text – Mishnah or baraita – do we follow as halakha? Although this question would have seemed of little import in a time when all women covered their hair, the question becomes fundamentally important in our times where women in general do not cover their hair. Since *dat Yehudit* is a socially determined category, the question becomes: In the absence of a *dat Yehudit* requirement, is there still a Torah law to contend with?

At this point, there seem to be three possible approaches to this question:

a. yes (following the baraita only)[40]
b. yes, but going out in kalta[41] would be sufficient (following Shmuel)
c. no (following the Mishnah only)

Modest Comportment

Before turning to the commentators and halakhic works (in the next chapters) to search for an answer to this question, we must look at one more set of important sources on hair covering and modesty in the Talmud.

B. KIDDUSHIN (70A–B)

The first source we will look at is a part of a story from the Babylonian Talmud. The context of the story is that a man from Nehardea went before the court of Rav Nachman to sue Rav Yehuda for having called him a "slave." Rav Yehuda goes to the house of Rav Nachman to deal with the claim, and a long dialogue occurs in which Rav Yehuda critiques everything Rav Nachman says and does. As a part of their back and forth, they touch upon the question of what is proper and improper in male-female interactions.

> [Rav Nachman] said to him: "Let Donag[42] come and serve us a drink." [Rav Yehuda] replied: "Shmuel said: 'One should not
>
> אמר ליה: תיתי דונג תשקינן,
> אמר ליה, הכי אמר שמואל:
> אין משתמשים באשה. קטנה

---

40. This position is only theoretical and does not seem to find support in the poskim.
41. Whether understood as coiffed or with a hairnet. For more discussion, see Rabbi Yechiel Yaakov Weinberg in *Responsa Seridei Eish* 1:78.
42. His daughter.

make use of a woman.'" [Rav Nachman responded:] "She is a minor." [Rav Yehuda retorted:] "Shmuel said explicitly: 'One should not make use of a woman' – at all, whether she be an adult or a minor!" [Rav Nachman said:] "Let us greet Yalta."[43] [Rav Yehuda responded:] "Shmuel said: 'The voice of a woman is considered suggestive (*erva*).'" [Rav Nachman responded:] "We can [send the greeting] by messenger." [Rav Yehuda] responded: "Shmuel said: 'One should not send greetings to a woman.'"[44] [Rav Nachman responded:] "But this greeting] is through the conduit of her own husband!" [Rav Yehuda] replied: "Shmuel said: 'One should not send greetings to women' – at all!" [Rav Nachman's] wife sent him a message: "Finish up with his case already, before he makes you look like an average simpleton."

היא! בפירוש אמר שמואל: אין משתמשים באשה כלל, בין גדולה בין קטנה. נשדר ליה מר שלמא לילתא, א"ל, הכי אמר שמואל: קול באשה ערוה. אפשר ע"י שליח! א"ל, הכי אמר שמואל:]דף ע עמוד ב[אין שואלין בשלום אשה. על ידי בעלה! אמר ליה, הכי אמר שמואל: אין שואלין בשלום אשה כלל. שלחה ליה דביתהו: שרי ליה תגרייה, דלא נישוויך כשאר עם הארץ.

In this passage there is a dispute between Rav Yehuda and Rav Nachman about proper interaction with women. It would seem that Rav Nachman has a much laxer attitude about what type of interaction would be considered appropriate. Rav Nachman does not believe that having his minor daughter serve them drinks, or allowing his wife to receive a greeting from the guest and offer greetings in return, would be inappropriate. Rav Yehuda does. Both Rav Nachman and Rav Yehuda are students of Shmuel. How can one explain the disparity in positions between these two authorities?

It is, of course, possible simply to claim that Rav Nachman was unaware of the statements of Shmuel or at least the "proper interpretation" of these statements. Conversely, one could argue that Rav Yehuda was exaggerating his claim and reading Shmuel in the strictest possible light. Although either of these interpretations may be true, it would appear that there is an additional factor at play: geography.

---

43. His wife.
44. Literally, "to inquire after a woman's welfare." This could be understood to mean "one should not ask about a woman's health," but the idiom denotes a greeting. It is clear that the Talmud is discussing whether one may greet a woman. It does not mean that one cannot ask one's friend if his wife is healthy.

Rav Nachman was a rabbi and leader in the Nehardea community and Rav Yehuda was a rabbi and leader in Pumbeditha. These two cities and Jewish communities were very different. As Yaakov Elman has noted in a number of studies, Pumbeditha was a very closed community.[45] The Jews who lived there were conservative and did not interact extensively with the larger Persian community. Nehardea was much more metropolitan and the Jews there were often part of the upper-crust society. The stories about Rav Nachman in this Bavli text certainly give one this impression.

Perhaps the different understandings of Shmuel offered by these two Amoraim are less reflective of their respective memories about their teacher's sayings and more about the actual practices of their respective communities. In other words, it may have come down to the fact that Rav Yehuda cannot picture Shmuel having been so lenient as to allow interaction with women and Rav Nachman cannot imagine he could have been so strict as to forbid it entirely. This would then be yet another example of the phenomena explored above. Rules of proper modest behavior, including dress, are sociologically determined.

MISHNAH – CHALLAH

The issue of inappropriate exposure comes up again in a sugya with a very different context, that of women reciting blessings and performing mitzvot. The primary Tannaitic text to which the sugya is attached is a mishnah in tractate Challah (2:3).

| A woman may sit and separate *challah* in the nude, since she can cover herself [by sitting], but not a man. | האשה יושבת וקוצה חלתה ערומה מפני שהיא יכולה לכסות עצמה אבל לא האיש |

In deciding what sort of nudity constitutes inappropriate exposure during one's own performance of the mitzvah and/or reciting of the blessing, the Mishnah seems to believe that only the exposure of actual genitalia would be problematic. The definition of private nudity is, of course, something wholly different than the definition of nudity in the company of others. However, this Mishnah is analyzed in both Talmuds

---

45. See for example, Yaakov Elman, "A Tale of Two Cities: Mahoza and Pumbedita as Representing Two Halakhic Cultures," in David Golinkin, et al., eds., *Torah le-Shamma: Essays in Jewish Studies in Honor of Professor Shamma Friedman* (Jerusalem: Makhon Schechter, 2007), 3–38 (Hebrew).

to determine its relevance to the question of defining nudity when in the presence of others.

JERUSALEM TALMUD

The Yerushalmi (y. Challah 2:4) discusses this case further.

This would mean that the [exposure of the] buttocks do not count as exposure.	הדא אמרה עגבות אין בהן משום ערוה.
This applies to the recitation of blessings, but insofar as [men] ogling her, anything would be forbidden.	הדא דאת אמרה לברכה אבל להביט אפילו כל שהוא אסור.
As it was taught: "One who gazes upon a woman's ankle it is as if he is gazing at her uterus,[46] and one who gazes at her uterus, it is as if he has slept with her."	כהדא דתני: "המסתכל בעקיבה שלאשה כמסתכל בבית הרחם, והמסתכל בבית הרחם כילו בא עליה."
Shmuel said: "The voice of a woman is considered suggestive."	שמואל אמר: "קול באשה ערוה."
Why is this? [For it states:] "And it will be that due to the voice of her fornication the land will be compromised..."[47]	מה טעם? 'והיה מקול זנותה ותחנף הארץ וגו'.'

In this sugya, a clear distinction is made between two areas of halakha. In the context of the recitation of the blessing over *challah*, nudity is defined as exposure of genitalia. Anything less than this is not a problem for the recitation of blessings, since the person is not considered to be naked. However, there is another area of halakha where the definition is totally different: this is the prohibition of a man to ogle a woman. The point here is that this prohibition has nothing to do with whether a woman is properly "naked." If a man is attracted to a woman's ankle, a spot not generally considered particularly provocative, then gazing upon it would be a violation of the prohibition equal to gazing at her if she was actually naked.

The baraita continues and states that looking at a woman naked would itself be the equivalent of sleeping with her. Here one can see that the baraita isn't using technical halakhic categorization but is trying to drive home a point with some midrashic hyperbole; a person who looks at a married woman naked could certainly not be charged with adultery and executed.

---

46. A euphemism for the vulva.
47. Jer. 3:9.

The point seems to be that the prohibition of ogling a woman has to do with the man's perspective and the man's thoughts. Since a man could be attracted to anything, it is up to him not to look at that which excites him; it is not the woman's job to make sure she is completely hidden from his view. Furthermore, the baraita warns, if he disregards this prohibition and gazes on her with lewd thoughts, philosophically (not halakhically) speaking, this act resembles fornication, perhaps even adultery.

The sugya ends with one additional observation. Shmuel claims that it isn't only the sight of a woman that could excite a man. Rather, the above prohibition would apply even if he was excited by the sound of her voice. The Talmud then supports Shmuel's position with a verse from Jeremiah.

In this context, Shmuel can be understood as extending the baraita's prohibition of ogling a woman to listening to her voice. However, from the discussion of Shmuel's position in the previous section one can see that the Yerushalmi's use of his view does not fit perfectly with both interpretations offered in b. Kiddushin.

In the discussion of Shmuel's position between Rav Yehuda and Rav Nachman, it would seem that Rav Yehuda believes that Shmuel's rule is an absolute prohibition, in force whether the man knows himself to be attracted to this woman, and, more importantly, enforced by not allowing the woman to talk to the man.

Rav Nachman's belief that there would not necessarily be a problem with Yalta greeting Rav Yehuda fits much better with the use of Shmuel in the y. Challah passage. Both agree that the "attraction" problem is really the man's problem and it would be his responsibility to maintain control of himself. There is no reason for Yalta to worry about this and not greet her guest.[48] This is the overall sense one gets from the Yerushalmi as well. The women should behave normally, and the men should adapt as necessary.

To summarize, the sugya in the Yerushalmi is rather simple. Technical nudity, at least insofar as the recitation of blessings is concerned, is defined by the exposure of genitalia. The prohibition of ogling, however, has no set definition and depends entirely on the subjective reaction of the man, which is why it is solely his responsibility to avoid it.

---

48. Of course, Rav Yehuda could invoke an ironic halakhic twist and say that with visual attraction the man can avoid looking, but what can he do if the woman's voice is attracting him other than to either leave or tell her to stop talking? In his case, he could not leave as he was there for court.

What is interesting is that no middle category is discussed; the middle category being behaviors or areas of the body that when exposed would constitute provocative behavior on the part of the woman since the average man would be aroused by it. This is a somewhat subjective category, but one would imagine that in most if not all societies it would take less than full nudity to catch the attention of the average man. This is the category which forms the basis of most of the sugyot we have looked at thus far, for this is exactly what the Mishnah and Tosefta are discussing with the list of behaviors that violate *dat Yehudit*.

BABYLONIAN TALMUD

The Bavli discusses the definition of inappropriate exposure (b. Berachot 24a) as well, also related to the mishnah in m. Challah and the recitation of blessings while naked. The overall context of the sugya in the Bavli is the question of when does it become forbidden for a man to recite the Shema due to the presence of women inappropriately exposed; as pointed out earlier, a very different context from that of the mishnah in m. Challah where the woman is by herself.

The first part of the sugya that we will look at is discussing a case where two men are in bed together undressed, as was the standard way of sleeping in those days for single men when travelling and sharing hotel accommodations.[49]

Rav Yosef son of Rav Nechuniah asked Rav Yehuda: "If two [men] sleep together in one bed, can each one turn his face the other way and recite the Shema?" [Rav Yehuda] replied: "This is what Shmuel said: 'Even if he is with his wife [in bed].'" Rav Yosef attacked this idea: "His wife and 'obviously' anyone else? It's the opposite, a man's wife is like his own flesh, but someone else is not."	בעי מיניה רב יוסף בריה דרב נחוניא מרב יהודה: שנים שישנים במטה אחת, מהו שזה יחזיר פניו ויקרא קריאת שמע, וזה יחזיר פניו ויקרא קריאת שמע? אמר ליה הכי אמר שמואל: ואפילו אשתו עמו. מתקיף לה רב יוסף: אשתו ולא מיבעיא אחר? אדרבה! אשתו כגופו, אחר לאו כגופו!

---

49. This was apparently standard practice all the way through the 19th century. Herman Melville even plays with this reality in *Moby Dick* where he has Ishmael and Queequeg unknowingly book the same room and end up sharing a bed. (Found in Chapter 3 of the above work, commonly entitled "The Spouter-Inn".)

Let us ask: [One source states:] "If two [men] sleep together in one bed, each can turn his face the other way and recite [the Shema]." But a different source states: "If one is sleeping in bed, and his children and family are next to him, he may not recite the Shema unless he has a sheet that physically separates them from him. However, if his children and family were minors, it would be permitted." If one follows Rav Yosef, there is no problem, as one baraita refers to his wife and the other to other people. However, according to Shmuel, there is a problem.

מיתיבי: שנים שישנים במטה אחת - זה מחזיר פניו וקורא, וזה מחזיר פניו וקורא; ותניא אחריתי: הישן במטה ובניו ובני ביתו בצדו - הרי זה לא יקרא קריאת שמע אלא אם כן היתה טלית מפסקת ביניהן. ואם היו בניו ובני ביתו קטנים - מותר.⁵⁰ בשלמא לרב יוסף לא קשיא: הא - באשתו, הא - באחר. אלא לשמואל קשיא!

Shmuel would say to you: "And do you think that the [Tannaitic texts] work well for Rav Yosef?" Does it not state: "If He was sleeping in bed and his wife was next to him – he may not recite the Shema unless there is a sheet physically separating them." What can you say about that? Only that according to Rav Yosef the case of [saying Shema while in bed with] one's wife is a dispute among the Tannaim. According to me there is also a dispute among the Tannaim.

אמר לך שמואל: לרב יוסף מי ניחא? והתניא: [היה ישן במטה ואשתו בצדו]⁵¹ - לא יקרא קריאת שמע אלא אם כן היתה טליתו מפסקת ביניהן! אלא מאי אית לך למימר - אשתו לרב יוסף תנאי היא, לדידי נמי תנאי היא.⁵²

---

50. Later on in the Talmudic pericope there will be a discussion of what the actual definition of minor should be.

The master said: 'If his children and the members of his household were minors, it is permitted [to recite the Shema without a physical separation between their bodies]. Until what age? R. Chisda said: "For a girl, three years old, for a boy, nine years old." There are those that say: "For a girl, eleven years old and for a boy, twelve years old." Both would agree that the minor status ends at 'breasts being formed and hair sprouting' (Ezekiel 16:7).

אמר מר: אם היו בניו ובני ביתו קטנים - מותר. ועד כמה? - אמר רב חסדא: תינוקת בת שלש שנים ויום אחד, ותינוק בן תשע שנים ויום אחד. איכא דאמרי: תינוקת בת אחת עשרה שנה ויום אחד, ותינוק בן שתים עשרה שנה ויום אחד, אידי ואידי עד כדי 'שדים נכונו ושער צמח'.

51. This is the text of the Paris 671 and the Florence II.1.7 manuscripts, and the line is found in the Munich manuscript as a variant. The passage makes little sense in the standard printing, since it is only an exact repetition of the previous baraita.
52. The Talmudic pericope will later discuss whether the law should follow Shmuel or Rav Yosef.

The debate between Rav Yehuda and Rav Yosef here is very telling. The basic problem each is dealing with is whether or in what circumstances a man may recite the Shema if his body is in physical contact with the naked body of someone else. The question that the sugya opens with is can he say Shema if he is in bed naked with another man? Again, the assumption here is not that this was a situation of homosexuality, but that this was the norm for travelling men.

Rav Yehuda offers an analogy to a man being in bed with his wife. He argues that since Shmuel allows a man to recite the Shema while he and his wife are both naked in bed, he certainly would allow a man to recite the Shema while in bed with another man. The logic seems to be that generally speaking a man is attracted to his wife. Hence, if this attraction poses no problem for the recitation of the Shema, it should certainly pose no problem when the man is in bed with someone he is not attracted to at all.

Rav Yosef disputes this logic. He says that a man is so used to being in bed with his wife that this situation would not be considered halakhically problematic. Being in bed with someone else could still be a problem, however, even if one were to accept Shmuel's principle that a man can recite the Shema while in bed with his wife.

At first, Rav Yosef's opinion sounds bizarre. He can't possibly think that a man would be more attracted to another man than to his own wife.[53] The answer would appear to be that Rav Yosef is not talking about attraction per se; he is talking about distraction. Rav Yosef would say that, of course, if a man is feeling aroused by his wife, or by anyone, he could not recite the Shema. This, he would say, is obvious and not something halakha would need to specify. The issue here is that a man is so used to having his wife next to him in bed that, assuming he is not feeling aroused, the situation feels normal. Her body is considered by him as if it were

---

> Rav Kahana said to Rav Ashi: "In a different case Rava said that even though Shmuel's position is refuted, the law still follows Shmuel, so what is the rule here?" [Rav Ashi responded:] "Do we weave everything out of the same cloth? Rather, where such a thing is stated, it is stated; when it is not stated, it is not stated!"

אמר ליה רב כהנא לרב אשי: התם אמר רבא אף על גב דתיובתא דשמואל הלכתא כוותיה דשמואל, הכא מאי? - אמר ליה: אטו כולהו בחדא מחתא מחתינהו? אלא: היכא דאיתמר איתמר, והיכא דלא איתמר לא איתמר.

53. Since there is no reason that the Talmud here should be seen as questioning the aphorism (b. Kiddushin 82a) לא נחשדו ישראל על משכב זכור.

his own. However, for the travelling man who finds himself in bed with another man, the situation may not be arousing but it may very well be distracting. The men are cognizant of each other's bodies, making the recitation of the Shema feel as if he is reciting Shema in the presence of nudity.

The Talmud next turns to the original case posed as a question by Rav Yosef son of Rav Nechuniah, i.e., that each man turns to the side to say the Shema.

| The master said: "This one should turn his head and recite the Shema..." – but there is still [the proximity of the other man's] buttocks![54] This supports Rav Huna, for Rav Huna said: "the [exposure of the] buttocks does not count as exposure." Let us support Rav Huna's assertion with a source: "A woman may sit and separate *challah* in the nude, since she can cover her genitals[55] with the ground, but not a man." Rav Nachman bar Yitzchak explained: "This is referring to when her genitals are covered over[56] by the ground." | אמר מר: זה מחזיר פניו וקורא קריאת שמע. והא איכא עגבות! מסייע ליה לרב הונא, דאמר רב הונא: עגבות אין בהם משום ערוה. לימא מסייע ליה לרב הונא: האשה יושבת וקוצה לה חלתה ערומה מפני שיכולה לכסות פניה בקרקע, אבל לא האיש. תרגמה רב נחמן בר יצחק: כגון שהיו פניה טוחות בקרקע. |

The parallels between this treatment of the sources and that of the Yerushalmi are clear. Both texts are concerned with the technical definition of nudity and are attempting to determine whether it extends further than only genitals to include even the buttocks. There is an important difference between the two treatments, however. The Jerusalem Talmud is only considering the question of whether exposure of buttocks is considered nudity where the person is alone. It does not at all discuss whether exposure of buttocks would be considered nudity for another in the room. The Bavli, however, at least in this pericope, is arguing that Rav Huna would admit that the physical proximity of another man's buttocks would not hinder the first man from reciting the Shema.

Accepting that physical proximity should be considered at least somewhat analogous to seeing, it appears that there are three distinct categories of nudity relevant to the recitation of Shema: 1. one's own

---

54. Ostensibly the two men's bodies are touching; see Rashi ad loc.
55. Literally "her face" but this is a euphemism.
56. Literally "plastered."

nudity; 2. the presence of non-arousing nudity; 3. the presence of arousing nudity. Insofar as the first category, this was explored by the Mishnah in m. Challah. The only time that one's own nudity poses a problem is with actual genital exposure. Rav Huna maintains that even the buttocks do not count as nudity. Rav Yosef seems to want to include a man's wife in the category as well, at least for physical proximity. The Talmud will also discuss the question of whether pubic hair and/or body hair sticking out from clothing is considered nudity.

> Rav Mari said to Rav Pappa: "If hair is sticking out of his clothing, what is the rule?" [Rav Pappa] called this: "Hair, hair (i.e., it's only hair)."
>
> אמר ליה רב מרי לרב פפא: שער יוצא בבגדו מהו? קרא עליה: שער, שער.

Rav Pappa states clearly and emphatically that hair never has the status of "nudity," and should be considered irrelevant with regard to a person saying *Shema* in its presence. It is reasonable to assume that Rav Pappa is working with the premise that male body hair is not going to be arousing for anyone saying Shema,[57] which is what separates this case from the ones that will immediately follow: about exposed parts of women where men are saying Shema, and an example of the third type of nudity – nudity that arouses others who are in the vicinity of the incompletely clad woman.

The third type of nudity is subjective, as it has less to do with actual exposure and more about the state of mind of the reciter. Hence, thus far, no set parameters or definition have been offered for this type of nudity. This will be the subject of the next piece of this sugya.

> Rabbi Yitzchak said: "A handbreadth of a woman's [exposed flesh] is considered suggestive (*erva*)."
>
> אמר רבי יצחק: "טפח באשה ערוה."
>
> With regard to what?
>
> למאי?
>
> If this is meant to prohibit [a man's] gazing at it –
>
> אילימא לאסתכולי בה –
>
> Did not Rav Sheshet [already] say: "Why does the verse list regular jewelry together
>
> והא אמר רב ששת: "למה מנה הכתוב תכשיטין שבחוץ עם

---

57. The above interpretation is that of Rashi, but, as will be seen in Chapter 4, R. Chananel (quoted in the *Or Zarua*, 1:133:1) believes that Rav Mari is referring to female body/pubic hair, which makes this pericope more complicated.

with erotic jewelry?[58] This is to teach you that anyone who gazes at the little finger of a woman is considered as if he were gazing at her private parts."

תכשיטין שבפנים? לומר לך: כל המסתכל באצבע קטנה של אשה כאילו מסתכל במקום התורף.״

Rather, it must be in reference to a person's own wife, and in regard to the recitation of the Shema.

אלא: באשתו, ולקריאת שמע.

Rav Chisda said: "A woman's calf (*shok*)[59] is considered suggestive, for [the verse] states: '*Reveal* the *shok*, pass through the rivers,'[60] and it is written: 'Your nudity shall be *revealed*, even your disgrace shall be seen.'"[61]

אמר רב חסדא: ״שוק באשה ערוה, שנאמר: ׳גלי שוק עברי נהרות׳, וכתיב: ׳תגל ערותך וגם תראה חרפתך׳.״

Shmuel said: "The voice of a woman is considered suggestive, as it states: 'for your voice is sweet and your appearance attractive.'"[62]

אמר שמואל: ״קול באשה ערוה, שנאמר: ׳כי קולך ערב ומראך נאוה׳.״

Rav Sheshet said: "The hair of a woman is considered suggestive, as it states: 'Your hair is like a flock of goats.'"[63]

אמר רב ששת: ״שער באשה ערוה, שנאמר: ׳שערך כעדר העזים׳.״

The main thrust of this source is a list of four examples of suggestive dress or behavior. The common denominator seems to be that all four examples are meant to be surprising or, at least, not obvious; up until this point in the sugya, only exposure of or proximity to genitals and buttocks have been discussed.

R. Yitzchak begins with the statement that a handbreadth of exposed flesh, presumably at the periphery of the woman's covered areas, should be considered provocative. His point seems to be that although it would

---

58. This is referring to Exodus 35:22 and/or Numbers 31:50, which includes in its list of jewelry the *kumaz*. The rabbis understand this to be a sort of erotic adornment.
59. The commentaries debate whether the *shok* refers to the thigh or the calf. See below note 67 on page 76 and note 48 on page 195.
60. Isaiah 47:2.
61. Isaiah 47:3. This is a *gezera shava* based on the word "reveal." In one place it states that the calf will be revealed and in another it states that the woman's nudity "*erva*" will be revealed – hence calf equals "*erva*."
62. Song 2:14.
63. Song 4:1.

be overly fastidious of halakha to count centimeters and a certain amount of reasonable ambiguity exists with clothing and coverage, nevertheless, at the point where an entire handbreadth "extra" is exposed, the ambiguity has ended, and the woman can be understood to be dressed suggestively.

Rav Chisda, Shmuel and Rav Sheshet then go on to list three more unexpected examples of suggestiveness: calf, voice, and hair. For our purposes, the inclusion of hair in this list is telling. Firstly, it demonstrates that exposure of hair is considered provocative, but less so than regular sorts of nudity that did not require listing in this source. This "sociological truth" can be seen expressed in some of the sources in the previous chapter as well.[64]

The editor's problem with, at least, the first statement – if not the entire list – stems from the same dichotomous principle seen in the Yerushalmi. It cannot be referring to the woman vis-à-vis herself, since the law there includes only genital exposure. However, it cannot refer to being in the presence of non-arousing nudity either, since this too is limited to genital exposure or proximity. Conversely, it cannot refer to the prohibition of ogling, since this prohibition is purely subjective and has no limits – even the pinky finger can be a problem for this halakha.

The editor then suggests an entirely new category: this is the type of exposure before which a man should not recite the Shema. According to this, a wife's less than perfect coverage can be seen as problematic. This seems to be in tension with the position of Rav Yosef that a wife's nudity is considered by a man to be like his own. One can solve this in one of two ways. Either one can suggest that this pericope does not follow Rav Yosef or one can suggest that Rav Yosef would distinguish between seeing and physical proximity when it comes to arousing nudity.

If this latter suggestion is correct, the Talmud here is suggesting that there is some sort of general standard of dress, below which the woman's appearance can be considered provocative. This is, of course, not a

---

64. For example, one can see this principle operating in the story of the woman who uncovered her hair to gather up the oil (infra text accompanying footnote 31 on page 18). This may have been crass behavior, but it is difficult to imagine that she would have done the same if it required removing her dress. Another example is the Sifre (on page 3) in which the question is posed about why the uncovering of hair was mentioned specifically. The answers range from "even hair" to "only hair," implying that exposure of hair is something essentially different (less) than exposure of body.

problem for one's wife to be dressed this way at home, unless the person is trying to recite the Shema; but it brings up the possibility that if she were dressed this way in public, it could be considered problematic. This possibility brings us full circle back to the other sources analyzed in these chapters discussing just this issue.

BERACHOT VERSUS KETUBOT

When considering this source in light of the discussion in B. Ketubot, one can't help but notice a certain tension. Why would Rav Sheshet use a verse in Song of Songs to demonstrate the semi-erotic nature of exposed hair when this has already been learned from a midrash on a verse in Numbers?[65]

The simplest interpretation of this quasi-contradiction in sources is to state that all of these insights in b. Berachot are not really derivations of halakha from a text (*derasha*) but are really the projection of sociological realities upon the text (*asmachta*). This is why the verses quoted are all in reference to parts of the body or actions that were considered *somewhat* provocative at the time. None of the verses referring to obviously sexual parts are used in this text,[66] and neither are verses that refer to obviously non-sexual parts.[67] This proves that the *derashot* here are not verse-driven but stem from a pre-existing notion of what parts of a woman's body (or what behaviors) are borderline erotic. Since the verses in Song of Songs describe almost every part of a woman's body (as well as a man's), this was clearly a conscious choice.

Having established the sociologically driven reality of this text, it follows logically that the actual halakhic application of it would be

---

65. This odd trend to back up the midrash from Numbers with another midrash has already been noted in the previous chapter's discussion of the Sifre, where the verse in 2 Samuel about Tamar is used as a "backup" verse.

66. E.g., breasts, abdomen, thighs, etc.

67. E.g., eyes, nose, feet, etc. A unique solution is offered by Rabbi Chaim Hirschenson (*Nimukei Rashi – Chiddushei Rav Chaim Hirschenson, Nasso* 69). Noting that there are parts of the body described romantically in Song of Songs that are not defined as *ervot*, such as the eyes, lips and teeth, he concludes that the fact that hair is mentioned in Song of Songs cannot indicate conclusively that it is an *erva*. Thus, he suggests that the Gemara must be referring specifically to pubic hair, which is indeed proximate to the genitalia, as is the *shok* mentioned in this same passage. Rabbi Hirschenson's position will be addressed later in Chapter 8. It is worth noting that this radical suggestion is contradicted by the many Rishonim cited in this work.

EXPOSED HAIR IN AMORAIC SOURCES

contingent upon society. This means that the exact same principle is at work here as was at work in almost all of the other Tannaitic and Amoraic discussions of women's hair.

The only exception is the baraita quoted in the sugya of B. Ketubot, where the requirement for a woman to cover her hair is referred to as a Torah law. It would appear that this position is an outlier, and that Shmuel's attempted resolution of the tension between the Mishnah and the baraita in that sugya should be taken as an important piece of theoretical Torah, but not a normative statement reflective of the general tenor of the Talmudic discussion of hair covering.[68]

From the discussion of the Talmudic editor in b. Berachot, it would seem that the Talmud does not believe that there is a specific technical prohibition for women to dress immodestly. Oddly enough, this fits well with the sugya in b. Ketubot, in a certain sense. In b. Ketubot, b. Sotah and b. Gittin, the significance of a woman dressing or behaving inappropriately is tied to the right of her husband to divorce her without paying her ketubah. In b. Berachot, the only halakhic significance the Talmud can find in a statement about what is considered provocative dress or behavior for women has to do with men reciting Shema. Why does the Talmud not simply suggest that the significance is that a woman would not be permitted to appear this way in public regardless of her husband's ketubah payments or a man's ability to say Shema in their presence? It would seem that this is not a halakhic category the Talmud recognizes.[69]

Men Whose Passions Are Under Control

There are a number of Talmudic passages which describe rabbis in scenarios that seem to be questionable from the perspective of proper behavior with the opposite sex. The most surprising example comes from b. Ketubot (17a):

Rav Acha would place [the bride] on his shoulders and dance. Some other rabbis inquired [of him]: "May we do this as well?" He replied to them: "If they are	רב אחא מרכיב לה אכתפיה ומרקד, אמרי ליה רבנן: אנן מהו למיעבד הכי? אמר להו: אי דמיין עלייכו ככשורא –

---

68. In fact, as was pointed out in the previous section, it may not even be reflective of the final outcome of that very sugya!
69. It is possible to argue that this is only true of liminally provocative dress, but that actual nudity is forbidden according to the Torah, with some not-as-yet specific definition of this. Later chapters will discuss this possibility.

> like a wooden-beam to you then yes, otherwise no." Rabbi Shmuel bar Nachmani said in the name of Rabbi Yonatan: "It is permitted to gaze upon the bride's face all seven days [of the marital feasting] in order to make her more beloved to her husband." However, the halakha is not in accordance with him.
>
> לחיי, ואי לא – לא. א"ר שמואל בר נחמני א"ר יונתן: מותר להסתכל בפני כלה כל שבעה, כדי לחבבה על בעלה. ולית הלכתא כוותיה.

In this story, Rav Acha does more than just gaze upon a woman's hair, he actually physically touches her in a rather unusual way, by picking her up and placing her upon his shoulders. Although this is by no means a sexual act, it still goes well beyond standard decorum and by all rights should be forbidden. Rav Acha's explanation, when asked about the permissibility of his action, is to say that the matter is personally subjective. In other words, it isn't a question of social norm or acceptability but of a given individual's emotional makeup. If a man is aroused by such behavior he may not engage in it; otherwise it is permissible.

The Talmud then references Rabbi Yonatan's position which, although not involving any physical contact, is, in fact, a step further than that of Rav Acha. Rabbi Yonatan allows men to gaze upon a bride in such a way as to make it obvious to her groom that they find her beautiful. In doing so, it seems impossible to say that men – with no exceptions – would not find gazing upon a woman they find beautiful arousing. Nevertheless, Rabbi Yonatan grants carte blanche permission as a special dispensation in order to bring some joy to her husband. The Talmud, however, rejects this lenient view. Nevertheless, it does not reject that of Rav Acha.

A similar principle to that of Rav Acha appears in b. Kiddushin (81b–82a):

> Rav Acha bar Abba went to the house of Rav Chisda his son-in-law. He picked up his granddaughter and put her on his lap. [Rav Chisda] said to him: "Doesn't the master know that she is betrothed?" [Rav Acha] responded: "You have violated the principle of Rav, for Rav Yehuda said in the name of Rav – some say it was Rabbi Elazar: 'It is forbidden for a man to betroth his daughter while she is a minor until she is old
>
> רב אחא בר אבא איקלע לבי רב חסדא חתניה, שקליה לבת ברתיה אותבוה בכנפיה. אמר ליה: לא סבר לה מר דמקדשא? אמר ליה: עברת לך אדרב, דאמר רב יהודה אמר רב, ואיתימא רבי אלעזר: אסור לאדם שיקדש את בתו כשהיא קטנה, עד שתגדיל ותאמר בפלוני אני רוצה.

enough to say "that is the person I want."'" [Rav Chisda responded]: "The master has also violated the principle of Shmuel, for Shmuel said: 'One may not interact with a woman.'" [Rav Acha] replied: "I follow the other principle of Shmuel, for Shmuel said: 'All for the sake of heaven.'"

מר נמי עבר ליה אדשמואל, דאמר שמואל: אין משתמשים באשה! אמר ליה: אנא כאידך דשמואל סבירא לי, דאמר שמואל: "הכל לשם שמים".

In this case the "violation" seems trivial to our eyes, as it does to Rav Acha bar Abba himself. Rav Acha bar Abba, visiting his daughter's house, puts his minor granddaughter on his lap and is rebuked by his son-in-law since the girl is betrothed and, anyway, she is a girl. Rav Acha bar Abba replies by rebuking his son-in-law for betrothing such a young girl and ends with an important principle. Quoting Shmuel, Rav Acha bar Abba claims that it is all dependent on a person's intention. He is just being playful and affectionate with his little granddaughter – the behavior is harmless[70] and, consequently, not a matter for concern, halakhically speaking.

A somewhat different kind of scenario comes from a story in b. Berachot 20a and b. Bava Metzia 84a:

Rabbi Yochanan would go and sit at the gates where women would immerse in the mikvah. He said: "When the Jewish women come out from their immersion they will come upon me [and see me]. [I do this] so that they will have good looking children like me and ones learned in Torah like me." The Rabbis asked him: "But doesn't the master worry about the evil eye?" He replied to them: "I am a descendent of Joseph upon whom the evil eye can have no power."

רבי יוחנן הוה אזיל ויתיב אשערי טבילה, אמר: כי סלקן בנות ישראל מטבילת מצוה לפגעו בי, כי היכי דלהוו להו בני שפירי כוותי, גמירי אורייתא כוותי. אמרו ליה רבנן: לא מסתפי מר מעינא בישא? אמר להו: אנא מזרעא דיוסף קאתינא, דלא שלטא ביה עינא בישא.

In this story, R. Yochanan puts himself in a situation where he sees women going in and out of the mikvah building. R. Yochanan claims that he does this so that the women, upon seeing his good looks and his intense

---

70. Rashi in Kiddushin 82a suggests a second reason for his behavior, one also cited by Ran, in his commentary on Rif. They suggest that he was doing it to make his own daughter, the girl's mother, happy, as she would enjoy seeing her father being affectionate with her daughter / his granddaughter.

study, will think about him and desire that their children be like him. His students and colleagues, hearing this, ask him if he is not worried about the evil eye in this situation, to which he replies that, as a descendant of Joseph, he is immune to such concerns.

However, the reader may ask, that only solves the problem of the women looking at him, but what about his looking at them? He is sitting in the vicinity of a mikvah, and sees the women going in and out. One would imagine that this could bring up sexual thoughts. Apparently, Rabbi Yochanan was not concerned with this possibility. Perhaps, as will be suggested by Ritva (see Ch. 5), this is for the same reason that Rav Acha was unconcerned about the bride on his shoulders: Rabbi Yochanan was master of his passions and the goings and comings of the women was of no sexual interest to him.

Taking Advantage

In line with some of the modesty discussions referenced above, the rabbis discuss the possibility that a man may unfairly take advantage of a woman's innocent behavior to invade her modesty.

WALKING AND PASSING

In b. Berachot 61a, there is a collection of baraitot that discuss interactions that are innocent on the woman's part but problematic on the man's part.

It was taught: "A man should not walk behind a woman on the road, even behind his wife. If he comes upon a woman on a bridge, he should let her pass on one side, and anyone who crosses a river behind a woman, has no share in the World to Come."	תניא: לא יהלך אדם אחורי אשה בדרך ואפילו אשתו, נזדמנה לו על הגשר - יסלקנה לצדדין, וכל העובר אחורי אשה בנהר - אין לו חלק לעולם הבא.
Our Rabbis taught: "One who passes money from his hand to a woman's in order to gaze upon her, even if he had Torah learning and good deeds like our teacher Moses, he will not clear himself of judgment in *Gehinnom*, as it says (Prov. 11:21): 'hand to hand he will not be cleared of evil' – he will not be cleared of the judgment of *Gehinnom*."[71]	תנו רבנן: המרצה מעות לאשה מידו לידה כדי להסתכל בה - אפילו יש בידו תורה ומעשים טובים כמשה רבינו - לא ינקה מדינה של גיהנם, שנאמר (משלי י״א) יד ליד לא ינקה רע - לא ינקה מדינה של גיהנם.

---

71. A version of this line appears in m. Kallah 1:6, m. Kallah Rabbati 1:6, and *Midrash Aggadah* Lev. 19:2 (ed. Buber), in *Parashat Acharei Mot* (2).

The first set of cases deals with a man walking near or behind a woman. The rabbis imagine that this could be titillating for the man, and the woman would be none the wiser. Hence the man is told that he may not walk behind a woman and ogle her body, and he may not cross a bridge that a woman is crossing; ostensibly this would make them pass close to each other. Most problematic would be crossing a river behind her, since by the nature of this activity there is a good chance her modesty would be compromised, through no fault of her own, and the man, instead of taking advantage of this, should keep his distance.

The second baraita deals with a case where the man and woman are engaged in an activity that is objectively neutral but that the man is receiving secret enjoyment from. The man passes the woman something – money in this case – but in such a way or with the intention of getting a better look at her. The rabbis are particularly bothered by this and see such behavior as taking advantage and hyperbolize the sin and the punishment to get their point across.

THE MAN WHO WOULD "DIE WITHOUT HER"

The Jerusalem Talmud, in two different places (y. Shabbat 14:4 and y. Avodah Zarah 2:2), discusses the rule prohibiting a person from receiving healing at the expense of committing one of the big three sins – idolatry, murder and certain sexual sins. Discussing the sexual sins, the Talmud writes:

This is not only applicable to a case where a man says: "Bring me that married woman," but even [for him] to listen to her voice. Like the case of a certain man who fell in love with a woman in the days of R. Elazar, and [his love-sickness] became dangerous. People came and asked [R. Elazar] what can be done to save this man's life? [R. Elazar] said: "Let him die, and do nothing." [They asked]: "May he be allowed to listen to her voice and thereby avoid death?" [R. Elazar] replied: "Let him die and do nothing."	לא סוף דבר בשאמר לו הבא לי אשת איש אלא אפילו לשמוע את קולה. כהדא חד בר נש רחם איתא ביומי דרבי אלעזר וסכן. אתון שאלון ליה מהו תיעביד קומוי וייחי. אמר ימית ולא כן. מהו ישמע קלה ולא ימות. אמר ימית ולא כן.
What was the case? R. Yaakov bar Iddi and R. Yitzchak bar Nachman: One said: "She was a married woman." The other said: "She was single."	מה הוות. רבי יעקב בר אידי ור' יצחק בר נחמן. חד אמר אשת איש. וחורנה אמר פנויה.

According to the position that she was married, [R. Elazar's reaction] is understandable. But according to the position that she was single, didn't Bar Kocha the carpenter fall in love with a woman in the days of R. Elazar and he allowed him [to marry her]? In one case she must have been single and the other married. [No,] even if one says that they were both single, one can explain this by suggesting that in one case he began to notice her while she was still married.

מאן דאמר אשת איש ניחא. ומאן דאמר פנויה והא בר כוחא נגרא רחם איתא ביומוי דר׳ אלעזר ושרא ליה. כאן בפנויה וכאן באשת איש. ואפי׳ תימר כאן וכאן בפנויה. תיפתר שנתן עיניו בה עד שהיא א"א.

There are those who suggest that this was an important woman and she would not marry him, and anything that he would end up doing with her would have been in sin, therefore, [R. Elazar] forbade him [to pursue her].

ואית דבעי מימר איתא רבה הוות ולא מנסבא. וכל מה דהוא מעבד באיסור הוה מעבד. בגין כן אסר ליה.

In this context, the Talmud cites a story about a man who felt that he needed to be with a certain woman (not his wife) in order to survive. What stands out is that there was a suggestion that the man could receive sufficient satisfaction just from hearing her voice, and even this was forbidden to him. The Talmud then goes on to suggest that this extended prohibition may even apply to unmarried women. It would seem that once the man makes it clear that he is deriving sexual satisfaction from the woman, even if the act is not sexual on her part at all, R. Elazar considered this to be an invasion of the woman's modesty and that the man has no right to do this, even if not doing it could cost him his own life.

This same basic story and analysis appears in the Babylonian Talmud as well (b. Sanhedrin 75a).

Rav Yehuda said in the name of Rav:

אמר רב יהודה אמר רב:

"It once happened that a man cast his eyes upon a certain woman and his heart was filled with black bile.[72] They came and

"מעשה באדם אחד שנתן עיניו באשה אחת, והעלה לבו טינא.

---

72. Black bile (in Greek μέλαινα χολή) was one of the four "humors" of Hippocrates, which, in great abundance, was believed to cause love-sickness. This translation of the term was first suggested by Barry Wimpfheimer. For more on this midrash in general, and the translation of the term in specific, see: Barry Scott Wimpfheimer,

asked doctors, and they said: 'There will be no cure unless he sleeps with her.'

The Sages said: 'Let him die rather than sleep with her.'

'What if she just stands before him nude?'

'Let him die and she not stand before him nude.'

'What if she speaks to him from behind a barrier?'

'Let him die and she not speak to him from behind a barrier.'"

R. Yaakov bar Iddi and R. Shmuel bar Nachmani debated this.

One said: "The woman was married."

The other said: "The woman was single."

The position that she was married makes sense, however with regard to the position that she was single, why [were the Sages] so strict?

Rav Pappa said: "Because of embarrassment to the family."

Rav Acha son of Rav Iyka said:

"So that Jewish women not become promiscuous."

Let him marry her?! It wouldn't have helped, following R. Yitzchak's argument, for R. Yitzchak said: "From the day the Temple was destroyed the joy of sex was taken away and given to sinners, for it says: 'Stolen water is sweet, and secret bread is pleasant' (Prov. 9:17)."

ובאו ושאלו לרופאים, ואמרו: 'אין לו תקנה עד שתבעל.'

אמרו חכמים: 'ימות, ואל תבעל לו.'

'תעמוד לפניו ערומה?'

'ימות ואל תעמוד לפניו ערומה.'

'תספר עמו מאחורי הגדר?'

'ימות ולא תספר עמו מאחורי הגדר.'"

פליגי בה רבי יעקב בר אידי ורבי שמואל בר נחמני.

חד אמר: "אשת איש היתה."

וחד אמר: "פנויה היתה."

בשלמא למאן דאמר אשת איש היתה - שפיר. אלא למאן דאמר פנויה היתה מאי כולי האי?

רב פפא אמר: "משום פגם משפחה."

רב אחא בריה דרב איקא אמר:

"כדי שלא יהו בנות ישראל פרוצות בעריות."

ולינסבה מינסב! לא מייתבה דעתיה, כדרבי יצחק, דאמר רבי יצחק: "מיום שחרב בית המקדש ניטלה טעם ביאה וניתנה לעוברי עבירה, שנאמר (משלי ט:יז): 'מים גנובים ימתקו ולחם סתרים ינעם.'"

Narrating the Law: A Poetics of Talmudic Legal Stories (Divinations: Rereading Late Ancient Religion; Philadelphia: University of Pennsylvania Press, 2011), 32–62 [54].

Although the ending suggestion for why he doesn't marry her is different, the overall sugya is the same. Again, the Sages do not allow the man to pursue her, even just to hear her voice; and again, there are some who believe that this should even apply to single women. This demonstrates how seriously the rabbis took the prohibition for a man to sexually invade a woman even in a way known only to him. These accounts parallel the prohibitions referenced above of passing something to a woman just to gaze at her or gazing at her little finger or at colored clothing.

Which Women Cover Their Hair?

An issue that comes up later in the Rishonim, but is not dealt with explicitly in the Talmudic literature, is which women need to cover their hair? Is hair covering a requirement only for married women, or is it just that since the consequence of public exposure of hair is vulnerability to divorce without the ketubah payment, only married women are discussed?

There is no explicit source about this, but there are passages that seem to have possible relevance to the question.

NEDARIM

As part of a discussion of precise understanding of colloquial terms, the Mishnah (m. Nedarim 3:8) writes:

| One who vows [to receive no benefit] from black-haired people is forbidden [to benefit from] the bald and the grey haired, but is permitted [to benefit from] women and children, as they are not referred to as black-haired; only men are. | נודר משחורי הראש אסור בקרחין ובעלי שיבות ומותר בנשים ובקטנים שאין נקראין שחורי הראש אלא אנשים. |

The Mishnah clearly considers the expression "black-haired people" to be a colloquial reference to men. The Babylonian Talmud analyzes this (b. Nedarim 30b).

| Why is this? Men sometimes cover their hair and sometimes reveal their hair, but women always cover, and minors always reveal. | מ"ט? אנשים זימנין דמיכסו רישייהו וזימנין דמגלו רישייהו, אבל נשים לעולם מיכסו, וקטנים לעולם מיגלו. |

Although one cannot offer a definite proof from this passage, it would seem that the working assumption of the passage is that all adult women, regardless of marital status, would cover their hair in this society.

NUMBERS RABBAH

A similar implication to that of B. Nedarim can be found in one of the comments from Numbers Rabbah on the sotah verse (*Nasso*, 9:16).

> And he should expose – Why? Since it is the practice of Israelite women to cover their hair. Therefore, [the kohen] would expose her hair and say to her: 'You have separated yourself from the ways of the Israelite women, whose custom is to go out with their heads covered. And you went out like the idolatrous women, who go out with their hair exposed. Now you have what you wanted!'
>
> ופרע - למה? שדרך בנות ישראל להיות ראשיהן מכוסות. ולכך היה פורע ראשה ואומר לה: 'את פרשת מדרך בנות ישראל שדרכן להיות מכוסות ראשיהן והלכת בדרכי העובדי כוכבים שהן מהלכות ראשיהן פרועות. הרי לך מה שרצית!'

Again, there is no explicit statement in this passage about which Jewish women need to cover their hair, but one gets the impression that it was adult Jewish women as a whole, not just the married ones; however, this source is more ambiguous than the first. The question will be discussed more fully in the section on Rishonim, since another of these authorities will bring it up explicitly. (This is also discussed in excursuses five and six.)

Two Righteous Women

We will end this chapter with a look at two "cases" of women and their hair coverings discussed in rabbinic literature.

KIMCHIT

The first hair covering story worth noting is the account of Kimchit the righteous woman. The story is found in multiple places in rabbinic literature. The dominant version is the one found in the Yerushalmi, with which we will begin.

JERUSALEM TALMUD

In the first halakha of the first chapter of Yoma,[73] the Yerushalmi records this story:

---

73. y. Yoma 1:1. The story is also found in y. Megillah 1:10; y. Horayot 3:2; Leviticus Rabbah, Acharei Mot 20; Pesiqta de-Rav Kahana, 26 (*Acharei Mot*); Numbers Rabbah, Bamidbar 2.

> It happened with Shimon ben Kimchit that he went to speak with the king on the eve of the Day of Atonement. A spray of spittle fell [from the king's] mouth onto [Shimon's] cloak and made him impure. Yehuda, his brother, took his place and served as the high priest [for that day]. So, their mother got to see two of her sons serve as high priests on the same day.
>
> Kimchit had seven sons and all of them served as high priests. The Sages sent a message to her asking: "What good deeds have you done?"[74] She said to them: "May [a curse] fall upon me if the walls of my house have ever seen the hairs of my head or the seam of my cloak."
>
> They said: "All flour (*kemach*) is flour, but the flour of Kimchit is fine flour."[75] They applied [this verse] to her: 'All the glory of the king's daughter is internal; her dress is of embroidered gold' (Psalms 45:14).

> מעשה בשמעון בן קמחית שיצא לדבר עם המלך ערב יום הכיפורים ונתזה צינורה של רוק מפיו על בגדיו וטימתו ונכנס יהודה אחיו ושימש תחתיו בכהונה גדולה וראת אימן שני בניה כהנים גדולים ביום אחד.
>
> שבעה בנים היו לה לקמחית וכולן שימשו בכהונה גדולה. שלחו חכמים ואמרו לה: "מה מעשים טובים יש בידך?" אמרה להן: "יבא עלי אם ראו קורות ביתי שערות ראשי ואימרת חלוקי מימיי."
>
> אמרון: "כל קימחיא קמח וקמחא דקמחית סולת." וקרון עלה: ד'כל כבודה בת מלך פנימה ממשבצות זהב לבושה.'

On the one hand, it seems clear that the rabbis are complimenting Kimchit for her exemplary behavior in the realm of modesty. Even more than this, the compliment of the sages was simply a reflection of the reality of her life's spiritual success with regard to her children. On the other hand, the story needs to be read in its proper genre, i.e., a story about exceptional piety. If one were to attempt to learn halakha from this story, one would come to the surprising conclusion that it would be forbidden for a woman to undress at all, even in the privacy of her own house!

BABYLONIAN TALMUD

This same account appears in the Babylonian Talmud in Yoma (47a) as well, with some small differences.

> Our rabbis taught: Kimchit had seven sons and all of them served as high priests. The

> תנו רבנן: שבעה בנים היו לה לקמחית וכולן שמשו בכהונה

---

74. I.e., to deserve this honor.
75. A play on her name.

| Sages said to her: "What have you done such that you merited this?" She said to them: "My walls have never seen the braids of my hair." They said to her: "Many have behaved thus, but to no avail." | גדולה. אמרו לה חכמים: "מה עשית שזכית לכך?" אמרה להם: "מימי לא ראו קורות ביתי קלעי שערי". אמרו לה: "הרבה עשו כן, ולא הועילו". |

Although the story is virtually identical, the valence of the conversation between Kimchit and the Sages is very different. Kimchit believes that her merit is that she never uncovered her hair in the privacy of her house; even leaving her hair in braids was considered insufficiently modest by her. Ironically, the Sages seem unimpressed by this statement. On the one hand, they tell her that she is far from the only person to have such standards. On the other hand, they point out that she is still the only woman that merited having all of her sons serve as high priests. The implication is that not even Kimchit really knows the actual source of her merit.

From the reaction of the Sages, one might argue that since they considered Kimchit's "meritorious behavior" somewhat banal, perhaps they believe that Kimchit's behavior is actually an example of what would be standard practice for women – thereby making it normative *dat Yehudit*. However, looking at the statement closely, it is clear that that is not the point. The Sages do not mean to imply that uncovering one's hair alone in one's own house is forbidden or immodest, only that the behavior of Kimchit, although exceedingly modest, was not uniquely so, and therefore cannot explain her unique reward.

It would seem that there is nothing one can learn about the normative requirements for modesty, or even just the normative behavior of observant Jewish women, from the exceptional case of Kimchit.

HAIR COVERING – THE WIFE OF ON BEN PELET

In the Babylonian Talmud (b. Sanhedrin 109b), there is a story of a woman who exposed her hair in public in order to save her husband's life.[76]

| Rav said: The wife of On ben Pelet saved him. She said to him: "What are you getting out of this [rebellion]? If one side becomes master, you will be the student, and if the other side becomes master, you will | אמר רב: און בן פלת אשתו הצילתו, אמרה ליה: מאי נפקא לך מינה? אי מר רבה – אנת תלמידא, ואי מר רבה – אנת תלמידא. אמר לה: מאי |

---

76. The story also appears in Numbers Rabbah (*Korach* 18:20), *Midrash Tanchuma* (Buber; *Korach* 24), and the Yalkut Shimoni (*Mishlei* 950).

be the student." He replied to her: "What can I do? I was at the first meeting, and I swore to join them." She said to him: "I know that the entire congregation is holy, for it says 'for the entire nation is holy' (Num. 16)." She said to him: "Go back, and I will save you." She made him drink wine, made him drunk, and made him lay down inside [the house]. She sat at the door and undid her hair. Anyone who came and saw her turned back. As this was occurring, the [rebels] were swallowed [by the earth].

אעביד, הואי בעצה, ואשתבעי לי בהדייהו: אמרה ליה: ידענא דכולה כנישתא קדישתא נינהו, דכתיב (במדבר ט״ז) כי כל העדה כלם קדשים. אמרה ליה: תוב, דאנא מצילנא לך. אשקיתיה חמרא, וארויתיה, ואגניתיה גואי, אותבה על בבא, וסתרתה למזיה, כל דאתא חזיה, הדר. אדהכי והכי אבלעו להו.

According to this story, despite the fact that there was a serious dispute between Korach, Datan, and Aviram on one side and Moshe and Aharon on the other, nevertheless, the people as a whole were still strictly scrupulous. For this reason, On's wife knew that no one would enter their house if she were not dressed appropriately. In her – correct – estimation, it would take nothing more than fully exposing her hair in order to keep the rebels from entering the house and reminding On of his promise.

There are a number of elements to this story worth noting. The first is that the term used for exposing her hair is סתר, undoing. This would imply that her hair was not only uncovered but fully undone, i.e., not in braids or coiffed. This is the term used in the Mishnah and Tosefta of Sotah discussed in the first chapter.

Secondly, one gets the impression that On's wife's behavior, although immodest, was not properly "sinful." The sin would have been on the men who, seeing her unclad, were attracted and therefore turned away as required to avoid sin. This fits with the model described in m. (and y.) Challah and b. Berachot, as per the analysis suggested above, that it is the requirement of the man to avoid looking at parts of a woman that catch his eye.

Of course, one could say that it fits into the rules of b. Ketubot and b. Sotah as well, insofar as appearing in this way would be a violation of her marital obligations not to appear in a provocative way before other men. However, it would seem obvious that, given the circumstances, On would have little to complain about in court.

SUMMARY AND CONCLUSION

From the various sugyot analyzed in this chapter, it would seem that the overall perspective on the proper dress and comportment of women found in both Talmuds is that it is sociologically determined. The argument made in this chapter is that despite the fact that the Gemara in Ketubot seems to present a biblical source for the obligation for married women to cover their hair, it may in fact be a function of societally dependent norms – as other Talmudic sources make clear. There is only one text in the Babylonian Talmud suggesting that a woman's appearing with fully uncovered hair is a Torah prohibition and objective: the Ketubot source. Furthermore, as is widely acknowledged, not everything presented as Torah law in the Talmud is in fact biblical,[77] further contextualizing the

---

77. The notion that not everything presented as Torah law is in fact biblical is developed in the following systematic comments by *Sedei Chemed* (*Maarekhet dalet, Kelal* 19):

Biblical: We have found this expression used for matters which are not, in fact, biblical obligations; the Talmud in fact means to say that this rule has some support in the Torah. So wrote our master the *Beit Yosef* (see beginning of *Yoreh Deah* 184, s.v. *u-vi-she'at*) with regard to the rulings of Tosafot, Rosh, and the Semag that separation from one's spouse before the anticipated time of menstruation is biblical. Similarly, the *Derisha* wrote (see beginning of *Yoreh Deah* 183) regarding the view of the *Tur* that such is a biblical obligation. A similar comment appears in the *Beit Yosef* (*Orach Chayyim* 418, s.v. *ve-yachid* [at the end]) regarding the Talmud's statement that *Rosh Chodesh* is biblical, that the Talmud means to say that the law is hinted at through a biblical association. See also *Shakh* (*Choshen Mishpat* 28:14), that according to both R. Isaac Levin (author of the *Megillat Esther*) and the *Shakh* himself, when the Talmud unequivocally states that something is "biblical," rather than asking it as a question, it is biblical... [otherwise] it need not be a proof to a Torah rule (but perhaps merely an association). R. Judah Ayash, in his *Afra de-Ara* commentary to Israel Jacob Algazi's *Ara de-Rabanan* (42:142), also indicated that what Rashi on the Rif (Beitzah 37) wrote regarding commercial activity on Shabbat, that it is a biblical prohibition, is not necessarily so, for that certainly is only rabbinic.... Regarding work on the intermediate days of a festival, the Talmud (b. Moed Katan 11b) states: "Mourning is rabbinic; work on the intermediate days of a festival is biblical," but some Rishonim explained that this means to say that there is an allusion to it in the Torah; see *Yeraim* 113, *Hagahot Maimoniyot, Hilkhot Yom Tov* ch. 7, Rosh, beginning of tractate Moed Katan, and Tosafot, b. Hagigah 18a, s.v. *holo*.

(Elsewhere in the *Sedei Chemed* (*Maarekhet Ha-dalet, pe'at hashulchan, Kelal* 12 page 129 in original edition), he writes: "Biblical – in many places we find this expression used to describe laws which are only rabbinic.")

Ketubot source. The main import of the discussion is that a woman dressed immodestly or behaving inappropriately is at risk of divorce without ketubah payment. Although this text may be understood as reflecting normative halakha, it is not representative of the positions taken in the majority of Bavli and Yerushalmi sugyot.

CHAPTER 3

Uncovered Hair in the Geonim and Rif: Three Models of Modesty in the Immediately Post-Talmudic Commentaries

CHAPTER 3, WHICH REVIEWS THE DISCUSSION OF immodest behavior and exposed hair in the Geonim (and the Rif), examines the possible ways to address diverse Talmudic sources. There are three competing models to explain the Talmudic tension surrounding hair covering. The first assumes the Talmudic source in Ketubot is not the normative one and that no Torah rule is present. The second approach assumes that the Ketubot rule is correct and that uncovered hair constitutes a violation of Torah law. The third resolves the tension in the Talmudic sources by validating them all, in their respective context and situation. Per this final approach, the source in Ketubot sets forth a rabbinic obligation for women to dress modestly.

Introduction

As noted in the previous chapter, there is a certain amount of tension with regard to female hair exposure. On the one side is the baraita in Ketubot and the position of Shmuel. On the other are all the other sugyot that examine this topic. According to the former, the prohibition against exposed hair is actually Torah law, derived from a verse in Numbers. The other sugyot seem not to base their holdings on Torah law. Nonetheless, some of these discussions instead suggest alternative midrashic proof texts, such as Song of Songs (b. Berachot 24a) and the Book of Samuel (*Sifre* Numbers, *Nasso* 11). These may well be fine and correct proof texts, but neither would make resolution of the hair covering issue a matter of Torah law.

This situation begs the question: How should a halakhist deal with this type of ambiguity? With regard to hair covering, there are three obvious models for addressing the topic, and all three are present in the Geonim (the post-Talmudic commentators living in Babylonia):

1. Follow the majority.
2. Follow the baraita and Shmuel.
3. Reconcile the competing text.

This chapter will examine how each of these three models operates in the works of the Geonim.

Model 1: Follow Majority
BEHAG

The Behag wrote the *Halakhot Gedolot* (32, *Miun*, p. 344), one of the earliest books on halakha, which codifies the Mishnah in Ketubot without comment:

| The following [category of women] may be divorced without receiving the ketubah payment: One who violates *dat Moshe ve-Yehudit*. | ואלו יוצאות שלא בכתבה: העוברת על דת משה ויהודית. |

What [violates] *dat Moshe*?
a. Feeding [her husband] untithed food,
b. Having intercourse with him during her menstrual period,
c. Not setting apart the dough offering,
d. Making vows and not fulfilling them.

ואיזו היא דת משה?
א. מאכילתו שאינו מעושר,
ב. ומשמשתו נדה,
ג. ולא קוצה לה חלה,
ד. ונודרת ולא מקיימת.

What [violates] *dat Yehudit*?
a. Going out with her hair exposed,
b. Weaving in the marketplace,
c. Conversing with random men.
d. Abba Shaul says: "Also cursing his parents in front of his face."
e. Rabbi Tarfon says: "Also a loudmouth."

ואיזו היא דת יהודית?
א. יוצאה וראשה פרוע,
ב. וטוה בשוק,
ג. ומדברת עם כל אדם.
ד. אבא שאול אומר: "אף המקללת יולדיו [בפניו]."
ה. רבי טרפון אומר: "אף הקולנית."

What is a loudmouth? Rav Yehuda said in the name of Shmuel: "One who speaks about sexual matters."

מאי קולנית? אמר רב יהודה אמר שמואל: "במשמעת קולה על עסקי תשמיש."

The Behag offers no explanation or modification of the various categories set forth in the Mishnah, although he does clarify the intent of R. Tarfon's category of loudmouth by quoting the Babylonian Talmud's interpretation of it. Given this, how is one to understand the Behag's position vis-à-vis hair covering? Presumably, for all the other categories, the Behag feels that no clarification is necessary since the Mishnah is self-explanatory. However, in light of the tension surrounding this issue of exposed hair, should one assume that the Behag believes there is a Torah rule for women to cover their hair (despite him not mentioning it)? Alternatively, should one assume that he discounts this baraita and Shmuel's attempt at reconciliation as not in accord with normative halakha?

Further complicating matters is the one other time (1, *Berachot*, p. 44) Behag discusses hair covering. There he summarizes and slightly rewrites the Talmudic sugya from b. Berachot discussed in the previous chapter:

Rabbi Yitzchak said: "A handbreadth [of exposed flesh] is considered suggestive (*erva*)."	אמר רבי יצחק: "טפח באשה ערוה".
With regard to what?	למאי?
If this is meant to prohibit [a man's] gazing at it –	אילימא להסתכל בה –
Did not Rav Sheshet [already] say: "Why does the verse list regular jewelry together with erotic jewelry, i.e., the *atz'adah* and the *kumaz*? This is to teach you that anyone who gazes at the little finger of a woman is considered as if he were gazing at her private parts"! Rather, it must be in reference to a person's own wife, and in regard to the recitation of the Shema, since even when a man's own wife reveals a handbreadth [of flesh] it is forbidden [for him] to recite the Shema in her presence…	והא אמר רב ששת: "למה מנה הכתוב תכשיטין שבחוץ עם תכשיטין שבפנים אצעדה וכומז? לומר לך: כל המסתכל באצבע קטנה של אשה כאילו נסתכל במקום התורף". אלא: באשתו, ולקרית שמע, דאפילו אשתו כי מגלי טפח מינה אסור לקרות קרית שמע כנגדה…
Rav Chisda said: "The calf is considered suggestive,	אמר רב חסדא: "שוק באשה ערוה,
for [the verse] states: '*Reveal* the calf, pass through the rivers' (Isaiah 47:2),	דכתיב: 'גלי שוק עברי נהרות',
and it is written: 'Your nudity shall be *re-*	וכתיב: 'תגל ערותך'".

vealed, even your disgrace shall be seen' (Isaiah 47:3)."

Rav Sheshet said: "The hair of a woman is considered suggestive, | אמר רב ששת: "שער באשה ערוה,

as it states: 'Your hair is like a flock of goats' (Song 4:1)." | דכתיב: 'שערך כעדר העזים.'"

Shmuel said: "The voice of a woman is considered suggestive, | אמר שמואל: "קול באשה ערוה,

as it states: 'for your voice is sweet and your appearance attractive' (Song 2:14)." | שנאמר: 'כי קולך ערב ומראך נאוה.'"

There is much ambiguity in the Behag's presentation of the last three examples of "suggestiveness." Are they meant to describe what a husband cannot see or hear during the recitation of Shema? From the beginning of the sugya, it would seem that this is the correct interpretation. Moreover, this is how the Behag's position was understood by Ra'aviah (b. Berachot 76).[1] Nonetheless, it is possible to view the last three examples of "suggestiveness" as self-standing statements about what a man should not look at. In other words, this sugya is positing that a man should not look at anything on a woman if it causes him to have improper thoughts (a standard which itself is a subjective one).

How, then, can we use this second sugya to determine the Behag's view on whether there is a level of hair covering demanded as a matter of Torah law? Looking only at his book as the sole source of halakha (which was presumably the intent of the book), one would conclude that a woman's hair covering is *dat Yehudit* and that it is to be understood to be quasi-erotic in accordance with Rav Sheshet. This would mean that men should not look at women's hair if it causes them lewd thoughts. Again, limiting our discussions to the Behag alone, there would be no indication that any form of hair exposure could be considered a violation of a Torah prohibition. Furthermore, there is no indication that there are "levels" of hair exposure at all. Similarly, there are no guidelines as to what the status of a woman with her hair done up or wearing a hairnet would be.

Where does this leave us? We can only assume that the Behag presented this issue as he did so that a reader following his decisions would

---

1. Ra'aviah also references R. Chananel as holding this position.

feel confident he was keeping Torah law properly. That is, after all, the goal of all halakhists and codifiers.[2]

While this seems a reasonable and correct read of the Behag, it is not without its problems. Why would the Behag, without explanation, discount a baraita and a prominent Amora's defense of it? Perhaps the Behag felt that the derasha was not halakha and that the rest of the sugya, which may be interpreted as an attempt to reconcile the derasha with the Mishnah, was unnecessary. This possibility is strengthened if one assumes that, contrary to the interpretation offered in the previous chapter of this book, the Behag understood R. Yochanan as an attempt to reconcile the baraita with the Mishnah as well. Otherwise, it is hard to understand why the Behag does not at least quote the second half of the sugya based on R. Yochanan and the Amoraim who interpret him, since these positions are not academic, but practical.

It is further possible that the Behag believes this derasha is not in accord with normative halakha because of the alternative derasha about hair in b. Berachot, which the Behag does include. Apparently, the Behag understood the existence of two derashot about women's hair as evidence of a debate between the pericopes (*machloket hasugyot*), and he understood the derasha in b. Berachot to be the one reflecting normative halakha.

Model 2: Following Ketubot

R. YITZCHAK ALFASI

In his own work on halakha, apparently modeled after the *Halakhot Gedolot*, R. Yitzchak Alfasi (Rif) takes the exact opposite approach to the Behag. Unlike in the Behag's use of the sugya in Ketubot, Rif (*Ketubot* 32b) includes a synthesis of the Ketubot passages from the Bavli and Yerushalmi – albeit leaving out the first half of the Yerushalmi and R. Zeira's question in the Bavli:

---

2. It is possible to push back and argue that the Behag does believe in some sort of Torah requirement for hair covering, but that he felt that this was a strictly academic point, since women in his time were covering their hair fully, in line with *dat Yehudit*. In other words, he could have reasoned that since a violation of *dat Yehudit* would be considered a serious enough breach of propriety such that the woman could be divorced without a ketubah payment, it could be argued that there is little need to discuss the question of what is technical halakha and what is accepted practice.

What [violates] *dat Yehudit*?	אי זו היא דת יהודית?
Going out with her hair exposed:	יוצאה וראשה פרוע.
[Going out with] her hair exposed is a Torah prohibition! For it is written: "And he shall expose the hair of the woman" (Num. 5:18);	ראשה פרוע דאורייתא היא! דכתיב: "ופרע את ראש האשה"!
And R. Ishmael taught:	ואמר רבי ישמעאל:
"This is a warning to the daughters of Israel not to go out with their hair exposed!"	"אזהרה לבנות ישראל שלא תצאנה בפריעת ראש".
Rav Yehuda said in the name of Shmuel: "With a *kalta*."	אמר רב יהודה אמר שמואל: "בקלתה".
As a matter of Torah law, a *kalta* would be sufficient, [according to] *dat Yehudit*, even a *kalta* would be insufficient.	דאורייתא קלתה שפיר דמי, דת יהודית אפילו קלתה נמי אסור.
R. Assi said in the name of R. Yochanan: "[One who goes out in] *kalta* has not violated [the prohibition of going out with] her hair exposed."	א"ר אסי א"ר יוחנן: "קלתה אין בה משום פריעת ראש".
Abaye, or alternatively Rav Kahana, stated:	אמר אביי, ואיתימא רב כהנא:
"[R. Yochanan's ruling is meant to apply to a woman who goes] from one courtyard to another by way of a thoroughfare."	"מחצר לחצר ודרך מבוי".
Yerushalmi: A courtyard that many people use as a pass-through is [considered] as a thoroughfare; a thoroughfare through which people generally do not pass is [considered] as a courtyard.	ירושלמי: חצר שהרבים בוקעין בו הרי הוא כמבוי, מבוי שאין הרבים בוקעין בו הרי הוא כחצר.

It seems that Rif accepts the idea of gradations within the rules of hair covering.[3] Since he believes that R. Yochanan's position (as modified by Abaye and the Yerushalmi) is binding, Rif holds that it is forbidden for a woman to go into an area used as a thoroughfare with her hair exposed

---

3. See the responsa of Rif (73) where he quotes the Mishnah as is, and references exposure of hair as a *dat Yehudit* without further comment. However, this is probably just a case of a shorthand quote since his main point is to discuss conversing with men.

in any way unless it is a short trip to get to another semi-private area. Additionally, it would be forbidden for her to enter an outside area rarely used by people unless she is wearing a kalta.

The only unresolved element is whether Rif believes a woman going out with fully exposed hair into the public thoroughfare is in violation of a Torah law. Although he makes no explicit statement either endorsing or disregarding the baraita, from the fact that he quotes it one may presume he believes it to be normative. This understanding is buttressed by the fact that Rif, unlike the Behag, leaves out the discussion in b. Berachot entirely. This omission was noticed by R. Zerachiah HaLevi in his *HaMaor HaKatan*, and by Ra'avad in his *Katuv Sham*.

That which Rav Pappa said,[4] that a handbreadth [of exposed flesh] is considered suggestive, and we establish this as referring to a person's own wife during the recitation of the Shema, and that the calf of a woman, and her voice and her hair are all suggestive, and it is forbidden to gaze at them – the Rif left all this out. (*HaMaor HaKatan*, Berachot ad loc.)	הא דאמר ר' פפא טפח באשה ערוה אוקימנא באשתו ולק"ש ושוק באשה וקול באשה ושער באשה הכל ערוה ואסור להסתכל בהן והרי"ף ז"ל השמיט כל זה.
Abraham said: It is unknown why the Rabbi left them out, as they make good sense. (*Katuv Sham*, Berachot ad loc.)	אמר אברהם: לא ידע זה על מה הניחם הרב, ויש להם טעם,

In a rare case of agreement, R. Zerachiah and Ra'avad are puzzled that Rif would simply leave this sugya and its consequent halakhot out of his book. The simplest explanation for this, and the inverse of what we suggested for the Behag, is that Rif does not believe this sugya to be normative.

The sugya in b. Berachot seems to believe that laws of modesty in general, and the laws of hair covering in particular, derive from Song of Songs. The sugya in b. Ketubot believes that the rules against exposure of hair are derived from a verse in Numbers and that all other forms of indecent exposure (e.g., weaving in public, wearing tattered clothing, bathing in the men's bathhouse, etc.) are *dat Yehudit* and derived from common sense. Although they need not be, these two presentations may be seen as contradictory, with Behag deciding on b. Berachot and Rif following b. Ketubot.

---

4. In our texts it is R. Yitzhak who says this.

Model 3: Reconciling the Competing Text

Finally, as implied in the comments of R. Zerachiah and Ra'avad, one can also see the two sugyot as mutually complementary, and discussing different rules.

R. HAI GAON

An approach to the text in b. Berachot as independent of and complementary to the regular laws of modesty referenced in b. Ketubot and b. Sotah was quoted by the students of R. Yonah in the name of R. Hai Gaon (Glosses on Rif; Ber. 17a).

R. Hai Gaon wrote that this is true with regard to any handbreadth of a woman's flesh that is generally covered, that when it is in view it is forbidden to recite the Shema in her presence, for a handbreadth of a woman's [exposed flesh] is considered suggestive (*erva*). Additionally, one should not recite the Shema when a woman is singing, since the voice of a woman is considered suggestive.	וכתב רבינו האי גאון ז"ל דהוא הדין לכל אשה שמגלה טפח במקום מכוסה שבה שאסור לקרוא כנגדה דטפח באשה ערוה וכן אין לו לקרות בשעה שמנגנת דקול באשה ערוה.
However, [reciting the Shema] in the presence of her face or any other part of her which is generally exposed, or while she is speaking regularly – this is permitted.	אבל כנגד פניה או כנגד מקום שאין דרך לכסות או בשעה שמדברת כדרכה מותר.
In fact, even if she is singing, but he can pay attention to his prayers such that he isn't really hearing her and not paying her any mind – this is permitted, and he should not stop his recitation. Also, when a handbreadth of her flesh is exposed, it would only be forbidden [to recite the Shema] while he was looking at her, but if she just happens to be in view, this would be permitted.	ואפי' בשעה שמנגנת אם הוא יכול לכוין בלבו לתפלתו בענין שאינו שומע אותה ואינו משים לבו אליה מותר ואין לו להפסיק קריאתו וכן כשממגולה טפח אינו אסור אלא כשמסתכל בה אבל בראייה בעלמא מותר:

Here R. Hai Gaon suggests that, insofar as the rules of proper concentration during the recitation of the Shema are concerned, there are three categories of exposure to erotic stimuli:

1. Paying attention to unusual erotic stimuli.
2. Being in the presence of unusual erotic stimuli but not paying attention.
3. Being in the presence of a woman with the usual level of exposure to her skin and voice.

To R. Hai Gaon, it is clear that the prohibitions recorded in b. Berachot are referring to unusual erotic stimuli, and not to being in the presence of the mundane. This is because to R. Hai, the entire sugya is about proper focus during the recitation of the Shema. There is no reason to think that a man cannot focus when in the presence of a woman dressed normally and speaking regularly.

And should he find himself in the presence of a woman with exposed flesh beyond the usual places or when she is singing? What then is the proper course of action?

R. Hai maintains that it really depends upon the person. Presumably, the average person would be distracted and should, therefore, not recite the Shema under such a circumstance. However, if the person feels that he can be in the presence of this woman dressed or behaving in this manner and not be distracted, he may recite the Shema.

To complicate things a bit, in a responsum in *Shaarei Teshuva* (29), R. Hai seems to offer an entirely different interpretation of this pericope. The responsum is a discussion of types of sins, and the relevant section is his discussion of the fifth type.[5]

| The fifth category is [sins] based on sight – like a man looking at women who are forbidden to him, as it says "a handbreadth of a woman's [exposed flesh] is considered erotic" and "a woman's hair is considered | הה'. הראייה והוא כגון ראיית העריות שהן אסור וכדאמרינן טפח באשה ערוה ושער שבאשה ערוה קול באשה ערוה ומיהו איסורה רבה איכא |

---

5. This responsum is quoted by R. Avraham Av Beit Din (Ra'avad II) in his *Sefer HaEshkol* (Albeck), Avodah Zarah 192a. While this article was in galleys, Gershon Klapper noted that this text is not listed in Tzvi Groner's רשימת תשובות רב האי גאון (Alei Sefer 13), which allows one to posit that this is a work of a Gaon, albeit not Rabbi Hai. He also notes that Gershom Scholem in *Major Trends in Jewish Mysticism* (p. 200) writes that the 13th-century Castilian pseudepigraphers are responsible for the Kabbalistic material attributed to Hai Gaon in *Shaarei Teshuva*. Indeed, it is possible that this is not a formal responsum but just analysis by a Gaon who lived before Avraham Av Beit Din. It seems that Gershon Klapper is correct in his claim that "the version in the Eshkol is the original, from which the *Shaarei Teshuva* redactors excerpted it, shortened it, and added the frame question on top."

erotic" and "a woman's voice is considered erotic." However, there is a greater sin with forbidden women, like those who have the prohibited status of *erva*, than with single women who are unrelated to the person. As it states: "A person should not gaze at a pretty woman even if she is single, or a married woman even if she is unattractive."

בעריות כגון האסורות אסור ערוה ממה שאין בפנויות רחוקות וכדתניא לא יסתכל אדם באשה נאה ואפילו פנויה, באשת איש ואפילו מכוערת.

Rav Hai seems to understand the list of prohibited parts of a woman as having to do with the prohibition of ogling a woman. This would appear to be an entirely different understanding than that offered in his first piece.

The important point for R. Hai is that the sugya in b. Berachot is relevant to men and how they behave. It is forbidden for men to look at erotic stimuli while saying the Shema. Additionally, it is forbidden for them to ogle women who are forbidden to them, even in places and ways that are not particularly erotic, such as looking at her hair or listening to her voice.

If one understands b. Berachot in this way, the sugya in b. Ketubot would cover the other side of this equation: women bear religious obligation to dress modestly. The sugya in b. Ketubot is clarifying what sort of behavior will disqualify her from any eligibility to claim her ketubah upon divorce. The derasha (interpretation) further teaches that a woman must cover her hair, at least partially (or perhaps coif it or braid it in some way). Hence, according to this understanding, one can accept both sugyot as correct, with one being focused on men's responsibility and the other on women's.

Conclusion: Three Models

This chapter outlines the emergence of the division of Jewish law authorities into competing understandings of the central Talmudic texts. One view posits that the Ketubot source is not normative and the modesty prohibitions are subjective and rabbinic. The second holds the objective rule of Ketubot is normative and that hair covering is a biblical obligation and objective. The third approach seeks to accept both rules as valid depending on the circumstance. It thus understands one approach as mandating that men not see that which is erotic and the other as creating an obligation (but not necessarily a Torah obligation) for women to dress modestly.

CHAPTER 4

Uncovered Hair in the Rishonim, Model 1: A Torah Prohibition and *Dat Moshe*: Modesty as an Objective Prohibition Among Some Rishonim

CHAPTER 4 REVIEWS ALL OF THE RISHONIM WE ARE aware of that adopt the view that hair covering is a Torah obligation (a *dat Moshe* requirement) or otherwise make it clear that the Ketubot source is addressing a biblical violation. This would make it immutable as a matter of Jewish law, and these Rishonim frame their views as the normative ones in Jewish law.

There are thirteen Rishonim who take the position that the obligation for women to cover their hair in some form is a Torah law and a *dat Moshe* requirement. This chapter offers a survey of these Rishonim in more or less chronological order and describes their positions in textual detail. Although there is some overlap between these positions, there are a number of important differences between the views posited by these Rishonim. We will examine these differences at length; but in brief, they touch upon the following:

- The relationship between the Ketubot source (b. Ketubot 72a–b) and the Berachot source (b. Berachot 24a)
- Whether hair covering is essentially sotah-related or modesty-related
- Whether all *dat Moshe* prohibitions are also Torah violations and vice-versa
- How much hair needs to be covered
- The connection between the obligation to cover one's hair and one's marital status

- Whether this issue is driven by payment issues
- Whether the obligation for a woman to cover her hair is driven by public location[1]

1. Rivan

The view that the prohibition for a woman to go out with her hair exposed is in fact a Torah law found support with R. Yehuda ben Nathan (Rashi's son-in-law, known as Rivan) and is quoted by R. Betzalel Ashkenazi in the *Shita Mekubetzet* (b. Ketubot 72a).[2]

"And he [the kohen] shall expose her [the suspected adulteress's] hair." – The Talmud in tractate Sotah (8a) states: "She revealed her hair for him (her alleged lover); therefore, the kohen reveals her hair [as part of the *sotah* ceremony]." We thus see that it was inappropriate for her to have revealed her hair, and from here [we derive a warning] to the daughters of Israel that they should not go out with exposed hair.	ופרע את ראש האשה. ואמרינן במסכת סוטה: היא גלתה לו את ראשה לפיכך הכהן מגלה את ראשה.אלמא דלא היה לה לגלות את ראשה ומכאן לבנות ישראל שלא יצאו בפריעת ראש
In other words, because the Torah specifically instructs the revealing of the *sotah*'s hair, we infer that all other women are obligated not to go about with their hair exposed. From here we thus adduce that this is a Torah prohibition, for it is derived from an inference from a Scriptural verse. How then, [the Talmud in Ketubot asks], can this be considered *dat Yehudit*?	כלומר מדאמר רחמנא גבי סוטה לגלות ראשה משמע שששאר הנשים צריך שלא ילכו בפרועת ראש אלמא שמעינן מהכא דמדאורייתא הוי דהא מדיוקא דקרא נפקא לן והיאך אתה קורא אותו דת יהודית
The Talmud responds: Shmuel answered, "with a *kalta*." In other words, when the	ומהדרינן אמר שמואל בקלתא כלומר הא דתנן דיוצאה

---

1. In considering this topic, we include the Rambam among the Rishonim who advance this view. Nonetheless, in a future chapter, we will explore the extent to which later halakhists believe this to be the Rambam's actual position or not.
2. R. Ashkenazi refers to this as "Rashi in an earlier version," but it is actually from Rivan's lost commentary on this tractate (or from his glosses on Rashi). See Ephraim Urbach, *Baalei HaTosafot* (fifth enlarged edition, 1984) at pages 39–41. Although I referenced this correctly in my Hebrew *Techumin* article, I mistakenly referred to this position in the English article in *Tradition* as "Rashi in an earlier version" (following R. Ashkenazi). I thank R. Yehuda Henkin for pointing out this error which I now correct.

UNCOVERED HAIR IN THE RISHONIM, MODEL I

> Mishnah states that a woman who goes with her hair exposed violates *dat Yehudit*, it means to say a woman who goes out wearing a *kalta*, for going out without even a *kalta* is a Torah prohibition. However, [going out] with a *kalta* would be permitted according to the Torah, and would not be [considered to be tantamount to going out in public with] exposed hair. However, following the dictates of *dat Yehudit*, even going out with [only] a *kalta* would be forbidden.
>
> וראשה פרוע העוברת על דת יהודית מיירי שיוצאה בקלתא דבלא קלתא אסור מן התורה ועם קלתא מותר מן התורה ואין בה משום פרוע ראש אבל דת יהודית אפילו קלתא נמי אסור
>
> The meaning of the term *kalta* is the *kippah* (covering) she puts on her head in order to cover her hair.
>
> ופי' קלתא כפה שמנחת על ראשה לכסות בה את השער

Although Rivan's interpretation of the sugya seems rather straightforward, it stands out as unusual and problematic in one aspect. Instead of simply spelling out the derasha in Ketubot, Rivan makes reference to a baraita in b. Sotah that explains why the woman's hair is publicly exposed. This presents us with two difficulties.

First, by incorporating the text from b. Sotah into the text from b. Ketubot, Rivan is implying that the text in Ketubot is insufficient to demonstrate that a woman going out in public with her hair exposed has violated a Torah prohibition. Second, the baraita in b. Sotah does not in fact say what Rivan says that it does, at least not in our text or in the text of any other authority who quotes it. The text is as follows:

> She covered her hair with beautiful ribbons; therefore, the priest removes the covering from her hair and places it between her feet.
>
> היא פרסה לו סודרין נאין על ראשה, לפיכך כהן נוטל כפה מעל ראשה ומניחו תחת רגליה.
>
> She coiffed her hair for him; therefore, the kohen undoes her hair.[3]
>
> היא קלעה לו את שערה, לפיכך כהן סותר את שערה.

One can see from this quote that the main concern of the author of this baraita is that the woman is accused of having done two things to her hair to make herself more attractive. First, she is accused of putting decorative ribbons in her hair. Second, she is accused of having coiffed or done her

---

3. The text was dealt with in Chapter 1.

hair up. These behaviors are not about exposure – that is, allowing her lover to see her undressed. Rather, they are about the woman dressing up for her lover in order to attract him.

Although it is true that both of the kohen's punishments are meant as reactions to these behaviors, in this source's estimation, the emphasis in each punishment is quite different. In reaction to the first behavior, the kohen is said to remove the *kippah*/covering from her head (in Rivan's definition this would be the kalta) and throw it onto the ground at her feet. The emphasis seems to be on discarding a decorative piece and trampling it on the ground – not the public exposure of her now-uncovered hair. The punishment for the second behavior is undoing or messing up her hair. Again, it does not seem to be the exposure per se that is of interest to the author of this source, but rather the fact that her once beautifully done hair is now wild and unattractive. This of course begs the question: to what end?

As was pointed out in a previous chapter, women would not go out publicly with undone hair. Rather, their hair was always coiffed or covered in some way. Thus, we see that the emphasis is not on making the woman appear indecent in public; it is designed to make them publicly unattractive. Admittedly, this is not the only possible interpretation of the punishment of the sotah, but it is the one the author of the baraita suggests and it is the one that Rivan looks to for support.

It is hard to know why Rivan decides to support the derasha in b. Ketubot with this passage in b. Sotah, as it seems to harm the case for a biblical prohibition more than it does help it. In short, Rivan seems to believe that the passage in b. Ketubot is in need of some reinforcement if it is to demonstrate that the prohibition is biblical, and he looks to b. Sotah for that reinforcement. Unfortunately, we neither have the same text he had nor are we privy to his interpretation of the words such that they would fit with his explanation.[4] Therefore, we must leave this position with a *tzarikh iyyun* – a need for further study.

---

4. If it is not too bold, perhaps one could suggest that either Rivan himself or the copyist whose Talmud manuscript Rivan was using got confused between the opening statement of the Mishnah "היא גלתה" (she revealed) and the statement as found in Rabbi's baraita "היא קלעה" (she coiffed), creating the hybrid text quoted in this piece.

2. Rambam (Maimonides)

The position of Rambam on hair covering is a matter of great dispute, as will be seen in a later chapter.[5] This dispute is driven by two factors. First, he does not explain his reading of certain sources but instead codifies them in his own words. Second, his treatments of different passages seems to imply different things. We will look at each of his various treatments of the subject and try to paint as complete a picture as possible.

MISHNAH KETUBOT

In his commentary on Mishnah Ketubot 7:6 (written as a young man), Rambam explains the nature of the married woman's various protocol violations.

It seems clear that she violated *dat Moshe* if [her husband] relies upon her in these above-listed matters and he asks her about them and she says they are permitted, but when he looks into the matter he finds that they are forbidden. In all of these cases there need to be witnesses and warning, only then will she lose her ketubah rights.	יתברר שהיא עוברת על דת משה אם סומך עליה בדברים אלו המנויים ושאל אותה ואמרה לו מותר, וכאשר חקר מצא שהוא אסור. וצריך בכל הדברים הללו עדים והתראה ואז תפסיד כתובתה.
And they said: "Exposed hair," even if she had a kerchief on her head, assuming she goes out like this to the market or to an open thoroughfare.	ואמרו ראשה פרוע, ואפילו היתה מטפחת על ראשה, ובתנאי שתצא בה לשוק או למבוי מפולש.
And they said: "Weaving in public" when she exposes her arms to people or if she was weaving while rose petals or *raychan* or the like were placed upon her forehead or cheek, and other such acts of lewdness and lack of modesty.	ואמרו טווה בשוק, במראה זרועותי' לבני אדם או שהיתה טווה כשעלי ורדים או "ריחאן" וכדומה להן צמודין לה על פדחתה או בלחייה וכיוצא בזה מן הפריצות ומיעוט הצניעות.
And they said: "She speaks with any man," they understood this as being playful with young men.	ואמרו מדברת עם כל אדם, אמרו משחקת עם הבחורים.

---

5. See the discussion of *Terumat HaDeshen* in Chapter 5 for a contrary reading of Rambam.

"She curses his parents before his face" – [meaning] she curses the father of her husband in front of her husband in whatever manner the curse or deprecation presented itself.	ומקללת יולדיו בפניו, שמקללת אבי בעלה בפני בעלה באיזה אופן שיהיה מן הקללה והחירוף.
"And the loudmouth" – she demands intercourse in a loud voice such that her neighbors hear her.	וקולנית, תובעת תשמיש בקול רם עד ששומעים אותה שכניה.
All of these examples are practical law, but only after she has been warned, as we explained.	וכל הדברים האלו לפסק הלכה, ודוקא אחרי התראה כמו שביארנו.

In his commentary on the Mishnah, Rambam's explanation of the text echoes the Bavli's understanding of it. Regarding hair exposure, Rambam makes clear that the Mishnah should be understood as including a case where a woman goes out in public with only a kerchief. He does not suggest that the category of *dat Moshe* would include going out with hair fully exposed.

If this were Rambam's only treatment of the passage, one could argue that he categorizes all violations of public hair exposure into the category of *dat Yehudit*. However, from Rambam's codification of this Mishnah in his *Mishneh Torah*, a slightly different picture emerges.

MISHNEH TORAH, "HILKHOT ISHUT" 24:11–13

In his *Mishneh Torah* (his later and generally more authoritative Code of Law) Rambam codifies the passages in m. and b. Ketubot as follows.

11) If a woman has done one of the following, she is considered to have violated *dat Moshe*:	יא] ואלו הן הדברים שאם עשת אחד מהן עברה על דת משה:
a. Going out in the marketplace with her head *uncovered*,[6]	א. יוצאה בשוק ושער ראשה גלוי,
b. making vows or taking oaths and not fulfilling them,	ב. או שנודרת או נשבעת ואינה מקיימת,

---

[6]. Ostensibly, he means here "totally bare" as opposed to exposed, which he defines later as with a kerchief but not with complete coverage. Rambam seems to be the first to introduce this term into the discussion of the halakhot of women's hair covering.

c. having intercourse with her husband during her niddah period,

d. not setting apart the dough offering,

e. or feeding her husband forbidden foods – not only insects, reptiles, and the carcasses of unslaughtered beasts, but even foods that are untithed.

How is [her husband] to know?

For instance, if she said to him:

"These fruits were tithed for me by such-and-such kohen [priest]," or "such-and-such woman set aside the offering from this dough for me," or "such-and-such sage ruled this [menstrual] blood-spot to be pure." Then after he ate or had relations with her, he inquired of that person, and the person informed him that such an incident never took place. Or if she was assumed to be in her niddah period by the local women but she told her husband that she was pure, and he had relations with her.

12) What is considered to be *dat Yehudit*? Those are the modest practices with which the daughters of Israel comport themselves.

If a woman has done one of the following, she is considered to have violated *dat Yehudit*:

a. Going out in the marketplace or in a through-alley with her hair exposed, and without the full-covering that all other women wear, even though her hair is covered by a kerchief.

b. Spinning [yarn] in the marketplace with red or the like on her face – on her forehead or cheeks, in the manner of the promiscuous non-Jewish women.

ג. או ששמשה מטתה והיא נדה,

ד. או שאינה קוצה לה חלה,

ה. או שהאכילה את בעלה דברים אסורים,

ואין צריך לומר שקצים ורמשים ונבלות, אלא דברים שאינן מעושרין.

והיאך יודע דבר זה?

כגון שאמרה לו:

פירות אלו פלוני כהן תקנם לי, ועיסה זו פלוני הפריש לי חלתה,

ופלוני החכם טיהר לי את הכתם,

ואחר שאכל או בא עליה שאל אותו פלוני ואמר לא היו דברים מעולם,

וכן אם הוחזקה נדה בשכנותיה ואמרה לבעלה טהורה אני ובא עליה.

[יב] ואיזו היא דת יהודית?

הוא מנהג הצניעות שנהגו בנות ישראל.

ואלו הן הדברים שאם עשת אחד מהן עברה על דת יהודית:

א. יוצאה לשוק או למבוי מפולש,

וראשה פרוע, ואין עליה רדיד ככל הנשים, אע״פ ששערה מכוסה במטפחת,

ב. או שהיתה טווה בשוק ורד וכיוצא בו כנגד פניה על פדחתה או על לחיה כדרך שעושות הגויות הפרוצות,

c. Spinning [yarn] in the marketplace and in such a way as it shows her bare arms to the onlookers.

d. Being playful with young men.

e. Demanding sex from her husband in a voice so loud that her neighbors hear her talking about sex.

f. Cursing her husband's father in front of her husband's face.

ג. או שטווה בשוק ומראה זרועותיה לבני אדם,

ד. או שהיתה משחקת עם הבחורים,

ה. או שהיתה תובעת התשמיש מבעלה בקול רם עד ששכנותיה שומעות אותה מדברת על עסקי תשמיש,

ו. או שהיתה מקללת אבי בעלה בפני בעלה.

13) Ezra established that a woman should wear a belt at all times in her house, for modesty's sake. [However,] if she does not wear it, she is not in violation of *dat Moshe* and does not lose her ketubah. Also, if she went out with her hair exposed from courtyard to courtyard by way of a thoroughfare, since her hair was covered by a kerchief, she is not in violation of *dat*.

[יג] עזרא תקן שתהיה אשה חוגרת בסינר תמיד בתוך ביתה משום צניעות, ואם לא חגרה אינה עוברת על דת משה ולא הפסידה כתובתה, וכן אם יצתה בראשה פרוע מחצר לחצר בתוך המבוי, הואיל ושערה מכוסה במטפחת אינה עוברת על דת.

The simple understanding of Rambam is that a woman who goes out with her hair completely uncovered violates *dat Moshe*. However, it must be noted that Rambam is of the opinion that the category of *dat Moshe* includes violations which are only rabbinic in nature. For example, he includes menstrual spotting, something that is certainly rabbinic according to all opinions. He also includes failing to separate dough and tithes, which, according to Rambam, are also considered rabbinic violations. Hence, it is impossible to ascertain whether in principle Rambam is of the view that uncovering of the hair is a rabbinic or a biblical violation.

Nevertheless, it is clear that Rambam accepts the basic idea of gradations of coverage. Hair covered by only a kerchief (his interpretation of the term *kalta*) represents a lower level of "immodest comportment" than fully uncovered hair, and only violates *dat Yehudit*, while fully uncovered hair violates *dat Moshe*.

To make matters more complicated, the exact meaning of *redid*, which was translated above as "full-covering," is unclear. Although it may just mean full head covering, like a turban or shawl, it may actually mean covering one's face with a veil. If this is true, Rambam's *dat Yehudit* is significantly stricter than other versions of this concept, and may reflect the reality of women's dress in medieval Muslim society.

MISHNEH TORAH – BERACHOT

Rambam codifies the passage in b. Berachot piecemeal. In the context of the laws of Shema, (*Mishneh Torah, Keriat Shema* 3:16), Rambam records the rule about an uncovered handbreadth of a woman being an erotic stimulus:

Just as it is forbidden to recite [the Shema] in the presence of feces and urine unless he distances himself, so too it is forbidden to recite [the Shema] in the presence of nudity unless he turns his face – even if [the nudity] is of a gentile or a minor, he should not recite [the Shema] before their nudity. Even if a wall of glass separates them, since he can see it, it is forbidden unless he turns his face.	כשם שאסור לקרות כנגד צואה ומי רגלים עד שירחיק כך אסור לקרות כנגד הערוה עד שיחזיר פניו אפילו כותי או קטן לא יקרא כנגד ערותן אפילו מחיצה של זכוכית מפסקת הואיל והוא רואה אותה אסור לקרות עד שיחזיר פניו.
The entire body of a woman is nudity, therefore a man should not look at a woman's body when he is reciting [the Shema]; even his wife, if a handbreadth of her body is exposed, he should not recite [the Shema] facing her.	וכל גוף האשה ערוה לפיכך לא יסתכל בגוף האשה כשהוא קורא ואפילו אשתו ואם היה מגולה טפח מגופה לא יקרא כנגדה.

From Rambam's codification of this source, he appears to be concerned only with the male gaze and not with the woman's comportment at all. The point of this text seems to be that reciting Shema is the sort of activity that should not be done while looking at any part of a woman's body, even if such looking is permitted, i.e., when the woman is the person's wife.

It would further seem from this source that the woman's body is only subjectively determined as nudity, most probably because of some assumed sexual attraction. This can be demonstrated from the fact that there is also an objective standard in cases of no attraction (minors, same gender), where the rule is simply not to say Shema in the presence of a person's exposed genitals.

What stands out here is that Rambam makes no mention in this halakha of calf, voice or hair. One could suggest that Rambam included calf as part of the category of body, but this would be more difficult to argue for hair or voice. However, these two (unlike calf) are dealt with in a different section of the *Mishneh Torah*.

Chapter 21 of the laws of forbidden unions begins by describing the prohibition to do anything that comes near to relations with a forbidden sexual partner,[7] which Rambam understands as a biblical prohibition to engage in sexual acts short of coitus with a forbidden partner. In this context, Rambam moves on to describing behaviors that would violate rabbinic extensions of this prohibition (21:2).[8]

> It is forbidden to allude [to something inappropriate] with his hands or feet, or to wink his eyes [flirtatiously] at one of the forbidden sexual partners, or even to have playful banter with her or act in a lighthearted manner. Even just to smell her perfume or gaze at her beauty is forbidden. Anyone who behaves this way purposefully
>
> ואסור לאדם לקרוץ בידיו וברגליו או לרמוז בעיניו לאחת מן העריות, וכן לשחק עמה או להקל ראש. ואפילו להריח בשמים שעליה או להביט ביפיה אסור. ומכין המתכוין לדבר זה מכת מרדות. והמסתכל אפילו

---

7. Leviticus 18:6 states לא תקרבו לגלות ערוה.
8. The simplest understanding of Rambam is that these extensions are rabbinic. This interpretation is taken by R. Vidal of Tolosa in *Maggid Mishneh*, where he argues that one who violates these prohibitions would only receive rabbinic lashes, *malkut mardut*. This is also the position of Rabbi Shlomo Levi (*Biur Chadash Maspik* on Rambam above). However, the Ramban (*Hasagot* to the *Sefer HaMitzvot* 353) seems to believe that the Rambam would include even these actions in the biblical prohibition, though the Ramban himself does not accept the Rambam's understanding of the prohibition. The *Lev Sameach* in his comments to the *Sefer HaMitzvot* rejects this interpretation, favoring that presented by *Maggid Mishneh*. Rabbi Moshe Feinstein (*Iggerot Moshe Even HaEzer*, 4:60) claims that these prohibitions are biblically prohibited, a position he attributes to both Rabbeinu Nissim (Ran) and Rabbi Shabbtai HaKohen (Shakh). Rabbi Shmuel Wosner (*Shevet HaLevi* 5:197) agrees with this interpretation as well, on the basis of the Talmud's understanding of the prohibition against straying after one's eyes, which the Talmud (b. Berachot 12b) understands as following promiscuity. Rabbi Wosner notes that it is hard to imagine a case where one would flirt with a forbidden sexual partner and it would not qualify as straying after one's eyes. Similar debates arise concerning the later prohibitions discussed in this law. While most authorities assume that listening to a woman's (singing) voice is a rabbinic prohibition, there are several authorities who understand that this prohibition is biblical. For example, see the *Shoshanat HaAmakim* 9 from the author of the *Peri Megadim*, Rabbi Yosef ben Meir Teomim. See also Rabbi Avraham HaLevi, *Gan HaMelech* Responsa 100 with the footnotes (Yismach Lev 5768, on Otzar). See also *Sedei Chemed, Maarechet HaKuf*, 42 who discusses both opinions.

is given the rebel's lashes. One who gazes at a woman – even at her little finger – it is as if he is gazing at her private parts. Even listening to the voice of a prohibited relation or looking at her hair is forbidden.

באצבע קטנה של אשה ונתכוון ליהנות כמו שנסתכל במקום התורף. ואפילו לשמוע קול הערוה או לראות שערה אסור.

The category Rambam here discusses as being forbidden according to rabbinic law is receiving sexual benefit, broadly defined, without physical contact. He seems to have two general categories of this. The first is flirting. This includes any sort of inappropriate gestures or banter. The main premise is that both the man and the woman are actively involved. The second type is a man attempting to receive some sort of erotic pleasure from a woman without her involvement. This could be by smelling her perfume, gazing at her or even listening to her voice. This behavior is entirely the man's, as there is no implication in Rambam's words that she is participating in this – at least not knowingly.

This latter category appears to be drawn from the pericope in b. Berachot, as this is the source for the categorization of hair and voice as erotic and the strong language used to condemn looking at any part of a woman, no matter how sexualized. The fact that Rambam discusses hair and voice[9] only in the context of the rabbinic prohibition of not approaching a forbidden relation in an inappropriate manner, and not in the context of reciting the Shema, suggests that he understands the pericope in b. Berachot to, in fact, contain two different types of halakhot in its list.

Whereas an exposed part of the body that is usually covered would make it forbidden for a man to recite the Shema in that woman's presence, even if that someone was his wife and seeing this part of her body would be neither novel nor forbidden, this would not apply to hair or voice. These areas are not part of the body and would not interfere with a man saying Shema unless, of course, he was actually aroused by them at the moment. Instead, the categorization of hair and voice as *erva* applies to a man's interaction with women forbidden to him. He should not try to derive sexual pleasure from any forbidden women, even just by looking at them – any part of them, including their hair or little finger – or by listening to their voice.

This interpretation can be strengthened by comparing Rambam's

---

9. And not "thigh" or "leg" or "calf." See the Maharam Al-Ashkar discussed in Chapter 7.

treatment of women's voices in another context. In a responsum (that is printed as part of the standard Rambam *Shu"t Rambam: Laws of Fasting* 5:14), Rambam was asked whether it would be permitted to listen to Arabic music or to music in general. Rambam begins his responsum with a discussion of why, according to his understanding, listening to music in general is prohibited, unless it be part of prayer. Almost as a side point, Rambam includes the following argument.

And if the one singing is a woman there would be a violation of yet a fifth prohibition, in accordance with the words [of the Sages]: "The voice of a woman is nudity" – how much more so if she is actually singing.	ואם משמיע הזמירות היא אשה הנה יש כאן אסור חמישי על פי מאמרם ז"ל קול באשה ערוה ומכ"ש אם מזמרת בקולה.

Rambam believes that any man who listens to a woman's voice violates the prohibition of *kol be'isha erva*. From his phrasing of the prohibition, it seems clear that Rambam interprets the prohibition as being about the woman's speaking voice; hence his comment that if the Talmud forbids even hearing a woman's speaking voice, certainly her singing voice must be forbidden. As was discussed in Chapter 2, this is the meaning of the phrase as spoken by Rav Yehuda in b. Kiddushin 70a, and there is little reason to assume that Rambam would believe the prohibition in b. Berachot 24a (or even y. Challah 2:1) would have any different meaning.

Rambam references a prohibition regarding women's hair one more time in Chapter 21 of the Laws of Forbidden Relations (21:17). This time, Rambam includes going out with uncovered hair as part of a list of forbidden behaviors for the woman. This point is altogether different and more akin to his discussion of hair in the laws of marriage.

Daughters of Israel may not go out into the marketplace with their hair exposed, whether they be single or married. Also, a woman may not go out into the marketplace with her son behind her; this is a [rabbinic] decree, lest they take her son and she go after them to get him back and the evil men who took [the boy] as a trick assault her.	לא יהלכו בנות ישראל פרועי ראש בשוק אחת פנויה ואחת אשת איש, ולא תלך אשה בשוק ובנה אחריה גזירה שמא יתפשו בנה ותלך אחריו להחזירו ויתעללו בה הרשעים שתפסוהו דרך שחוק.

Concentrating on the rule about hair, at first glance this is not surprising. As discussed above, Rambam wrote in the laws of marriage that a woman going out with her hair exposed violates *dat Yehudit* (or *dat*

Moshe if fully uncovered) and opens herself up to possible divorce without payment of the ketubah. In that sense, the fact that her doing so is actually a violation of halakha is not particularly novel. What appears surprising is that, according to Rambam, the rule applies to all women, married or not. Apparently, in Rambam's view, there is no connection between the requirement for a woman to cover her hair and said woman being married. Covering hair is simply a norm of female modesty. A married woman who violates such a norm, thereby humiliating her husband, is subject to the loss of her ketubah. A single woman who violates the norm cannot be subject to this penalty, but she is still considered as having violated the norms of modesty, whether they be *dat Moshe* or *dat Yehudit*.

Considering Rambam's overall view of the laws of modesty, one is left wondering whether any of the rules are subject to societal norms or whether they are rigidly defined. This will be debated by the commentators on Rambam as we will see in a later chapter. However, it is worth noting that, if Rambam's norms are fixed, his standards are much stricter than any by which normative Orthodoxy lives. All women, married and single, would need to cover their hair, perhaps their faces as well, and even hearing a woman's speaking voice would be forbidden to men.

3. R. Yehonatan of Lunel

Another Rishon who takes a strict view of the sugya on hair covering is R. Yehonatan ben David haKohen of Lunel (c. 1135–after 1210). In his commentary on Rif's Halakhot, R. Yehonatan discusses both the Mishnah and Gemara in Ketubot (b. Ketubot 72a; Rif pages, 32b). In his comments on the Mishnah, he writes:

The following [category of women] may be divorced without receiving the ketubah payment: One who violates *dat Moshe* – such as a commandment found explicitly in the Torah, as [the Mishnah] goes on to elaborate. *Dat Yehudit*, matters that are not forbidden according to Torah law but rather the practices that the daughters of Israel follow out of modesty, and this woman violates such a practice.	אלו יוצאות שלא בכתובה. דת משה, כגון מצוה הכתובה בתורה כדמפרש ואזיל. דת יהודית, דברים שאינן אסורין מן התורה אלא מן מנהג בנות ישראל הן לצניעות בעלמא והיא עוברת על אותו מנהג.
These examples [of *dat Moshe*] teach us that even though the woman is not forbid-	ואשמעינן הני דאע״פ שאינה נאסרת עליו הואיל ומחטיאתו

den to her husband, since she causes him to sin she may be divorced without her ketubah payment, as we say (b. Kiddushin 68a): "All agree that when a man sleeps with a woman who had not immersed following her period of menstruation, the child born from the union is not a *mamzer* (illegitimate)," [and yet the woman is divorced without receiving her ketubah payment]; thus certainly when a woman commits adultery and becomes forbidden to her husband, [as it states,] "After she has become defiled [to him]" (Deut. 24:4), she is divorced without receiving her ketubah payment.

And moreover this never needed to be stated explicitly because it had already been taught [in the Mishnah] that a woman is to be divorced without receiving her ketubah payment for brazenness alone, such as for going out with her hair exposed, which is a [rabbinic] decree to prevent a greater sin.

Her hair exposed – her head uncovered and thus all the hair of her head can be seen, as is the practice of a bride going to the wedding canopy. [The Talmud asks]: [Is that not] a Torah prohibition, as it is written, "And he shall uncover her head"? Rather, even were she to place a cap on her head, if some of her hair were to protrude from under the cap, it would be a violation of *dat Yehudit*, such as if she were to go [thus] to the public marketplace.

She spins [thread] in the marketplace – such that when she lifts up [her arms] the sleeves fall back towards the shoulders and her flesh is visible underneath.

Converses with random men – meaning men she doesn't really know, neither her neighbor nor her relative. It would be un-

תצא בלא כתובה כדאמרינן [קידושין ס"ח ע"א] 'הכל מודים בבא על הנדה שאין הולד ממזר' וכ"ש במי שזינתה תחתיו שנאסרת עליו [כדכתיב] [דברים כ"ד] 'אחרי אשר הוטמאה' שתצא בלא כתובה.

ועוד דלא איצטריך למיתני דהא תני דמשום חוצפא לחודה תצא שלא בכתובה כגון יוצאה וראשה פרוע שהיא גזירה משום עבירה גמורה.

ראשה פרוע, ראשה מגולה ונראה כל שער ראשה כמנהג כלה הנכנסת לחופה, [ומקשי בגמ'] דאוריתא היא כדכתיב [במדבר ה'] ופרע את ראש האשה אלא אפילו תניח כפה על ראשה קצת שערה מבחוץ מתחת הכיפה הוי דת יהודית כגון שיוצאה בשוק של רבים.

[וטווה] בשוק, שכשמגבהת בגדי זרועותיה נופלין למטה כלפי הקבורת ובשרה נראה מתחת.

ומדברת עם כל אדם, כלומר שאינו רגיל עמה ולא שכנה ולא קרובה ולא מיבעיא אם

UNCOVERED HAIR IN THE RISHONIM, MODEL I

necessary to state about playful banter, meaning speaking about unnecessary matters, that she may be divorced without a ketubah payment. Rather even if she speaks with him about necessary matters she may be divorced without a ketubah payment for why should she be speaking with men she doesn't know? This is excessive brazenness!	משחקת עמו כלומר שמדברים דברים שאינם צריכים דתצא שלא בכתובה אלא אפילו מדברת עמו דברים הצריכים לה תצא דמה לה לדבר עם אנשים שאינן רגילין ואין זה אלא חוצפא יתירא.
And the loudmouth – the Talmud explains that this refers to making her voice heard about sexual matters, meaning that she declines to go to the mikvah and refuses marital intimacy to the point where he berates her and this is heard [by neighbors] and he is embarrassed.	אף הקולנית, מפרש בגמ' דמשמעת קולה על עיסקי תשמיש כלומר ממאנת לילך על בית הטבילה ומסרבת בתשמיש עד שמרבה עליה רעים והקול נשמע וחרפה היא לו.

Two points seem evident from the text. First, R. Yehonatan has nearly unique and very strict interpretations of a number of passages in the Mishnah. Conversing with random men applies even to necessary, business-like conversations and the "loudmouth" becomes a wife who refuses marital intimacy. Second, his discussion of hair covering is somewhat confusing. He initially writes that exposed hair is a violation of a decree, ostensibly to prevent lewdness. However, in the next sentence he adopts Rambam's view that fully uncovered hair violates a Torah prohibition, and that *dat Yehudit* refers to women wearing caps that do not fully cover their hair. But if it is a Torah prohibition, in what sense is it a "decree"?

R. Yehonatan expands on his interpretation of these rules in his comments on the passage in the Gemara.

"And he shall uncover her head," It is taught in tractate Sotah (8b): She uncovered her head for [her suitor], therefore the kohen shall uncover her head – we thus see that she was not to reveal her hair. From here we derive that the daughters of Israel are not to go with their hair exposed.	ופרע את ראש האשה, ואמרינן במסכת סוטה [ח' ע"ב] היא גלתה לו את ראשה לפיכך הכהן מגלה לה את ראשה אלמא דלא היה (לו) [לה] לגלות את ראשה ומכאן לבנות ישראל שלא יצאו בפריעת ראש.
Kalta – a basket in which she rests her spindle [marginal gloss: and the flax] and	קלתה, סל שמנחת בו את הפלך [גליון, ואת הפשתן]

which she places on her head when she is [otherwise] bare-headed. [Whereas according to] *dat Yehudit*, going out with a *kalta* on her head would be insufficient for the purposes of modesty.

ומניחתו על ראשה כשהיא פרועת ראש. ודת יהודית אפילו קלתה נמי לא, משום צניעות.

From one courtyard to another by way of an alley – since for those dwelling in the alley her hair is exposed; however, since she has a *kalta* on her head this is sufficient, for she doesn't remain there for any length of time and it would be difficult for the men in the alley to see her hair through the holes in the basket.

מחצר לחצר ודרך מבוי, דמשום בני מבוי איכא משום פריעת ראש וכיון דקלתה על ראשה שפיר דמי שהרי [אינה] שוהה שם כלום ואין שערותיה נראין כל כך (לפי) [לבני] מבוי בין הנקבים.

Exposing her arms to men – meaning, her sleeves are wide and when she lifts her arms they fall and her arms are visible.

במראה זרועותיה לבני אדם, כלומר שבתי זרועותיה רחבים וכשמגבהת זרועותיה נופלין ונראין זרועותיה.

Spinning red near her face – she spins something red colored literally next to her face so that her face will redden and brighten through the redness of the thread.

בטווה וורד כנגד פניה, שטווה דבר צבע אדם כוורד כנגד פניה ממש כדי שיאדימו פניה ויאורו באדמימות החוט.

Acting playfully with young men – meaning speaking about nonsense.

במשחקת עם בחורים, כלומר מדברת דברים בטלים.

In his analysis of the Talmudic passage, R. Yehonatan softens some of his previous statements. For example, speaking to men becomes speaking about nonsense and the cap becomes a kalta. Nevertheless, he maintains that totally uncovered hair is a violation of a Torah rule. Interestingly, his phrasing of this rule is a little softer than that of the Talmud (he does not have the word *azhara*/warning), but he still includes the proof from the sotah.

It is possible to reconcile R. Yehonatan's contradictory statements. One could argue that he sees the requirement for a woman to cover her hair as one detail in the overarching requirement that she not behave in a lewd manner, since this could lead to adultery and the like. In this scenario, one could imagine a Torah law prohibiting lewd behavior but leaving the list of such behaviors subjectively determined. In turn, the *dat*

Yehudit laws would be an outgrowth of the Torah laws one step removed, and also subjectively determined.

Given all this, would speaking with random men about business be a violation of *dat Yehudit*? It would depend on the social realities. Perhaps the same would be true of hair covering. Meaning, R. Yehonatan would be saying: *We see from the Torah that women covered their hair and doing so must be part of the overall prohibition on lewd behavior. Nevertheless, this specific behavior will only remain forbidden as long as it is considered lewd.* This is one way to view R. Yehonatan's position, which is difficult to pin down with any certainty.

4. & 5. Rid and Riaz

Further examples of Rishonim who take the derasha of the school of R. Yishmael and Shmuel's endorsement of it at face value are the great Italian halakhists R. Isaiah (ben Mali) di Trani the Elder (Rid) and his grandson, R. Isaiah (ben Elijah) di Trani the Younger (Riaz).

RID

In his *Piskei HaRid* on the passage in b. Ketubot, Rid rewrites the section on *dat Yehudit* as follows:

What [violates] *dat Yehudit*? Going out with her hair exposed – meaning, matters which are not forbidden but which women are accustomed not to do as a sign of modesty.	ואי זו היא דת יהודית יוצאה וראשה פרוע. פי' דבר שאין בו איסור אלא שהנשים נהגו דרך צניעות.
[The Talmud] poses a difficulty: "[Going out with] her hair exposed is a Torah prohibition! For it is written: 'And he shall expose the hair of the woman' (Num. 5:18); And the school of R. Yishmael taught: 'This is a warning to the daughters of Israel not to go out with their hair exposed!'" Meaning, since it says, "and he shall expose," clearly until then [her hair] wasn't exposed. Alternatively, since this is done to the *sotah* in order to degrade her, clearly it is degrading to a woman to go out with exposed hair.	ומקשה: "ראשה פרוע מדאוריתא הוא! דכת[יב]: 'ופרע את ראש האשה', דבי ר' ישמעאל תנא: 'אזהרה לבנות יש[ראל] שלא יצאו בפריעת ראש.'" פי' מדכת[יב] 'ופרע' אלמ[א] עד השתא לא הוה פרוע, אי נמי בסוטה שעושין כן כדי לנוולה אלמ[א] ניוול הוא לאשה לצאת בפריעת הראש.

Rav Yehuda says in the name of Shmuel: "As a matter of Torah law, if there is a *kalta* on her head that would be sufficient. As a matter of *dat Yehudit*, [going out] with a *kalta* would be a violation." Rav Assi said in the name of R. Yochanan: "[One who goes out in] *kalta* has not violated [the prohibition of going out with] her hair exposed."

אמ[ר] רב יהוד[ה] אמ[ר] שמואל: "דאוריית[א] קלתה על ראשה שפיר דמי, ודת יהודית בקלתה נמי אסיר." אמ[ר] רב אסי אמ[ר] ר' יוחנן: "קלתה אין בה משום פריעת הראש."

R. Zeira took issue with this: "Where [are we talking about]? If you were to say in the marketplace – this would be [a violation of] *dat Yehudit*; but if you were to suggest instead in a courtyard, if so, you have not left a single daughter of our patriarch Abraham who remain married to her husband!"

הוי בה ר' זעירא: "היכא? אילימ[א] בשוק - דת יהודית היא! אלא בחצר, אם כן לא הנחתה בת לאברהם אבינו שיושבת תחת בעלה!"

Abaye, or alternatively R. Kahana, stated: "[R. Yochanan's ruling is meant to apply to a woman who goes] from one courtyard to another by way of a thoroughfare." Meaning, because people from the public are not generally there.

אמ[ר] אביי ואיתימ[א] רב כהנא: "מחצר לחצר ודרך מבוי." פי' דלא שכיחי [ביה] בני רשות הרבים.

Spinning [thread] in the marketplace – Rav Yehuda said in the name of Shmuel: "She exposes her arms to the men." Rav Chisda said in the name of Avimi: "She spins and [the thread] goes down to her face." Meaning, the thread goes down to her "lower face" (a euphemism for the pelvic region), and it is vulgarity to do this in front of people.

וטווה בשוק, אמ[ר] רב יהודה אמ[ר] שמואל: "במגלה זרעותיה לבני אדם." רב חסדא אמ[ר] אבימי: "בטווה ויורד כנגד פניה." פי' החוט יורד כנגד פניה של מטה, והוא פריצו[ת] לעשות כן בפני בני אדם.

Conversing with random men – Rav Yehuda said in the name of Shmuel: "Being playful with young men."

ומדברת עם כל אדם, אמ[ר] רב יהודה אמ[ר] שמואל: "במשחקת עם הבחורים."

From the above presentation it is clear that Rid understands *dat Yehudit* violations to be expressions of vulgarity. He implies this by calling *dat Yehudit* "modest behavior" and makes it even more explicit in his discussion of the dangling thread, which he explicitly calls a vulgar habit. Ostensibly, he would agree with many of the other Rishonim who interpret *dat Yehudit* this way, meaning examples of *dat Yehudit* violations are by necessity subjectively determined.

Nevertheless, unlike some of those Rishonim, Rid still quotes the derasha of the school of R. Yishmael and Shmuel's support of that derasha, implying that a Torah law regarding hair covering is a viable option. In fact, as will be seen in the next subsection, his grandson Riaz, who follows his grandfather's overall interpretation of the passage, actually decides the halakha in accordance with Shmuel and the school of R. Yishmael.

RIAZ

In his *Piskei Riaz* (Ketubot 7:2), Riaz codifies the laws of *dat Moshe* and *dat Yehudit*.

The following [category of women] may be divorced without receiving the ketubah payment or the supplementary payment: One who violates *dat Moshe* – and these are the matters about which we are commanded in the Torah of Moses – or one who violates *dat Yehudit* – this refers to the modest customs that Jewish women have taken upon themselves.	אילו יוצאות שלא בכתובה ובלא תוס[פת], העוברת על דת משה, והם דברים שנצטווינו עליהם מתורת משה, או העוברת על דת יהודית, שהוא מנהג צניעות שנהגו בנות ישראל בעצמם.
What [violates] *dat Yehudit*? Going out with her hair exposed, even if she had a *kalta* on her head; since her head was not covered with a veil, this is considered lewd, and she should be divorced with no ketubah payment or the supplementary payment.	ואי זו היא דת יהודית? יוצאה וראשה פרוע, ואפילו היתה קלתה על ראשה הואיל ולא היתה מכוסה בצעיף הרי זה מדרכי הפריצות, ותצא בלא כתובה ובלא תוספת.
If she was going from one courtyard to another by way of an alley with a *kalta* on her head, this would not be considered lewd. But if the alley is a through-street on both sides, it is the same as a public area and using it has the same restrictions as in a public area.	היתה יוצאה מחצר לחצר דרך מבוי בקלתה על ראשה אין בזה משום פריצות, ואם היה המבוי מפולש משני צדדיו הרי הוא כרשות הרבים והיוצאה בו כיוצאה ברשות הרבים.
But if she were to go out without [even] a *kalta* on her head, this would violate a prohibition of the Torah, as it says (Num. 5:18) "And he shall expose the hair of the woman." This is a warning to the daughters of Israel not to go out with their hair exposed.	ואם לא היתה קלתה על ראשה הרי זו אסורה מן התורה, שנאמר: "ופרע את ראש האשה" אזהרה לבנות ישראל שלא יצאו בפריעת הראש.

> Even in a courtyard it is forbidden [for her] to go out without a *kalta* on her head – this is the position of the Talmud of the Land of Israel, as is explained in my *Kuntres Ha-Re'ayot*, in the fourth proof.[10]
>
> ואפילו בחצר אסורה [לצאת] בלא קלתה על ראשה, וכך היא שטת תלמוד ארץ ישראל, כמבואר בקונטרס הראיות בראיי' ד'.
>
> Similarly, if she was spinning [thread] in public and exposing her arms to people, or if she was spinning and the thread goes down between her thighs opposite her "lower face" (a euphemism for the pelvic region), or if she acts playfully with young men, or if she speaks loudly about sex – all of these matters violate *dat Yehudit*, and she may be divorced without a ketubah payment or the supplementary payment.
>
> וכן אם היתה טווה בשוק ומגלה זרועותיה לבני אדם, או שהיתה טווה והחוט יורד בין ברכיה כנגד פניה שלמטה, או שהיתה משחקת עם הבחורים, או שהיתה משמיש משמעת קולה על עסקי תשמיש, בכל אלה עוברת על דת יהודית ותצא בלא כתובה ובלא תוספת.

Riaz takes a very strict position on hair covering. First, he explicitly states that going out with totally uncovered hair violates a Torah law, and thus, following his own definition at the beginning of the section, violates *dat Moshe*. Second, he seems to follow Rambam's interpretation of full covering, which includes a veil. Third, Riaz takes the unique position that women must have their heads covered in their own courtyards, albeit only with a kalta. He rejects R. Zeira's assertion that no married woman does this by citing the Jerusalem Talmud. However, this interpretation of the Jerusalem Talmud appears to be a stretch, or at least a very strict reading. Although the Jerusalem Talmud does say that the prohibition of exposed hair applies to courtyards, it goes on to say that exposed hair means totally exposed, and would not apply to a woman whose hair was coiffed. Moreover, it would certainly not apply to a woman partially covering her hair. As far as I know, this interpretation of the Jerusalem Talmud and, consequently, the halakha, is unique to Riaz.

6. *Sefer Mitzvot Gadol* (Semag)

Although a French rabbi from the Tosafist school, R. Moshe of Coucy (13th century) was very influenced by the work of Rambam. This is clear from many different halakhot in his *Sefer Mitzvot*, and is certainly

---

10. Unfortunately, the *Kuntres HaRe'ayot* for Ketubot has yet to be published. If this proof is in the four volumes which have been published, I have been unable to find it.

true for his treatment of hair covering. For example, in his Positive Commandment 48, R. Moshe reproduces Rambam's discussion from the *Mishneh Torah* almost verbatim.

A woman who was unfaithful to her husband receives no ketubah payment, whether from the main funds or the additional funds, and this doesn't only apply to an adulteress, but even a woman who violates *dat Moshe* or *dat Yehudit* receives no ketubah payment.	מי שזינתה תחת בעלה אין לה כתובה לא עיקר ולא תוספת. ולא המזנה בלבד אלא [אף] העוברת על דת משה או על דת יהודית אין לה כתובה.
If a woman has done one of the following, she is considered to have violated *dat Moshe*, as it states in the seventh chapter of Ketubot:	ואילו הן הדברים שאם עשתה אחת מהן עברה על דת משה, כדאיתא בפרק המדיר:
a. Going out in the marketplace with her head uncovered, for the school of R. Yishmael taught: "And he shall expose the hair of the woman' (Num. 5:18) – This is a warning to the daughters of Israel not to go out with their hair exposed,"	א. יוצאה בשוק ושער ראשה גלוי, דתנא דבי רבי ישמעאל (שם) ופרע [את] ראש האשה אזהרה לבנות ישראל שלא יצאו בפריעת ראש,
b. or she makes vows or takes oaths but doesn't fulfill them,	ב. או שנודרת ונשבעת ואינה מקיימת,
c. or she has intercourse with her husband during her niddah period,	ג. או ששמשה מטתה והיא נדה,
d. or she does not set apart the dough offering,	ד. או שאינה קוצה לו חלה,
e. or she feeds her husband forbidden foods – not only insects, reptiles, and the carcasses of unslaughtered beasts, but even foods that are untithed.	ה. או שהאכילה את בעלה דברים אסורים ואין צריך לומר שקצים ורמשים ונבילות אלא אפילו דברים שאינם מעושרים.
What is considered to be *dat Yehudit*? Those are the modest practices with which the daughters of Israel comport themselves. These are the behaviors that if a woman has done one of them she is considered to have violated *dat Yehudit*:	[ו]איזוהי דת יהודית? הוא המנהג הצניעות שנהגו בנות ישראל. ואילו הן הדברים שאם עשתה אחת מהן עברה על דת יהודית:
a. Going from one courtyard to another	א. היוצאה מחצר לחצר דרך מבוי וראשה פרועה ואין עליה

by way of an alley with her hair exposed, without the *redid* as found in the Targum Yerushalmi [of the Torah[11]] for the word 'veil' (Gen. 24:65) – that all other women wear, even though her hair is covered by a kerchief. But this is not completely exposed, for the Jerusalem Talmud states that, "One who goes out with her hair coiffed has not violated [the prohibition of going out with] her hair exposed." And that which it says there: "This refers to in a courtyard, but in a thoroughfare, it would violate [the prohibition of going out] with her hair exposed," – this means when her intention is to remain in the thoroughfare,

b. or if she was spinning [yarn] in the marketplace with red or the like, according to R. Chananel [this means] on her face, on her forehead or cheeks, in the manner of the promiscuous non-Jewish women,

c. or she was spinning [yarn] in the marketplace in such a way that it shows her bare arms to the onlookers,

d. or she was being playful with young men,

e. or she would demand sex from her husband in a voice so loud that her neighbors hear her talking about sex,

f. or she would curse her husband's father in front of her husband's face.

[רדיד, רדיד תרגום ירושלמי של] צעיף, כשאר כל הנשים אף על פי ששערה מכוסה במטפחת. ואין בזה פרועת ראש לגמרי דהא אמרינן בירושלמי "היוצאה בקפליטין שלה אין בה משום פריעת ראש," ומה שאומר שם "הדא דאת אמר בחצר אבל למבוי יש בה משום פריעת ראש" – התם כשרוצה לשהות במבוי,

ב. או שהיתה טווה בשוק ורד או כיוצא בו, לדברי רבינו חננאל (שם עב, ב תד"ה בטווה), כנגד פניה על פדחתה או על לחיה כדרך שעושות הגויות הפרוצות,

ג. או שטווה בשוק ומראה זרועותיה לבני אדם,

ד. או שהיתה משחקת עם [ה] בחורים,

ה. או שהיתה תובעת התשמיש מבעלה בקול רם [עד] ששכנותיה שומעין אותה מדברת על עסקי תשמיש,

ו. או שהיתה מקללת אבי בעלה בפני בעלה.

Like Rambam, R. Moshe assumes that the derasha of the school of R. Yishmael is accepted as halakha, and that the distinction between with a kalta and without a kalta – which he, like Rambam, interprets as a veil – is a difference between a *dat Moshe* violation and a *dat Yehudit* violation.

---

11. This text of the Semag is taken from the Bar Ilan CD 26 and the words in brackets are not present in other editions. This issue is not central to our work and is therefore not discussed.

R. Moshe also treats the "handbreadth of flesh" passage in b. Berachot in a similar way to Rambam as being mainly a reference to the rules of reciting Shema (Commandment 18).

If a person was washing in sullied water, which did not have a foul smell, such that the person could not see his nudity, he may remain in his seat and recite [the Shema]. But if the person was bathing in clear water, he must cover himself with a cloth upon his heart, and this was the practice of R. Jacob.	היה רוחץ במים עכורין שאין ריחן רע \עד\ שאינו רואה את הערוה יושב במקומו וקורא ובצלולין מתכסה \בבגד\ כנגד לבו וכן היה נוהג רבינו יעקב (ע"פ תוספות ריה"ח כה, ב).
So too do we say in b. Berachot (24a) that a handbreadth of flesh on a woman is an erotic stimulus when exposed and a person should not recite [the Shema] until he turns his face away from her, even if she is his wife.	וכן אמרינן שם בברכות (כד, א) שטפח באשה ערוה כשהוא מגולה ולא יקרא עד שיחזיר פניו ממנה אף על פי שהיא אשתו.
If a man was sleeping in bed with his wife, his wife is considered as an extension of his body; even if they are undressed and their flesh is touching down below, he need only turn his face in the other direction and place his blanket underneath his heart and recite.	היה ישן עם אשתו, אשתו כגופו דמי ואף על פי שנוגעין בקירוב בשר מלמטה הופך פניו וחוצץ טליתו מתחת לבו וקורא,
The same goes for his children and extended family when they are minors, but not once they are grown up. This refers to a girl of eleven years or a boy of twelve years – [with children this age in the bed] it would be forbidden for the person to recite with them [undressed] next to him unless his blanket divides between them. Once they arrive at puberty they are considered adults. This was the decision of Rav Alfas as well as the *Halakhot Gedolot*.	וכן בניו ובני ביתו הקטנים אבל לא הגדולים, \והם\ תינוקת מבת אחת עשרה שנה ותינוק מבן שתים עשרה שנה אסור לו לקרות עמהם עד שתפסיק טלית ביניהם וכיון שהגיעו לשדים נכונו ושער צומח נחשבים כגדולים וכן פסקו רב אלפס (דף טו, א) והלכות גדולות (ל"מ):

R. Moshe's view aligns with that of the Talmud save for one detail: he does not suggest that the handbreadth was meant to reference the man's wife, as the Talmud states. Other than this, he follows the Talmud's suggestion that the prohibition of seeing an exposed handbreadth of flesh on a woman refers to looking at her while reciting Shema.

The prohibition of ogling a woman is included in the Semag in a totally different section, Prohibition 126, and this also follows Rambam's precedent.

Therefore, the Sages said that it is forbidden for a person to have playful banter with women or to allude [to something inappropriate] with his hands or feet, or to wink his eyes [flirtatiously] – even listening to their voices, or gazing at them or looking upon their hair is forbidden.[12] For this reason, being alone with forbidden sexual relations is also prohibited, since these behaviors lead to forbidden sexual practices.	לפיכך אמרו חכמים שאסור לו לאדם לשחוק עם הנשים ולא לקרוץ בידיו ורגליו ולא לרמוז בעיניו ולא להסתכל בהן ואפילו לשמוע קולה[ן] \ולהרהר\ [ומהרהר] בהן ולראות שערן אסור. וגם מטעם זה אסור להתייחד עם העריות שהדברים האלו מביאין לידי גילוי ערוה,
The Sages even forbade looking upon a single woman with lewd intentions, for it says (Job 31:1): 'I have made a covenant with my eyes – why should I look upon a virgin?' They also forbade looking upon the colorful used clothing of a woman one knows, even if they are just lying on a wall, as it says in the first chapter of b. Avodah Zarah (20b), for this will lead him to fantasize about her. And it also says, in the final chapter of b. Yoma (74b) [referencing Eccl. 6:9]: '"The sight of one's eyes is better' – regarding women, than doing a deed."[13] Therefore, a person must be very careful with this. But if he is gazing at her with intent to marry her if he likes her – this is permitted; it is even obligatory to do so, as we already explained in the laws of Kiddushin that it is forbidden for a man to betroth a woman until he sees her.	ואפילו בפני אשה פנויה אסרו חכמים להסתכל דרך זנות, הרי הוא אומר (איוב לא, א) ברית כרתי לעיני ומה אתבונן על בתולה, וכן אס[רו] להסתכל בבגדי צבע ישנים קצת של אשה שהוא מכיר ואפילו שטוחים על גבי כותל כדאיתא בפרק קמא דעבודה זרה (כ, ב) שעל ידי כן מהרהר בה, ואומר [נמי] בפרק בתרא דיומא (עד, ב) טוב מראה עינים באשה יותר מגופה של מעשה (קהלת ו, ט) לפיכך צריך ליזהר \מאד מאד\ בדבר. ואם נתכוון להסתכל בה כדי לישא אותה אם תישר בעיניו מותר וגם חייב הוא לעשות כן כאשר בארנו במצות קידושין (עשין מח) שאסור לאדם לקדש אשה עד שיראנה (קידושין מא, א).

R. Moshe throws in the prohibition against listening to women's voices or gazing at their hair as part of this discussion. This prohibition

---

12. A paraphrase of Rambam's halakha quoted above.
13. In the Talmud, this is cited as the derasha of Resh Lakish.

is clearly inspired by two of the three other examples of erotic stimulus in the b. Berachot passage (only the calf is missing). According to this interpretation, it is the men who are prohibited from deriving sexual satisfaction through their interactions with women. The burden does not fall on women to avoid talking or showing their hair.

Regarding the issue, it is possible that Rambam and Semag may have a difference of opinion. Although both forbid men from gazing sexually at women's hair, Rambam believes that all women must be veiled, even unmarried girls. Semag, on the other hand, does not record such a rule, and it seems reasonable to assume that R. Moshe of Coucy followed the Franco-German custom of single girls/women having their hair uncovered.

7. Ramban (Nachmanides)

As described in Chapter 2, b. Gittin 89a cites Rabbi Akiva's view that a man may even divorce his wife over impropriety that is known only through gossip. Rabbi Yochanan ben Nuri reacts by saying that no daughter of Abraham would be safe from divorce if this were correct. He maintains that infidelity must be objectively determined in order to create grounds for divorce. Ra'avad (quoted in Ramban ad loc.) comments on R. Yochanan ben Nuri's position:

Rabbi Avraham had a difficulty with this; doesn't R. Yochanan ben Nuri accept [the Mishnah], "These women are divorced without a ketubah payment: Those who violated *dat Moshe* and *Yehudit*"?[14]	קשיא ליה לרב ר' אברהם הנזכר ז"ל דלר' יוחנן בן נורי לית ליה הא דתנן ואלו יוצאות שלא בכתובה העוברת על דת משה ויהודית,
But this is not really a difficulty at all, since even though she may be divorced without a ketubah payment, since she did not behave like a modest woman, nevertheless she is not forbidden to him because of this; rather it is a mitzvah for a righteous man to divorce her.[15] Even R. Meir[16] would ad-	ולאו קושיא היא כלל שאע"פ שיוצאת שלא בכתובה שלא נהגה כמנהג הצנועות אינה אסורה לו בשביל כך אלא מצוה עליו לגרשה לבעל נפש. ואפילו לר"מ נמי אינה נאסרת בדת יהודית שאם יוצאת

---

14. Ra'avad asks this in slightly different words (glosses on Rif, b. Gittin 50a).
15. Ramban makes this point again, i.e., that the husband is not *required* to divorce his wife because of *dat Moshe* or *dat Yehudit* violations, but that if he wishes to do so he need not make the ketubah payment – in his gloss on b. Yevamot 24b.
16. R. Meir's position is that even if the woman were eating, drinking, or nursing in public she can be divorced, ostensibly without ketubah payment.

> mit that she is not forbidden due to *dat Yehudit* concerns, such that if she were to go out to the marketplace with only a *kalta* she would not be forbidden, even though she is violating *dat Yehudit*.

> בקלתה לשוק אינה נאסרת ואף על פי שהיא עוברת על דת יהודית.

Ra'avad observes that R. Yochanan ben Nuri's position appears to contradict the Mishnah, which holds that a woman can be divorced for violating public modesty laws. This contradiction is based on the fact that the Mishnah never references a need for real witnesses and testimony. However, Ramban (1194, Gerona – 1270, Jerusalem) responds to this observation by saying that the cases are not really comparable. R. Yochanan ben Nuri is discussing accusations of adultery. In such a case the man would be obligated to divorce his wife. It is in this case – where the divorce would be obligatory and not just optional – that R. Yochanan ben Nuri demands a higher level of proof, including witnesses and court testimony. Conversely, according to the Ramban's logic, R. Yochanan ben Nuri would accept the husband's option to divorce his wife without payment of her ketubah if she were to violate *dat Yehudit* publicly, without court testimony.

Ramban's illustration of the *dat Yehudit* violation is interesting. He gives the example of a woman going out to the marketplace only with a kalta. It is noteworthy that he uses this as an example of *dat Yehudit* and does not simply say that her hair is exposed. This implies that Ramban believes a woman going out with fully uncovered hair in public violates *dat Moshe*.

Ramban makes his understanding of the status of uncovered hair clear in his *Sefer HaZechut* as well (Yevamot 2b in the *Sefer HaZechut*).

> …One who violates *dat* does not lose her ketubah or become forbidden to her husband at all after one incident. For instance, if she leaves her house to go out to the market with only a *kalta* or if she acts playfully with young men once, but before that and after that she is a modest woman and behaves in accordance with *dat Yehudit* – it is certainly forbidden to divorce her and she does not lose her ketubah; for if one does not take this position, no daughter of Abraham will be left married to her husband!

> ... העוברת על דת אינה מפסדת כתובתה ולא נאסרת על בעלה כלל בפעם אחת שאם נזדמן לה ויצאה בקלתה לשוק או שחקה עם הבחורים ומתחלה וכן לאחר כן היא צנועה ומתנהגת יפה בדת יהודית ודאי זו אסור לגרשה ולא הפסידה כתובתה שאם לא תאמר כן לא הנחת בת אברהם אבינו יושבת תחת בעלה

Even if she violates *dat Moshe*, feeding her husband untithed food or being intimate with him while she is a niddah, or making vows she doesn't keep – if he knows that she has repented, and that she tithes the food and keeps her vows properly, she is permitted [to her husband] and she does not lose anything [from her ketubah settlement] – if only her husband could be like her, that if he were to sin but once he would immediately repent and turn away from it.	ואפילו כדת משה נמי האכילתו שאינו מעושר ושמשתו נדה ונדרה ולא קיימה אם יודע שעשתה תשובה מעשרת ומתקיימת נדריה יפה הרי זו מותרת ולא הפסידה כלום הלואי שיהא בעלה כמוה שאם פשע פעם אחד מיד יעשה תשובה ויחזור בו.
This is why the [Mishnah] uses present tense, "She goes out with her hair exposed; she spins [thread] in the marketplace; she speaks with random men." Additionally, this is why she must receive a warning [before she loses her ketubah]. Additionally... if her husband wishes to remain married to her he may; the court says nothing to him unless he comes and asks their advice, then they would suggest that he divorce her.	וזו היא ששנינו בהן לשון הווה יוצאה וראשה פרוע טווה בשוק ומדברת עם כל אדם ועוד נמי צריכה התראה. ועוד... אם רוצה בעלה לקיימה מקיימה ואין ב״ד אומרים לו כלום אלא א״כ בא לישאל עליה והכא אמרינן תצא.

In this piece, Ramban proposes a definition of a woman who violates *dat Moshe* and *dat Yehudit* as one who does so consistently as a pattern of behavior. She is not a woman who violates it once nor does she repent from her behavior. For our purposes, it is important to note that when Ramban speaks of going out with hair exposed as a violation of *dat Yehudit*, he specifically describes the woman as having gone out with a kalta. In sum, it seems reasonable that Ramban accepts the derasha and Shmuel's interpretation of the Mishnah, and believes that a woman going out without any hair covering would violate *dat Moshe*.

8. Rabbi Menachem HaMeiri

Another example of a Rishon who believes that minimal hair covering is a Torah requirement is R. Menachem HaMeiri (1249–c. 1310, Perpignan). In his commentary on Ketubot 72a–b, he quotes the Mishnah in Ketubot about *dat Moshe ve-Yehudit* and then explains the Talmudic analysis of the terms. His discussion of *dat Yehudit* is significant.

Afterwards, [the Talmud] explains the particulars regarding *dat Yehudit*. All of them are surrounding the issue of modesty, for they are all lewd acts and they lead down various paths towards fornication.

It explains: "She goes out to the marketplace with her hair exposed" – the Gemara explains that doing so would actually violate a Torah law, for it is written: 'and [the priest] shall expose the woman's hair' – meaning, this [woman] but not a different [woman]. The school of Rabbi Yishmael taught: "From here we learn a warning to all the daughters of Israel not to go out with their hair exposed." Rather [the Gemara] explains that what is meant by a *dat Yehudit* violation as opposed to a *dat Moshe* one is not if she goes out with her hair totally uncovered; rather she has a *kalta* on her head. According to the Torah this does not count as fully exposed hair even in the marketplace, however for *dat Yehudit* it is insufficient, even in an alley that functions as a thoroughfare for masses of people, unless she covers her hair with a kerchief. Nevertheless, this rule applies specifically if she is going out to the marketplace this way; but if she is going between courtyards through a closed alley it is permitted. If she is in her own yard, even though this is deplorable behavior, she would not even violate *dat Yehudit* if her hair were fully uncovered.

In the Western Talmud (=Yerushalmi), they said that if she goes out *capillatus*[17] she does not violate [the *dat Yehudit* prohibition] of going out with her hair exposed. This refers to a courtyard; but in a

ואחר כך פירש פרטים שבדת יהודית וכלם ענינים של צניעות ומתורת שהם דברים של פריצות ויוצאים מהם דרכים ושבילים לזנות.

ופירש בהם יוצאה בשוק וראשה פרוע ופירשו בגמרא שזו מן התורה היא ובכלל דת משה וכדכתיב ופרע את ראש האשה כלומר זאת ולא אחרת ותנא דבי ר' ישמעאל: "מכאן אזהרה לבנות ישראל שלא יצאו בפירוע הראש". אלא שפירשו זו שנכללה בדת יהודית ולא בדת משה שאינה יוצאה בגלוי שיער לגמרי אלא שהניחה קלתה על ראשה ומן התורה אין זה פרועת ראש לגמרי אף בשוק אלא שבדת יהודית אין זה מספיק בשוק או אף במבוי מפלש שבקיעת רבים מצויה בו עד שיתכסה שערה במטפחת ומכל מקום דוקא שתצא לשוק כן אבל מחצר לחצר דרך מבוי סתום שאין בו בקיעת רבים מותר ובחצירה מיהא אף על פי שהדבר מגנה אין כאן אפילו משום דת יהודית אף בפירוע הגמור

ובתלמוד המערב אמרו היוצאה בקפליטין שלה אין בה משום יוצאה וראשה פרוע הדא דתימא לחצר אבל למבוי יש בה חצר שרבים בוקעין בה

---

17. Literally, this means coiffed (see Chapter 2 for discussion); but that is not how Meiri will understand the term.

thoroughfare, [it would violate the prohibition of going out with her hair exposed]. There is a [type of] courtyard that is like an alley, and there is a [type of] alley that is like a courtyard. A courtyard that many people use as a pass-through is [considered] as an alley; an alley through which people generally do not pass is [considered] as a courtyard.

Capillatus is the same thing as *kalta* referenced in this passage in our Talmud. Even though in most places the meaning of the term is a small basket into which she places her thread, nevertheless in this case it seems that it refers to a kind of hat from thick cloth which she wears at night but during the day girds herself with it, so that the hat hangs between her thighs and she places her thread into it… There are others who interpret this as a cloth she puts on her head when she wishes to carry something heavy…

Spinning [thread] in the marketplace – the Gemara explains this as showing her arms in a brazen fashion, or that she ties a rose or some other flower near her cheeks or her forehead, like the lewd women are accustomed to do.

Speaks with random men – this means that she acts playfully with them in a brazen manner.

Similarly, any example like this [would also violate *dat Yehudit*]; it all depends on how the judge sees it. The Great Rabbi (=Rashi) interprets in a different manner, and it is all true, since it all follows the nature of the brazen behavior…

---

18. Meiri next deals with the cursing of the husband's parents, but I will skip over this section as it is too tangential to the discussion of modesty and hair covering.

Rabbi Tarfon says: "Also the loudmouth." What is a loudmouth? Any woman who speaks inside her house and her neighbors hear her voice. The Gemara explains this as her voice being audible when discussing sexual matters.

The Great Posek (=Rif) and [the Great] Compiler (=Rambam) interpret this as referring to a woman who demands [sex] verbally and immodestly, such that she does not refrain from doing so in earshot of her neighbors who can hear her.

The Great Rabbi (=Rashi) interprets this as her refusing to engage in intercourse or refusing to dip in the mikvah at the appropriate time, for no reason except to refuse him, to the point where he feels the need to heap insults and other rebukes upon her, and even to express his suffering in public.

Both of these interpretations are true when it comes to deciding halakha; however any woman whose voice while having intercourse in [her room adjoining] one courtyard can be heard in a different courtyard, whether because of some medical problem or some other reason – this is not a *dat Yehudit* issue but a blemish issue.

You should know that in all cases where the woman is violating *dat*, this specifically refers to women who do this consistently. However, if a woman does one of these once or twice, this does not apply. This is why the language is present tense, "she feeds him," "she is intimate with him," "she spins [thread] in the market," "she speaks with random men" – but it doesn't say [for instance], "she fed him," "she spun"...

ר' טרפון אומר אף הקולנית ואי זו היא קולנית כל שמדברת בתוך ביתה ושכניה שומעין את קולה, ופירשוה בגמרא שמשמעת קולה על עסקי תשמיש.

ופירשוה גדולי הפוסקים והמחברים בתובעת בפה ובפריצות שאינה נמנעת מצד שכנים השומעים

וגדולי הרבנים מפרשים שמסרבת בתשמיש או שממאנת לטבול בשעתה שלא לשום סבה אלא דרך סרוב עד שהוא צריך להרבות עליה רעים ורעות וצריך להודיע צערו לרבים

והכל אמת לענין פסק ומכל מקום כל שמשמשת בחצר זו ונשמע קולה בחצר אחרת מצד סבת חולי או אי זה סבה אין זה נכלל בדת יהודית אלא במומין

וצריך שתדע שבכל אלו שבעוברת על דת דוקא כשמתמדת בכך הא כל שנזדמן כן אחת ושתים לא והוא שתופשה בלשון זה מאכילתו וכו' ומשמשתו וכו' טווה בשוק ומדברת עם כל אדם ואינו אומר שהאכילתו וכו' ולא שטותה בשוק...

According to Meiri, *dat Moshe* hair violations are qualitatively different from *dat Yehudit* hair violations. *Dat Yehudit*, Meiri writes, is a subjectively determined category that every judge needs to decide about on his own. This is why Meiri can quote the interpretations of both Rambam and Rashi on a given example, even when they directly contradict each other. They can both be correct if both behaviors are, in fact, questionable in nature and can be reasonably described as violating decent social norms for married women. This can change, of course, depending on each generation and the society in which the behavior occurs.

However, when it comes to *dat Moshe*, Meiri is strict. He assumes the Talmud communicates an absolute prohibition for a woman to go into the public square with her hair fully uncovered. This division between an absolute requirement for minimal hair coverage versus a socially mediated/subjective prohibition for all other forms of modest dress and behavior, including the remaining hair requirements, points to the probability that Meiri does not believe that the Torah requirement to cover hair is actually an issue of modesty. (This position is actually quite a prominent one among contemporary Jewish law authorities and was adopted by R. Moshe Feinstein, as will be seen in a later chapter.)

Meiri also discusses hair covering in the context of the passage in b. Berachot (24a):

A man needs to be careful when he recites the Shema or he prays, that he not focus his eyes upon something that may bring him to have sexual thoughts. Even regarding his wife, the Sages said that seeing a handbreadth of exposed flesh which she does not normally expose would prohibit him from reciting the Shema, even though this would not prohibit him studying Torah, for gazing upon her will cause sexual thoughts.	צריך לאדם שיזהר כשיקרא את שמע או יתפלל שלא יפנה עיניו לשום דבר המביא לידי הרהור אפי' באשתו אמרו חכמים ראיית טפח באשתו בכל מקום שאין דרכו להגלות אוסרת בק"ש אף על פי שאינה אוסרת לדברי תורה שהראייה גורמת הרהור
Similarly, a woman's calf or a woman's hair which should be covered, and the singing voice of a woman are all considered *erva* with regard to reciting the Shema, assuming these are not things to which he is accustomed. However, her face, hands, and feet, and her speaking voice, as opposed to singing voice, and the hair which sticks out from the side of the covering – there is no reason to be concerned about these.	וכן שוק באשה ושער באשה הראוי להתכסות וקול של זמר באשה ערוה לענין ק"ש ובלבד במה שאין רגיל בה אבל פניה וידיה ורגליה וקול דבורה שאינו לזמר ושער היוצא חוץ לצמתה אין חוששש להם

The same is true regarding a man, if his pubic hair sticks out from his clothing, there is no reason to be concerned.[19]	וכן באיש יצא שער ערותו דרך בגדו אינו חושש
Similarly, the Later Rabbi (=R. Tam) wrote that the hair of virgins, even if entirely exposed, is permitted – this refers to gazing [at her]. And with another woman [not his wife], even if [he was only gazing at] her little finger, since he is intentionally gazing at her or listening to her voice, even if it isn't her singing voice, [this would be forbidden]. It is like what we said in b. Kiddushin (70a) regarding Rav Nachman, who said to Rav Yehuda: "Let the master send greetings to Yalta," and he responded "No, because the voice of a woman is *erva*." "Nevertheless," [Rav Nachman responded] "greetings are permitted." [Rav Yehuda] replied that it is no different than a singing voice...	וכן כתבו אחרוני הרבנים ששער הבתולות אף על פי שכלו מגולה מותר אין הכונה אלא למסתכל ובאשה אחרת אפי' באצבע קטנה כל שהוא מכוין לראות או לשמוע אסור בכל שעה להסתכל בה ולשמוע קולה אפי' קול שאינו של זמר וכמו שאמרו קדושין ע' א' ברב נחמן שאמר לרב יהודה לישדר מר שלמא לילתא ואמר ליה לא סבר לה מר קול באשה ערוה ומ"מ אפשר לומר בשאלת שלום והשבתו כעין זמר הוא...

In this passage, Meiri identifies three kinds of erva that create a prohibition to recite the Shema when facing them. The first is a permitted erotic stimulus (gazing at his wife). The second is forbidden erotic stimuli, such as a woman whose calf or hair is exposed when it usually is not, or listening to a woman singing. Both of these erotic stimuli are socially subjective in that they are dependent on how women usually are (or are not) dressed in public. The third category is personally subjective and depends on what may cause any given man to become aroused.

When defining the parameters of the first prohibition, Meiri references what is usually covered, without reference to any difference between Torah requirements and socially acceptable behavior. The significance of this point becomes clearer with Meiri's invocation of the position of Rabbeinu Tam (which will be analyzed in detail in the next chapter). Rabbeinu Tam believes that single women do not need to cover their hair – a position in direct contradiction to that of Rambam. Meiri explains R. Tam's position further by arguing that since a single woman may go out with her hair uncovered, all may look at her. This is true not only in life but even when reciting Shema (when one may not even gaze upon one's wife's hair, which is still erva, since she is a married woman.)

---

19. This is a ruling that Meiri seems to have adapted from the *Sefer HaHashlama*.

Meiri's position is striking, due to the tension it creates between two positions. He believes that some form of hair covering is a Torah requirement for women while simultaneously subscribing to R. Tam's view that this requirement only applies to married women. The solution to this tension lies – as it did in the explanation offered above in his commentary on b. Ketubot – in Meiri's belief that the *dat Moshe* requirement of some hair covering (for married women) is not about modesty but is instead a separate law – a *chok* – that exists irrespective of societal norms. Married women must cover their hair because this is what the Torah means to imply in its description of the sotah ritual.

It is important to note that this understanding seems to have led married women – at least in the Talmudic period – to wear a fuller hair covering. The relevance of this societal norm should be obvious. The prohibition of reciting the Shema in the presence of erva applies to men in the presence of women in a state of dress (or voice) in which they would not generally appear in public. It thus applies to women who do not have their hair covered in line with *dat Yehudit*. However, since no custom or halakha requires unmarried women to cover their hair at all – if one follows R. Tam – their hair would not constitute a problem for the Shema-reciting male.

As stated above, this compromise of Meiri is reflective of the view of many poskim in modern times – that there is a *dat Moshe* requirement for some sort of hair covering for married women which exists irrespective of societal norms, but all *dat Yehudit* rules, including those of hair covering, are societally determined since modesty rules in general are societally determined. This presentation of the halakha will be dealt with at length in a later chapter, where the position of R. Moshe Feinstein is analyzed.

9. Zohar

The Zohar [widely considered a late 13th-century kabbalistic work compiled by R. Moses de-Leon and his colleagues (c. 1240–1305)], is exceedingly strict with regard to the prohibition of women going with uncovered hair. The Zohar writes (*Parashat Nasso*, pp. 125b–126a):

R. Chizkiyah stated: A stupor shall befall the man who allows his wife to let her hair be seen protruding forth. This is one of the modest practices of the home.	א"ר חזקיה תונבא ליתי על ההוא בר נש דשבק לאנתתיה דתתחזי משערה דרישה לבר ודא הוא חד מאינון צניעותא דביתא,

A woman who exposes some of her hair for self-adornment causes poverty for her household, causes her children to be unimportant in their generation, and causes a foreign spirit to dwell in her house. What causes all this? The hair of her head that is visible from the outside. If this is true within the home, how much more so in the marketplace. And how much more so [could it lead to] even further brazenness. Thus the verse, "Your wife shall be as a fruitful vine in the innermost parts of your house" (Psalms 128:3).

ואתתא דאפיקת משערא דרישה לבר לאתתקנא ביה גרים מסכנותא לביתא וגרים לבנהא דלא יתחשבון בדרא וגרים מלה אחרא דשריא בביתא מאן גרים דא ההוא שערא דאתחזי מרישה לבר, ומה בביתא האי כ"ש בשוקא וכ"ש חציפותא אחרא ובגין כך אשתך כגפן פוריה בירכתי ביתך,

R. Yehuda stated: The hair of the head of a woman being exposed causes "other hair" [i.e., the powers of impurity] to be revealed and harm her. Thus, a woman is required to ensure that even the beams of her house not see a single hair of her head, and all the more so outdoors.

אמר ר' יהודה שערא דרישא דאתתא דאתגלייא גרים שערא אחרא לאתגלייא ולאפגמא לה בגין כך בעיא אתתא דאפילו טסירי דביתא לא יחמון שערא חד מרישא כ"ש לבר,

Come and see how just as hair is of paramount importance for men, the same is true for women. Go and see how much harm a woman's hair causes: it causes [harm] above, and causes [harm] below, it causes [harm] to her husband who is cursed, and it causes poverty, it causes *another matter*[20] in her house, and it causes her children's importance to depart, let the Merciful One save us from such impudence.

ת[א] חז[י] כמה בדכורא שערא הוא חומרא דכלא הכי נמי לנוקבא, פוק חמי כמה פגימו גרים ההוא שערא דאתתא, גרים לעילא גרים לתתא גרים לבעלה דאתלטייא גרים מסכנותא גרים מלה אחרא בביתא גרים דיסתלק חשיבותא מבנהא, רחמנא לישזבון מחציפו דלהון,

For this reason, a woman must cover her hair even in the corners of her own house. And if she does so, this is written (Psalms 128:3) "your sons like olive saplings." Why olive saplings? Just as olive saplings do not lose their significance either in the winter or in the summer, and they are always con-

ועל דא בעיא אתתא לאתכסייא בזיוותי דביתא ואי עבדת כן מה כתיב (תהלים קכח) בניך כשתילי זיתים, מהו כשתילי זיתים, מה זית דא בין בסתווא בין בקייטא לא אתאבידו טרפוי ותדיר

---

20. This is a euphemism for sexual matters.

sidered more important than other trees, so too will [her sons] grow in importance in comparison with other people.

Not only this, but her husband will be blessed with everything, with blessings from above and blessings from below, wealthy in children and grandchildren. This is what is written (Psalms 128:4), "So shall the man who fears the Lord be blessed," and it is written (ibid., 128:5–6), "May the Lord bless you from Zion; may you share the prosperity of Jerusalem all the days of your life, and live to see your children's children. May all be well with Israel!"

אשתכח ביה חשיבות יתיר על שאר אילנין, כך בהא יסתלקון בחשיבו על שאר בני עלמא

ולא עוד אלא דבעלה מתברך בכלא בברכאן דלעילא בברכאן דלתתא בעותרא בבנין בבני בנין, הדא הוא דכתיב (שם) הנה כי כן יבורך גבר ירא יי' וכתיב (שם) יברכך יי' מציון וראה בטוב ירושלים כל ימי חייך וראה בנים לבניך שלום על ישראל (ישראל סבא קדישא):

The Zohar is strict in a number of ways. First, it requires hair covering even in the home. Second, it never directly discusses whether the rule is from the Torah or rabbinic. However, considering the seriousness of the curses one receives for not adhering to the rule, one can only imagine that the Zohar views it as a prohibition of divine origin. Third, it seems to require all hair on a woman's head with no exception, in contrast to what we will see in later chapters from Ra'avad and those who follow him.

Nevertheless, the Zohar never says this obligation applies to single women, and it consistently discusses the problems exposed hair causes to a woman's husband and children. Therefore, it seems that the Zohar does not apply this law before marriage.[21]

10. Aharon HaKohen

Rabbi Aharon ben Jacob HaKohen was a rabbi from Narbonne in Provence,[22] who in 1306 was forced to leave France during the expulsion

---

21. I recognize that the listing of the Zohar in the group of Rishonim is problematic both to some academics and to some Talmudists albeit for different reasons. The Zohar is not written as a legal text or commentary on the Talmud and its status in halakhic discussions has always been much debated. Nonetheless, numerous halakhic authorities treat the Zohar like a Rishon, in that it cannot be legally binding when it contradicts the Talmud but helps us understand Talmudic disputes and resolve them practically.

22. The idea that he was from Lunel, as recorded by David Conforte in *Kore*

of Jews. Following his evacuation from Provence, he emigrated to Majorca in the Spanish archipelago where he wrote his magnum opus, *Orchot Chayyim* (*The Ways of Life*) circa 1337. Rabbi Aharon takes up the issue of women's hair covering in a number of sections.

In the laws of Ketubot (33/34), R. Aharon follows the outline of the *Mishneh Torah* and the Semag:

> If a woman has done one of the following, she is considered to have violated *dat Moshe*:
> a. Going out in the marketplace with her head uncovered,
> b. making vows or taking oaths and not fulfilling them,
> c. having intercourse with her husband during her menstrual period,
> d. not setting apart the dough offering,
> e. or feeding her husband forbidden foods – not only insects, reptiles, and the carcasses of unslaughtered beasts, but even foods that are untithed.
>
> אלו הן הדברים שאם עשתה [אחת מהן] עברה על דת משה:
> א. יוצאה בשוק ושער ראשה גלוי
> ב. או שנשבעת ונודרת ואינה [מקיימת]²³
> ג. או ששמשה [מטתה] והיא נדה
> ד. או שאינה קוצה לה חלה
> ה. או האכילה לבעלה דברים האסורים ואין צריך לומר שקצים ורמשים ונבלות אלא אפילו האכילתו דברים שאינן מעושרין.
>
> What is considered to be *dat Yehudit*? Those are the modest practices with which the daughters of Israel comport themselves.
>
> ואי זו היא דת יהודית? [הוא מנהג] הצניעיות שנהגו בנות ישראל.
>
> If a woman has done one of the following, she is considered to have violated *dat Yehudit*:
> a. Going out in the marketplace or in a through-alley with her hair exposed, and without the full covering that all other women wear, even though her hair is covered by a kerchief.
> b. Spinning [yarn] in the marketplace with red or the like on her face – on her forehead or cheeks, in the manner
>
> ואלו הן [הדברים] שאם עשתה [אחת] מהם עברה על דת יהודית:
> א. יוצאה לשוק או למבוי מפולש וראשה פרוע ואין לה רדיד כשאר הנשים אף על פי ששערה מכוסה במטפחת,
> ב. או שהיתה טווה בשוק וורד וכיוצא בו נגד פניה

HaDorot, seems to be a mistake. Perhaps the error was inspired by confusion with another Rabbi Aharon (ben Meshullam) who did hail from Lunel a century earlier, and whose works have been lost, but this is just speculation.

23. Some texts have משלמת.

of the [promiscuous] non-Jewish women. c. Spinning [yarn] in the marketplace and in such a way as it shows her bare arms to the onlookers. d. Being playful with young men. e. Demanding sex from her husband in a voice so loud that her neighbors hear her talking about sex. f. Cursing her husband's father in front of her husband's face.	על פדחתה או על לחיה כדרך שעושות הגויות [הפרוצות], ג. או שטווה בשוק ומראה זרועותיה לבני אדם, ד. או שהיתה משחקת עם הבחורים, ה. או שהיתה תובעת תשמיש מבעלה בקול רם עד ששכנותיה שומעות אותה מדברת על עסקי תשמיש, ו. או שהיתה מקללת אבי בעלה בפני בעלה.
Ezra established that a woman should wear a belt at all times in her house, for modesty's sake. [However,] if she does not wear it, she is not in violation of *dat Moshe* and does not lose her ketubah. Also, if she went out with her hair exposed from courtyard to courtyard by way of a thoroughfare, since her hair was covered by a kerchief, she is not in violation of *dat* [*Yehudit*].	עזרא תקן שתהיה אשה חוגרת בסינר תמיד בתוך ביתה משום צניעות ואם לא חוגרת אינה עוברת על דת משה ולא הפסידה כתובתה. וכן אם יצתה וראשה פרוע מחצר לחצר בתוך המבוי הואיל ושערה מכוסה במטפחת אינה עוברת על דת [יהודית].[24]

Although R. Aharon somewhat abridges Rambam's presentation, it seems clear that he accepts Rambam's overall distinction between *dat Moshe* hair covering and *dat Yehudit* hair covering. Moreover, in an earlier section of the laws of Ketubot (7/8) regarding the *Mishneh Torah*'s formulation (Laws of Forbidden Relations, 21:17) regarding minors, R. Aharon adopts the Rambam's hardline approach.

Jewish women should not go out with their hair exposed, whether married or single…	ולא יהלכו בנות ישראל פרועות ראש בשוק אחת נשואה ואחת פנויה…

---

24. Some texts have משה. This discrepancy probably reflects different scribes adding in an ending, each according to his own understanding. Rambam, whom R. Aharon is copying here, includes neither in the *Mishneh Torah* (just *dat*) and this was probably the case in the *Orchot Chayyim* as well. See the note in the Frankel Rambam entitled על דת משה.

Considering the above, it appears that R. Aharon believes there is a Torah prohibition for all women to go out with their hair uncovered, and that even the *dat Yehudit* requirement of fuller coverage would apply to unmarried women. In other words, R. Aharon fully follows the formulation of Rambam.

However, if this is the case, R. Aharon's formulation in the laws of *gittin* (1) seems rather surprising.

Rabbi Isaac of Corbeil wrote: It is a commandment to divorce one's wife with a document, as it is written, "If a man finds evidence of sexual misconduct on her part, he shall write her a bill of divorce and place it in her hand" (Deut. 24:1).	כתב הר"י מקורב"ל ז"ל מצות עשה לגרש האשה בספר כדכתיב כי מצא בה ערות דבר וכתב לה ספר כריתות ונתן בידה.
Evidence of sexual misconduct –	ערות דבר –
such as violating *dat Moshe*:	כגון עוברת על דת משה:[25]
a. Feeding [her husband] untithed food,	א. מאכילתו דבר שאינו מעושר
b. Having intercourse with him during her menstrual period,	ב. ומשמשתו נדה
c. Not setting apart the dough offering,	ג. ולא קוצה לה חלה
d. Making vows and not fulfilling them.	ד. ונודרת ואינה מקיימת.
Or such as violating *dat Yehudit*:	וכן עוברת על דת יהודית:
a. [Going out] to the marketplace with her hair exposed, even with a *kalta* on her head if she goes out into the public domain,	א. [יוצאת] בשוק וראשה פרוע, ואפילו קלתה על ראשה אם יוצאה לרשות הרבים.
R. Peretz added a gloss: In our society, the hairnet is called *kupia* instead of *kalta*.	[וכתב]] הר"ף ז"ל: 'ולדידן שבכא שקורין קופי"א הוי כמו קלתה.'
But it is permissible to go from one courtyard to another by way of an alley.	אבל מחצר לחצר דרך מבוי מותר.
b. Weaving with red (rouge?) on her face.	ב. וטווה וורד כנגד פניה,
c. Being playful with the young men.	ג. ומשחקת עם הבחורים.

R. Aharon repeats the list of *dat Moshe* and *dat Yehudit* in the laws of divorce (*gittin*). In this case he decides to follow the formulation of R. Isaac of Corbeil which is found in the *Sefer Amudei Golah*. The problem

---

25. Some texts add ויהודית.

is, as will be pointed out in the section dealing with this work, R. Isaac specifically rejects Rambam's formulation and returns to the formulation of the Mishnah. How is it that R. Aharon could quote the *Mishneh Torah* in Ketubot and the *Amudei Golah* in Gittin without dealing with the discrepancy between the two formulations? It is puzzling.

R. Aharon references hair covering in one other place, the laws of reciting Shema (36/37). There, he reverses himself and follows the permissive position of Ra'avad popular among Provençal poskim, which we will discuss in the next chapter. In this case, he seems to be aligning himself with another permissive ruling – that of R. Tam (also to be discussed in the next chapter).

It is forbidden to recite [the Shema] in the presence of nudity unless he turns his face – even if [the nudity] is of a gentile or a minor, he should not recite [the Shema] before their nudity. Even if a wall of glass separates them, since he can see it, it is forbidden unless he turns his face.	ואסור לקרות כנגד הערוה עד שיחזיר פניו. ואפי׳ כנגד ערות עכו״ם [או][26] קטן לא יקרא אפי׳ היתה מחיצה של זכוכית מפסקת כיון שהוא רואה את הערוה וצריך להחזיר פניו.
The entire body of a woman is nudity, even a man's wife; if a handbreadth of her body is exposed, he should not recite [the Shema] facing her, but her face, hands, feet and the hair that sticks out of the covering and is never covered – these one should not be concerned about since he sees them regularly. However, it would be forbidden for him to gaze at these when they are of another woman.	וכל גוף האשה ערוה אפי׳ היא אשתו אם רואה ממנו טפח מגולה לא יקרא כנגדה אבל פניה וידיה ורגליה ושערה מחוץ לצמתה שאינו מתכסה אין חוששין להם מפני שהוא רגיל בהם אבל אשה אחרת אסור להסתכל בהם.
R. Tuviah said in the name of R. Tam: Specifically, this refers to gazing upon her – this is the [forbidden] erotic stimulus, but insofar as reciting [the Shema] when her hair is exposed, this is permitted, for it is an everyday occurrence that we are not strict	וכתב ה״ר טוביה בשם ר[בינו] ת[ם]: "דוקא להסתכל היא ערוה אבל לקרות כנגד שערה מותר שהרי מעשים בכל יום שאין נזהרים מלקרות כנגד שער הבתולות."

---

26. I added in this word. The text actually reads "a gentile minor" but this makes little sense. As R. Aharon is simply copying the *Mishneh Torah* here, it seems safe to assume that the word "or" is missing due to a copyist error. The word appears in the *Kol Bo* as well.

about reciting [Shema] in the presence of the hair of virgins.

In this section, R. Aharon establishes the existence of two different prohibitions. First, there is the prohibition of reciting Shema in front of an erotic stimulus, which he defines as anything exposed that is usually covered. Second, there is the prohibition of gazing upon any part of a woman, other than the man's wife, whether or not it is usually exposed. This he forbids because the man is treating the woman as an erotic stimulus, even if there is nothing unusual about her dress.

R. Aharon ends by saying that the rule about hair being an erotic stimulus when exposed, which would forbid a person from reciting Shema in that woman's presence, only applies to married women for two reasons: One, since single women always expose their hair; two, as R. Tam states, men always recite Shema in their presence. This statement is surprising, since it seems to contradict the claim in the laws of b. Ketubot that all women must cover their hair, married or not! Unless one wishes to say that R. Aharon is simply quoting two contradictory positions, Rambam and R. Tam, one must say that he considers hair covering, and *tzniut* in general, to be subjective. Given that R. Aharon considers hair covering to be *dat Moshe*, this would mean that even the Torah aspect of *tzniut* must be seen in social context. In other words, minimal *tzniut* is *dat Moshe*, but what minimal *tzniut* means is dependent on social norms.

A NOTE ON THE POSITION OF THE *KOL BO*

It is worth briefly mentioning the popular abridgment of the *Orchot Chayyim*, called the *Kol Bo*. There, the formulation from b. Gittin is quoted (76), whereas the formulation from b. Ketubot is skipped entirely (75). This *might* mean that the (unknown) author of the *Kol Bo* follows the position that there is no *dat Moshe* rule about hair, whereas R. Aharon was either undecided on or unclear about whether the possibility of a *dat Moshe* requirement to cover hair was halakha. Nevertheless, since the *Kol Bo* itself is a very selective work, often leaving out halakhot entirely, the above deduction must be considered tentative. Finally, *Kol Bo* quotes only the first section of the rules about reciting Shema in the presence of an erotic stimulus, but skips the second half of the discussion, including any reference to hair. For this reason, the laws of Shema do not really shed much light one way or the other on the position of the *Kol Bo*.

11. R. Yerucham ben Meshullam

A uniquely strict position is taken by R. Yerucham ben Meshullam in his *Sefer Meisharim* (23:8).

The following [category of women] may be divorced without receiving the ketubah payment: One who violates *dat Moshe ve-Yehudit*, and one who makes vows but doesn't keep them, and one who curses [her husband's] parents in front of his face, and a loudmouth.	אלו יוצאות שלא בכתובה עוברת על דת משה ויהודית, ונודרת ואינה מקיימו[ת], ומקללת יולדיו בפניו וקולנית.
Dat Moshe – such as: a. Feeding [her husband] untithed food, b. Having intercourse with him during her menstrual period, c. Not setting apart the dough offering. For instance, if she said to him: "Such-and-such a person tithed this pile of grain for me" or "looked at my [menstrual] spots" or "separated the *challah* for me," or "freed me from my vows," and her husband then went and asked the sage in question and it turned out to be false.	דת משה כגון: א. מאכילתו שאין מעושר, ב. ומשמשתו נדה, ג. ולא קוצה לה חלה. וכגון דאמרה פלוני תקן לי כרי זה או ראה כתמי או תקן לי חלתי או התיר לי נדרה ושאלו לו לחכם ואשתכח שקרא.
Dat Yehudit – a. Going out with her hair exposed, b. Spinning [yarn] in the marketplace, c. Conversing with random men.	ודת יהודית - א. יוצאה וראשה פרוע, ב. וטווה בשוק, ג. ומדברת עם כל אדם.
Exposed hair refers to a woman whose hair is covered with a kerchief, without the full covering that all other women wear – and even so, she loses her ketubah. For if [her hair] were entirely uncovered, it would be obvious, since [going out in such a way] is forbidden even according to the Torah, as Scripture states, "And he shall expose the woman's head."	'ראשה פרוע' כגון שערה מכוסה במטפחת על ראשה ואין עליה רדיד כשאר הנשים ואפילו הכי אבדה כתובתה דאי מגולה מכל וכל פשיטא דאפילו מן התורה אסור מדכתיב: 'ופרע את ראש האשה'.
Spinning [yarn] in the marketplace refers to spinning red on her forehead opposite her face in the manner of harlots, or showing her bare arms to the onlookers, and being playful with young men.	'וטווה בשוק' כגון טווה וורד על פדחתה כנגד פניה כדרך הזונות או מראה זרועותיה לבני אדם ומדברת עם כל אדם ומשחקת עם בחורים.

Additionally, going out with her hair exposed means that she goes [this way when travelling] from courtyard to courtyard by way of a thoroughfare; for if it were to refer to going into the marketplace with hair exposed, or into a thoroughfare, this would violate *dat Moshe*, for, in any case, a woman's hair is *erva*.

וכן נמי 'ויוצאה וראשה פרוע' שיוצאה מחצר לחצר ועוברת דרך מבוי כי בפריעת הראש לשוק או למבוי הרי זו עובר על דת משה ומכל מקום 'שער באשה ערוה'.

'One who curses [her husband's] parents in front of his face' – for example, if she said to him: 'Let a lion eat your grandfather' in front of his son, and this would be one who curses [her husband's] parents in front of his children.

'והמקללת יולדיו בפניו' כגון דאמרה יאכל הארי אביך בפני בנו וזה מקללת יולדיו בפני מולידיו.

'Loudmouth' – she makes her voice heard regarding sexual matters, meaning, she demands [sex] explicitly, with a loud voice.

'וקולנית' דמשמעת קולה על עסקי תשמיש פי' שתובעת בפה בקול רם.

'One who makes vows but doesn't keep them' – because of the consequences to his children.

'ונודרת ואינה מקיימת' – בשביל עונש בניו.

Warning is needed in order for her to lose her ketubah. He is not forced to make her leave if he wishes her to stay. Nevertheless, it is a mitzvah for him to divorce her.

וצריכה התראה להפסידה כתובתה ולא כייפי' לו להוציא אם רוצה לקיימה ומיהו מצוה לגרשה.

A few unique features stand out here. First, although the common reading of the Mishnah is that all of the examples fit into the categories of *dat Moshe* or *dat Yehudit*, R. Yerucham assumes that vowing without fulfilling, cursing the husband's parents, and the loudmouth are all separate categories. This does not affect the issues of interest to this book but it is a unique reading of the text nonetheless.

Second, R. Yerucham does more than just follow Rambam's formulation here. He goes a step further. Rambam, followed by R. Moshe of Coucy and R. Aharon HaKohen, believes fully exposed hair is a violation of *dat Moshe*. However, all other examples of partially exposed hair are in violation of *dat Yehudit*. In contrast, R. Yerucham believes that even going out with partially covered hair would violate *dat Moshe* if she was going to a marketplace or a public thoroughfare for more than just a moment – only the latter would violate *dat Yehudit*. To support this ruling, he quotes the phrase from b. Berachot that a woman's hair is considered *erva*.

In his larger work, *Toledot Adam ve-Chava*, R. Yerucham does not return to the issue of *dat Moshe* and *dat Yehudit* in any detail; instead he merely references (23:2) his analysis in *Sefer Meisharim*:

The rules about a lewd wife, like one who violates *dat Moshe* and *Yehudit*, I wrote them up in *Sefer Meisharim* in the laws of the ketubah.	דיני הפרוצה כגון עוברת על דת משה ויהודית כתבתיו בספר מישרים בדין כתובה.

Even from this short description, one can see that R. Yerucham believes that women who violate *dat* are broadly defined as "lewd." In this sense, even though R. Yerucham takes a stricter view of uncovered hair than other Rishonim, he sees the point of the rule in the same light: violation of modesty rules in public implies infidelity at some level.

In his *Toledot*, R. Yerucham does discuss the passage in b. Berachot. To understand how R. Yerucham reads this passage, it is essential to understand it in the larger context of his discussion of halakhot related to men looking at women (*Toledot* 23:1).

It is forbidden to gaze upon an unmarried woman, even if she is attractive, or a married woman, even if she is ugly, nor at her colorful garments, even if they are spread out [to dry] on a wall, and this applies when he knows their owner.	אסור להסתכל באשה פנויה ואפילו נאה ובאשת איש ואפילו כעורה ולא בבגדי צבע שלה אפילו שטוחים על גבי הכות[ל], ובמכי[ר] בעליהן.
A man should not fantasize during the day lest he come to sin [i.e., spill his seed] at night – this is clear in b. Avodah Zarah (20b).	ולא יהרהר אדם ביום ולא יבא לידי עבירה בלילה פשוט בעבודה זרה.
A woman's [exposed] handbreadth [of flesh] is *erva*. The voice of a woman is *erva*. A woman's hair is *erva* – this is made clear in b. Berachot (24a). Not only a handbreadth, but even looking at her little finger is forbidden, and they only mentioned a handbreadth for when reciting Shema or praying, and were referring to the man's wife.	טפח בא[שה] ערוה קול באשה ערוה שער באשה ערוה פשוט בברכות. ולאו דוקא טפח אלא להסתכל אפילו באצבע קטנה שלה אסור ולא אמרו טפח אלא לקריאת שמע ולתפלה ולאשתו.

The beginning of the halakha describes the laws against a man gazing at a woman in a sexual way. These laws come from tractate Avodah Zarah and are standard fare in halakhic works. However, what is unusual about the treatment in the *Toledot* is that R. Yerucham puts the passage from

b. Berachot about the handbreadth, voice, and hair into the context of the passage in b. Avodah Zarah about gazing. This demonstrates that for R. Yerucham, the primary point of the passage in b. Berachot is to discuss the rule forbidding men to gaze at women. Nevertheless he does not ignore the Talmud's suggestion that the rules of reciting Shema are under discussion here. He simply offers an interesting compromise reading: It is forbidden to gaze upon a woman with sexual desire; even gazing at her hair, her clothes, or her little finger, even just to listen to her voice, can be forbidden if done in a way that arouses the man. Still, it is not forbidden to recite the Shema or pray in the presence of any of these (her hair, voice, clothes, etc.) unless a handbreadth of (usually covered) flesh is actually exposed.

12. R. Nissim of Gerona (Ran)

In a virtually identical analysis of the passage in b. Gittin 89a offered by Ramban, Ran (Rabbeinu Nissim ben Reuven) makes his understanding of *dat Yehudit* and hair covering clear. As described earlier in the section on Ramban, both Ramban and Ra'avad question the position of R. Yochanan ben Nuri that women may only be divorced for lewd behavior if actual witnesses to something are brought, by contrasting this statement with the rule about *dat Moshe ve-Yehudit*. Ran will quote this question and answer in the identical way Ramban does.

Rabbi Avraham ben David had a difficulty with this: doesn't R. Yochanan ben Nuri accept [the Mishnah], "These women are divorced without a ketubah payment: Those who violated *dat Moshe* and *Yehudit*"?[27]	קשיא ליה לרב ר' אברהם ב"ר דוד ז"ל: לית ליה לר' יוחנן בן נורי הא דתנן: 'ואלו יוצאות שלא בכתובה העוברת על דת משה ויהודית'!?
But this is not really a difficulty at all, since even though she may be divorced without a ketubah payment, since she did not behave like a modest woman, nevertheless she is not forbidden to him because of this, rather it is a mitzvah for a righteous man to divorce her. Even R. Meir[28] would admit that she is not forbidden due to *dat*	ולאו קושיא כלל היא, שאע"פ שיוצאת שלא בכתובה שלא נהגה כמנהג הצנועות אינה אסורה בשביל כן, אלא מצוה עליו לגרשה לבעל נפש. ואפילו לר"מ נמי אינה נאסרת בדת יהודית שאם יצאת בקלתה לשוק אינה נאסרת

---

27. Ra'avad asks this in slightly different words (glosses on Rif, b. Gittin 50a).
28. R. Meir's position is that even if the woman were eating, drinking or nursing in public she can be divorced, ostensibly without ketubah payment.

> *Yehudit* concerns, such that if she were to go out to the marketplace with only a *kalta* she would not be forbidden, even though she is violating *dat Yehudit*.
>
> אף על פי שהיא עוברת על דת יהודית.

As Ran's piece is virtually identical to that of Ramban, I will not repeat the analysis of the position here, but I will again note the key observation for the argument in this chapter.

One important piece of Ran's presentation is how he illustrates the case of violating *dat Yehudit*. Ran uses the example of a woman going to the marketplace only with a kalta to illustrate *dat Yehudit*. Since he uses this as the example and doesn't simply say that she goes out with her hair exposed, this implies that Ran, like Ramban, believes that a woman going out with fully uncovered hair in public violates *dat Moshe*.[29]

In fact, in his glosses on Rif's restating of the Mishnah and Talmud in Ketubot (32b), Ran explains the kalta question in exactly this way. Glossing the Talmud's question "but it is a Torah law" that a woman must not go out with her hair exposed, Ran writes:

> So why didn't [the Mishnah] refer to it as *dat Moshe*?
>
> ואמאי לא קרי ליה דת משה?

13. Rabbi Shimon bar Tzemach Duran

In his commentary on Shlomo ibn Gabirol's list of mitzvot (Positive Commandment 137), Rabbi Shimon bar Tzemach Duran discusses the fact that not all Torah laws need to be listed as one of the 613 commandments. As one of his examples of Torah laws that are not/should not be listed, he references hair covering.

> Similarly, [the Talmud] states in the seventh chapter of Ketubot: 'Exposed hair is a biblical [prohibition].'
>
> וכן אמר בפרק המדיר: 'פריעת הראש דאורייתא.'

Although the comment is short, it seems relatively clear that R. Shimon believes that a woman going into the public domain with fully uncovered hair would violate *dat Moshe*.

---

29. See also pseudo-Ran Shabbat 60b:

ותיהוי כבירית טהורה ותשתר. פי' בירית כלי הוא לקשר כל אחד ואחד מבתי השוקים שלא יפלו על רגליה ויוצאין בהן בשבת דלא חיישי' דילמא שלפא ומחויא שהרי מיד יפלו בתי שוקי' לארץ ומיגניא בי', ודכוותה במחט שאינה נקובה שהיא אישפי' קלא לצניעותא היא נותנת שלא תצא שער ראשה ולא מחויא דשער באשה ערוה.

Rabbi Duran also touches upon the concept of *dat Yehudit* briefly in a responsum discussing a rebellious wife (*Tashbetz* 2:103). In a responsum sent to a Rabbi Mordechai HaKohen, Rabbi Duran writes:

You asked: Reuven married the virgin Rachel, and wrote her a ketubah. But Rachel does not behave towards Reuven in the manner of modest Jewish women, but she curses him to his face and curses his father and mother morning and night to his face, and she does this because he tells her that she should behave more modestly like a Jewish woman, and she should not go up on roofs or windows, and she should not go to inappropriate places, because of the generation's lewdness – so she does this just to infuriate him. For this reason, Reuven wishes to divorce her. Teach us, master, the rules regarding this arrangement, whether he needs to pay her, what is the deal with the dowry and the extra, and what the rule is regarding her.	שאלתם ראובן נשא רחל בתולה וכתב לה כתובה. ורחל אינה עומדת עם ראובן כדין בנות ישראל הצנועות אלא מקללתו בפניו ומקללת אביו ואמו בקר וערב בפניו וזה היא עושה בשביל שהוא אומר לה שתהא צנועה כבנות ישראל ואל תעלה בגגות ובחלונות ולא תלך למקום שאינו ראוי לה ללכת עמהם משום פריצות הדור והיא עושה ביותר להכעיסו. וכיון שראה ראובן כך רצה לגרשה. ילמדינו רבינו דין ההסכמות מהו חייב לתת לה ומעניין הנדוניא והתוספת גם כן דינה כדין ישראל:
Answer: If it is true that she is as debauched as you describe in your question, and that this is due to her husband warning her to act more modestly, which brings her to curse his father in front of his face, the law dictates that she may be divorced without a ketubah payment for two reasons: because she violated *dat Yehudit*, and because she cursed his father in front of his face...	תשובה אם אמת הי' הדבר שזו כל כך היא פרוצה כמו שנזכר בשאלה ומפני שבעלה הוא מזהירה על הצניעיות והיא מקללת אביו בפניו. הדין נותן שתצא שלא בכתובה מפני שני דברים מפני שהיא עוברת על דת יהודית. ומפני שהיא מקללת יולדיו בפניו...

In this piece, R. Duran describes the wife's behavior as violating *dat Yehudit* even though no specific violation is described. In fact, other than the cursing (which R. Duran categorizes separately), there are only vague descriptions – such as going up on roofs, standing in front of windows, or going to inappropriate places. None of these are listed in the Mishnah as violations of *dat Yehudit*, and yet Rabbi Duran believes that they are. This demonstrates that R. Duran sees the category of *dat Yehudit* as a general notion equaling modest behavior. Nevertheless he is forced to admit that the specifics are defined by the culture. Otherwise, he would have needed to ask about the specifics of her actions and whether the woman violated any of the specific listed examples of *dat Yehudit*.

In short, although R. Duran does have fully uncovered hair as an example of a Torah prohibition, his overall approach to *dat Yehudit* is to consider it a subjective law which applies to contextually understood immodest behavior.

Conclusion

There are a considerable number of Rishonim who understand the codified Jewish law as mandating that hair covering by a (married) woman is an objective Torah-based obligation without any subjective component to the central obligation. While this school of thought acknowledges there is also a subjective and rabbinic obligation (*dat Yehudit*), these scholars recognize that there is a core obligation to cover hair grounded in an immutable obligation that functions independently of any societal norm. Other aspects of modesty should be generally understood in this school of thought in the same way. Furthermore, it really does not matter whether this obligation is biblical, hinted at in the Torah, or rabbinic. These authorities classify the obligation as immutable and independent of social norms in the time and place the Jewish community is living in.

CHAPTER 5

Uncovered Hair in the Rishonim, Model II: A Subjectively Determined Custom: Embracing a Societal Conception of Modesty Among Other Rishonim

CHAPTER 5 REVIEWS AT LEAST TWENTY-FOUR RISHONIM who either adopt the view that uncovered hair is a subjectively determined violation (and a *dat Yehudit*) or otherwise present this topic in a way that implies that hair covering is no different than any other aspect of subjective modesty and is thus subject to the cultural norms of community.

Introduction

In contrast to the Rishonim discussed in Chapter 4, there is a large group of Rishonim who see the requirement for a woman to cover her hair to be, like the laws of modesty in general, subjectively determined. How they come to this conclusion and how they deal with the Talmudic passage in b. Ketubot differs somewhat from Rishon to Rishon. We will explore these Rishonim and their positions in this chapter. Six differences emerge:

1. There is a significant group of Rishonim who infer sociological context from the way they understand single women not covering their hair.
2. There is a group who directly connect the obligation of hair covering to arousal and not to any objective obligation.
3. There is a group who seem to consider the b. Berachot source as more central than the b. Ketubot source and as rabbinic. They thus simply do not codify the Ketubot *dat Moshe* source.

4. There is a group who seem to codify the b. Ketubot source, but who adopt the Mishnah positing that uncovered hair is a *dat Yehudit* and not *dat Moshe*.
5. Related to the previous group is a group who understand the b. Berachot source as limited to prayer and view the Ketubot sources as similarly subjective.
6. Finally, there is a group who advance many somewhat conflicting rationales, but are overall inclined to see their view as subjective and not objective.

1. Rashi

Rashi's view of this matter is complex and needs to be teased out of his comments on a number of different sugyot. One can only understand Rashi's opinion by examining the totality of his relevant commentaries.

SOTAH

As we saw in Chapter 2, the Talmud in b. Sotah 25a asks two questions about a woman who violates "*dat*." Does she require warning? Must her husband divorce her? However, the Talmud never specifies the type of *dat* to which it is referring. Rashi attempts to clarify this ambiguity in his commentary:

| A woman who violates *dat Yehudit*, in that she is not modest: she goes out with her head uncovered, spins in the marketplace, or converses with random men, for which according to the seventh chapter of Ketubot, she must leave without receiving the ketubah payment. | עוברת על דת יהודית שאינה צנועה יוצאה וראשה פרועה וטווה בשוק ומדברת עם כל אדם דאמר בכתובות בפרק המדיר דיוצאה שלא בכתובה. |

Rashi specifies here that the *dat* under discussion is *dat Yehudit*. In his list of examples of what constitute violations of *dat Yehudit*, Rashi includes exposed hair. Of course, one could counter that this is simply an example of Rashi referencing a mishnah without explaining further. Nevertheless, this will be a useful data point when looking at Rashi's analysis in other sugyot.

KETUBOT

In the main passage about exposure of hair in b. Ketubot 72a, Rashi explains how the derasha from Numbers works according to the baraita.

A warning –	אזהרה –
a. From the fact that we do this to sully her looks, a tit for tat since she did the same in order to improve her looks for her lover, we can deduce that doing so [for any other purpose] is forbidden.	א. מדעבדינן לה הכי לנוולה מדה כנגד מדה כמו שעשתה להתנאות על בועלה מכלל דאסור
b. Alternatively, since the verse states "and he shall expose," one can deduce that up until that point [her hair] was not exposed. One learns from this that it was not the way of Israelite women to go out with their hair exposed – this is the main point.	ב. א״נ מדכתיב ופרע מכלל דההוא שעתא לאו פרועה הות שמע מינה אין דרך בנות ישראל לצאת פרועות ראש וכן עיקר.

Rashi offers two interpretations of how this derasha works. The first assumes that the humiliating punishment of the woman resembles some forbidden behavior on her part. Hence, since her hair is undone, this must have been forbidden for her to do and the punishment mimics her forbidden behavior. The second explanation argues that the derasha is picking up on the reality that the kohen is, in fact, exposing her hair. If so, her hair must have been covered or done up in some way; otherwise, what is the kohen in fact doing? Hence, one can learn from this that Israelite women covered their hair.

Although one could read Rashi's comment as suggesting two different understandings of this derivation as a Torah law, there is some ambiguity in his explanations. Rashi never explicitly says that a woman with exposed hair is violating Torah law. Furthermore, both of his proofs only prove either that it was forbidden, at least at the time, to uncover her hair (first explanation) or that it was the practice at the time for Israelite women to keep their hair covered (second explanation). Although the differences between these views may seem to be nuanced, it is nevertheless important to take note of this now, since the ambiguities between both views will be the source of alternative explanations of Rashi that will be suggested by various Acharonim.

B. BERACHOT

Rashi's glosses on the passage in b. Berachot are particularly important. As was discussed in our analysis of this passage, the Talmud considers two basic interpretive options for the rules the Amoraim are stating: either they are meant to apply to ogling or to the recitation of Shema. For the latter, the Talmud specifically states that the problem would extend even to the person's wife. However, to whom does the prohibition of looking at or ogling extend? Rashi answers this question in two separate glosses.

To look upon her – if she is married.	לאסתכולי בה - אם אשת איש היא.
Calf – of a married woman.	שוק - באשת איש.

Rashi believes seeing a woman's calf, hair, or any other exposed handbreadth of her flesh, and ostensibly even listening to her voice, are all prohibited if the woman in question is married. All the examples cited here involve minimally erotic body parts. It would seem that Rashi understands there are three distinct categories of women's anatomy modesty. At one extreme are things that are so sexually charged that they should be seen only by the woman's husband. This would be nudity in the classical sense. The other extreme includes those things that can be revealed by any woman at any time, such as her hands or face, as they are never erotic.

Between these two extremes exists a middle area, comprising those parts listed in this sugya. Although a man's looking at a woman's hair or calf is not considered sexually arousing behavior per se, it is inappropriate for him to look at these parts on a married woman as it violates the couple's marital space. Following this interpretation, one can see that, for Rashi, the texts of b. Ketubot, b. Gittin and b. Sotah are the exact inverse of this rule. Just as men may not look at these spots on a woman, women may not expose these spots publicly to men. Both actions violate the marital bond.

Rashi's school of thought has a certain halakhic insight to it. First, it explains the historical practice with regard to hair: unmarried women did not cover their hair, notwithstanding the apparently clear directive of b. Berachot 24a that uncovered hair is immodest. Second, it recognizes that when one is single, somewhat enticing conduct of various sorts is part of the process of courting. According to this view, men in the process of dating are allowed to look at a woman's hair or calf, or listen to her voice and ask, "Is that hair/calf/voice appealing to me?" A healthy attraction is part of being happily married, which is why it is permitted in this context.

More significantly, this view recognizes that single women are allowed to reveal more of themselves than married women precisely because they are *seeking* to get married, and in order to get married, a certain amount of otherwise inappropriate interaction is considered necessary. A man may look at potential brides in a way that one may not normally look at other women. But once a woman is married, the mere act of revealing these areas is a significant breach of marital norms, as this is conduct only single people engage in.

NUMBERS

One further piece of evidence supporting the notion that Rashi may not have viewed the exposure of a woman's hair as a violation of a Torah law comes from his commentary on the Torah. As in the derasha recorded in b. Ketubot, Rashi attempts to make a deduction from the fact that the kohen exposes the woman's hair (Numbers 5:18).

And exposes – he undoes the braids of her hair in order to humiliate her. From here we learn that the revealing of Jewish women's hair publicly is an affront to them.	ופרע - סותר את קליעת שערה כדי לבזותה, מכאן לבנות ישראל שגלוי הראש גנאי להן:

This comment is surprising for two reasons. First, in his glosses on b. Ketubot, Rashi explains the concept of kalta as a work basket. If Rashi is working with a two-tiered concept of covering, with partial coverage being the wearing of a work basket and full coverage being a full headdress of some sort, why does he mention in Numbers the undoing of braids, a totally different reading of kalta (=*capillatus*)? Second, unlike the derasha in the Bavli, Rashi does not say that one can deduce from this verse that the Torah forbids women to go out with their hair undone, only that their doing so would be considered humiliating.

The most likely suggestion is that Rashi does not consider the baraita in the Bavli to be the authoritative interpretation of the verse in Numbers. At least in his commentary on the Torah, Rashi seems to prefer the formulation of the derasha in the Sifre, as that formulation has the first tier of covering as braided or coiffed hair,[1] and it understands the entire concept of hair covering as a Jewish custom.[2]

SUMMARY

It is always difficult to say with certainty how Rashi viewed a given halakha, since Rashi mainly explicates the Talmudic texts and rarely codifies the

---

1. As was pointed out in Chapter 1, this is also the opinion of the baraita quoted in b. Sotah 8a.
2. See Aryeh Frimer, "Women Covering Hair," *Ḥakirah* 12 (2011): 20–24, for an alternative analysis in the name of R. Aaron Soloveichik.

law. It appears from the above texts that Rashi understood exposed hair to be a violation of marital norms and that looking at a married woman's hair is sinful precisely because it is normally not accessible to the eyes of men other than her husband. This is also why a sotah's hair is publicly undone, since this would embarrass her and make her feel publicly exposed.

The only commentary of Rashi's that could be understood as reflecting the idea of hair exposure as a violation of Torah law is his interpretation of the baraita in b. Ketubot. However, this is mitigated by three factors. First, Rashi is a commentator and explains all passages whether or not they are eventually codified as halakha. Second, Rashi's interpretations there are ambiguous, especially his second interpretation, and it is not entirely clear that even in these comments he believes that the practice of hair covering is a Torah requirement. Finally, in his commentary on the Torah, Rashi ignores this baraita in favor of the interpretation of the Sifre and the baraita in b. Sotah 8a. Therefore, it would seem that although one cannot completely determine Rashi's position, the entirety of his corpus pushes one towards the belief that Rashi understood the prohibition of hair exposure to be a custom and, consequently, societally determined.

2. Rabbeinu Tam

Perhaps the single most important observation relevant to the position that hair covering must be considered a subjectively determined rule comes from Rashi's grandson, Rabbeinu Tam (R. Jacob ben Meir of Ramerupt, 1100–1171). Discussing the reference in tractate Berachot to women's hair being considered erva, he writes:

> That which they said: "The hair of a woman is considered an erotic stimulus," this refers to gazing at it, but not reciting [Shema] – for it is a daily occurrence that we are not careful to avoid reciting [Shema] in the presence of the hair of virgins – this was the explanation of R. Tuvia in the name of R. Tam.[3]
>
> והא דאמרו שער באשה ערוה היינו להסתכל בה אבל לקרות לא דמעשים בכל יום שאין אנו נזהרין מלקרות כנגד שער הבתולות כך פי' רבינו טוביה בשם ר"ת.

Rabbeinu Tam begins with a sociological fact. Religious people in his society would recite the Shema in the presence of virgins whose hair was uncovered. This sociological fact points us to another sociological fact that

---

3. Referenced in Menachem Rekanati 26 and Rabbi Moshe Orbino *Ohel Moed, Shaar "Keriat Shema"* 5:5 and *Orchot Chayyim "Keriat Shema"* 36 (the above text is from Rekanati).

Rabbeinu Tam took for granted: unmarried women didn't cover their hair in his society. Confronting these sociological facts, R. Tam decided that this situation must not be the one to which the Talmud refers, since that would mean that the average religious man reciting Shema in France was sinning, at least on occasion. Therefore, he decided, it must be that not all examples of uncovered hair are the same. How does one distinguish between hair that is erva and hair that is mundane? Apparently, what is mundane is not erva and what is erva is not mundane. This observation forms the bedrock of many of the later interpretations of these passages, especially among the Ashkenazi Rishonim.

3. Rabbi Isaac ben Samuel the Elder of Dampierre (Ri)

Similar to the position taken by his uncle, R. Tam, R. Isaac ben Samuel the Elder of Dampierre (1115–1184), known as Ri, believes that the prohibition of reciting the Shema in the presence of erva does not apply to exposed hair. Ri's position is quoted in the *Agudah*'s treatment of the b. Berachot (3:73) passage:

The hair of a woman is an erotic stimulus; the voice of a woman is an erotic stimulus. Ri explained that all of these rules refer to [a prohibition upon a man] to gaze upon them, but insofar as the recitation of the Shema it is permitted for a man to recite Shema in the presence of a woman with uncovered hair.	שער באשה ערוה קול באשה ערוה פירש ר"י כל זה איירי להסתכל בה, אבל לענין קריאת שמע שרי לקרות אם ראש אשה מגולה.

Although Ri does not differentiate between married women and unmarried women, it seems reasonable that he has in mind women who do not cover their hair. In his society, that would have been unmarried women. It is further worth noting that Ri considers this rule, as well as the rule about voice, to be relevant to the prohibition of ogling.

4. Sefer Al HaKol

The author of *Sefer Al HaKol*, a student of R. Moshe ben R. Shneur of Evreux, quotes his teacher's discussion of the passage in b. Berachot (18), which follows the contours of Ri's position.

The voice of a woman is an erotic stimulus; the hair of a woman is an erotic stimulus – these were not said with reference to reciting the Shema. Additionally, we are not	קול באשה ערוה, שער באשה ערוה, ולא לענין ק"ש איירי, וגם אין אנו נזהרי' לקרות ק"ש אם מסתכלין בה דהא

> strict about reciting the Shema while looking at [a woman], for that which it said "a handbreadth of a woman's [exposed flesh] is an erotic stimulus" was only when the handbreadth of flesh was in a place which she would generally not reveal, other than face, hands, and feet – the words of Ram (i.e., R. Moshe of Evreux).[4]
>
> דאמ' טפח באשה ערוה היינו טפח מבשרה שאינה רגילה לגלות לבד מבפנים ידים ורגלים, לשון הר"ם.

Like Ri, R. Moshe of Evreux strikes an interesting balance. On the one hand, he excludes voice and hair from the discourse about what men can be in the presence of while reciting the Shema. On the other hand, in his discussion of the exposed handbreadth and the recitation of the Shema, he states clearly that the rule applies only to parts of the body that are generally exposed.

Putting these two points together, it remains unclear whether R. Moshe believes in an objective requirement for women to cover certain parts. Are hair and voice examples of areas men are forbidden to look at because they are generally covered? Or are they examples of places women are required to cover, and thus men are forbidden to look at them uncovered? The matter is unclear from this brief presentation.

Nevertheless, if we understand R. Moshe of Evreux as following the position of Ri, then his position would be that it is forbidden to ogle a woman's hair or listen to her voice in such a way as to be aroused. The prohibition exists because a man may come in contact with these things, but they are generally more hidden than hands, feet, and face, which are mundane and less prone to being sexualized.

---

4. Most references to "Ram" in the *Al HaKol* seem to refer to Rabbi Moshe of Evreux. However, many of those positions overlap with positions of Rabbi Meir of Rothenberg, who can also be referenced as "Ram," often making it unclear who is being referenced. This may be because Rabbi Meir of Rothenberg also studied in Evreux. Thanks to Rabbi Dr. Ephraim Kanarfogel for his insight. This is not beyond dispute, as the Weiss edition from Berdichiv 1908 of this work proposes that the actual author of this work is Rabbi Moshe of Evreux and "Ram" is Rabbi Meir of Rothenberg. See also Jacob Epstein "Al Hakol" (in Hebrew), *Sinai*, 94:3/4: 123–136 (5744). It is worth adding that the Bar Ilan CD notes the more common view as the consensus when it states in the bibliographic entry for this work that "The identity of the author is unknown, although he was apparently a disciple of R. Moses ben Shneur of Evreux, one of the late Tosafists." We have followed that view. Thank you to Rabbi Dr. Kanarfogel and Dr. Marc Shapiro for helping work through this issue.

5. Sefer HaIttur

In his *Sefer HaIttur*, R. Yitzchak ben Abba Mari (c. 1122–1193) discusses the issue of the inappropriately behaving wife under the category "rebellious" (מרד, letter מ at p. 69a).

Section 1 – Women who may be divorced without payment of the ketubah or the *tosefet* (voluntary additional payment), and who only receive what remains intact from their dowries – nine examples are recorded in our Mishnah:	השער הראשון - שיוצאות בלא כתובה ותוספת ואין נוטלות אלא מה שהוא בעין מנדונייתן תשעה מהן במשנתינו
For it was taught: One who violates *dat Moshe ve-Yehudit*. What [violates] *dat Moshe*?	דתנן: העוברת על דת משה ויהודית. ואיזו היא דת משה?
1. Feeding [her husband] untithed food,	א. מאכילתו שאינו מעושר
2. Having intercourse with him [during her menstrual period],	ב. ומשמשתו
3. Not setting apart the dough offering,	ג. ואינה קוצה לה חלה
4. Making vows but not fulfilling them.	ד. ונודרת ואינה מקיימת
What [violates] *dat Yehudit*?	ואיזו היא דת יהודי'?
5. Going out with her hair exposed, etc. We established that even with a *kalta* this is forbidden. R. Yossi said in the name of R. Yochanan: "[One who goes out in] *kalta* has not violated [the prohibition of going out with] her hair exposed." Abaye said: "From courtyard to courtyard by way of a thoroughfare." Yerushalmi: "A courtyard through which many people pass is like a [thoroughfare]."	ה. יוצא' וראשה פרוע וכו'. ואוקימנא אפי' בקלתה אסור. וא"ר יוסי אמר רבי יוחנן: "קלתה אין בה משום פריעת הראש." ואמר אביי: "מחצר לחצר ודרך מבוי." ירושלמי: "חצר שהרבים בוקעין בו הרי הוא [כמבוי].⁵"
6. Weaving in the marketplace thus exposing her arms to the men. Rav Chisda said in the name of Avimi: "She spins red wool before her face."	ו. וטווה בשוק ומראה זרועותיה לבני אדם, ורב חסדא אמר אבימי: "בטווה וורד כנגד פניה."
7. Conversing with random men – Being playful with young men.	ז. ומדברת עם כל אדם במשחקת עם הבחורים

---

5. The text says כחצר but this makes no sense and must be a misprint. Thank you to Gershon Klapper who highlighted that there are many variations in this text making determining the exact text unclear, even as its basic approach is spelled out.

8. Abba Shaul says: "Even one who curses his parents in front of his children."

ח. אבא שאול אומר: "אף המקללת יולדיו בפני מולידיו."

9. R. Tarfon says: "Even the loudmouth" –

ט. ר' טרפון אומר: "אף הקולנית."

One who speaks about sexual matters. Rav Alfas wrote: "She asks [her husband for sex] explicitly." Yerushalmi: Shmuel said: "Any woman who when she speaks her neighbors hear her." Rav said: "Any woman whose voice bounds from bedroom to bedroom during sex." Rash[6] explained: "Any woman who objects to going to the mikvah and her neighbors hear her."

במשמעת קולה על עיסקי תשמישה. כתב רב אלפס: "כגון דתבעה ליה בפה."

ירושלמי: שמואל אמר: "כל שמדברת ושכינותיה שומעות." רב אמר: "שקולה הולך ממטה למטה בשעת תשמיש."

ופר"ש: "כל שאינה רוצה ללכת לטבילה ושכינותיה שומעו'."

In essence, R. Yitzchak is quoting the Mishnah with a partial summary of the Talmudic discussions. It seems reasonable to assume that R. Yitzchak quoted the passages in the Talmud that he considered authoritative. Hence, the fact that he quoted only R. Yochanan (as well as the subsequent discussion) lends credence to the analysis of this text proffered in the second chapter – Shmuel and R. Yochanan should be seen as arguing, with R. Yitzchak accepting R. Yochanan's view as authoritative.

Of course, it is possible that R. Yitzchak reads the two positions as in agreement, but skips over Shmuel's since he views it as having no halakhic significance. The former reading seems the most straightforward. The problem with the second reading can be seen by looking closely at R. Yitzchak's language. R. Yitzchak does not say that one should read the Mishnah as referring to a woman going out with a kalta, which would have implied that without a kalta, the violation would be more severe. Instead, he says that the Mishnah refers also to a woman going out with a kalta, implying that the violation would be the same with or without a kalta. There is, in fact, no evidence at all that R. Yitzchak believes that a woman who goes out in public with her hair fully undone or uncovered is in violation of *dat Moshe* or a Torah prohibition. If this analysis is correct, then R. Yitzchak in his *Sefer HaIttur* is another example of a Rishon who believes the entire requirement for hair covering to be *dat Yehudit*.

---

6. This refers to Rabbi Samson of Sens.

6. Sefer HaYereim

In his *Sefer HaYereim* (392 (12)), R. Elazar of Metz – a student of R. Tam – discusses the issue of erva in general, bringing up a category called erva of non-sexual organs. The basis for his discussion is the Talmudic passage in b. Berachot.

Subsidiary category: Non-sexual organs, meaning not genitals –	תולדות: עריות שאינן נשכבות שאינן אותו מקום -
R. Yitzchak said: "A handbreadth of [exposed flesh] of a woman is nudity."	דאמר ר' יצחק [ברכות כ"ד א'] "טפח באשה ערוה."
and we establish this statement, in the third chapter of Berachot, as referring to during the recitation of the Shema, that even the man's wife, when she reveals a handbreadth of herself, it is forbidden for her husband to recite the Shema in her presence. This [problematic] handbreadth refers only to areas which she generally covers.	ומוקמינן בברכות פ' מי שמתו לק"ש דאפילו אשתו כי מגלה טפח מינה אסור לקרוא ק"ש כנגדה פי' טפח שדרכו להתכסות
Rav Chisda said: "The calf is considered nudity, for [the verse] states: 'Reveal the calf, pass through the rivers,' and it is written: 'Your nudity shall be revealed, even your disgrace shall be seen.'"	ואמר רב חסדא: "שוק באשה ערוה דכתיב 'גלי שוק עברי נהרות' וכתיב 'תגל ערותך גם תראה חרפתך.'".
Rav Sheshet said: "The hair of a woman is considered suggestive, as it states: 'Your hair is like a flock of goats.'"	ואמר רב ששת: "שער שבאשה ערוה דכתיב 'שערך כעדר העזים.'".
Shmuel said: "The voice of a woman is considered suggestive, as it states: 'for your voice is sweet and your appearance attractive.'"	ואמר שמואל: "קול באשה ערוה דכתיב 'כי קולך ערב.'".
– meaning, her singing voice.	פי' קול של שיר
All of these matters were explained by R. Yehudai Gaon[7] as referring to the recitation of the Shema. Therefore, it is forbidden to recite the Shema, or any one of the prayers requiring a minyan,[8] while hearing	וכל הני פירש רב יהודאי גאון ז"ל לענין ק"ש הלכך אסור לומר ק"ש או דבר קדושה בשמיעת קול שיר של אשה ובעונותינו בין הגוים אנו

---

7. Most probably, R. Elazar of Metz is referring to the passage in the Behag discussed in the previous chapter.
8. Literally, a matter of holiness, *devar kedusha*.

> the voice of a woman singing. However, in our many sins, we live among the gentiles, and "it is a time to act for God by abrogating your Torah." Therefore, we are not strict about learning [Torah] if we can hear the voice of gentile women.
>
> יושבים ועת לעשות לה' הפרו תורתך הלכך אין אנו נזהרים מללמוד בשמיעת קול נשים ארמיות.

There are several worthwhile points in the *Yereim*'s discussion. First, he completely accepts the reading of the sugya as relating only to what is forbidden to do while reciting the Shema. He does take this one step further to forbid a man to study Torah while gazing at a woman's non-sexual organs (including uncovered hair) or while hearing her voice. However, he sees no general prohibition against seeing these parts or hearing the voice of a woman. Second, like R. Tam, the *Yereim* references day-to-day reality. In his world, the gentile women would sing in public and it could be heard by others, including men. For this reason, the *Yereim* makes the shocking assertion that he and his community would learn Torah despite hearing women's voices. Otherwise, they would rarely be able to study.

In short, the *Yereim* seems to believe that a man should not be exposed to the hair, voice and calf of a woman when praying or learning Torah. He does not say whether he believes that women should not expose these things to men in general nor does he say whether the list would change depending on circumstances. Given that he references gentile women singing and not Jewish women, one may imagine that the practice in his community was for Jewish women not to sing in public. His opinion regarding a society where even Jewish women sang in public is not clear from this source.

7. Sefer Chasidim

The *Sefer Chasidim* has a unique approach to the rules of modesty. First, the *Sefer Chasidim* (#110, ed. Margoliot) believes that the examples found in the passage in b. Berachot are only examples. The principle, however, is that any body part mentioned in the Song of Songs must be considered erva, assuming it is generally covered.

> The hair of a woman is an erotic stimulus when it is revealed, as well as anything referenced in Song of Songs, like "your belly is a pile of wheat" or "his calves are pillars of marble, "your two breasts, etc." And ev-
>
> שער באשה ערוה לגלות וכל האמור בשיר השירים כגון בטנך ערימת חטים שוקיו עמודי שש שני שדיך וכו' וכל שדרך לכסות ערוה לאשה

erything which is generally covered would be an erotic stimulus [and forbidden] for women to reveal.

לגלות.

If this were the only text in the *Sefer Chasidim* about hair covering and modesty, one could argue that it fits in with the position of R. Tam and others, who believe that social norms determine what is or what is not appropriate to expose in public. One example in this source, however, points to the unique viewpoint of the *Sefer Chasidim*. He quotes the verse "his calves are pillars of marble" – which references a man. Does this mean that the *Sefer Chasidim* believes that men must also avoid exposure of their flesh in a provocative way to women and that women are forbidden to gaze at men? The answer is yes, as evidenced by #614 (ed. Margoliot) of *Sefer Chasidim*:

One must be careful with any body part mentioned in the Song of Songs, even hearing the voice of a woman; the same applies to a woman that she should not hear the voice of a man, for anything that a man is commanded to avoid a woman is commanded to avoid as well.	מכל מה שכתוב בשיר השירים צריך להזהר שלא ישמע קול אשה והוא הדין לאשה שלא תשמע קול איש שמכל שהאיש מוזהר אשה מוזהרת.
Know this, any woman who walks in front of a man's house and instead of lowering her voice when she passes his house she raises her voice – her intentions are for the bad. The same is true for a man. Therefore, all who behave this way generally, upon them was said (Is. 65:14): "Behold my servants will sing out from happiness of heart, but you will scream out from pain of heart, and from broken spirit will you wail."	ודע שכל אשה שהיא הולכת לפני בית איש ומתחילה לא הרימה קולה אבל כשהולכת לפני בית איש משמעת קול הרי כונתה לרעה וכן האיש לכך כל הרגילים בזה עליהם נאמר (ישעי' ס"ה י"ד) הנה עבדי ירונו מטוב לב ואתם תצעקו מכאב לב ומשבר רוח תילילו.
A woman's hair is an erotic stimulus – as it says (Song 4:1): "Your hair is like a flock of goats." Also, [he that gazes at the woman's hair] will not merit seeing "the hair of His head, like lamb's wool" (Dan. 7:9).	ושער באשה ערוה שנאמר (שה"ש ד' א') שערך כעדר העזים גם לא יזכה לראות שער רישיה כעמר נקא (דניאל ז' ט').
If one is careful not to gaze at women, he will merit seeing the glory, as is written (Is. 33:17): "The King in his beauty your eyes will see."	ואם נזהר מלראות באשה יראה את הכבוד כדכתיב (ישעי' ל"ג י"ז) מלך ביפיו תחזינה עיניך.

Furthermore, if a man has nice hair and he is not careful with it[9] he will be stricken like Absalom, who was hung by his hair. In fact, for any part of his body that a man isn't careful about [flaunting], he will be stricken in [that part of] the body.	וגם אם שער ראשו יפה ואינו נזהר בו לוקה כאבשלום שנתלה בשערו ובכל דבר שאינו נזהר ילקה בגופו.
One who is careful not to gaze at women, but does gaze at the women's lovely clothes, will be stricken in his clothing, and will not experience being dressed in respectable clothing.[10]	ומי שנזהר מלהסתכל באשה ואינו נזהר מבגדים חמודות של נשים הרי ילקה בבגדיו ולא יראה במעשה לבושו של כבוד.

Even after reading the above passage some matters remain unclear; indeed, *Sefer Chasidim* does not discuss women looking at men's hair. How is it that the rules of modest comportment are parallel between men and women, but, as he wrote in the previously quoted rule, it depends on what is usually covered? What happens when the social conventions surrounding men's and women's dress differ in this regard? The answer to this question is unclear. Nevertheless, it seems clear that the *Sefer Chasidim* conceived of modest dress as incumbent on men and women. Such an outlook is unparalleled in the halakhic literature and deserves more detailed study.[11]

8. Sefer HaRokeach

In his *Sefer HaRokeach* (Berachot 345), R. Elazar of Worms codifies the discussion in b. Berachot similarly to R. Tam.

---

9. Ostensibly, he means careful not to show it off.
10. Alternatively, this could mean "clothes of glory" and have a kabbalistic connotation; as the author here makes no reference to verses about God, as he did for his other examples, it is difficult to know what he means here.
11. It is worth noting that Rabbi David Bigman, Rosh Yeshiva of Yeshivat Maaleh Gilboa, in *A New Analysis of "Kol B'Isha Erva"*, advocates accepting the Ra'aviah's subjective perspective and permits men to listen to women singing in non-provocative contexts. Based on the same logic, he advocates, though not as a matter of strict law, following the position of the *Sefer Chasidim* and prohibiting women from listening to men sing in circumstances that would be forbidden in the reverse. See this in translation here: https://www.jewishideas.org/article/new-analysis-kol-bisha-erva. In his response to Rabbi Bigman, in an article, *Reaction to Rabbi Bigman on Kol B'Isha Erva*, Rabbi Baruch Gigi, Rosh Yeshiva of Yeshivat Har Etzion, also advocates following this strict position as well. Both were published in Hebrew on January 11, 2017. See https://tinyurl.com/y2ngqhfm.

In the third chapter of [b.] Berachot R. Yitzchak said: "If a woman [reveals] a handbreadth [of flesh], it is forbidden to recite [Shema] in her presence." Also if her hair is revealed, or her arms, he should stop, whether he is reciting Shema or praying or making the grace after meals blessings. If the woman is not his wife, even any amount [of revealed flesh or hair should cause him to stop].

בפ' ג' דברכות (דף כד) אמר ר' יצחק טפח באשה ערוה אסור לקרות כנגדה. או אם שערותיה מגולות. או בתי זרועותיהן יש לו לפסוק אם קורא קרית שמע או מתפלל או מברך ברכת המזון. ובאשה אחרת אפילו כל שהוא.

This appears as well in the Jerusalem Talmud, in the second chapter of tractate Challah: "The hair of a woman is an erotic stimulus. The voice of a woman is an erotic stimulus."

ואיתא נמי בירושלמי בפ' ב' דמס' חלה שער באשה ערוה. קול באשה ערוה.

Any spot that a woman generally covers, if it is revealed, it is forbidden [to recite Shema in her presence], even if it is his wife. If her hands are visible, it is permitted [to recite in her presence].

כל מקום שדרך האשה להתכסות אם הוא נגלה אסור אף אם היא אשתו וידיה מגולות מותר.

Two details are worth noting here. First, the *Rokeach* reads the entire text as being in reference to the recitation of blessings in general. Expanding out from the usual reference to Shema, he also speaks about praying or reciting the grace after meals. He supports this by referencing the parallel passage in the Jerusalem Talmud, tractate Challah, which includes hair and voice. Second, in his summary of the rule, the *Rokeach* specifically states that the rule applies to areas that are generally covered. In other words, in line with R. Tam's position, he believes that erva is defined sociologically as parts of the body (including voice, apparently) that a man would not usually see (or hear).

9. Rabbi Eliezer ben Yoel Halevi (Ra'aviah)

Although Ra'aviah does not discuss the Ketubot sugya in detail, he refers to it in his work (919) as part of his discussion of the term "the law of Moshe and Israel" used in the marriage ceremony and the ketubah.[12]

---

12. Unlike many Rishonim, there are substantial differences between the four competing editions of the Ra'aviah. The first published version (and the one most commonly used, including on Bar Ilan) is by Chaim N. Dembitzer (Cracow, 1882).

Like the law of Moshe and Israel – for her father gave her to the husband's agents of his own accord, as is stated in the fifth chapter of Ketubot, [the term] should not be understood as it was in the case in Narash (b. Yevamot 110a) where [the suitor] stole her from [her father], where it was concluded that anyone who marries does so on the authority of the rabbis, i.e., "like the law of Moshe and Israel," and the rabbis can undo his marriage.

It was further necessary to use this phrase [in the ketubah] to inform us that he is only writing this ketubah on behalf of a woman who behaves with him "like the law of Moshe and Israel." For it was taught

כדת משה וישראל,[13] שמסרה האב לשלוחי הבעל מרצונו, כדאיתא בפרק אף על פי, ולא כההיא עובד' דנרש דחטפה מיני,' דמסיק[14] כל דמקדש אדעתא דרבנן מקדש, פי'[15] כדת משה וישראל, ואפקע[ינהו][16] לקידושין מיניה.

ועוד הוצרכנו לכתוב זה,[17] להודיענו שלא כתב לו[18] כתובה אלא להתנהג עמו כדת משה וישראל, דתנן בפ' המדיר אילו יוצאת בו[לא][19]

The second edition of the material was published by Avraham Sulzbach in a work entitled *Chosen Yeshuot* (Frankfurt am Main, 5666), and remains obscure. The third edition was published by Avigdor Aptowitzer, who published a two-volume edition with a well-respected introduction, which was updated and revised and expanded in 1965 (by Rabbis She'ar Yashuv Cohen and Eliyahu Prisman in Jerusalem). This edition is substantially superseded by the recent edition by Rabbi David Dublitzky, *Sefer Ra'aviah* (Bnei Brak, 5765). It is usually best to compare Ra'aviah's position with that of his grandfather, Ra'avan. In this case, however, it cannot be done. Although both the sugya in b. Ketubot and that in b. Berachot are each referenced briefly in Ra'avan's *Even HaEzer* (Ketubot, towards the end; Berachot, 164), the reference is so general in character that it is impossible to offer any insight into how Ra'avan read these texts. In the next many notes we contrast the text between the Sulzbach and Aptowitzer editions in a few places with the letters "S" and "A".

13. S. כלומר.
14. S. דאסיק.
15. S. כלומר.
16. A. ואפקעא.
17. S. ועוד צריך לכתוב(ות); Sulzbach apparently understands this passage in Ra'aviah as explaining the purpose of the sugya in b. Ketubot as opposed to Aptowitzer who understands this as a second explanation for why the phrase דת משה וישראל appears in the ketubah. The latter interpretation appears to be preferable, both because of the context in Ra'aviah's discussion as well as because Sulzbach is forced to amend his text in order to make his case.
18. The term here is an ethical dative "for himself," Sulzbach reads לה, i.e., a regular dative "for her."
19. A. בכתובה, but this seems to be a mistake.

in the seventh chapter of Ketubot: "Who is divorced without a ketubah payment? Whoever violated *dat Moshe ve-Yehudit*. What [violates] *dat Moshe*? Feeding [her husband] untithed food, having intercourse with him during her menstrual period, not setting apart the dough offering.[21] What [violates] *dat Yehudit*? Going out with her hair exposed, weaving in the marketplace, conversing with random men."[22] There are those who believe he should be forced to divorce such a woman, as was discussed there.

כתובה העוברת על דת משה ויהודית. [ואיזהו עוברת על דת משה, מאכילתו שאינו מעושר ומשמשתו נידה ולא קוצה לו חלה. ואיזו היא דת יהודית, יוצאת וראשה פרוע וטווה בשוק ומדברת על כל אדם].[20] וגם יש שכופין להוציא כדתנן התם.

In the Jerusalem Talmud, it reads: "A woman who exposes her hair, or [stops being intimate with him] [stops adorning herself for him][27] in order to make her husband angry – R. Avin HaLevi says: 'She is a rebellious wife and she loses the additional parts of her ketubah.' The Rabbis say: 'Rip up her ketubah, whether she is betrothed or married, she receives no payment and she leaves the marriage with a *gett*' – and the law follows the rabbis."

ובירושלמ' גרסי' איתתא דפרעא לרישא אי נמי ד[ובטלה תיקון מיניה][23] [נטלה תיקון עדיה מיניה][24] אגב לאכעוסי בעלה ר' אבין הלוי אמ' מורדת הויא ופסידה תוספת כתובתה ורבנן אמרי [תיקרע][25] כתובתה בין ארוסה בין נשואה לית לה פורנא[26] ונפק' בגיטה, והילכת' כרבנן.

The starting point of Ra'aviah's analysis is "the law of Moses and Israel" phrase found in the ketubah. Ra'aviah argues that in the context of the ketubah, the term has two meanings. The primary meaning is that the

---

20. Instead of this whole quote, Sulzbach simply reads וכו'.
21. Ra'aviah here leaves out the woman who makes vows but does not fulfill them.
22. Ra'aviah leaves out one that curses his parents (Abba Shaul's case) and the loudmouth (R. Tarfon's case).
23. Aptowitzer.
24. Sulzbach.
25. Aptowitzer has תיקוע, but this seems like a mistake, as it makes no sense. Aptowitzer himself writes in the notes that he prefers Sulzbach's text for this word as well.
26. S. כתובה.
27. The textual difference between the first and second version is important here; the meaning of the latter as not adorning is certain, the meaning of the former version less so.

marriage was done legally with the consent of all parties. Ra'aviah believes that there is reason to worry. Specifically if the witnesses did not validate this claim, when a man marries a minor, the husband would be left open to a charge that he married this girl without her father's permission.

Ra'aviah also mentions a secondary meaning to the term: that the ketubah only remains when the marriage is conducted in accordance with the laws of Moses and Israel. Ra'aviah uses this as an opening to discuss *dat Moshe* and *dat Yehudit*. His point is that if a woman violates either *dat Moshe* or *dat Yehudit*, then she is not fulfilling her marital obligations to her husband and thereby forfeits her right to the ketubah payment upon divorce.

In quoting the Mishnah, Ra'aviah makes no reference to any of the Talmud's discussion of these terms, including the claim that fully uncovered or undone hair would be a violation of a Torah law. This could be evidence that, like the Behag, Ra'aviah does not see this text as authoritative. Nevertheless, this is not a conclusive argument, since Ra'aviah may just be quoting shorthand here.

In addition to the question of the ketubah payment, Ra'aviah states that some authorities even believe that men must, in fact, divorce their wives if they violate these norms of behavior, although this point is debated. To further illustrate this controversy, Ra'aviah quotes from the *Sefer Yerushalmi*.[28] The quote references a woman engaging in two problematic activities: going out with her hair exposed or refusing *"tikkun"* for him out of spite.

The word *tikkun* here is problematic and it is unclear what, exactly, is meant by the term. Unfortunately, as the original *Sefer Yerushalmi* has been lost for centuries, Ra'aviah's quote is the only witness to this text. In Avraham Sulzbach's edition of the text, he has the phrase as נטלה תיקון עדיה מיניה, meaning that she stops adorning herself with makeup or jewelry. Victor Aptowitzer has a slightly different text: בטלה תיקון מיניה. The meaning of this phrase is more uncertain. It could be understood

---

28. Although Ra'aviah quotes this as the Talmud Yerushalmi, it has been demonstrated by a number of scholars that the German Tosafists actually had an expanded work, based upon the Yerushalmi, referred to by scholars as *Sefer Yerushalmi*. As Yaakov Sussman has demonstrated in a number of articles, this work seems to be the source for many of the Yerushalmi quotes from this community that are not to be found in any extant manuscript or printing of this Talmud. See Yaakov Sussman, "The Ashkenazi Yerushalmi MS – 'Sefer Yerushalmi,'" *Tarbiz* 65 (1995): 37–64 [Hebrew].

the same way as Sulzbach's text, that she stopped wearing jewelry. More likely, it could be understood as a euphemism for refusing to be intimate with her husband.

However one understands the phrase, it is meant to be one of two examples. The other marital breach on the woman's part that causes her to lose her ketubah payment in case of divorce is uncovered hair. Although there is a debate between the sages and R. Avin about what the penalty for such behavior would be – R. Avin believes it is the loss of part of her ketubah in case of divorce; the stricter approach of the sages insists upon the loss of her entire ketubah and a mandatory divorce to boot – for our purposes, the important thing to note about the *Sefer Yerushalmi* quote is that exposure of hair is considered to be analogous to refusal to wear makeup (or refusal to be intimate).

If the *tikkun* case refers to refusal of intimacy, the meaning is clear. Any man would find it intolerable to remain married to someone who refuses to be intimate with him for no reason other than spite. The more extreme case, and the more interesting one for our purposes, is a wife who refuses to adorn herself with jewelry or makeup. Unlike refusing intimacy, where it could be argued that the behavior is sinful as it abrogates a marital obligation (although this would be a stretch), refusing to wear jewelry is not a sin at all. The behavior described is purely a spiteful attempt on the wife's part to annoy her husband in some way. If her husband did not care for jewelry, her lack of adornment would be meaningless and inoffensive.

If uncovering of hair is considered as analogous to either of these, then one would have to assume that the reason it is considered a serious violation is because it is intolerable to a husband to have his wife appear in this way in public. If this is correct, then one must assume that this is a sociological reality, and that in a society where married women expose their hair in public, a husband may not be embarrassed and this would not be sufficient cause to penalize her with the loss of her ketubah.

B. BERACHOT

Like Rabbeinu Tam, Ra'aviah sees public modesty requirements as being subjectively determined. This can be seen from his treatment (Berachot 76) of the sugya in b. Berachot.

| The *Halakhot Gedolot* concluded that all of the cases referenced here, like the [exposed] handbreadth [of a woman's flesh] | פסק בהלכות גדולות דכל הני דאמרינן הכא טפח באשה ערוה ואפילו היא אשתו |

being considered inappropriate exposure – this refers even to a man's wife, for another woman even less than a handbreadth [would be inappropriate] – and the calf of a woman being inappropriate exposure, and the hair of a woman [and the voice of a woman] – in the presence of any of these a man may not recite the Shema. R. Chananel wrote similarly. Moreover, I say that the reason [that even a voice can be included in this list] is that even though one cannot see a voice, nevertheless it can cause a man to have inappropriate thoughts.

ובאשה אחרת אפילו דבר קטן מטפח וכן שוק באשה ערוה וכן שער באשה ערוה [וכן קול באשה ערוה] כל הני אסור לקרות ק"ש כנגדם, וכן פר"ח. ואומר אני דטעמא דאע"ג דאין הקול נראה לעין מיהו הרהור איכא.

All of these things [that we referenced above] as being inappropriate exposure – this applies specifically to things that women do not generally expose, but for [a man to recite the Shema in the presence of] a virgin who generally exposes her hair does not concern us, for there will be no inappropriate thoughts. The same goes for a woman's voice [that he is used to hearing].[29]

וכל הדברים [שהזכרנו למעלה] לערוה דווקא בדבר שאין רגילות להגלות, אבל בתולה הרגילה בגילוי שער לא חיישינן, דליכא הרהור, וכן בקולה [לרגיל בו].

In tractate Challah, the Jerusalem Talmud has the following, in reference to the Mishnah that discusses a woman who is sitting and taking *challah* in the nude:

ובמסכת חלה גרס בירושלמי: אהא דתנן האשה יושבת וקוצה לה חלתה ערומה]. [:

This would mean that the [exposed] buttocks do not count as exposure. This applies to the recitation of blessings, but inso-

הדא אמרו עגבות אין בהם משום ערוה הדתימר לברכה אבל להביט אפילו [כל שהוא]

---

29. At this point Ra'aviah moves into a short discussion relevant only to the prohibition of hearing the woman's voice.

Now one should not compare the case of hearing a woman's voice to the case [of feces] in glass, in front of which one is permitted to recite Shema, for in this case the voice, which is the inappropriate stimulus, is out in the open, only it isn't visible, so it is more comparable to exposed [feces] before a blind person; this is my opinion.

וקול ליכא לדמויי [לצואה] בעששית שמותר לקרות ק"ש כנגדה, דהכא הקול שהוא הערוה גלוי אלא שאין העין שולטת בו לראות ודמיא [לצואה] מגולה לפני סומא, כן נראה לי.

far as [men] ogling her, [anything] would be forbidden. Like that which was taught: "One who gazes upon a woman's ankle it is as if he is gazing at her uterus,[31] and one who gazes at her uterus, it is as if he has slept with her." Shmuel said the voice of a woman is an erotic stimulus. What is the reason? [For it is written (Jer. 3:9):] 'And it will be that due to the voice of her fornication the land will be compromised.'

אסור[30] כהדא דתניא המסתכל בעקיבה כמסתכל בבית הרחם והמסתכל בבית הרחם כאילו בא עליה [שמואל אמר קול באשה ערוה מה טעם והיה מקול זנותה ותחנף ⟨את⟩ הארץ וגו' (ירמיהו ג"ט),

There are those that interpret [Shmuel's prohibition] as being due to the fact that men will often look at her while she is singing. This implies that for saying a blessing there is no prohibition [to be in her presence while she is singing] if one does not look at her, but it is forbidden to look at her [while she is singing].

ויש מפרשים מפני שדרכו להביט בה כשמנגנת]. משמע דלברכה אינו אסור בשאינו מביט, אבל להביט אסור.

For the purposes of this analysis, there are two key elements to Ra'aviah's understanding of the sugya. First, following the Behag and R. Chananel (at least how he understands them), Ra'aviah believes that the

---

A proof for this comes from the Jerusalem Talmud (y. Berachot. 3:5; y. Sanhedrin 10:1): R. Eyla and his fellows were sitting before a hostel one night. They suggested: "May we speak a little Torah?" [R. Eyla] responded: "Since if it were daytime we would see [the waste] that is before us, therefore now it is forbidden [to speak Torah]." And even though [it would appear that] one may be lenient by voice since it cannot be seen ever, not by him or anyone else, nevertheless one should be strict.

וראייה דגרסינן בירושלמי הכא:ר' אילא וחברייא הוו יתבין קמי פונדקיא ברמשא אמרי מהו מימר מילי דאורייתא אמר ליה מכיון דאלו הוו(ה) איממא הוינן] חזינן מה קומ(י)נן] ברם כדון אסור. ואף על פי [שנראה)] להקל בקול שאינו ראוי בשום ענין לראיה לא לו ולא לאחרים, אפילו הכי ראוי להחמיר.

It seems that Ra'aviah was responding to some halakhic authorities who did not believe that any prohibition regarding a woman's voice was sustainable. As will be seen, Ra'aviah seems to be of two minds on this subject, and his ambivalence manifests itself in his citing of an alternative interpretation to Shmuel, namely that the prohibition of hearing a woman's voice is a secondary decree to avoid the possibility that the hearer will look (inappropriately) at the singer.

30. Some manuscripts have this line here: ויש 'וגו הארץ ותחנף זנותה מקול והיה דכתיב מפרשים מפני שדרכו להביט בה כשמנגנת, but it appears out of place here and fits better after Shmuel.

31. A euphemism for the vulva.

entire text in b. Berachot and y. Challah only relates to the recitation of the Shema and other blessings. Of course, a man is not permitted to gaze at a woman to whom he is attracted; but this, as both Talmuds make clear, would apply even to parts of the woman that are not generally thought to be erotic, such as a finger (Bavli) or an ankle (Yerushalmi).

The second, and perhaps more important, point made by Ra'aviah is that even the areas of a woman listed as erotic are only considered so because they are usually covered. Hence, Ra'aviah writes, a man could recite the Shema in the presence of an unmarried woman with her hair uncovered, since this would not be considered erotic but normal.

SUMMARY

Taken together, Ra'aviah does not seem to have an actual list of required clothing for women to wear in public. In b. Ketubot he argues that any behavior that humiliates the husband – ostensibly because it implies lewdness or breaks public convention – makes a wife subject to divorce. In b. Berachot he argues that any erotic stimulus, defined as parts of a woman that are usually covered, prevent a man from saying the Shema and other blessings. Finally, these two pericopes also include the prohibition for a man to gaze upon a woman sexually, irrespective of what she is wearing or what part is attracting him.

What all three of these halakhot have in common is that they are subjectively determined. Behavior which embarrasses the average husband is context- and society-specific. The concept of "areas of a body usually covered" is dependent on societal norms. It would seem that for Ra'aviah, subjectively determined rules of modesty are the only ones halakha knows or uses. In this sense, Ra'aviah's treatment of the subject is the fullest and most robust example of the Rabbeinu Tam model.

10. Tosafot and Tosafot HaRosh

The Tosafot's positions may be gleaned from their final comment in b. Gittin (90b).[32] This comment is a gloss on a line in the b. Gittin sugya analyzed in the second chapter. In this sugya, R. Meir lists types of men based on how they interact with their wives. The wicked man, R. Meir says, allows all sorts of questionable behaviors of his wife and makes no

---

32. This gloss of the Tosafot is restated (without attribution) word for word by Ran in his commentary of Rif's *Halakhot*.

comment. One of those behaviors is that she "bathes with men." The editors of the Talmud are bewildered by this suggestion; could R. Meir really be discussing a married woman that bathes with other men?! They suggest that it means that she uses the same bathing area as men, but not at the same time.

The Tosafot begins by quoting Rashi's gloss on the question.

| "Do you really mean to say [he sees her] bathe with other men?" – Rashi explained: "If that were the case, there would be circumstantial evidence that she is unfaithful and thus forbidden [to her husband] and he *must* divorce her, it is not merely a mitzvah." | עם בני אדם סלקא דעתך - פירש בקונטרס: "אם כן רגלים לדבר שזונה היא ואסורה לו, וחובה לגרשה ולא מצוה." |

According to Rashi, the reason R. Meir's suggestion seems so problematic is because such behavior would be tantamount to her admitting marital infidelity. In such a case the man would be obligated to divorce his wife. Hence, the example doesn't fit the overall paradigm of improper behaviors for which it is a mitzvah for a husband to divorce his wife. The Tosafot challenge Rashi's interpretation based on the sugya in b. Sotah 25a, also discussed in Chapter 2.

| This seems difficult, for one must also divorce a woman who spins in the marketplace or goes out with her head uncovered – not just that one *should* divorce her, yet the question in b. Sotah (25a) as to whether or not a husband may choose to stay married to a woman who violates *dat Yehudit*[33] remains unresolved – why did the Talmud not raise this issue there [by bringing these cases as clear proof]? | וקשה, דהא טווה בשוק ויוצאה וראשה פרוע נמי חובה לגרשה ולא מצוה! דבעיא היא בסוטה (דף כה.) אי עוברת על דת יהודית מותר לקיימה או לא - ולא איפשיטא. ואמאי לא פריך נמי עלה? |

The Tosafot assume that the statement of R. Meir should be understood as listing cases where a husband would be required to divorce his wife, and not, as Rashi suggests, cases where it is merely a mitzvah to do so. Tosafot's proof is that when the passage in b. Sotah is attempting to prove, one way or the other, whether a man must divorce a wife who acts inappropriately, it does not turn to R. Meir's statement in an attempt to

---

33. The Gemara in b. Sotah does not use the expression "*dat Yehudit*"; this is an interpretive gloss by Tosafot.

prove that this is not a requirement – something the Tosafot believe the Talmud would have done if Rashi's understanding of R. Meir was correct. The Tosafot offer two possible answers to this question.

One may answer that because the question in b. Sotah was only in regard to a rabbinic violation, it is reasonable for the Talmud to posit that one ought to divorce such a woman, but here [in Gittin], one is biblically obligated to divorce [a woman who bathes with other men].	ויש לומר דכיון דבעיא בסוטה לא הויא אלא מדרבנן קאמר שפיר דמצוה לגרשה, אבל זו חובה לגרשה מן התורה
Another possible interpretation: "Do you really mean to say that she bathes with other men?" – even a wicked person would not stand for this from his wife, or even the laxest of women would not do this.	ועוד יש לפרש רוחצת עם בני אדם סלקא דעתך אפילו אדם רע אינו סובל זה מאשתו או אפילו קלה שבקלות אינה עושה כן.

The second answer sidesteps the issue by offering an alternative, simpler understanding of the Talmud's question. According to this approach, the Talmud is simply incredulous and denies R. Meir would ever have suggested something so improbable as a husband knowing his wife literally bathes with other men but does not divorce her. No woman would do this, Tosafot argues, and if one did, certainly no husband would stand for it.

The first answer, however, is Tosafot's attempt to make sense of Rashi's comment. Tosafot answers that, of course, Rashi knows that, according to R. Meir, one is obligated to divorce one's wife for any of these infractions. However, all of these infractions are rabbinic in nature, as they are all *dat Yehudit* violations. Although the Talmud doesn't say this explicitly, both Rashi and Tosafot interpret the term *dat* in b. Sotah as *dat Yehudit*. The Talmud there is asking whether we follow R. Meir's position that it is a requirement for a man to divorce his wife if she violates *dat Yehudit*. Perhaps it is only a mitzvah.

However, if a woman were literally bathing with other men, Rashi argues this would be evidence of an affair. In such a case there would be a Torah requirement to divorce his wife. That, says Tosafot, is Rashi's point here. This example would not fit the paradigm of *dat Yehudit*/rabbinic violations, since the behavior implies that she has committed adultery, something far more serious than a violation of modest behavioral norms.

For the purposes of this book, we note that one of Tosafot's examples for *dat Yehudit* is "exposed hair" (ראשה פרוע). We see that the case the Talmud in b. Ketubot views as a Torah law is understood by Tosafot to be rabbinic in nature.

R. Asher ben Yechiel (Rosh), in his *Tosafot HaRosh* (ad loc.), offers a virtually identical interpretation of this passage to that of Tosafot.

"Do you really mean to say that she bathes with other men?"	[עם] בני אדם סלקא דעתך?!
– Rashi of blessed memory explained that if that were the case, there would be circumstantial evidence that she is unfaithful and thus forbidden [to her husband], and the Talmud would not have said that in that case one ought to divorce such a woman, but rather one *must* divorce her.	פירש"י ז"ל: אם כן, רגלים לדבר שזונה היא ואסורה! ועל זה לא יאמר מצוה לגרשה אלא חובה לגרשה.
If you challenge this by saying, if that is true, then certainly one must also divorce a woman who goes out with her hair exposed because she violates *dat Yehudit*, yet it is an unresolved question in b. Sotah (25a) as to whether or not a husband may choose to stay married to such a woman.	ואם תאמר: אם כן, יוצאה וראשה פרוע נמי חובה לגרשה, דעוברת על דת יהודית! ובעיא היא בסוטה בפ' ארוסה אם רצה הבעל לקיימה אי שרי אי אסיר ולא איפשיטא.
One may answer that there [in b. Sotah] the violation was rabbinic [and so one need not in fact divorce such a woman], but here [actually bathing with other men] would be a biblical violation.	ויש לומר דהתם מדרבנן והכא מדאורייתא.
Another possible interpretation: *"Do you really mean to say that she bathes with other men?"* – There is no husband who would stand for that.	אי נמי הכי פירושו: [עם][34] בני אדם סלקא דעתך - אין לך אדם שיסבול דבר זה.

Like Tosafot, Rosh in his gloss on this passage is of the view that a woman who goes out with her hair exposed violates *dat Yehudit* (and not *dat Moshe*). Furthermore, while Rosh initially entertains the possibility that a man must divorce a woman who violates *dat Yehudit*, he ultimately concludes that one may divorce her but need not do so.

---

34. The print says "בפני," but this makes little sense in context.

The subjective nature of the hair covering rules, and of *dat Yehudit* in general, fits well with Tosafot and *Tosafot HaRosh*'s interpretations of Rav Acha bar Abba's comment at the end of b. Kiddushin (referenced in Chapter 2), explaining why it was acceptable for him to put his granddaughter on his lap, "all for the sake of heaven." On this line, Tosafot comment:

> | All for the sake of heaven – this is what we rely upon nowadays, since we interact with women on a regular basis. | הכל לשם שמים – ועל זו אנו סומכין השתא שאנו משתמשים בנשים. |
> |---|---|

Tosafot HaRosh offers a similar comment:

> | All for the sake of heaven – upon this we rely to interact with women. | הכל לשם שמים. אהא סמכינן להשתמש באשה. |
> |---|---|

The Tosafot are acutely aware that in their society men do business with women. However, one could argue that interacting with women is forbidden, as Shmuel says explicitly. For this reason, Tosafot and *Tosafot HaRosh* follow Rav Acha bar Abba's lead and suggest that since this is "business as usual" in their society, there should be no problem. The Tosafot are stretching the principle somewhat, since Rav Acha bar Abba was using it to defend playing with his granddaughter, which could be seen as a mitzvah of kindness. Here, the Tosafot apply it to run-of-the-mill activity because in their society, this behavior is not at all sexual or provocative.

11. Sefer HaEshkol

In his *Sefer HaEshkol* (ed. Albeck, Avodah Zarah 192a), Rabbi Avraham ben Isaac Av Beit Din (Ra'avad 2) quotes the responsum by R. Hai Gaon found in the *Shaarei Teshuva* 29. The responsum is a discussion of types of sins, and the relevant section is his discussion of the fifth type.

> | The fifth category is [sins] based on sight – like a man looking at women who are forbidden to him, as it says "a handbreadth of a woman's [exposed flesh] is considered erotic" and "a woman's hair is considered erotic" and "a woman's voice is considered erotic." However, there is a greater sin with forbidden women, like those who have the prohibited status of *erva*, than | הה'. הראייה והוא כגון ראיית העריות שהן אסור וכדאמרינן טפח באשה ערוה ושער שבאשה ערוה קול באשה ערוה ומיהו איסורא רבה איכא בעריות כגון האסורות אסור ערוה ממה שאין בפנויות רחוקות וכדתניא לא יסתכל אדם באשה נאה ואפילו |
> |---|---|

with single women who are unrelated to the person. As it states: "A person should not gaze at a pretty woman even if she is single or at a married woman even if she is unattractive..."

פנויה, באשת איש ואפילו מכוערת...

Here Rav Hai seems to understand the list of prohibited parts of a woman as having to do with the prohibition of ogling a woman. As noted in Chapter 3, this would appear to be an entirely different understanding than that offered in the piece quoted by the students of R. Yonah. In that chapter, I suggest a way of reading both of Rav Hai Gaon's comments as one, but this may be unnecessary here. As the *Sefer HaEshkol* only quotes this responsum and not the other, it is possible that R. Avraham Av Beit Din understood the passage in b. Berachot to be primarily about ogling and not Shema, and this includes the statement about hair.

12. Sefer HaManhig

In his *Sefer HaManhig* (Laws of Prishut, Tahara and Kedusha), R. Avraham ben Natan Even HaYarchi (known as Ra'avan; 12th century Provence) interprets all the erva and separation from women laws through the prism of the man avoiding erotic stimuli.

The Sages taught in Pirkei Avot (1:5): "Do not converse overly much with a woman, and this refers to one's own wife, how much more so to the wife of one's friend," for this would lead to possible sin. In Avot of R. Nathan (Ch. 7) it says: "This refers to one's wife when she is forbidden due to menstruation, how much more so with the wife of a friend as it may lead to adultery."[35]

ושנו חכמי' בפרקי אבות, [פ"א מ"ה] אל תרבה שיחה עם האשה באשתו אמרו קל וחומר באשת חבירו, דאיכא הרגל עבירה, ובפרקי אבות דר' נתן [פ'[ז] באשתו נידה אמרו כו', ומפני הרגל עבירה קל וחומר באשת חבירו שלא יבוא לידי ניאוף,

For anyone who gazes upon women will end up sinning, as it says in b. Nedarim (20a), and anyone who gazes at a woman's ankle will end up having wayward children. This applies even to one's wife when she

שכל הצופה בנשי' סוף בא לידי עבירה, בנדרי' פרק ואלו מותרי,' [כ' ע"א] וכל המסתכל בעקבה שלאשה הוויין לו בנים שאינן מהוגנין,

---

35. A number of Rishonim quote this text (Rashi, *Rokeach*, Tashbetz), but it does not appear in our versions of Avot of Rabbi Nathan. The text may be a modified version of Avot of Rabbi Nathan based on the Talmudic pericope in b. Nedarim 20a, which R. Even HaYarchi will quote next.

is a niddah, how much more so does it apply to a married woman; and by "ankle" it means literally an ankle.

In the first chapter of b. Sotah [it says]: "Anyone who passes money from his hand to a married woman's hand in order to gaze upon her will never free himself from the judgment in *Gehinnom*, as it says (Prov. 11:21): 'hand to hand he will not be cleansed of wickedness,' and it says (Prov. 6:27): 'Will a man set a fire in his bosom?' So too any [man] who sleeps with the wife of his fellow, all who touch her will not be cleansed."[36]

In the sixth chapter of b. Shabbat (64b) [it says]: "Why did the verse include hidden jewelry, as it says (Num. 31:50): 'ring, bracelet and *kumaz*'?[37] This is to teach you that anyone who looks at the little finger of a woman is considered as if he were looking at her private parts." 'And we brought the offering of the Lord' (Num. 31:50) – Moses said to them: "Why this sacrifice? Is it that you have returned to your original sinfulness?" They responded (Num. 31:49): "We have lost no one." [Moses responded:] "If so, why this offering?" They said to him: "Even though we did not sin, we still had inappropriate thoughts." Thereupon "we brought the offering of the Lord."

ואפי' לאשתו נידה, קל וחומר לאשת איש ועקבה עקב רגלה ממש.

ובפ' המקנא, כל המרצה מעות מידו ליד אשת איש כדי להסתכל בה לא ינקה מדינה שלגיהינם, שנ' יד ליד לא ינקה רע, וכתי' היחתה איש אש בחיקו וגו', כן הבא אל אשת רעהו לא ינקה כל הנוגע בה.

ובשבת פרק במה אשה יוצ', למה מנה הכתו' תכשיטי' שבפנים שנ' טבעת עגיל וכומז וגו', לומר לך כל המסתכל באצבע קטנה שלאשה כאילו מסתכל במקום התורף. ונקרב את קרבן י', אמ' להם משה קרבן זה למה שמא חזרתם לקלקולכם הראשון, אמרו לו לא נפקד ממנו איש אם כן קרבן זה למה, אמרו לו אם מידי עבירה יצאנו מידי הרהור לא יצאנו, מיד ונקרב את קרבן י'.

---

36. The text, as it appears here, does not exist in the Talmud as we have it. The tractate he references, b. Sotah, does not have this statement at all, although it does contain a midrash on the verse in Proverbs, but it understands the referent as a man who sleeps with a married woman. The statement about passing things to a married woman as an excuse to look at her appears in b. Berachot 61, but without the second verse; this is also how it appears in the minor tractates, Kallah (1:6) and Kallah Rabbati (1:9). In *Midrash Aggadah* (ed. Buber), in *Parashat Acharei Mot* (2), the midrash appears as being from "our rabbis," but the second verse is different (Prov. 11:22).

37. The rabbis understand the *kumaz* to be a sort of erotic adornment as noted above in note 58 on page 74.

And the Sages said (b. Berachot 24a): "A handbreadth of a woman is an erotic stimulus, the voice of a woman is an erotic stimulus, the hair of a woman is an erotic stimulus." ואמ' חכמי', [ברכות כ"ד ע"א] טפח באשה ערווה, קול באשה ערוה, שער באשה ערוה.

The *Sefer HaManhig*'s approach to all of these halakhot is consistent. The rule is that men must avoid any possible erotic stimulus in their interaction with women. Moreover, the *Sefer HaManhig*'s examples of acts that could bring about arousal are very broadly defined, as they includes regular conversation and seeing a woman's ankle.

13. Ra'avad and Provençal Rishonim (HaHashlama, Meorot, and Mikhtam)

One specific issue that becomes very important in the discussions of the Acharonim is the status of hair that comes out from underneath a woman's head covering. The first authority to discuss this detail is the Ra'avad (R. Avraham ben David of Posquières, ca. 1125–1198). Although we do not have Ra'avad's original work, his views are quoted by a number of authorities. Thus, we could consider them all as one group of Rishonim.

SEFER HAHASHLAMA

The earliest extant quote comes from the *Sefer HaHashlama*, a commentary on the Rif authored by R. Meshullam ben Moshe of Béziers (ca. 1165–1238). In his glosses on the Rif's text of tractate Berachot, he writes:

Rabbi Yitzchak said: "A handbreadth of a woman's [exposed flesh] is considered *erva*." With regard to what? If this is meant to prohibit [a man's] looking at it – Did not Rav Sheshet [already] say, "Why does the verse list regular jewelry together with erotic jewelry?"[38] This is to teach you that anyone who looks at the little finger of a woman is considered as if he were looking at her private parts."! Rather, it must be in reference to a person's own wife. But if it

אמר ר' יצחק טפח באשה ערוה. למאי, אילימא לאסתכולי בה הא אמר רב ששת למה מנה הכתוב תכשיטין שבחוץ עם תכשיטין שבפנים לומר לך כל המסתכל באצבע קטנה של אשה כאילו מסתכל במקום התורף, אלא באשתו. ובדברי תורה אמאי לא? אלא באשתו ובק[ריאת] ש[מע].

---

38. This is referring to Exodus 35:22 and/or Numbers 31:50, which includes in its list of jewelry the *kumaz*. The rabbis understand this to be a sort of erotic adornment as noted above in note 58 on page 74.

is while studying Torah, why can he not? Rather, it is referring to his wife, and in regard to the recitation of the Shema.

> Rav Chisda said: "A woman's calf is considered *erva*, for [the verse] states: '*Reveal* the calf, pass through the rivers' (Isaiah 47:2)." Shmuel said: "The voice of a woman is considered *erva*, as it states: 'for your voice is sweet [and your appearance attractive']' (Song 2:14)." Rav Sheshet said: "The hair of a woman is considered suggestive, as it states: 'Your hair is like a flock of goats' (Song 4:1)."

> אמר רב חסדא שוק באשה ערוה שנאמר גלי שוק עברי נהרות. אמר שמואל קול באשה ערוה שנאמר כי קולך ערב. אמר רב ששת שער באשה ערוה שנאמר שערך כעדר העזים.

The above is the familiar passage in b. Berachot, except with an added line. This line demonstrates that, according to R. Meshullam (it is unclear if this was in his version of the Talmud or if it just represents his own opinion), not reciting Shema in the presence of nudity is specific to that mitzvah and has no application to Torah study in general. Other than this single but critical line, the passage is more or less what appears in the Talmud. *Sefer HaHashlama* quotes it in its entirety because the Rif skipped it entirely in his halakhot (as noted in Chapter 3 of this book). Thus, R. Meshullam feels it necessary to assert that these rules are to be taken as authoritative:

> All of these are the halakha.

> כולהו הני הלכתא נינהו.

R. Meshullam next tries to tackle why it is one might think it is not halakha, and respond to it:

> And even according to Rav Huna, who says that the buttocks do not count as nudity, this is referring to the buttocks [of a couple in bed back to back] that are touching each other, or, alternatively, about a person's own buttocks, but not about looking at someone's [buttocks], for it is clearly forbidden [for a man to recite the Shema] while looking [at his wife's buttocks].

> ואפילו לרב הונא דאמר עגבות אין בהם משום ערוה הני מילי עגבות דנגעי אהדדי אי נמי עגבות דנפשיה ומגולות ולא מסתכל בהו אבל לאיסתכולי ודאי אסור.

R. Meshullam realizes that if Rav Huna's claim is taken at face value, that a woman's buttocks are not considered nudity, then it would make no sense to count her hair or calf as nudity. In fact, this is one explanation given for why the Rif skips it, and why R. Meshullam feels compelled to respond to it. Thus, he argues, Rav Huna cannot be taken at face value, as the Talmud already notes, and that he must instead mean something else, either about a person's own buttocks or how couples' bodies touch in bed. In brief, Rav Huna's statement has no bearing on whether calf, hair, and voice should be considered nudity in the context of looking at a woman or reciting Shema.

The *Sefer HaHashlama* then quotes the Ra'avad's reading of this passage:

| And regarding that which we said, that a handbreadth of [exposed body] on a woman is nudity, and we establish that this principle is in reference to a man's wife while he is reciting the Shema – the Ra'avad explained that this is specifically in reference to a private part, and Rav Chisda comes to teach that a calf is a private place on a woman even if it is not a private place on a man, but her face, her hands, and the hair that comes out from underneath her covering, which she does not usually cover, there is nothing to be concerned about, because he is used to them and they will not distract him. | והא דאמרינן טפח באשה ערוה ואוקימנא באשתו ובק[ריאת] ש[מע] - פירש הראב"ד דוקא ממקום צנוע, ואתא רב חסדא למימר דשוק מקום צנוע באשה ואף על פי שאינו צנוע באיש, אבל פניה וידיה ושערה מחוץ לצמתה שאינה מתכסה אין חוששין להן מפני שרגיל בהן ולא טריד. |

The Ra'avad here establishes an important principle, one that will be widely quoted in the halakhic works of the Acharonim: The list in b. Berachot is meant to clarify a sociological fact, namely that these are places that a woman generally keeps covered, even if men do not. Thus, even if Rav Sheshet specifically mentions hair, this does not apply to the hair that women do not generally cover. Of course, Ra'avad and the *HaHashlama, et alia*, never imagined a society in which women do not cover their hair at all, let alone sing in public or expose their calves. Nevertheless the principle leaves open the strong possibility that none of these can be considered nudity in such a culture, since they are generally exposed.

As the rules above are applicable specifically to men saying the Shema in the presence of their wives, Ra'avad continues by discussing the rule about other women:

> With regard to another woman, it is certainly forbidden to gaze upon any part of her, even her little finger and her hair, and it is forbidden to even listen to her speaking voice, as we said in b. Kiddushin: "[Rav Nachman said to Rav Yehuda:] 'Let the master send greetings to [my wife] Yalta.' [Rav Yehuda] said to him: 'Rav Huna said: 'the voice of a woman is *erva*.'" This is because it is a greeting.[39] Rather whatever is done for the sake of heaven [is fine]. This is what Ra'avad wrote.
>
> ובאשה אחרת ודאי אסור להסתכל בשום מקום אפילו באצבע קטנה ובשערה ואסור לשמוע קול דבריה, וכדאמרינן בקדושין לשדר לן מר שלמא לילתא אמר ליה הכי אמר רב הונא קול באשה ערוה. ומשום שלום קאמר אלא הכל לשם שמים. כל זה כתב הראב"ד.

Ra'avad ends with a strong contrast: When it comes to other women, everything is forbidden if he is doing it to enjoy their attractions, even their little finger or their speaking voice. In fact, even sending a greeting through her husband is forbidden. Though the sources he quotes do not say that this has anything to do with attraction, Ra'avad ends with the quote from b. Kiddushin that anything for the sake of heaven is permitted, thus presenting a clear dichotomy: When it comes to other women, anything done because of attraction is forbidden, while anything done for "the sake of heaven" is permitted.

SEFER HAMEOROT (B. BERACHOT AD LOC.)

Another Provençal scholar who bases his discussion on Ra'avad's is the student of R. Meshullam of Béziers, R. Meir ben Shimon HaMeili (early 13th century), in his *Sefer HaMeorot*. Like the *Sefer HaHashlama*, he begins with the fact that Rif left this discussion out of his book entirely, and opens with a quote from the *Baal HaMaor* (which we saw in Chapter 3):

> The Rabbi, author of the *Maor*, wrote: כתב הרב בעל המאור
>
> "A handbreadth [of exposed flesh] on a טפח באשה ערוה, אוקימנא

---

39. The line makes little sense and the next sentence seems to be a non sequitur. Jackson Gardner suggested that "shalom" here means empty greetings that are not really generating anything important like business and thus they are "hevel" and unnecessary; rather, only speech for the sake of heaven should be used. The editor (Blau) suggests in note 64 that this is a copyist error and replaces the line with what we find in the *Sefer HaMeorot*, "and nowadays we do send greetings to women, and speak about necessary matters, and it is all [ok] when for the sake of heaven" (והאידנא נהגי בשאילת שלום ובדברי צורך, הכל לשם שמים). This is possible, though it is difficult to understand mechanically how one would have turned into the other.

> woman is *erva* – this applies to a man's wife and during his recitation of the Shema. While a woman's calf, a woman's voice, and a woman's hair are all *erva* to gaze at. But the Rif left all this out."
>
> באשתו ולק[ריאת] ש[מע] ושוק באשה וקול באשה ושער באשה הכל ערוה להסתכל בהם. והרי"ף השמיט כל זה עד כאן.
>
> Ra'avad [in his *Katuv Sham*] and the *Ha-Hashlama* wrote the same.
>
> וכן כתבו הראב"ד וההשלמה.
>
> But if his buttocks are touching that of [his wife] or, alternatively, if he is by himself and his buttocks are exposed but he is not looking at them, this does not constitute *erva*.
>
> ועגבות דנגעי אהדדי, אי נמי עגבות דנפשיה ומגולות ולא מסתכל בהו אין בהם משום ערוה.

This latter point is essentially a paraphrase of the *Sefer HaHashlama*, emphasizing the reverse, that the buttocks do not generally constitute an erva problem. At this point, the Meili turns to Ra'avad:

> The Ra'avad wrote: This [permissive attitude to contact with the buttock while reciting Shema] is specifically a reference to his wife, since he is used to her. But contact with the buttocks of anyone else, whom he is not used to, would constitute a problem of *erva*.
>
> וכתב הראב"ד דדוקא עגבות דאשתו דגייסא בה, אבל דאחר דלא גייס אי נגעי אית בהו משום ערוה.
>
> Moreover, looking at them [his wife's buttocks while reciting Shema] is certainly forbidden, for it was taught: A woman may sit naked and remove *challah* since she can cover her genitals[40] with the ground, but this is not true of a man. And the Talmud establishes this case as one in which her entire bottom is covered by the ground, meaning that even her buttocks are covered.
>
> אבל לאסתכולי ודאי אסור. דתניא אשה יושבת וקוצה לה חלה ערומה מפני שיכולה לכסות פניה בקרקע אבל לא האיש. ואיקימנא כגון שהיו כל פניה טוחות בקרקע, פרוש שהעגבות מכוסות.

Ra'avad's distinction here is between physical contact with the buttocks, which can be ignored on the assumption that a husband is used to feeling his wife next to him in bed, and looking at it, which is always erotic and thus its being exposed is considered erva even if the person is alone. The Meili next moves on to quote the rest of Ra'avad, about what

---

40. Literally "her face" but this is a euphemism.

constitutes private areas of the body (other than obvious places such as the buttocks) and what constitutes public areas:

"A handbreadth of [exposed flesh] on a woman is *erva*" – and we establish that this principle is in reference to a man's wife while he is reciting the Shema – the Ra'avad wrote that this is specifically in reference to a private part, and a calf is a private place on a woman even if it is not a private place on a man, but her face, her hands, and the hair that comes out from underneath her covering, which she does not usually cover, there is nothing to be concerned about, because he is used to them and they will not distract him.	וטפח באשה ערוה דאוקימנא אפילו באשתו ולק[ריאת] ש[מע] - כתב הראב"ד דדוקא ממקום צנוע, ושוק באשה הוי מקום צנוע אבל באיש לא הוי מקום צנוע. אבל פניה ידיה ושערה מחוץ לצמתה שאינה מתכסה אין חוששין להן מפני שרגיל בהם ולא טריד.
With regard to another woman, it is certainly forbidden to gaze upon any part of her, even her little finger and her hair, and it is forbidden to even listen to her speaking voice, as we said in Kiddushin, and this applies even to sending a greeting. But nowadays, we greet women and discuss necessary matters, and whatever is done for the sake of heaven [is fine], as we see there.	ובאשה אחרת ודאי אסור להסתכל בה בשום מקום ואפילו באצבע קטנה ובשערה. ואסור לשמוע דבריה כדאמרינן בקדושין ואפילו לשאלת שלום. והאידנא נהגי בשאילת שלום ובדברי צורך, הכל לשם שמים כדאיתא התם.

Meili's quote of Ra'avad is more or less the same as that of the *Sefer HaHashlama*. Even though the text says hair is erva, since women tend to leave some hair exposed, ("hair that comes out from under the covering"), the prohibition cannot apply to it.

SEFER HAMIKHTAM

R. David ben Levi of Narbonne (late 13th century) also discusses this passage in Berachot 24a, but only the first part.

The Rif z"l wrote: We establish [the law] in accordance with Rav Joseph, that a man's wife is considered part of his own body. And a verse supports him for it says (Gen. 2:24): "and they shall be as one body." And he may thus recite the Shema while in bed	כתב הריא"ף ז"ל קיימא לן כרב יוסף דאשתו כיון שכגופו היא, וקרא מסייעו דכתיב והיו לבשר אחד, קורא קריאת שמע במיטתו עמה ובלבד שיחזיר פניו לצד אחר, ואע"פ שנוגע

| with her, as long as he turns his face to the other side. Even though their buttocks are touching, this doesn't matter. | עמה בעגבות אין בכך כלום. |

Like Rif, and unlike his Provençal teachers, he ignores the rest of the passage. Nevertheless, it is possible that we may be missing part of his treatment, since Maharam Al-Ashkar, in his responsum (#35 discussed in Chapter 7) quotes the *Mikhtam* as agreeing with Rashba and *Orchot Chayyim*, both of whom quote the second part of Ra'avad's treatment about hair outside the covering and what constitutes private parts of the body.

| I heard that the author of the *Mikhtam* wrote the same thing. | וכן שמעתי שכתב בעל המכתם. |

That said, since he merely states that "he heard the author of the *Mikhtam* said this," it is clear that he does not have the text in front of him. Thus, it is also possible that he is referring to another work by the same author (now lost), or, more probably, he is confusing the *HaHashlama* or the *Meorot* with the *Mikhtam*.

14. Sefer Amudei Golah – Sefer Mitzvot Katan

Sefer Amudei Golah (also known as *Sefer Mitzvot Katan* or *Katzar*, meaning *The Short Book of Mitzvot*, and known by the acronym *Semak*) is a work of halakha written by R. Isaac of Corbeil (ca. 1210–1280). He wrote the book as a reaction to the Semag, with two goals in mind. First, he wanted to produce a shorter book that would be useful to the average Jew. Second, he wanted to advance the halakha as understood in France and counteract the powerful influence that Rambam's work had on the Semag and thereby in his native France. The Semak's treatment of *dat Moshe* and *dat Yisrael* is a classic example of this latter phenomenon.

In mitzvah 184 (standard edition; 181 Oxford; 182 Constantinople), R. Isaac deals with the passage in b. Ketubot:

| To divorce one's wife, as it is written, "If a man finds evidence of sexual misconduct on her part, he shall write her a bill of divorce and place it in her hand" (Deut. 24:1). | לגרש את האשה דכתיב 'כי מצא ערות דבר וכתב לה ספר כריתות ונתן בידה'. |
| *Evidence of sexual misconduct* – such as violating *dat Moshe*: | ערות דבר – כגון עוברת על דת משה: |

a. Feeding [her husband] untithed food,	א. מאכילתו שאינו מעושר,
b. Having intercourse with him during her menstrual period,	ב. ומשמשתו נדה,
c. Not setting apart the dough offering,	ג. ולא קוצה לו חלה,
d. Making vows and not fulfilling them.	ד. ונודרת ואינ[ה] מקיימת.
Or such as violating *dat Yehudit*:	וכגון עוברת על דת יהודית:
a. Going out to the marketplace with her hair exposed, even with a *kalta* on her head if she goes out into the public domain – in our society, the hair net is called *kupia* instead of *kalta* – but it is permissible to go from one courtyard to another by way of an alley.	א. שיוצאה בשוק וראשה פרועה, אפילו קלתה על ראשה אם יוצאה לרשות הרבים, ולדידן שבכה שקורין קופי״א[41] במקום קלתה.[42]
b. Weaving with red (rouge?) on her face – R. Chananel explained that she spins red wool near her face so that it casts a red glow on her cheeks.	אבל מחצר לחצר דרך מבוי שרי ב. וטוה ורד כנגד פניה, פירש רבינו חננאל שטווה צמר אדום כנגד פניה וכדי שיפול אדמומית על פניה
c. Acting flirtatiously with the young men.	ג. ומשחקת עם הבחורים.

From the above, one can see that R. Isaac of Corbeil believes that all of the laws of hair covering belong to the category of *dat Yehudit*. The Semak had R. Moshe of Coucy's *Sefer Mitzvot Gadol* (Semag) in front of him, which explicitly rules that uncovering one's head entirely is a violation of *dat Moshe*, as is the view of Rambam as expressed in the *Mishneh Torah*. R. Isaac does not rule in accordance with the Semag. Instead, he maintains that the prohibition of uncovering hair is entirely within the category of *dat Yehudit*, returning to the language of the Mishnah itself and, like the Tosafot, ignores the gloss in the Talmud as well as the rewrite of the halakha as presented in the *Mishneh Torah* and the Semag.

R. Isaac also deals with the passage in b. Berachot:

---

41. The Oxford MS has הוטלי״ן.
42. I indented this line since R. Aharon of Lunel refers to this line as being a gloss of Rabbeinu Peretz. It is well known that the glosses on *Sefer Amudei Golah* were often incorporated into the text of the work without comment and it is incredibly hard to disentangle glosses from the original.

That there not be seen in you some base matter – as it says (Deut. 23:15): 'and no base matter should be seen [by God] in you.' The Sages said: "If a person was washing in sullied waters where his nudity cannot be seen, he can sit in his spot and recite [the Shema], but if the waters were clear and he can sully them he should do so, if not he should cover himself with his garment against his chest." This was the practice of R. Tam, and the same applies to the Grace after Meals, and similar things.

Similarly, if a handbreadth of a woman's [flesh] is exposed, a man should not recite [blessings] until he turns his face away from her, even if she is his wife, as we said in the third chapter of b. Berachot, if a man was sleeping in bed with his wife – and a man's wife counts as if she is an extension of his own body – even if their bodies are touching skin to skin, he just turns his face and places the blanket against his breast and recites [the Shema].

The same rule applies for his minor sons and daughters, but not if they are adults, like the girl when she turns twelve years of age, until the blanket divides between them.

It is forbidden to recite [the Shema] in the presence of nudity covered by something transparent, since either way it can be seen. The same goes of women's hair.

שלא יראה בך ערות דבר שנאמר 'לא יראה בך ערות דבר.' ואמרו חכמים: היה רוחץ במים עכורים שאין ערותו נראית יושב במקומו וקורא ואם צלולין הם ויכול לעכרן עוכרן ואם לא מתכסה בבגד כנגד לבו. וכן היה נוהג ר"ת וכן לענין ברכת המזון וכיוצא בו.

וכן טפח באשה ערוה אם הוא מגולה. ולא יקרא עד שיחזיר פניו ממנה ואפילו היא אשתו כדאמרינן בפרק מי שמתו. היה ישן עם אשתו אשתו כגופו ואף על פי שנוגעים בקרוב בשר מלמטה הופך פניו וחוצץ בטליתו כנגד לבו וקורא.

וכן בניו ובנותיו הקטנים אבל לא הגדולים כגון תינוק בן י"ב שנה ויום אחד עד שיפסיק כל הטלית ביניהם.

וערוה בעששית אסור לקרות כנגד' דמכל מקום נראית היא. וכן שער באשה ערוה.

In this text, R. Isaac makes clear that he understands the passage in b. Berachot to be referring to the laws of reciting the Shema. As such, these laws do not reflect on what the required norms might be, only that given certain areas are generally covered, a man may not recite the Shema in the presence of said areas when uncovered. Thus, since there is no attempt either here or in the discussion of hair covering in the laws of divorce to argue for this law being a Torah law or *dat Moshe*, it seems clear that the entire obligation is rightly categorized as *dat Yehudit* and is dependent on the practices of modest Jewish women.[43]

15. Or Zarua

In his *Or Zarua* (*Taharat Keriat Shema ve-Tefillah* 133), R. Isaac of Vienna quotes a number of interpretations. Nevertheless, the thrust of the interpretations limits the scope of the laws either to areas that are usually covered or to during the recitation of the Shema.

Rav Mari said to Rav Pappa: "If hair is sticking out of her clothing, what is the rule?" [Rav Pappa] called this: "Hair, hair." R. Chananel explained: "If hair was sticking out of her clothing, but her flesh was covered, this is not an issue of improper exposure, because it is hair and not flesh. And the fact that Rav Kahana[44] called Rav Mari: 'Hair,' this means that the hair is just hair and not flesh, similar to when someone was called 'Gentile, gentile.'"[45] – This was the interpretation of R. Chananel.	אמר לי' רב מרי לרב פפא שער יוצא לה בבגדה מהו קרי עלי' שער שער. פי' ר"ח הי' שער יוצא מתוך בגדה ובשרה מכוסה אין בו משום ערוה כי שער הוא ולא בשר וזה שקרא רב כהנא על רב מרי שער שער כלו' השער שער הוא ולא בשר כיוצא בו קרי' עלי' גוי גוי ע"כ פי' ר"ח.
That which Shmuel said, that a woman's hair is an erotic stimulus, for it says "Your hair is like a flock of goats" – My teacher, R. Yehuda bar Yitzchak said that this was not	והא דאמר שמואל שער באשה ערוה שנאמר שערך כעדר העזים פי' מורי רבינו יהודה בר יצחק דלאו לעניו

---

43. R. Peretz. As a comment on the above halakha, R. Peretz writes:

8) In the *Book of Mitzvot* (Semag) it says: "This means specifically gazing at it, but to read Shema in its presence would not be [forbidden], as we are not strict about reciting [Shema] in the presence of the hair of virgins, who keep their hair exposed.	ח) יש בספר מצות דוקא להסתכל בה אבל לקרות כנגדן לא שאין אנו נזהרין לקרות כנגד שער בתולות פרועות ראש.

To put this comment in perspective, I think it is important to note that whereas this leniency, i.e., following Rabbeinu Tam's point about hair of non-married women, would be novel for the Semag, since that work is strict like Rambam, for the *Amudei Golah* it is already a given. Most probably R. Isaac did not reference it because he did not need to; certainly, it seems most logical to believe that the *Amudei Golah* would agree with this statement.

44. Above it was Rav Pappa; there seems to be some textual confusion here.
45. The reference is to b. Chullin 19b, where R. Yochanan calls R. Elazar this after he asks him a certain question about the difference between two different slaughtering mistakes.

said in reference to the recitation of Shema, and we are not strict to avoid saying Shema before the exposed hair of virgins. This is in contrast to the explanation of R. Yosef, who explained [Shmuel's statement] to be in reference to the recitation of the Shema.

R. [Yitzchak] said: "A handbreadth of a woman's [exposed flesh] is an erotic stimulus." With regard to what? If this is meant to prohibit [a man's] looking at it – did not Rav Sheshet [already] say: "Why does the verse list exposed jewelry together with hidden jewelry? This is to teach you that anyone who looks at the little finger of a woman is considered as if he were looking at her private parts."! This is not a problem; one is in reference to being in the presence of another woman, and the other is in reference to a person's own wife, and in regard to the recitation of the Shema.

R. Chananel explained that exposed jewelry means the ring, the armlet and the bracelet, which are jewelry worn on the arms. The hidden jewelry refers to the *atz'adah*, which is worn on the legs, and the *kumaz*, which adorns the private parts, which is the place of harlotry. Therefore, it is forbidden to recite the Shema before an exposed handbreadth of the flesh of a man's wife in a place which is generally covered, until she covers it, but it is forbidden to recite the Shema before any other woman, even if less than a handbreadth of flesh in a place that is generally covered is exposed.

Rav [Chisda] said: "A woman's calf is considered erotic stimulus, for [the verse] states: '*Reveal* the calf, pass through the rivers,' and it is written: 'Your nudity shall be *revealed*, even your disgrace shall be seen.'" – This was stated with regard to the recitation of the Shema.

ק״ש איירי וגם אין אנו נזהרין לקרות ק״ש לפני בתולות פרועות ראש ודלא כפי׳ ה״ר יוסף שפי׳ דלענין ק״ש איירי:

א״ר [יצחק] טפח באשה ערוה. למאי אילימא לאסתכולי בה והא אמר רב ששת ״למה מנה הכתוב תכשיטין שבחוץ כנגד תכשיטין שבפנים לומר לך כל המסתכל באצבע קטנה של אשה כאלו מסתכל במקום התורף.״ ל״ק הא לאחרת הא לאשתו ולק״ש.

פי׳ ר״ח תכשיטין שבחוץ הן טבעת עגיל וצמיד שהן תכשיטי ידים תכשיטין שבפנים אצעדה וכומז אצעדה ברגלים והכומז במקום התורף שהוא מקום זמה הלכך טפח מבשר אשתו שמגולה במקום שרגיל להיות מכוסה אסור לקרות ק״ש עד שתכסה ובאשה אחרת אפי׳ בפחות מטפח שנתגלה מבשרה במקום הראוי להיות מכוסה אסור לקרות ק״ש עד שתכסה:

אמר רב [חסדא] שוק באשה ערוה שנא׳ גלי שוק עברי נהרות וכתי׳ תגל ערותך גם תראה חרפתך לענין ק״ש איתמר.

> Shmuel said: "The voice of a woman is considered suggestive, as it states: 'for your voice is sweet and your appearance attractive'" – This was not stated with regard to the recitation of Shema, since she herself recites the Shema.
>
> אמר (רב ששת) [שמואל] קול באשה ערוה שנא' כי קולך ערב ומראך נאוה. לאו לענין ק"ש איתמר דהיא גופה קורא ק"ש:

In the paragraph about hair, the *Or Zarua* records a debate between R. Yehuda and R. Yosef. R. Yosef believes that the statement calling hair erva refers to its status during the recitation of the Shema. R. Yehuda bar Yitzchak of Paris, however, believes that this quote is not related to recitation of the Shema at all. His proof for this is telling. He argues that it cannot refer to the recitation of the Shema since we do, in fact, recite the Shema before the exposed hair of unmarried women.

This point fits well with the *Or Zarua*'s final point. He argues that a woman's voice being erva also cannot refer to during the recitation of the Shema since, inevitably, she hears her own voice when she recites it. In other words, the *Or Zarua*, following his teacher R. Yehuda of Paris, sees the Shema prohibition as relating to objective nudity. He does not feel that it is about attraction but appropriateness. Therefore, if we are allowed to recite Shema in the presence of the hair of unmarried women or their voices, these things cannot be erva objectively speaking. Furthermore, hair is "just hair" as the *Or Zarua* states in the name of R. Chananel. Objective erva is flesh that is generally covered, even less than a handbreadth.[46] What is left, then, is the prohibition of ogling. It is forbidden for men to ogle women, since that is the kind of looking that brings on *hirhur* (sexual thoughts). This prohibition extends to ogling her hair or even listening to her voice.

16. R. Asher ben Yechiel (Rosh)

As already demonstrated above, Rosh, in his *Tosafot*, describes a woman going out with her hair uncovered as being in violation of *dat Yehudit*, as opposed to *dat Moshe*. This description fits well with his overall interpretation of the Mishnah on hair covering in Ketubot. Rosh, in his comments

---

46. How the calf is supposed to fit into this is hard to say, since the *Or Zarua* doesn't tell us. The simplest explanation is that the reality of his time and that of the Talmud is that the calf was generally covered and that this derasha would not have been offered in a society where the calf was generally exposed.

on this pericope (m. Ketubot 7:9), begins by quoting the Mishnah. He then offers an overall interpretive framework for it:

> The rule that a woman who violates *dat Moshe* and *dat Yehudit* does not receive her ketubah payment applies specifically to cases in which she causes her husband to sin, such as those in our Mishnah and the like – for instance, feeding him forbidden fats or blood, or making vows and not fulfilling them, for one's children [die on account of this sin]. However, if a woman violates other prohibitions, such as if she herself were to consume a forbidden item, she does not forfeit her ketubah. But with regard to *dat Yehudit*, it is on account of her brazenness and on account of the suspicion of infidelity that [her husband] is able to deprive her of her ketubah.
>
> האי דעוברת על דת משה ויהודית אין לה כתובה היינו בדבר שהיא מכשילתו כי הנך דמתניתין וכיוצא בהם כגון שהאכילתו חלב או דם וכן נודרת ואינה מקיימת בשביל בניו. אבל אם היתה עוברת בשאר עבירות כגון שהיא עצמה אכלה דבר איסור לא הפסידה כתובתה. ודת יהודית משום חציפותא ומשום חשד זנות הוא דמפסדה.

In this analysis, Rosh offers a clear distinction between *dat Moshe* and *dat Yehudit*. *Dat Moshe* is about causing the husband to sin, or, as in the case of the broken vows, endangering the lives of his children. However, *dat Yehudit* is about humiliating the husband, by dressing provocatively or acting flirtatiously in public and with other men. From this we see that, according to Rosh, a woman having her hair uncovered should not be considered to have violated *dat Moshe* because she is not causing her husband to sin; rather, she should only be considered to have violated *dat Yehudit* (and only in a time and place that uncovered hair would indicate impudence and cause suspicion of infidelity). However, Rosh continues to quote the Talmudic pericope almost as is, following Rif's shortened version of the text.

> "*Dat Yehudit* – going out with her hair exposed." [Going out with] her hair exposed is a Torah prohibition! For it is written: "And he shall expose the hair of the woman" (Num. 5:18); And the school of R. Yishmael taught: "This is a warning to the daughters of Israel not to go out with their hair exposed"! R. Yehuda said in the name
>
> דת יהודית יוצאה וראשה פרוע. ראשה פרוע דאורייתא הוא! דכתיב: 'ופרע את ראש האשה.' ותנא דבי רבי ישמעאל: "אזהרה לבנות ישראל שלא יצאו בפריעת ראש." אמר רב יהודה אמר שמואל: "דאורייתא בקלתה

of Shmuel: "As a matter of Torah law a *kalta* would be sufficient, but regarding *dat Yehudit* even a *kalta* would be insufficient."[47] R. Assi said in the name of R. Yochanan: "[One who goes out in] *kalta* has not violated [the prohibition of going out with] her hair exposed." Abaye, or alternatively R. Kahana, stated: "[R. Yochanan's ruling is meant to apply to a woman who goes] from one courtyard to another by way of a thoroughfare." Yerushalmi: A courtyard that many people use as a pass-through is [considered] as a thoroughfare; a thoroughfare through which people generally do not pass is [considered] as a courtyard.

שפיר דמי, דת יהודית אפי' בקלתה נמי אסור." א"ר אסי א"ר יוחנן: "קלתה אין בה משום פריעת הראש." אמר אביי ואיתימא רב כהנא: "מחצר לחצר ודרך מבוי." ירושלמי (בפירקין הלכה ז) חצר שהרבים בוקעין בו הרי הוא כמבוי שאין הרבים בוקעין בו הרי הוא כחצר.

'Weaving in the marketplace' – Rav Yehuda said: "She exposes her arms to the men." Rav Chisda said in the name of Avimi: "She spins red wool before her face." 'Conversing with random men' – Rav Yehuda said in the name of Shmuel: "Being playful with young men."

וטווה בשוק - אמר רב יהודה: "במראה זרועותיה אל בני אדם." אמר רב חסדא אמר אבימי: "בטווה ורד כנגד פניה." ומדברת עם כל אדם - אמר רב יהודה אמר שמואל "במשחקת עם בחורים."

We concluded in the 4th chapter of Sotah (25a) that one is required to warn a woman who violates *dat* before her ketubah payment can be cancelled, and if her husband wishes to remain with her, the question is posed there whether he is permitted to remain with her or not, and it is never answered, so we do not force him to leave her; however it is a *mitzvah* to divorce her. Thus wrote Ra'avad.

ומסקינן בסוטה פרק ארוסה (דף כה א) דעוברת על דת צריכה התראה להפסידה כתובתה ואם רצה הבעל לקיימה מיבעיא התם אם יכול לקיימה אם לאו ולא איפשיטא ולא כייפינן ליה להוציא ומיהו מצוה לגרשה. כך כתב הראב"ד ז"ל:

---

47. On this line, the *Hagahot HaAsheri* (R. Israel of Krems, late 14th to early 15th century) records the following comment in the name of R. Chezekiah of Magdeberg (13th century):

> This is so in the public domain, but in a courtyard, even the absence of a *kalta* is not considered a violation, even of *dat Yehudit* – Maharich.

> והיינו ברשות הרבים, ובחצר לא הוי אפילו דת יהודית, אפילו בלא קלתא - מהרי"ח.

It is difficult to know how Rosh understands Shmuel's position here. If one assumes that Rosh follows Shmuel as a matter of halakha, this would imply that a woman going out with totally uncovered hair would violate *dat Moshe*, despite the fact that Rosh explains *dat Moshe* as being exclusively about either causing the man to sin or endangering the life of his children. There are a number of solutions to this problem. One could suggest that the explanation Rosh gives for *dat Moshe* is his overall thinking, but that totally uncovered hair would be an exception. Alternatively, one can assume that Rosh is offering what he thinks is the meaning of *dat Moshe*, but includes Shmuel's position anyway, even though he and the rest of the text follow R. Yochanan and not Shmuel.

Although the interpretation by Rosh's son, R. Jacob, of his father's comment does not provide a definitive answer, it is surely instructive to see how R. Jacob interprets his father's comment as a matter of halakha. In his short work summarizing his father's rulings, the *Kitzur Piskei HaRosh* (m. Ketubot 7:9), R. Jacob writes:

These [women] may be divorced without a ketubah payment: One who feeds [her husband] forbidden food, which he finds out about afterwards. If she is known to be menstruating but she tells him that she is pure and he sleeps with her, she is divorced. So too, if she makes vows but does not keep them. Additionally, if she goes out with a *kalta* on her head, without a veil, to the marketplace or to a through-alley or to a courtyard which the masses use to cross through. However, if [she goes out to a courtyard that] the masses do not use as a cut-through, or to an alley that is not a through-street, she may not be divorced [without payment]. Additionally, if she spins red before her face or speaks with random men – also if she curses his father before his face or before his children. Also, if she demands sex in a loud voice or, when she is demanding it, she fights with him to the point that others hear her voice – in all of these cases she may be divorced without a ketubah payment.	ואלו יוצאות שלא בכתובה: המאכילתו דבר איסור ונודע לו אחר כך....הוחזקה נדה בשכנותיה ואמרה לו שהיא טהורה ובא עליה תצא, וכן נודרת ואינה מקיימת. וכן יוצאה בקלתה על ראשה בלא צעיף לרשות הרבים ובמבוי המפולש או בחצר שרבים בוקעין בו, אבל אם אין רבים בוקעין בו ומבוי שאינו מפולש לא תצא. וכן אם היא טוה בשוק שמראה זרועותיה לבני אדם או שטוה ורד כנגד פניה וכן מדברת עם הבחורים. וכן מקללת אביו בפניו או בפני בניו. וכן תובעת תשמיש בקול רם או כשתובעה לתשמיש מריבה עמו עד שנשמע קולה – בכולם תצא בלא כתובה.

The text here is ambiguous. R. Jacob does not include the terms *dat Moshe* or *dat Yehudit* in this presentation. Nevertheless, he seems to group hair covering as it is grouped in the Mishnah, with the second list. On the other hand, he only mentions going out with a kalta. What if she were to go out without a kalta? Would that be a greater violation? Or is he just saying "even with a kalta, but certainly without a kalta" without implying that there is a Torah law/Jewish custom dichotomy? It is unclear, but it is worth pointing out that in his own book, the *Tur* (which we will look at in the next chapter), he explicitly supports the latter.

Rosh also deals with this text in a responsum (32:8). The case Rosh is presented with deals with a number of Jewish women who "converted" to Christianity out of fear during a time of persecution. Now that the persecution has ceased, they wish to return to their Jewish lives and their husbands. After discussing the question of whether the women should be allowed to return to their husbands (there was a fear that they may have had relations with other men consensually while they were among the gentiles), Rosh turns to the question of whether they should be considered to have the status of women who violated *dat*, such that they could be divorced without payment of their ketubah.

There are those who wish to argue that she should be considered to have violated *dat* such that she forfeits her ketubah payment.... Nonetheless, it seems to me that she does not forfeit her ketubah payment, because a woman is only considered to have violated *dat Moshe* if she [actively] caused her husband to sin, similar to those [actions] listed in the Mishnah (b. Ketubot 72a): feeding him untithed food, not setting apart the dough offering, making vows and not fulfilling them, or having intercourse with him during the period of her menstruation.	ויש רוצין לומר, שיש להן דין עוברת על דת להפסיד כתובתה...מ"מ נראה לי דלא הפסידה כתובתה; דלא מיקריא עוברת על דת משה אלא בדברים שמכשלת בהם הבעל, כדברים המפורשים במשנה (כתובות עב): מאכילתו שאינו מעושר ולא קוצה לו חלה ונודרת ואינה מקיימת ומשמשתו נדה.
The proof to this proposition is that the Talmud states regarding a woman who makes vows and does not fulfill them – "As our master stated, on account of the sin of [unfulfilled] vows, one's children die." We see that the sin of not fulfilling her vows is itself not sufficient for her to be considered	תדע לך, דקאמר בגמרא, בנודרת ואינה מקיימת: דאמר מר: בעון נדרים בנים מתים; אלמא, בשביל העון שאינה מקיימת נדרה לא מיקריא עוברת על דת להפסידה כתובתה, אלא שגורמת תקלה

to have violated *dat* [*Moshe*] such that she would forfeit her ketubah payment – only because her actions cause harm to her husband by leading to the death of his children [is she considered such]. In the Jerusalem Talmud this is stated very clearly.

לבעלה שבניו מתים. ובגמרא ירושלמית מפורש היטב.

Here again, Rosh reiterates his overall theory that *dat Moshe* is about causing the husband to sin or hurting him in some way. Although one could argue that by going out with uncovered hair a woman humiliated her husband and hurt him, this does not seem to resonate with Rosh. The reason this humiliation encompasses the nature of all *dat Yehudit* violations, as Rosh explained in his comments on Ketubot, is due to its brazenness; Rosh claims that it brings about suspicion of infidelity. There is no categorical way to distinguish fully uncovered hair from partially uncovered hair along this axis, as it would seem that fully uncovered hair still fits better with *dat Yehudit* (brazen and implied infidelity) than *dat Moshe* (causing him to sin or endangering his children).

To complete the picture being painted by Rosh, it is important to look at his comments on the pericope in b. Berachot as well (3:37).

Rabbi Yitzchak said: "A handbreadth of a woman's [exposed flesh] is considered an erotic stimulus (*erva*)." With regard to what? If this is meant to prohibit [a man's] looking at it, did not Rav Sheshet [already] say: "Why does the verse list regular jewelry together with erotic jewelry? This is to teach you that anyone who looks at the little finger of a woman is considered as if he were looking at her private parts."

א[מר] ר[בי] יצחק: "טפח באשה ערוה." למאי הלכתא? אילימא לאסתכולי בה, והאמר רב ששת: "למה מנה הכתוב תכשיטין שבפנים עם תכשיטין שבחוץ? לומר לך כל מי שמסתכל באצבע קטנה של אשה כאילו מסתכל במקום התורפה."

This is not a problem, one is referring to [a man in the presence of] another woman and one is referring to a man [in the presence of] his wife, and during his recitation of the Shema. In addition, it refers to a part of the woman that is usually covered, and specifically when she is with someone else, but if she is by herself, we said above that a woman may sit and separate her *challah* in the nude.

לא קשיא הא באחרת והא באשתו ולק[ריאת] ש[מע]. ודבר שרגיל להיות מכוסה באשה ודוקא באחרת אבל בעצמה הא אמרי[נן] לעיל האשה יושבת ערומה וקוצה חלתה.

Rav Chisda said: "A woman's calf is considered an erotic stimulus, for [the verse] states: '*Reveal* the calf, pass through the rivers' (Isaiah 47:2), and it is written: 'Your nudity shall be *revealed*, even your disgrace shall be seen'(Isaiah 47:3)."	ואמר רב חסדא: "שוק באשה ערוה, שנאמר: 'גלי שוק עברי נהרות,' וכתיב: 'תגל ערותך.'".
Shmuel said: "The voice of a woman is considered an erotic stimulus, as it states: 'for your voice is sweet [and your appearance attractive]' (Song 2:14)." This means that to hear [her voice at all is forbidden] and not [just] regarding reading the Shema.	אמר שמואל: "קול באשה ערוה, שנאמר: 'כי קולך ערב.'" פירוש - לשמוע ולא לענין קו[ריאת] ש[מע].
Rav Sheshet said: "The hair of a woman is considered an erotic stimulus" – [This applies to] the hair of [married] women who normally cover their hair, but it is permitted to recite [the Shema] in the presence of virgins, who normally go with their hair exposed.	אמר רב ששת: "שער באשה ערוה." - בנשים שדרכן לכסות שערן אבל בתולות שדרכן לילך פרועות מותר לקרות כנגדן.

In Rosh's recapitulation of the pericope in b. Berachot, he makes two adjustments in explaining the passage. First, he explains that the exposed handbreadth causes a problem only because what is exposed is generally covered. This is why the rabbis were so strict when they forbade even the woman's husband from reciting the Shema in her presence when she is dressed this way. Second, Rosh explains that Rav Sheshet's declaration that a woman's hair is considered an erotic stimulus only applies to a woman who usually covers her hair. However, the hair of virgins (or unmarried women) is not considered to be an erotic stimulus, since these women generally go around with their hair exposed.

Rosh's understanding of this pericope can be clarified even further when looking at his glosses on the passage in the *Tosafot HaRosh* (ad loc.).

A handbreadth [of exposed flesh] on a woman is an erotic stimulus – meaning, that which is generally covered on a woman, if a handbreadth of it is exposed it is an erotic stimulus.	טפח באשה ערוה. פי' מה שרגיל להיות מכוסה באשה אי הוי טפח ממנו מגולה הוי ערוה,
[The Talmud] asks with regard to what [was this said]? If regarding gazing upon	ופריך למאי אי לאסתכולי בה הא אפילו באצבע קטנה

her, it would even be forbidden to gaze upon her pinky, which is not generally covered.

שאין דרכו להיות מכוסה אסור להסתכל בו.

Rather the rule applies to a man's wife and refers to the recitation of the Shema. And this rule only affects other people [who are with her] but if she is by herself we already stated above that a woman may separate out *challah* sitting while in the nude.

לא צריכא אלא באשתו ולק"ש. ודוקא לאחר אבל היא עצמה הא אמרינן לעיל האשה יושבת ערומה וקוצה חלתה.

Rav Chisda said: "A woman's calf is an erotic stimulus." For one should not say that since sometimes a woman pulls up her dress she isn't always covered, we learn from this that it is considered an erotic stimulus.

ואמר רב חסדא שוק באשה ערוה. דלא תימא פעמים שהאשה מגבהת בגדיה ואין דרכה להיות מכוסה קמ"ל דהוי ערוה.

A woman's hair is an erotic stimulus – for married women, who generally cover their hair, but [this does not apply] to virgins who generally go out with their hair exposed, it would be permitted to recite Shema in their presence.

שער באשה ערוה. בנשים נשואות שדרכן לכסות שערן אבל בתולות שדרכן לילך פרועות ראש מותר לקרות ק"ש כנגדן.

A woman's voice is an erotic stimulus – this was not said regarding the reciting of Shema but as a general prohibition for a man to listen to women's voices.

וקול באשה ערוה. לאו לענין ק"ש קאמר אלא שאסור לשמוע קול הנשים.

Rosh's comments in the *Tosafot HaRosh* are virtually identical to his comments in his halakhot, except in the former he adds an explanation for R. Chisda's position. He claims that the reality which Rav Chisda addresses is that women generally wore dresses long enough to cover their calves, but that they would lift them above their calves at times, presumably when walking over rough terrain or areas that were wet or muddy.[48] Rav Chisda's point, according to Rosh, is that even though it would be usual for men to see women doing so, this would not, ipso facto,

---

48. This comment supports what I have argued in a number of places, that "*shok*" in Rabbinic literature always means "calf" and not "thigh" as it is often mistranslated. Whereas it seems reasonable that women in Talmudic times would, as a general practice, lift their dresses over their calves in order to avoid getting wet, or dirty, or to avoid tripping on rough terrain, it seems well-nigh impossible to imagine that

define calves as "generally exposed." It seems safe to assume, then, that in a society where women's calves were, in fact, generally exposed, Rav Chisda's point would not apply, and the calf would no longer be defined as an erotic stimulus.

Rosh believes that the problem of reciting the Shema before an erotic stimulus applies to women who are dressed in such a way that they expose more than they customarily would. The only exception in this passage is Shmuel's comment about voice. Rosh does not believe that this rule is part of the rules about Shema but understands it as a statement of independent force – i.e., it is forbidden for a man to listen to a woman's voice irrespective of whether he is reciting the Shema.

Rosh's opinion is summarized by his son, R. Jacob, in the *Kitzur Piskei HaRosh*.

| An exposed handbreadth on a man's wife is considered an erotic stimulus, and it is forbidden to recite the Shema in her presence, even though she may sit in the nude and separate her *challah* and recite the blessing. The calf of a woman is considered an erotic stimulus, as is the hair of a married woman but not of a virgin. The voice of a woman is an erotic stimulus, and it is forbidden to listen [to it]. | טפח מגולה באשתו ערוה, ואסור לקרות קריאת שמע כנגדה, אבל היא יושבת ערומה וקוצה לה חלתה ומברכת. שוק באשה ערוה, וכן השער בנשואה ולא בבתולה, וקול באשה ערוה, ואסור לשמוע. |

In summary, Rosh should be understood as holding that categorization of a woman's body part as erva depends entirely on societal practice. This is how he reads the text in b. Berachot about the laws of Shema and the pericope in b. Ketubot about *dat Yehudit*.

17. Rekanati

R. Menachem Rekanati (c. 1250–1310) mentions this rule in three separate works. First, in his *Ta'amei HaMitzvot*, in the section dealing with sotah,[49] at the end of a long discussion of the Zohar he says the following:

| The text requires that [the priest] undo | והצריך הכתוב לסוטה פריעת |

---

modest women – in any period of time – would lift their skirts above their thighs in public as a standard practice. See note on page 419.

49. *Sefer Ta'amei HaMitzvot LehaRekanati im chelufai nuschaot*. London: Rabbi Simcha Bunim Lieberman, 1962, 72a.

> the hair of the *sotah*. And the rabbis say in b. Ketubot (72a):
>
> "And he shall undo the hair of the woman" – The school of R. Yishmael taught: "This is a warning to the daughters of Israel not to appear in public with their hair undone."
>
> Understand this.
>
> הראש, וארז"ל בכתובות (עב.)
>
> ופרע את ראש האשה - תאנה דבי ר' ישמעאל: מכאן אזהרה לבנות ישראל שלא יצאו בפריעת הראש,
>
> והבן זה.

Rekanati's comment is cryptic. Although it follows a long quote from the Zohar, it is clearly a separate treatment since he neither connects it to the Zohar nor does he quote the passage in the Zohar about hair covering from this same parasha (which we saw in the previous chapter).

We learn what Rekanati is likely hinting at here from his commentary on the Torah dealing with Bamidbar 5:7:

> And the reason for "and you shall undo the woman's hair" hints at the intention to uncover a space upon which the attribute of justice may fall upon her if she is unclean, the same as the intention behind [the verse about the man with leprosy/*tzaraat*] (Lev. 13:45) "and his hair will be undone," for the same spirit of impurity that flows upon him.
>
> In order [for women] to stay far away from this attribute, our rabbis say (b. Ketubot 72a):
>
> "And he shall undo the hair of the woman" – The school of R. Yishmael taught: This is a warning to the daughters of Israel not to appear in public with their hair undone.
>
> וטעם ופרע ראש האשה רומז על העניין המכוון להמציא מקום למדת הדין לחול עליה אם היא טמאה, כטעם וראשו יהיה פרוע (ויקרא יג:מה) לרוח הטומאה השופעת עליו
>
> ולהתרחק ממדה זו אמרו רבותינו (כתובות עב.)
>
> ופרע את ראש האשה, תאנא דבי רבי ישמעאל: מכאן אזהרה לבנות ישראל שלא יצאו בפריעת ראש.

Undone hair, according to Rekanati, has the kabbalistic meaning of allowing the spirit of impurity or God's punishment for sinful behavior, to have access to the person and flow upon him/her. Thus, he explains, the Rabbis deduced (or decreed) that all women, or at least married women, must cover or do up their hair. Whether he means that such behavior symbolically pushes away that spirit of impurity or that it has some metaphysical effect in protecting a woman from it is unclear, but this is likely what he was hinting at in his *Ta'amei HaMitzvot* as well.

Interestingly, Rekanati's halakhic treatment of hair covering is devoid of such considerations, and his approach, at least in his halakhic work, (26), generally follows the Ashkenazi poskim.

R. Elazar of Metz wrote that it is forbidden to recite any of the sanctified prayers while hearing the singing voice of a woman, but 'it is a time to act for God, abrogate your Torah' therefore we are not strict [about this law] when hearing the singing voice of women.	כתב הר"א ממיץ דאסור לקרות דבר שבקדושה בשמועת קול שיר של אשה ועת לעשות לה' הפרו תורתך הלכך אין אנו נזהרין מלשמוע שמועת שיר הנשים
The handbreadth of a woman's [exposed flesh] is an erotic stimulus only if it is a handbreadth that is generally covered, and applies even if she is his wife.	וטפח באשה ערוה היינו טפח שדרכו ליכסות ואף על פי שהיא אשתו.
That which they said that a woman's hair is an erotic stimulus, this refers to gazing upon her, but insofar as reciting [the Shema], it is an everyday occurrence that we are not strict about reciting Shema in the presence of the hair of virgins – this was the explanation of R. Tuviah in the name of R. Tam.	והא דאמרו שער באשה ערוה היינו להסתכל בה אבל לקרות לא דמעשים בכל יום שאין אנו נזהרין מלקרות כנגד שער הבתולות כך פי' רבינו טוביה בשם ר"ת.
Possibly the rule about the exposed handbreadth of a woman's [flesh] has the same application, and this seems clear from the *Sefer HaMitzvot HaKatzar* that wrote: "So too for the rule that a handbreadth of a woman's [flesh] is an erotic stimulus if exposed, and you may not recite [the Shema] until one turns his head from her" – from here it seems that if one does turn one's head it would be permitted to recite the Shema without a separation.	ושמא דאף טפח באשה ערוה ה"פ וכ"מ מספר המצות הקצר שכתב וכן טפח באשה ערוה אם היא מגולה שלא יקרא עד שיחזור פניו ממנה משמע כשמחזיר פניו שרי בלא הרחקה.
The Ra'avad wrote: "This applies specifically to a private area on her, and specifically to others because of lewd thoughts, but on her own it would not be a problem, for we have established that a woman may separate her *challah* in the nude while seated."	וכתב הראב"ד דדוקא במקום צנוע שבה ודוקא לאחרים משום הרהור אבל לעצמה לא דהא קיי"ל האשה יושבת וקוצה לה חלתה ערומה:

Rekanati understands the entire text from b. Berachot to be referring to men reciting the Shema. Next, he references three Ashkenazi leniencies. First, he quotes R. Elazar of Metz, in the *Yereim*, explaining that it is permitted to recite Shema when hearing a woman sing because it is impossible to avoid. Next, he references R. Tam, quoted by R. Tuviah, that the rule does not apply to the hair of unmarried women, since they expose their hair as a matter of course. Third, he quotes the *Sefer Amudei Golah* (Semak), who says that turning one's head away from the exposed hair is sufficient. He concludes by quoting Ra'avad, who points out that the entire definition of nudity in this passage is in reference to men; it has nothing to do with how women should dress when reciting blessings alone. In short, according to Rekanati, the rules in b. Berachot are only relevant to prayer, are meant to be practical, and are sociologically determined.

18. The Mordechai and the Hagahot Maimoniyot

The lenient interpretations of the passage in b. Berachot had a strong effect on Ashkenazi Jewish law, as can be seen by the two major complementary works of German halakha in the 13th century.

R. Mordechai ben Hillel (c. 1250–1298) published his seminal work, compiling Ashkenazi *pesak* (decision), as a compendium to R. Alfasi's *Halakhot*. In his gloss on the passage in b. Berachot (Ch. 3, #80), he writes:

It is forbidden to recite the Shema in the presence of a naked gentile – and we further say here in the Talmud that a handbreadth of a woman's [exposed flesh] is an erotic stimulus, even when it is the person's wife. This means a handbreadth [of flesh] that is generally covered. Similarly, the calf and the voice of a woman is an erotic stimulus. R. Hai Gaon explained that all of the above is in reference to reciting the Shema.	נכרי ערום אסור לקרות קריאת שמע כנגדו והכא נמי אמרינן הכא בתלמודא טפח באשה ערוה אפילו באשתו פי' טפח שדרכה להתכסות וכן שוק וקול באשה ערוה ופי' רב האי גאון דכל הני לענין ק"ש.
And R. Elazar of Metz, in the *Sefer HaYereim* wrote: "Therefore, it is forbidden to recite the Shema, or any one of the sanctified prayers while hearing the voice of a woman singing. However, in our many sins,	וכתב הר"א ממיץ בס"י: "הלכך אסור לומר דבר שבקדושה בשמיעת קול שיר של אשה ובעונותינו בין העובדי ככובים אנו יושבים

we live among the gentiles, and 'it is a time to act for God by abrogating your Torah.' Therefore, we are not strict about learning [Torah] if we can hear the voice of Aramean women." The Behag also explained the matter in line with R. Hai Gaon, as did R. Chananel.

ועת לעשות לה' הפרו תורתך הלכך אין אנו נזהרין מללמוד בשמיעת קול שיר נשים ארמאות." וכו[ך] פ[ירש] בה"ג וכו[ך] פ[ירש] ר[בינו] ח[ננאל] כדברי ר' [הא]י[50] גאון.

And Ra'aviah wrote: "All of these things that we referenced above as being inappropriate exposure – this applies specifically to areas that women do not generally expose, but for [a man to recite Shema in the presence of] a virgin who generally exposes her hair does not concern us, for there will be no inappropriate thoughts."

וכתב ראב"ה: "כל הדברים שהזכרנו למעלה לערוה דוקא בדבר שאין רגילות להגלות אבל בתולה הרגילה בגלוי שער לא חיישינן דליכא הרהור."

First, R. Mordechai believes that the entire passage is referring to rules for men reciting Shema. In reading the passage this way, R. Mordechai follows the lead of R. Hai Gaon, R. Chananel and the Behag (as discussed in Chapter 3). Furthermore, R. Mordechai adds the leniency of the *Sefer HaYereim*, that when there is no choice, one can learn Torah – the equivalent of reciting Shema halakhically – in the presence of the singing voice of gentile women. Finally, R. Mordechai records the leniency of Ra'aviah (the same as that of R. Tam) that the rule applies only to that which is unusual. This is an even more lenient ruling than that of the *Yereim*, since Ra'aviah doesn't use the language of "abrogating Torah" but simply records this as the halakha.

A similar treatment appears in the glosses of R. Meir ben Yekutiel HaKohen (c. 1260–1298)[51] on the *Mishneh Torah* called *Hagahot Maimoniyot* (*Mishneh Torah, Keriat Shema* 3:16).[52] He writes:

---

50. Some texts read Yehudai.
51. Both men died in the Rindfleish massacres, which is why they share the same death year.
52. In that passage, Rambam writes:

The entire body of a woman is nudity, therefore a man should not look at a woman's body when he is reciting [the *Shema*]; even his wife, if a handbreadth of her body is exposed, he should not recite [the *Shema*] facing her.

וכל גוף האשה ערוה לפיכך לא יסתכל בגוף האשה כשהוא קורא ואפילו אשתו ואם היה מגולה טפח מגופה לא יקרא כנגדה.

The Behag explained that this [law] applies to a man's wife, but with another woman, even less than a handbreadth, and similarly for a woman's calf, hair and voice – it is forbidden to recite Shema in the presence of any of these. R. Chananel explained it this way. Regarding the voice, even though it cannot be seen with the eyes, [hearing] it may still bring about lewd thoughts.

All of these apply specifically to areas that women do not generally expose, but for [a man to recite Shema in the presence of] a virgin who generally exposes her hair does not concern us, for there will be no inappropriate thoughts. And the same applies to the voice which he is accustomed to hearing.

60) ופי' בה"ג הני מילי אשתו אבל באשה אחרת אפילו דבר קטן מטפח וכן שוק באשה ושער וקול באשה כל הני אסור לקרות ק"ש כנגדן וכו' פי' רבינו חננאל וקול אף על גב דאין נראה לעינים הרהור מיהא איכא.

וכל אלה דוקא שאין רגילות להגלות אבל בתולה הרגילה בגלוי שער לא חיישינן דליכא הרהור וכן בקול הרגיל בו.

Like his colleague R. Mordechai, the *Hagahot Maimoniyot* invokes the interpretation of the Behag and R. Chananel. Thus he also believes that the passage in b. Berachot is only relevant to men reciting the Shema. Although he does not invoke the leniency of the *Sefer HaYereim*, he does reference Ra'aviah and the idea that the prohibition applies only to seeing parts of women usually covered, as Ra'aviah (based on R. Tam) said about the hair of unmarried women.

19. The Agudah

The halakhic work *Sefer HaAgudah* is organized to follow the order of the Talmud. R. Alexander Suslin HaKohen (d. 1349) analyzes the passages from b. Berachot and b. Ketubot in turn. In his treatment of the b. Berachot (3:73) passage, the *Agudah* makes two points.

A handbreadth of [exposed flesh] on a woman is an erotic stimulus; the calf of a woman is an erotic stimulus, on the spots that she usually covers. The hair of a woman is an erotic stimulus; the voice of a woman is an erotic stimulus. Ri explained that all of these rules refer to [a prohibition upon a man] to gaze upon them, but

טפח באשה ערוה, שוק באשה ערוה במקום שדרך לכסות. שער באשה ערוה קול באשה ערוה. פירש ר"י כל זה איירי להסתכל בה, אבל לענין קריאת שמע שרי לקרות אם ראש אשה מגולה.

> insofar as the recitation of the Shema it is permitted for a man to recite Shema in the presence of a woman with uncovered hair.

First, the *Agudah* interprets the statements about the exposed handbreadth and the calf to be about areas that are usually covered. In other words, the rules about both (including the calf) are subjectively determined. Something is an erotic stimulus if it is usually covered but uncovered in front of the man reciting the Shema.

Second, the *Agudah* interprets the statements about hair and voice in line with Ri. As described above, Ri believes these two rules have to do with gazing. Hence, there would be no prohibition of reciting Shema before a woman's hair because hair is often uncovered. (As described above, it is unclear if he refers here to the hair of unmarried women or all women.) The same applies to a woman's voice. The fact that Jewish men in this period heard women singing as a matter of course is referenced specifically by the *Sefer HaYereim*.

The *Agudah* discusses hair again in his treatment of the passage in b. Ketubot (7:103–104).

> What is [a violation of] *dat Moshe*? Feeding him untithed food. Having relations with him during her menstrual period. Not removing *challah* when preparing dough. Making vows she does not keep. What is [a violation of] *dat Yehudit*? Going out with her hair exposed from a courtyard to another courtyard by way of an alley. Spinning [thread] in the marketplace and showing her arms. Speaking with random men. Cursing his parents in front of his children. R. Tarfon said: "Also the loudmouth, whose voice can be heard on intimate matters." Yerushalmi: Regarding women about whom it is said that they may be divorced without a ketubah payment – they need to receive prior warning.

ואיזו דת משה? מאכילתו שאינו מעושר. משמשתו נידה. ולא קוצה לה חלה. ונודרת ואינה מקיימת. איזה דת יהודית? יוצאה וראשה פרועה מחצר לחצר דרך מבוי. וטווה בשוק ומראה זרועותיה. ומדברת עם כל אדם. ומקללת יולדיו בפני מולידיו. רבי טרפון אמר אף הקולנית משמעת על עסקי תשמיש. ירוש' [ה"ו] נשים שאמרו יוצאות בלא כתובה צריכה התראה.

It is hard to gauge the position of the *Agudah* here. In the *Sefer HaAgudah*, no prohibition regarding hair covering is listed under *dat Moshe*; however, the prohibition of entirely uncovering one's head is not found at all in the *Agudah*, neither in the category of *dat Moshe* nor that of *dat Yehudit*. From the fact that the *Agudah* references women with uncovered hair in b. Berachot as a matter of course, it would appear difficult to imagine that he believed in an objective prohibition against uncovering hair as in Rambam's works.

20. Talmidei Rabbeinu Yonah

The position of R. Hai Gaon (discussed in Chapter 3) was quoted by the students of R. Yonah Gerundi (d. 1263) in their glosses on Rif (Berachot 17a).

R. Hai Gaon wrote that this is true with regard to any handbreadth of a woman's flesh that is generally covered, that when it is in view it is forbidden to recite the Shema in her presence, for a handbreadth of a woman's [exposed flesh] is considered *erva*. Additionally, one should not recite the Shema when a woman is singing, since the voice of a woman is considered suggestive.	וכתב רבינו האי גאון ז"ל דהוא הדין לכל אשה שמגלה טפח במקום מכוסה שבה שאסור לקרוא כנגדה דטפח באשה ערוה וכן אין לו לקרות בשעה שמנגנת דקול באשה ערוה.
However, [reciting the Shema] in the presence of her face or any other part of her which is generally exposed, or while she is speaking regularly – this is permitted.	אבל כנגד פניה או כנגד מקום שאין דרך לכסות או בשעה שמדברת כדרכה מותר.
In fact, even if she is singing, but he can pay attention to his prayers such that he isn't really hearing her and not paying her any mind – this is permitted, and he should not stop his recitation. Also, when a handbreadth of her flesh is exposed, it would only be forbidden [to recite the Shema] while he was looking at her, but if she just happens to be in view, this would be permitted.	ואפי' בשעה שמנגנת אם הוא יכול לכוין בלבו לתפלתו בעניין שאינו שומע אותה ואינו משים לבו אליה מותר ואין לו להפסיק קריאתו וכן כשמגולה טפח אינו אסור אלא כשמסתכל בה אבל בראייה בעלמא מותר:

As explained in Chapter 3, R. Hai Gaon's lenient position is also adopted by the students of R. Yonah. Regarding the rules of proper concentration during the recitation of the Shema, there are three categories of exposure to erotic stimuli:

1. Paying attention to unusual erotic stimuli.

2. Being in the presence of unusual erotic stimuli but not paying attention.
3. Being in the presence of a woman with the usual level of exposure to her skin and voice.

According to R. Hai Gaon, it is clear that the prohibitions recorded in b. Berachot are referring to unusual erotic stimuli, and not to being in the presence of the mundane. This is because to R. Hai, the entire sugya is about proper focus during the recitation of the Shema. There is no reason to think that a man cannot focus when in the presence of women dressed normally and speaking regularly.

However, R. Hai argues, what one should do when in the presence of a woman with exposed flesh beyond the usual places or when she is singing really depends upon the person. Presumably, the average person would be distracted and should, therefore, not recite the Shema. However, if the person feels that he can be in the presence of a woman dressed or behaving in this manner and not be distracted, he may recite the Shema. This last point is similar to the Semak's opinion that turning one's head should be sufficient.

21. Ohel Moed

In his halakhic work, *Ohel Moed* (*Keriat Shema* 5:5), R. Samuel b. Meshulem Yerundi (b. 1335) follows the contours of R. Tam's pesak.

It is forbidden to recite Shema in the presence of a naked gentile, for the term *erva* is used in reference to the sons of Noah, as it says (Gen. 9:23): "And they did not look upon their father's nudity (*erva*)."	גוי ערום אסור לקרות ק״ש כנגדו דהא כתי[ב] ערוה בב״נ דכתיב וערות אביהם לא ראו
And a handbreadth of a woman's exposed [flesh] which she generally covers is like *erva*, and even if it is his wife it is forbidden for him to recite the Shema in her presence.	וטפח מגולה באשה במקום שדרכה לכסות הרי הוא כערוה ואפי׳ היא אשתו אסור לקרות את שמע כנגדה.
A woman's calf is an erotic stimulus, and the voice of a woman, if it is a greeting, is forbidden. A woman's hair – it is forbidden to gaze upon it but it is permitted to recite the Shema in its presence. Similarly, R. Jacob wrote that it is an everyday occurrence that we recite [the Shema] in the presence	שוק באשה ערוה. קול באשה אם היא שאלת שלום אסור. שער באשה אסור להסתכל בו אבל לקרוא את שמע נגד שערה מותר וכן כתב רבי׳ יעקב ומעשים בכל יום שאנו קורים כנגד שער הבתולות

of the hair of virgins. And with hair that sticks out of her covering which is never covered, we are not concerned, since he is used to that hair. The singing voice of a woman, even his wife, is an erotic stimulus.

ובשערה שחוץ לצמתה שאינו מתכס' אין חוששין משום שהוא רגיל באותו שער. קול של זמר אפי' באשתו ערוה.

The *Ohel Moed* seems to read the passage as being primarily about the recitation of the Shema, at least insofar as the exposed handbreadth and the hair are concerned. Insofar as calf and voice, he isn't clear where this fits in, although it is worth noting that he takes a strict interpretation of voice as referring to greeting with a speaking voice and not singing.

Regarding the Shema-related rules, he makes two interrelated points. He begins by describing the exposed handbreadth of a woman's flesh as areas which she generally uncovers. Second, he references R. Jacob (=Tam), stating that uncovered hair is only relevant to married women, since unmarried women don't cover their hair anyway. Thus, he seems to interpret these two rules as being subjective in nature. How this fits with the calf and voice rules is unclear.

22. Tzedah LaDerekh

The author of the work *Tzedah LaDerekh* (R. Menachem b. Aaron b. Zerah), a student of R. Yehuda, son of Rosh writes (3.2:14):

The following are to be divorced without receiving their ketubah: a wife who violates *dat Moshe* or *dat Yehudit*.

אלו יוצאות שלא בכתובה. העוברת על דת משה ויהודית.

And what is *dat Yehudit*? Going out to the marketplace or through an alley or courtyard which many people frequent in the manner of promiscuous women. Also, weaving in the marketplace and showing her arms there to people. Also weaving with red on her face in the manner of promiscuous women. Also, speaking and acting playfully with young men. Also cursing [her husband's] father in front his face or his son's face. Also, demanding intercourse in a loud voice such that the neighbors hear.

איזו היא דת יהודית היוצאת כפרוצות לרשות הרבים או למבוי מפולש או בחצר שהרבים מצויין. וכן הטווה בשוק ומראה שם זרועותיה לבני אדם. וכן בשטווה ויש על פניה ורד כדרך שעושות הפרוצות. וכן המדברת ומשחקת עם הבחורים וכן המקללת אביו בפניו או בפני בנו וכן התובעת מבעלה תשמיש בקול גדול עד ששומעין השכנים.

The list of prohibitions here follows the Mishnah without the addition of basic hair covering to the biblical prohibition. Moreover, the *Tzedah LaDerekh* clarifies that the problem with going out with uncovered hair or wearing red on the face is that it is "in the manner of promiscuous women." In other words, the behavior itself is not the problem but what such behavior conveys. Logically, such a prohibition must be dependent on social norms as well as the practice of modest and promiscuous women in a given society.

23. Rashba

The position of Rabbi Shlomo ben Adret (Rashba, 1235–1310) on whether hair covering is a Torah requirement is difficult to ascertain, since he never discusses this question explicitly. There are two responsa that offer a clue to his thinking.

CASE 1: THE ANGRY WIFE WHO EXPOSED HER HAIR

In a letter to Rabbi Chayyim Or Zarua (Responsa 1:571), Rashba offers his take on a case that was dealt with in Germany. He begins by summarizing the case and the decision of the German rabbinic court and goes on to offer his critique of their decision.

Germany, to Rabbi Chayyim ben Rabbi Isaac z"l, Or Zarua, from the city of Vienna.	אשכנז, אל הרב רבי חיים בן הרב רבי יצחק ז"ל אור זרוע מעיר ויאינא.
You say that Mrs. Arloga is quarreling with her husband R. Yonah. As a result of this quarrel, she burst out [of her home] into the public market and called out in a loud voice that her husband was a sectarian, and that she saw him acting sordidly with his slave, and that once he even did so with his son, and that he further acted sordidly with/before witnesses that she had obtained. So she went out into the public market and screamed this out before gentiles and Jews. And as she was doing this she exposed her hair and her arms, and even slightly below her arms.	אמרת כי מרת ארלוגה מתקוטטת על בעלה רבי יונה. ומתוך הקטטה פרצה ויצאה בשוק ואמרה בקול רם לבעלה שהיה מין. וראתה אותו מקלקל עם עבדו ופעם אחת עם בנו ועוד קלקל עם עדים שהיו לה. ויצאה בשוק וצעקה על זה בפני גוים וישראלים רבים. ומתוך כך פרעה ראשה ונתגלו זרועותיה וקצת תחת זרועותיה.

Now I have looked through the words of these rabbis and that which they have decreed regarding her, and from all of their words I see that they judged her in the precedent somewhat as a rebellious wife, and that they judged her as having violated *dat Moshe ve-Yehudit*, since she revealed her hair and her arms.

I will review in general the main reasons they dealt with regarding whether the husband should pay or withhold paying her ketubah.

…Regarding their claim that she should be forced to leave without her ketubah payment since she violated *dat Moshe ve-Yehudit*, since she went out with her hair exposed and her arms somewhat exposed as well – this [rule] only applies if she violated *dat Moshe* and [*dat*] *Yehudit*. Additionally, the [sages] only said this regarding a woman who does this consistently, but if she revealed or exposed her hair randomly, or if she conversed with random young men once, haphazardly, she certainly does not lose her ketubah. That is what the Mishnah means by, "she *goes out* with her hair exposed, or she *spins* [thread] in the marketplace."

Furthermore, this was a moment of anger, and in a moment of anger she is like an insane person, and neither God nor God's mitzvot are before her at such a time, as they said in b. Nedarim (22b), that when a person is angry, even the divine presence has no significance before him.

ואני עמדתי על דברי הרבנים ואת אשר נגזר עליה. ומדברי כלם ראיתי שדנו אותה במסורת וכן דנו אותה במקצת כמורדת. ושכן דנו אותה כעוברת על דת משה ויהודית מפני שגלתה ראשה וזרועותיה.

הריני חוזר דרך כלל על כל עיקרי הדברים שדנו אותה לשלם או להפסידה כתובתה.

…במה שבאו לחייבה לצאת שלא בכתובה מדין עובר על דת משה ויהודית בשפרעה ראשה וקצת זרועותיה. זה אינו אלא כשעוברין על דת משה ויהודית. ועוד שלא אמרו אלא ברגילה בכך. אבל אם גלתה ופרעה ראשה באקראי או שדברה עם הבחורים פעם אחת דרך מקרה ודאי לא הפסידה כתובתה. וזה ששנו במשנתי' (כתובות פ"ז דף ע"ב) יוצאה וראשה פרוע וטווה בשוק.

ועוד שבשעת הכעס היה ובשעת הכעס הרי היא כשוטה ואין השם ומצותיו כנגדו באותה שעה. כמו שאמרו בנדרים (דף כ"ב ע"ב) שהכועס אפילו שכינה אין חשובה כנגדו.

The German rabbis concluded that by running outside with her hair exposed and with her arms partially exposed, Mrs. Arloga violated *dat Moshe ve-Yehudit* and, therefore, lost the right to her ketubah payment upon divorce. Rashba disagrees for three reasons. The second and third reasons are simple to understand. The second reason is that a woman only loses her ketubah if she behaves this way consistently, but this case involves a one-time offense. The third reason is that the woman was not in her right mind, because she was angry, so the behavior should not be held against her.

The first reason is more difficult to understand. Rashba seems to be saying that the woman only loses her ketubah if she violates both *dat Moshe* and *dat Yehudit*, whereas in this case, ostensibly, she only violated one – *dat Yehudit*. Here he differs from the German rabbis he quoted whom he presents as thinking she violated both – *dat Moshe* by exposing her hair and *dat Yehudit* by exposing her arms; at least that is what the parallelism in the line describing their position seems to imply. This would seem to mean that Rashba himself thinks that the exposing of hair only violated *dat Yehudit*. This could be because he rejects the derasha and Shmuel's interpretation of the Mishnah, but it could also be because he imagines that the woman's hair was partially covered or done up in some way.

CASE 2: THE MAN WHO TRIED TO BACK OUT OF THE MARRIAGE

Rashba touches on the term *dat Moshe ve-Yehudit* in another responsum (5:246). The context of this responsum is that a man took an oath to marry a girl once she became a little older. However, once she reached the agreed age, the man decided that he did not wish to marry her. He claimed that his oath does not bind him, since as part of the language of the oath, he said that he would marry her "according to the law of Moses and Israel," and now, since her father is deceased, he cannot marry her "according to the law of Moses and Israel," since the proper form according to the Torah would be for her father to accept the *kiddushin* (betrothal). Rashba views this man's claim as nonsense, since the phrase includes all of halakha, even rabbinic ceremonies. As part of this responsum, Rashba touches upon the version of the phrase which appears in Mishnah Ketubot.

For everything that the Sages legislated is like *dat Moshe ve-Yisrael*, and when a man betroths a minor girl, this is the language he uses for the betrothal. The reason is that the Torah said (Deut. 17:11): 'Do not veer from what they tell you.' The Torah stated this as a general rule, that we should not	כי כל מה שתקנו חכמים, כדת משה וישראל היא. ומי שמקדש את הקטנה, בו בלשון הוא מקדשה. והטעם, שהתורה אמרה: לא תסור מן הדבר אשר יגידו לך. דרך כלל אמרה תורה, שלא נסור

UNCOVERED HAIR IN THE RISHONIM, MODEL II

veer from what [the Sages] tell us, whether in interpreting the Torah and whether in creating new rules. Whoever does not listen to them is defined as violating *dat*.

Now even though we were taught in the 7th chapter of Ketubot: "The following [category of women] may be divorced without receiving the ketubah payment: One who violates *dat Moshe ve-Yehudit*. What [violates] *dat Moshe*? Feeding [her husband] untithed food, having intercourse with him during her menstrual period, not separating her challah, and making vows and not fulfilling them. What [violates] *dat Yehudit*? Going out with her hair exposed, spinning [thread] in the marketplace, and conversing with random men." From here it seems that *dat Moshe* only applies to laws that are literally from the Torah, but this is not so.

Over there, one can say that whether she violates the Torah laws themselves, or whether she violates the practice that the Jews require Jewish women to practice for modesty, she goes out without her ketubah. Therefore, it lists what she violates and causes him to violate among the Torah laws. Therefore, over there, it means *dat Moshe* literally and *dat Yehudit* as the modesty customs among Jews.

However, in our case, *dat Moshe* refers even to rabbinic betrothal, for *dat* requires a person to accept the laws of the [Sages].

ממה שיגידו לנו, בין בפירושי התורה, בין בתקנותיהם. ומי שאינו שומע להם, עובר על דת הוא.

ואף על פי ששנינו בפ' המדיר (דף ע"ב ע"ב): אלו יוצאות שלא בכתובה: העוברת על דת משה ויהודית. איזו היא דת משה? מאכילתו דבר שאינו מעושר, ומשמשתו נדה, ואינה קוצה לה חלה, ונודרת ואינה מקיימת. ואיזו היא דת יהודית? יוצאה וראשה פרוע, וטווה בשוק, ומדברת עם כל אדם. דאלמא: לא תקרא דת משה, אלא מה שהוא ממש מדאורייתא. לא היא!

דהתם, איכא למימר דבין עוברת על מצות התורה ממש, בין עוברת על מה שנהגו היהודי' לנהוג בנות ישראל בצניעות, דיוצאה שלא בכתובה. לפי' פרט מה שעוברת ומעברת אותו על מצות התורה. והלכך התם, על הכוונה כדת משה, ממש; ודת יהודית, במה שהיהודים נוהגים בצניעות.

אבל כאן, דת משה אפי' בקידושין דרבנן, שהדת צותה לשמוע לתקנותיהן.

In discussing the Mishnah, Rashba makes it clear that in the context of Ketubot, *dat Moshe* means making her husband violate a Torah law, and *dat Yehudit* means behaving in a way that does not fit with the modest customs of Jewish women. Additionally, Rashba quotes the Mishnah as is, without adding uncovered hair into the *dat Moshe* category. One could suggest that Rashba quotes the Mishnah as is for simplicity, and that he would maintain that fully uncovered hair violates a Torah law. Nevertheless, it is also possible that he does not follow the *derasha* of the school of R. Yishmael or the position of Shmuel. This would fit with what appears to be his position in the previously cited responsum.

GLOSS ON GITTIN – ANSWERING RA'AVAD'S QUESTION

A third place Rashba references this phrase appears in his gloss on b. Gittin 89a, where he quotes Ra'avad's question on R. Yochanan ben Nuri, who says that accusations of adultery require witnesses.

The Ra'avad asked, doesn't R. Yochanan ben Nuri accept [the Mishnah]? "These women are divorced without a ketubah payment: Those who violated *dat Moshe* and *Yehudit*"?	הקשה הראב"ד ז"ל לר' יוחנן בן נורי לית ליה הא דתנן ואלו יוצאות שלא בכתובה העוברת על דת משה ויהודית,
One can suggest that even though she may be divorced without a ketubah payment, since she did not behave with modesty, nevertheless, if her husband wishes to remain with her he may, only it is a mitzvah to divorce her.	ואיכא למימר שאע"פ שיוצאות בלא כתובה לפי שלא נהגו כמנהג הצנועות מ"מ אם רצה הבעל לקיים יקיים אלא שמצוה עליו לגרשה.

In answering Ra'avad's question, Rashba offers the same answer as Ramban with one difference. Unlike Ramban, Rashba does not offer an example of a violation of modesty. This is significant since Ramban's example was a woman wearing only a *kalta*, implying that this was less of a sin than fully uncovered hair, which was the proof that Ramban used to demonstrate that fully uncovered hair was a violation of *dat Moshe*. Again, Rashba's not quoting the *kalta* case does not prove that he feels that there is no difference; it may be that he wanted to make his gloss shorter than Ramban's and felt that offering an example would be superfluous. Nevertheless, this is the third example where Rashba avoids saying or explaining *dat Moshe* as including any form of hair covering, even when the sources he quotes do.

Rashba's position is unclear. However from the sources analyzed above, the evidence points towards a strong possibility that he did not think that fully uncovered hair violated a Torah law. This is reinforced by one additional source.

CHIDDUSHEI HARASHBA (B. BERACHOT 24A) – INVOKING RA'AVAD'S PRINCIPLE

We saw above that Ra'avad, as part of his treatment of the difference between what counts as private parts of a body and what does not, declared that hair outside the covering is not considered private since women generally exposed it. Although the Ra'avad's original gloss is lost, it was maintained in the Provençal works *HaHashlama* and *Meorot* – but these works were relatively obscure. Consequently, the principle became well known only when it was quoted and adopted by Rashba:

That which Rav Isaac said: "A handbreadth [of exposed flesh] on a woman is considered nudity" – which we establish as referring to a man who recited the Shema in the presence of his own wife, the Ra'avad explained that it is possible that this only refers to private places, and in this context, R. Chisda added that a woman's calf is a private place and thus nudity, even for her husband, even though this is not a private place on men. However, her face, hands, and feet, her speaking voice, and the hair that comes out from under her covering and which she does not cover – we are not concerned about them, since he is used to them and seeing them will not distract him.	והא דאמר רב יצחק טפח באשה ערוה ואוקימנא באשתו ובק"ש פירש הראב"ד ז"ל דאפשר דוקא ממקום צנוע שבה ועלה קאתי ר"ח למימר דשוק באשה מקום צנוע וערוה הוא ואפילו לגבי בעלה אף על פי שאינו מקום צנוע באיש, אבל פניה ידיה ורגליה וקול דבורה שאינו זמר ושערה מחוץ לצמתה שאינו מתכסה אין חוששין להם מפני שהוא רגיל בהן ולא טריד,
When it comes to another woman, however, he is forbidden to gaze at her at all, even at her little finger or her hair, and it is forbidden to hear even her speaking voice, as it says in b. Kiddushin (70a): [Rav Nachman asked Rav Yehuda]: 'Would you like to send greetings to [my wife] Yalta?' [Rav Yehuda] responded: 'This is what Shmuel said: "The voice of a woman is nudity."' Though it appears that this is specifically a reference to offering or returning greetings, for this is an act that brings people closer.	ובאשה אחרת אסור להסתכל בשום מקום ואפי' באצבע קטנה ובשערה ואסור לשמוע אפי' קול דבורה כדאמרינן בקדושין [ע' א'] לישדר מר שלמא לילתא אמר ליה הכי אמר שמואל קול באשה ערוה, ואלא מיהו נראה דדוקא קול של שאלת שלום או בהשבת שלום כי התם דאיכא קרוב הדעת,
With regard to Rav Alfasi, who mentions none of this [in his book], Ra'avad sug-	והרב אלפסי ז"ל שלא הזכיר מכל זה כלום כתב הראב"ד

gests that perhaps because it says the buttocks are not considered nudity, the Rabbi reasoned that certainly a handbreadth, a calf, hair, or voice cannot be. But [Ra'avad] wrote that these are not really comparable; here it is because he sees and is distracted, but with the buttocks we explained that it either refers to his own or his wife's [when a man is in bed with his wife and they are not dressed] and he cannot see it, only that their bodies are touching. And in any circumstance in which he doesn't see anything but only their bodies are touching he will not be distracted since he is used to this.

ז"ל דאפשר דמשום דאמרינן לעיל עגבות אין בהן משום ערוה סבור הרב ז"ל דכ"ש טפח ושוק ושערה וקול, וכתב הוא ז"ל דלא מן השם הוא זה אלא הכא משום דמטריד וברואה, ועגבות הא פרישנא דוקא דנפשיה ובאשתו בשאינו רואה ואף על פי שנוגע, דכל שאינו רואה משום נגיעה לבד לא מטריד הואיל וגס בה.

The treatment of Ra'avad here is the fullest extent, and from here the principle made it into the Rama's glosses on the *Shulchan Arukh* (as we shall see). It fits well with Rashba's other treatments of the question, since Ra'avad's bottom line seems to be that what is or is not private is dependent not on an objective statement in the Talmud but on the reality of what women in a given society do. Since they cover some hair and not other hair, the hair that is usually covered is erva; the hair that is usually exposed is not. We will see in Chapter 7 that Maharam Al-Ashkar builds his permissive ruling on this observation.

24. Sefer HaShulchan

One of Rashba's students, R. Chiya bar R. Shlomo of Barcelona (late 13th to early 14th century), also mentions Ra'avad's principle in his halakhic work, *Sefer HaShulchan* (Laws of Shema, Gate 3).

All of a woman's body is considered *erva*, even that of a person's wife. And if a man is in the presence of a handbreadth of exposed flesh from a woman's body he may not recite the Shema, as they said "a handbreadth of a woman's [flesh] is *erva*," and so is her hair and voice, for anyone looking at her.

The author of the *Halakhot Gedolot* z"l ex-

כל גוף האשה כערוה ואפילו אשתו וכל שהוא מגולה טפח מגופה לא יקרא כנגדו, וכמו שאמרו טפח באשה ערוה, וכן שער וקול באשה ערוה לרואה אותה,

ופירש בעל הלכות גדולות

plained that any handbreadth exposed on her that he can see is *erva*, but R. Avraham ben David z"l wrote that this may only apply to places on a woman that are private but her face, hands, feet, speaking – not singing – voice, and the hair that is outside her covering that she doesn't cover, a person need not worry about these for his wife, since he is used to seeing them and this would not distract him, and he can read Shema in her presence.

ז"ל כל טפח שהוא מגולה ממנה והוא רואה אותה ערוה, אבל הרב אברהם בן דוד ז"ל כתב דאפשר דדוקא ממקום צנוע שבה, אבל פניה ידיה ורגליה, וקול דבורה שאינו זמר, ושערה מחוץ לצמתה שאינו מתכסה, אין חוששין להן באשתו, מפני שרגיל בהן ואינו טרוד וקורא קריאת שמע כנגדן:

The *Sefer HaShulchan* here sets up a clear distinction between the Behag's approach and that of Ra'avad. Whereas Behag considers all parts of a woman *erva*, such that a handbreadth of any part of a woman becomes problematic for a man for the recitation of Shema, Ra'avad holds that it all depends on whether or not such an area is generally covered. Thus, the *Sefer HaShulchan* offers a concise description of the two basic approaches, objective and subjective *erva*.

25. Ritva

As described in Chapter 2 and again in Chapter 4, b. Gittin 89a has a statement recorded in the name of Rabbi Akiva that even if a woman's impropriety is known only through gossip, this is sufficient reason for her husband to divorce her on these grounds. To this statement, Rabbi Yochanan ben Nuri reacts by saying that no daughter of Abraham would be safe from divorce if this were correct. Rather, infidelity must be objectively determined in order to create grounds for divorce.

Rabbi Yom Tov ben Avraham of Seville (c. 1250–1330), known as Ritva, here asks Ra'avad's question, although without attribution:

But this seems difficult to me, for didn't R. Yochanan ben Nuri have the Mishnah which states: "These [women] may be divorced without a ketubah payment: Those who violate *dat Moshe ve-Yehudit*."? However, it seems possible to argue that this is not a problem, for that case was specifically addressing the loss of her ketubah, but her husband may remain with her [if he

וק"ל וכי ר' יוחנן בן נורי לית ליה הא דתנן (ע"ב א') ואלו יוצאות שלא בכתובה העוברת על דת משה ויהודית, ואיכא למימר דלא קשיא דהתם דוקא להפסידה כתובתה אבל בעלה רשאי לקיימה דאין אוסרין על בעלה אלא בדבר ברור,

chooses], since a woman is only forbidden to her husband when [the adultery] is clear.

In other words, divorcing one's wife for violating *dat Moshe ve-Yehudit* is optional. However, if he does so, he need not pay her the ketubah settlement, since she is considered at fault.

Ritva makes the same point about the divorce being optional in his gloss on b. Yevamot 24b, dealing again with a case of a woman who was involved in "base behavior."

| ...If he wishes to divorce her because his heart pushes him [to do so], she may be divorced against her will, just like a woman who violates *dat Moshe ve-Yehudit*, who is divorced without a ketubah payment if her husband so desires; what is more, [a woman who violates *dat Moshe ve-Yehudit*] requires a warning before she may be divorced, as was stated in b. Sotah (25a), but this woman, where there is the implication of base behavior, requires no warning. | ... אם רצה להוציא מפני שלבו נוקפו תצא ממנו בעל כרחה כעוברת על דת משה ויהודית שהיא יוצאה בלא כתובה אם רצה הבעל להוציא, ולא עוד אלא דההיא צריכה התראה להפסידה כתובתה כדאסיקנא במסכת סוטה (כ״ה א׳) אבל זו שיש בה דבר מכוער מאבדת התראתה. |

Ritva's most extensive discussion of this point, and the difference between base behavior and violating *dat Moshe ve-Yehudit*, comes in his gloss on b. Kiddushin 81a.

| That which was taught in Mishnah, tractate Ketubot: "One who violates *dat Moshe ve-Yehudit* may be divorced without payment of her ketubah," this does not mean that the court forces him to do this against his will; rather if he wishes to divorce her she is divorced without a ketubah payment. The same is true regarding that which we said in b. Yevamot (24b): "A merchant leaving her house while the woman is putting on her undergarment, overturned shoes under the bed – since such is evidence of a base matter, and she may be divorced without her ketubah [payment]," this means only if he wishes to divorce her; this is also the interpretation of the Geonim. | והא דתנן במסכת כתובות (ע״ב א׳) העוברת על דת משה ויהודית תצא שלא בכתובה, לאו דמפקי לה בי דינא מיניה בעל כרחו אלא שאם רצה מוציאה שלא בכתובה, וכן נמי הא דאמרינן ביבמות פרק כיצד (כ״ד ב׳) רוכל יוצא ואשה חוגרת בסינר ומנעלים הפוכים תחת המטה הואיל ומכוער הדבר תצא שלא בכתובה, היינו שאם רצה להוציא יוצאה בלא כתובה לא שיוציאוה ממנו בית דין בעל כרחו, וכן פירשו שם הגאונים ז״ל. |

And this makes sense, for we hold (b. Ketubot 9a) that a woman is not forbidden to her husband except when he has expressed jealousy (about a particular man) and she is then alone with him. However, if she had only been alone with a man but there had been no jealousy about him beforehand, she is not forbidden. And even if he expressed jealousy on his own or due to the account of one witness and he said to her: "Do not be alone with so-and-so," and she then went off with so-and-so – witnessed by two witnesses – into a hidden place or an abandoned place, and they stayed there long enough to have been intimate – she still isn't forbidden to her husband, as it says in tractate Sotah (2a). There is no behavior baser than that!

...any case where a person believes based on his own experience or based on the testimony of gentiles that his wife is forbidden to him, he is obligated to divorce her if he is to do what is right in the eyes of heaven. If he admits as much (i.e., that he believes she has been unfaithful) in court they will require a divorce... except that in these cases, where there are no witnesses that she was alone [with another man] or witnesses to any other base behavior, only that he is forbidding her to himself [based on his belief that she has been unfaithful] he is still obligated to pay the ketubah payment, for if one did not rule this way no daughter of our father Abraham would ever receive her ketubah![53]

ודין הוא דהא קיימא לן (כתובות ט' א') אין האשה נאסרת על בעלה אלא על עסקי קינוי וסתירה אבל בסתירה בלא קינוי אינה נאסרת, ואפילו במקנא לה על פי עצמו או במקנא לה על פי עד אחד ואמר לה אל תסתרי עם פלוני ונכנסה עמו בפני עדים לסתר או לחורבה ושהתה עמו כדי ביאה אינה נאסרת על בעלה כדאיתא במסכת סוטה (ב' א') והרי אין לך דבר מכוער גדול מזה.

...כל שלבו מאמין על פי עצמו או אפילו על פי גוים שאסורה לו אשתו חייב להוציאה בבא לצאת ידי שמים, ואם הודה בבית דין בכך מוציאין אותה ממנו. אלא דבכי האי גוונא דליכא עדי ייחוד ולא עדי דבר מכוער אלא שהוא אוסרה על עצמו חייב לפרוע לה כתובתה, שאם אין אתה אומר כן לא הנחת בת לאברהם אבינו שיהא לה כתובה.

---

53. I.e., every man who wants a divorce would lie and say he believes that she has cheated. We are aware of the fact that the Ritva's commentary on Kiddushin is suspect; there are two versions and neither is fully complete. This appears in the "first version" (apparently the later of the two). See the Mossad HaRav Kook in the introduction to this work.

From here we see that there are three rules in this matter: 1. If [the charge] comes from himself or a single witness whom he believes, she is forbidden to him and he must divorce her in order to do what is right in the eyes of heaven, and the court can force him to divorce her based on his statement, but he still needs to pay the ketubah payment.

2. If a woman violates *dat Moshe ve-Yehudit* or if there are witnesses to base behavior, if he wishes to divorce her he may do so without payment of her ketubah, assuming the witnesses warned her in advance, as is stated in tractate Sotah (25a). However, this [last point] is limited to cases of violating *dat*; but when there are witnesses to base behavior there is no need for the witnesses to have warned her in advance. That which we inquired about [in b. Sotah], regarding a woman who violates *dat* if the husband wishes to stay with her whether that is permitted or not, and the question was not answered where it was asked, but it was answered somewhere else, for we hold that if a husband dismisses his jealous command before she goes off alone with the man, the jealous command is considered dismissed, all the more so in a case of violating *dat*, if he wishes to remain with her he may remain with her and the court will not force a divorce. Thus did our rabbis explain: since he remains with her even after he could have gone to court and divorced her [without payment], yet he did not divorce her, he makes it clear that he has dismissed the issue and she is no longer in danger of losing her ketubah payment.

3. If there are witnesses that she has been unfaithful, or witnesses that she had been

נמצאת אומר כי שלשה דינין בדבר דעל פי עצמו או על פי עד אחד שמאמין בו אסורה לו וחייב להוציאה בבא לצאת ידי שמים, ובית דין גם כן מוציאין ממנו על פיו וחייב לפרוע לה כתובתה.

ובעוברת על דת משה ויהודית או בעדי דבר מכוער אם רצה להוציא מוציא שלא בכתובה, והוא דאיכא התראה כדאיתא במסכת סוטה (כ"ה א'), מיהו דוקא בעוברת על דת אבל בעדי דבר מכוער אינה צריכה התראה, והא דאיבעיא לן התם בעוברת על דת ורצה הבעל לקיימה אם מותר אם לאו ולא איפשיטא התם במקום בעיא, הא איפשיטא מאידך דקיימא לן דבעל שמחל על קנוייו קודם שנסתרה שהוא מחול, וכל שכן לעוברת על דת שאם רצה לקיים מקיים ואין בית דין מוציאין מידו, וכן פירשו רבותינו ז"ל, וכיון שקיימה לאחר שהיה יכול למיקבל בבית דין ולהוציאה ולא הוציאה גלי אדעתיה דמחל ותו לא מפסיד לה כתובתה.

איכא עדי טומאה ממש או עדי קינוי וסתירה שהוא

warned not to be alone with a certain man and she was [afterwards] alone with him, which is the equivalent to witnesses seeing her cheat, the court forces him to divorce her without a ketubah payment. Even if she has a number of offspring there is no need even for a warning at all. Regarding witnesses to adultery, we follow Shmuel (b. Makkot 7a) that even for punishments it is sufficient that it looks like they are fornicating, and one does not need to see actual penetration.

כעידי טומאה בית דין מוציאין ממנו בעל כרחו שלא בכתובה, ואפילו יש לה כמה בנים ואינה צריכה התראה כלל, ועדי טומאה קיימא לן כשמואל (מכות ז' א') דאפילו לעונשין סגיא משיראו כמנאפין ולא בעינן כמכחול בשפופרת.

From the above we see that, according to Ritva, violating *dat Moshe ve-Yehudit* is in the same halakhic category as behaving basely. In other words, there is a continuum. Adultery is the sin that ends marriage; base behavior implies adultery but comes with no absolute proof. Violating *dat* insults a husband in a way similar to but less than being unfaithful to him. However, since Ritva consistently discusses *dat Moshe* and *dat Yehudit* here, even though his emphasis is clearly on the latter, it is impossible to tell from these examples how he categorizes totally uncovered/undone hair.

Turning to the passage in b. Ketubot (72a–b) regarding *dat Yehudit*, Ritva writes:

Exposed hair is a violation of Torah law, for it is written: 'and [the kohen] shall expose the hair of the woman.' Rashi explains that one can deduce from this that her hair has been covered. Furthermore, since the Torah says to expose her hair in order to make her appear base, one can deduce that exposed hair is a kind of vulgarity for a woman.

ראשה פרוע דאורייתא היא דכתיב ופרע את ראש האשה. פרש"י ז"ל מדכתיב ופרע מכלל דמעיקרא מכוסה היה, ועוד דכיון דאמרה תורה לפרוע האשה כדי לנוולה מכלל דפריעת הראש פריצות הוא לאשה.

Rather [the *dat Yehudit* violation refers to a woman] in a courtyard. If so, you have not left a single daughter of our patriarch Abraham who could live with her husband – Rashi of blessed memory explained, that in a courtyard there is a prohibition of uncovering hair. The meaning of his explanation

אלא בחצר אם כן לא הנחת בת לאברהם אבינו יושבת תחת בעלה. פרש"י ז"ל א"כ דבחצר יש בה משום פריעה, פירוש לפירושו דכיון דאמר רבי יוחנן קלתה אין בה משום פרוע ראש בחצר מכלל דבלא

is that since according to this suggestion R. Yochanan's ruling that when a woman goes with a *kalta* on her head, she is not considered to be of uncovered head applies in a courtyard, we infer that without a *kalta* there would be a prohibition against uncovering hair even in a courtyard – if so, you have not left a single daughter of our patriarch Abraham who could live with her husband, since most Jewish women go with their heads entirely uncovered in their own courtyards, as no one is there to see. [The Talmud] concludes that R. Yochanan was referring to one who goes from one courtyard to another by way of an alley.

Thus there are three rules with regard to this law: In a courtyard, even without a *kalta*, there is no prohibition against exposed hair; in the marketplace, going even with a *kalta* is a violation of *dat Yehudit*; and in an alley, it is permissible to go with a *kalta* but not without one. The Jerusalem Talmud adds: Some courtyards can be like alleys and some alleys can be like courtyards. A courtyard which many people use as a pass-through has the status of an alley; an alley through which many people do not pass has the status of a courtyard.

Spinning red near her face – Rashi explains that this means the she weaves with her hand in her lap and the string hangs down before her "lower face" (a euphemism for the pelvic region). This is a forced interpretation and the language does not support it. The correct interpretation is that of Rambam, who explains that she places the red near her forehead or weaving near her face, literally, and the red gives her face a ruddy complexion, which is what the daughters of the gentiles do [i.e., they use rouge], and this is a vulgar behavior.

קלתה יש בה משום פריעת הראש אפילו בחצר, וא"כ לא הנחת בת לאברהם אבינו יושבת תחת בעלה שרובן הולכות בחצרן בפרוע ראש כיון שאין שם רואין, ואסיקנא מחצר לחצר ודרך מבוי.

ושלשה דינין בדבר, דבחצר אפילו בלא קלתה אין בה משום פריעת ראש, ובשוק אפילו בקלתה דת יהודית היא, ובמבוי בקלתה אין שלא בקלתה לא, ואמרו בירושלמי (ה"ו) יש חצר שהוא כמבוי ויש מבוי שהוא כחצר, מבוי שאין הרבים בוקעים בו דינו כחצר וחצר שהרבים בוקעים בו דינו כמבוי, ע"כ.

בטווה ורד כנגד פניה. פרש"י ז"ל טווה בכפה על ירכה והחוט מתרדד כנגד פניה של מטה, ופירוש דחוק הוא מאוד ואין הלשון מודה לו, והנכון כמו שפירש הרמב"ם ז"ל (פכ"ד מהל' אישות הי"ב) שנותנת ורד סמוך לפדחתה או בפילכה כנגד פניה ממש והורד נותן אדמימות בפניה וכדרך שעושות בנות הגוים וזה דרך פריצות.

> Acting playfully with young men – this implies that both [conditions] are necessary. That which is said in a nearby passage, that she speaks with random men, is speaking of the same woman. Even though over there it doesn't say "acting playfully," they didn't really mean flirting but rather walking around and speaking of frivolous topics – this is how I see it.
>
> במשחקת עם הבחורים. משמע דתרוויהו בעינן והא דאמרינן בסמוך מדברת עם כל אדם אמר בה ואף על גב דהתם לא שחקה, לא משחקת ממש אמרו אלא מטיילת ומדברת דברי בטלה, כנ"ל.

Ritva seems to take two positions that are in some small tension with each other. In the above passage, Ritva seems to accept the Talmud's claim that a woman going out to the marketplace with fully uncovered hair violates a Torah prohibition. That would seem to imply an objective definition of modest behavior on halakha's part – namely, fully uncovered hair in public is considered immodest irrespective of social norms. On the other hand, in his discussion of the passages in b. Sotah and b. Yevamot, he seems to see the entire focus of the modesty rules for *dat Moshe ve-Yehudit* as being about humiliating her husband, even allowing her husband to dismiss the behavior as irrelevant to the marriage. If so, what sense would it make for the Torah to legislate forbidden behavior and dress? If halakha wants to spare the husband shame, should not the prohibitions be flexible such that in any given society immodest behavior would be forbidden but normal behavior ignored?

It seems likely that Ritva's understanding of these passages derives from his understanding of yet a third passage, towards the end of tractate Kiddushin (82a). This passage, which is discussed in Chapter 2, ends with a statement by Shmuel that interaction with women is permissible, "all for the sake of heaven." On this, Ritva comments:

> All is dependent on the wisdom of heaven[54] – This is the normative rule of Jewish law, that all is dependent on what a person sees in himself. If he needs to distance himself from his inclination more, he must do so, even such that he not look at women's colorful [garments even when they are being washed], as was stated in Avodah Zarah (20b). So too, if he sees in
>
> הכל לפי דעת שמים - וכן הלכתא דהכל כפי מה שאדם מכיר בעצמו, אם ראוי לו לעשות הרחקה ליצרו עושה ואפילו להסתכל בבגדי צבעונין של אשה אסור כדאיתא במסכת עבודה זרה. ואם מכיר בעצמו שיצרו נכנע וכפוף לו ואין מעלה

---

54. Ritva's text is slightly different from that of the Talmud we have.

himself that his inclination is under control and he has no erotic thoughts at all, he can look at and speak with a woman prohibited to him sexually and can greet a married woman.

This explains the conduct of Rabbi Yochanan who sat by the gates of immersion (b. Bava Metzia 84a), without concern for any erotic intent, and Rabbi Ami who spoke with the king's mother (b. Ketubot 17a), and other rabbis who spoke with various matrons, and Rav Ada bar Ahava[55] who danced with the bride on his shoulders at a wedding and danced with her and was not afraid of erotic thoughts for the reason stated above.

However, one should not be lenient on these matters unless one is a greatly pious person, and acutely aware of one's own desires. Not every learned man feels confident in his dominance over his inclinations, as we have seen in the various quotes and accounts referenced above. Happy is the man who has control over his instincts and whose energy and drive are devoted to Torah, for the words of Torah will stick with a man from his youth and give him purpose and hope in his old age, as it says (Psalms 92:15): "In old age they still produce fruit; they are full of sap and freshness."

טינא כלל מותר לו להסתכל ולדבר עם הערוה ולשאול בשלום אשת איש,

והיינו ההיא דרבי יוחנן (ב"מ פ"ד א') דיתיב אשערי טבילה ולא חייש איצר הרע, ורבי אמי דנפקי ליה אמהתא דבי קיסר (כתובות י"ז א'), וכמה מרבנן דמשתעי בהדי הנהו מטרונייתא (לעיל מ' א'), ורב אדא בר אהבה שאמרו בכתובות (שם) דנקיט כלה אכתפיה ורקיד בה ולא חייש להרהורא מטעמא דאמרן,

אלא שאין ראוי להקל בזה אלא לחסיד גדול שמכיר ביצרו, ולא כל תלמידי חכמים בוטחין ביצריהן כדחזינן בשמעתין בכל הני עובדין דמייתינן, ואשרי מי שגובר על יצרו ועמלו ואומנתו בתורה, שדברי תורה עומדים לו לאדם בילדותו ונותנין לו אחרית ותקוה לעת זקנתו, שנאמר עוד ינובון בשיבה דשנים ורעננים יהיו.

From the above passage, we can see that Ritva includes a category midway between modest and immodest behavior. According to Ritva, there are behaviors that would be arousing to the average man but would be considered irrelevant to a sage who has control of his passions. This is a step beyond the Tosafot's use of this passage to defend the modern practice of doing business with women. According to the Tosafot, this just means that nowadays business in mixed company should not be

---

55. Our Talmudic texts have "Rav Acha."

considered inappropriate because it is normal. According to Ritva, even some inappropriate behaviors can be seen as benign interactions for men with more self-control. Halakhically speaking, this is a complicated position to hold, since it would mean that the same behavior that could be considered lewd to one man could be fine for another in that same time and place. Yet this is what Ritva appears to be saying.

Considering this, one can reasonably suggest a solution to the above referenced tension. On one hand, halakha offers overall guidelines for what is considered modest behavior and dress for women. On the other hand, such rules may be overridden when the men involved are sure that nothing untoward will occur in act or thought due to her behavior. For example, it would seem to be a relatively safe assumption that dancing with a married woman – especially dancing that includes physical contact – would be forbidden. However, since Rav Ada bar Ahava had no sexual thoughts or issues with this behavior it was permitted for him to put the bride on his shoulders and for the bride to allow him to do so. Similarly, with hair covering, the Torah lays out a basic suggested practice, which would be for women to cover their hair. However, in a society where the average man feels that uncovered hair is not lewd, and the average husband feels neither shamed nor threatened by his wife's going out with exposed hair, Ritva may argue "all for the sake of heaven" – that as long as the behavior is not considered lewd by any of the players it should not be considered a violation of halakha.

26. Terumat HaDeshen

R. Yisrael Isserlein (1390–1460, Neustadt) has two important responsa that touch on hair covering and *dat Moshe/dat Yehudit*, in his *Terumat HaDeshen*. In responsum 10, R. Isserlein records a question about head covering for men wishing to recite blessings or pray.

Question: There is a common saying among the people: Those hats made of interlaced straw are insufficient to be considered hair covering in order to allow a man to pray or even to mention God's name in a blessing, when the man's head is covered only with that hat. Should one be strict about this or not?	שאלה: מרגלא בפומייהו דאינשי, שאותן כובעים שהן קלועין מקש, לא חשיבי כיסוי לראש להתפלל בהן, או להזכיר הברכה בשם, כשאין הראש מכוסה אלא באותו כובע, יש ליזהר מזה או לאו?

Although the question really has little to do with the laws of modesty and female head covering, the *Terumat HaDeshen* touches upon this issue in his answer:

Answer: It seems that there is no requirement to be strict about this. In fact, I once heard from someone that an important person was asked about this and he ruled there to be no requirement to be strict about this, but he never gave reason or proof for his words.	תשובה: יראה, דאין דין להקפיד בדבר הזה. וכן שמעתי, מאדם אחד, שגדול אחד נשאל על זה, והורה דאין קפידא בדבר, וטעמא וראיה לא הגיד לדבריו.
It seems one could bring a proof from the passage in the seventh chapter of Ketubot (72a), with regard to the uncovering of a woman's hair. There is a basis in the Torah [for a woman to cover her hair], for she is warned regarding the prohibition [of going out with her hair uncovered], and yet it says there that with a *kalta* on her head it would be permitted, even in a public area, and if moving from a courtyard to another courtyard through a thoroughfare, doing so [with only a *kalta*] would not even violate *dat Yehudit*. From this we see that even a basket,[56] which is not even remotely similar to a cloth covering, for it has holes in many places since it is not interlaced tightly, [is a sufficient covering according to Torah law]; this should be all the more so with straw hats which are intertwined tightly without holes, and offer similar coverage to cloth.	ונראה להביא ראיה, מהא דאיתא פרק המדיר (כתובות עב ע״א), לגבי גילוי ראש דאשה, יש לה סמך מן התורה דמוזהר עלה, ואפ״ה קאמר התם, דמדאורייתא בקלתה על ראשה שריא, ואפילו ברה״ר, ומחצר לחצר דרך מבוי, ואפי׳ משום דת יהודית לית לה בה. הא קמן, דאפי׳ סל, דאינו דומה כלל לכיסוי הבגד, שהרי הוא חלול בכמה מקומות, לפי שאינן קלועין יפה, וכ״ש כובעין של קש, הוא קלוע מרוצף ומהודק היטב, ודומה לכיסוי של בגד.
And [this is so] even though there is a distinction to be made between uncovered hair as it is discussed there versus here, for there we say that in a courtyard a woman requires no head covering. However, regarding an uncovered head for reciting blessings, we are strict about this even in	ואף על גב ד{ב}לאו הכי יש חילוק, בין גילוי הראש, דהתם להכא, דאמרינן התם דבחצר, האשה אינה צריכה שום כיסוי. וגילוי הראש לענין ברכה, קפידא אפי׳ בבית, י״ל דודאי איסור גילוי הראש

---

56. This is apparently the interpretation of the word *kalta* preferred by R. Isserlein.

the privacy of one's home. Nevertheless, one may suggest that the nature of the prohibition of uncovered hair in the context [of women] is based solely on the lewdness of men. Hence, where people are not generally found, like in a person's yard, there is no reason for the prohibition. However, the prohibition of having an uncovered head [for blessings] is out of fear of [the person reciting the blessing] having a frivolous attitude towards heaven, for he is invoking the name of God without fear and awe. There is no reason [in this case] to distinguish between private and public domains, since the world is filled with God's glory.

Nevertheless, we can learn from rules of headcovering there to here, each in its own relevant context. Even covering with a shawl is considered hair covering for a woman, as was stated in the final chapter of Eruvin, "Covering like a mourner." Rashi interprets this to mean, "[The mourner] does not go out with his [or her] hair exposed."

It seems reasonable to bring a further proof as well, from the 16th chapter of Shabbat (120b), for it was taught there: "If the name [of God] was written on his arm and he must dip in a ritual bath, since the mitzvah is upon him, he should wrap reeds around the name." The reason for this is explained there: "For it is forbidden to appear naked before the name of God, so he wraps reeds around it to cover it." So one can see that reeds are sufficient as a covering and the same should apply to straw, for what is the difference?

However, we could push back against this proof that certainly covering in that scenario is sufficient when using anything, much more so than for the recitation of

דהתם, איננו אלא משום פריצות דגברי, והיכא דלא שכיחא רבים, כגון בחצר אין קפידא; אבל איסור גילוי ראש דהכא, משום קלות ראש כלפי שמיא, דמדכר שם מקום ב"ה שלא באימה וביראה; ואין לחלק בין בית לרשות הרבים דמלא כל הארץ כבודו.

מ"מ ילפינן מגילוי הראש דהתם, האי כדיניה והאי כדיניה. ואפי' עטיפה קרי ליה לכיסוי ראש דאשה, כדאיתא פרק בתרא דעירובין: עטיפה כאבל; ופרש"י משום דאינו יוצא בפרועת ראש.

ועוד היה נראה להביא ראיה, מפ' כל כתבי (שבת קכ ע"ב) דתניא התם: הרי שהיה שם כתוב על בשרו, ונזדמן לו טבילה של מצוה, כורך עליו גמי. ומסיק דהטעם הוא: מפני דאסור לעמוד לפני השם ערום, ולכך כורך עליו גמי לכסותו. אלמא דגמי מהני לכיסוי, וה"ה קש, דמ"ש?

אך דקשה לן עלה דע"כ, כיסוי דהתם סגי לן בכל דהו, טפי מכיסוי דלענין ברכה בהזכרת השם, דפריך התם ונינח ידיה

God's name in a blessing, for over there [the Talmud] asks: "Let him put his hand over the name, why does he need to use reeds?" And it answers: "Because he might forget and move his hand." So one sees that if it were not for this, covering with a hand would have been sufficient. However, with regard to blessings, one of the Sages has copied from a responsum of *Or Zarua* that it would not be sufficient to cover one's head with one's hand in order to make a blessing, but one must use a cloth. He brought a proof for this from the fact that when Rabbeinu Tam would wash in hot water and drink he would cover himself with a cloth up to his chest so that his heart would not see his nakedness – which implies that he used a cloth and not his hands.

עלויה דשם, ולמה לי גמי? ומשני: משום דלמא מישתלי ושקיל ליה לידיה, הא לאו הכי סגי בכיסוי היד. ולענין ברכה, העתיק אחד מהגדולים מתשובת א"ז, דלא מהני, אם משימין ידים על גילוי הראש לברך כך, אם לא יכסנו בבגד, והביא ראיה, מהא דעבד ר"ת כשהיה רוחץ בחמין והיה שותה, היה מתכסה בבגד כנגד לבו, שלא יהא לבו רואה את הערוה, משמע דוקא בבגד ולא בידים.

Nevertheless, one could suggest that using one's hand is sufficient for covering up the name of God but insufficient for saying God's name in a blessing, not because one type of covering is better than the other, but rather the reason it is insufficient to place one's hand on one's head or to put one's arm in between one's chest and one's nakedness is because the head, the chest and the arm/hand are all part of the same body, and the body cannot cover itself. However, this is not true for God's name, since the hand is not trying to cover the body but to cover the name which is not part of the body. Nevertheless, one may learn from there that covering with reeds counts as covering, and the same should be true for straw.

אמנם י"ל, דהא דלגבי כיסוי השם מהני מה שהניח ידו עליו, ולגבי הזכרת הברכה לא מהני כיסוי הידים, לאו משום דהאי כיסוי חמיר מהאי, אלא היינו טעמא דלא מהני, שמניח ידיו על ראשו, או אם יהא חוצץ בהן כנגד לבו, משום דהראש והלב והיד חד גוף אינון, ואין הגוף יכול לכסות את עצמו, משא"כ לגבי כיסוי השם, שהיד אינה באה לכסות הגוף, אלא לכסות שם שאינו מן הגוף. ומ"מ שמעינן מהתם, דכיסוי [ג]מי חשיב כיסוי, וה"ה כיסוי קש.

Although the *Terumat HaDeshen* focuses on covering one's head for blessings, he leaves some clues as to his understanding of the prohibition of a (married) woman exposing her hair in public. He begins by giving reasons for the prohibition. He states that the issue has to do with the lewdness (*peritzut*) of men. Since men will be aroused by her hair, it is forbidden for her to expose it in public. Assuming that the *Terumat HaDeshen* believes this rule applies only to married women – as was the common understanding among Ashkenazi poskim – this must be understood as a sociologically determined explanation. Why would men be aroused only by the hair of married women? Since it cannot be based on levels of attractiveness, it must be based on social cues. Since married women cover their hair, exposing it has a provocative quality. One may reasonably assume, then, that in a society where uncovered hair is not provocative, the rule would not apply, and a public place would be equivalent to a courtyard.

The other noteworthy aspect is that the *Terumat HaDeshen* appears to accept the Talmudic position (of Shmuel) that there is a *dat Moshe* aspect to hair covering, since he states that wearing a kalta/basket would be sufficient to remove the Torah prohibition. How does this point work with the previous one? It seems that the *Terumat HaDeshen* must believe the Torah prohibition, although discussing exposed hair specifically, is really just a synecdoche for modesty laws in general. In other words, it is a violation of Torah law for a woman to dress provocatively, and fully uncovered hair in biblical society would be an example of that. However, in theory, in a society where exposed hair is not considered provocative at all, there would be no violation of a prohibition, whether biblical or rabbinic.

That this is the reasoning behind the *Terumat HaDeshen*'s position is borne out by another responsum (242) where he discusses a woman who was repeatedly alone with gentile men. The question with which he deals is as follows:

Question: A certain married Jewish woman has accustomed herself to be alone in gentile homes, sometimes even at night, since she does various forms of business with these gentiles. It is her way to go to their villages and often can spend eight days or more together with them. She is also accustomed to receiving credit from these gentiles when she doesn't have cash for purchases, and through this she often ends up	שאלה: אשה אחת אשת ישראל רגילה להתייחד בבתי נכרים לפעמים בלילה כמו ביום ע"י סרסרות ומשא ומתן שיש לה עם נכרים, ודרכה ללכת לכפרים ולשהות הרבה פעמים יחידה בין הנכרים כמו ח' ימים ויותר, ורגילה להקיף מן הנכרים מה שאין לה לפרוע ועי"כ באתה הרבה

confined alone among the gentiles for days or weeks. Is she permitted to her husband or not, and, at the very least can she be categorized as in violation of *dat*?	פעמים לידי תפיסה שנחבשה יחידית בין הנכרים ימים ושבועים, שריא לבעלה או אסורה או נקראת לכל הפחות עוברת על דת או לאו?

The *Terumat HaDeshen* begins with the question of whether the woman is forbidden to her husband, ostensibly implying a belief that she has been unfaithful to him. For our purposes, the second question is more important. The *Terumat HaDeshen* ends his description of the case with the question of whether the woman should be considered as violating *dat*. He does not describe which "*dat*" she may be violating or how this behavior should, in theory, fit in with the list of behaviors in rabbinic sources that violate *dat*. This he will take up in the answer.

Answer: It would appear that she is not forbidden to her husband because of the above referenced behaviors in which she has been wrongly engaged. Just because she has been alone with gentiles night and day of her own free will she should not be forbidden, for since she was not actually incarcerated among them we do not worry about rape, and she would be permitted even to a kohen, as has been put forward by Tosafot (*AZ* 23a) and the *Sefer HaTerumah* quoting Ri. If this were not so, no daughter of our father Abraham would be fit for a kohen since it is impossible that she hasn't been alone with a gentile at least once. [57]	תשובה: יראה דאין לאוסרה על בעלה בשביל כל המעשים הללו שהריעה לעשות. דמשום דנתייחדה מרצונה עם הנכרים גם לילה גם יום לא אסרינה מש"ה, דכיון דאינה מסורה בידם כמו הנחבשת לא חיישינן אפי' לאונסין, ושריא אפי' לכהן כמו שמחלקים התוס' פ"ב דע"ז (דף כג ע"א ד"ה ותו), וכן ספר התרומה בשם ר"י, דאל"כ לא הנחת בת לאברהם אבינו שכשירה לכהונה, דאי אפשר שלא תתייחד עם הנכרים פעם א'.
...However, it would seem that the woman described in our case, although it is true that she is not forbidden to her husband, as we clarified above, nevertheless, she should be categorized as violating *dat* since she was alone among gentile [men] of her own free will a number of times.	...אפס נראה דהך איתתא דנ"ד נהי נמי דאינה נאסרת על בעל כדברירנא לעיל, מ"מ עוברת על דת מיקרי הואיל ונתיחדה מרצונה כמה פעמים בין הנכרים.

---

57. The *Terumat HaDeshen* continues with a lengthy discussion of the debate among the Rishonim about what circumstances exactly would cause the woman to be forbidden to a kohen or to her husband. This discussion lies well out of the scope of this book, so we will skip to the more pertinent section of the responsum.

UNCOVERED HAIR IN THE RISHONIM, MODEL II

For the Talmud, in Ch. 7 of Ketubot, poses the question [about the Mishnah's reference to exposed hair as a violation of *dat Yehudit*], "but going out with exposed hair to the public area violates a Torah law! For it is written, 'and he shall expose the hair of the woman.'" Rashi explains [the question]: "Why call it *dat Yehudit*, it is *dat Moshe*!" And the prohibition of a married woman being alone with a man is also a Torah law, as is clear in the second chapter of Tractate Avodah Zarah [hence, by analogy it should also be a violation of *dat Moshe*]. Even though Rambam wrote that the origin of [the prohibition against seclusion with another man] is only ancient tradition (*divrei kabbalah*), he also wrote that uncovering of hair is *only a rabbinic admonition*, as evidenced by the language of his formulation. Presumably, [Rambam would explain] that the Talmud uses the term "Torah violation" only to mean that there is a hint to this rule in the Torah, and if so, seclusion also [is hinted at in the Torah].

The same is implied in Rashi's comments on b. Sotah (25a), for the Talmud notes [in commenting on a baraita that states that neither a betrothed woman nor one awaiting levirate marriage can be asked to drink the *sotah* waters]: "She doesn't drink but her husband can still claim offense [at her inappropriate behavior]. To what purpose? Is it not to make her lose her ketubah payment? Abaye said: 'No, it is to make her forbidden to her husband.'" And Rashi explains: "'To what purpose? Is it not to make her lose her ketubah payment' – this refers to violating *dat*, for she was alone among men." Meaning, even though this is only about making her lose her ketubah payment, it requires the husband to claim of-

דהא פריך תלמודא פ' המדיר (כתובות דף ע"ב עמוד א') הלכה בשוק וראשה פרוע דאורייתא היא דכתיב ופרע את ראש האשה כו', פרש"י אמאי קרית ליה דת יהודית דת משה היא, ויחוד אשת איש נמי דאורייתא כדאיתא פ' אין מעמידין.

ואף על גב דרמב"ם כתב דאינו אלא מדברי קבלה הא איהו נמי כתב דפריעת ראש באשה אינו אלא זהירות מדרבנן כדמוכח מלשונו, וממסמא (וּמִסְתָּמָא) ס"ל הא דפריך תלמודא דאורייתא ר"ל רמז דאורייתא יש לה, וא"כ ה"ה יחוד נמי.

וכן משמע פרש"י נמי פ' ארוסה במס' סוטה דפריך תלמודא מישתא הוא דלא שתיא הא קנוייה מקניא לה מאי לאו להפסיד כתובתה, אמר אביי לא לאוסרה עליו, ופרש"י מאי לאו להפסיד כתובתה דזו היא העוברת על דת שנסתרה עם אנשים כלומר אף על פי שאינו אלא להפסיד כתובתה בעי קנוי והתראה, ודחה אביי לא לאוסרה כלומר דווקא לאוסרה בעי קנוי והתראה אבל להפסיד כתובתה לא.

fense and warn her. But Abaye dismisses this interpretation: "No, it is to make her forbidden to her husband." Meaning, the need for a claim of offense and warning applies specifically to forbid her to her husband, but it is not necessary to make her lose her ketubah payment.

From this we can see that a married woman secluding herself with a man of her own will is called a violation of *dat* – all the more so if she is alone with gentiles, who are drowning in promiscuity. This needs little elaboration since it requires little demonstration.

הא קמן דמתייחדה מרצונה מקרי עוברת על דת כ"ש הנסתרת עם הנכרים דשטופי זמה הם, ואין זה צריך פנים דא"צ כ"כ ראייה.

Even if she hadn't been alone and secluded herself with men of her own will, but she caused it to come about a number of times because of debt or confusion, for she was held captive by gentiles without a guard, and this is sufficient to consider her seclusion purposeful, as we said in b. Gittin (46b), with regard to certain men from Mikhsi who borrowed money from gentiles [and could not pay it back] and the gentiles came and indentured them. [The Talmud/Rav Huna] decides there that since they [=the Jews] did this [borrowed money from gentiles] regularly, two or three times at least, it is as if they gave themselves over [to the gentiles as slaves].

אפי' אי לא הוי נסתרה ומתייחדת מרצונה, אלא שגרמה כמה פעמים ע"י הקפותה ובלבוליה שנחבשת בין הנכרים בלתי שומר, ומעיד להחשיבה כמזיד להתייחד כדאמרינן פ' השולח (גיטין מו ע"ב) גבי הנהו דבני מכסי דהוי יזפי מנכרים ואתי וגרבי להו, ומסיק כיון דרגילי בהכי כמו שמסרו את עצמם מרצונם ושנו ושלשו.

Therefore, since [her seclusion] is considered a violation of *dat*, it is a mitzvah for him to divorce her. And if he does not remove her [from his house] he is considered wicked. Clearly, with regard to this case the Gaon did not make his decree, as can be seen in *Hagahot Maimoniyot* and in *Mordechai*, Ch. 7 of Ketubot, in the name of Maharam. However, with regard to cancelling her ketubah payment, we require a

וא"כ הואיל וחשיב עוברת על דת מצוה לגרשה, ואם אינו מוציאה נקרא רשע, ופשיטא דאכה"ג לא תיקן הגאון כדאיתא בהגה"ה במיימון ובמרדכי פ' המדיר בשם מהר"ם. אלא דלענין להפסיד כתובתה בעינן התראה כדמסיק במס' סוטה פ' ארוסה /דף כה ע"א/ דעוברת על

warning, as was decided in b. Sotah (25a), that a woman who violates *dat* needs to have received a warning if her husband is to cancel her ketubah payment.

In truth, it seems somewhat possible to argue that for a woman like this who is accustomed to being alone among the exceedingly promiscuous gentiles, and who behaves in many different extremely brazen ways, there would not be a need for a warning to cancel her ketubah payment.

There is a possible proof for this from the above quoted passage from b. Sotah, for the Talmud decides there, with regard to the wife of a person who became a deaf-mute or who was incarcerated, that the court can claim offense on his behalf, but cannot force her to drink *sotah* waters or cancel her ketubah payment, and we learn from this that she requires warning [in order to lose her ketubah]. The Talmud then asks: "How come everyone didn't prove it from this example? The answer is that this case is different since she has no fear of her husband at all." Rashi explains that this is the reason why it is not considered flagrant behavior unless he warns her; however, for a woman who does have fear of her husband, one could argue that even without warning there is flagrant behavior, since she is ignoring him.

From this we see that the reason for requiring a warning is because of brazenness and impudence. Now it is true that the Talmud does decide to settle the matter from the case of the wife of a person who became a deaf-mute, and it does not make a distinction between a woman who has fear of her husband and a woman who has no such fear. This, however, can be ex-

דת צריכה התראה להפסיד כתובתה.

אמנם היה נראה קצת דאיתתא דכה"ג דרגילה להתייחד בין הנכרים שטופי זמה בכמה גווני קעבדית כמה מיני חוצפות יתירא לא בעי התראה להפסיד כתובתה.

ונראה ראייה לזה מפ' ארוסה דלעיל דקפשיט התם במסקנא מאשת מי שנתחרש או חבוש בבית האסורים דב"ד מקנין אותו לאשתו ולא להשקותה אלא לפוסלה מכתובתה, אלמא בעי התראה ש"מ. וקאמר תלמודא וכולהו מ"ט לא פשטא מהא דשאני התם דלית לה אימתא דבעל כלל, ופרש"י דמש"ה לא חשיב פריצותא אא"כ התרה בה, אבל איתתא דאית לה אימתא דבעל איכא למימר דבלא התראה איכא פריצותא מדלא אשגחה אבעלה.

הא קמן דטעם דהתראה משום פריצותא וחציפותא הוא, נהי נמי דמסיק תלמודא ופשט מאשת /מי/ שנתחרש ולא מפליג בין היכא דאיכא אימתא דבעלה ובין היכא דליכא אימתא, נוכל לומר דהיינו משום דסבר דלא חשיב פריצותא כ"כ הא דלא

plained by suggesting that ignoring one's husband is not really all that brazen. Nevertheless, these earlier Amoraim do not totally discount the idea that the matter remains dependent on exceptional brazenness, and one can argue that whenever there is a case of exceptional brazenness, the suggestion that she does not need to have been warned in advance stands in such an instance. However, since we are only arguing by analogy, we do not suggest acting upon this.

אשגחה אבעלה, אבל מ"מ סברו אמוראי קמאי דלא מדחינן לגמרי דבפריצותא חוצפה תליא מילתא, ואימא כל היכא דאיכא פריצותא יתירתא נשארת הסברא דלא בעי התראה בכה"ג, ומפני שאנו מדמין לא נעשה מעשה.

Much of this responsum is dedicated to the technical question of whether being alone with a man constitutes a violation of *dat*, and the *Terumat HaDeshen* argues that it should actually be considered a violation of *dat Moshe*. The responsum also deals with the question of whether such a woman even requires a warning to penalize her with the loss of her ketubah payment. Although these matters are mostly tangential to the topic of this book, the above responsum does make one very surprising statement.

As part of his comparison of Rambam's views on seclusion and violation of *dat*, Rabbi Isserlein claims that neither prohibitions are Torah laws according to Rambam. A woman secluding herself with another man is forbidden according to tradition (*divrei kabbalah*) and *dat Moshe* is only rabbinic in nature. This is a very surprising reading of Rambam. Although as discussed in Chapter 4, the simplest reading of Rambam is to say that he believes fully uncovered hair to be a violation of a Torah prohibition; nevertheless, as pointed out in the discussion there, Rambam does include rabbinic violations in his list of violations under *dat*.[58] Menstrual

---

58. In fact, no less a modern authority than Rabbi Mordechai Willig has embraced the *Terumat HaDeshen*'s reading of Rambam as correct (see note 60 on page 256. 231). See also the comment of R. Judah Rosanes (1657–1727) in *Mishneh LeMelekh, Hilkhot Sotah* 2:1, who writes,

...There is no doubt that a married woman who secludes herself with a man violated *dat Moshe*, for we hold that seclusion is forbidden according to the Torah, as was stated in the second chapter of Avodah Zarah. Now even though our master [Rambam], in the second chapter

...אין ספק דאשת איש שנתייחדה עוברת על דת משה היא דהא קי"ל דיחוד אסור מן התורה וכדאיתא פ"ב דע"ז ואף על פי שרבינו בפכ"ב מהלכות איסורי ביאה דין ב' כתב ואיסור

spotting, for example, generates only a rabbinic prohibition according to all views. Furthermore, according to Rambam, the dough offering (and Levitical tithe) are only rabbinic obligations nowadays, and tithes on fruit are rabbinic obligations at all times.[59]

One can tie this reading of Rambam in with the first responsum. Rambam believes that a woman (any woman – even a single woman) who goes out with her hair totally uncovered has violated *dat Moshe*. However, he believes that *dat Moshe* is not necessarily coterminous with violating a Torah law. Assuming that R. Isserlein factors Rambam's view into his overall perspective, it is easier to understand how on one hand he believes that a woman with fully uncovered hair violates *dat Moshe,* and on the other hand believes that this rule applies subjectively – to situations or societies where such behavior is likely to arouse the "lewd" men.[60]

| of *Hilkhot Issurei Biah*, law 2, writes that the prohibition of seclusion with *arayot* is from tradition, that is because of his general theory that anything that is not written explicitly in the Torah cannot be called biblical, and this is exactly how he describes the passage in Avodah Zarah, where it says that seclusion for *arayot* level forbidden relations is forbidden in the Torah. Furthermore, even if one were to accept that the law was only rabbinic, nevertheless, it is clear that seclusion is no less forbidden than a woman having her head covered with a *kalta*, which according to all opinions is only a rabbinic prohibition.... | יחוד העריות מפי הקבלה זהו לפי סברתו דכל דבר שאינו מפורש בכתוב לא קרי ליה דבר תורה וה"ה שם העתיק סוגיא דע"ז דאמרינן דיחוד עריות מן התורה ועוד דאף דנימא דאין איסורו כי אם מדרבנן מ"מ פשיטא דלא גרע יחוד מראשה פרוע בקלתה דאליבא דכ"ע אין איסורו כי אם מדרבנן ואפ"ה יוצאה שלא בכתובה. |

Reading between the lines, if all consider a woman wearing a *kalta* in public to be only a rabbinic violation, not all consider a woman without a *kalta* to be a Torah violation. In other words, the *Mishneh LeMelekh* maintains that there are Rishonim who ruled that hair covering is only rabbinic. Presumably, he believes this is Rambam's view, especially since he claims that Rambam considers anything not explicitly referenced in the Torah "tradition" and it is unclear whether the passage about the sotah can be considered "explicitly referenced in the Torah." See also *Responsa VaYashev Moshe, Yoreh Deah* 2; *Yechaveh Daat* 5:62.

59. See the comments of R. Vidal of Tolosa in the *Maggid Mishneh* (ad loc.):

| Our master [Rambam] explained that when the Talmudic sages stated "feeding him untithed food," they certainly meant to include all other types of forbidden foods, for nowadays tithes are only a rabbinic obligation, as noted in the first chapter of *Hilkhot Terumot*. | ביאר רבינו שכשאמרו מאכילתו שאינו מעושר כל שכן שאר דברים האסורין שהרי המעשר בזמן הזה אינו אלא מדבריהם כנזכר פרק ראשון מהלכות תרומות. |

60. Note the following fascinating comment by Rabbi Mordechai Willig of Yeshiva

The *Terumat HaDeshen*, like the Ritva, writes that the laws of *tzniut* are dependent on time and place. As Rav Yehuda Herzl Henkin[61] notes, Rabbi Yosef Y. Ostreicher (*Sefer Leket Yosher* 37b), a student of Rabbi Isserlein, cites Rabbi Isserlein as having permitted walking behind women, in line with the position of the Ritva above.

Excursus Two: The Observation of Rabbi Sinzheim as Proof to the Views Found in This Chapter

A further proof that many Rishonim are of the view that there is no biblical prohibition against going with one's hair uncovered can be found in the writings of R. Yosef David Sinzheim (author of the *Yad David*) in his *Minchat Ani* (Volume 1 pg. 176) in the section entitled "*Gilui se'ar be-isha*":

> The *Terumat HaDeshen* notes in the course of Responsum 242 that Rambam maintains that for a woman to go with uncovered head is only a rabbinic prohibition.... However, the writings of all the other decisors indicate that uncovering of hair is a biblical prohibition, as Rabbeinu Yerucham wrote explicitly. With regard to going with one's hair uncovered in a courtyard, the *Beit Shmuel, Even HaEzer* 21:5 wrote

---

University in a class entitled "Kol Isha and the Requirement of Women to Cover their Hair" (April 28, 2010).

The Rambam maintains that all women have to cover their hair: single and married. It's a simple read of the Rambam [Ishut 24:11]. Jewish women should not go out to the market with their hair undone, whether single or married. As a matter of fact, the *Terumat HaDeshen* [10], one of the later Rishonim, says that according to the Rambam, the entire requirement for covering the hair is only rabbinic, even though the Gemara says *deoraita* and *dat Moshe*; *Terumat HaDeshen* still insists it is rabbinic. How did he know? Rambam doesn't say so. You know how he knew? Because the Rambam equates the obligation of single women and married women in the area of hair covering. And it is inconceivable that a single woman should have to cover her hair by Torah law. If the Rambam equates them, then the whole enterprise is rabbinic in nature...

See, https://tinyurl.com/y5buktqw (44:00–46:00). (Transcribed and edited slightly stylistically, with Hebrew translated.)

61. *Understanding Tzniut: Modern Controversies in the Jewish Community* (NY: Urim Publications, 2008), 80–88. I would be remiss if I did not note my deep sadness in the passing of Rabbi Henkin צז״ל whilst this book was in preparation. Many times, he communicated to me his view that my basic opinion was in error on this matter. He always did so with respect and calm and kindness. He will be sadly missed in our community.

that such is not prohibited but only a practice of modesty... this seems to be missing the obvious.

See *Even HaEzer* 115, where he wrote regarding the dispute there[62] that even according to those who maintain that it is forbidden to go with one's hair uncovered in a courtyard, such is only a rabbinic prohibition. Accordingly, if one is to accept that going without even a work-basket (i.e., with one's hair fully uncovered) in a public domain is biblically prohibited, then the Rabbis enacted legislation forbidding doing so in a courtyard, lest one come to do so in a public domain. However, if going with one's hair fully uncovered in a public domain is only forbidden rabbinically, why would they have outlawed this in a courtyard – it would be considered one preventive decree on top of another?! Indeed, one may suggest that those who maintain that it is permissible to go out in a courtyard with one's hair fully uncovered in fact maintain that this is only rabbinic, just as the *Terumat HaDeshen* maintains is the view of Rambam. Therefore, the Sages did not enact a decree about going into a courtyard, but only in an alleyway which resembles a public domain. The same seems to be the view of the *Beit Yosef*, who only forbade going with a kerchief on one's head rather than a full headscarf in a courtyard which many use as a pass-through or in an alley.[63]

Who are the Rishonim who maintain that it is permissible for a woman to go out in a courtyard with her hair fully uncovered? Tosafot,[64] Rosh, Ran, Rashi, Rif, Ritva, *Ittur*, and many others (including, as we will explore, the *Tur* and *Shulchan Arukh*).[65] When R. Yochanan maintains "When a woman goes with a basket [on her head], she is not considered to be [going with] an uncovered head," his view is predicated on the assumption that there is no biblical prohibition at all. Many Rishonim

---

62. The editor notes: "In our edition of the *Beit Shmuel*, the emendation he suggests already appears."
63. R. Yosef David Sinzheim (Chief Rabbi of Strasbourg), *Minchat Ani* 1:44–45.
64. Tosafot, b. Ketubot 72b, s.v. *chatzer* ("In a courtyard – meaning, even without a basket there still is no prohibition of going with an uncovered head; for if this were not the case, then you have not left a single daughter of our patriarch Abraham.")
65. See *Beit Yosef, Even HaEzer* 115, s.v. *u-mah she-katav ve-davka*, which quotes the views of the Rishonim on this matter. The *Beit Yosef* is himself unsure as to what the view of the *Tur* is, but the *Be'er Sheva* (Responsum 18) maintains that the *Tur* in fact agrees with this position.

in fact rule this way, as we have seen. We thus understand why so many Rishonim cite the passage in the Yerushalmi stating that some courtyards are considered as alleys, and some alleys are considered as courtyards. Since no biblical prohibition is involved here at all (this is the view of the Yerushalmi),[66] one must keep in mind that not every courtyard is the same, and that the Talmudic Sages enacted a decree with regard to an alley through which many people pass just as they enacted a decree regarding the public domain (and they did not rely, for instance, on the definitions from the laws of *eruv*).[67]

---

66. This seems to be the simple understanding of the position of R. Yochanan in the Jerusalem Talmud (y. Ketubot 7:6 [42b]): "R. Chiyyah stated in the name of R. Yochanan: When a woman goes out with her *kaplitin* [on her head], she is not considered to be [going with] an uncovered head. That which you have said must be with regard to going into a courtyard, but in an alleyway, it is considered to be going with an uncovered head." See also *Penei Moshe*, y. Gittin 9:11, s.v. *ve-ha tani*.

See the comments of the *Nimukei Yosef* to b. Ketubot 72, who writes: "One may suggest that the Talmud mentioned going from one courtyard to another by way of an alley with regard to a completely uncovered head" (like the Yerushalmi). The statement of R. Yishmael does not appear in the Yerushalmi at all. R. Yosef Trani (Responsa Maharit 1:76) writes:

> The Yerushalmi states that a courtyard which many people use as a pass-through is [considered] as an alley; an alley through which many people do not pass is [considered] as a courtyard. And even though we say that going in an alley with a basket is not considered to be going with uncovered head nor a violation of *dat Yehudit*, it seems that here [the Yerushalmi] is speaking of an alley which is a thoroughfare, that the courtyard through which many people pass means that many residents of the entire region, who do not live in the courtyard, need to pass through – for instance, in order to access the many stores there. However, an alley which is used as a pass-through only by residents of the adjoining courtyards, even if there are many of them, but all others go there for no reason other than if they have business with the residents of those courtyards, then it is not considered to be an alley through which many people pass, and is no different from an alley which is not a thoroughfare.

67. According to this school of thought, the Gemara would be explained as follows: When R. Yehuda stated in the name of Shmuel that "biblically, her work-basket is satisfactory, but according to *dat Yehudit* even a basket is [insufficient and] prohibited as well," their view is that according to R. Yehuda, it is biblically prohibited to go out in the marketplace without any head covering at all, and the Rabbis decreed that rabbinically, one is required to have more of a head covering than the Torah required. R. Yochanan states that a woman who covers her hair with only "a basket, she is not considered to be going with an uncovered head"; in other words, she violates no prohibition – neither biblical nor Rabbinic. Abaye explains that there is no prohibition, according to R. Yochanan, when a woman wears only a basket in an

Conclusion

This section collects many Rishonim – and it is particularly inclusive of the vast majority of Ashkenazi medieval authorities – who rule that there is no Torah obligation for a married woman to cover her hair in situations where modest women in the society in which they are living also do not. These Rishonim constitute the giant rabbinic authorities of this era (other than Rambam) and include dominant Jewish law authorities such as Rashi, Rabbeinu Tam, Ri, Rosh, Rashba, Ritva and the *Terumat HaDeshen*, as well as other lesser known names. They do this in a variety of different ways and with a variety of different textual nuances, but the flow of these authorities – and they are most of the Rishonim – is that neither hair covering specifically nor modesty generally is determined by an objective list of what has to be covered and what does not. Rather, it is driven by an idea that immodest behavior is to be avoided and immodest behavior is a violation of halakha.

---

alley. But in a through-alley or a courtyard through which many people pass (both of which are legally equivalent to the marketplace according to R. Yochanan; see *Tur, Even HaEzer* 115 and compare the rules with regard to a marketplace, through-alley, and courtyard through which many pass), R. Yochanan maintains that wearing only a basket is prohibited, since their status is equivalent to that of a marketplace. According to R. Yochanan, there is never a biblical prohibition even in a marketplace, but there is a prohibition based on the rules of modesty (*dat Yehudit*) to go with one's head uncovered in the marketplace (which is the statement of R. Yishmael), and the sages further decreed, in his view, a prohibition to go out with only a basket (which in their time was considered immodest) in the marketplace or anywhere resembling a marketplace. But they made no such decree with regard to going out into a courtyard or anywhere resembling a courtyard, as there is no possibility of a prohibition based on rules of modesty applying there. Thus, the view of R. Yochanan in the Bavli is harmonized with the view of R. Yochanan in the Yerushalmi, as well as with the Yerushalmi's statement that "a courtyard which many people use as a pass-through is considered as an alley, while an alley through which many people do not pass is considered as a courtyard," which many Rishonim include (as they also infer from R. Yochanan that it is permissible to go with one's head uncovered in a courtyard). Likewise, those who maintain that there is a biblical prohibition to go with one's head uncovered also maintain that it is forbidden to go out in a courtyard without at least a basket; see, e.g., *Piskei Riaz*, b. Ketubot 72. According to this explanation, there is a dispute among the Rishonim as to whether we rule in accordance with R. Yehuda/Shmuel or R. Yochanan.

CHAPTER 6

Tur, Shulchan Arukh, Rama, and *Levush* as well as the Various Commentaries: The Primary Codes Adopt the Subjective View and the Commentaries Endorse the Objective Understanding

CHAPTER 6 SURVEYS THE VIEWS OF THE PRIMARY CODifiers of Jewish law after the period of the Rishonim ends: *Tur, Shulchan Arukh*, Rama, and *Levush*, each of whom adopts the view that uncovered hair is a subjectively determined violation (and a *dat Yehudit*) or otherwise presents this topic in a way that implies that hair covering is no different than any other aspect of modesty and subject to the cultural norms of the community. This chapter then reviews the many different commentaries on these texts. The commentators almost uniformly and without exception reject the positions of the Rishonim and adopt the view that the prohibition is objective and a Torah violation. This chapter concludes with a long excursus on the word *hynuma*.

Introduction

In the previous two chapters, I detailed the positions of the Rishonim. In Chapter 4, I dealt with the Rishonim who understand the rule for married women to cover their hair as objectively determined, such that it remains in place irrespective of how women dress in any given society. In Chapter 5, I discussed those Rishonim who see the rule as subjectively determined, the application of which must be determined based on women's practice in any given society. In this chapter, I will discuss what appears to be a key turning point in the way this halakha has been understood.

In Part One, I will trace how this halakha was decided in three central books of halakha: the *Tur*, the *Shulchan Arukh* and Rama, and the *Levush*.[1] In Part Two, I will discuss how this understanding was (forcefully) shifted by the classic commentaries on the *Shulchan Arukh*.

For reasons that are beyond the scope of this book, Jewish law – broadly speaking – entered into a period of codification that started with the writing of the *Tur* by Rabbi Jacob ben Asher in the beginning of the 14th century and continued until the 19th century (and maybe beyond). This codification, focused on the writing of the rules of Jewish law, allows one to see how exactly the rules of modesty and head covering were formulated.[2]

Part 1 – Explaining the *Tur*, *Shulchan Arukh*, Rama, and *Levush*

THE *TUR*

In Chapter 5, we discussed the position of R. Asher ben Yechiel (Rosh) at length, in two different places. His son, R. Jacob ben Asher (c. 1250–1327) takes up the issue of hair covering in three places in the *Tur*. The subject comes up twice in *Even HaEzer* and once in *Orach Chayyim*. Beginning with *Even HaEzer*, the first mention of hair covering (*EH* 21) mimics the Rambam's rule (*Mishneh Torah, Hilkhot Issurei Biah,* 21:17), and seems to apply to all women.

> Jewish women should not go out to the market with their hair undone, whether single or married.
>
> לא ילכו בנות ישראל פרועות ראש בשוק אחת פנויה ואחת א[ושת] אי[ש].

According to the simple reading of this paragraph, all Jewish women are forbidden to go to a public place with their hair undone; whether undone means covered or coiffed is not clear from the text. As we said in the section on the Rambam's position, this rule explicitly applies to all women, married or not, which is quite different than the way the rule is understood in most sources.

---

1. Although the *Tur* would belong in Chapter 5, chronologically speaking, the *Tur* and *Shulchan Arukh* are so central and interconnected that I thought it best to present them together, particularly since it is the first law code after the Rambam.
2. It is beyond the focus of the work to discuss why this happened, or its details. For more on this, see Michael J. Broyde and Shlomo C. Pill, "Setting the Table: An Introduction to the Jurisprudence of Rabbi Yechiel Mikhel Epstein's Arukh HaShulhan" (Academic Studies Press 2021).

The *Tur* (*Even HaEzer* 115) brings up the rule again when discussing the laws of the ketubah.

The following are to be divorced without receiving their ketubah: a wife who violates *dat Moshe* or *dat Yehudit*.	אלו יוצאות בלא כתובה העוברת על דת משה ויהודית.
And what is *dat Yehudit*? Going out with her hair undone; even if it is not entirely undone but only covered by her *kalta* – since she was not covered with a head-scarf, she is to be divorced. Rambam wrote that even though a woman's hair is covered with a kerchief, since she is not wearing a full covering like all women, she is to be divorced without receiving her ketubah. This is particularly if she goes out to a public thoroughfare, or a through-alley, or a courtyard which is crossed by the public. But [if she goes] to a regular alley or courtyard, she is not to be divorced.	ואיזו היא דת יהודית יוצאת וראשה פרוע אפי׳ אין פרוע לגמרי אלא קלתה בראשה כיון שאינה מכוסה בצעיף תצא כתב הרמב״ם אף על פי שמכוסה במטפחת כיון שאין עליה רדיד ככל הנשים תצא בלא כתובה ודוקא שיוצאת כן ברשות הרבים או במבוי המפולש או בחצר שהרבים בוקעים בו אבל במבוי שאינו מפולש וחצר שאין הרבים בוקעים בו לא תצא
So too, the woman who spins [yarn] in the marketplace, since she shows her arms to people. Also, she who spins red near her face. Rashi explains that this means that she weaves with her hand in her lap and the string hangs down before her "lower face" [a euphemism for the pelvic region]. Rambam wrote: Spinning [yarn] in the marketplace, spinning with red or the like on her face – on her forehead or cheeks, in the manner of the promiscuous [non-Jewish] women.	וכן הטווה בשוק שמראה זרועותיה לבני אדם וכן הטווה ורד כנגד פניה ופירש״י שטווה בכפה על ירכה והחוט מחוח כנגד פניה של מטה והרמב״ם כתב בשטווה בשוק וטווה ורד וכיוצא בו כנגד פניה על פדחתה או לחייה כדרך שעושין הפרוצות
Also if she speaks with or acts playful with young men. Also, if she curses [her husband's] father in front of his face or in front of his son. Also, one who demands sex from her husband in a loud voice such that her neighbors hear, or if she fights with him such that her voice is heard when demanding things of a sexual nature – in all	וכן המדברת והמשחקת עם הבחורים וכן המקללת אביו בפניו או בפני בנו וכן התובעת מבעלה התשמיש בקול רם עד ששכנותיה שומעות אותה או שמריבה עמו עד שנשמע קולה כשתובע על עסקי תשמיש בכל אחד מאלו תצא

of these cases she is divorced without receiving a ketubah payment. בלא כתובה

If one only had the two sources in *Tur Even HaEzer*, one would understand that all Jewish women, married or not, are forbidden to go out with their head uncovered, and were a married woman to do so, she should be divorced without payment of her ketubah due to her lewd behavior. The discussion in *OC* 75, however, complicates matters, as it states rather clearly that single women need not cover their hair.

If a handbreadth of a woman's flesh, which she usually covers, is exposed, it is forbidden to recite the Shema before her, even if she is one's wife. Likewise, if her calf is exposed, it is forbidden to recite [the Shema] before her. So too with the hair of a woman which it is her way to cover – it is forbidden to recite [the Shema] before it. However, for virgins whose way it is to go with their hair undone, it is permitted.	טפח המגולה באשה במקום שדרכה לכסותו אסור לקרות קריאת שמע כנגדה אפילו היא אשתו וכן אם שוקה מגולה אסור לקרות כנגדה ושער של אשה שדרכה לכסותו אסור לקרות כנגדו אבל בתולות שדרכן לילך פרועות הראש מותר.

How is one to explain this discrepancy? The simplest explanation is that the *Tur* believes modest practice is defined by local custom: virgins may uncover their hair only in a place and time where the social norm is that they may, and only because the social custom is such. In *EH* 21 he follows the Rambam's prescription of modest dress, which was the standard in Sephardic countries (including Spain, where he lived), namely that married and single women covered their hair. In *OC* 75, he references the Ashkenazic practice of single women going with their hair uncovered, explaining if that is their custom, then their hair would not be considered "exposed," and it would not be a problem for the man reciting the Shema.[3] It seems obvious from the *Tur*'s formulation that in a place where single women generally cover their hair (Sephardic countries), it would be forbidden to recite the Shema before them with their hair exposed.

With this formulation in mind, *EH* 115 is rather simple to explain as well. The woman loses her ketubah payment because she is behaving immodestly. The behavior is lewd not because it is unconditionally

---

3. The line is taken from Ra'aviah which is cited in the Mordechai commenting on b. Berachot 24a, note 80 and the *Bach* on *Tur* 21. All of this is nearly explict in the Ra'aviah discussed above in Berachot *siman* 76 and Dublitzky (n. 84) notes that there is evidence to this in the various manuscripts.

forbidden, but because proper women[4] in that society do not go out with their hair uncovered. *Tur EH* 21 states what to him was the socially normal rule and *OC* 75 references what he knows is the standard in other communities; he does not know of any society where married women go with their hair uncovered, so the possibility is never mentioned. Nevertheless, it would seem that he would agree that in such a society a woman would not be in violation of *dat Yehudit* if she went out this way, since the behavior is not lewd.

It is possible to argue that the *Tur EH* 21 refers to an "objective" prohibition, one not driven by societal norms, and that *OC* 75 is relevant only to the recitation of the Shema. In this approach, the *Tur* would be claiming that all women, single or married, are required to cover their hair. However, in a country where single women do not do so, their uncovered hair would not be considered a "distraction" to the man reciting the Shema. However, this interpretation is difficult to accept since the *Tur* does not at all imply that the single women he describes as uncovering their hair in *OC* 75 are doing something forbidden.

Another way to answer the problem in theory would be to suggest that in *EH* 21 when the *Tur* says *penuyah* (unmarried women), he is referring only to single women who have been married in the past, as opposed to virgins, who would not cover their hair. However, this interpretation seems very unlikely, since in the next line he says:

But it is permitted to gaze upon a single woman in order to determine whether he finds her attractive, for the purpose of marriage – whether a virgin or a non-virgin.	ומותר להסתכל בפני הפנויה לבודקה אם היא יפה שישאנה בין שהיא בתולה או בעולה.

Here he says explicitly that a *penuya* can refer to a virgin or a previously married woman. It strains one's credulity to claim that the *Tur* could mean two different things by the same word in the same sentence!

Rather, it seems clear the *Tur* believes that it is the normative practice for all women, married or not, to cover their hair, but he is aware that in certain countries the practice is different for single women, and he is comfortable acknowledging that in a place where single women do not cover their hair, in fact there is no violation of Jewish law. Because of this, the formulation in *EH* 21 that "A Jewish woman should not go bareheaded in the market whether she is single or married," can no more be the source

---

4. Married in Ashkenazic countries, all in Sephardic ones.

for the objective prohibition for married women to cover their hair than it is the source for the objective prohibition for single women to cover their hair. If such an objective prohibition is neither in *EH* 21 nor in *EH* 115, it certainly is not found in *OC* 75. Hence, one may conclude that it is not present in the *Tur*.

THE *SHULCHAN ARUKH*

The above formulation is not unique to the *Tur*. In the *Shulchan Arukh*, R. Joseph Karo (1488–1575, Safed) offers substantially the same formulation.

In *Even HaEzer* 115:4, the *Shulchan Arukh* classifies uncovered hair as a violation of *dat Yehudit*.

The following are to be divorced without receiving their ketubah: a wife who violates *dat Moshe* or *dat Yehudit*... What is considered to be *dat Yehudit*? Those are the modest practices with which the daughters of Israel comport themselves.	אלו יוצאות שלא בכתובה: העוברת על דת משה ויהודית... איזו היא דת יהודית, הוא מנהג הצניעות שנהגו בנות ישראל.
If a woman has done one of the following, she is considered to have violated *dat Yehudit*:	ואלו הם הדברים שאם עשתה אחת מהם עברה על דת יהודית:
a. Going out in the marketplace, a through-alley, or a public courtyard with her hair undone, and without the full covering that all other women wear, even though her hair is covered by kerchiefs.	א. יוצאת לשוק או למבוי מפולש או בחצר שהרבים בוקעים בו וראשה פרוע ואין עליה רדיד ככל הנשים, אף על פי ששערה מכוסה במטפחות,
b. Spinning [yarn] in the marketplace with red or the like on her face – on her forehead or cheeks, in the manner of the promiscuous non-Jewish women.	ב. או שהיתה טווה בשוק ורד וכיוצא בו כנגד פניה על פדחתה או על לחיה, כדרך שעושות העובדי כוכבים הפרוצות,
c. Spinning [yarn] in the marketplace and in such a way as it shows her bare arms to the onlookers (and she does this often) (Rashba 571).	ג. או שטווה בשוק ומראה זרועותיה לבני אדם (ורגילה בכך) (רשב"א סי' תקע"א),
d. Being playful with young men.	ד. או שהיתה משחקת עם הבחורים,
e. Demanding sex from her husband in a voice so loud that her neighbors hear	

her talking about sex. f. Cursing her husband's father in front of her husband's face.	ה. או שהיתה תובעת התשמיש בקול רם מבעלה עד ששכנותיה שומעות אותה מדברת על עסקי תשמיש, ו. או שהיתה מקללת אבי בעלה בפני בעלה.

In *Even HaEzer* 21:2, the *Shulchan Arukh* mandates that both married and single women cover their hair.

Jewish women should not go out to the market with their hair undone, whether single or married.	לא תלכנה בנות ישראל פרועות ראש בשוק אחת פנויה ואחת אשת איש.

Finally, the same apparently contradictory ruling regarding the recitation of Shema in front of the uncovered hair of single women appears in *Shulchan Arukh Orach Chayyim* 75:1–2.

a If a handbreadth of a woman's flesh which she usually covers is exposed, even if she is one's wife, it is forbidden to recite the Shema before her...	א טפח מגולה באשה במקום שדרכה לכסותו, אפי׳ היא אשתו אסור לקרות ק״ש כנגדה...[5]
b The hair of a woman which it is her way to cover, it is forbidden to recite before it. [*A gloss: even if she is one's wife.*] However, virgins whose way it is to go with their hair undone, it is permitted. [*A gloss: The same is true about the hair of (married) women which generally stick out from under the covering (Beit Yosef in the name of Rashba) and certainly this holds true for the hair of a non-Jewish woman (=a wig), even if she generally covers it (Hagahot Alfasi HaChadashim).*]	ב שער של אשה שדרכה לכסותו, אסור לקרות כנגדו. הגה: אפי׳ אשתו, אבל בתולות שדרכן לילך פרועות הראש, מותר. הגה: וה״ה השערות של נשים, שרגילין לצאת מחוץ לצמתן (ב״י בשם הרשב״א) וכ״ש שער נכרית, אפי׳ דרכה לכסות. (הגהות אלפסי החדשים).

A close look at these three sources together demonstrates that the *Shulchan Arukh* cannot reasonably be interpreted as establishing an objective requirement for women to cover their hair. Let's take the sources one by one.

---

5. Rama has a comment here, but it is not relevant to our subject.

Following the lead of the *Tur*, and thus having removed hair covering from the category of *dat Moshe* in EH 115, *Shulchan Arukh EH* 115 cannot be the source of an objective prohibition to cover hair. *Dat Yehudit* is a subjective category, and the *Shulchan Arukh* says that himself explicitly when he describes this category as "the modest practices with which the daughters of Israel comport themselves."

EH 21:2 could at most be the source of an objective requirement for *all* women, married or single, to cover their hair; the text gives us no way to distinguish between married and unmarried women. Moreover, it cannot be the source for an objective prohibition since this would put it in contradiction to *OC* 75, which makes it clear that single women do not have to cover their hair when modest single women in broader society do not.

Finally, *OC* 75 clarifies that common practice is the determining factor, as it describes the obligation to cover in reference to the social norm (*derech*) to cover. *OC* 75 states that in a place where any particular group of women covers their hair, all women in that group must cover their hair. Conversely, when single women do not cover their hair as a matter of fact, they need not as a matter of halakha, either.

The glosses added by Rama (R. Moshe Isserless, 1530–1572, Cracow) sharpen this point by linking the halakhic category of married women's hair (which need not be covered as a matter of halakha when it is not actually covered as a matter of social norm) to the halakhic category of single women's hair – the obligation to cover is driven by the social norm and nothing else.

LEVUSH

Finally, R. Mordechai Yoffe (c. 1530–1612), in his *Levush Malchut*, substantively echoes this formulation as well. In *Even HaEzer* 115:4, the *Levush* classifies uncovered hair as a violation of *dat Yehudit*.

1 The following are to be divorced without receiving their ketubah: a wife who violates *dat*, meaning she causes her husband to violate *dat Moshe* or *dat Yehudit*...	1 אלו יוצאות בלא כתובה העוברת על דת, פירוש המעבירה את בעלה על דת משה ויהודית....
4 What is considered to be *dat Yehudit*? Those are the modest practices with which the daughters of Israel comport themselves. If a woman has violated one of them, she	4 איזה היא דת יהודית, הוא מנהג צניעות שנהגו בו בנות ישראל, ואם עברה על אחת מהן עברה על דת יהודית

is considered to have violated *dat Yehudit*, and she must leave without her ketubah. And these are they:

a. Going out in the marketplace or in a thoroughfare with her hair undone, and without the full covering that all other women wear, even though her hair is covered by kerchiefs.
b. Or spinning [yarn] in the marketplace with red or the like on her face – on her forehead or cheeks, in the manner of the promiscuous non-Jewish women.

c. Or spinning [yarn] in the marketplace and in such a way as it shows her bare arms to the onlookers, and she does this often.
d. Or being playful with young men.
e. Or demanding sex from her husband in a voice so loud that her neighbors hear her talking about sexual matters.

All of these things are examples of promiscuity, and her husband is humiliated by her. Therefore, she must leave without receiving her ketubah payment.

In *Even HaEzer* 21:2, the *Levush* mandates that both married and single women cover their hair:

Jewish women should not go out in the marketplace with their hair undone, no matter if they are single or married, for this is promiscuous for a woman, and there is also a deeper meaning according to the Kabbalah.

Finally, the same apparently contradictory ruling regarding the recitation of Shema in front of the uncovered hair of single women appears in the *Levush, Orach Chayyim* 75:1–2.

1 An exposed handbreadth of a woman's flesh which she usually covers is nudity, and it is forbidden to recite the Shema before her, lest one come to have lewd thoughts, even if she is one's wife. Even her calf, which men usually expose (i.e., men's own calves are exposed), is considered nudity for a woman, and it is forbidden to recite the Shema before her. But her face, hands and feet which are generally exposed, it is permitted to recite before them, since they will not engender lewd thoughts as he is used to them…

א טפח מגולה באשה במקום שדרכה לכסות הוי ערוה ואסור לקרות קריאת שמע כנגדה דלא ליתי לידי הרהור, אפילו היא אשתו, ואפילו שוקה שדרך להיות באיש מגולה, באשה הוי ערוה ואסור לקרות כנגדה, אבל פניה ידיה ורגליה שדרכן להיות מגולין מותר לקרות כנגדן, דלא אתי לידי הרהור הואיל ורגיל בהן …

2 The hair of a woman which it is her way to cover, it is forbidden to recite before her, even if she is one's wife. However, virgins whose way it is to go with their hair undone, it is permitted. The same is true about [married] women's hair which is generally exposed, like with the hair that generally sticks out from under the covering, it is permitted, and this is even more obviously permitted for a wig, which isn't her hair, even if she usually covers it.

ב שער של אשה שדרכה לכסותה, אסור לקרות כנגדה אפילו באשתו, אבל בתולות שדרכן ללכת פרועות הראש מותר, והוא הדין שערות של נשים שדרכן להיות מגולין כגון שערות הרגילות לצאת חוץ לצמתן מותר, וכל שכן פאה נכרית שאינה שלה אפילו דרכה לכסותו מותר:

Again, as we saw in the *Tur* and the *Shulchan Arukh* and Rama, the *Levush* in one place states that all women, married or unmarried, must cover their hair in public, and in another, states that unmarried women do not generally cover their hair. The best explanation for this contradiction is that the differences between the rules connects to the differences in normative practice between communities. The main objective of these sources is to delineate between generally accepted practice and lewd or promiscuous behavior.

The counter-argument is that even unmarried women should cover their hair according to the rules of the *Tur, Shulchan Arukh*, Rama, and *Levush*. While reasonable at first glance, an objective obligation to cover simply cannot be sustained after a close read of *OC* 75 or *EH* 21 in any of these works.

Therefore, it would seem that according to the *Tur, Shulchan Arukh* and the *Levush*, in a society in which even married women going out with their heads uncovered is not considered lewd behavior, there should be no prohibition for a married Jewish woman to go out with her hair uncovered.

Part 2 – The Commentators on the Tur and Shulchan Arukh (Nos'ei Keilim)

Despite what seems to be the simple meaning of these texts presented above, most of the commentators on these books (the *nos'ei keilim*) answer the contradiction between *EH* 21 and *OC* 75 differently.

MODEL 1: TWO TYPES OF *PENUYOT*

The most common approach among the *nos'ei keilim* is to suggest that the word *penuya* (unmarried) in *EH* 21 refers specifically to divorced or widowed women, and not women who have never been married (virgins), whereas in *OC* 75, the reference is to all single women, regardless of their past marital or sexual history.

I reject this reading because it would mean interpreting the word *penuya* in two different ways in the same halakha, since in the next line, the *Tur* is explicit that *penuya* can refer to virgins. Nevertheless, many of the key commentators make this argument.

COMMENTARIES ON THE *TUR*

In his commentary on the *Tur*, the *Perisha*, R. Joshua Falk-Katz (1555–1614) offers the following interpretation of *EH* 21 (#3):

"Jewish women should not go out to the market with their hair undone, whether single [or married]" – It would seem that by "single" he means to say a widow or a divorcée, but virgins are permitted to go out [without their hair uncovered] as is our custom.	לא ילכו פרועות ראש [בשוק] אחת פנויה וכו'. לכאורה נראה דפנויה רצה לומר כמו אלמנה או גרושה אבל בתולות מותרות להלך כמנהגינו:

According to this, when the *Tur* says single women may not go out with their hair uncovered, it only refers to previously married women. A similar interpretation of *EH* 21 was offered by the *Bach* (R. Joel Sirkes, 1561–1640):

It must be said that by single is meant a non-virgin woman, but virgins are not included in this prohibition.	וצריך לומר דבפנויה בעולה קאמר אבל הבתולות אינן באזהרה:

The *Bach*'s position is substantially the same as the *Perisha*'s, but he uses the term "non-virgin" instead of "widow or divorcée." Although it is possible that he means the term as a synonym for previously married, it is also possible that there is a halakhic difference between the two positions, and that the *Bach* would require a non-virgin to cover her hair whereas the *Perisha* would not.

COMMENTARIES ON THE *SHULCHAN ARUKH*

BEIT SHMUEL

The same approach of distinguishing between two types of *penuyot* can be found among the commentators on the *Shulchan Arukh* as well. The *Perisha*'s position is taken by R. Shmuel ben Uri Shraga Phoebus (latter half of 17th century) in his *Beit Shmuel* (EH 21:2):

> Whether single – this means a widow or a divorcée, but a virgin is permitted...
>
> א[חת] פנויה - היינו אלמנה או גרושה אבל בתולה מותר...

TAZ AND *CHELKAT MECHOKEK*

The *Bach*'s position, in contrast, is taken by his son-in-law R. David HaLevi Segal (1586–1667), in his *Taz* (*Turei Zahav*) on the *Shulchan Arukh* (ad loc.):

> Whether single or married – not included in this category is a single virgin since she generally goes in public with uncovered hair.[6]
>
> אחת פנויה ואחת אשת איש - אין בכלל זה פנויה בתולה דהיא רגילה בגילוי שער.

This is also the opinion of the *Taz*'s older brother, R. Isaac HaLevi Segal (as we will see in the next chapter on responsa). A similar comment is made by R. Moshe ben Yitzhak Yehuda-Lima (c. 1615–1670), in his *Chelkat Mechokek* (EH 21:2):

> Whether single or married – This refers to a single woman who was once married, but regarding a virgin, we say that she goes out with her *hynuma* and her hair uncovered. This is the position of the *Bach*, and see further in the *Mordechai*.
>
> א[חת] פנויה וא[חת] א[שת] א[יש] - פנויה בעולה קאמר אבל בתולה אמרי' דיוצאה בהינומ' וראשה פרועה וכן הוא בב"ח ועיין במרדכי:

---

6. The comment does not appear in the standard version, but it has been included in updated printings that make use of manuscripts.

BEIT HILLEL

The difference between these "virgin versus non-virgin" and "previously married versus maiden" positions was not always noticed or insisted upon. Many commentators are unclear on which side they fall, or make the assumption that both positions are the same. One commentary that does not clarify his stance on the question of whether he believes the *Shulchan Arukh* is distinguishing between previously married and never married, or virgin and non-virgin, is R. Hillel ben Naphtali Hertz (1615–1690), in his *Beit Hillel* on *EH*:

> Virgins are permitted to go out [in public] with their hair uncovered as it says in the *Shulchan Arukh OC* 75:3?! Because virgins generally go out with their hair undone, this is permitted.
>
> והנה בתולות מותר לילך פרועות ראש כדאיתא בש"ע בא"ח בסימן ע"ה ס"ג אבל בתולות שדרכן לילך פרועות הראש מותר.

Although he uses the word "virgin," this term can double for "never before married" and he offers no clear terms such as a "non-virgin" or "widow" to offer a contrast. Thus, *Beit Hillel*'s view on that question is unknown.

AMBIGUOUS ELISION

NACHALAT TZVI

One commentator who elides the point entirely is R. Tzvi Katz (early 17 century), a student of the *Bach*, in his *Nachalat Tzvi*:

> "Whether single" – my teacher (*Bach*) and R. Falk-Katz (*Perisha*) wrote that this refers specifically to widows and divorcées but not to virgins.
>
> אחת פנויה - וכתבו מ"ו ורפ"ך דוקא כגון אלמנה או גרושה אבל בתולה מותר, ע"ש.

By quoting the *Bach* and the *Perisha* as if they were saying the exact same thing, the *Nachalat Tzvi* implies that this is all one position, though it is unclear which one.

STRICT ELISION

BA'ER HEITEIV

R. Judah ben Simon Ashkenazi of Tykocin (d. 1723), in his *Ba'er Heiteiv*, also elides these two positions:

> Single – single here refers to a widow or divorcée or a non-virgin, but a virgin is per-
>
> פנויה - פנויה היינו אלמנה או גרושה או בעולה, אבל

mitted [to go out with her hair undone]. Bach, Chelkat Mechokek, Beit Hillel, Beit Shmuel.

בתולה מותר; ב"ח, ח"מ, בית הילל, ב"ש.

By putting *Bach*, *Chelkat Mechokek* and *Beit Shmuel* in the same camp, *Ba'er Heiteiv* like *Nachalat Tzvi*, elides the two camps and makes them into one. Unlike those before him, however, he is explicitly putting all the previous authorities into the stricter camp that forbids non-virgins, even if they were never before married, from appearing in public with their hair undone.

DAGUL MERVAVAH

R. Ezekiel Landau (1713–1793), in his *Dagul Mervavah* (EH 21:2), also elides the two positions in favor of the stricter one. He begins by using the language of the *Beit Shmuel*, but ascribes it to both him and the *Chelkat Mechokek*:

The *Chelkat Mechokek* and the *Beit Shmuel* have understood correctly that [*penuya*] refers here to a widow or divorcée.

יפה כיוונו החלקת מחוקק והב[ית] ש[מואל] דהיינו אלמנה וגרושה

The *Dagul Mervavah* continues his gloss by attempting to show that a non-virgin who had never been married falls into the category of widow and divorcée for the purposes of hair covering. To do so, he makes reference to a passage in the Yerushalmi (y. Ketubot 2:1). The passage is commenting on a mishnah (m. Ketubot 2:1) describing a case in which a woman is trying to prove that she had been a virgin when she got married:

A woman was widowed or divorced: She says: "I was a virgin when you married me."[7] He says [or his heirs say][8]: "No, you were a widow when I married you." – If there are witnesses that she went out at her wedding and her hair was undone, her ketubah is two hundred [*zuz*]. R. Yochanan ben Baroka says: "The passing out of parched grain is also a proof [that she was a virgin when married]."

האשה שנתארמלה או שנתגרשה היא אומרת בתולה נשאתני והוא אומר לא כי אלא אלמנה נשאתיך אם יש עדים שיצאת בהינומא וראשה פרוע כתובתה מאתים ר' יוחנן בן ברוקא אומר אף חלוק קליות ראיה:

---

7. The issue here is not virginity per se (how would the heirs know?), but whether it was a first or second marriage.
8. Heirs are not mentioned here explicitly, but the Talmud takes it for granted and it is obvious: by definition, a widow cannot debate with her late husband.

The Yerushalmi offers the following analysis:

Shouldn't there be a concern that perhaps she was a virgin from *nissuin*? This shows that a virgin from *nissuin* does not go out with her hair undone.	וחש לומר שמא בתולה מן הנישואין היא זאת אומרת בתולה מן הנישואין אינה יוצאת וראשה פרוע

The Yerushalmi suggests that the fact that the woman went out with her hair undone at her wedding might not be a proof that she had never been married before. Perhaps she had been married before and her husband died before they could consummate the marriage, and thus she was still a virgin. This, theoretically, would lead to her going out with her hair undone but still only able to collect a ketubah payment of 100 zuz, since she had been married previously. The Yerushalmi answers that we can learn a rule from this, namely that the Mishnah assumes that women who were once married, even if they remained virgins, do not go out with their hair undone.

The Yerushalmi continues with another problem:

Should there be no concern that she may have had her hymen ruptured through an accident (i.e., and not coitus; literally, "struck by wood")? Rather, [the Mishnah] follows R. Meir, for R. Meir said that a woman whose hymen was ruptured by accident receives a ketubah of two hundred zuz. R. Yochanan said: "They were not concerned about unusual cases."	וחש לומר שמא מוכת עץ היא אלא כר' מאיר דר' מאיר אומר מוכת עץ כתובתה מאתים וא״ר יוחנן לא חשו על דבר שאינו מצוי.

Here the concern is that even if she had never before been married, and even if she is a virgin, perhaps she lacks a hymen for some other reason, which would lower her ketubah payment but not require her to have her hair done up or covered. The Talmud offers two answers: First, it may be that the Mishnah follows the position of R. Meir, that a virgin lacking a hymen still receives a ketubah of 200 zuz. Second, it may be that the Mishnah simply is not taking into account exceptional cases, but if she really was a virgin without a hymen, the free-flowing hair at her wedding would be a false proof. Such a case is too unusual to make rules to avoid this possibility.

The *Dagul Mervavah* uses this passage to support his contention that a non-virgin falls into the same category as a widow and divorcée:

This comes from the words of the Yerushalmi, y. Ketubot Ch. 2, at the end of the first halakha [that states]:

"And her head uncovered ... and we should be concerned and say perhaps she is a virgin even though once married (i.e., the marriage wasn't consummated). This implies that a virgin after marriage should not go out with her hair uncovered."

See discussion there.

That text also provides proof that a non-virgin, even if she has never been married before, is not permitted to go out with her hair undone, for the Yerushalmi there asks,

"Perhaps she had her hymen broken in an accident? It follows R. Meir, who says that her ketubah payment should be 200 *zuz*."

But this is still a problem, since she could be a non-virgin in any case. Rather, it seems clear that a non-virgin may not go out with her hair undone.

והוא מדברי הירושלמי בפ"ב דכתובות סוף הלכה א'

וראשה פרוע וכו' וחש לומר שמא בתולה מן הנישואין היא זאת אומרת בתולה מן הנישואין אינה יוצאה וראשה פרוע.

ע"ש

וגם משם ראיה דגם בעולה אפילו לא נישאת עדיין כלל אינה רשאית לצאת בראש פרוע שהירושלמי הקשה שם

ושמא מוכת עץ היא כר"מ דאמר כתובתה מאתים

וקשה אכתי שמא בעולה היא אלא ודאי דבעולה אסורה לצאת ראשה פרוע:

The *Dagul Mervavah* argues that the Yerushalmi's answer to the second question is, on the face of it, insufficient. Even if a woman who suffers the accidental rupture of her hymen gets 200 zuz, the woman who went out with her hair undone at her wedding may not have been a virgin at all, even if she had never been married before. Why does the Yerushalmi discuss only the unlikely scenario of a ruptured hymen and not the more likely scenario of premarital sex?

For this reason, the *Dagul Mervavah* argues that the Yerushalmi must be assuming that non-virgins must do up or cover their hair. This proves, to his mind, that a non-virgin fits in the category of widow and divorcée, and that she may not go around with her hair undone, unlike a virgin who may.

ROSH PINAH

Another commentator who elides the two positions in favor of the stricter approach is Rabbi Shmarya Shmeril Brandris of Harlimov (1780–1857) in his *Rosh Pinah*, a super-commentary that is split into one on the *Chelkat*

Mechokek (called *Chelkat HaSadeh*) and the other on the *Beit Shmuel* (called *Ikvei HaBayit*). In *Chelkat HaSadeh*, he comments on why *Chelkat Mechokek* uses the word "non-virgin":

> "'Whether single, etc.' – this means a non-virgin" – this phrasing implies that he is referring to illicit sex and not specifically a divorcée or widow. And I saw in the *Dagul Mervavah*, who quoted a Yerushalmi... And he is certainly picturing illicit sex, for if he was thinking of a widow or a divorcée, this would be obvious, for this is exactly the sign [that distinguishes virgins from previously married women], since a widow or divorcée do not have undone hair [in public].
>
> אחת פנויה כו' - בעולה קאמר - משמע מלשון זה אפילו בעולה בזנות, ולאו דוקא גרושה או אלמנה. וראיתי בספר דגול מרבבה הביא בשם הירושלמי... והיינו ודאי כונתו על בעולה בזנות דאי על אלמנה וגרושה פשיטה, דהא היינו הוא הסימן, שאלמנה וגרושה אין ראשה פרוע,
>
> According to this, it is a bad thing that is done, in our many sins, by allowing unmarried harlots not to cover their hair until they are ready to give birth...
>
> ולפי זה לא יפה עושים במה שאין מכסים ראשי הזונות פנויות בעו"ה עד מלאת ימיה ללדת...

This analysis is not surprising, since *Chelkat Mechokek* does seem to take a strict position. However, in his *Ikvei HaBayit*, the *Rosh Pinah* makes the argument that the *Beit Shmuel* also meant to take the strict position:

> "'Whether single etc.' – but a virgin is permitted" – this phrasing implies, as I said in my *Chelkat HaSadeh*, that a single woman who had illicit sex is forbidden [to appear in public with her hair undone] and that only a virgin is permitted. And that which the *Beit Shmuel* wrote "this refers to a widow or a divorcée" – this is certainly not meant exclusively, rather the law also applies to a non-virgin.
>
> אחת פנויה וכו' אבל בתולה מותר - מלשון זה משמע גם כן כמו שכתבתי בח"מ דבעולה בזנות אסור, ודוקא בתולה מותרת. ומ"ש הב"ש היינו אלמנה וגרושה ודאי לאו דוקא אלא הוא הדין בעולה.

Thus, the *Rosh Pinah* argues that the *Beit Shmuel* and *Chelkat Mechokek* actually adopt the same position and that *Beit Shmuel* means to include any non-virgin in the category of "widow and divorcée." Despite the *Rosh Pinah*'s claim about what the *Beit Shmuel* "certainly" means, he offers no reason why this must be the case. In fact, if anything, the opposite is more likely to be the case, and that "non-virgin" is just shorthand for "previously married" as has been argued by a minority of commentators.

LENIENT ELISION

PITCHEI TESHUVA

In his *Pitchei Teshuva*, R. Abraham Tzvi Hirsch Eisenstadt of Bialystok (1812–1868) takes umbrage with this eliding of positions presenting all the commentators as being in agreement that only an actual virgin may appear in public with her hair undone:

> ... That which the *Ba'er Heiteiv* wrote "[single here] refers to a widow or divorcée or a non-virgin [but a virgin is permitted]" – from this phrasing it is clear [that by "non-virgin"] he is referring to a woman who had illicit sex, which follows the position of the *Shevut Yaakov* that he quoted later.
>
> ... ומ"ש הבה"ט היינו אלמנה או גרושה או בעולה כו' מלשון זה מבואר דבעולה בזנות קאמר והיינו כהשבו"י שהביא לקמן.

> But in truth he did not copy down [the halakhic position] correctly, when he listed all three together, since these three were not mentioned together in one place, for the *Bach* and the *Chelkat Mechokek* do not mention the widow and divorcée, only the non-virgin, while the *Beit Shmuel* does not mention the non-virgin, but only the widow and divorcée.
>
> אך באמת לא העתיק כראוי במה דנקט אלו הג' יחד כי אלו שלשתן לא הוזכרו במקום א' כי בב"ח וח"מ לא הוזכר אלמנה וגרושה רק בעולה ובב"ש לא הוזכר בעולה רק אלמנה וגרושה

> Thus it is clear that the words of the *Beit Shmuel* imply that a non-virgin who is single but has had illicit sex is not prohibited [from going in public with her hair undone] (and this is also what the *Pri Megadim* deduces from his language in *OC* there).
>
> והא ודאי דמדברי הב"ש משמע דבעולה פנויה שזינתה אין איסור (וכן מדייק מדבריו הפמ"ג בא"ח שם)

Ironically, the *Pitchei Teshuva* goes on to elide the positions himself, but in the opposite way:

> And even the *Bach* and the *Chelkat Mechokek* who use the term non-virgin, it could be argued that they just mean
>
> ואף הב"ח וח"מ דנקטו בעולה י"ל דכוונתם נמי בעולה ע"י נשואין דהיינו אלמנה וגרושה

non-virgins from a previous marriage, namely a widow or a divorcée from *nissuin* (consummated marriage), as opposed to from *erusin* (betrothal), who would not fall under this prohibition. But loss of virginity from illicit sex does not bring about a prohibition of going in public with undone hair. My grandfather, in his *Panim Meirot* 1:35 wrote thus as well . . . [9]

מן הנשואין ולאפוקי מן האירוסין דלא אבל ע"י זנות י"ל דאין איסור בפריעת ראש. גם בתשו' אא"ז פנים מאירות ח"א סי' ל"ה דעתו כן . . .

The *Pitchei Teshuva* also believes that only one position exists among the early *nos'ei keilim*, only he believes the agreement falls out on the lenient side. According to the *Pitchei Teshuva*, the "non-virgin" in the *Beit Shmuel* (and presumably the *Perisha* as well) is simply shorthand for previously married. Women who have never been married do not need to cover their hair in public irrespective of any possible sexual history.

ARUKH HASHULCHAN

R. Yechiel Michel Epstein, in his *Arukh HaShulchan* (EH 21:4) adopts the lenient position of the *Perisha* and *Beit Shmuel* as the baseline, but leaves open whether the halakha follows the *Bach* and *Chelkat Mechokek*.

> "Jewish women should not go out to the market with their hair undone, whether single" – such as a widow or divorcée – "or married" – [For these women,] going out in a public place with their hair undone is forbidden according to the Torah, for it says with regard to the *sotah*, "and her hair should be undone" which shows that she does not generally go out like that. This will all be explained in *siman* 115.
>
> לא תלכנה בנות ישראל פרועות ראש בשוק אחת פנויה כגון אלמנה וגרושה ואחת אשת איש וילך פרועת ראש ברה"ר אסור מן התורה דכתיב בסוטה ופרע את ראש האשה מכלל דאינה הולכת כה ובסי' קט"ו יתבאר בזה
>
> With regard to an unmarried woman (lit. a virgin) who had relations or who was betrothed but not yet married, there are those who say she must cover her hair and those who say she does not.
>
> וכן בתולה שנבעלה או נתקדשה ולא נשאת עדיין י"א שתכסה ראשה וי"א שא"צ:

---

[9]. The responsum of the *Panim Meirot* will be discussed at length in the next chapter.

This reading of the *Shulchan Arukh*, irrespective of whether non-virgin refers only to previously married women or any single woman who has had sex, is the dominant interpretation among the commentators, but not the only one.

Model 2a – Braiding versus Covering (Magen Avraham)

MAGEN AVRAHAM

A less popular solution to the problem of *EH* 21 versus *OC* 75 was put forward by R. Avraham Gombiner (1633–1683) in his *Magen Avraham*. Commenting on the reference to virgins whose practice it is to go with their hair uncovered, he says the following (*OC* 75:3):

> "Virgins whose practice it is, etc." – This is a problem, since in *Even HaEzer* 21:1, he (=the *Shulchan Arukh*) wrote that "Jewish women should not go out with their hair undone in the market place, whether they are single or married." This is also what the Rambam wrote in Chapter 21 of the laws of forbidden relations. Moreover, in Ketubot, towards the beginning of the second chapter, it states: "If she went out to her wedding day with her hair undone," this is a sign that she is a virgin.

> בתולות שדרכן כו'. ק[שיא] דבא"ע סי' כ"א ס"א כ' לא תלכנה בנות ישראל פרועי' ראש בשוק א' פנויות וא' אשת איש וכ"כ הרמב"ם פכ"א מהא"ב ועוד דאי' בכתובות רפ"ב אם יצאה בהינומ' וראשה פרועה זהו סי' שהיתה בתולה.

Here the *Magen Avraham* lays out the contradiction clearly, noting that the *Shulchan Arukh* is following the Rambam in *Issurei Biah* 21, to forbid any woman, single or married, to go in public with her hair undone. However, this rule contradicts the premise in *OC* 75 that at least in some communities, single women do not cover their hair, and that this custom is explicitly supported by the Talmud in b. Ketubot which assumes that free-flowing hair is a sign that the woman is a virgin.

In his commentary on the *Magen Avraham* called the *Machatzit HaShekel*, R. Samuel ben Natan HaLevi Loew Kelin (1720–1806) clarifies the *Magen Avraham's* problem even further:

> "'Virgins etc.' – Moreover, in Ketubot, etc." – If so, this contradicts the *Shulchan Arukh* in *Even HaEzer* and Rambam, who wrote that single women are forbidden to go in

> בתולות כו'. ועוד דאיתא בכתובות כו'. וא"כ קשיא על שו"ע אה"ע ורמב"ם דכתבו דפנויות אסורות לילך בגילוי

public with their hair revealed. For the opposite is the case! This behavior is the [social] sign that she is a virgin!

ראש, הא אדרבא זהו הסימן שהיתה בתולה:

This gloss states the problem quite clearly. The *Magen Avraham* is aware of the direction taken by the *Perisha* and the *Bach*, that the rule in EH 21 only applies to previously married women or non-virgins, but he rejects this approach outright – for the same reason I rejected it above:

It is unreasonable to suggest that the "single women" referred to [in EH 21] means widows, for if that were the case he should have clarified explicitly.

ודוחק לומר דפנויות דקתני היינו אלמנה דא״כ ה״ל לפרש[10]

Nevertheless, the *Magen Avraham* does not assume, as I did, that the difference between EH 21 and OC 75 is based on communal practice, and that which women in a given community – if any – cover their hair is based only on communal norms and not objective standards. Instead, he takes a third approach, namely that we are speaking of two different kinds of hair covering:

One might suggest that the "undone hair" about which he writes in *Even HaEzer* means that they undo their hair entirely, and go out [with it free-flowing] in the market place, for this is forbidden even for a single woman. And Rashi said as much in his commentary on *Nasso*, on the phrase "and he will undo the hair of the woman" [referring to the law of the *sotah*] (Num. 5:18).

וי״ל דפרוע׳ ראש דכתב בא״ע היינו שסותרות קליעות שערן והולכות בשוק דזה אסור אפי׳ בפנויה וכן פירש״י פ׳ נשא על ופרע ראש האשה

The *Machatzit HaShekel* explains the deduction from Rashi:

"Rashi said as much in his commentary on *Nasso*, etc." – This is what he says: "'And [the priest] shall make wild' – he undoes the braids of her hair in order to humili-

פירש רש״י פרשת נשא כו׳. וז״ל, ופרע סותר קליעת שערה כדי לבזותה, מכאן לבנות ישראל שגילוי הראש

---

10. The *Machatzit HaShekel* explains:

"It is unreasonable to suggest" – But this is what the *Bach* in *Even HaEzer* (ad loc., s.v. "lo") suggests, that [single] there refers to a widow.

ודוחק לומר כו׳. והב״ח באה״ע [שם ד״ה לא] מפרש כן דמיירי התם באה״ע באלמנה:

Admittedly, the *Machatzit HaShekel* is being imprecise here and eliding the suggestion of the *Perisha* with that of the *Bach*.

ate her. From here we learn that revealed hair is a humiliation for Jewish women." If this is the case, it implies that it is specifically unbraided (or uncoiffed) hair that is the humiliation.

גנאי להם, עכ"ל. א"כ משמע דוקא סתירת הקליעה גנאי:

At first glance, it would seem that the *Magen Avraham* solved the problem here by positing that a minimal coiffing or braiding is a Torah requirement for all Jewish women. This would mean that the discussion of virgins with their hair undone should not be taken literally – it does not mean it was uncovered, but rather that it was braided or coiffed and not free-flowing. Nevertheless, *Magen Avraham* realizes that such a solution brings up further problems, and he backtracks a bit:

Nevertheless, we must admit that a single woman is not forbidden with a Torah prohibition [to go with her hair free-flowing], for if we were to say that the verse [in Numbers] also includes single women, then she would also be prohibited from going in public with her hair uncovered, for it is from this verse that Ketubot Ch. 7 learns the prohibition for Jewish women to go in public with their hair uncovered. Rather, we must say that the verse is not referring to single women, only that it is modest behavior for even virgins not to go out in public that way (i.e., with their hair free-flowing).

ומ"מ צ"ל דפנויה לא מתסרי מדאוריי' דא"ת דקרא איירי גם בפנויה א"כ גם בגילוי הראש תהא אסור' לילך דמהכא ילפינן בכתובות פ"ז שלא תלכנה בנות ישראל בגילוי הראש אלא ע"כ קרא לא איירי בפנויה רק שמדת צניעות היא לבתולות שלא לילך כן:

The *Magen Avraham* is stuck because both the basic requirement to braid the hair and the extended requirement to cover the hair are learned from the same verse. Thus he cannot split the difference and argue that the former is a requirement for all women and the latter only for married women. Thus, *Magen Avraham*'s answer really turns out to be only half an answer. Ultimately, he must say that the requirement for the single woman to go with her hair done up is not a real prohibition but a suggestion about modest behavior, while for the married woman (referenced in the same sentence) it is forbidden to go out this way.

MACHATZIT HASHEKEL

This is not the only problem with the *Magen Avraham*. The *Machatzit HaShekel* points out another one:

"Only that it is modest behavior" – If so, Rashi on the Pentateuch [who says that undone hair is a humiliation to Jewish women] is either only referring to married women or he is including single women but only as an *asmachta* (a mnemonic connection).	רק שמדת צניעות כו'. וא"כ רש"י בחומש או איירי דוקא בנשואה, או בפנויה ודבריו אסמכתא.
Nevertheless, even according to the words of the *Magen Avraham*, that a virgin is nonetheless forbidden to go out with free-flowing hair, in other words, with her braids undone, if so, there is still a problem from [the Talmudic text which states] that if a woman went out at her wedding [with her hair undone, it is clear she was a virgin]. For Rashi explains there at the beginning of the chapter (b. Ketubot 15b): "Hair undone means that her hair flows freely onto her shoulders." And this means that her hair is unbraided, and that is the customary practice [even now].	עכ"פ גם לפי דברי מ"א דעכ"פ גם בתולה אסורה בפריעת ראש דהיינו קליעת שערה מסותרים, א"כ עדיין קשיא מהא דאם יצאה בהינומא כו', דהא פירש רש"י ריש פרק האשה שנתארמלה [כתובות טו, ב] וז"ל, וראשה פרוע שערה על כתפה, עכ"ל. והיינו קליעתה סתורה, וכן המנהג:

Admittedly, the *Machatzit HaShekel* overstates his question, since the *Magen Avraham* admits that there cannot be an actual prohibition against virgins going out with their hair undone, because the requirement to cover is learned from this same verse and only applies to married women. Nevertheless, the *Machatzit HaShekel*'s point is well taken. It seems strange to say that the rule in *Even HaEzer* 21 is meant to strongly push virgins to dress modestly by having their hair coiffed or braided when in public, when the Talmud is explicit that free-flowing hair is the sign of a woman's having never been married, and that such behavior was and is the customary practice of Jewish maidens.

PRI MEGADIM – ESHEL AVRAHAM

Another commentary on the *Magen Avraham*, the *Pri Megadim* of R. Joseph ben Meir Teomim (1727–1792), tries to make sense out of *Magen*

Avraham's claim. In the *Eshel Avraham* section, he starts by outlining what we know about the halakhot here from the Talmud and Rashi's commentary on the Torah:

> The words of the master require elucidation. For in b. Ketubot 72b, it states that undone hair is a biblical prohibition [and not merely a custom of Jewish women as the Talmud implies], from the verse (Num. 5:18) "and he shall undo her hair," this is a warning... And [the Talmud] answers that from the Torah, going with a *kalta* would be sufficient. See [*Shulchan Arukh*] EH 115:4.
>
> ודברי האדון צ"ב. כי הנה בכתובות ע"ב א' וראשה פרוע דין תורה הוא, ופרע ראש האשה (במדבר ה' י"ח) אזהרה כו', ומשני דין תורה קלתה שרי, ועיין אה"ע [סימן] קט"ו סעיף ד'.

> And Rashi on the Pentateuch [explains] "undo" as unraveling her braids, and as R. Eliyahu Mizrachi wrote [in his supercommentary on Rashi] there that [what Rashi is noticing on that verse is that] the word "head" is superfluous, for [not only is her hair uncovered but] her entire body is uncovered [so why single out her head?] We learn from this that the revealing of her hair is a step beyond [the revealing of her body], namely that her braids are unraveled.
>
> ורש"י בחומש ופרע "סותר" קליעת שערה, וכמו שכתב הרא"ם ז"ל שם דראש מיותר, דגופה נמי סותר, שמע מינה שמגלה ראשה עוד "וסותר" קליעת שערה.

Having laid this out, the *Pri Megadim* first explains what he feels cannot be the *Magen Avraham*'s intention here:

> One cannot suggest here that unravelling braids is actually a biblical prohibition that would apply to a virgin as well, and that this is what EH 21:2 means [that both virgins and married women must not go out with their hair unbraided] but that here [in OC, in which the *Shulchan Arukh* refers to single women who uncover their hair] it means while wearing braids, since that which is the custom of Jewish women [not to do] is permitted for virgins. For
>
> וליכא למימר דסותר אסור דין תורה בבתולה נמי וזה שכתוב באה"ע [סימן] כ"א סעיף ב', וכאן בלא סותר קליעת שערה, דבאשה דת יהודית ובתולות מותר, דהא בורכא דבאשת איש כל שכן שאין קלתה הוה דין תורה כמבואר בגמרא שם [ע"ב] ואה"ע [סימן קט"ו שם],

such would be scandalous for a married woman [i.e., going out with her hair uncovered] – and all the more so without a *kalta* [he means coiffing or braiding] – is a [violation of] Torah law, as the Talmud there and *EH* state explicitly.

The *Pri Megadim* seems to understand that *EH* 21 means the rule requiring single and married women not to go out to the marketplace with their hair undone implies that the two women share the same prohibition. As *Pri Megadim* notes, once the *Magen Avraham* has suggested that the category of single women here includes virgins, this makes such a parity impossible. Whereas unbraided hair for married women is a Torah prohibition and scandalous behavior, this is not the case for virgins. This explains the *Magen Avraham*'s backtracking at the end of his comment, a point the *Pri Megadim* reinforces:

> Rather it is certain that the simple meaning of the verse is that undoing simply means uncovering, which is a humiliation for a married woman, and that the midrashic explanation of the extra word is similarly adding humiliation upon humiliation [for the married woman], but that the sages made a rule about virgins [not unbraiding their hair] since [being in public with free-flowing hair] is a big humiliation, but that here [in *OC*], the case is that she does not have unbraided (or uncoiffed) hair.

> אלא דוודאי פשטיה דקרא ופרע משמע גילוי ראש לחוד גנאי באשת איש, ומיתורא דריש שסותר ג"כ, גנאי על גנאי, וחז"ל גזרו בבתולה בסותר דהוה גנאי גדול, וכאן באין סותר.

In the end, the *Pri Megadim* supports the basic distinction implied by the *Magen Avraham* that *EH* 21 encompasses women with unbraided hair and *OC* 75 women with braided hair. Furthermore he shows why *Magen Avraham* cannot claim that this is a Torah law for virgins derived from the book of Numbers, but at most a rabbinic decree.

The *Pri Megadim* seems more willing to entertain this possibility, even if it implies that virgins must all have their hair done up in some way. This point is used by the *Machatzit HaShekel* to prove the *Magen Avraham*'s interpretation wrong, since virgins, in the time of the Talmud and in his day, wore their hair free-flowing, at least to their weddings.

MAGEN GIBBORIM

Another commentator who disagrees with *Magen Avraham*'s reading here is the *Magen Gibborim/Shiltei HaGibborim* by R. Mordechai Ze'ev Ettinger (1794–1863). In his gloss on *OC* 75:2, he begins by summarizing the *Magen Avraham*'s overall approach:

> With regard to the [reference to unmarried women with] uncovered hair, the *Magen Avraham* noted a contradiction with that which is explicit in *EH* 21:2, that women, whether single or married, are prohibited [to go in public with their hair undone]. Moreover, [this latter prohibition contradicts] what is stated in b. Ketubot 15b [that a virgin] goes out at her wedding with hair undone.
>
> בפריעת ראש המ"א הקשה מהא דמבואר באהע"ז סי' כ"א סעיף ב' דאחת פנוי' ואחת א"א אסור ועוד הא מבואר בכתובות דף ט"ו ע"ב דיוצאת בהינומא וראשה פרוע

> And it is difficult to suggest that the single women [in *EH* 21:2] refer to widows, as [the *Shulchan Arukh*] should have made this explicit. Therefore, it must be that the undone hair in *EH* 21 refers to unbraided hair, and that it is, in fact, forbidden even for single women (i.e., even virgins) [to go out in public in this manner].
>
> ודוחק לומר דפנויות דקתני היינו אלמנה דהוה לי' לפרש וע"כ כ' דפריעת ראש דמבואר באהע"ז שם היינו שסותרות קליעת שערה וזה אסור אף בפנוי' ע"ש

The *Magen Gibborim* first notes, as *Pri Megadim* did, that this requires the *Magen Avraham* to reinterpret the passage in b. Ketubot about how women getting married for the first time would appear at their weddings:

> According to his understanding, it is necessary to posit that [the reference in b. Ketubot about] a woman going out at her [first] wedding with her hair undone must be assuming that her hair is braided [or coiffed]. But in truth, Rashi interprets there that her hair is on her shoulders [i.e., free-flowing]. This implies that it is permitted for women never before married to appear in public with their hair unbraided.
>
> ולדבריו צריך לומר דהא דיוצאת בהינומא וראשה פרוע היינו גילוי ראש בלא קליעת שער ובאמ' רש"י פירש שם ושערה על כתפה משמ' דאף קליעת שערה מותר

The *Magen Gibborim* is bothered that the passage in b. Ketubot seems to state almost explicitly that maidens may appear in public with their hair free-flowing. Indeed, this is how Rashi understands the passage. Rashi's question is based on women who appeared at their weddings with their hair undone and also appeared in other public contexts with their hair undone. This is implied but not stated outright. In fact, the *Magen Gibborim* notes that the *Shevut Yaakov* actually suggests otherwise in order to defend the *Magen Avraham*'s reading, but he (*Magen Gibborim*) rejects this approach:

The *Shevut Yaakov* (1:103) quotes the *Magen Avraham* and explains that the Mishnah allows the woman's hair to be entirely undone [when she goes out at her wedding] because at this moment her *shoshvinim* (bridesmaids) as well as many relatives are with her, and there is nothing to fear. But this is a stretch. Moreover, according to *Shevut Yaakov*, it is unclear what would have been bothering the *Magen Avraham* about the Mishnah in the first place.	(ובשו"ת שבות יעקב חלק א' סי' קג[11] הביא דברי המ"א אלו וכתב דראשה פרועה דמתני' הוא לפי שבאותו הפעם הולכות עמה שושביני' והרבה קרובים וליכא למיחש וזה דחוק וגם דלדבריו יקשה מאי מקשה המ"א מהמשנה)

Having rejected the *Shevut Yaakov*'s suggestion about how the *Magen Avraham* might read the passage in b. Ketubot, the *Magen Gibborim* continues with more problems:

There is a further problem with the *Magen Avraham*'s understanding. If he is correct, then a married woman is not actually prohibited from going in public with uncovered hair, only with unbraided hair. For according to him, there is no distinction between a single woman and a married woman [insofar as the basic halakha].	וגם קשה לפי דברי המ"א דא"כ אף בנשואה לא יהי' איסור בגילוי ראש רק בקליעת שער דהרי לדבריו אין חילוק בין פנוי' לנשואה
But the truth is that for married women, even exposed hair [in public] is prohibited, as the *Magen Avraham* himself says, for [the Rabbis] say in b. Ketubot 72, [that the verse in Numbers is] a warning to Jewish women not to go in public with hair undone.	ובאמת בא"א אף בגילוי ראש איכא איסורא כמ"ש המ"א עצמו דהרי אמרו בכתובי' דע"ב אזהרה לבנות ישראל שלא תצא בפריעת ראש

---

11. The text here actually reads קיג (113), but this is a slip of the pen.

The *Magen Gibborim* realizes that he has not proved his case, since the Talmudic passage he quotes does not use the term "uncovered hair" but "undone hair." This phrase can be interpreted as unbraided, so he tries to preemptively refute this objection:

> Now even though the *Shevut Yaakov* explains the phrase "undone hair" to mean "[undoing] braided hair," in truth the Talmud's phrase does not seem to mean this but rather, the *kalta* [which married Jewish woman are supposed to have minimally when they go in public] is a basket and not braiding [or coiffing]. See Rashi and the *Shita Mekubetzet* there.
>
> ואף דבשו"ת שבות יעקב שם פירש דפריע' ראש דהתם היינו קליעת שער באמת לשון הש"ס שם אינו משמע כן דקלתה היינו סל ולא קליעת שער וע' ברש"י ובשטה מקובצת שם,

Here again the *Magen Gibborim* is aware that his objection is weak, especially since one of the sources he uses to counter the *Shevut Yaakov*'s interpretation is Rashi in his Torah commentary, who actually reads the verse in Numbers that way. The *Magen Gibborim* tries to deal with this as well:

> And even though Rashi, in his commentary on [the verse in] *Nasso* "and [the priest] undoes the woman's hair" [states that] this means he undoes her braids, we must say that even so, the Talmud (Sota 8a) learns from here [the rule that a married woman may not go out in public with] exposed hair. For the language of "and he shall undo" implies that it was covered before and now it has been exposed, and this then means exposing her hair. It is only that from the inclusion of superfluous reference to the woman's "head," they [the Rabbis] derive through midrashic means that [the priest] should also unbraid her hair, as the Mizrachi already explained. And thus, the words of the *Magen Avraham* are puzzling.
>
> ואף דפרש"י פ' נשא ופרע הינו סתירת קליעת שערה צ"ל דאפ"ה יליף בש"ס מכאן לגילוי ראש דלשון ופרע משמע דהי' מכוסה קודם ומגלה עכשיו והיינו גילוי ראש ורק דמלשון ראש האשה דמיותר דרשו גם קליעת שער כמ"ש המזרחי שם וע"כ דברי המ"א תמוהי'

Having dismissed the *Magen Avraham*'s interpretation, the *Magen Gibborim* then goes on to reject the *Magen Avraham*'s question on the *Shulchan Arukh*:

In truth, *Magen Avraham*'s difficulty [with the passage in *OC*] based on *EH* is not really a problem. For that which the *Magen Avraham* considered to be an unreasonable interpretation, namely that single here refers to widows and divorcées, is, in fact, what it means. This is the interpretation of the *Bach*, and the *Chelkat Mechokek*, and the *Beit Shmuel* in *Even HaEzer* ad loc. And they brought a proof from the Mishnah in which [the single girl] goes out at her wedding [with her hair undone].[12]

ובאמ' גוף קושייתו מהאע"ז [מאהע"ז] לא קש' דמה שחש' המ"א לדוחק דפנויות היינו אלמנה וגרושה, כן הוא האמת כמ"ש הב"ח והח"מ והב"ש באהע"ז שם והביאו ראי' זו ממשנה דיוצאת בהינומא.

With that, the *Magen Gibborim* brings us full circle. The *Magen Avraham* rejects the "two types of *penuyot*" approach and thus suggests distinguishing between unbraided and exposed hair. The *Magen Gibborim*, however, rejects this distinction as an interpretation of *EH* 21, and argues for the preferability of the main view, that the *Shulchan Arukh* (and the *Tur*) mean only never-before married women when they use the term *penuyot* in this context.[13] Nevertheless, the *Magen Gibborim* does not really push this interpretation forward in a substantial way. Specifically, he does not explain why the term would be used this way here but then used to refer to all single women later, previously married or not.

---

12. He continues this thought by quoting the *Shita Mekubetzet*:

    And this is what the *Shita Mekubetzet* wrote in the beginning of the second chapter of Ketubot, that hair undone means exposed, and that this applies specifically to unmarried women but for married women it is forbidden, based on the verse that says "and [the priest] shall undo her hair," see further there, that he states this in the name of a collection from Geonic works.

וכ"כ בשטמ"ק ריש פ"ב דכתובות דראשה פרועה היינו מגולה ודוקא פנוי' אבל נשואות אסורות מקרא דופרע ראש האשה ע"ש שכתב כן בשם ליקוטי הגאונים.

    It is unclear why he believes this passage supports the interpretation of *penuyah* as never-before married. Perhaps the quote is out of place and he meant this to connect to one of his earlier points, either about only married women having to cover their hair or about undone hair meaning exposed hair.

13. Note that the *Magen Gibborim* does not discuss here the distinction in the sources he quotes between never-before married and non-virgins, but he does bring it up further on in his gloss, when he discusses the *Dagul Mervavah* (analyzed above in this chapter).

ROSH PINAH – IKVEI HABAYIT

Another commentator who argues for the preferability of the two types of *penuya* interpretation over and against that of the *Magen Avraham* is the *Ikvei HaBayit* section of the *Rosh Pinah* (EH 21):

See *Shulchan Arukh OC* 75 in the *Magen Avraham* (#3), who asked the question there based on what the author [of the *SA*] wrote here "whether single" which implies that a single woman is prohibited [from appearing in public with her hair undone]. He (=*Magen Avraham*) wrote that it is difficult to claim that single means a widow, for if so, he (=*SA*) should have clarified.	ועיין בשו"ע או"ח סימן ע"ה במגן אברהם סק"ג דהקשה שם ממ"ש המחבר כאן אחת פנויה דמשמע דגם פנויה אסור, וכתב דדוחק לומר דפנויה היינו אלמנה, דאם כן הו"ל לפרש, ע"ש.
But it seems that there was certainly no need [for the *SA*] to clarify, for there is an entire Mishnah [devoted to this] which states: "If there are witnesses that she went at her wedding with her hair undone." So we see that a virgin may [appear in public with her hair undone]. Thus, there is no choice but to assume that [the *SA*] is referring to a widow or divorcée.	אבל נראה דודאי א"צ לפרש, דמשנה שלימה שנינו אם יש עדים שיצתה בהינומה וראשה פרוע, הרי דבתולה מותרת, וע"כ דחיק ומוקי נפשיה באלמנה וגרושה...

The *Rosh Pinah* makes an argument based on the halakha in the Mishnah (one also implied in *OC* 75), that virgins are permitted to appear with their hair undone in public. Thus, he states, there is no choice but to assume the *Shulchan Arukh* was using the word *penuya* here as a reference to non-virgins or previously married women but not to virgins even though in the next sentence he uses it to mean all unmarried women, even virgins. Like the *Magen Gibborim*, however, the *Rosh Pinah* offers no reason why the *Shulchan Arukh* would write this way, except to state that what he means should be obvious, so he didn't have to be careful with his terminology.

Model 2b – With or Without a *Kalta* (Yaavetz)

In his commentary on *Tur Orach Chayyim* called *Mor u-Ketzia*, R. Jacob Emden (1697–1776), known as Yaavetz (an acronym of Jacob Emden ben Tzvi), takes a similar, though not identical, approach to that of the *Magen Avraham*. He begins by briefly restating the problem:

With regard to the [question of] virgins going in public with their hair undone, see the *Magen Avraham* who had difficulty with the contradiction between the Mishnah in the second chapter of Ketubot and that of the seventh chapter (7th mishnah). And other later authorities, commenting on *Even HaEzer* 21, have similar difficulties.

ולענין פריעת ראש דבתולה, עמ"א שנדחק בסתירה שבין המשנה דרפ"ב דכתובות ודפ"ז שם (מ"ז), וכן נתקשו בו האחרונים באה"ע (סי' כ"א).

As opposed to the *Tur* or *Shulchan Arukh* who have two contradictory chapters in the *Shulchan Arukh* (*EH* 21 and *OC* 75), the *Mor u-Ketzia* references two contradictory mishnayot. He frames the problem differently than the *Magen Avraham* did, which, as we will see, is connected to how he wants to address and solve the problem. In citing his commentary on the Mishnah, called the *Lechem Shamayim*, Yaavetz does not note that he has shifted the discussion from the *Tur* to the Mishnah, and continues as if the *Magen Avraham* et al. had been discussing the Mishnah:

Indeed, in my humble opinion, all of them have misunderstood the Mishnah, as I explained there [Ch. 2] in my *Lechem Shamayim*, with God's help, and the matter is clear without any need to make stretched or complicated arguments, and I made the words of all the Sages sensible.

אמנם לענ"ד כולם שגו בהבנת המשנה, כמ"ש שם [ריש פ"ב] בלח"ש בס"ד והוא דבר ברור בלי שום דוחק ופקפוק, וקיימתי כל דברי חכמים,

To understand this point, we should look carefully at the mishnayot in question and Yaavetz's analysis in *Lechem Shamayim*.

One of these mishnayot, the sixth mishnah in the seventh chapter of m. Ketubot, is familiar to us from the first chapter of this book, and is the core text upon which the prohibition for married women to go in public with their hair undone derives, listing it as one of the *dat Yehudit* violations.

The other mishnah to which Yaavetz refers is the first mishnah of Ketubot, discussed by many of the above commentators such as the *Dagul Mervavah* and the *Magen Avraham*. The mishnah discusses the question of the ketubah payout. The woman, divorced or widowed, wishes to collect her ketubah money from her ex-husband or his heirs, but apparently has no documentation of how much money she was promised. The standard for first marriages is 200 zuz, and she claims this was her first marriage and she is thus entitled to that sum. Her ex-husband (or his heirs) claim that this was a second marriage. The standard for second marriages is 100 zuz;

therefore she would only be entitled to that sum. Without documentation, how can this be proven one way or the other?

The mishnah suggests that certain procedures are different in first marriage ceremonies than in second ones. Specifically, in a first marriage, she goes out in *hynuma* (i.e., at her wedding) with her hair undone. R. Yochanan ben Baroka says that, in addition to this custom, parched grain was passed around at first marriages but not second marriages. Thus, if witnesses can attest to one of these things having occurred at the wedding, we could resolve this question. The tenth mishnah clarifies that testimony is even valid if such witnesses had been minors at the wedding and they say, "I remember that so-and-so went out in *hynuma* with her hair undone" (זכור הייתי בפלונית שיצתה בהינומא וראשה פרוע).

In *Lechem Shamayim* in m. Ketubot 2:1, Yaavetz lays out the contradiction and his interpretation:

"With her hair undone" – the difficulty is clear to everyone, for according to the Torah this is forbidden, as we see later in Chapter 7 mishnah 2, in line with Rambam who explains that this includes even single women.	וראשה פרוע - הקושיא נגלית בכאן. דהא מן התורה אסור. כדלקמן פרק ז משנה ב. וכר״מ [=רמב״ם] בפירוש שגם הפנויה בכלל האיסור.

This is a fundamental point for Yaavetz that warrants highlighting. According to him, the requirement for all women, married or single, to have their hair done up or covered is biblical and he supports this from the verse in Numbers and the mishnah in m. Ketubot (which most authorities take for granted refers to married women). His proof is that the Mishnah is in accord with the view of Rambam in "Laws of Forbidden Relations" 21:17 (discussed in Chapter 4):

Daughters of Israel may not go out into the marketplace with their hair exposed, whether they be single or married...	לא יהלכו בנות ישראל פרועי ראש בשוק אחת פנויה ואחת אשת איש...

It is this law upon which the *Tur*, *Shulchan Arukh* and *Levush* base their language in *EH* 21, that women may not go out in public with their hair undone "whether married or single."

Admittedly, Rambam does not say he believes this prohibition to be biblical. Yaavetz deduces this from the fact that Rambam equates single and married women in this law, and that the prohibition for a married woman to do so comes from a *derasha* on a verse in Numbers. Thus, one can offer the syllogism, if single is like married and married is biblical then single is biblical. Yaavetz continues by briefly mentioning other approaches to the problem:

Therefore, [some authorities] wish to distinguish between virgins and unmarried widows.	לכן רוצים לדחוק ולחלק בין בתולה לאלמנה פנויה.

Like the *Magen Avraham*, Yaavetz does not think that this phrase can reasonably be read to be only about women who were previously married. Thus, he offers a different suggestion:

To my mind, there is no problem [with m. Ketubot 2:1] to begin with. With all due respect, the Acharonim struggled mightily here for no reason. For in their quick reading, they did not comprehend the meaning of the Mishnah, namely they did not realize that it requires two things: "She goes out with a *hynuma* and her hair undone." And a *hynuma* (according to both interpretations)[14] is certainly not less than a *kalta*, with which she is permitted to go out in public according to the Torah. It is forbidden [for Jewish women to go out in public with a *kalta*] only according to *dat Yehudit* that women accepted as a stringency upon themselves, but this stringency does not apply to single women at all.	ולדידי מעיקרא לא קשיא מידי. ובמ[חילת] כ[בודם] בכדי טרחו כל האחרונים בכך. כי לא עמדו על פירוש משנתנינו לפום ריהטייהו. ולא שערו דהכא תרתי בעינן. יוצא בהנומא וראשה פרוע. והנומא (לשני הפירושים) ודאי לא גרע מקלתא דשריא בדאורייתא ואסירא רק מדת יהודית. שהחמירו הנשים על עצמן. אבל לא חלה חומרא זו על הפנויות לגמרי.
With that, all the words of the sages stand firm. And those of Rambam – "They are the covenant – the words said to Moses at Sinai."[15] For insofar as the undone hair in the biblical verse, there is no difference between single and married women.[16] But insofar as the *dat Yehudit*, there is certainly	נמצאו כל דברי חכמים קיימים. ודר"מ ברית הן הדברים שנאמרו למשה מסיני. שאין חלוק בפריעת ראש דקרא בין שום פנויה ובעולה. אלא בדת יהודית ודאי יש חילוק ביניהן. שזו

---

14. He means the interpretations in the Bavli, which he understands as a head covering of myrtle leaves or a veil that extends from the head downwards. We will discuss this at length in the next subsection.
15. This is an expression, found in b. *Pesachim* 38a.
16. He uses the word "non-virgin" here, which is confusing, as this usually refers

> a difference between them, for one can go out in public with her hair undone, only wearing a *kalta*, and the other is forbidden to do this. And without this distinction, there would be no easy way to distinguish between them and to recognize married women from a distance and to know which women are single[17] and fit to marry, so that the men can pursue them and marry them.
>
> הולכת בשוק פרועת ראש עם קלתא. וזו נאסרה מכל וכל. ולא סגי בלאו הכי. כדי להבדיל ביניהם ולהכיר הנשואות להתרחק מהן. ולידע הבתולות הראויות להנשא. דלקפצו עליהו אינשי לנסובינהו.
>
> All this is clear, with God's help, without any confusing arguments. See also the *Mor u-Ketzia* on *OC* (75), and what I wrote about this in my responsum [2:2], with God's help.
>
> זה דבר ברור בס"ד בלי שום גמגום. ועיין עוד מו"ק א"ח (סע"ה) ומ"ש בתשו' בס"ד.

Yaavetz's reading hinges on the interpretation of the word *hynuma* in the Mishnah, which he understands as some kind of head covering, based on his reading of the Bavli (that will be discussed in the next subsection). Thus, in his view, all women – including virgins – must cover their hair in some way in public, and the only distinction is between full covering for married women and partial covering for single women. Thus, what the Mishnah here means is that at the wedding, the men saw her with her hair partially covered.

Returning to the commentary on the *Tur*, he makes the same argument in his *Mor u-Ketzia*, where, by answering the apparent contradiction in the Mishnah, he aims at neutralizing the problem in the *Tur* (and *Shulchan Arukh*) as well:

> For certainly the opinion of Rambam is correct that there is no distinction with regard to the prohibition to appear in public with undone hair, for virgins are included. However, [this applies] specifically [to going out in public] without a *kalta* or any covering at all, but [the requirement to wear] a *kalta* is *dat Yehudit* only for married women. In fact, for single women/virgins,
>
> דודאי דעת ר"מ אמת שאין חלוק באסור פריעת ראש שגם הבתולות בכלל. מיהו דווקא בלי קלתה ובלי שום כסוי, אבל קלתה מדת יהודית היא בנשואה בלבד. אכן בפנויה בתולה אין שום איסור כלל אלא התר גמור.

---

to single women who were previously married or who had premarital sex, but here he seems to use it to refer to married women.

17. He uses "virgins" here, but he means unmarried women.

there is no prohibition whatsoever [to appear in public with only a partial covering] and it is totally permissible.

And it is nice for them to have a clear sign that they are available for marriage, and she should not be allowed to make herself look bad and be wrapped up like a mourner, but rather braided like a bride, and see there [in *Lechem Shamayim*] with clear proofs.

Thus we learn, in connection to our topic, that even virgins who go out in public with their hair entirely undone without any covering upon it, that this is certainly a forbidden form of nudity, and that there is no distinction with women's hair in this regard.

Rather [a single woman can show] specifically [the hair] that can be seen under her head covering and the cloth upon her, as well as [the hair] outside on the edges, that are permitted even to a married woman, and this should not be added to.

A married woman, a single woman, and a virgin are all equal in this regard. And this is correct and clear, with the help of God.[18]

וכך נאה להן להיות להן הכר שעומדות להנשא ואינה רשאה לנוול עצמה להיות עטופה כאבלה, אלא קלועה ככלה ויע״ש בהוכחות נכונות.

נמצינו למדין לעניננו שגם הבתולות כשהולכות פרועות ראש גלוי לגמרי בלי שום מכסה עליו ודאי הוי נמי ערוה, ואין לחלק בשער אשה לענין זה,

אלא דווקא במה שנראה ממנו מתחת כפה שבראשה ורדיד שעליה חוץ לצמתה הוא דשרי כמו באשה, הבו דלא לוסיף,

ואין חלוק בין אשה לאשה, נשואה ופנויה ובתולה כולן שוות בענין. זהו הנכון והמחוור בס״ד.

---

18. For completion's sake, here is the paragraph that treats this subject in *She'eilat Yaavetz* (2:2):

The Acharonim who wrote with one voice with regard to the contradiction between the mishnayot in chapter 2 and chapter 7 of Ketubot became very entangled in the matter. In my humble opinion, they struggled and shook their heads to no purpose, for there is no contradiction here at all. And that which Rambam wrote is certainly in line with their meaning, [namely,] that it is forbidden according to the Torah for any single woman to go in public with her hair undone, as I already wrote clearly in the *Lechem Shamayim* with the help of God.

מ״ש האחרונים פה אחד בענין הסתיר׳ מרפ״ב דכתובות לפ״ז. שנסתבכו בה מאד. לענ״ד בכדי טרחו וטרייהו לרישייהו על לא דבר. כי אין כאן סתירה לגמרי. ודר״מ ג״כ כמשמעם ודאי. שכל פנויה אסור׳ בפ״ר ד״ת =בפריעת ראש דבר תורה=. כמ״ש בלח״ש. דבר ברור בס״ד.

In his overall approach to the problem, Yaavetz follows the contours of the *Magen Avraham*, that the distinction between *EH* 21 and *OC* 75 is that each is referring to a different level of hair covering. According to *Magen Avraham* it is braiding/coiffing versus covering, and according to Yaavetz it is partial covering versus full covering.

By shifting the discussion to Mishnah Ketubot instead of the *Tur* or *Shulchan Arukh* Yaavetz focuses the discussion on what turns out to be his major *chiddush* (novel suggestion), and the point he claims all missed before him: that the Mishnah says she goes out with a *hynuma* which means with a *kalta* or partial head covering. The problem with this suggestion is that *hynuma* almost certainly does not mean a head covering. The reason no one else thought of this *chiddush* is because it is not correct. To demonstrate this, we need to offer a brief excursus on the meaning of this mishnah.

Excursus Three: On the Meaning of *Hynuma*

The word *hynuma* is a Hebrew adaptation of a Greek word, but the question is, which word exactly?[19]

WEDDING

The simplest translation of the word *hynuma*, and the one I used above in translating the Mishnah, is "at her wedding." This is the literal meaning of the Greek word *hymenaios* (ὑμέναιος), related to the same root as the Greek god of weddings, Hymen. (The English word "hymen" derives partially from this root as well, and we will say something further on that later on.) This translation requires a metathesis here, namely, that the letters moved around in the transfer from Greek to Hebrew. An example of this phenomenon is how the Greek word *limein* (λιμήν: harbor) became the Hebrew *namal* (נמל: harbor). This happens in the development of purely Hebrew words as well – *simlah* (שמלה) and *salmah* (שלמה) both mean "dress;" *keves* (כבש) and *kesev* (כשב) both mean "sheep" – and is actually a common linguistic phenomenon in all languages. Thus, the meaning of the Mishnah would be that she came to her wedding (נישואין), that is to her *chuppah* or her husband's house, with her hair undone.

---

19. I thank Dr. Zev Farber for helping me with the Greek and Arabic here and in other places in this book. This section could not have been written without his help.

BRIDE'S WEDDING LITTER

It is possible that the Mishnah has a specific wedding practice in mind. If so, it is likely referring to the Jewish custom of bringing the bride to her wedding/her new home on a litter or sleeping couch (אפריון, from the Greek φόρημα; m. Sotah 9:14, t. Sotah 15:9). In the Roman period, wealthy women would be carried in a litter and not walk on the ground. This was done for brides at Jewish weddings during this period. If so, the idea here would be that people saw her coming to her wedding on her litter with her hair undone. "Litter" is in fact how Marcus Jastrow translates *hynuma* here in his dictionary, namely, "slumbering couch" or "curtained litter," assuming that the Greek word for "wedding" became a colloquial synecdoche (what he calls a "popular adaptation") in rabbinic Jewish parlance for this practice.

This is also how the Yerushalmi translates the term (y. Ketubot 2:1):

"In *hynuma*" – There [in Babylonia] they translate as *nimnuma* ("a sleeper," probably a sleeping couch). The rabbis here say, *priyoma* (i.e., *apiryon*, "litter").	בהינומה. תמן נמנומה רבנין דהכא אמרין פיריומא.

In Babylonia, where Greek was less well known, the rabbis looked for an Aramaic etymology for the term. They opted for the root נ.ו.מ, meaning "sleep." In Israel, they understood it was simply the Greek word for wedding and noted that in Jewish parlance it referred to the litter. Either way, both opinions recorded in the Yerushalmi seem to have understood the practice the same way, as a reference to the woman appearing on her litter coming to her wedding.

WEDDING HYMNS

Another possible translation for *hynuma*, adopted by Shmuel Safrai and Tal Ilan, connects it to the other meaning of the Greek term *hymenaios* (ὑμέναιος), namely the wedding song (from which the English word "hymn" derives).[20] This is Chanoch Albeck's interpretation in his commentary on the Mishnah:

---

20. See Tal Ilan, *Jewish Women in Greco-Roman Palestine: An Inquiry Into Image and Status* (Texts and Studies in Ancient Judaism; Tübingen: Mohr Siebeck, 2006), 95; Shmuel Safrai, "Home and Family" in *The Jewish People in the First Century*, II (eds. Shmuel Safrai and Menachem Stern; Assen: Van Gorcum, 1976), 758.

> "That she went out in *hynuma*" – that at the time of *nissuin*, she would go out from her father's house to her husband's house with hymns and songs.
>
> שיצאת בהינומא - שבשעת הנישואין יצאה מבית אביה לבית בעלה בהימנון ובשיר.

According to this translation, the bride was coming in – whether on a litter or by foot – "accompanied by wedding songs" and her hair undone.

LAW (*NOMOS*) OF VIRGINS

R. Chananel suggested an entirely different translation based on a different Greek word. His commentary here is not extant but his gloss appears in the dictionary of R. Nathan ben Yechiel (1035–1106) called the *Arukh* on the entry *hynuma*:

> R. Chananel explained that *hynuma* in Greek is "law," i.e., the law (or practice) of the virgins.
>
> פירוש ר' חננאל הינומא ל"י הוא תורתא כלומר חוק הבתולות.

R. Chananel is picturing not the word *hymena* (marriage), but the word *nomos* (νόμος), i.e., law. This suggestion avoids the metathesis need for the *hymena* explanation, but it leaves the opening syllable "*hy*" unexplained. It seems likely that R. Chananel did not know Greek but was patching together an argument from a Greek word he knew together with the context.

THE DEBATE IN THE BAVLI

Much of the debate in the *meforshim* derives from an attempt to understand the two opinions mentioned in the Bavli (b. Ketubot 17b):

> What is *hynuma*? Surchav bar Pappa said in the name of Zeiri: "A *tanura* made of myrtles." Rabbi Yochanan said: "A cover in which a bride can sleep."
>
> מאי הינומא? סורחב בר פפא משמיה דזעירי אמר: תנורא דאסא, רבי יוחנן אמר: קריתא דמנמנה בה כלתא.

Here the Bavli offers two possible explanations. Let's start with the second one.

R. YOCHANAN: COVER FOR THE SLEEPING BRIDE

The simple understanding of R. Yochanan is familiar to us as it is the opinion the Yerushalmi refers to as "what they say over there,"[21] namely,

---

21. Ironically, R. Yochanan is not from Babylonia but from Israel.

that the term derives from the root נ.ו.מ, and means a place the bride can sleep, ostensibly referring to a covering for a litter. The bride would then get rest on the way to her husband's house while people carry her on her covered litter.

The *Otzar HaGeonim* records a number of Geonic interpretations of this phrase. For example, one Gaon, picturing the more common oriental custom of travelling on an animal as opposed to the Roman practice of being carried in a litter, suggests that it refers to a howdah (a carriage which was positioned on the back of a camel or a donkey):

"A *karita* for napping" – another text says, "for a bride to nap in." This is what is referred to in Arabic as *al-hodj* ("the howdah").	(חריתא) [קריתא] דמנמנמא נ"א דמנמנמא בה כלתא הוא הנקרא בלשון ערבי אל הודג׳ (الهودج)

A similar interpretation, quoted in the name of R. Chananel but more likely from Rav Hai Gaon, states:

[A cover] in which a bride sleeps – this refers to a *chuppah* that they would make for a bride that looked like a multicolored city, and she sleeps inside it. And because she nods off inside it, it is called a *hynuma* (=a sleeper).	(חריתא) [קריתא] דמתמנמנמא בה כלתא - פי׳ חופה שהיו עושין לכלה כדמות עיר ממיני צבעונין והיא ישנה בתוכה משום דמנמם בגוה קרי לה הינומא.
And it appears that when they were walking her from her father's house to her husband's house, they would take her out in this, for if not, what could the phrase "she went out with her *hynuma*" mean?	ונראה שכשהיו מוליכין אותה מבית אביה לבית בעלה היו מוציאין אותה בתוכה שאם לא כן יקשה לשון יצאתה בהינומא.
Alternatively, it could be suggested that she would stand in it at the groom's home. And that which we are taught, "if she goes out in *hynuma*" – means to say if she stepped outside of it publicly.	אי נמי אפשר לומר שבבית החתן היתה עומדת בתוכה. ומאי דתנן אם יצאתה בהינומא רצה לומר אם יצאת בפני העם.

This Geonic source offers two possibilities. Either it is some type of covered device for travelling – whether a litter or a howdah is unclear; or it is the *chuppah* itself, set up in the husband's home.

Another interpretation, offered by the Gaon who suggested the howdah, is that it is a wrapping:

And there are those who say it is a covering.	וי"א מחפה.

It is unclear, however, if he means a type of tent, like a *chuppah*, or a type of gown, akin to a body covering (we will discuss the possibility of a gown in the discussion of Surchav bar Pappa's position), or possibly (in line with Yaavetz) a hair covering, although this last position seems very unlikely, since it is juxtaposed with the term "and her hair undone."

An entirely different interpretation of R. Yochanan's words appears in Rashi's gloss (ad loc.):

| "*Kiryata* (a coverer)" – a veil that folds over her eyes, like they do in our community. Sometimes, she falls asleep in it, since her eyes are covered. Therefore, it is called a *hynuma*, from the word *"tenuma"* ("sleep"). | קריתא - צעיף על ראשה משורבב על עיניה כמו שעושין במקומינו ופעמים שמנמנמת בתוכו מתוך שאין עיניה מגולין ולכך נקרא הינומא על שם תנומה. |

The key words in Rashi are "like they do in our community." Rashi is trying to interpret the term in a way familiar to him from Jewish weddings in which women wear veils (as they still do today). Needless to say, Rashi does not know Greek and, though he certainly knows the Mishnah about litters (*apiryon*), he does not immediately connect this practice with the term *hynuma* as the Yerushalmi does, nor does he live in a Muslim society where a Roman litter could easily be pictured as an oriental howdah.

SURCHAV BAR PAPPA: A *TANURA* OF MYRTLES

The first position recorded in the Bavli, that of Surchav bar Pappa, is also unclear. He makes no explicit suggestion of an etymology, as R. Yochanan does, and the Aramaic term he uses, *tanura*, is also open to interpretation. The most common translation of the term is "oven," which is certainly not its meaning here.

The *Otzar HaGeonim* quotes one Gaon who suggested the term referred to a tent:

| A tent of myrtles in which the bride naps. | קובה מן אסא דמנמנמא בה כלתה. |

This would make Surchav bar Pappa's view a variation on the second view, that it is a structure in which a bride can nap. Although he does not say if this is meant to happen during the transport to her husband's house, it is likely what he means.

One authority who grappled with the phrase "*tanura* of myrtles" is R. Yosef ibn Migash (Ri Migash, 1077–1141), who writes:

| A *tanura* of myrtles – Meaning: like a tent made from myrtles and they sit the bride in it when they are bringing her to her husband's house, and it is like what they call in Arabic *amaraya* [camel saddle, perhaps a howdah]. The reason it is called "an oven" (*tanura*) is because a tent is similar to an oven since an oven is wide on the bottom and narrow on the top until [it reaches the width] of a finger. | תנורא דאסא - פירוש: כמו קובה שעושין אותה מן ההדס ומושיבין בה הכלה בשעה שמוליכין אותה לבית בעלה, והוא כמו זו שקורין אותה בלשון ערבי עמאריא (عمارية) לפי שקורין לה תנורא הוא מפני שהקובה דומה לתנור שהרי התנור רחב הוא מלמטה וצר מלמעלה עד כאצבע. |

Ri Migash also understands the term as a reference to a tented howdah, but his tortured attempt to make sense of the word *tanura* shows how difficult it is to understand the term.

In his *Dictionary of Babylonian Jewish Aramaic*, Michael Sokoloff explains that the term actually derives from the Iranian (Persian) term *tanu-vara*, meaning body covering. The term is often used in Syriac as a reference to a soldier's body armor, but in this case, the reference is to a corselet (or perhaps a gown), which Surchav bar Pappa claims is made of myrtle branches (or, if it's a gown, decorated with myrtle leaves).

Surchav bar Pappa is likely picturing a known custom for Jewish weddings in Babylonia, but a myrtle corselet or gown is in no way a translation of *hynuma*, a word whose meaning may have been lost among the Babylonian Jews, most of whom knew no Greek and were unfamiliar with Roman customs.

A GREEK WORD FOR VEIL?

In his glosses on the *Arukh* called *Musaf He-Arukh* R. Benjamin Musafia (1606–1675) responds to R. Chananel's suggestion (quoted above) that despite what the Talmud says, he believes *hynuma* derives from the Greek word *nomos* and means "law." The *Musaf He-Arukh* writes:

| From the words of R. Chananel we learn to explain foreign words even if the meaning veers somewhat from the Gemara – not to argue with them [the sages] but to bring the root of the word to light. | מדברי ר"ח נלמוד לבאר המלות שהן נכריות אף כי הפירוש נוטה קצת מדברי הגמרא לא לחלוק עליהם כי אם להוציא לאור עקר המלה. |
| And it seems to me that *hynuma* in Greek means veil placed on the face and covering | ונ"ל שפי' הינומא בל"י מסוה נתון על הפנים ומכסה |

the eyes, and this is how virgins generally go out [on their wedding days].	העינים, וכן נהגו הבתולות לצאת בו.

As he does not quote the Greek word, we do not know if he was basing this on an etymological argument or if he just guessed that it must be from Greek, and assumed Rashi's view referring to it as a veil must be correct. Nevertheless, an argument from Greek to this effect was made by R. Israel Lifschitz (1782–1860) in the *Yachin* section of his *Tiferet Yisrael* (ad loc.):

In a *hynuma* – *hymenas* in Greek is a veil ["schleier" (in Yiddish)] to cover her eyes. The sages twisted the word, slicing it up as they saw fit to make it related to Hebrew, [suggesting that] since her eyes are covered [by the veil] she sleeps underneath it and that that is why it is called *hynuma*... There are those who make the *hynuma* from cloth and others from myrtles.	בהינומא. "הומענאס" בלשון יון הוא צעיף [שלייער] לכסות עינים, וחז"ל הסיבו המלה וסרסוהו כפי הנאות בלשון קודש, דע"י שעיניה מכוסים היא מנמנמת תחתיו, ולכן קראוהו הנומא...ויש עושין הנומא זה מבגד ויש מהדסים:

The *Tiferet Yisrael* is picking up on the Greek word *hymen* (ὑμήν) which means "thin membrane" and by extension "a garment of fine texture." It is not actually the standard Greek word for a veil, which is *kalumma* (κάλυμμα), but *could* be a derivative usage, especially since the word *hymen* is a homonym for the name of the wedding god Hymen; and this combination (hymen meaning both thin membrane and wedding deity) is almost certainly because a woman's thin vaginal membrane, the hymen (a term derived from this confluence of terms), is lost after a wedding and is needed to prove her virginity before the wedding night. Nevertheless, it is more likely that *hynuma* is not actually connected to a Greek word for veil, certainly not in the rabbinic period at least, but that Rashi's interpretation pushed the *Tiferet Yisrael* to look for a way of making it work in Greek.

STANDARD INTERPRETATIONS

If we look at the standard commentaries on the Mishnah, we see that the views supported by the traditional commentators surveyed above dominate. Rambam (1135–1204), in his commentary on the Mishnah, defends the litter/howdah view:

> *Hynuma* – a silken tent. It was their custom to take the virgins from their father's house to their husband's house in one.
>
> הינומה, אוהל של משי היה מנהגם שלוקחין בו הבתולות מבית האב לבית הבעל.

It is unclear where he gets the idea of a silken tent. Perhaps he is picturing a covered litter or howdah in an elegant, oriental style.

R. Ovadiah of Bartenura (ca. 1445–1515) simply paraphrases the Bavli:

> *Hynuma* – there are those who say that [this refers to] a canopy of myrtles made for virgins. There are those who say that it refers to a veil put over her eyes, under which she can sleep.
>
> הינומא - איכא מאן דאמר חופה של הדס שעושים לבתולות. ואיכא מאן דאמר צעיף שנותנים על העינים ומתנמנמת בו:

Clearly, he reads R. Yochanan like Rashi, picturing a veil, and Surchav bar Pappa as either a covered litter or howdah, or a *chuppah*, perhaps a travelling one for her to walk under.

Finally, R. Yom Tov Lipman Heller (1579–1654), in his *Tosafot Yom Tov*, simply quotes R. Chananel and Rashi:

> In *hynuma* – The *Arukh* writes: R. Chananel explained: "This is Greek for "law" (*nomos*), meaning, the law of the virgins." And Rashi explains that according to the one who says [a covering] – a veil etc., she falls asleep in it, since her eyes are covered. Therefore, it is called a *hynuma*, from the word *"tenuma"* ("sleep").
>
> בהינומא - כתב הערוך פי' ר"ח הינומא לשון יון הוא תורה כלומר חוק הבתולות ע"כ. ורש"י פי' למ"ד [קריתא] צעיף וכו' ומתנמנמת בו מתוך שאין עיניה מגולין ולכך נקרא הינומא על שם תנומה:

NOT A HAIR COVERING – RESPONSE TO YAAVETZ

At this point, we return to Yaavetz to make the following point. *Hynuma* is a complicated word to translate. We have shown that philology takes us to wedding or wedding hymn; Chazal take us to litter, corselet or gown; and traditional commentaries take us to howdah, veil, *chuppah*, or even law. But what *hynuma* does not mean according to any of the above is *kalta* or head covering. It is not something all virgins wear until they are married but rather a special wedding practice. Thus, Yaavetz's "clear and correct" solution is anything but.

The reason *Magen Avraham* focuses on solving the tension in the *Tur* and *Shulchan Arukh* and does not turn to the Mishnah about the *hynuma* is because this Mishnah does not help, since it does not describe a woman wearing something on her head, as Yaavetz believes it does. Instead, as Rashi states clearly, the woman at this wedding has her hair entirely undone, even down to the shoulders, and this practice thus fits with that recorded in *OC* 75 of virgins with their hair undone. It also contradicts *EH* 21, where their hair is said to require covering (or coiffing/braiding). In sum, it adds no new elements with which to solve the problem.

Without his *hynuma* point, Yaavetz is stuck in the same quandary as *Magen Avraham*. He is claiming that all women, even virgins, need to cover their hair partially, with a *kalta*, even though the Mishnah he quotes and the practice in *OC* 75 clearly assume that virgins do not cover their hair at all. *Magen Avraham* tries to solve this problem by saying that the requirement for virgins is only a custom and ostensibly ignored in certain circles – as cited in the Mishnah and the *Tur/Shulchan Arukh*! – but this is merely an assertion. Yaavetz is in an even worse predicament, since he needs to claim that these women are not just braiding/coiffing their hair but covering it with a *kalta*, even though nothing in these texts imply this at all: In fact, they virtually state the opposite. His creative translation of *hynuma* is the only defense he can muster, and as we have seen, there is no place in either etymology or Chazal and the Rishonim for such a reading.

Nevertheless, Yaavetz is not the only commentator who reads *hynuma* in this way. Another such authority is R. Baruch Fränkel-Te'omim (1760–1828), in his *Imrei Baruch* on the *Shulchan Arukh*, who critiques the *Chelkat Mechokek* with the following:

| "We say that she goes out with *hynuma* and her hair undone, etc." – *Nota bene*: According to Rashi's commentary there, which states "And her head is undone, with her hair down to her shoulders, etc." there is no proof [that a virgin may go in public with her hair undone], for it is not true that her hair [is (really) undone, for] it is covered with a *hynuma,* and only the hair that extends from under her kerchief and falls down to her shoulders can be seen; see Maharam Schiff. | אמרינן דיוצאה בהינומא וראשה פרוע כו' – נ"ב – לפי פירש"י שם בזה"ל וראשה פרוע ושערה על כתיפה כו' ע"כ אין ראיה, דאמת אין ראשה [פרוע דהא] מכוסה בהינומא ואין נראה השער רק חוץ לצמתן ומונחים על כתיפה, ויעוין במהר"ם שי"ף. |

The comment to which *Imrei Baruch* makes reference can be found in the glosses of R. Meir ben Jacob HaKohen Schiff (1608–1644), known as Maharam Schiff, on the Talmud, in which he offers the following analysis of Rashi:

In Rashi, *sub versa* "her hair is undone" [he states:] "her hair goes down to her shoulders, etc." For the *hynuma* covers her head and extends over her eyes. Or perhaps, the point of "her head undone" is that her hair isn't wild but only her head itself is wild, in the sense that hairs are hanging on this side and that, and it requires further study.	ברש"י בד"ה וראשה פרוע שערה על כתיפה וכו'. כי הינומא היא מכסה על הראש ומשרבב על עיניה. או ר"ל ראשה פרוע לא שערה פרוע רק הראש בעצמו פרוע ע"י שהשערות תלויין לכאן ולכאן ודו"ק:

Saying that "hair down to her shoulders" means "the top of her head is covered" is a *very* forced reading of Rashi. Nevertheless, although it seems exceedingly difficult to translate *hynuma* as a head covering, it must be admitted that it is not only Yaavetz who translates this way, but also Maharam Schiff and the *Imrei Baruch*. Presumably, they would approach the contradictions in the *Tur* and *Shulchan Arukh* in the same way as Yaavetz, that *OC* is assuming partial covering and *EH* 21 no covering at all.[22] Nevertheless, as noted above, the translation of *hynuma* is almost certainly not "head covering," making this a difficult position to accept.

DAUGHTERS OF ISRAEL – *ALL GIRLS?

Before moving to a conclusion, we should look at one outlying position. R. Elijah ben Shlomo Zalman of Vilna, known as the Vilna Gaon or the Gr"a (1720–1797), offers this terse comment in his glosses on the *Shulchan Arukh* called *Biur HaGra* (#11):

"Whether a *penuyah*" – since the term used is "daughters of Israel" and not "a woman."	אחד פנויה. מדקאמר לבנות ישראל ול"ק לאשה:

From the terseness of the comment, it is difficult to discern his point, but the super-commentary on the *Biur HaGra* by R. Baruch Rakover (1917–2002) called *Birkat Eliyahu* offers some clarification:

---

22. R. Isaac Segal, in his responsum (see Ch. 7), also translates *hynuma*, as head covering; but he does not solve the contradiction in this way, but in the more common way of translating single women in such a way as to exclude virgins.

> It says in b. Ketubot 72a "A warning to the daughters of Israel not to go out in public with their hair undone." Since the term used is "daughters of Israel" and not "a woman" it is clear that single women are warned not to go out in public with their hair undone.
>
> איתא בכתובות עב א: אזהרה לבנות ישראל שלא יצאו בפרוע ראש. ומדקאמר: "לבנות ישראל" ולא קאמר "לאשה" מוכח שגם פנויות מוזהרות לא לצאת בפרוע ראש.

Apparently, the Gr"a read the word "daughters" as meant to include unmarried girls still living in their fathers' homes. If anything, this implies that the Gr"a takes the line in *Even HaEzer* 21, and ostensibly Rambam's ruling in the *Mishneh Torah* upon which it is based, at face value. All women must cover or do up their hair. Although this means that he does not solve the contradiction the way the *Bach/Chelkat Mechokek* or *Perisha/Beit Shmuel et alia* do, it is unclear whether he would agree with *Magen Avraham* or Yaavetz that the answer is two kinds of hair covering, or with my solution, that it all depends on local practice.

Unfortunately, his even briefer gloss on *OC* 75 does little, if anything, to clarify the matter. Commenting on the *Shulchan Arukh*'s statement about virgins who are not in the practice of covering their hair, he writes (#5):

> "But, etc." – as it is written at the beginning of the second chapter of Ketubot, "and her hair is undone, etc."
>
> אבל כו'. כמ"ש ברפ"ב דכתובות וראשה פרועה כו':

Again, the *Birkat Eliyahu* clarifies the Gr"a's meaning:

> As it is written at the beginning of the second chapter of Ketubot 15b, "A woman was widowed or divorced: She says: 'I was a virgin when you married me.' He says [or his heirs say]: 'No, you were a widow when I married you,' – If there are witnesses that she went out in *hynuma* and her hair was undone, her ketubah is two hundred [*zuz*]." Clearly, undone hair is a sign of virginity, since that is how they used to go out [in public]...
>
> כמ"ש ברפ"ב דכתובות טו ב: האשה שנתארמלה או נתגרשה, היא אומרת בתולה נשאתני והוא אומר לא כי אלא אלמנה נשאתיך, אם יש עדים שיצאת בהינומא וראשה פרוע כתובתה מאתים. אלמא דפרועה ראש זהו סימן לבתולה, שכן היו הולכות...

The Gr"a's point is this: the passage in b. Ketubot is clear proof that virgins are allowed in public with their hair undone. But how does this fit with the rule in *EH* 21 that all women, married or single, must have their hair covered (or coiffed/braided) when in public? The Gr"a doesn't say. From this comment, the solution could be any of the three models.

Excursus Four: Why Is Violating Dat Yehudit Prohibited and What Is Dat Yehudit?

It is worth highlighting an important, but very technical, dispute between two (and maybe three) schools of thought about why violating the *dat Yehudit* rules are prohibited as well as what exactly is prohibited by the term *dat Yehudit*. One school of thought seems to insist that the term *dat Yehudit* is a reference to rabbinic violations and *dat Moshe* to biblical violations. Per this approach, either can cause divorce. A second school of thought posits that *dat Yehudit* is limited to those violations of social norms that give rise to a fear of sexual impropriety, whereas *dat Moshe* is all other violations that impact the husband (but are not sexual). A third school of thought limits the term *dat Moshe* to violations of Torah law (sexual and otherwise), and *dat Yehudit* to sexual violations only. This approach recognizes that there are categories of sinful violations but not grounds for divorce.

Consider, for example, the *Tzemach Tzedek* (Menachem Mendel Schneerson, 1789–1866).

The following is found explicitly in *Responsa Tzemach Tzedek, Even HaEzer* 151:

| And if you are bothered by the question of how can we write "in accordance with *dat Moshe*, etc." when we are speaking only of a rabbinic enactment? And the Talmud (end of b. Ketubot 72a), asks [Is not going out with an] uncovered head a biblical prohibition? To which Rashi comments: why is it therefore not considered *dat Moshe*? That seems to imply that a rabbinic violation cannot be classified as *dat Moshe*. This seems to support the position of the *Shevut Yaakov* [no. 206] who in his text uses the expression "in accordance with rabbinic decree." But *in fact all that this indicates is that a biblical violation certainly cannot be classified as dat Yehudit, for dat Yehudit* | ואי קשיא האיך יכתבו כדת משה כו' מאחר שהוא רק תקנתא דרבנן. ובכתובות (דף ע"ב סע"א) פרוע ראש דאורייתא הוא פי' רש"י ואמאי לא קרי לה דת משה משמע לכאורה דדבר דרבנן לא נקרא דת משה וזה ראי' לכאורה לדעת השבו"י שבנוסח רי"ו כתוב כתקנתא דרבנן כו'. אך באמת ז"א דודאי דבר דאורייתא לא יתכן לקרותו דת יהודי' דפי' דת יהודי' הוא דמנהג צניעות שנהגו בנות ישראל אבל בדת משה נכלל גם דבר דרבנן |

> means that it is a custom of modesty that Jewish women have become accustomed to. However, *dat Moshe* also includes rabbinic violations that are not customs, as the *Maggid Mishneh* explained with regard to one who feeds her husband untithed produce (See *Beit Shmuel*, beginning of *Even HaEzer* 115),[23] that it even includes feeding him the dough-offering from dough made of grain grown outside the land of Israel, which has no basis in Torah law at all, like the ability a deaf-mute has to divorce.
>
> שאינו מנהג וכמ"ש המ"מ בפי' מאכילתו שאינו מעושר עב"ש רס"י קט"ו ומשמע אפי' בחלה בח"ל שאין לו עיקר מהתורה כלל דומי' דגט חרש.
>
> And even though the authorities there raise doubts with regard to *eruv*, which has no basis in Torah law as well, we may infer that in our case, with regard to something she feeds him, she is to be divorced without receiving her ketubah payment – that [feeding rabbinically prohibited food] is categorized as *dat Moshe*, and thus it is fine to include [the phrase "in accordance with *dat Moshe*"] in a *gett* for a deaf person and nothing more is needed.
>
> וע"ש שנסתפקו גבי עירוב שאין לו עיקר מהתורה מכלל דבכה"ג במידי דבר אכילה יוצא' שלא בכתובה הרי שזה נכלל בדת משה וא"ש לכתוב כן גם בגט חרש ותו לא מידי.

The point of the *Tzemach Tzedek* is that *dat Moshe* is a general term for violations of Jewish law, whether they be from the Torah or not, whereas *dat Yehudit* is limited to matters of modesty and sexuality.

Slightly different sentiments are also found in R. Avraham b. Mordechai HaLevi of Cairo's Responsa *Ginat Veradim, Even HaEzer* 4:11:

> In the seventh chapter of Ketubot, the Mishnah teaches that a wife who violates *dat Moshe* or *dat Yehudit* is to be divorced without receiving her ketubah. *Dat Moshe*
>
> בפרק המדיר תנן שהעוברת על דת משה ויהודית שיוצאה שלא בכתובה ודת משה היינו דברים שהם מפורשים

---

23. It is possible that the *Tur* disagrees and thinks that there is not a single rabbinic prohibition categorized as *dat Moshe* nor any biblical prohibitions labeled *dat Yehudit*. This is why the *Tur* in *EH* 115 changes the words from the Rambam of כתם to דם. (The former is rabbinic and the latter is biblical.) In the *Tur*'s model, like the model of many others, there seems to be no category of leading him astray on rabbinic matters. If I had to guess why, I would speculate that this is because it is no sin on the husband's part to unintentionally violate a rabbinic decree in this way.

are those things which are *explicitly prohibited in the Torah of Moshe*, particularly matters which involve the husband as well. For instance, if she feeds him untithed produce and lies to him and says they have been tithed; or she has intercourse with him during the period of her menstruation and says that she is pure but in fact has the presumptive status of being a menstruant by dint of her conduct among her neighbors; similarly, if she makes vows but does not fulfill them, for one's children die on account of this sin. In all of the above instances, he too sins and loses out on account of her. But if she is intentionally lax in other prohibitions which have nothing at all to do with her husband, we pay no attention. *Dat Yehudit* are those matters of *modesty and dignity which the daughters of Israel practice*, such as not to go out with one's head uncovered and the like. These, too, are relevant to the husband, for a man is particular about such conduct by his wife.[24]

בתורת משה ודוקא במידי דשייך איהו ג"כ בהם כגון שמאכילתו טבלים שמכזבת לו ואומרת שהם מתוקנים או שמשמשתו נדה שאומרת לו שהיא טהורה והיא הוחזקה נדה בשכנותיה וכן ג"כ אם נודרת ואינה מקיימ' דבעון נדריה ימותו בניו שבכל דברים אלו הוא נכשל ומפסיד בעבורה אבל אם מזלזלת בשאר איסורין לעצמה ולא שייך בעלה בהן ל"ל בה. ודת יהודית היינו מילי דפרישות וסלסול שנהגו בו בנות ישראל כגון שלא לצאת וראשה פרוע וכיוצא בזה והני נמי שייך בהו הבעל כי האדם מקפיד על אשתו בזה.

Per this view, everything that is expressly written in the Torah is not categorized as *dat Yehudit*, and *dat Yehudit* is limited to matters that are

---

24. He adds:

> One is only required to give forewarning to a woman who violates *dat Yehudit*, whose sin is relatively minor; but one who violates *dat Moshe*, whose sin is great, requires no forewarning at all, for we penalize her. There is some support for this from Rashi (b. Sotah 25a), who in commenting on the Talmud's question of whether a woman who violates *dat* requires forewarning [before losing her ketubah payment], defines such a woman as: "a woman who violates *dat Yehudit*, who is immodest, who goes out with her head uncovered or spins in the marketplace, and speaks with any man, [activities] which the Talmud in b. Ketubot (72a) rules as being grounds for divorce without receiving her ketubah." He explicitly states that the question in the Gemara is with regard to one who violates *dat Yehudit*, and not *dat Moshe*.

When he cites the opinion of Rashi that one who violates *dat Yehudit* requires forewarning, he also cites Rashi's view that hair covering is *dat Yehudit* and not *dat Moshe*. See also Responsa *Yakhin u-Voaz* 1:122.

related to modesty and the like. Matters that do not cause him to sin are of no importance in this classification system. Furthermore, rabbinic violations she causes him to do are not relevant for these purposes, as they are neither matters of modesty nor Torah law.[25] Indeed, *Ginat Veradim* is clear that there is no violation of the marriage rules if she is lax in matters of Jewish law that do not impact her husband.

R. Baruch Fränkel-Te'omim, in his notes on the *Beit Meir* (*Even HaEzer* 115), disagrees with this position. He writes that *dat Moshe* includes only those actions which lead the husband to sin as well (whether they are a Torah or a rabbinic violation). Conversely, anything which does not cause him to sin is only *dat Yehudit*. In his view, seclusion with another man and hair covering are considered *dat Yehudit* even though they might be considered biblical prohibitions.[26] All of this is based on the language of Rosh (m. Ketubot 7:9) who states that "With regard to *dat Yehudit*, the husband is able to deprive his wife of her ketubah on account of her impudence and on account of the suspicion of infidelity." This insight is important as it is used by some[27] to explain that a married woman who does not cover her hair is only violating a *dat Yehudit*, even if there is an undergirded Torah prohibition. Nonetheless, her sin is an immutable violation of Torah law. To clarify, per this construct, a woman violating either hair covering or *yichud* would not be a violation of the rules of modesty. However, such conduct would still be a ritual violation of Jewish law but not of the rules of the marriage. Thus, it would not be the husband's concern as a marital matter.[28]

There is no fundamental disagreement between Rosh and other authorities with regard to "what is considered *dat Yehudit*." Indecent

---

25. See note 64 on page 233 above for an explanation of this. While at first glance this seems counterintuitive – why should the rabbis not penalize through the loss of the ketubah when she causes him to violate rabbinic law? – one can see echoes of that in the phrase b. Ketubot 72b אם כן, לא הנחת בת לאברהם אבינו שיושבת תחת בעלה. The idea that not every violation of Jewish law is relevant in a divorce proceeding makes sense. Rabbinic law is complex; even ignorant people are entitled to be secure in their marriage.

26. A suggestion along these lines can be found in R. Yehuda Herzl Henkin's *Responsa Bnei Banim* 3:22.

27. Eli Baruch Shulman, Exchange: Hair Covering and Jewish Law: A Response, *Tradition* 43:2 (73-88) (2010) at https://traditiononline.org/exchange-hair-covering-and-jewish-law-a-response/.

28. See *Iggerot Moshe EH* 1:114 who states simply ובגופו הדבר כיון שבזה"ז אין להחשיבה פרוצה בזה כיון שהרבה מזלזלות בזה אין להפסידה כתובתה.

actions which give rise to "the suspicion of infidelity" are those matters which are dependent on the "practices of the modest daughters of Israel."[29]

What, then, is under dispute? If there are actions which in no way detract from a woman's modesty but are still biblically prohibited for some other reason – how are those actions to be classified? According to the commentary of Rabbi Fränkel-Te'omim on the *Beit Meir* and Rosh, these are another class of sins entirely. They are neither *dat Moshe* nor *dat Yehudit*, but simply sins unrelated to marriage. However, nowhere in Rosh can one find a biblical prohibition (other than *dat Moshe* or *dat Yehudit* and modesty) that is the biblical source for hair covering.

R. Moshe Feinstein, in his *Iggerot Moshe, Even HaEzer* 1:69, writes the following with regard to what is considered to be a violation of *dat Yehudit* and promiscuous behavior:

[T]here is another prohibition outlined in b. Ketubot 72 for women under the rubric of *dat Yehudit* not to act in a promiscuous manner. However, in this regard it is limited to where she alone acts this way. But when all the women of her city act that way, it is not at all appropriate to consider such conduct promiscuous. It makes no difference that the conduct of these women might have originally been promiscuous behavior at one time; *nonetheless, since such is now the manner of dress and walking, one ought not consider it promiscuous conduct and forbid it.* [Avoiding such clothing or activity] is regarded as the conduct of the pious and exceedingly modest – may blessing come to such a person.[30]	אך יש איסור אחר בנשים מדין דת יהודית שלא להתנהג בפריצות בכתובות דף ע״ב אבל מצד זה הוא רק כשהיא עצמה עושה כך אבל כשדרך כל הנשים בעירה כן אין שייך להחשיב זה לפריצות ואין חלוק מה שנעשה דרך הנשים שבעיר היה משום פריצות דעכ״פ כיון שכן הוא דרך לבישתן והלוכן אין להחשיב זה למעשה פריצות ולאסור עליהן אלא מדרך חסידות לצניעות יתירא ותע״ב

---

29. Among the Rishonim and Acharonim, nearly all are unanimous in rejecting this opinion and taking the view that *dat Yehudit* only includes rabbinic prohibitions; see *Sedei Chemed*, s.v. *dat*, and Encyclopedia Talmudit, s.v. *dat Yehudit* and *dat Moshe*, who cite numerous Rishonim and Acharonim who say that "*dat Yehudit*" is equivalent to "rabbinic prohibition" (*issur derabbanan*). (See note 77 on page 89.)
30. See also what my esteemed teacher R. Mordechai Willig wrote on this topic in his work *Am Mordechai* Berachot 16:3 (pp. 67–68).

A similar ruling is found by R. Ovadia Yosef in *Responsa Yabia Omer*, Vol. 4, *Even HaEzer* no. 3:

> Today, it has become widespread practice for God-fearing women to go out with only a kerchief or hat, without a headscarf or veil, and no one makes a fuss. It thus seems that the essential concept of women covering their hair is biblical in nature, and is obligatory irrespective of changes in practice, and is unchanging for all time. However, with respect to the modest practices of Jewish women, we accept any established practice to be lenient. This accords with the ruling of Maharam Al-Ashkar (no. 35) who permits women, in places where the practice is for all to do so, to go about with hair protruding from under their hat.
>
> והנה היום פשט המנהג שהנשים יראות ה' יוצאות במטפחת או בכובע בלבד בלי צעיף או רביד /רדיד/, ואין פוצה פה ומצפצף. וע"כ דדוקא עצם כיסוי הראש שהוא דאורייתא הוא מחוייב המציאות לעולם ולא ישתנה בשום זמן, אבל מנהג בנות ישראל שנהגו לצניעות כל שהמנהג בכל העיר להקל אזלינן בתר מנהגא. ודמי למ"ש מהר"ם אלשקר (סי' לה) להתיר במקום שנהגו הנשים לצאת בשערות שחוץ לצמתן.

So too, R. Yehuda Herzl Henkin describes the concept of *dat Yehudit* thusly:

> It seems to us that *dat Yehudit* is dependent on local practice, as evidenced by Rambam.... It is also widely accepted among the Rishonim that *dat Yehudit* is based on common practice, as Rashi explained: "which the daughters of Israel practice *even though it is not expressly written in Scripture.*" R. Isaiah di Trani, in his commentary (*Tosefot Rid*) to the phrase, "There is no prohibition" explained: "*rather, the women follow those practices in a modest manner*" – in the present tense.[31]

What we have here are three models of *dat Yehudit*:

1. All Torah violations are *dat Moshe*, and all rabbinic violations are *dat Yehudit*. This is one explanation of the Rambam and is directly found in many others (such as *Beit Shmuel*), who insist that full uncovering of hair is a Torah violation and a *dat Moshe*.[32]

---

31. See R. Henkin's article, "*Shi'ur Kisui Rosh Shel Nashim,*" *Techumin* 13, p. 290–298, and particularly at 297.

32. R. Yonah Landsofer, in his Responsa *Me'il Tzedakah* 61, writes that while *dat Moshe* includes prohibitions that are not biblical, it only includes prohibitions that have at least an allusion in the Torah:

> Seclusion of a married woman with another man is a biblical violation, as the

2. Any violations of Torah law that impact the husband are *dat Moshe*, and *dat Yehudit* is limited to situations of immodest behavior (and nothing else).
3. Any violation of Jewish law is a *dat Moshe,* and *dat Yehudit* is limited to violations of customs of modesty in a particular time and place.

Conclusion: Interpreting or Arguing? Comparing the Three Models

A simple read of the *Tur, Shulchan Arukh,* Rama, and *Levush* drive one to conclude that none of them recorded a self-standing prohibition for women – married or single – to cover their hair in a time and place where other modest women do not cover. There is, in my view, no other reasonable way to read the rules they codify that properly explain both the single woman exception and its placement in the various codes.

The commentators generally argue with this reading of these works and interpret the *Tur* and *Shulchan Arukh* differently, but I would argue that this does not fully solve the problem. The *Tur* and *Shulchan Arukh* contain a contradiction and everyone is struggling to resolve that contradiction. One could leave it at that and say that we do not know how to solve it, but I believe that the solution is clear.

To reiterate, briefly, I do not see the solution of either the *Perisha/Beit Shmuel* or *Bach/Taz/Chelkat Mechokek* as resolving the contradiction found in the *Tur* and *Shulchan Arukh*. This attempted solution does not arrive at the true intent of the *Tur* and *Shulchan Arukh* since, irrespective of how one comes out halakhically on whether non-virgins who have never been married need to cover their hair, the *Tur* and *Shulchan Arukh* use the word *penuyah*, which refers to all single women, when discussing the obligation. Indeed, there are 22 times when the *Shulchan Arukh* uses the term *penuyah* and not a single one of them can be reasonably understood solely as a reference to a single woman who has already been married. Furthermore, it is used this way in the same *siman* (*EH* 21) in the very next sentence. In the *Tur* it is the same sentence.

Talmud, Avodah Zarah 36b, concludes. And though Rambam in his book of general principles wrote that such is only rabbinically forbidden, nonetheless with regard to matters such as this we consider it to be of *dat Moshe*, just as the Talmud in b. Ketubot (72) counters that going out with uncovered hair is a biblical prohibition – though this, too, according to his general principles, is only rabbinic as well; we must therefore explain that because there is some allusion to it in the Torah, we consider it as *dat Moshe*.

Thus, I agree with *Magen Avraham* that such an interpretation of the *Tur* and *Shulchan Arukh* is very difficult. In reality, these commentators are not interpreting the *Tur* and *Shulchan Arukh* at all, but rather arguing with them. They are essentially saying that the *Tur* and *Shulchan Arukh* cannot be saying what they are saying, and thus, their words must mean something other than what they seem to.

The *Magen Avraham's* interpretation, which is that *EH* refers to braiding or coiffing hair and *OC* to covering hair, is a more plausible reading of the words. The problem is that it seems to be inconsistent with the text of the *Tur, Shulchan Arukh,* and *Levush*. Nothing in these works implies that these single women have their hair braided or coiffed, and this is not the practice of Ashkenazi Jewish women either then or now. Thus even if the Talmudic text can be read this way, it is certainly not what these works mean.

The problem with Yaavetz's version of the position is even stronger. If single women do not feel the necessity of braiding their hair when appearing in public, they certainly do not feel the need to cover it with a kalta. Moreover, his proof is that this halakha comes from the Mishnah about virgins appearing at their weddings with their hair uncovered. Frankly, it is no proof it all, since his translation of *hynuma* is incorrect. Even worse, his reading of "with hair undone" in that Mishnah along with Rashi's "hair down to the shoulders" as meaning "hair covered with a kalta" is a stretched reading that is trying to force the Mishnah and Rashi to say the exact opposite of what they say.

Consequently, the only interpretation left to us is what I suggested at the beginning. In *Even HaEzer* 21, the *Tur, Shulchan Arukh* and *Levush* are quoting Rambam, and working with a baseline practice from Sephardic countries where all girls and women, single or married, cover their hair when appearing in public. However, in *OC* 75, they are quoting from an Ashkenazi source, which assumes a baseline practice of single women going out with their hair undone and married women covering their hair. This follows the subjective model of *dat Yehudit* and hair covering discussed in Chapter 5; namely, that modest behavior is judged by the standards of normative practice in a given society. Thus, I would add that according to *Tur, Shulchan Arukh* and *Levush*, in a society in which no women, even married women, cover their hair, appearing with uncovered hair would not be considered a violation of *dat Yehudit*. Granted, none of them say this explicitly, but that is simply because they had never heard of any such society, since, in their day and age, no Christian or Muslim society had such a practice. The practice – and thus the halakhic problem – is a distinctly modern one.³³

---

33. The central claim of this chapter, namely the position that hair covering is societally defined, is adopted not only by some authorities but by Rabbi Yosef Karo and is critical to assessing the weight of this argument for practical halakha. A critique made against this claim is that this view does not appear explicitly in the *Beit Yosef*, the more thorough encyclopedia of Jewish law that *Shulchan Arukh* is meant to summarize. In several exchanges with Rabbi Yehuda Herzl Henkin, this has been his central critique. However, as he himself notes, without interpreting *Shulchan Arukh* in such a way, a seeming contradiction remains. Rabbi Henkin writes as follows:

> Shulhan Arukh, Even ha-Ezer 115, lists *peru'at rosh* under *dat Yehudit* in paragraph 3 but not under *dat Moshe* in paragraph 1. This recently led a colleague to claim that according to the *Shulchan Arukh* even going completely bareheaded in public violates only *dat Yehudit*, which is a matter of minhag and subject to change. But such a view is (1) impossible according to those who view *peru'at rosh* as a Torah violation, (2) found nowhere in the Rishonim, and (3) it contradicts R. Yosef Karo's own Bet Yosef. The problem is that the *Shulchan Arukh* combined two incompatible positions. In par. 1 he copied the language of the Tur who followed the mishnah in m. Ketubot which does not list *peru'at rosh* under *dat Moshe*; see above, "Dat Moshe and Yehudit," and in *Bnei Banim*, vol. 2, no. 22. In par. 3, however, the *Shulchan Arukh* copied the language of Rambam in *Hilkhot Ishut* (24:12) that the source of *dat Yehudit* is minhag, which is nowhere mentioned in the Tur. The two are contradictory, and the intent of *Shulhan Arukh* remains obscure. However, I think the problem is not in halakha. Rambam wrote that a woman violates *dat Yehudit* if she goes out to market "*ve-rosha paru'a veen aleha redid.*" This must mean that she is considered *peru'at rosh* inasmuch as she is not wearing a redid, even though she is wearing a *kalta*. It does not mean that if her head is completely uncovered she violates only *dat Yehudit*, for Rambam wrote in the previous halakha that going out completely bareheaded violates *dat Moshe*! Since in par. 3 the *Shulchan Arukh* copied Rambam's exact wording, it presumably meant the same thing by it that Rambam did. The difficulty is that, if so, the Shulhan Arukh nowhere mentions the prohibition of going out completely bareheaded. That women are forbidden to do so, however, is incontestable. (emphasis added)

This note appears in Rabbi Henkin's "Contemporary Tseni'ut," *Tradition* 37:3, n. 115, republished in *Understanding Tzniut: Modern Controversies in the Jewish Community* (NY: Urim Publications, 2008), p. 43 n. 120.

Rabbi Henkin's methodological assumptions as I understand them are:
1. No position can be held in *Shulchan Arukh* if not mentioned in *Beit Yosef* explictly.
2. It is preferable to assume a contradiction in *Shulchan Arukh* or at least leave a question unresolved, than to posit that *Shulchan Arukh* introduces a position not developed in *Beit Yosef*.

3. Seeming contradictions can occur when *Shulchan Arukh* borrows the language of Rishonim whose positions are not compatible with each other.
4. Despite the above, we assume that as much as possible, *Shulchan Arukh* accommodated the positions of the Rishonim he quoted.

Thus, in this case, Rabbi Henkin, while he recognizes the problem in interpreting *Shulchan Arukh*, relies on the Rambam to interpret the intent of Rabbi Yosef Karo.

My position, however, is that:

1. *Shulchan Arukh* was intended as an integrated code and we should assume consistency when possible.
2. It is possible that *Shulchan Arukh* will accept a view developed elsewhere in *Beit Yosef*, even if not mentioned in the local discussion. In this case, the basic idea of subjectivity in defining many of the *ervot* is discussed in *Orach Chayyim* 75 and adopted by *Beit Yosef* in his ruling that unmarried women do not have to cover their hair when the custom is not to cover.
3. In this case, therefore, consistency can be easily shown since in *OC* 75 he adopts and incorporates Ra'aviah (which as noted above, he does not think is inconsistent with Rambam).

Thus, my basic view is that his claim that "women who normally go with their hair uncovered" is not about virgins or single women, but about anyone who has this practice. This helps resolve the contradictions in *Shulchan Arukh* very nicely. My contention in this chapter has been that *Shulchan Arukh* takes hair covering out of the category of *dat Moshe* because he thinks it does not belong there. As a general rule, I assume that when *Shulchan Arukh* tinkers with the formulation of the Rambam, he does so for halakhic reasons, reflecting his disagreement with the Rambam in some way. My view explains why *Shulchan Arukh* removes hair covering from the category of *dat Moshe*, while other views do not.

CHAPTER 7

Partial Uncovering and Hair Covering by Betrothed Women: Two Important and Relevant Debates; The Subjective School and the Objective Disagree About Some Pre-Modern Cases

CHAPTER 7 SUMMARIZES LITERATURE WITH REGARD TO the cases of uncovering hair, albeit only partially. The first case we discuss is the case of a woman who only covers part of her hair and the second is the case of a woman who is only partially married. Both of these cases have elaborate discussion in the pre-modern literature and they provide an important intellectual foundation for any discussion of full uncovering of hair by married women. Indeed, this literature produces the first source actually acknowledging that uncovered hair could be permitted as a matter of Jewish law.

Introduction

Before any halakhic discussion of married women and uncovered hair takes place or can take place, this chapter collects very detailed discussion of two cases that address initial cases of hair uncovering by married women: partial uncovering and uncovering by betrothed brides. Each of these situations introduces important concepts to the conversation in the classical sources.

Hair Outside the Covering (Maharam Al-Ashkar)

Maharam Al-Ashkar (R. Moses ibn Al-Ashkar 1466–1542), who lived in Egypt and then Israel, was one of the prominent Sephardic poskim in the transition period from the Rishonim to the Acharonim. His responsum (number 35) on the question of the permissibility of exposing hair that comes out of the sides of a head covering took the earlier permissive positions a step further:

> Tlemcen (Algeria) – My friend asked me this question: Should we be concerned about those women whose practice it is to let their hair show outside their veils, for aesthetic reasons? According to what we heard, he who taught, saying that these women have inherited lies from their mothers whose practice is to reveal it, for it is totally forbidden, for our Sages said explicitly that a woman's hair is forbidden nudity, and therefore it would be fitting for us to rebuke them and warn them not to reveal it.

> תלמסאן שאלה שאלת ממני הידיד אם יש לחוש לאלו הנשים שנהגו לגלות שערן מחוץ לצמתן להתנאות בו לפי מה ששמענו מי שהורה ואמר כי שקר נחלו אמותינו הנוהגות לגלותו כי הוא איסור גמור ובפי' אמרו ז"ל שער באשה ערוה ולכן ראוי להוכיחן ולהזהירן שלא לגלותו.

The questioner takes the rabbinic description of hair as "forbidden nudity" literally and exactly. He further assumes that Maharam Al-Ashkar will agree that despite the fact that these women inherited this practice from their mothers, the local Jewish leadership should do whatever they can to stop it. It turns out that Maharam Al-Ashkar sees the matter in a very different light:

> Response: The truth is that there is nothing to be concerned about with this hair at all, since they are accustomed to show it, and this holds true even for [men] reciting the Shema in [their presence].

> תשובה איברא דאין בית מיחוש לאותו שער כלל כיון שנהגו לגלותו ואפילו לק"ש.

Maharam Al-Ashkar begins the responsum strongly, staking out the exact opposite position as that assumed by the questioner: the women are behaving properly by following their mothers' practice to leave the hair that comes out of the covering uncovered, and there is nothing to be concerned about. To clarify this point, Maharam Al-Ashkar turns to an analysis of the Talmudic passage:

> And that [Talmudic rule stating] "the hair of a woman is forbidden nudity" refers only to women who generally cover it,

> וההיא דשער באשה ערוה לא מיירי אלא בשער שדרך האשה לכסותו דומיא דטפח

PARTIAL UNCOVERING AND HAIR COVERING

along the lines of the handbreadth rule [in the same passage].

And this is what the Gemara says (b. Berachot 24a):

> Rabbi Yitzchak said: "A handbreadth of a woman's [exposed flesh] is considered forbidden nudity."

This means a handbreadth [of exposed flesh] that is generally covered. Then we ask,

> With regard to what? If this is meant to prohibit [a man's] looking at it...

Meaning to say that if this is a married woman, and his intention is to derive pleasure from looking at her,

> then even her pinky,

which is generally not covered,

> is forbidden to look at, etc.

The Gemara answers:

> Rather, it must be in reference to a person's own wife, and in regard to the recitation of the Shema.

Meaning to say, that if a handbreadth of [usually covered flesh] is exposed on her, he (her husband) should not recite the Shema in her presence.

And we also say there:

> Rav Chisda said: "A woman's calf is considered forbidden nudity..." Shmuel said: "The voice of a woman is considered forbidden nudity..." Rav Sheshet said: "The hair of a woman is considered forbidden nudity..."

There are those who explain all of the above as referring to [nudity before which a woman's husband may not] recite the Shema, and this is the interpretation of Rav Hai Gaon, z"l.

והכי איתה בגמרא
אמ"ר יצחק טפח באשה ערוה
פי' טפח שדרכה לכסות ואקשינן
למאי אילימא לאסתכולי בה כלומר דאם אשת איש היא ומתכוין ליהנות
אפילו באצבע קטנה
שאין דרכו להיות מכוסה
אסור להסתכל וכו'
ומשני
לא צריכא לאשתו ולק"ש
פירוש דאם טפח מגולה בה לא יקרא ק"ש כנגדה.

ואמרינן נמי התם
אמר רב חסדא שוק באשה ערוה.... אמר שמואל קול באשה ערוה... אמר רב ששת שער באשה ערוה....

ואיכא מאן דמפרש דכל הני נמי לענין ק"ש אמרינן להו. וכן פירש רבינו האיי גאון ז"ל.

And there are those who say that the only rule above that was stated with regard to Shema is that of the handbreadth [for this is the only place the Gemara specifically applies this interpretation] and where it is said. This appears to be the view of Rambam z"l, since he only forbids a husband from reciting the Shema in the presence of an exposed handbreadth [of his wife's flesh], and the rest of the above he includes in the list of forbidden gazing at a married woman, in Chapter 21 [law 2] of the Laws of Forbidden Relations.

ואיכא מאן דמפרש דלא איירי לענין ק"ש אלא טפח דוקא והיכא דאיתמר איתמר. ונראה כי זה דעת הרמב"ם ז"ל מדלא אסר באשתו לק"ש אלא טפח דוקא והני אחריני אסר להו לגבי אשת איש בפרק כ"א מהלכות איסורי ביאה.

Rashi z"l, however, even though he explains the passage as being about gazing at married women, wrote that the rule applies as well to a person's wife when reciting the Shema, because anything forbidden for a married woman to expose is forbidden for a husband to look at while reciting Shema.

אבל רש"י ז"ל אף על גב דקא מוקים להו באשת איש כתב דהוא הדין נמי באשתו לק"ש דדבר ערוה באשת איש אסור באשתו לק"ש.

The Rif z"l left out all of the above in his discussion of the Shema rules, even the law about the exposed handbreadth, which [the Gemara] explicitly explains as relevant to the recitation of Shema. The Ra'avad z"l explained this by suggesting that it is possible that since an earlier part of the passage declares that the buttocks are not considered forbidden nudity, the Rabbi z"l [=Rif] assumed that certainly a handbreadth, a calf, hair and voice could not be.

והריא"ף ז"ל השמיט כל זה מענין ק"ש ואפילו ההיא דטפח דאוקמוה בהדיא בק"ש. וכתב עליו הראב"ד ז"ל דאפשר דמשום דאמרינן לעיל עגבות אין בהם משום ערוה סבור הרב ז"ל דכ"ש טפח ושוק ושער וקול ע"כ.

Maharam Al-Ashkar lays out the pericope in b. Berachot and outlines four interpretations:

1. All four rules apply only to men reciting Shema in the presence of their wives (Rav Hai Gaon).
2. The rule about the handbreadth applies only to husbands during Shema, and the other two (hair and voice)[1] are about what men may look at on married women (Rambam).

---

1. Rambam does not mention calf in this halakha – see my discussion of Rambam in Chapter 4.

3. All four rules apply both to husbands reciting Shema and to married women in the presence of other men (Rashi).
4. All of these rules were meant to apply to husbands reciting Shema near their wives, but none of them count as halakha (Ra'avad's interpretation of Rif).

Maharam Al-Ashkar then moves to explain what can be learned about hair covering and modesty rules from this passage:

We find here that according to all these positions, there is no thought about a prohibition regarding [appearing in public with] this hair at all. For according to those who understand it to be relevant to married women [only] – we are not speaking about [men gazing at] married women here. And according to those who read it as relevant to a man's wife – this only applies when he is reciting the Shema, and even then, only to areas that are generally covered, since it will catch his eye [lit. "he is strict about it"] and he could come to fantasize. But something that she usually exposes, since he is used to it, he may even recite Shema [in her presence when it is exposed], as was explained.	אשתכח השתא דלדברי כולם אין באותו שער שום חשש איסור כלל דמאן דמוקים להו באשת איש אנן לאו באשת איש עסקינן ומאן דמוקים לה באשתו לא נאסר אלא לק״ש ודבר שדרכו להיות מכוסה דמקפיד עליה ואתי לידי הרהור. אבל דבר שדרכו להיות מגולה דלבו גס ביה מותר ואפי׳ לק״ש כדפרישית

Maharam Al-Ashkar points out here that however one understands the passage, it will not lead to an absolute prohibition against women to appear in public with any of their hair exposed. Maharam's phrasing here leaves the point somewhat obscure but seems to be saying as follows: the Talmud is not discussing how women may appear in public but rather what men may gaze upon (i.e., with the intent of enjoying the woman's beauty). As such, the Talmud makes it clear that these rules cannot apply to married women, since it is forbidden for any man (other than her husband) to gaze sexually at any woman for any purpose.

Thus, the passage is merely describing what may be in the presence of a man reciting the Shema and is also speaking only about his wife. Furthermore, even when it comes to a man's own wife, the prohibition falls only on parts of her that she doesn't show in public. A man in the presence of his wife dressed as she would be in public has nothing to be concerned about. This means, Maharam argues, that the list of erva spots is a subjective listing, depending on what women in any given society wear in public. He buttresses this point by quoting Ra'aviah, which we saw in Chapter 5:

> And this is what the commentators z"l have said, and this is what Ra'aviah z"l said:
>
> All of these things that we referenced as being inappropriate nudity – this applies specifically to things that women do not generally expose, but for [a man to recite Shema in the presence of] a virgin who generally exposes her hair does not concern us, for there will be no inappropriate thoughts.
>
> And the author of the Mordechai and the Rosh z"l agreed with this. All goes according to local practice.

> וכן כתבו המפרשים ז"ל וכן כתב רבי' אבי"ה ז"ל
>
> כל אלו שהזכרנו לערוה דוקא בדבר שאין[ן] רגילות להגלות אבל בתולה הרגילה בגילוי השער לא חיישינן דליכא הרהור ע"כ.
>
> וכן הסכים בעל המרדכי והרא"ש ז"ל והכל כפי המנהגות והמקומו'.

Maharam continues by quoting the Ra'avad's comment about hair outside the covering that we also saw in Chapter 5 and notes those who agree with this ruling:

> And the Rashba wrote in his commentary on b. Berachot as follows:
>
> That which Rabbi Yitzchak said: "A handbreadth [of exposed flesh] on a woman is considered nudity" – which we establish as referring to a man reciting the Shema in the presence of his own wife, the Ra'avad z"l explained that it is possible that this only refers to private places, and in this context, R. Chisda added that a woman's calf is a private place and thus nudity, even for her husband, even though this is not a private place on men. However, her face, hands, and feet, her speaking voice, and the hair that comes out from under her covering and that she does not [generally] cover – we are not concerned about, since he is used to them and seeing them will not distract him. When it comes to another woman, however, he is forbidden to gaze at her at all, even at her little finger or her hair.

> וכתב הרשב"א ז"ל בחדושיו בברכות זה לשונו
>
> והא דאמר רבי יצחק טפח באשה ערוה ואוקימנא באשתו לק"ש פי' הראב"ד ז"ל דאיפשר במקום צנוע שבה ועלה קאתי רב חסדא למימר דשוק מקום צנוע וערוה הוא אפי' לגבי בעלה אף על פי שאינו מקום צנוע באיש. אבל פניה ידיה ורגליה וקול דברה שאינו זמר ושערה חוץ לצמתה שאינו מתכסה אין חוששין להם מפני שהוא רגיל בהם ולא טריד ובאשה אחרת אסור להסתכל אפילו באצבע קטנה ובשערה ע"כ.

PARTIAL UNCOVERING AND HAIR COVERING

> And this is also what the author of the *Orchot Chayyim* wrote:
> But her face, hands, and feet, and the hair that comes out from her covering that she doesn't [generally] cover – we are not concerned about, since he is used to them.
> I heard that the author of the *Mikhtam* wrote the same thing.

> וכן נמי כתב בעל אורחות חיים
> אבל פניה ידיה ורגליה ושערה מחוץ לצמתה שאינו מתכסה אין חוששין להם מפני שהוא רגיל בהן.
> וכן שמעתי שכתב בעל המכתם.

Here Maharam Al-Ashkar has a source that explicitly mentions the case he was asked about: hair that sticks out of the hair covering that a woman doesn't cover in public. Of course, Ra'avad is discussing a woman sitting in the presence of her husband, but Maharam notes the obvious deduction – if her husband is not drawn to seeing her this way because this is how she generally appears, then this must be what she wears in public and in the presence of other men as well. And thus, if Ra'avad, Rashba, *Orchot Chayyim*, and the *Mikhtam* all take this for granted, how can the questioner even consider rebuking these women?

Maharam next attempts to show that the positions of Ra'aviah and Ra'avad are far from being radical or counter-intuitive interpretations of the Talmud. Rather, the idea that women appear in public this way was obvious and well known:

> And this does not really need much support, since according to all of the above Sages, there is no prohibition at all. Quite the contrary, they explicitly permit this, even for [their husbands] reciting the Shema, and they testify that it was the practice for women to expose [this hair], and it is certain that girls would do so in the times of the Mishnaic and Talmudic Sages.

> ואין זה צריך לפנים דלדברי כולם אין בו צד איסור כלל אדרבה שהתירוהו בפירוש ואפילו לק״ש והעידו שנהגו לגלותו ובודאי כי כן היו נוהגות בנות ישראל בימי חכמי המשנה והתלמוד ז״ל

Having established that this was the practice in Talmudic times, Maharam suggests that it goes back even farther, to Second Temple times:

> And it seems possible [that this was the practice] even when [Jews] lived in their own land during the time when the Temple stood, as it says explicitly in the third chapter of Bava Batra (60b) [in the context of mourning rituals for the loss of the Temple]:

> ואיפש׳ דאפילו בעודן על אדמתן בזמן שבית המקדש קיים כדאיתא בהדיא בפרק חזקת הבתים דאמרינן התם

> A woman can wear all her jewelry but leave out something small. To what does this refer? Rav said: "Her depilation of her temple (*bat tzid'a*), as it says (Ps 137:5–6): 'If I forget you, Jerusalem [may I forget my right hand. Let my tongue stick to my palate if I do not mention you, if I do not place Jerusalem at the head of my happiness.]"
>
> עושה אשה כל תכשיטיה ומשיירת דבר מועט. מאי היא רב אמר בת צדעא שנ' אם אשכחך ירושלם [תשכח ימיני תדבק לשוני לחכי אם לא אזכרכי אם לא אעלה את ירושלם על ראש שמחתי]

> The author of the *Arukh* z"l explained that it was written in responsa that when a woman braids her hair, she leaves out a small amount between her ears and her forehead, opposite her temples. Then she brings mixed lime, which has been pressed, and she applies it to this hair, and doesn't braid it, but keeps it on her face – this is what poor women do. But rich women comb it through with perfume and rich oils, so that these hairs stick together and so that they do not appear like mourners, and [instead] look beautiful.
>
> ופירש בעל הערוך ז"ל דכתיב בתשובות כשהאשה קולעת שערה משיירת ממנו דבר מועט בין אזניה לפדחתה כנגד צדעתה ומביאה סיד טרוף כשהוא חבוט וטחה אותו שער ואינה קולעת אותו אלא מטילה כנגד פניה זה עושה בת עניים. אבל עשירה שורקתו בבשמים ובשמן טוב כדי שיתחברו שערות זו בזו ולא תהיה כאבלות ויתיפו. ע"כ.

According to this, women who wish to show mourning would depilate the hair that would otherwise have been decorated and allowed to lie unbraided against her temples. If this is the case, Maharam Al-Ashkar argues, then the women in pre-destruction times must indeed have left this lock of hair out. In fact, according to the *Arukh* they would even have decorated this hair with perfume and oil. It is thus impossible to argue that allowing some hair to show is somehow objectively forbidden according to the Torah. With that, Maharam continues his defense of these women:

> And this [pre-destruction] practice is exactly the custom of women today. For a woman braids all her hair and leaves out some hair by her temples, that fall down across her face, and this is what the sages called *bat tzid'a* as was explained. And they are further accustomed to brush this hair with perfume and oils just as the wealthy women in the past, even though it is not
>
> וזה המנהג בעצמו הוא מנהג הנשים היום שהאשה קולעת כל שערה ומשיירת שער הצדעים יורד על פניה והוא הנקרא בלשון חכמים בת צידעא כמו שנתבאר ונוהגות גם כן לשרוק אותו בבשמים ושמן הטוב כעשירות של אותו הזמן אף על גב דלא

PARTIAL UNCOVERING AND HAIR COVERING

really proper to do this, because of the necessity to mourn the Temple, as [the Gemara] states there.

חזי למיעבד הכי זכר לחרבן הבית כדאיתא התם.

Maharam's point here is that the women in his day, about whom the questioner is complaining, do their hair exactly as women in ancient times did. Even if there is a problem with decorating this lock of hair, since it means the women are not acknowledging their mourning over the destroyed Temple, this has nothing to do with laws of modesty.

Maharam then pushes against the trend to be extra strict for kabbalistic reasons:

And everything you find in the Zohar that is particularly strict about a woman revealing hair, it is possible that this is referring to hair that she usually covers, for the Gemara [also] simply [refers to hair] and we say that it is only referring to that which she usually covers and [in front of her husband] reciting Shema. And if it means something else – we rely on the Talmud and the customs.

וכל מה שתמצא בספר הזוהר מקפיד על גלוי שער האשה איפשר דבשער שדרכה לכסותו משתעי דבגמר' סתמא נמי קאמר ואמרינן דלא איתמר אלא במה שדרכה לכסות ולק״ש. ואם יש שם דבר אחר אנן אתלמודא ואמנהגא סמכינן.

Here Maharam Al-Ashkar takes a two-pronged approach: First, it is likely the Zohar simply means what the Talmud means, and that its severe prohibition of exposing hair only refers to hair that is usually covered. Second, even if the Zohar means something more than this, we follow the Talmud and not the Zohar when the two contradict.

From here, Maharam makes an offensive move, and essentially attacks the questioner:

So let us go and scream at those who are forbidding a woman from showing this hair in her own house based on the text that says "a woman's hair is forbidden nudity" without knowing what hair it is referring to and what halakha it is dealing with in the Gemara. For, in line with their approach, it should also be forbidden to expose eyebrows, for the Torah also refers to them as hair, in the passage in which [someone being purified from *tzaraat*] must shave all

ובואו ונצווח על אלו האוסרים אותו שער לאשה בתוך ביתה מההיא דשער באשה ערוה בבלי דעת באי זה שער אמרו ולמאי הילכתא איתמ' בגמ' ואלא מעתה לפי דרכם שער גבות עיניה נמי היה להם לאסור דשער קרייה רחמנא נמי דכתיב יגלח את כל שערו את ראשו ואת זקנו ואת גבות עיניו וגומ'

the hair on his head, beard, and eyebrows (Lev. 14:9).

The point being made here is that the focus on hair sticking out from under the covering makes little sense. Although it seems to come from a literalist reading of the Talmud, which, Maharam points out, is mistaken anyway, it is an inconsistent literalist reading, since it doesn't include eyebrows, which are also hair. He further points out that the focus on hair seems random considering other parts of herself that women expose and which don't seem to bother the questioner:

> All the more so should they forbid [her exposing] her face, hands, and feet. Why are they only concentrating on this hair (i.e., the hair that comes out from the covering)? If it is because they are generally exposed, so are these [eyebrows, faces, etc.].

> וכל שכן פניה ידיה ורגליה דהוה להו נמי למיסרן ומאי שנא אותו שער ואי משום דדרכן להיות מגולין האי נמי דרכו להיות מגולה.

Maharam, for rhetorical effect, reintroduces the possibility that the prohibition can be interpreted as dealing with men gazing at married women, but he then shows how this is wrong and irrelevant.

> And if the text is only speaking about married women, and a fear that men will gaze upon them with the intention of enjoying their beauty, are we really speaking about married women and wicked men? The sages said clearly that it is forbidden [for me] to gaze even upon [a married woman's] pinky or colorful clothing, so certainly at her hair!

> ואי לא איירו אלא באשת איש ובמסתכל ומתכוין ליהנות אטו באשת איש וברשיעי עסקינן ובבירור אמרו זכרונו לברכה דאפלו באצבע קטנה אסור להסתכל ואפילו בבגדי צבעונין שלה נמי אסור וכל שכן בשערה

> For we were taught (b. Avodah Zarah 20a): "'Be careful to avoid any bad thing' (Deut. 23:10) – A man should not gaze upon an attractive woman, even if she is single, or at any married woman, even if she is ugly, nor at the colorful clothing of a woman, etc. Rav Yehuda said in the name of Shmuel: 'Even if they are spread out over a wall [to dry].' Rav Pappa said: 'Assuming he knows their husbands.'"

> דת"ר ונשמרת מכל דבר רע שלא יסתכל אדם באשה נאה ואפילו פנויה באשת איש ואפילו מכוערת. ולא בבגדי צבע של אשה וכו' ואמר רב יהודה אמר שמואל ואפי' שטוחין ומונחין על גבי הכותל. אמר רב פפא ובמכיר את בעליהן

Having made this point again, this time with another strong Talmudic prooftext, Maharam returns to the offensive, using harsh language about the premise of the question:

> Rather, the words of those [forbidding the woman from appearing with some hair outside the covering] are nullified, for they are without substance.
>
> אלא שדברי אלו בטלין הם דלית בהו מששא כלל.
>
> How much worry and anxiety are this person spared, who says such a thing![2] For since [women] have exposed this [hair] since ancient times, and in most places in the Diaspora under Muslim rule, and he has no power to stop this – how did it enter his head to forbid it?
>
> וכמה לא חלי ולא מרגיש האי גברא דקאמר לה להאי מילתא דכיון שנהגו לגלותו מימי עולם ומשנים קדמוניות ברוב תפוצות הגולה שתחת יד ישמעאל ואין בידו למחות איך עלה בלבו לאוסרו?

Maharam now moves to a new point – that even if it were forbidden for women to expose this hair, the questioner should still not have attempted to stop them:

> In fact, even if it was forbidden as a Torah violation, we say "Let Jews be, it is better if they sin unintentionally and they not become intentional sinners" as we conclude in the fourth chapter of [b.] Beitzah (30b)...[3]
>
> ואף אם היה אסור דאפילו באיסורא דאוריתא אמרינן הנח להם לישראל מוטב שיהיו שוגגין ואל יהו מזידין כדאסיקנ' בביצה פרק המביא....

Thus, even if there were a prohibition, the questioner should still not try to stop people from acting in a way that everybody acts, since they will

---

2. This is a Talmudic expression (b. Yoma 22b; b. Bava Kamma 20b), highlighting how some people are lucky such that their mistakes don't destroy them, since God appears to be on their side.

3. At this point, the Maharam goes off on a tangent, attempting to prove that this principle applies even to Torah laws:

וכדאיתא שם בהלכות הרי"ף זכרונו לברכה. ואף על גב דבשבת ריש פרק שואל בכולהו נוסחי דווקני אוקימנא לדברבנן אמרינן הנח להם לישראל וכו' ובדאוריתא אין מניחין וקשו תרויהו אהדדי כבר אמרו רבותינו ז"ל דההיא דפרק המביא דמסקי' דאפילו בדאוריתא שבקי' להו דוקא במידי שהוא דבר תורה מהלכה למשה או מדרשא ואיסורו אינו ברור וניכר שהוא מדאורית' דהא מאי דאיתא התם דאוריתא היינו תוספת יום הכפורים דילפינן לה מערב עד ערב תשבתו שבתכם ואין לו זמן קבוע וניכר לאיסורו וכשהן אוכלין ושותין הם סבורים שעדיין לא קדש היום אבל בשאר איסורין הניכרים כגון חלב ודם ושבת וגזל וכיוצא בהן לא אמרינן הנח להם לישראל

not listen, and such rebuke violates the Talmudic principle of "let them be." Maharam then takes this to the next, rhetorically charged level:

> And if the principle of "let [Jews be]" applies to Torah and rabbinic laws, certainly it applies to matters that are permitted, and which the people have treated as permitted, such that anyone who rebukes them for this is not speaking wisely and may even be, God forbid, bringing them to sin, and will pay the penalty in the future.
>
> והשתא אם בדאוריתא ובדרבנן אמרינן הנח להם כל שכן בדבר המותר שנהגו בו היתר שכל המוכיחן בזה לא בדעת ידבר ונמצא מכשילן ח״ו ועתיד ליתן את הדין.

It is hard to imagine a stronger statement than this, as Maharam turns the table on the questioner, making him into the sinner, and not the women. With that Maharam turns to his final point, that the permissibility of such behavior should extend even to newcomers from stricter communities. This is the one argument about which Maharam expresses some hesitancy:

> And if I weren't afraid, I would suggest that perhaps even women who have come as refugees from Christian countries, where they were accustomed to cover this hair when they lived there, should not be admonished not to uncover it, since they have established their homes here, and it cannot reasonably be said that they plan to return to their native lands.[4]
>
> ואלמלא דמסתפינא הוה אמינא דאפילו אותן הנשים שבאו מגורשות מארצות הערלים שהיו נוהגות לכסותו כשהיו שם אין להזהירן שלא לגלותו כיון שקבעו דירתן בכאן ואין לומר בהן דעתן לשוב לארצם.

Maharam is living in the period immediately after the expulsion of Jews from Christian Spain and Portugal. Many of the Jews took refuge in North African countries, such as where the questioner is writing from.

---

4. Here Maharam attempts to prove this point, by outlining the halakhic discussion about changing customs after moving:

ובהדיא אמרינן בחולין כי סליק רבי זירא לארץ ישראל אכל מוגרמתא דרב ושמואל. פירוש רב ושמואל היו אוסרין בבבל משפיר כובע ולמטה ואף על פי שנשאר מטבעת גדולה מלא החוט על פני רובה. ורבי זירא כשהלך לארץ ישראל אכל מה שהיו אוסרין רב ושמואל בבבל. ואקשינן והיכי עביד הכי והא תנן נותנין עליו חומרי מקום שיצא משם. ומתרצינן רבי זירא אין דעתו לחזור לבבל ומתוך כך לא חשש למנהגם. ומתניתי׳ דקתני נותנין עליו חומרי מקום שיצא משם בשדעתו לחזור למקומו וכן הסכימו המפרשים ז״ל. וגדולה מזאת כתב הרא״ש ז״ל בפסקיו דאפילו שהולך ממקום שמחמירין למקום שמקילין ואפילו דעתו לחזור יש לו לנהוג כקולי המקום שהלך לשם ואל יחמיר כמנהג מקומו מפני המחלוקת בדבר שיש בו שנוי מנהג ע״כ.

Apparently, in these Christian countries, the protocol for hair covering was stricter due to local (Christian) mores.

Thus, it occurs to Maharam that halakha might be stricter with such women, and demand they maintain their previous stricter standards. Nevertheless, this is not Maharam's inclination. Instead, he hesitantly suggests that such women should be allowed to dress in the same way as the local women, without comment by the local rabbinic authorities.

After discussing the halakhic position that even people who might return to their homelands one day may take on the lenient practices of the place where they are currently living, Maharam concludes his responsum with some further mitigating points about these refugee women:

How much more so these women [who were expelled from their countries], for it cannot reasonably be claimed that they intend on returning to the homelands, as we already wrote. And how much more so, since even in their homelands, they didn't cover this [hair] because of a prohibition [of exposing it] but because most non-Jewish women tended not to reveal this [hair].	וכל שכן באלו הנשים דליכא למימ' בהו דעתן לשוב לארצם כמו שכתבנו וכל שכן דאפי' בארצן לא היו מכסות אותו משום איסור אלא שלא היה מנהג ארצן לגלותו דאפילו רוב הגויות לא היו נוהגות לגלותו.
Therefore, it is fitting to allow even those women who used to cover this hair in the home countries to present themselves in the way customary in their current countries. And the holy behavior of their mothers (i.e., ancestors) is in their own hands, as we proved from Bava Batra above.	הילכך אפי' לאותן שהיו נוהגות לכסותו בארצן ראוי להניחן לנהוג כמנהג הארץ אשר גרו בה. ומעשה אמותן הקדושות בידיהן כמו שהוכחנו מההיא דפרק חזקת הבתים דלעיל
And in many instances the Rabbis were lenient so that a woman not become unattractive in her husband's eyes, and I do not need to write about this at length. The words of he who is wrapped up in love of you, and whose heart pounds in response to your separation from him – Moshe ibn Al-Ashkar, may the Merciful one protect him.	ובכמה וכמה דברים הקילו רבותינו ז"ל כדי שלא תתגנה האשה על בעלה. ואין צורך באורך. נאם המעוטף באהבתך ולפרידתך קירות לבו מקרקר. משה ן' אל אשקר. נ"ר.[5]

---

5. I assume this is נטריה רחמנא.

The upshot of Maharam Al-Ashkar's strongly worded responsum is clear: what is permitted and what is forbidden with regard to exposing hair hangs entirely on what is standard in the community. Maharam lived at a time when a married woman appearing in public with totally exposed and free-flowing hair would have been unthinkable, so we do not know for sure what he would say about whether married women must cover any of their hair in modern and western societies. Nevertheless, the ethos of his responsum is strongly in favor of letting women dress in such a way as to appear like the average modest woman in her community.

His ending, which compares the strict Christian practice with the more liberal Muslim one in his time, strengthens this impression, since it clarifies that part of what makes a practice "normal dress" is connected with the behavior of the gentile community in which a given Jewish community is embedded.[6]

R. Isaac HaLevi Segal

MUST A BETROTHED WOMAN COVER HER HAIR?

R. Isaac ben Samuel HaLevi Segal (ca. 1580–1660), the older brother of the *Taz*, was asked about whether an *arusah* – a woman who has performed the *erusin* or betrothal ceremony and is technically married, but has not performed the *nissuin* ceremony and is not yet living with her husband in a physical relationship – must cover her hair (*Responsa Mahari HaLevi* #9):

> A virgin who was married through *erusin*, is it prohibited for her to appear in public with uncovered hair like a fully married woman, and thus it is forbidden to recite the Shema in the presence of her uncovered hair, or is she not prohibited from appearing in public with her hair uncovered until after *nissuin*, and if so, it would be permitted to recite the Shema in the presence of her exposed hair while she is merely an *arusah*?
>
> בתולה שנתארסה אם אסורה מן הדין ללכת פרועת ראש כמו נשואה וא"כ אסור לקרות ק"ש כנגד שערות ראשה, או אינה אסורה מדינא בפריעת ראש עד אחר הנשואין וא"כ מותר לקרות ק"ש כנגד שערות ראשה בעודה ארוסה.

---

6. I recognize that others take a narrower read of the Maharam Al-Ashkar (see material on pages 312 and 427). However, the read adopted here is a more natural understanding of the text.

The question R. Segal receives, though it is about the proper public appearance of a betrothed woman, is focused exclusively on the question of the Shema recitation. R. Segal responds with a detailed and multi-pronged answer, beginning with the passage in b. Ketubot about a virgin's appearance at her wedding:

Answer: At first glance it would appear that a betrothed woman is permitted to appear in public with her hair undone, from the fact that we were taught in a mishnah in the second chapter of Ketubot (15b):	תשובה, לכאורה היה נראה דארוסה מותרת לצאת אף בפני רבים בפריעת ראש, מדתנן בריש פרק ב' דכתובות [טו ע"ב]
A woman who is widowed, she says I was a virgin when I married.... If there are witnesses that she went out with *hynuma* and her hair was undone, her ketubah is two hundred.	האשה שנתארמלה היא אומרת בתולה נשאתני וכו' אם יש עדים שיצתה בהינומא וראשה פרוע כתובתה מאתיים,
We see from this that in their days, she would appear in public with her hair undone before her *chuppah*, even though she had already been betrothed earlier.	הא קמן דבימיהם יצאה בפני רבים פרועת ראש קודם החופה אף שהיתה ארוסה קודם לכן,

R. Segal's opening assumption is that if she showed up to her wedding (*nissuin*) with her hair undone, that means she is permitted to have her hair undone in general. And since, presumably, the average woman getting married is already betrothed, as that was the practice in Talmudic times, betrothed women clearly do not need to cover their hair.[7]

R. Segal then discusses the alternative understanding of that Talmudic passage – namely, that the woman's appearance at her wedding was a one-time matter and not reflective of how she would usually appear in public before her wedding, and rejects it:

---

7. Next, R. Segal discusses a tangential question: namely, whether a woman may continue to have her hair uncovered even during the first day of her seven days of post-wedding parties:

ומדברי הרא"ש שם [פ"ב סימן ג'] משמע דאפי' אחר החופה ביום ראשון מז' ימי המשתה מותרת בפריעת ראש בפני רבים, שכתב וז"ל יש אומרים דכל שבעה אסור להסתכל בכלה אבל יום ראשון שהוא עיקר החיבוב אצל בעלה מותר, דאל"כ מי יעיד שיצתה בהינומא וראשה פרוע. ולית בדאפילו שעה אחת אסור להסתכל, אלא כיון שרואין ההינומא שעשו ואומרים זו היא של כלה פלונית היינו עדותה א"נ ראיית ההינומא כשהיא עליה או פריעת הראש אין זה הסתכלות בפניה עכ"ל, הא קמן שהיתה בפריעת ראש בפני רבים ביום ראשון מז' ימי המשתה שהן אחר החופה, כדמשמע ממ"ש הרא"ש יום ראשון שהוא עיקר החיבוב אצל בעלה, וה"נ מוכח בכמה דוכתי דז' ימי המשתה הן אחר החופה.

Now if you argue that they only permitted her to appear publicly with her hair undone at her wedding, so that people would know she was a virgin, this is not the case. For they had other, halakhically permissible signs such as *hynuma* (m. Ketubot 2:1), passing around parched wheat in Judah (ibid.), or dripping oil in Babylonia (b. Ketubot 17b), and other such things; thus, hair undone is not a unique [indicator], but rather anything that is a custom that virgins do as a sign of their virginity during their weddings, as is clear there in the Gemara. And this is what the Rambam wrote in his commentary on the Mishnah (ad loc.) and what he wrote in Chapter 16 of the Laws of Marriage (law 25). If so, why would they have allowed a prohibited action, such as undone hair, for no reason?! Rather, we learn from this that [a virgin appearing in public with her hair undone] is permitted.

וכי תימא דלא התירו לה ללכת פרועת ראש אלא בעת הנישואין כדי שידעו שהיא בתולה, הא ליתא שהרי היו להם סימנים אחרים המותרים כמו הינומא [שם במשנה], וחלוק קליות [שם] ביהודא, ודרדוגי דמשחא כו' בבבל [שם יז ע"ב] וכיוצא בהן, דפרועות ראש לאו דוקא אלא ה"ה כל דבר שהמנהג לעשות להבתולות סימן בעת נישואיה להראות שהיא בתולה וכדמוכח התם בגמ', וכ"כ הרמב"ם בפירוש המשנה שם, וכ"כ בפי"ו מהלכות אישות [הכ"ה], וא"כ למה להם לנהוג להתיר דבר איסור דהיינו פריעת ראש ללא צורך, אלא ש"מ דשריא.

Having established that it was permitted for a virgin to appear in public with her hair undone, R. Segal turns to a discussion of the passage in b. Berachot about uncovered hair, which would imply the opposite:

That which R. Sheshet stated (b. Berachot 24a), that the hair of a woman is considered *erva*, one may suggest that was with regard to a married woman, who regularly goes with her hair covered. But with a virgin who regularly goes with her hair exposed there is no concern for improper sexual thoughts, as Rosh and the Mordechai, citing Ra'aviah, wrote in the third chapter of Berachot.

והא דאמר רב ששת [ברכות כד ע"א] שער באשה ערוה, י"ל דהיינו בנשואה שדרכה לילך בכיסוי שערה, אבל בתולה הרגילה ללכת בגילוי ראש ליכא למיחש להרהור וכמ"ש הרא"ש [סימן לז] והמרדכי בשם ראבי"ה בפ"ג דברכות.

And even though they said this with regard to the recitation of the Shema, as they explain the passage according to R. Hai Gaon, that all these laws were said with regard to one's own wife and the recitation of the

ואף על גב שהם כתבו זה לענין ק"ש דמפרשי כרב האי דכולהו מיירי באשתו ולק"ש, מ"מ מדכתבו דליכא למיחש להרהור בגילוי ראש הבתולה

PARTIAL UNCOVERING AND HAIR COVERING 309

Shema, nevertheless, from the fact that they wrote that there is no need to be concerned about improper sexual thoughts from [seeing] the uncovered head of a virgin, there is also no prohibition to look at her, as the one rationale applies to the other.

תו ליכא איסורא נמי להסתכל בה וחד טעמא לתרוייהו.

In short, at this point in his responsum, R. Segal argues that the prohibition of looking at a woman only applies if she appears improperly dressed, and this is determined by norms. Virgins in the Ashkenazi communities in Germany, where Mordechai and Ra'aviah were from, would generally appear in public with their hair undone, and just as there is no problem reciting Shema in their presence, so too there is no prohibition to look at them. (To be clear, he is not speaking about active gazing with sexual intent, which the Gemara said is forbidden even if he is only looking at her pinky.)

R. Segal's point here is ostensibly that the passage in b. Berachot is not meant as a clear prohibition on uncovered hair, but only as a subjective prohibition on reciting Shema or looking at a woman's hair, assuming it is usually covered.[8] In communities in which only some women cover their hair (married) and others don't (virgins/unmarried), the prohibition would only apply to the former group.

Nevertheless, R. Segal moves on to reject the above conclusions and offers an entirely different approach to the passage about the virgin getting married that takes the matter in a different direction:

But if we read carefully, we will see that the above is not correct. From the fact that Rashi felt the need to explain there at the beginning of the second chapter of Ketubot:

אבל כדדייקינן חזינן דלאו הכי הוא, דמדאיצטריך ליה לרש"י לפרושי התם בריש פ"ב דכתובות

"'Hair on her shoulder' – this is how they used to take the virgins out of their fathers' homes to their husbands' homes."

שערה על כתיפה, כך היו נוהגים להוציא את הבתולות מבית אביהן לבית בעליהן, ש"מ דכל שעת אירוסין לא

---

8. As he does not cite the passage from b. Ketubot here, we see that in his understanding the prohibition against a (married) woman appearing in public with her hair undone is based on the verse in Song of Songs and the Talmudic passage in b. Berachot, not from the verse in Numbers and the passage in b. Ketubot.

> We can deduce from this that while she was an *arusah* she would not go out with her hair undone.
>
> היתה יוצאה בפריעת ראש,
>
> For if this were not the case, why would Rashi have described this as the customary way of taking [a virgin] from her father's house to her husband's house?
>
> דאי לא תימא הכי למה ליה לרש״י למיתלי במנהג יציאתן מבית אביהן לבית בעליהן
>
> Thus the Mishnah reads well according to its simple meaning: since people testified that she went out with her hair undone, she was certainly a virgin; since if she had been a widow or divorcée, she would not have gone out with her hair undone.
>
> הא אתיא מתני׳ שפיר כפשטה שכיון שהעידו שיצאה וראשה פרוע ודאי היתה בתולה, דאי היתה אלמנה או גרושה לא יצאה בראשה פרועה,

Having taken the step to say that the Talmud is actually describing a special appearance of a virgin getting married, R. Segal must next explain why it is that this woman would not appear in public with her hair undone other than at her wedding. Here he takes a new approach:

> Rather, it is certain that a betrothed woman, even if she is a virgin, does not appear with her hair undone in a courtyard, and certainly in a thoroughfare, just as a married woman would not. For with both women, we must be concerned about [men having] improper thoughts about them.
>
> אלא ע״כ שגם בתולה ארוסה אינו יוצאה בראש פרועה לחצר וכ״ש למבוי כמו נשואה דבתרווייהו איכא למיחש להרהור,

R. Segal argues that betrothed women should be treated the same as any married woman. In other words, un-betrothed virgins would have appeared in public with their hair undone, but betrothed virgins would not have. The reason R. Segal gives for this is concern about men having sexual thoughts.

Logic indicates that this cannot be based on the subjective argument that betrothed women always cover their hair, because that would be circular (if they were all allowed to appear with hair undone then it would not be a problem in the first place). And thus, R. Segal either means that we are more concerned about betrothed (and married) women because of the level of sin involved, or because undone hair communicates availability, and mixing "available" with "betrothed" sends a problematic message. (As we will see shortly, he means the latter.)

Once R. Segal has taken this step, he needs to explain why the Talmud focuses on how this woman appears with her hair exposed:

For this reason Rashi z"l was forced to explain:	ומשום הכי הוכרח רש"י ז"ל לפרש וז"ל:
Her hair is undone – on her shoulders, etc.	וראשה פרוע שערה על כתיפה כו',
Meaning, that which it says [in the Mishnah] "her hair is undone" means that she allows some of the ends of her hair to fall onto her shoulders behind her.	כלומר הא דקתני ראשה פרוע היינו שמניחה קצת סופי השערות לאחריה על כתיפה,
And because [one might think that] even this is forbidden, as Rav Sheshet said: "The hair of a woman is *erva*," which implies even a small amount of her hair, for they said there that [the prohibition] of gazing at her applies even to her little finger, and this is referring to after the *chuppah*, as is clear from the words of the Rosh quoted above.	ומשום דאפי' בכה"ג איכא איסורא כדאמר רב ששת שער באשה ערוה, והיינו אפילו במעט משערותיה, דהא לאיסתכולי בה אמרו שם אפי' באצבע קטנה אסור, והכא מיירי לאחר החופה וכדמוכח נמי מדברי הרא"ש דלעיל,
Therefore, Rashi explains:	לכן פירש"י וז"ל
This was their practice to bring the virgins out from their fathers' houses to their husbands' houses.	כך היו נוהגין להוציא את הבתולות מבית אביהן לבית בעליהן ע"כ,
Meaning that exposing a little hair like this is not prohibited; for since they were accustomed to reveal some hair, there is no concern about improper thoughts.	כלומר שאין איסור בגילוי קצת כזה מפני שכך נהגו לגלות אותו קצת מהשער לית ביה חשש הרהור.

Here R. Segal makes his understanding of the situation clear. Rav Sheshet's prohibition is subjective and applies only to hair that is not exposed in public. Nevertheless, the prohibition cannot be haphazard; it has to work with what various forms of garments *mean* in a given society.

Thus, in a culture that differentiates how married or single women appear in public, it would make no sense to have betrothed women dress like single women. The point of distinguishing between single and married, he believes, is to communicate marital status. Since uncovered hair communicates availability, why would a betrothed woman be permitted to send this message with her public appearance?

To explain the hair that she exposes at the nissuin ceremony, R. Segal argues that most of her hair is covered and only a little comes out the back. The reason this is not prohibited, he argues, is because all women – even married women – dress this way. In other words, this hairstyle does not communicate availability and thus a betrothed woman can certainly appear this way. To support this point, R. Segal turns to the responsum of Maharam Al-Ashkar analyzed at length above:

| And I saw this claim in the responsa of Maharam Al-Ashkar, number 35, that there is no prohibition against the practice of [married] women to expose some of the hair that comes out from under their covering. And he brought proofs for this, see there. | וכן ראיתי בתשובות מהר״ם אלשק״ר בסי׳ ל״ה שאין איסור במה שנהגו לגלות שערן חוץ לצמתן והביא ראיה לדבר ע״ש. |

Having supported his point with an earlier authority, he turns back to the wedding practice described in the Gemara:

| So too [here], since the practice for women to appear this way was only once, at the time when they are leaving their fathers' homes, etc., and she is in no way intending to be provocative, rather all of them appear this way when they leave their fathers' homes, etc., a small amount of exposure like this violates no prohibition at all. | וגם כיון שלא נהגו שתלך כך אלא פעם אחת בעת הליכתן מבית אביהן כו׳, ולא נתכוונה בזה לפריצות אלא כולם נהגו כך בעת יציאתן מבית אביהן כו׳, בקצת גילוי כזה אין כאן שום איסור, |

R. Segal does not seem to have clear, objective criteria to determine whether a given amount of exposed hair is prohibited. Since he already discounted Rav Sheshet's rule as encompassing a blanket prohibition against exposed hair in all scenarios, he turns instead to context. Noting that the Talmudic passage is describing what seems to have been a specific hairstyle for weddings, he argues that this context by definition is not meant to be lewd.

Instead, it communicates the same message as a modern-day wedding dress – this woman is getting married. The fact that it is meant to be attractive is understood by all as part of how a bride likes to appear. Moreover, such a small amount of exposure does not violate the spirit of the prohibition, since it can hardly be considered lewd dress. The combination of these factors, R. Segal argues, makes this practice permitted.

He further supports his reading by drawing an analogy to a point made by Rashba (this responsum is dealt with in the Rashba section in Chapter 5):

> And this is in line with what the Rashba said in his responsum [1:]575, that that which we were taught in the Mishnah regarding a woman who violates *dat* [*Yehudit*] by going out with her hair undone – this is specifically referring to a woman who does this consistently, but not if she happened to do it only once. Because the prohibition here is only when she intends to behave lewdly and violate the practice (*dat*) of Jews (*Yehudim*).
>
> וכמ"ש הרשב"א בתשו' [ח"א] בסי' תקע"ה דהא דתנן [כתובות עב ע"א] בעוברת על דת יוצאת וראשה פרוע היינו דוקא ברגילה בכך אבל לא בעשתה כך באקראי פעם אחת בלבד, משום דליכא איסורא אלא במתכוונת לפריצות ולעבור על דת יהודים.

> Even though in that case [of Rashba] the point was that she does not lose the ketubah payment on that account, nevertheless, it is clear that such behavior constitutes neither a prohibition nor lewd behavior.
>
> ואף על גב דהתם מיירי לענין כתובה שלא הפסידה בכך, מ"מ מוכח דליכא איסור ופריצות בכך.

Here R. Segal brings up a new criterion for determining whether a given appearance is a violation of *dat Yehudit*: happenstance versus frequency. He notes that according to Rashba, if a woman happened to go out without a head covering once, it should not be interpreted as violating Jewish norms, but just as a random occurrence with no meaning. Perhaps she was rushed or preoccupied? Clearly, Rashba would not apply this to someone who went out naked, but the fact that the violation is slight and not reflective of her usual behavior makes the interpretation that she was not intending to act lewdly more probable.

Applying this to the case about a wedding, R. Segal's point is that a slight violation, like hair coming out from under the covering – combined with the fact she was doing this because it was her wedding – also argues against this being a violation of *dat Yehudit*.

> And now that which it says in the Mishnah about going out in *hynuma* (covering)[9] while her hair is undone makes sense, for it doesn't say "or her hair is undone"; rather both are required, for the *hynuma* covers
>
> והשתא אתי שפיר הא דקתני שיצאתה בהינומא וראשה פרוע ולא קתני להדיא או ראשה פרוע, אלא דתרתי בהדדי נהגי, שההינומא כיסתה

---

9. We discussed previously that this is not the original intention of the Mishnah, but

some of the hair on her head, and some of what was left over she allowed to fall on her shoulders [at her wedding] during that time, according to the customary practice.	קצת שערות ראשה וקצת הנשאר הניחה על כתיפה בעת ההיא כפי המנהג.

R. Segal's premise, of course, is that in the Talmud's society, such a hairstyle would generally be considered a violation in other contexts; otherwise, if all married women went out this way, why would it be a sign of anything on a bride?[10]

. . . Rather, throughout her days as a betrothed woman, it is forbidden for her to appear in public with her hair undone – this we learn from Rashi, as I have written.	. . . אבל כל ימי אירוסיה אסורה לצאת בפריעת ראש כדמשמע מפירש״י כדכתיבנא.

R. Segal then turns to a long alternative proof that betrothed women may not appear in public with their hair undone from the Talmudic passage discussing the rule that a betrothed woman cannot participate in the sotah ritual. Throughout the Talmud's back and forth, it never mentions the problem that the priest would not be able to uncover her hair, since her hair is already uncovered, which demonstrates, in R. Segal's thinking, that the Talmud must assume that her hair is covered,[11] discounting the possibility that the Talmud merely assumes that the uncovering of hair is not an essential step and that it would just be skipped.[12]

---

this is how many authorities especially among the Acharonim understood the term.

10. Here, R. Segal returns briefly to the tangential point (see earlier footnote) to discuss whether she is allowed to appear this way on the first day of her *sheva berachot* as well:

וכה״ג הוא דכתב הרא״ש שיצאת פרועת הראש ביום ראשון אחר החופה.

11. As he notes:

ועוד נראה להביא ראיה לזה מהא דאיתא בריש (פ״ג) [פ״ד] דסוטה [כד ע״ב] דארוסה אינה שותה, ויליף לה מקראי לחד מ״ד מתחת אישך, ולאידך מתחת אישה, ופריך טעמא דכתיבי הני קראי הא לאו הכי הו״א ארוסה שותה והא ר' חנינא איתי מתניתא בידא מבלעדי אישך מי שקדמה שכיבת בעל לבועל ולא שקדמה שכיבת בועל לבעל, אמר רמי בר חמא משכחת לה כגון שבא עליה ארוס בבית אביה (כצ״ל ולא גרסינן חמיה) ע״כ, והשתא אי איתא דארוסה מותרת לצאת בפריעת ראש אכתי קשה הא בלאו הני קראי א״א לומר דארוסה שותה מדכתיבא גבי סוטה ופרע ראש האשה והיינו כדי לבזותה, כדילפינן בפ' המדיר [כתובות עב ע״א] דיוצאה וראשה פרועה היא עוברת על דת מדאמרה רחמנא ופרע ראש האשה כדי לבזותה, וזה אין שייך בארוסה שהרי יוצאת תמיד בפריעת ראש.

12. As he notes:

וכי תימא כיון דופרע ראש האשה לאו יתירה הוא דאיצטריך לגופיה ס״ד אמינא דאף ע״ג דהאי פריעת ראש בסוטה נשואה כתיב מ״מ בארוסה אינה מעכבת אלא שותה אף שאין בה

He then turns to precedent that he found in a work describing contemporary minhag:

This can also be found in the *Glosses* on our *Minhagim* (customs) in the laws of marriage (customs of all year round, #14) regarding a man who went with his daughter and her fiancé to the house of Maharan, and Maharad was there as well as other students, and Maharan told her that she should no longer appear in public with her hair uncovered, etc., and this was even though she was not set to be married for quite some time, as it says there.	וכן נמצא בהגהות מנהגים שלנו בדיני נישואין [ומנהג כל השנה אות יד] באחד שהלך עם בתו ועם המשודך לבית מהר"ן, והיה שם גם כן מהר"ד ושאר לומדים, וקידש החתן את הכלה, וצוה לה מהר"ן שלא תלך עוד בגילוי שערה כו' ואף שלא נישאת אלא זמן רב אח"כ כדאיתא התם ע"ש.

The book he is quoting is the anonymous glosses on the *Sefer Minhagim* of R. Isaac Tyrnau of Austria, who lived in the 15th century. The glosses were not written all by one person, and likely derived from different scholars who wrote on the margins of their own copies of the book. These were then collected and published together. Such a practice was standard in Ashkenazi lands, and we see the same thing with the glosses on the *Sefer Amudei Golah* (Semak) and on the *Shaarei Dura*.

The actual case is hard to follow from this brief description, so below is the case as presented in the glosses:

A man engaged his daughter [to someone] and let that person live with them. Some time later, the father of the bride wanted to travel abroad and take the groom and bride with him. The groom did not want to go on the trip, for he said, "Perhaps when I go with you abroad, you won't give me your daughter [in marriage] and no one there will speak up for me." They wanted to leave early the next day, so that night the	אחד שידך בתו ולקח החתן אליו ואחר ימים רבים היה רוצה לילך אבי הכלה למרחקים ולהוליך את החתן והכלה עמו. והחתן לא רצה לילך כי אמר שמא כשאבא עמכם למרחקים אינך נותן לי בתך ואין מי שידבר בעדי. ולמחר בהשכמה היו רוצין לילך, ובאותו לילה הלכו

פריעת ראש. הא ליתא דהא קרא דמבלעדי אישך נמי לאו מיותר הוא דאיצטריך לגופיה בנבעלה לבעלה, שא"א להשביע סתם שלא שכב שום איש אותה, ובהכרח צריך למכתב מבלעדי אישך. ולא מצי נמי למכתב ויתן איש פלוני בך את שכבתו, שהרי משביעה ג"כ משאר כל אדם כדילפינן גלגול שבועה מהך דסוטה, ואפ"ה פריך דניליף מינה דארוסה אינה שותה מדלא קרינן ביה מבלעדי אישך כו', ה"נ איכא למילף מדלא קרינן בארוסה ופרע את ראשה. אלא ש"מ דארוסה אסורה לצאת בגילוי ראשה.

father of the bride, with the bride and groom, went to the house of Maharan. There they found Maharan (probably R. Natan Eiger), Maharad (probably R. David Landeshut), and some students.

The bride's father and the groom made a formal acceptance of the *tenaim* (financial agreement between families before a marriage) that night. Maharan took a full glass in his hands, and made the blessing over betrothal, and then officiated over the bride and groom's kiddushin.

The father of the bride did not actually know whether she was yet an adult (i.e., whether she had begun puberty), so [Maharan] told [the father] to take his daughter's hand in his when the groom betroths the bride. Then the groom said, "Behold, you are [betrothed to me]"...but the groom did not break the glass. {And [Maharan] told the bride that she should not go out in public with her hair exposed.}[13]

Afterwards, the groom was in his father-in-law's house for a long time, as he was before, and no one bothered them since they said this is not really forbidden. And they stayed and did not travel abroad. And when they got married, they said the seven blessings and no more.

אבי הכלה והכלה והחתן לבית מהר״ן. והיה שם מהר״ן (=נתן איגר?) ומהר״ד (=דוד לנצהוט?) ובחורים.

ואבי הכלה והחתן קבלו קנין על תקון התנאים באותו לילה. ולקח מהר״ן זכוכית מלא בידו ובירך ברכת אירוסין ואח״כ קידש החתן את הכלה.

ואבי הכלה לא ידע אם היא גדולה או קטנה וצוה לו ליקח יד בתו בתוך ידו בשעה שקידש החתן את הכלה. ואמר החתן הרי את [מקודשת לי] וכו׳ ולא שיבר החתן את הזכוכית. [וצוה על הכלה שלא תלך עוד בגילוי שערה]

ואח״כ היו החתן ג״כ בבית אחד זמן רב כמו בתחילה ולא מיחו בהן כי אמרו שאין איסור בדבר. ונשארו שלא הלכו למרחקים. וכשעשה הנשואין ברכו ז׳ ברכות ולא יותר.

With the quote from Maharan, likely a reference to the 16th-century scholar R. Nathan Eiger,[14] R. Segal has essentially proven his case that, at least in their community, betrothed women must cover their hair.

---

13. As this is in brackets in the Machon Yerushalayim edition, this means it is not found in all the editions but is likely original. Certainly, it was in the edition R. Segal was using.

14. This obscure scholar is best known for his lenient position on a woman remarrying within two years of her husband dying in certain circumstances. Maharam Padua (Meir Katzenellenbogen) polemicized against this position in his responsa (#21). See discussion in Howard Tzvi Adelman, *Women and Jewish*

PARTIAL UNCOVERING AND HAIR COVERING

To soften the blow somewhat, he reminds the questioner that hair covering applies only in public, not in one's personal courtyard and certainly not in one's own house, as is clear from the passage in b. Ketubot.[15] But this point brings him back to the Ashkenazi sources about the hair covering passage in b. Berachot, which seem to be in some tension with this point:

But that which the Rosh wrote, as well as what the *Mordechai* wrote in the name of Ra'aviah in the third chapter of Berachot, regarding that which Rav Sheshet said: "The hair of a woman is *erva*," that,	והא דכתב הרא״ש וכן המרדכי בשם הראבי״ה בפ׳ מי שמתו אהא דאמר רב ששת שער באשה ערוה דהיינו
This refers specifically to [non-virgin] women who cover their hair but virgins, who are accustomed to appear in public with their hair undone – it is permitted to recite the Shema in their presence.	דוקא בנשים שדרכן לכסות שערן אבל בתולות שדרכן לילך פרועות מותר לקרות ק״ש כנגדן עכ״ל,
The recitation of Shema generally takes place in one's home or courtyard, yet even so they wrote that the way of women is to cover their hair.	וסתם ק״ש הוא בבית או בחצר, ואפ״ה כתבו שדרך נשים לכסות שערן.

In short, interpreting the b. Berachot passage to be about the recitation of the Shema, and adding the leniency about this only applying to women who cover their hair, seems to bring with it an unintentional stringency, namely that Rosh and Ra'aviah are assuming they cover their hair at home as well, something that flies in the face of the passage in b. Ketubot. As R. Segal is sure that this cannot be what they mean, he offers a way out:

It must be that this is what is meant: Since women cover their hair when they go out	צ״ל דה״פ כיון שדרך הנשים לכסות שערן ביציאתן בפני

Marriage Negotiations in Early Modern Italy: For Love and Money (Routledge, 2018) at Chapter 6.

15. See:
מיהו כל זה הוא לענין שלא תצא פרועת ראש לשוק או למבוי של רבים או אף לחצר אם רבים בוקעין בו דהו״ל כמבוי כדכתב הרא״ש בפרק המדיר בשם ירושלמי, אבל בחצר שאין רבים בוקעין וכ״ש בביתה אפילו נשואה אין בה משום פריעת ראש, כדאמרינן בהמדיר [עב ע״ב] ואלא בחצר א״כ לא הנחת בת לאברהם אבינו שיושבת תחת בעלה, (ופירשו התוס׳ [שם ד״ה ואלא בחצר] אפי׳ בלא קלתה נמי אין בה משום פריעת ראש שא״כ לא הנחת בת כו׳), ומסיק התם דמחצר לחצר דרך מבוי מתיר ר׳ יוחנן דוקא בקלתה, משמע להדיא דבחצר שרי אפילו בלא קלתה, וכ״כ הגהות אשר״י שם [סימן ט], והוא פשוט מהסוגיא שם.

> in public, and even in their own houses they generally cover their hair, for this reason when their hair is exposed [their husbands] could be distracted and have sexual thoughts even at home if their hair is exposed. But this is not the case with virgins, whose practice is to appear in public with their hair exposed – in front of them it is permitted to recite the Shema in one's house.
>
> רבים וגם בביתם מכסות ראשן ע״פ הרוב, משום הכי איכא טרדות והרהור בעת שקורא ק״ש כנגדן אף בביתן אם הן פרועות ראשן, משא״כ בבתולות דדרכן לצאת אף בפני רבים בגלוי ראש מותר לקרות כנגדן ק״ש בבית.

Here R. Segal makes it clear that concerns about distraction or sexual thoughts are almost entirely a product of social habit. Since women tend to cover their hair even at home, even though they do not have to, when their hair is exposed it seems to the man as if she is not fully dressed. If they didn't tend to cover their hair at home, it would not seem this way. This is all irrespective of the halakha dictating when they should cover their hair. Similarly, with virgins, it isn't that hair is not erva because they don't need to cover it; it is because they don't happen to cover it – i.e., to men, they do not appear partially undressed, but appear to be dressed normally – and thus, nothing stands out and halakha doesn't worry about sexual thoughts.

SOLVING THE CONTRADICTION IN THE TUR

R. Segal moves to his final point, which is to solve the contradiction in the *Tur* we discussed in the previous chapter. Although he solves this – just as his brother did – in what is the most common way, distinguishing between virgins and previously married women, he is unique in offering linguistic support for this interpretation. He starts by laying out the *Tur*'s deduction in *Even HaEzer* 21.

> And if you say that in the seventh chapter of Ketubot, the house of R. Ishmael says: "'And you shall undo the woman's hair' – this is an admonition to the daughters of Israel not to appear in public with their hair undone." And the *Tur* learns from this in [*Even HaEzer*] 21 that this admonition applies to married and single women alike, from the fact that it simply says "daughters
>
> וא״ת הא בהמדיר תני דבי ר׳ ישמעאל ופרע ראש האשה אזהרה לבנות ישראל שלא יצאו פרועות ראש, ויליף הטור מהא בסי׳ כ״א דאזהרה זו היא בין בנשואה בין בפנויה, מדנקט סתמא בנות ישראל א״כ נילף נמי מהאי סתמא דבנות ישראל דאפי׳

of Israel." Therefore, we should learn from this that any daughter of Israel, even a virgin who is not engaged, is forbidden to appear in public with her hair undone.

בתולה שאינו ארוסה אסורה לצאת בפני רבים פרועת ראש.

Although it is unclear why he calls this the *Tur*'s deduction rather than Rambam's, he makes the point clear. In *Even HaEzer* 21, the *Tur* says all women, single and married, are prohibited from appearing in public with their hair undone. R. Segal brings this up as a problem for his argument that the requirement for hair covering starts only at betrothal. But as part of his answer, he distinguishes between different types of unmarried women (and thus, without stating it, solves the contradiction in the *Tur*).

It seems possible that the teaching of R. Ishmael's school is of necessity interpreting the verse, which says "and he shall undo the woman's hair" and the term "woman" is not used with regard to virgins. But any (non-virgin) woman, even if she is single, can easily fit into the verse's category of "and you shall uncover the woman's hair." For this reason, the *Tur* forbids even a single woman, such as a widow or divorcée [from appearing this way in public].

י״ל דתנא דבי רבי ישמעאל ע״כ קאי אקרא דכתיב ופרע ראש האשה ואין בתולה נקרא אשה, אבל אשה בין נשואה בין פנויה שייך בה שפיר קרא ופרע ראש האשה. ומשום הכי אסר הטור אף לפנויה כגון אלמנה או גרושה.

R. Segal makes a linguistic argument here, namely that "woman" refers only to non-virgins. If so, even the most maximal reading of the derasha, as the *Tur* offers, can only extend the prohibition to unmarried women who are not virgins. Thus, the *Tur*, even if he says single, never meant to include virgins. R. Segal then responds to a possible objection:

And note, that if you want to claim that the school of R. Ishmael prohibits even a virgin [from appearing this way in public], there is a difficulty. From where would they learn this? For the verse is about a *sotah*, who is certainly not an unmarried virgin! And this is easy to understand.

ותדע דאי תימא דתנא דבי ר״י אוסר אף לבתולה פנויה, קשיא מנ״ל למילף הכי דהא האי קרא כתיב גבי סוטה דודאי אינה בתולה פנויה וק״ל.

This claim is difficult to understand, since his objection that sotahs are by definition married would negate the *Tur*'s reading as well. Be that as it may, his basic point is clear: for the *Tur*, saying that "all women, single or married, must cover their hair in public" is not meant to include virgins. With that, R. Segal turns to the conclusion of his responsum:

> We learn from this that a betrothed woman is like a married woman, and it is forbidden for her to appear in public with her hair undone. And just as it is prohibited to recite the Shema before a married woman whose hair is exposed, even in one's own house, even though she is not required to cover her hair there, the same rule applies in the presence of a betrothed woman exposing her hair, before whom it is forbidden to recite the Shema, even in her house or courtyard.
>
> נמצינו למידין דארוסה דינה כנשואה שאסורה לצאת בפריעת ראש בפני רבים, וכי היכי דבנשואה אסור לקרות ק"ש כנגד שערות ראשה אף בבית אף על פי דאין בה איסור פריעת ראש, ה"ה נמי כנגד שערות ראש ארוסה אסור לקרות ק"ש אף בבית או בחצר.

> I have said what appears to me to be correct, Isaac Levi.
>
> הנלע"ד כתבתי יצחק לוי

In short, according to R. Segal, betrothed women are the same as married women. For our purposes, there are two main takeaways. First, even though he points to the derasha as the source of the prohibition in *Tur Even HaEzer* 21, he is clear that what underpins this rule in b. Berachot is the sociological reality that exposed hair implies availability. And thus, unlike the *Tur*, he only speaks about betrothed and married women, not single women. Second, he is clear that sexual thoughts derive from seeing what is unusual to see on a given woman, and not from any prohibition.

One wonders what R. Segal would say about how such a prohibition would function in a society in which uncovered hair does not communicate availability, and exposed hair is standard for all women – married or not, inside the home or out.

Maharam Chaviv

R. Moshe ibn Chaviv (Maharam Chaviv, 1654–1696), Chacham Bashi and Rishon LeTzion in Jerusalem, was asked about French women who even after erusin (betrothal) do not cover their hair (*EH* 149):

> Question: If we should be concerned about those women betrothed with kiddushin, living in the cities of Frankia, whose
>
> שאלה: אם יש לחוש לאלו הבתולות [המאורס]ות בקידושין שנהגו בערי

> practice is to appear in public with uncovered hair. Is it permitted or perhaps, [it falls under the category of] the hair of a woman is nudity. – May his reward be doubled from heaven.
>
> פארנקייה ללכת בגילוי שער אם מותר, או דלמא שער באשה ערוה, וש[כרו] כ[פול] מ[ן] ה[שמים].

Maharam Chaviv responds by saying that the question of whether betrothed women must cover their hair in public is simply based on local custom:

> Response: It seems simple, in my humble opinion, that since they have already developed the practice of going with their hair uncovered, there is no need for concern.
>
> תשובה: נ[ראה] לע[ניות] ד[עתי] דבר פשוט דכיון דכבר נהגו ללכת בגילוי שער דאין לחוש

To support this position, Maharam Chaviv quotes the Ashkenazi Rishonim, such as Ra'aviah and those who follow him, who read the passage in b. Berachot this way:

> As Rosh wrote at the end of the third chapter of Berachot, regarding the statement of R. Sheshet that the hair of a woman is considered *erva*, that this applies specifically to married women, who normally cover their hair, but for unmarried women to normally go with their hair uncovered is permissible.
>
> כמ"ש הרא"ש ז"ל [במסכת ברכות] שלהי מי שמתו [סי' ל"ז] אהא דאמר רב ששת שער באשה ערוה, דוקא בנשים שדרכן לכסות שערן אבל בתולות שדרכן לילך פרועות מותר.
>
> So also wrote the Mordechai, citing Ra'aviah; the *Hagahot Maimoniyot*, Laws of Reciting the Shema 3:[60]; *Tur, Orach Chayyim* 75; and so ruled the rabbi [the *Shulchan Arukh* ibid., 75:2].
>
> וכ"כ המרדכי בשם ראבי"ה [שם סי' פ'], וכ"כ הגהות מימון פ"ג דק"ש [אות ס'], וכ"כ הטור בא"ח סי' ע"ה וכן פסק הרב ז"ל [שו"ע סעיף ב'].

Having established this, Maharam Chaviv makes a particularly important argument:

> If you are inclined to dismiss this and say that there can be no proof from these sources, as they are all speaking about a single woman, but with a betrothed woman it would be forbidden – that argument is void. Consider the reasoning behind why the decisors ruled that it is permissible for single women: since they do so regularly, it
>
> ואם נפשך לדחות ולומר דאין מכאן ראיה, דכל זה מיירי בפנויה אבל במקודשת אסור, ליתא, דזיל בתר טעמא דלמה התירו הפוסקים בבתולות משום דכיון דרגיל ביה ליכא הרהור, ה"ה בנדון דידן.

does not arouse improper sexual thoughts, and the same is true in our case.

He notes that Ra'aviah and those who follow him are speaking about single women; how does he know that the argument can be applied to betrothed women? The answer, he says, is the reason for the law, which is that what counts as an erotic stimulus or "nudity" depends on what society considers normal. In other words, the distinction between married and unmarried is incidental; the point is how a particular group of women dresses in a given society. Social expectations determine what is considered nudity. Thus, if in France betrothed women have their hair uncovered, then this by definition is not a form of nudity.

Maharam's proof for this brings him to the discussion of Ra'avad's principle and the application to even married women:

A proof to our words comes from that which the *Beit Yosef* z"l in *Orach Chayyim* 75 wrote in the name of the Ra'avad, with regard to that which Rav Chisda said: "The calf of a woman is nudity," and the *Beit Yosef* asked: "What is Rav Chisda teaching us? Anything that is generally covered is nudity [when exposed], so why talk about the calf? And he wrote that the Rashba [in his glosses on b. Berachot 25a] brought down in the name of the Ra'avad z"l,	וראיה לדברינו אלה מהא דכתב הבית יוסף ז"ל בא"ח סי' ע"ה בשם הראב"ד אהא דאמר רב חסדא שוק באשה ערוה, והקשה הבית יוסף מאי קמ"ל רב חסדא, כל שדרך לכסותו הוי ערוה ומאי איריא שוק, וכתב שהביא הרשב"א [בחידושיו ברכות כ"ה ע"א] משם הראב"ד ז"ל,
that it is possible that [nudity] is only referring to a private place, and in that context Rav Chisda came to say that a woman's calf is a private place, even for her husband [when he is reciting Shema in her presence], even though it is not a private place for a man, but that her face, hands, and feet, and her speaking voice, which is not [her] singing [voice], and the hair that comes out from under her covering that is not generally covered – we are not concerned about them since he is used to them and it does not distract him.	דאיפשר דווקא ממקום צנוע שבה, ועלה קא אתי רב חסדא למימר דשוק באשה מקום צנוע וערוה הוי ואפי' לגבי בעלה ואעפ"י שאינו מקום צנוע באיש, אבל פניה ידיה ורגליה וקול דבורה [ש]אינו זמר ושערה מחוץ לצמתה שאינו מתכסה, אין חוששין להן מפני שהוא רגיל בהן ולא טריד, עכ"ל.

Having quoted Ra'avad's principle, Maharam Chaviv makes his point clear:

> We see here explicitly that even when it comes to a married woman, the Ra'avad says that once something is not generally covered, it is not considered nudity [when exposed].
>
> הרי בהדיא דאפי' באשת איש נשואה אמר הראב"ד כיון שהוא מקום שאינו מתכסה אין בו משום ערוה.

Thus, in Maharam Chaviv's understanding, the principle of subjectivity reigns supreme. It does not matter if the woman is single, betrothed, or even married; all that matters is what the practice is for any given group of women in any given community. Whatever they generally cover is nudity when exposed; whatever they generally leave uncovered is not. Thus, his answer to the questioner is simple: if in France, betrothed women do not cover their hair, then by definition, they don't have to.

Chavot Yair

In his responsa *Chavot Yair* (#196), R. Yair Chayyim Bacharach (1639–1702), deals with a question of a married man who wishes to perform erusin with a woman while his wife is dying, so that he does not lose her to another suitor. Although much of the responsum is not directly relevant to the question of hair covering, the responsum is short and quite interesting – not to mention widely referenced because of the importance of the *Chavot Yair* as a posek. So I will lay out the whole piece, starting with the question:

> Question: Reuven's sister is a servant in Levi's house. She is smart, very beautiful, knows how to do all sorts of things, and knows multiple languages. For this reason, many are chasing after her and asking to marry her, even forgoing any dowry at all.
>
> שאלה: אחות ראובן משרתת אצל לוי והיא משכלת ויפת תואר מאד ומכרת בכל חכמה ומלאכה ולשונות ומפני כך רבו הקופצים ומהדרים אחריה ומבקשים לישאנה חנם אין כסף
>
> So Levi, her employer, has no sons. He has a sickly wife who has been suffering with lung disease for many years. All the doctors have given up on her, and all of them say that she cannot live another year.
>
> והנה לוי בעל הבית שלה אין לו בנים ויש לו אשה חולנית בחולי הריאה כמה שנים וכל הרופאים נתייאשו ממנה וכלם עונים ואומרים כי לא תוכל להתקיים בחיים עוד שנה

Now Levi spoke with Reuven telling him not to marry off his sister in a hurry, for when his wife dies, he (Levi) would like to marry her. And to ensure this, he (Levi) requests a handshake and a document signed before witnesses.

ולוי דיבר עם ראובן שאל ימהר להשיא אחותו כי כשתמות אשתו ישאנה ועל זה יבקש ליתן ת[וקיעת] כ[ף] ויעשה ש[וטר] ח[וב] לפני עדים

But Reuven doesn't believe Levi's oath and promise, since he (Levi) is an extremely wealthy man, as well as a town bully, and thus he has asked to place one hundred reichsthalers[16] in Reuven's pocket, and to draw up a ketubah for his sister worth 1,000 reichsthalers, and to dress her like a princess.

וראובן אינו מאמין ללוי לאלתו ולשבועתו כי הוא עשיר מופלג ואלים בעירו והוא מבקש ליתן לראובן ק' ר"ט לכיסו ולעשות לאחותו כתובה אלף ר"ט ולהלבישה כבת מלך

And Reuven asked me, in my lowliness, to advise him about what is proper to do, since an important person in his town advised him to let Levi betroth the girl before witnesses, so that she will be his betrothed after his wife dies.

ושאל ראובן לשפלותי שאיעץ לו כדת מה יעשה כי ייעצו גדול שבעירו שיניח ללוי לקדשה לפני עדים שתהיה מקודשת אחר מות אשתו:

Reuven wants to know whether he can allow Levi to betroth his sister while his wife is still alive because he is worried that Levi will have second thoughts. The money Levi offers to pay does not convince Reuven, since Levi is wealthy, and does the oath, because Levi is (supposedly) dishonest and bullies everyone in town, so he can get away with anything.

The *Chavot Yair* begins by declaring the very question to be problematic:

Answer: Regarding your question – it is an inappropriate question.

תשובה וע[ל] ד[בר] שאלתך שאלה שאינה הוג[נ]ת[17] היא

Before answering it, he compares this question to another he once received:

I was asked a similar question from so-and-so, a widower, in whose community a poor and downtrodden married couple

ודוגמה לשאלה זו שאלני פב"פ אלמן אחד זה כמה שנים שהיה בקהלה שלו

---

16. The silver coins established as standard currency in the Holy Roman Empire at the Leipzig convention of 1566.
17. The Hebrew has הוגגת, but this is a typo.

PARTIAL UNCOVERING AND HAIR COVERING 325

had lived for years, and through work and great toil, the husband was able to supply his wife only with minimal bread and water. Their fighting and their separation have been growing for many years, to the point where it is reasonable to worry that she might sell her virtue for a loaf of bread, since she doesn't have any marketable skills. He would love to divorce her and she is willing, only she is asking him for just 50 gold pieces, so that she can dress herself [nicely] afterwards, with the hope that she would find another man [to marry her] so that she not die of starvation, for who would marry her barefoot and unclothed. But her husband lacks the means to fulfill her request here.

So the widower asked me, since he is taking care of his children and wishes to marry this woman after she is divorced with a *gett* from her husband, if he can send a message to the woman that if she wants to enter an arrangement with him, he too would like to arrange to marry her as she is now, and he can dress her [nicely]. Therefore, she should divorce her husband without a payment of silver.

He supported his words with the following: certainly, if the husband did not want to give a *gett* to his wife unless she gave him something from her own pocket, though she has nothing, and another man came and spoke to the woman, asking her if she wants to have an arrangement with him and marry him, and [to accomplish this] he would give her husband the amount he is asking for directly or he could give it to her – this would be a little grotesque. It is reminiscent of the account at the end of the story of the Temple's destruction.

איש ואשתו עניים מרודים וע״י טורח ועמל רב הי׳ בכחו להספיק לאשתו לחם צר מים לחץ וע״י זה רבתה המחלוקת והפירוד ביניהם כמה שנים עד כי יש לחוש לקלקולה על פת לחם כי אינה בעלת מלאכה כלל והוא מבקש ליתן גט וגם היא מרוצת רק שתבקש ממנו רק חמשים זהו׳ שתלביש עצמה אח״כ אולי תהיה לאיש אח״כ ולא תמות ברעב כי מי ישאנה ערום ויחף ואין באיש למלאות רצונה בזה.

ושאלני האלמן שמטופל בבנים ורצונו ליקח אותה אחר שילוחיה בגט מבעלה אם ישלח אל האשה באם תרצה להתקשר לישאנו גם הוא רוצה להתקשר שישאנה באשר היא וילבישנה לכן תתגרש מאישה בלי בצע כסף,

ונתן טעם לדבריו כי ודאי אלו לא רצה האיש לתת גט לאשתו אא״כ תתן לו מכיסה סך מה ואין לה ובא אחד ודיבר אל האשה אם תתקשר עמו שתנשא לו יתן הוא לבעלה סך שמבקש הבעל או יתנוהו לה שתתן לו היה קצת מכוער הדבר ויש לו דמיון מה למעשה שבסוף אגדת החרבן

The *Chavot Yair* is referring to the following story from b. Gittin 58a (Soncino trans.):

A certain man once conceived a desire for the wife of his master, he being a carpenter's apprentice. Once his master wanted to borrow some money from him. He said to him: "Send your wife to me and I will lend her the money." So he sent his wife to him, and she stayed three days with him. He then went to him before her. "Where is my wife whom I sent to you?" he asked. He replied: "I sent her away at once, but I heard that the youngsters played with her on the road." "What shall I do?" he said. "If you listen to my advice," he replied, "divorce her." "But," he said, "she has a large marriage settlement." Said the other: "I will lend you money to give her for her ketubah." So he went and divorced her and the other went and married her. When the time for payment arrived and he was not able to pay him, he said: "Come and work off your debt with me." So they used to sit and eat and drink while he waited on them, and tears used to fall from his eyes and drop into their cups.	מעשה באדם אחד שנתן עיניו באשת רבו, ושוליא דנגרי הוה. פעם אחת הוצרך (רבו) ללות, אמר לו: שגר אשתך אצלי ואלונה, שיגר אשתו אצלו, שהה עמה שלשה ימים. קדם ובא אצלו, אמר לו: אשתי ששיגרתי לך היכן היא? אמר לו: אני פטרתיה לאלתר, ושמעתי שהתינוקות נתעללו בה בדרך. אמר לו: מה אעשה? אמר לו: אם אתה שומע לעצתי גרשה. אמר לו: כתובתה מרובה, אמר לו: אני אלווך ותן לה כתובתה. עמד זה וגרשה, הלך הוא ונשאה. כיון שהגיע זמנו ולא היה לו לפורעו, אמר לו: בא ועשה עמי בחובך. והיו הם יושבים ואוכלים ושותין והוא היה עומד ומשקה עליהן, והיו דמעות נושרות מעיניו ונופלות בכוסיהן.

This is, of course, a terrible story which the Talmud includes to illustrate why Judea and the Second Temple were destroyed. The *Chavot Yair* is aware that he (or the man presenting his case) is overreaching, and thus pulls back a bit, having made his rhetorical point:

Even though it is certainly not the same thing, someone who hears of it may have bad things to say. Even more so this case, in which he did nothing other than speak to the woman and suggest that she accept the *gett* and forgo the pay without worry that she will afterwards be in an embarrassing and humiliating state, with no one to pull her out of her humiliation. And this *gett*	אף דודאי אינו עניין לו מ[וכל] מ[וקום] יש לזות שפתים לשומע מ[וכל] שכ[ון] זה דלא עביד מידי רק שידבר עם האשה שתקבל הגט חנם ולא תחוש שתהיה אח"כ לבזיון וחרפה ואין מי שיאסוף חרפתה והוא גט מצוה לכל היודע עסקיהם.

here is a mitzvah as anyone who knows their situation would know.

The above was apparently the man's pitch to Rabbi Bacharach, but he was unsympathetic.

> Nevertheless, I responded to him in fury, wrath, and great anger, that he should not appear in front of my face with a request for advice about how to carry off a matter that is against normal social behavior, since it is not right to speak to another man's wife about how he would like to marry her after she gets divorced.
>
> ומ"מ השבתי לו באף ובחמה ובקצף גדול שאל יוסיף לראות פני בבקשת עצה נגד מנהג עולם כי לא נכון לדבר עם אשת איש מענין נישואיה אחר גירושיה

Having explained the analogous case, the *Chavot Yair* returns to the question at hand:

> And even though your question is less problematic in one way, since the element of inappropriate behavior with a married woman is absent, [and his own status as a married man is not really comparable] since, technically speaking, a man may marry many women, nevertheless, it is worse in many other ways.
>
> ואף כי שאלתך קלה מצד שאין כאן לעז אשת איש שהרי ע"פ הדין נושא אדם כמה נשים מ"מ חמורה יותר מכמה צדדים

He now goes on to explain why the case at hand is worse:

> Even if it were actually possible (permitted?) to do this, which it isn't really, since if he betroths her and says to her, "Behold you are betrothed to me with this coin after my wife dies" – he can renege on this, as the *Tur* and other poskim write in *Even HaEzer* and *Shulchan Arukh*[18] number 40.
>
> אף אם היה אפשר לעשות כן מה שבאמת אי אפשר שאם יקדשה ויאמר לה ה"א מקודשת לי בפרוטה זו לאחר שתמות אשתי יכול לחזור בו כבטור ופוסקים בא[בן] ה[עזר] וש[ולחן] ע[רוך] סי' מ'

His first point is practical; even if such a thing as "future betrothal" in this scenario were permitted, it would not help Reuven, since Levi

---

18. The word *Shulchan Arukh* is out of place here, but clearly he means "*Tur* and *Shulchan Arukh* in *Even HaEzer* 40." He probably noticed that he forgot to mention the *SA* after he had already written *EH*, so he just added it in out of place on the assumption that everyone will know what he meant.

could always back out of the betrothal before his wife dies and it would be null and void.

> And if he says "[you are betrothed to me] now," which would not violate the ban of R. Gershom, since it does not cover betrothal, as is written in [*Even HaEzer*] #1, nevertheless, it is still impossible, for how could she appear in public with her hair undone considering she would be a married woman?!
>
> ואם יאמר מעכשיו את"ל דאין חשש חרם ר"ג דלא תיקון בארוסה כמ"ש שם סי' א' מ"מ אי אפשר דאיך תלך פרועת ראש והרי היא אשת איש

To the modern reader, the *Chavot Yair*'s point here likely comes as a surprise, since it would seem that the obvious problem with the suggestion is that Levi is already setting up his next wedding while his wife lies dying in the house and Reuven is cashing in on this by agreeing to let his sister accept this scandalous proposal. Undoubtedly, R. Bacharach is also bothered by the cruelty, which is why his response is so aggressive, but he is looking to anchor his objection in a halakhic argument and this is what he finds. Of course, Reuven could respond by saying that his sister would cover her hair in that case, but most likely R. Bacharach assumes that they would want to make this arrangement secretly, due to its scandalous and unpleasant nature.

For our purposes, what is important is that the *Chavot Yair* is treating the assumption that betrothed women must cover their hair as an absolute requirement. He knows this flies in the face of the Talmudic evidence, and turns to deal with that problem:

> Even if you wish to say that betrothed women in the time of the Talmud would appear in public with their hair undone, that is because in their times, the betrothal took place much earlier than the marriage, and there are differences in the laws pertaining to the two statuses, as the *Tur* and *Shulchan Arukh* wrote there ([*EH*] 54). Therefore, as long as she wasn't married, it is possible that her public appearance and dress was the same as what the virgins would wear, and this is what the Talmud implies. But this is not the case in our days, when the *nissuin* ceremony is performed
>
> ואפילו את"ל דארוסות בזמן הש"ס היו הולכות פרועות ראש היינו מפני שהיו בימיהם האירוס זמן רב לפני הנשואין ויש כמה חילוקי דינים ביניהם כמ"ש טור וש"ע שם סי' נ"ד לכן כל כמה שלא נישאת אפשר שגם בהילוכה ומלבושיה היה כמנהג הבתולות והכי משמע בש"ס מ[ה] ש[אינו] כן] בימינו דאין בין קידושין ונישואין כלום כל שנתקדשה ראוי שתתנהג כמנהג נשים

immediately following the *erusin* ceremony, so that once a woman is betrothed [in our times], it is fitting that she behave exactly like a married woman, and cover her hair with a kerchief.

ולהתכסות בצעיף

The *Chavot Yair*'s argument is essentially that *arusah* is no longer a kind of social status but has merged with *nesuah*, sociologically speaking. In other words, since the two ceremonies of erusin and nissuin are no longer separated, but conducted one after another on the same day, in contemporary reality, women are either married or unmarried; they are never "betrothed." Therefore, in the case he is being asked about, which would actually create a betrothed woman, she would need to "round" to the most relevant status, which is *nesuah* – and married women cover their hair.

His argument, therefore, is entirely sociological. He isn't claiming that erusin does not function anymore on a halakhic level, only that it doesn't exist as a social status. Since social status determines whether a woman covers her hair, then since married women cover their hair – and betrothed women in our society are essentially the same as married women – then betrothed women must cover their hair.

He then adds another telling caveat:

Even if she wishes to cover with a *redid* (veil or shawl), as is the custom of virgins, this violates *dat Yehudit*, as is written [in *Even HaEzer*] 115.	ואפילו תרצה להתכסות ברדיד כמנהג בתולות הוא נגד דת יהודית כמ"ש שם סי' קט"ו

The *Chavot Yair* notes that virgins also cover, but in a different way than married women. Thus, the fact that this woman would continue to wear a *redid*, which can mean either a veil or a shawl, is of no help. Even though it is a covering, it communicates to those who see her that she is not married.

The *Chavot Yair*'s citation of *Even HeEzer* 115 is at first quite surprising. In that text, the *Tur* and *Shulchan Arukh* are quoting Rambam, who says that if a married woman goes out in public without a *redid*, even though her hair is covered with a kerchief, it is grounds for her husband to divorce her without a ketubah payment. In other words, in these sources, a *redid* is something that married women wear. Yet the *Chavot Yair* is quoting this as a proof that unmarried women wear it!

To make sense of this reference, we must again posit that the specifics are culturally determined. In Rambam's time and place, a veil (or shawl) was worn by married women; appearing without it was effectively dressing like a single woman. In R. Bacharach's society, single women wore veils (or shawls) and married women wore head coverings; thus appearing with the *redid* was dressing like a single woman.

Rashbam, in his gloss on Genesis 38:14, seems to be making this point as well. When Tamar takes off her widow's garments, she also puts on a kerchief and veil. Rashbam comments:

> She covered her hair with a kerchief – be- ותכס ראשה בצעיף - שאין זה
> cause this is not the way of widows. דרך אלמנות

The *Chavot Yair* is making an important point. How is it that something can be nudity for one group of women and not for another in the same society? In most sources, the answer has been social expectation. A woman in a bathing suit on a beach looks normal; a woman in a bathing suit in an office building looks naked. The same is true about types of clothing: a woman in a bikini on a beach is considered dressed; but a woman in underwear on the same beach, even if the underwear is the same size or covers more than a bikini, is considered undressed. (I am not making a halakhic statement, only making an observation of sociological norms in the western world.) All this can only be explained by social expectation. More can be less if it sends the message of *this is something that is generally not seen in public.*

The *Chavot Yair*, however, is taking this in a different direction. Social expectations for married/unmarried are relevant only if one knows the person. If one knows a woman is married, but she appears dressed like an unmarried woman – for example, with her hair uncovered – then that would have the effect of her appearing to this man as not fully dressed. However, to an onlooker who did not know her, she would just appear as a standard unmarried woman.

This, R. Bacharach argues, is exactly the problem. Going out looking like a single woman when one is actually married is lewd behavior. Think about what it could mean if a woman wishes to appear in public without her wedding ring. This is not about nudity – nobody thinks of a woman without a ring as partially naked – but about communicating availability.

This, R. Bacharach argues, is why a married woman wearing a *redid* in his society is a problem. It is not because she isn't covered; it is because she is communicating availability. This, he argues, is the "lewdness" or "nudity" that the *dat Yehudit* rule is meant to cover. A married woman should communicate "married" to onlookers. As this is a purely social and subjective concept, it all depends on what "married" looks like in a given society.

The *Chavot Yair* makes clear in the next sentence that this is what he is worried about:

| Moreover, we must be concerned about problematic things that can happen, since it is the way of the promiscuous young Jewish men who behave wantonly with single women, which is not the case with married women, with whom they are strict (lit. they put up a fence) and none of them behave wantonly with them, lest they – God forbid – end up actually sinning with her. | ועוד יש לחוש לכמה חששות ותקלות כי מנהג בחורי ישראל הפריצים לנהג קלות ראש עם הבתולות מ[ה] ש[אינו] כו[ן] עם הנשואות גדרו גדר ואין מי שנוהג קלות ופן חלילה יכשילו בה לגמרי |

According to this, a married woman dressing like a single woman invites men to treat her like a single woman. And since this will often involve attempts to flirt and perhaps even to seduce, she should not put herself in such a situation. According to this, the primary concern about proper hair covering is not about nudity but about what a given type of public appearance represents about the person's marital status.

Considering this problem, the *Chavot Yair* tells the questioner that the idea of early and secret betrothal should not be considered.

| Therefore, back away from this approach and from this bad idea, for it was not with wisdom and fear of God that you suggested it. | לכן כלך מדרך זה ומזאת העצה הרעה אשר לא בדעת ויראת ה' יעץ כזאת |

Before ending the responsum, the *Chavot Yair* admits that there could be creative but still problematic alternatives that could get Levi the security he is looking for:

| Even so, there are a number of ways in which [Reuven] can make a connection with Levi in a permissible way. For example, he can give him a document with an obligation to pay Reuven 1000 reichsthal- | אף כי יש כמה דרכים אשר בהם נוכל להתקשר עם לוי בדרך היתר הלא יכול ליתן שטו[ר] חו[וב] שיתחייב לראובן אלף ר"ט וז[מן] פ[רעונו] |

ers and the date of payment would be set as one year after his wife dies or whenever he marries another woman, and that if he does marry the virgin so-and-so [=Levi's sister], he becomes exempt [from this payment] and the document of obligation is entirely canceled – which is how we write documents [for daughters who will inherit] half of the amount a son does. Alternatively, he can forbid upon himself [with a vow] all Jewish girls other than her. And there are other ways [Levi can get assurances from Reuven] if he does not wish to believe his oath.

יהיה אחר שנה אחר פטירת אשתו או בזמן נישואין שלו עם אשה אחרת אכן אם ישא בתולה פלונית פטור ומסולק משט״ח זה לגמרי באופן דכתבינן שטרי חז[וצין חו]לק[ו זכר] או שיאסור עליו כל בנות ישראל חוץ מזו ועוד כמה דרכים אם לא ירצו להאמינו על שבועתו.

But even these suggestions seriously bother R. Bacharach, and thus he ends his responsum by reiterating how he thinks it would be best if none of the above creative solutions were followed:

All of this would be done in hiding and secrecy because of the emotional pain. Therefore, if it were not for my fondness for you, which is great, I would not have written even these last suggestions.

וכל זה יהיה בהעלם וסתר מפני עגמת נפש ולכן לולי אהבתך כי רבה היא גם דברי האחרונים האלה לא כתבתי.

For all my life, I never wanted to express an opinion that would be outside the normal social behavior. And this is what we have established with regard to religious law, that it is forbidden for a sage to permit something that would be shocking to the masses, even if it is perfectly permissible, as the *Shulchan Arukh* wrote in *Yoreh Deah* 242:10.

כי מימי לא רציתי לטפל ולגלות דעתי בדבר שהוא חוץ לסדר ומנהג העולם והכי ק״ל גבי איסור והיתר שאסור לחכם להתיר דבר התמוה לרבים אפילו הוא היתר גמור כמ״ש בש״ע י״ד סי׳ רמ״ב ס״י

So too in this case, which is a shocking matter, and something outside normal practice and Jewish tradition, in which at least ten [men] should gather together like Boaz, and underneath a *chuppah* as is the normal practice. And did Rav decree a flogging for anyone who betrothed without first being engaged (b. Kiddushin 12b)?!

ה״נ נדון זה שהוא דבר תמוה וזר נגד מנהג ודת ישראל שנאספים יחד לפחות עשרה כבועז ותחת חופה כנהוג והרי רב מנגד אמאן דמקדש בלא שידוכי לכן ידי דעתי ועצתי אל תהא בזה ואי אישר חילי הייתי גוזר עליך שלא תעשה

For this reason, let my hand, my opinion, and my advice have no place in this act, and if I had the power, I would forbid you to do this – enough said. Signed the troubled Yair Chayyim Bacharach.

כן ודי בזה. נאם הטרוד יאיר חיים בכרך

The strong negative ending supports the point I made earlier: that his main objection is not the technical problem that the woman would be betrothed and thus obligated to cover her hair like a married woman while pretending to be single, but rather because this secret betrothal is a social aberration that R. Bacharach cannot countenance. Nevertheless, his position that betrothed women need to cover their hair was noted by other Sages and debated.

That said, for our purposes, the takeaway is that this obligation is based on a social reality – since the only two categories in his world are married and single, a betrothed woman would have to dress as married. And since married women cover their hair, this betrothed woman would need to do so as well. The *Chavot Yair* is explicit that this obligation is not objective in any way, since he himself notes that in Talmudic times, the practice was different.

It is, therefore, unclear what the *Chavot Yair* would say about a society in which no difference in appearance exists between married and single women. It is possible he would say that halakha requires that Jewish women make such a distinction regardless, though it is also possible that he would feel forced to admit that in such a society the rule of *dat Yehudit* for dress or hair has no application.

Shevut Yaakov's Responsum: Must a Raped Virgin Cover Her Hair (Coiffing or Covering: What Is a *Kalta*?)

A particularly difficult question that was discussed already in pre-modern responsa is whether a virgin girl who had been raped must cover her hair. On the one hand, she is no longer a virgin, and her ketubah is 100 zuz. Should her status not be reflected in her dress? On the other hand, wearing the head covering penalizes her for something she did not do willingly. It makes her less attractive to potential suitors and functions as a constant reminder of what she suffered. Must we really force her to do this?[19]

---

19. In our era – and maybe any other – focusing on the "hair covering" consequences of rape seems cold for such a compassionate rabbinic tradition. Indeed,

The classic responsum on this question, which we already saw quoted in the *nos'ei keilim* of the *Shulchan Arukh* in the previous chapter, appears in the *Shevut Yaakov* of R. Jacob ben Joseph Reischer (Prague, Bavaria and Germany ca. 1670–1733). The question was put as follows (1:103):

A virgin Jewish girl was raped, she cried out but no one came to her aid (Deut. 22:27) – may our rabbi teach us whether it is permitted for her to go in public with her hair exposed, the way virgins do, or must she cover her hair, as is the practice of married women?	בתולת בת ישראל שנאנסה כי צעקה ואין מושיע לה ילמדנו רבינו אי מותרת לילך בגילוי ראש כדרכן של בתול' או צריכה לכסות שערה כמנהג הנשים בעולת בעל:

The questioner is clearly sympathetic to the idea that the girl should not be forced to cover her hair, but he does not know the law. The *Shevut Yaakov* begins his answer by surveying the basic sugyot:

Response: The Talmud, in b. Ketubot, chapter *HaMadir*, page 72a, in the Mishnah, writes: "These are divorced without a ketubah payment: [A woman] who violates *dat Moshe* and *dat Yehudit*. (Rashi explains *dat Yehudit* as "the practice of Jewish women.") And what counts as *dat Yehudit*? A woman who appears in public with her hair undone." {The Talmud then poses the question: "Undone hair} is a Torah prohibition, for it says (Num. 5:18), 'and you undo the hair of the woman' and it was taught in the house of R. Ishmael: 'This is a warning to Jewish women not to appear in public with their hair undone.'" [The Talmud] answers, "[Going out with only] a *kalta* is sufficient according to the Torah. (Rashi explains that a *kalta* is a basket.) According to *dat Yehudit*, [going out with only] a *kalta* is also forbidden."	תשובה גרסינן בש״ס דכתובות פ' המדיר דף ע״ב ע״א במתני' ואלו יוצאת שלא בכתוב' העובר' על דת משה ויהודית פרש״י דת יהודית שנהגו בנות ישראל ואיזה דת יהודית יוצאה וראשה פרועה {ומקשי הש״ס ראשה פרועה}[20] דאורייתא היא דכתיב ופרע ראש האשה ותנא דבי ר' ישמעאל אזהרה לבנות ישראל שלא יצאו בפרועת ראש ומשני דאורייתא [קלתה][21] שפיר דמי (פרש״י קלתה סל) דת יהודית אפי' קלתה נמי אסיר ע״כ

---

this responsum itself is an attempt to address one set of the pastoral issues related to the rape.

20. These words do not appear in the text, but either them or something like them were lost by a copyist whose eye jumped from ראשה פרועה to פרועה ראשה (homeoteleuton), as the text makes no sense otherwise.

21. The text says קלתת but this is a merely a misprint or a slip of the pen.

The *Shevut Yaakov* then moves on to the halakhic codifications:

> The Rambam in Ch. 21 of the "Laws of Prohibited Sexual Relations" and the *Tur* and *Shulchan Arukh* in *Even HaEzer* 21 wrote: "Jewish women should not go out to the market with their hair undone, whether single or married."
>
> וכתב הרמב"ם בפ' כ"א מהא"ב והטור והש"ע בא"ה סי' כ"א וז"ל לא ילכו בנות ישראל פרועת ראש בשוק אחת פנויה ואחת אשת איש
>
> And the *Bach* wrote that that which [the *Tur* et al.] wrote "whether single or married" would appear to be derived from that which the Talmud says, "it was taught in the house of R. Ishmael: 'This is a warning to Jewish women not to appear in public with their hair undone.'" Ostensibly, both single and married women are included in this warning. And [the *Bach*'s] words are correct.
>
> וכתב הב"ח הא דכתב אחת פנויה ואחת א"א נרא' דנפקו להו מדאיתא שם בש"ס תנא דבי רבי ישמעאל אזהרה לבנות ישראל שלא ילכו פרועת ראש אלמא דאחת פנויה ואח' אשת איש באזהר' ודבריו נכונים.

Here the *Shevut Yaakov* has made two points. First, that the simple reading of the Rambam, *Tur*, and *Shulchan Arukh* here is that all women, regardless of marital status, must have their hair done up or covered, and that, as the *Bach* argued, this rule is derived from the baraita of R. Ishmael. But having noted that, the *Shevut Yaakov* moves to explore the problem that was the crux of Chapter 6:

> But the *Bach*, and Rabbi Falk-Katz [in the *Perisha*], and other late authorities, expressed bewilderment since it is the straightforward custom for virgins to go out into the market place with their hair undone, and this is stated explicitly in *OC* 75, see there. And all of these authorities "prophesize" [the answer] along the same lines, that when Rambam and *Tur* write that [the obligation of hair covering] applies to an unmarried woman, they mean to say a widow, for she is no longer a virgin.
>
> אך שתמהו הב"ח והרפ"ך ושאר כל האחרונים דהא המנהג פשוט שהולכין הבתולת פרוע' הרא' בשוק וכ"כ בא"ח סי' ע"ה יע"ש ועל זה מתנבאי' כול' בסגנון אחד דהא דכת' הרמב"ם והטור אחת פנוי' היינו אלמנה שהיא בעולה.

Shevut Yaakov notes the majority view, that single here means widowed or divorced, but he is clearly unhappy with this approach and argues against it:

> But in truth this seems forced, as the wording of Rambam and *Tur*, who simply wrote
>
> אך באמת דבריהם דחוקים דלשון הרמב"ם והטור שכתבו

"single woman," seems to apply to unmarried women in general. Moreover, the Talmudic source of this law, which states "the daughters of Israel," seems to include unmarried women.

סתם פנויה משמע דהכל בכלל כל שהיא פנויה וגם מקור הדין שבש"ס דקאמר בנות ישראל גם הבתולות בכלל

Unsurprisingly, then, his next move is to bring up the alternative approach of the *Magen Avraham*:

And in the *Magen Avraham* on *OC* 75.3, he writes: "This is a problem, since in *Even HaEzer* 21:2, he (=the *Shulchan Arukh*) wrote that Jewish women should not go out with their hair undone in the market place, whether they are single or married." This is also what the Rambam wrote in Chapter 21 of the laws of forbidden relations. Moreover, in Ketubot, towards the beginning of the second chapter, it states: "If she went out to her wedding day with her hair undone, this is a sign that she is a virgin."

ובמגן אברהם בא"ח סי' ע"ה ס"ק ג' כתב וז"ל קשה דבא"ע סי' כ"א ס"ב כתב לא תלכנה בנו' ישראל פרועת ראש בשוק אחת פנויה ואחת אשת איש וכ"כ הרמב"ם פכ"א מה' איסורי ביאה ועוד דאיתא בכתובת /בכתובות/ רפ"ב אם יצאה בהינומא וראשה פרוע' זה סימן שהיתה בתולה

It is unreasonable to suggest that the "single women" referred to [in *EH* 21] means widows, for if that were the case he should have clarified explicitly.

ודוחק לומר דפנויה דקתני היינו אלמנה דא"כ ה"ל לפרש

One might suggest that the "undone hair" about which he writes in *Even HaEzer* means that they undo their hair entirely, and go out [with it free-flowing] in the market place, for this is forbidden even for a single woman. And Rashi said as much in his commentary on *Nasso*, on the phrase "and he will undo the hair of the woman" [referring to the law of the *sotah*] (Num. 5:18).

וי"ל דפרועת ראש דכתב בא"ע היינו שסותרת קליעת שערן והולכת בשוק דזה אסור אפי' בפנויה וכן פרש"י בפר' נשא על ופרע ראש האשה

Nevertheless, we must admit that a single woman is not forbidden with a Torah prohibition [to go with her hair free-flowing], for if we were to say that the verse [in Numbers] also includes single women, then

ומ"מ צ"ל דפנויה לא מתסרי מדאורייתא דא"ת דקרא איירי בפנויה א"כ גם בגילוי הראש תהא אסורה לילך דמהכא ילפינן בכתובת פ"ז שלא

she would also be prohibited from going in public with her hair uncovered, for it is from this verse that Ketubot Ch. 7 learns the prohibition for Jewish women to go in public with their hair uncovered. Rather, we must say that the verse is not referring to single women, only that it is modest behavior for even virgins not to go out in public that way (i.e., with their hair free-flowing). – End quote.

תלכנה בנות ישראל בגילוי ראש אלא ע״כ קרא לא איירי בפנויה רק שמדת וצניעות הוא לבתולת שלא לילך כן עכ״ל המ״א

As noted in the previous chapter, *Magen Avraham* explains the contradiction between *OC* 75, which says single women go out with their hair undone, and *EH* 21, which says no women may appear in public with their hair undone, by positing that *OC* is referring to head coverings and *EH* is referring to coiffing or braiding. In other words, no women may appear in public with free-flowing hair, but unmarried women may appear in public with their hair braided or coiffed even though it is not covered by anything.

Not only does the *Shevut Yaakov* agree with *Magen Avraham* about the difference between coiffing/braiding hair and covering it with something else as an answer for this contradiction in the *Tur* and *Shulchan Arukh*, but he decides to take the point one step further and apply it to the Talmudic pericope itself:

Were it not that the explanations of Rashi to the Talmud and Rambam in his Commentary on the Mishnah give me pause, I would have explained the passage in b. Ketubot 72a–b in this manner as well: that when the Talmud states it is biblically prohibited for a woman to go with her head undone, it means that she undoes the braids (or coiffing) of her hair. The Talmud then questions this by noting that going with undone hair is a biblical violation, if the woman lets her hair flow freely, to which the Talmud appropriately responds that biblically, *kalta* is satisfactory, meaning that biblically it is forbidden for the daughters of Israel to go out in the marketplace with

ואי לאו דמסתפינא מפרש״י שבש״ס והרמב״ם בפי׳ המשניות הייתי מפרש גם סוגיא דש״ס דכתובת פ׳ המדיר על דרך זה דהא דקאמר יוצאת וראשה פרועה היינו שסותרת קליעת שערה ומקשה פריעת ראש דאורייתא היא אם סותר את שערה לזה שפיר משני הש״ס דאורייתא קלתה שפיר דמי פי׳ מדאורייתא שאסור לבנות ישראל לילך פריעת ראש בשוק היינו ששערותיה סתורות אבל קלתה פי׳ מלשון קליעת שער שפיר דמי אבל

> their hair undone; but *kalta*, as in braided hair (*keli'at sei'ar*), is sufficient. However, according to *dat Yehudit* and custom, even going out with braided hair and no other hair covering is prohibited as well for married women and non-virgins.
>
> דת ומנהג יהודית אפי' קלועין שערה ג"כ אסור לילך בגילוי באשת איש ובעולת בעל
>
> We thus find that Rambam, who codified only what was prohibited by law and not by custom, wrote that "the daughters of Israel should not go out in the marketplace with their heads uncovered, whether they are single...," meaning with their hair free-flowing and not braided, as it is even forbidden for an unmarried woman to go out that way in the marketplace.
>
> נמצא דהרמב"ם שלא כתב רק מה שאסור מדינא ולא מצד המנהג לכן כתב לא ילכו בנות ישראל פרועת ראש בשוק אחת פנויה וכולי דהיינו אם שערותיה סתורים ולא קלועים דאסור אפי' בבתולה לילך כך בשוק

For our purposes, this is the key point of the *Shevut Yaakov*. The Talmud distinguishes between a biblical requirement for women not to appear in public with their hair undone, and a *dat Yehudit* requirement for women to cover their hair. The Talmud explains that the biblical requirement is for women to go out at least with kalta but *dat Yehudit* requires more than just kalta.

The standard interpretation of kalta is an incomplete covering. However, *Shevut Yaakov* suggests that *Magen Avraham*'s insight can be fruitfully applied here as well. Perhaps the biblical rule is that no women may appear in public with free-flowing hair and that all women must coif or braid their hair before appearing in public. *Dat Yehudit*, then, was designed specifically for married women and requires that hair not merely be done up but covered by something else. The *Shevut Yaakov* continues by addressing the *hynuma* passage discussed at length in the previous chapter:

> That which we said at the beginning of the second chapter of Ketubot, that if there are witnesses that she appeared at her wedding with her hair undone, her ketubah is two hundred, this implies even in public. And this is our practice, that on the day of their wedding they go out with their hair free-flowing, and this is because at that time she is walking with her bridesmaids
>
> והא דאמרינןברפ"ב דכתובת אם יש עדים שיצאה בהינומא וראשה פרועה כתובתה מאתים משמע אפי' בשוק וכן הוא מנהגינו שהולכין כך ביום חתונתם עם שער' סתורי' היינו משו' שבאותו פעם הולכין עמה השושבני' והרבה קרובים ונשים ליכא

and many relatives, including women, such that there is no reason to worry about anything, for a bride would not be so base as to fornicate on her wedding day.	למיחש מידי ולא תהיה עלובה כלה לזנות ביום חופתה

In the *Shevut Yaakov*'s reading, the wedding day is unique in that the woman appears with her hair entirely undone, as opposed to the usual requirement for her to have her hair braided or coiffed. His explanation for why a virgin's wedding day should be the exception to hair modesty rules is unusual, since he argues that the doing up of hair is a way to avoid lewd behavior, as opposed to the more standard explanation that a woman's appearing with free-flowing (or uncovered) hair is itself lewd behavior.

He continues with describing the pesak:

Be this as it may, [this is the rule] according to the Rosh and the Mordechai quoting the Ra'aviah at the end of the 3rd chapter of Berachot.	ויהי' איך שיהי' [כך היא][22] לדעת הרא"ש והמרדכי בשם הראבי"ה סוף פ' מי שמתו
And such is our practice. And when the *Shulchan Arukh* ruled in *Even HaEzer* 75:2 that for all single women, because they regularly do so, it is permissible for them to go out in the marketplace with their heads uncovered, it is because we have no further concerns about giving rise to erotic thoughts so long as their hair is braided.	וכן הוא מנהגינו וכאשר פסק בש"ע א"ח סי' ע"ה דכל הבתולות כיון שרגילה בגילוי שער מותר להלך כן בשוק תו לא חיישינן משום הרהור אם שערותיה קלועים

In short, hair that is not free-flowing but done up in some way is not considered erotic or lewd dress, and is permitted for unmarried women. The *Shevut Yaakov* then returns to the case at hand, to argue that a raped woman should be treated like a virgin, and be allowed to appear with her hair done up but uncovered:

If so, then the woman who was raped should ostensibly be included in this category [of women who need only braid/coif their hair]. Since she is used to going out with hair uncovered, why should we	וא"כ גם זו שנאנסה לכאורה בכלל כיון שעדיין רגילה בגילוי למה נביישה בחנם והיא אנוסה

---

22. Something like this is missing from the line, otherwise the sentence has no meaning. I filled in based on standard usage and the similarity between this phrase and the previous one that could have caused the scribe to miss it.

embarrass her, just because she has been raped?

Despite this reading of the text, the *Shevut Yaakov* does not, in the end, rule permissively:

> Nevertheless, a proof can be offered that anyone who has had intercourse needs to cover her hair, in line with the *dat Yehudit* practice.
>
> אך יש להביא ראיה דכל שנבעלה צריכה לילך מכוסה בראש׳ כדת ומנהג יהודית,

His proof for the need to be strict comes from the same pericope he quoted above, the rule about the virgin bride at her wedding:

> For it states in the Talmud [tractate Ketubot], towards the beginning of the second chapter, that if witnesses testify that she appeared at her wedding with her hair free-flowing, her ketubah payment is two hundred *zuz*.
>
> דהא איתא בש״ס [מס׳ כתובו] ר״פ האשה שנתארמלה אם יש עדים שיצאה בהינומא וראשה פרועה כתובתה מאתים

He next moves to the Talmud's discussion of a related practice, namely the passing of a wine barrel before the bride. According to Rav Ada bar Ahava, if she is a virgin, the barrel is passed sealed and if she is not a virgin it is passed unsealed:

> And in the Gemara there, page 16b, [it states]: "Why do they do this? Why not just pass [the wine barrel] before a virgin, but don't pass it at all before a non-virgin? Because, at times, women have been known to claim two hundred [for their ketubah], and they say: 'I was a virgin, and the fact that they did not pass it before me is because I was raped.'" From this passage, we see that the rabbis were concerned even about an unusual claim, such as rape, for it is not common for a woman to ask for two hundred based on such a claim.
>
> ובגמרא שם דף י״ו ע״ב אמאי נעבריה קמי בתולה וקמי בעולה לא ניעבר כלל זימנין דתפסה מאתים ואמרי אנא בתולה הוי והאי דלא עברי קמאי איתנוסי הוא דאיתנס ע״כ הרי מסוגיא זו דחשו חכמי׳ אפי׳ לטענה דלא שכיח כגון אונסא דלא שכיח שיגבה מאתים היכי דתפסה ע״י טענה כזו

> Now if a raped woman need not cover her hair, just like any other virgin, then how could the Mishnah say "if there were witnesses that she appeared at her wedding with her hair undone" – what did the rabbis
>
> ואם אית׳ דאנוס׳ אין לכסות ראש׳ כמו שאר בתולות א״כ איך קאמר המתני׳ אם יש עדים שיצא׳ בהינומא וראש׳ פרוע׳ מה הועילו

> gain with their rule? For the ketubah of a raped woman is [only] 100 *zuz*, and her hair free-flowing.
>
> חכמים בתקנתם הלא בנאנסה דכתובת' מנה וראשה פרועה

The *Shevut Yaakov*'s point here is that from the rule about witnesses at a wedding we can deduce the rabbis' assumptions about who covers her hair and who does not. The background is as follows: if a man's widow is disputing with his heirs about how much the ketubah payment from the estate should be, with her claiming two hundred and the heirs claiming one hundred, without a document stating one or the other, the matter is hard to prove. How could anyone, other than herself, know whether she had been a virgin at the wedding? Thus, she could easily be lying to collect an extra hundred zuz.

The rabbis then state that in lieu of a document, people who were at the wedding testifying that she appeared with her hair free-flowing and uncovered is considered sufficient to support her claim. This is because only virgins appear at a wedding this way. Thus, the *Shevut Yaakov* argues, if non-virgins, including raped women, also appear at their weddings with their hair uncovered, then the rabbi's ruling here is of little value, since such women only receive *ketubot* of 100 zuz, not 200 zuz. In such a case, a woman who was married after having been raped could use her appearance at the wedding with her hair uncovered to force the heirs to pay out double what they are supposed to, which would be a problem. Thus, the *Shevut Yaakov* claims, clearly the rabbis are assuming that a raped woman covers her hair and could not make use of a claim about people at her wedding.

The *Shevut Yaakov* then continues the point by staving off an attempt to use his own *chiddush* against him:

> Even according to what I wrote, that the undone hair that the virgins appear with at their weddings, which refers specifically to unbraided (free-flowing) hair, and this is the sign that she is a virgin, which would not be the case with a raped woman, where she would not have her hair free-flowing and she would appear in public only with her hair braided – this is not the case,
>
> ואף לפי מה שכתבתי דדוקא ראשה פרועה שהולכין הבתולות בשעת חתונת' דהיינו סתירת שער' זה הוי ראי' שהיא בתולה משא"כ אנוס' אין סותרין את שערה ומוליכין אות' בשוק כשהי' קלועה גם זה אינו
>
> For it is explicit in the *Yalkut* [*Shimoni*] of *Parashat Nasso*, 107b, in the name of the Sifre:
>
> דהא להדי' אית' בילקוט פ' נשא דף ר"ז ריש ע"ב בשם ספרי וז"ל

> "Another matter: this teaches that Jewish women would cover their heads, even though there is no proof to the matter, there is an allusion to it, for it says (2 Sam 13:19): 'And Tamar put ashes on her head and the long-sleeved coat that was on her she tore.'"
>
> דבר אחר לימד על בנות ישראל שיהיו מכסות ראשן ואף על פי שאין ראיה לדבר זכר לדבר שנאמר ותקח תמר אפר על ראשה וכתונת פסי' אשר עליה קרעה ע"כ
>
> And that is a case of rape. So we see explicitly that [a raped woman] should cover her hair, and this goes all the more so for a seduced girl – any woman who had sex, her ketubah is one hundred *zuz*.
>
> והתם אנוסה הוי הרי להדיא דאפי' אנוסה יש לכסות ראשה וכ"ש מפותה כל שנבעלה וכתובתה מנה

The *Shevut Yaakov* realizes that, based on this novel argument, the following theoretical argument could be made: all women must have their hair coiffed or braided when appearing in public, but do not need to cover their hair until they are married. For virgin women, a special custom of her appearing at her wedding with her hair free-flowing existed, and this could be taken as a sign that she was a virgin. So, all that would need to be done to avoid the confusion problem mentioned above is for a raped (or seduced) woman to appear at her wedding with her hair braided or coiffed, but not free-flowing, and it would be clear she was not a virgin.

This works theoretically, but the *Shevut Yaakov* has a proof against it, namely the Sifre which we saw in Chapter 1 and which he found quoted in the *Yalkut Shimoni*. (Perhaps he did not have a Sifre.) According to this, the biblical evidence that women must cover their hair comes from what Tamar, the daughter of King David, does after she is raped by her half-brother Amnon. The fact that she does this after she was raped, argues the *Shevut Yaakov*, shows that a raped woman's status is like that of a married woman and that she must cover her hair – braids or coiffing being no longer sufficient.

The *Shevut Yaakov* ends his responsum by showing the flip side of this argument – that a virgin widow, i.e., a woman whose husband died while they had only done erusin and not nissuin, does not need to cover her hair:

> Indeed, a virgin who has received *kiddushin* but not *nissuin* is certainly permitted to walk in public with her hair uncovered, since even a woman widowed when only
>
> אכן בתולה שנתקדשה ועדיין לא נשאת מותרת להלוך פרועת ראש בודאי כיון שכתובת' מאתי' אפי'

an *arusah*, her ketubah payment is two hundred, as is stated explicitly in *Even Ha-Hezer* 67. And this is clear in the Talmud and is the implication in the poskim.

This is unlike what was stated in *Responsa Chavot Yair* 196, that even a virgin who received *erusin* should cover her hair. This is not correct, for if it were, we must pose this difficulty: How does the Mishnah say, "If witnesses testify that she appeared at her wedding with her hair free-flowing"? For she can always take two hundred and say that she was a virgin, [explaining] that the only reason she did not go out with her hair uncovered [at her wedding] is because she was widowed when only an *arusah* – just as the rabbis argued with regard to the passing of the cup. So what help did the rabbis accomplish with this enactment?

Rather it is certain that any woman who has not had sex is permitted to walk in public like any other virgin, in contrast to women who are no longer virgins, even due to rape. Go out and see what the people are doing. This is my opinion, Jacob the small.

אלמנה מן האירוסין כמבואר שם בא"ע ר"ס ס"ז ע"ש והוא פשוט בש"ס ומשמעות הפוסקים

דלא כמ"ש בתשובת חות יאיר סי' קצ"ו דאף בתולה שנתקדשה יש לילך בכיסוי ראש וזה אינו דא"כ תקשה איך קאמר המתני' אם יש עדים שיצא' בהינומא וראשה פרועה הלא זומנין [זימנין] דתפסה מאתים ותאמר אנא בתולה הזית/הוית/ והא דלא יצאה ראשה פרועה משום שהיתה אלמנה מן האירוסין וכדקאמר הש"ס גבי העברת כוס ומה הועילו חכמים בתקנתם

אלא ודאי כמ"ש דכל שלא נבעלה מותרת להלוך כמו כל הבתולות משא"כ בנבעלה אפי' באונס ופוק חזי מה עמא דבר כנ"ל ה"ק יעקב:

Thus the *Shevut Yaakov* ends with the following outline: According to Torah law (*dat Moshe*), all women must have their hair done up in coiffing or braids when appearing in public. In the Talmud, this doing up of hair is referred to as *kalta*. The one exception is that virgins may appear with their hair free-flowing at their weddings, as this is not considered lewd behavior, and it also functions as evidence in the future for the necessity of a full, 200 zuz, ketubah payment.

According to Jewish practice (*dat Yehudit*), however, women who are no longer virgins must cover their hair in public, and this applies even to women who were raped or had sex before marriage. It does not apply to women who were widowed before *nissuin*, since such women are still virgins. This distinction also serves as evidence for the ketubah amount, since any woman who is married with her hair covered gets only 100 zuz, as it is a sign that she was not a virgin, whereas any woman who gets married with her hair free-flowing gets two hundred, as it is a sign she was a virgin.

In sum, the *Shevut Yaakov* has three states in which a woman can appear in public:

- Free-flowing hair – only a virgin at her wedding;
- Hair coiffed or braided – biblically this is enough for all women but Jewish custom only allows virgins to appear this way;
- Hair covered – women who are not virgins (married or not).

This rubric brings up one final question: If it is biblically required for all women to have their hair done up, how is it that virgins are permitted to appear at their weddings with their hair free-flowing? Granted, there is no chance for lewd behavior, but isn't a prohibition a prohibition regardless of whether it will lead to problematic behavior?

In order to make sense of this position, it seems necessary to posit that according to the *Shevut Yaakov*, even the biblical requirement to braid or coif hair is really a subjective rule based on societal norms. Since the wedding day of a virgin is considered exceptional by society, then we treat it accordingly and the normal rules don't apply. The point is, apparently, that the biblical norms of braiding hair reflect a basic standard of propriety, while the Jewish practice of covering hair reflects an extra step towards modesty beyond just the basic standard. One wonders, however, what aspect of either rule would apply in a society in which no women cover their hair except for religious reasons, and that actual subjective propriety is no longer a real factor.

It seems that, at the very least, the biblical rules would no longer be in force, since in society at large, appearing in public with free-flowing hair would not be considered risky behavior, tempting impropriety as it once was. At most, one could say that hair covering is still "extra modesty," though at this point, one would have to underline the *extra* since it is, in reality, an order of magnitude beyond contemporary standards of modest dress.

Panim Meirot

Another rabbi who dealt with a related question – whether a non-virgin should have to cover her hair – was R. Meir ben Isaac Eisenstadt (Maharam Ash, 1670–1744), a dayan and rosh yeshiva, in his responsa *Panim Meirot* (1:35). His responsa became well known because many of them were included in the *Pitchei Teshuva*, the important commentary on the *Shulchan Arukh*, written by his descendant, Rabbi Avraham Tzvi Hirsch Eisenstadt (1812–1865). This one is referenced in the *Pitchei Teshuva* on *Even HaEzer* 21, as it is relevant to the major debate about whether a non-virgin who was never married needs to cover her hair.

The responsum begins with the author's summation of the question:

I was asked by the great rabbi, our master and teacher, R. Shlomo, the head of the beit din in the holy city of Ussia, in a matter in which it became known that a virgin had had sex, and the rabbi wants to force her to cover her hair with a scarf.	נשאלתי מהרב הגדול מהור"ר שלמה אב"ד דק"ק אוסיא בדבר שנתברר ויצא קול על הבתולה שנבעלה ורצה הרב לכופה שתכס' ראשה בצניף

The *Panim Meirot* begins his answer with a strong objection to the questioner's point:

And this is what I answered him: I do not have enough time to offer responses to that which he invented based on his personal theory – only, regarding that which he tried to support based on the Gemara in the 7th chapter of Ketubot, "'And he shall undo the woman's hair' – this is a warning to Jewish women [not to appear in public with their hair undone]," and the honorable Torah scholar wishes to say that there is no difference between married and single women in this regard, even though the practice of virgins is to appear in public with their hair undone, so that it would be clear [that they were available] – God forbid he should suggest this. For if this is a Torah law, how could Jews have established a custom against a law in our Torah?!	וזה אשר השבתי אין הזמן מספיק עמי להושיבו דבר על מה שרוצה להמציא מסברא דנפשי' רק מה שבנה יסוד על גמרא פ' המדיר ופרע ראש האשה מכאן אזהרה לבנו' ישראל ורצה מכ"ת לומר שאין חילוק בין אשת איש לפנויה אך שנהגו הבתולות לילך פרוע' ראש כדי שיהי' להם היכר חלילה לומר כן אי דבר זה דאורייתא איך יקבעו ישראל מנהג נגד דת תורתינו

The questioner's premise is impossible, he suggests, because it would mean that the Jewish custom of single girls appearing in public with their hair undone is actually a violation of Torah law. Having pointed out this flaw, however, the *Panim Meirot* continues by noting that the questioner does have some support in halakhic literature:

> In truth though, his theory is mentioned in *Even HaEzer* 21:2, which writes, "Jewish women should not walk around with their hair undone in the market place, whether they are single or married."
>
> ובאמת סברתו נזכר בא"ע סי' כ"א ס"ב כתב לא תלכנה בנות ישראל פרועו' ראש בשוק אחד פנוי' ואחד א[שת] א[יש].

At first glance, then, the *Shulchan Arukh* seems to be supporting the questioner's premise, that all women, no matter their marital status or sexual history, should have their hair done up or covered. Nevertheless, the *Panim Meirot* moves immediately to problematize this suggestion:

> But there is a problem with this rule itself, if it is a Torah prohibition [for any woman to appear in public with her hair undone], how is it that virgins in our communities do go out with their hair undone?
>
> ועל הדין זה גופי' קשיא אי דאורייתא איך בתולי' שלנו הולכו' פרועו' ראש

Reiterating his previous objection, the *Panim Meirot* is unwilling to accept that all the single Jewish girls in his society were sinners and takes their behavior as a proof that the questioner's understanding of halakha cannot be correct. He then supports this with the clear implication of the Talmud, that single women did not cover or coif/braid their hair:

> And in Ketubot, it is implied that in Talmudic times they went out this way, for we say that if she went out at her wedding [*hynuma*] with her hair undone this is a sign she was a virgin.
>
> ובכתובו' משמע שבזמן התלמוד היו הולכו' כן דאמרינן אם יצאה בהינומה וראש' פרועה זה סימן שהיתה בתולה

Next, the *Panim Meirot* strengthens his point by noting the contradiction discussed in the previous chapter between *Even HaEzer* 21 and *Orach Chayyim* 75:

> And in *OC* 75 it says "and virgins whose way it is to go out [in public] with their hair undone, it is permitted to recite the Shema in their presence." If so, the words of the *Shulchan Arukh* contradict each other!
>
> ובא"ח סי' ע"ה וכן בתולות שדרכן לילך פרועו' ראש מותר לקרו' ק"ש כנגדן וא"כ דברי הש"ע נראי' כסותרי' זה את זה

Instead of attempting to answer the contradiction, as was done by the many Acharonim surveyed in the previous chapter, the *Panim Meirot* quotes the *Magen Avraham* to make one specific point:

> Look at the *Magen Avraham* who agreed for a single woman it is not a Torah prohibition
>
> ועיי' במג"א שהסכים דבפנוי' לאו דאורייתא ובבתול' אין

and that for a virgin there is no concern about transgression at all, and his words are a peg [upon which to hang our analysis] that will not come loose.

חשש נידנוד איסור ודבריו הם יתר /יתד/ שלא תמוט

Certainly, the *Magen Avraham*, whose position we discussed at length in the previous chapter, states explicitly that single women are not covered by the Torah prohibition. Nevertheless, the *Panim Meirot*'s reading of the *Magen Avraham* as distinguishing between single women and virgins is a bit idiosyncratic. The pertinent quote reads as follows:

Nevertheless, we must admit that a single woman is not forbidden with a Torah prohibition [to go with her hair free-flowing], for if we were to say that the verse [in Numbers] also includes single women, then she would also be prohibited from going in public with her hair uncovered, for it is from this verse that Ketubot Ch. 7 learns the prohibition for Jewish women to go in public with their hair uncovered. Rather, we must say that the verse is not referring to single women, only that it is modest behavior for virgins not to go out in public that way (i.e., with their hair free-flowing).

ומ"מ צ"ל דפנויה לא מתסרי מדאוריי' דא"ת דקרא איירי גם בפנויה א"כ גם בגילוי הראש תהא אסור' לילך דמהכא ילפינן בכתובות פ"ז שלא תלכנה בנות ישראל בגילוי הראש אלא ע"כ קרא לא איירי בפנויה רק שמדת צניעות היא לבתולות שלא לילך כן:

Though the simple reading of this passage is that the *Magen Avraham* is using "single" and "virgin" synonymously, the *Panim Meirot* is picking up on the switch in language in the final sentence: "The verse is not referring to single women" versus "it is modest behavior for virgins." His understanding is that the first phrase means to say that single women, who have been married or who have had sex before, should – or even must – cover their hair, though this is not a Torah law but only a rabbinic one, whereas for virgins, doing so would only be an exceptionally pious or modest behavior, not required or expected.

Relying on the *Magen Avraham* that the Torah law is not applicable to any unmarried woman, virgin or not, the *Panim Meirot* goes on to clarify the halakha as he understands it:

If so, we can derive the law: If [the requirement] was from the Torah, it would be incumbent upon us to force her to cover her hair.

וא"כ זכינו לדין דאי הוי דאורייתא הי' מצוה עלינו לכופה לכסות ראשה

> Even if this is merely a negative commandment derived from a positive one, even so, we would enforce a positive commandment and even administer lashes until his spirit leaves him, as it states in the 9th chapter of b. Ketubot, 86a–b.
>
> אף דלאו הבא מכלל עשה עשה הוא מ"מ כייפינן אעשה ומכין אותו עד שתצא נפשו כדאית' בהכותב דף פ"ו
>
> But since it is clear that no Torah prohibition exists with regard to a single woman, why should we shove our heads [into her affairs] and strong-arm her into covering her hair?
>
> אבל כיון דנתברר דבפנוי' אין כאן איסור דאורייתא א"כ מה לנו להכניס ראשינו לילך עמה בגדולו' לכוף אותה שתכסה ראשה.

The *Panim Meirot* makes a novel point here. It isn't that he is sure that a non-virgin need not cover her hair. His point is that since there is no Torah law involved, and at most it is a rabbinic requirement, the local rabbis should leave the decision to her and not try to force her to fulfill the rabbinic requirement.

He next turns to a possible objection to his answer from a different angle:

> And if [you will respond] that it is for the ketubah [so that she not appear as if she is a virgin when she is not], but doesn't every man who is to marry a woman check into her background? And since it is well known that she has had sex, anything he decides to do for her in the ketubah is his own choice, and he has permission to add to it.
>
> ואם בשביל הכתובה הלא כל הנושא אשה בודק וחוקר אחרי' וכיון דנתפרסם שזנתה כל מה שיעשה לה כתובה מדעתו הוא ורשות בידו להוסיף.

This lack of concern about the ketubah is a uniquely lenient approach. From here, he turns to his last point, responding to another possible objection:

> And the fact that [non-virgins] tend to cover their hair is because it serves their own good, so that she will not be insulted by passers-by who see the bulge of her pregnant belly [and no hair covering] and they will know that she had illicit sex, but here, since she says explicitly that she does not want such assistance, we should listen to her.
>
> והא דנהגו לכסות ראשה עושים לטובתה שלא תהי' חרפה וגדופה לכל עובר אורח שיראה אותה כריסה בין שיני' וידע שזנתה אבל היכא שהיא אומרת שלא ניחא בתקנתה כגון דא שומעין לה

What appears to me to be correct I have written – Meir.	הנ[ראה] לע[ניות] ד[עתי] כתבתי מאיר

His final point is again quite novel and open-minded. He notes that non-virgins in his society tend to cover their hair. But instead of claiming that since this is the accepted practice all such women are required to follow it, he argues that this has nothing to do with appearing as a "proper non-virgin," but instead it is an attempt to appear married.

Implicit in his argument is the following: the reason people "know" that a given woman is not a virgin is because she got pregnant; otherwise, why would this be public knowledge? Thus, on a societal level, many of these women would feel less conspicuous if they dressed as if they were married by covering their hair. This being the case, if a given woman does not wish to dress as if she is married, and is not worried about being insulted, her choices should be respected.

In short, according to the *Panim Meirot*, virgins need not cover their hair, and single women who are not virgins are not absolutely required to cover their hair. Importantly, the *Panim Meirot* insists that we treat women's behavior as a norm, since he "proves" that single women are not required to cover their hair by pointing out that they do not. Finally, the *Panim Meirot* even notes that practices must be understood in context. It isn't just mechanically about whether a given group of women cover their hair, but *why*. Thus, he argues that since in his time covered hair is a sign of marriage, it is only married women who must cover.

Responsa Sefer Yehoshua: The Betrothal of Roiza

A particularly important responsum for the question of the nature of the prohibition for married women to appear in public with their hair undone appears as a tangent in a long responsum by R. Yehoshua Heschel Babad of Tarnopol (1754–1838) in his *Responsa Sefer Yehoshua* (#89). (He is the grandfather of the famous R. Yosef Babad, author of the *Minchat Chinuch*, and also the chief rabbi of Tarnopol in his day.)

The case the *Sefer Yehoshua* is dealing with is that a married man named Beryl, apparently – but not definitively – as a joke, betrothed a single woman named Roiza, referred to throughout as "a virgin." The main issue has to do with whether Roiza should be considered betrothed, or "possibly betrothed," to require Beryl to give her a *gett* and pay her a ketubah payment. (He cannot marry her, since he is already married.)

At one point, the responsum takes a long tangent to discuss the fact that the woman actually started covering her hair[23] when told to do so, and considers whether that could be used to claim that the betrothal should be treated as real (which is not how the *Sefer Yehoshua* thinks about the case):

> Regarding what his honor said that a certain man commanded her to cover her hair like a betrothed woman, that perhaps it should be suggested that the fact that she covered her hair like [married] women can be analogized to what the poskim wrote in *Yoreh Deah* 1:13 with regard to a butcher who made a sign on the head of a sheep [that it seemed to him the animal was *treif*], that if he can offer a plausible explanation [for why he did so and the animal is not *treif*] he is believed, whereas *Yoreh Deah* 185:3 implies that a woman who wears her niddah clothing is not believed [to claim that she is not really niddah] even if she gives a plausible explanation to her words – she is not believed [since wearing the clothing creates a presumption (חזקה) in the neighborhood]. If so, one would ostensibly say in this case that since she covered her hair, she has solidified the perception that she has been betrothed.
>
> ובאשר כתב כבודו שציוה איש אחד לכסות ראש כאשה המתקדשת, בזה יש לדבר לכאורה במה שכסתה את ראשה כדרך הנשים אולי דומה למאי שכתבו הפוסקים ביו"ד סי' א' [סעיף י"ג] גבי טבח שעשה סימן בראש הכבש דאם נתן אמתלא לדבריו נאמן, ובי"ד סי' קפ"ה [סעיף ג'] משמע דהיכי דלבשה בגדי נדותה דאינה נאמנת אפי' בנותנת אמתלא לדבריה, וא"כ יש לכאורה לומר כיון דכסתה ראשה אלמוהו אלמה לקלא דקדושין

Having offered this theoretical defense of the questioner's position, R. Babad rejects it outright:

> But this is not right either. For the *Bach* and the *Shakh* in his *Nekudot HaKessef* distinguish between the case of the butcher,
>
> גם זהו אינו, דהא כתבו הב"ח והש"ך בנקודות הכסף לחלק בין האי דטבח דמהני אמתלא

---

23. This same analysis appears almost word for word in a gloss on *Even HaEzer* 21 in R. Babad's *Sefer HaVatik*, a collection of glosses on the Talmud, *Mishneh Torah*, and *Shulchan Arukh* that is printed together with his *Sefer HaNaim*, a collection of glosses on the Torah. Neither of these are independent works; all of these glosses are taken from the *Responsa Sefer Yehoshua*, and compiled by a descendant of his, Gedaliah Daniel Babad, and were published in 1990. (Yehoshua Babad did write books with these names, but the manuscripts were lost in a fire and never published.)

where a plausible explanation would be sufficient, and the case of a woman wearing her niddah clothing, where it would not. And this is because in the butcher's case, there was no alternative, whereas in the case of a niddah, it would have been enough had she merely said: "I am impure."

ובין לבשה בגדי נדותה דלא מהני, היינו משום דכאן אי אפשר בענין אחר משא"כ גבי נדה די לה שתאמר טמאה אני,

If so, the same is true in this case, irrespective of circumstances. For if a betrothed woman needs to cover her hair in accordance with what the man mistakenly taught her, then she needed to cover her hair until such time as it became clear that she was not really betrothed; and once it is decided that she isn't really betrothed, then she was covering her hair in error, and there is no more plausible excuse than that.

א[ם] כ[ן] ה[כי] נ[מי] ממ[ה] נ[פשך], אם האשה המתקדשת צריכה לכסות ראשה כאשר הורה המורה בטעות, הרי היתה צריכה לכסות ראשה עד יוציא היתירה לאור, ואחר שיצא לאור משפטה שאין כאן קדושין הרי בטעות כסתה ראשה, ואין לך אמלתא גדולה מזו,

In short, the fact that the woman covered her hair because she thought she was betrothed does not turn her into being betrothed. Obviously, R. Babad argues, once she realizes that she is not betrothed and does not need to cover her hair she will just stop. The questioner, in other words, has it backwards. The question of whether the betrothal counted is paramount and the hair derivative; it cannot work the other way around.

The *Sefer Yehoshua* next tries to prove this point by turning back to the analogies with the *treif* animal and the niddah:

Take note, if a decisor were to declare a particular animal *treif*, and the butcher were to make a mark based on this, or if a woman were to show a stain to a rabbi and he were to tell her that she was impure, and she then put on her niddah clothing based on this, and afterwards, the same decisor realizes that he has made an error, and reverses the decision by declaring the animal kosher or the woman pure – would anyone say that we need plausible explanations here or offer any debate at all [that the animal is kosher or the woman pure]? Certainly, no one would debate this at all, and the animal would be considered

והגע עצמך, אם היה המורה אומר על בהמה שהיא טריפה ועשה הטבח סימן בזה, וכן באשה שהראתה כתמה להרב והורה שהיא טמאה ולבשה ע"ז בגדי נדותה, ואחר זה ראה המורה שהורה בטעות והכשיר הבהמה או טיהר דם האשה, היאמר בזה שצריכן אמתלאות או לפקפק בזה בשום פקפוק, בודאי לית מאן דחש ליה כלל, והרי הבהמה כשרה והאשה טהורה, וא"כ ה"נ דכוותיה,

kosher and the woman pure. If so, the same is true in this case.

Having pushed the point with the *treif* and niddah examples, he turns to a third analogy, a marriage that did not count:

For even a woman who was married by accident, we establish the halakha in *Even HaEzer*, at the end of #17, that she is considered to be as if she had been raped, so the matter would be even clearer in this case [where nothing was consummated]. And even though the *Beit Shmuel* there argues, in my humble opinion, even he would agree in our case. This is simple, and this is not the place to discuss it at length.	והא אף באשה שנשאת בטעות קיי״ל בא״ע ס״ס י״ז דהוי כאנוסה, מכל שכן הכא, ואף לבית שמואל שפקפק שם לענ״ד הכא מודה, וזהו פשוט ואין כאן מקומינו להאריך בזה.

R. Babad now returns to the question of the relevance of this woman's hair covering to those who think that betrothed women do not need to cover their hair anyway:

And if we say that a betrothed woman need not cover her hair, then certainly we need not be concerned [that she did so], since a betrothed woman need not cover her hair, as we will explain shortly is the law; if so, covering hair is not a sign of betrothal at all, since how can we say that since she covered her hair she must be betrothed since even if she were betrothed she would not need to cover her hair! Rather [covered hair] is only a sign of a sexual relationship [=*nissuin*], it is not a sign of betrothal. Thus, it is not relevant to say that hair covering strengthens the perception [of her as betrothed] at all.	ואם נימא דארוסה אינה צריכה לכסות ראשה, מכל שכן דאין לחוש, כיון דארוסה אינה צריכה לכסות את ראשה כאשר נבאר לקמן דכך הוא הדין א״כ אין הכיסוי סימן לארוסה כלל, דהאיך נימא כיון דכסתה ראשה על כרחך היא ארוסה, דאף אם היתה ארוסה אינה צריכה לכסות ראשה, ואין זה רק סימן בעולה ולא סימן ארוסה, א״כ לא שייך לומר דהכיסוי מאלמי לקלא כלל.

Having made the point that the fact that this woman covered her hair does not mean she was actually betrothed, he moves on to discuss the question of whether betrothed women are even required to do so – a topic discussed in a number of responsa we discussed earlier in this chapter.

But it is obvious that, in truth, a betrothed woman may appear in public with her	והנה זה דבר פשוט דבאמת ארוסה יכולה לצאת בפריעות

> hair undone from the first mishnah in the second chapter of Ketubot: that if she went out with *hynuma* and her hair undone her ketubah is two hundred, and in the time of the Mishnah, betrothal took place a long time before the marriage; and even so, she appeared with her hair undone. And I found also in the *Shita Mekubetzet* to b. Ketubot in the name of Rashba that he wrote the same explicitly as will be explained later on, with God's help.
>
> ראש מהאי מתניתין בפ"ב דכתובות במשנה א' דאם יצאה בהינומא וראשה פרועה כתובתה מאתים, והרי בזמן המשנה הקידושין היו זמן רב קודם הנישואין ואפ"ה יצאה בפריעת ראש, ומצאתי ג"כ בשיטה מקובצת לכתובות בשם הרשב"א ז"ל שכתב כך להדיא כאשר יתבאר לקמן בעזה"י.

The text that the *Sefer Yehoshua* brings as proof that betrothed women need not cover their hair is the same one that others used to prove the opposite; but as noted above, this is the simple meaning. The *Sefer Yehoshua* moves on from there to discuss the position of the *Panim Meirot* (quoted above) about an unmarried non-virgin covering her hair:

> Since I saw in the *Panim Meirot* 1:35, regarding this law, in a question about a single woman who became pregnant: Although it is the way of such women to cover their hair, this one did not want to. And he wrote that we should not force the promiscuous woman in this case, since [the practice] is only so that the promiscuous woman not be embarrassed to appear in public in the manner of a virgin while she is visibly pregnant and everyone who sees her will know she had sex out of wedlock. And in such a case, if she says "I am not interested in this form of assistance" we listen to her. And he quoted there the words of the *Magen Avraham* in OC 75, and he wrote there that the *Magen Avraham* is correct, see there.
>
> ולפי שראיתי בדין זה בפנים מאירות ח"א סי' ל"ה בשאלה באשה הרה לזנונים דדרכן של הנשים לכסות ראשן ואחת לא רצתה, וכתב שלא לכוף את הזונה בזה, כי אין זה רק שלא תבוש הזונה כי כריסה בין שיניה והיא כבתולה וכל הרואה ידע כי זינתה וגם היא הרה לזנונים, ובכה"ג שאמרה אי אפשר בתקנה כגון זו שומעין לה, והביא שם דברי המג"א באו"ח סי' ע"ה, וכתב שם דהעיקר כהמג"א, יעו"ש.

The *Sefer Yehoshua* is not happy with this analysis at all, and under the guise of a backhanded compliment, states that he will show how it is mistaken:

> But my inadequate mind and modest intelligence cannot cope with his words, therefore I feel it necessary to expand on
>
> והנה דבריו הנ"ל לא אוכל להולמן לפי קט שכלי ולפענ"ד, לכן מוכרח אני

this a bit, to clarify, since, in my limited understanding, it seems that the words of the early Sages did not delve deeply into this matter.

להאריך קצת בזה ולברר, כי לפי קוצר השגתי לא ירדו לעומק דברי הראשונים בזה.

From here, R. Babad launches into an analysis of the Talmudic pericope in b. Ketubot:

> The Gemara in b. Ketubot (72a) states [quoting the Mishnah's definition of a woman who violates *dat Yehudit*]:
>
> גרסינן בגמרא כתובות דף ע"ב [ע"א]
>
>> What is *dat Yehudit*? She goes out with her hair undone. [But going out with] her hair undone is a Torah prohibition! For it is written: "And he shall expose the hair of the woman" (Num. 5:18); and the school of R. Ishmael taught: "This is a warning to the daughters of Israel not to go out with their hair exposed"!
>>
>> ואיזה דת יהודית יוצאה וראשה פרוע ראשה פרוע דאורייתא הוא דכתיב ופרע ותנא ר' ישמעאל אזהרת לבנות ישראל לצאת בפרוע ראש
>
> [The Gemara] answers:
>
> ומשני
>
>> As a matter of Torah law a *kalta* would be sufficient, *dat Yehudit* even a *kalta* would be insufficient.
>>
>> דאורייתא קלתא שפיר דמי דת יהודית אפילו קלתא נמי אסור.
>
> This is the section we need for our analysis.
>
> ע"כ הצריך לעניננו.

Having quoted the key passage in the Talmud, he turns to the Rashba's analysis:

> Now, the *Shita Mekubetzet* – in his gloss on the second chapter of Ketubot, regarding the case in which she says "I was a virgin when you married me, etc." that if there are witnesses that she went out in *hynuma* with her hair undone, her ketubah is two hundred – brings the Rashba's challenge:
>
> והנה השיטה מקובצת בפרק האשה שנתארמלה בהאי דאמרינן דהיא אומרת בתולה נשאתני וכו' דאם יש עדים שיצאת בהינומא וראשה פרוע דכתובתה מאתים, מביא קושיא בשם הרשב"א וז"ל,
>
>> "Hair undone" means uncovered, and this is how a virgin would appear [at her wedding] but not a widow (=previously married woman). But that which we say [in a different Talmudic passage] "and he should undo the woman's hair" and the school of R. Ishmael taught: "This
>>
>> וראשה פרוע פירוש מגולה וכך היו נוהגין לבתולה ולא לאלמנה, והאי דאמרינן ופרע את ראש האשה ותנא דבי רבי ישמעאל אזהרה לבנות ישראל שלא יצאו בפרועות ראש איכא

is a caution to all Jewish women not to appear in public with their hair undone" [which implies all women, not just married women] – one could suggest it is only talking about married women. – This [point] is from a collection of Geonic writings.

למימר בנשואות קמיירי, ליקוטי הגאונים, עכ"ל.

According to Rashba in the name of the Geonim [as quoted in the *Shita Mekubetzet*], only married women must cover their hair, and that is clear from the simple meaning of the passage about weddings – which assumes that a virgin getting married appears with her hair undone. R. Babad next moves to the *Shulchan Arukh* and the *Magen Avraham*:

These are the words of the *Shulchan Arukh* in *OC* 75:2:

ז"ל המחבר באו"ח סי' ע"ה סעיף ב',

The hair of a woman which it is her way to cover, it is forbidden to recite Shema before it. [*A gloss: even if she is one's wife.*] However, virgins, whose way it is to go with their hair undone, it is permitted.

שער של האשה שדרכה לכסות אסור לקרות ק"ש כנגדן ⟨הג"ה רמ"א אפילו אשתו⟩ אבל בתולות שדרכן לילך פרועות הראש מותר,

And the *Magen Avraham* wrote (#3) *sub versa* "virgins, who generally, etc.":

וכתב המג"א ס"ק ג' ד"ה בתולות שדרכן כו', וז"ל:

This is a problem, since in *Even HaEzer* 21:1, he (=the *Shulchan Arukh*) wrote that Jewish women should not go out with their hair undone in the market place, "whether they are single or married." This is also what the Rambam wrote in Chapter 21 of the Laws of Forbidden Relations. Moreover, in Ketubot, towards the beginning of the second chapter, it states: "If she went out to her wedding day with her hair undone" [this is a sign that she is a virgin].

קשה דבא"ע סי כ"א ס"ב כתב לא תלכנה בנות ישראל פרועות ראש בשוק א' פנויות וא' אשת איש וכ"כ הרמב"ם ז"ל בפ' כ"א מהלכות א[סורי] בי[אה], ועוד דאיתא בכתובות רפ"ב אם יצאה בהינומא וראשה פרוע [וזהו סי' שהיתה בתולה],[24]

---

24. These words aren't quoted in the *Sefer Yehoshua*, but they are in the *Magen Avraham* and they are clearly being understood here as well, since otherwise the statement from the Talmud, which is what led to this *Magen Avraham* being quoted here, has no point.

It is unreasonable to suggest that the "single women" referred to [in *EH* 21] means widows, for if that were the case he should have clarified explicitly.

ודוחק לומר דפניות היינו אלמנות דא״כ הוי להו לפרש,

One might suggest that the "undone hair" about which he writes in *Even HaEzer* means that they undo their hair entirely, and go out [with it free-flowing] in the market place, for this is forbidden even for a single woman. And Rashi said as much in his commentary on *Nasso*, on the phrase "and he will undo the hair of the woman" [referring to the law of the *sotah*] (Num. 5:18).

וי״ל דפרועות ראש דכ׳ בא״ע היינו שסותרות קליעות שערן והולכות בשוק דזה אסור אפי׳ בפניות וכן פירש״י פ׳ נשא על ופרע ראש האשה,

Nevertheless, we must admit that a single woman is not forbidden with a Torah prohibition [to go with her hair free-flowing], for if we were to say that the verse [in Numbers] also includes single women, then she would also be prohibited from going in public with her hair uncovered, for it is from this verse that Ketubot Ch. 7 learns the prohibition for Jewish women to go in public with their hair uncovered. Rather, we must say that the verse is not referring to single women, only that it is modest behavior for even virgins not to go out in public that way (i.e., with their hair free-flowing).

ומ״מ צריך לומר דפניות לא מיתסרו מדאורייתא דא״ת דקרא איירי גם בפניות א״כ גם בגילוי הראש תהא אסורה דמהכי ילפינן בכתובות פרק ז׳ שלא תלכנה בנות ישראל בגילוי הראש אלא ע״כ קרא לא איירי בפניות רק שמדות צנועות הוא לבתולות שלא לילך כן עכ״ל.

Having quoted the *Magen Avraham*, whose argument we analyzed at length in the previous chapter, the *Sefer Yehoshua* moves directly to that responsum of the *Panim Meirot* discussed above:

And regarding this the *Panim Meirot* 1:35 wrote that his [the *Magen Avraham's*] words are an anchor that cannot be moved, and that no Torah prohibition exists for single women. Thus, in the case of a woman who became pregnant out of wedlock, covering her hair would only be for her

ועל זה כתב הפנים מאירות ח״א סי׳ ל״ה שדבריו הם יתד בל תמוט, ובפניות אין כאן איסור דאורייתא, ובהרה לזנונים אין זה כי אם לטובתה שלא תיבוש ושלא יהיה חרפה וגדופה לכל עובר אורח, והיכי

benefit, so that she not be embarrassed and not be an object of insult for any passerby. But if she says that she doesn't want this form of social assistance, we listen to her [and she need not cover her hair]. See there for more details.

דאומרת שלא ניחא לה בתקנה כגון זו שומעין לה, יע"ש.

With that, R. Babad has set up the *Magen Avraham*'s position that hair covering is not required for single women, adopted by the *Panim Meirot*, as the presumptive halakha. Of course, unlike the Geonic responsum brought above, this does not deal with the question of whether a betrothed woman counts as married, so it is not immediately clear why the *Sefer Yehoshua* brings this up. Instead of stopping to clarify this, however, he moves on to questioning one of *Magen Avraham*'s points:

I see two surprising claims in the words of the *Magen Avraham*. First, he wants to distinguish between women who coif (or braid) their hair and women who let their hair down. If so, there is a problem: Why does the Gemara in the 7th chapter of Ketubot need to force this distinction "according to Torah law a *kalta* is sufficient, but in *dat Yehudit* appearing with only a *kalta* is forbidden"? It is a forced reading of the Mishnah to interpret the phrase "undone hair" as referring to women whose head is covered with a *kalta*. In truth, "undone hair" implies that their head is entirely exposed. Instead, it could simply make [the *Magen Avraham*'s] distinction and say that according to Torah law, the prohibition is for women to have their hair free-flowing, but according to *dat Yehudit*, it applies even to women whose hair is coiffed, since it was the practice of Jewish women to appear modest and not lewd, and therefore, revealing their braided hair would violate *dat Yehudit*.

ותרי תמיה קא חזינא הכא בדברי המג"א, א' שרצה לחלק בין קליעות שערן לסותרת קליעות שערן, א"כ קשה, למה ליה להמציא בגמרא כתובות פרק ז' דאורייתא קלתא שפיר דמי דת יהודית קלתא נמי אסור, מה שהוא דחוק בלשון המשנה לומר דפריעות ראש היינו מכוסה בקלתה, ובאמת פריעות ראש משמע גילוי הראש, הוי ליה לחלק בזה גופה, דמדאורייתא דוקא בסותרת קליעות שערן הוא דאסור אבל בקליעות שער הוא דמותר, ודת יהודית הוא אף בקליעות שערן הוא אסור, כיון דדרך בנות ישראל לילך בצניעות ולא בפריצות ולכן הוי קליעות שערן מגולה עוברות על דת יהודית,

R. Babad challenges the *Magen Avraham*'s notion of braided hair conforming to Torah law (*dat Moshe*) by pointing out that the Talmud does not make this distinction but uses kalta. Apparently, he is unfamiliar with the *Shevut Yaakov* – since he does not discuss it – who suggests that kalta means braided and is thus exactly what the *Magen Avraham* is saying. In any event, the *Sefer Yehoshua* leaves that question unanswered and moves to a second question:

> Second, how can he answer his own question, and that which was asked by many Rishonim, regarding the opening of the second chapter [of Ketubot] about [a virgin] who goes out in *hynuma* with her hair undone, and Rashi explains "esjevelede" [in Old French], her hair down to her shoulders." It is thus explicit that her hair is exposed, and it would appear this means that her hair is undone. But how could they allow her to violate a Torah prohibition, or at the very least, take her in public in an immodest fashion?
>
> השנית, מה יתרץ על קושיתו וקושיות הראשונים ברפ"ב [דכתובות] דיצא בהינומא וראשה פרוע ובפרש"י איצטבליד"ה שערה על כתיפה, הרי להדיא שהיה מגולה, ולפי הנראה שהוא בסותרות קליעות שער, והאיך עברו על איסור דאורייתא, ועכ"פ הוציאה שלא כמנהג הצניעות.

This question was also dealt with in the *Shevut Yaakov*, who suggests that it is an exception to the rule because of context. (As we saw above, a number of other sources actually suggest that the top of her hair is covered and only the bottom is falling on her shoulders, but this would not help the *Magen Avraham* in any case.) Again, the *Sefer Yehoshua* leaves this question unanswered and moves on to yet a third question, this time on the Gemara itself:

> There is a further problem with trying to understand what the ancients themselves [referenced in the Gemara] were thinking. For this passage is writing about virgins and not previously married women, and we have already written that it would seem that the woman going out in *hynuma* with her hair undone occurred at the time of the marriage after the betrothal. But this is a problem, for why should it be that a betrothed woman may [appear in public with her hair undone] but a married woman may not? Should not a betrothed
>
> ועוד קשה לפי סברתם בדברי הקדמונים גופא, שכתב דברפ"ב מיירי מבתולות ולא מנשואות, הלא כבר כתבנו כפי הנראה דכך היתה הכלה יוצאות בהינומא וראשה פרוע בשעת נשואין ואחר אירוסין, וקשה מאי שנא ארוסה דמותרת ונשואה אסורה, האם אינו חמורה ארוסה כמו נשואה אידי ואידי חייבי מיתות ב[ית] ד[ין] המה. ואדרבה ארוסה בסקילה ונשואה בחנק, והיכן

> woman's [modesty] be treated as strictly as that of a married woman since both of them would receive the death penalty [for adultery]? In fact, a betrothed woman would be stoned [which is more severe] while the married woman would be strangled [which is less severe]. Where do we see a way to distinguish between them so as to allow one to appear in public with her hair undone but not the other?
>
> מצינו לחלק ביניהם שזהו מותרת לילך בפרועות ראש וזהו אסורה,

With this point, R. Babad seems to be moving in the opposite direction to where he started. He began by saying that betrothed women need not cover their hair and now says that this makes no sense since modesty is just as valuable to a betrothed woman as a married woman since they are both forbidden to any man other than their husbands/betrothed. However, he isn't actually backtracking, but laying the ground for his explanation of this rule. To do so, he first continues by showing how the law really doesn't apply to betrothed women despite the fact that on the face of it, it should apply:

> And yet, [the verse] "and you shall undo the woman's hair" is referring to a married woman, since it appears in the passage about the *sotah*, and by definition, she is not a virgin, since [according to halakha] sex with the husband must have preceded sex with the lover. And she also has to be married, since we do not give the drink to betrothed women.
>
> אף באמת ופרע ראש האשה מיירי בנשואה דהא בסוטה כתיב וסוטה על כרחך בעולה הוי, דצריך שתקדים שכיבות בעל לבועל, ונשואה הוית דארוסה אין משקין אותה,

> But even so, why don't we say that since a married woman is forbidden [to appear with her hair undone in public] the same is true of a betrothed woman? Where do we see any reason to distinguish between the two?
>
> מ"מ מדוע לא נימא כיון דנשואה אסורה ארוסה נמי אסורה, ומאין נמצא לחלק ביניהם,

In short, the verse about the sotah is only referring to married women, but ostensibly, the Sages should have extended it to betrothed women, and yet they did not. To make matters worse, he notes that according to at least some authorities, the law has been extended to widows and divorcées, even though their modesty is much less important than that of betrothed women:

> The problem is even worse if we follow the suggestion of the *Chelkat Mechokek* in *Even HaEzer* 21[:2], that "single women" means "widows [or divorcées]." How can we say that single widows are forbidden [to appear in public with their hair undone] but betrothed women, who are by marriage bonded to a man, are permitted? This is entirely backwards! [Literally, "the citizen is on the ground and the alien resident is up in heaven."]

> וביותר לפמ"ש החלקת מחוקק בא"ע סי' כ"א [ס"ק ב'] דפניות היינו אלמנות, האיך נימא דאלמנות פניות אסורות וארוסה דהיא אשת איש מותרת, יציבא בארעא [וגיורא בשמי שמיא].

Having built this edifice, the *Sefer Yehoshua* turns to the *Tur* and the Rosh, first to solidify the truth of his observation, though ultimately, this will allow him to explain the anomaly:

> But in truth, it would seem from the words of the *Tur*, whose words express in his own idiom the words and reasoning of the Rishonim, namely, Rosh, Mordechai and *Hagahot Maimoniyot*, who all had the same idea in mind [here]; it would seem that there is no room for doubt or argument, and it is as if it comes from Sinai, and the words of the Gemara were stated with great precision and one cannot veer from them at all. The words of the *Shulchan Arukh* are the same as those of the *Tur*, and they all have the same intention.

> אבל באמת היה יראה מדברי הטור שהביא דברי הראשונים במחק לשונו ובטעמן של ראשונים, הם הרא"ש והמרדכי והגמ"י, אשר כולם לדבר אחד נתכונו, יראה שאין בזה שום נדנוד ופקפוק, וכאילו ניתנו מסיני, ודברי הגמרא נאמרה בדקדוק גדול אשר אי אפשר לזוז, גם דברי המחבר הם כדברי הטור, וכונה אחת לכולם.

Having made this strident claim about the authority of the *Tur* in this case, the *Sefer Yehoshua* moves on to quote him:

> Here are the words of the *Tur* in *OC* 75:

> וז"ל הטור באו"ח סי' ע"ה,

>> If a handbreadth of a woman's flesh, which she usually covers, is exposed, it is forbidden to recite the Shema before her, even if she is one's wife. Likewise... with the hair of a woman which it is her

>> טפח המגולה באשה במקום שדרכה לכסותה אסור לקרות ק"ש כנגדה וכן וכו' שער של אשה שדרכה לכסותן אסור לקרות

way to cover – it is forbidden to recite [the Shema] before them. However, for virgins, whose way it is to go with their hair undone, it is permitted.

כנגדן[25] אבל בתולה שדרכן לילך פרועות ראש מותר עכ"ל

He repeats here thrice, with the revealed handbreadth, he wrote "which it is her way to cover" and regarding the hair as well he wrote "it is their way to cover," and regarding the virgin "it is their way to appear with hair undone."

הרי דשינה ושילש, בטפח המגולה כתב שדרכה לכסותה, והשער נמי כתב שדרכן לכסות, ובבתולה שדרכן לילך פרועות ראש.

Here the *Sefer Yehoshua* picks up on a key point: The *Tur* always phrases the prohibitions and permissions as expressing what the women generally do. This implies that what establishes the requirements is the standard practice of women and not an abstract dress code unrelated to time and place. Thus, the *Sefer Yehoshua* lays out the core principle:

The general principle at work here regarding what counts as [a woman] revealing nudity is that anything that women are expected to cover and she reveals counts as nudity. But if women do not generally cover something [and she reveals it], this does not count as nudity at all, since everyone is used to women appearing with that part uncovered.

והכלל כי בזה תלוי גילוי הערוה, אם הוא דרך לכסות בנשים והיא מגלה הרי זה ערוה, אבל באם לא היה דרכן לכסות לא הוי בגדר ערוה כלל כיון שכולם רגילים לילך בדבר א' מגולה.

R. Babad's maneuver here is both simple and revolutionary. It is simple since it expresses the essence of what the early Ashkenazi Rishonim stated about virgins not covering their hair that we analyzed at length in Chapter 5. It also fits with the analysis of Maharam Al-Ashkar, discussed at the beginning of this chapter. It is revolutionary because until the *Sefer Yehoshua*, no authority formulated this explicitly as a rule, and certainly not as the core principle upon which the laws of modesty as a whole are built.

To clarify what he is saying, the *Sefer Yehoshua* offers an example in addition to discussing hair covering, which, of course, is his main point:

---

25. The *Tur* actually says here כנגדו, before "it," meaning the hair, not the person. Maybe the word should be כנגדה based on the manuscripts.

For example, if they generally cover their hands or face, then if they reveal a handbreadth from these generally covered places, this counts as revealed nakedness, and one could not recite the Shema in their presence.

דרך משל, אם דרכן לכסותו ידיהם או פניהם אז אם מגלות טפח במקום שדרכן לכסות הוי גילוי ערוה ואסור לקרות כנגדן,

The same applies to hair; it counts as revealing nakedness assuming they generally cover it. But if [married] women would generally reveal their hair, or a handbreadth of their bodies, like virgins whose practice it is to appear in public with their hair revealed – this would not count as revealing nakedness.

וכמו כן בשערן הוי גילוי ערוה אם דרכן לכסות, אבל אם מנהגן לגלות שערן או טפח בגוף כמו הבתולות שדרכן לילך בגילוי הראש אין זה גילוי ערוה,

And the same is true in places where women appear in public with their face or hands uncovered; this is not nudity since this is their practice. But if it was not their practice to appear with these parts revealed, but one woman in particular would reveal her hidden parts, it would be forbidden to recite the Shema in her presence.

וכמו כן במקומות שנשים הולכות הפנים וידיהם מגולות אין זה ערוה כיון דדרכן בכך, ואם לא היה דרכן לילך בגילוי והיתה נמצאת אחת אשר גילתה מסתוריה היה אסור לקרות כנגדה משום ערוה,

R. Babad continues by stating that this is the exact intent of the *Tur* and the Ashkenazi Rishonim, and adds further quotes to support this:

Look there [in the *Tur*] carefully, and you will see these things are as clear as the sun at noon.

יעיין שם ויראה שדברים הללו ברורים כשמש בצהרים.

And this is explicit in the Rosh, Chapter 3 of Berachot, 24[a]:

וכן הוא להדיא בהרא״ש בפ״ג דברכות דף כ״ד [ע״א]

> R. Yitzchak said: "A handbreadth of [exposed flesh] on a woman [is nudity]," Rav Sheshet said: "A woman's hair is nudity," referring to those whose practice it is to cover their hair, but virgins, whose practice it is to appear in public with their hair undone – it is permitted to recite the Shema in their presence.

אמר ר' יצחק טפח באשה וכו' א״ר ששת שער באשה ערוה בנשים שדרכן לכסות שערן אבל בבתולות שדרכן לילך פרועות מותר לקרות כנגדן עכ״ל,

Similarly, in the *Hagahot Maimoniyot*, in Chapter 3 of the Laws of Reciting Shema,

וכן הוא בהגמיי׳ בפ״ג מהלכות ק״ש מציין שם בהלכה ט״ז

PARTIAL UNCOVERING AND HAIR COVERING

he notes there in law 16, *sub versa* "and the Behag explained...":

ד"ה ופי' בה"ג וכו'

> All these [cases of nudity] refer specifically to places that are not generally exposed. But we are not concerned about [reciting Shema before] a virgin, whose practice it is to appear in public with her hair uncovered, for it will not excite fantasy. The same is true for voice, when he is used to it.

> וכל אלה דווקא שאין רגילין להגלות אבל בתולה הרגילה לילך בגילוי שער לא חיישינן דליכא הרהור וכן בקול ורגיל בו,

The Mordechai also wrote the same thing, and the *Beit Yosef* quoted all this in summary fashion.

וכן כתוב המרדכי, והביא הבית יוסף הכל שם בקצרה.

With that, the *Sefer Yehoshua* has demonstrated that his principle is really that of the Ashkenazi Rishonim. And thus, he moves on to reiterating his position and summarizing its main features:

> The basic axiom upon which all depends is that any part of the body which is always seen, and which it is not the common practice [of women] to cover, and which men are used to seeing, is not considered *erva*; people are not stirred by such because they are used to seeing it, and no biblical prohibition is involved at all [in uncovering them]. But when body parts are customarily covered, then even if they are partially exposed, men find this stirring; therefore, these [parts] are considered *erva* and it is biblically prohibited [to uncover them].

> וזהו הוא יתד שהכל תלוי בו, שכל דבר הנראה תמיד ואין דרכן לכסותן ורגילין בהו אנשים, אין זה ערוה ואין בני אדם מתגרים בהם מפני שרגילין בכך, ואין כאן מדאורייתא איסור כלל, אבל במה שמנהג לכסותן אז בהתגלות קצת מתגרים בני אדם מהם אז ערוה מיקרי ואסור מדאורייתא,

Having reasserted his axiom, he moves back to his critique of the *Magen Avraham*'s distinction between free-flowing hair and uncovered hair:

> According to this, no essential distinction can be made between women who go out with braided hair or with their hair free-flowing; since women's practice [nowadays] is to cover their hair, [their uncovered hair even if coiffed or braided]

> ולפ"ז אין חילוק בין קליעות שער לסותרין קליעות שערן, כיון דדרך הנשים לצאת בכל שערותיהן מכוסה הוי בהו ערוה ואסור מדאורייתא,

is considered *erva* and it is a Torah prohibition to appear in public this way.

R. Babad rejects the idea that the Torah prohibition can be limited to an "objective" rule such as doing up one's hair, since everything depends on societal norms. Having established this, he turns back to the Talmudic pericope to deal with the question he posed earlier, that he claimed could not be answered according to the *Magen Avraham*'s reading:

This is why the question asked in b. Ketubot 72 is a good one, for how can [the Mishnah] say that undone hair is a violation of *dat Yehudit*, since women's practice is to cover their hair entirely, braided and pinned up in a *kalta* and covered in a cloth? If so, then their undoing their hair must be a violation of a Torah law!	ולכן מקשים שפיר בכתובות ע״ב דהאיך תאמר דפריעת הראש הוי דת יהודית כיון דדרכן של נשים לצאת מכוסה ראשיהם לגמרי אפילו קליעות בקלתה ובדדיד מכוסה, א״כ הוי פריעת ראשן פי׳ מקלעת שער איסור דאורייתא,
[The Gemara] was thus impelled to answer that according to Torah law, having one's hair exposed but in a *kalta* is sufficient, but according to *dat Yehudit* even in a *kalta* would be forbidden, since the practice of women was to go out with their hair covered by head scarves specifically, then in that era in particular going with only a *kalta* was considered to be brazen, and women who did so violated *dat Yehudit*. But were it the practice of all Jewish women to go with their heads entirely uncovered, there would be no prohibition at all, even for married women to go out this way.	ולכן הוכרח לתרץ דאורייתא פרועי ראש הא קלתא שפיר דמי ודת יהודית אפי׳ קלתא נמי אסורה כיון שנוהגין לצאת ברדידין דוקא אז הוי קלתא חציפות והוי עוברות על דת יהודית, אבל אי הוי נוהגין כל בנות ישראל לצאת בפרעיות לא הוי שום איסור אפילו בנשואות לצאת בכך,
It is only that the Gemara proves from that fact that the verse says "and he undoes the woman's hair" that this married woman must have had her hair covered before this, and that is how the women would practice. And this the authors of the Gemara knew as a fact, that women cover all their hair with a *kalta* and headscarves; if so, women exposing their hair violate a Torah prohibition and not merely *dat Yehudit*,	אלא דהגמרא מוכיח מדכתיב ופרע את ראש האשה מכלל שער עתה הכלה בכיסוי, והיינו כמו שנהגו כל הנשים, וכן הוא האמת ידעו בעלי הגמרא שמכסים כל שערותיהן בקלתא וברדידין, א״כ הוי פריעות ראשן ערוה אסור מדאורייתא ולא מדת יהודית, לכן צריך לומר דדת

therefore, [the Gemara] had to say that *dat Yehudit* applied if they were wearing only a *kalta*, and this has been made clear with God's help.

יהודית היינו קלתא, וזהו ברור בעזה"י,

Having explained the Talmudic passage to his satisfaction, the *Sefer Yehoshua* moves on to make his most extreme statement:

Even were the opposite to be the case, that married women went with their heads uncovered and single women covered their hair, it would be forbidden for single women to go without their heads covered, but permissible for married women.

ואף אם היה בהיפוך שתלכו נשואות בגילוי ובתולות מכוסין היו בתולות אסורה ונשואות מותרות,

According to this formulation, women's practice is the only factor for determining when hair covering is required; thus if the practice ended up being the opposite, this would be the halakha as well, and this goes for the Torah prohibition as well as the *dat Yehudit* prohibition.

Having established this principle, R. Babad can now answer his question about why halakha distinguishes between betrothed and married women for hair covering:

According to this, there is no problem at all with why a betrothed woman is treated not like a married woman but like a single woman [for hair covering], since it is all dependent on how women dress in practice; note this carefully.

ולפ"ז אין כאן שום קושיא מארוסה לנשואה ופנויה, דהכל תלוי במנהג הנשים, ודוק היטב.

In other words, the very premise of the question was off. There is no reason other than social habit for covering or uncovering hair, as a general rule. Betrothed women don't happen to cover their hair, so no specific betrothed woman has to. The only rule is that a woman should appear in public the way the average woman appears in public in her society. Totally flouting those norms would violate a Torah prohibition and partial flouting violates *dat Yehudit*.

Armed with this understanding of the halakha, the *Sefer Yehoshua* turns back to the position of the Geonim quoted (in the name of Rashba) above:

And now the words of the Geonim which the *Shita Mekubetzet* quoted above are

ומהשתא דברי הגאונים שהביא השיטה מקובצת ברורים

as clear as day: the case of going out with *hynuma* while her hair is exposed is referring specifically to virgins, since virgins would appear in public with their hair exposed. Similarly, betrothed women would appear in public with their hair exposed until their marriage. Since that is how they would appear, [their hair] would not be considered *erva* at all, and there is no prohibition in this behavior, which is not the case with married women, whose practice it was to cover their hair, and thus, exposed hair for them would be *erva* and a violation of Torah law.

דהאי דיצאת בהינומא וראשה פרוע בבתולות מיירי ובתולות דרכן לילך פרועי ראש, וכמו כן ארוסות דרכן לילך בפריעות ראש עד עת נישואין שלהם, וכיון שדרכן לילך כך לא הוי לגבייהו ערוה כלל ואין כאן שום איסור בהו, משא"כ נשואות דדרכן לכסות הוי פרועות ראש לגבייהו ערוה ואסור מדאורייתא,

The *Sefer Yehoshua* next notes how this answers the strange law applying the requirement of hair covering to widows and divorcées but not to betrothed women:

According to this, since it is the way [of] married women, even if they are single because of being widowed or divorced, since their practice is to cover their heads with a scarf, it is a Torah prohibition for them to appear in public with their hair uncovered, since in their case, since they are not accustomed to appear this way, it is considered *erva* when they reveal their hair, and this is forbidden according to the Torah.

ולפ"ז כיון דדרכן [של] נשואות אף שהם אלמנות וגרושות פנויות כיון שכבר נהגו לכסות ראשן בצעיף, אסורים מדאורייתא לילך בפריעות ראש, דלגבייהו כיון שאינן הרגילות בכך ערוה מקרי כשמגלין שער ראשן ואסורין מדאורייתא,

In short, the practice itself need not make sense: the only rule is that women follow it and appear dressed "normally," i.e., in whatever way the average women in their situation in society would appear in public. This, R. Babad, believes, solves all the problems he mentioned earlier:

Thus, all the problems [mentioned above] are solved, and this is certainly the intention of the *Shulchan Arukh* in [OC] 75. And anyone who looks at the matter will judge properly that what I argued above is the *Shulchan Arukh*'s intention, and my words do not veer from those of the Rishonim at all, as everything flows in the same direction.

וסרו כל התלונות ובוודאי גם זו כוונת המחבר בסי' ע"ה, וכל מעיין בצדק ישפוט שלדברים הללו כיון המחבר ולא זז מדברי הראשונים כלל, והכל הולך אל מקום אחד.

And now you will see that the words of the *Chelkat Mechokek* in [EH] 21 are correct and clear, in which he wrote: "whether single or married refers to a woman who is not a virgin, etc." and the *Beit Shmuel* wrote: "whether single refers to a widow or divorcée." And these fit with what I have written, and it all makes the same point.	ועתה תראה שדברי החלקת מחוקק בסי' כ"א נכונים וברורים במה שכתב אחד פנויות ואחד אשת איש היינו בעולה קאמר וכו' עכ"ל, והבית שמואל כתב פנויה היינו אלמנה וגרושה, והיינו כמ"ש והכל אחד הוא.

This last point reflects what we called the "strict elision" model in Chapter 6, except its basis is not an abstract connection between non-virgins and previously married women, but a [presumed] reality that both sets of women do, in fact, cover their hair.

Having solved the halakhic sources, including the *Shulchan Arukh* and its commentarties, to his own satisfaction, the *Sefer Yehoshua* returns to the position of the *Panim Meirot* quoted above that a single woman who became pregnant need not cover her hair since she isn't technically married:

For this reason, there is no room for the theory put forward by the *Panim Meirot* referenced above, for women who have become pregnant out of wedlock always cover their hair, and that being the case it is as a consequence, forbidden according to the Torah [for them to appear in public with their hair uncovered], as we explained.	ומטעם זה אין מקום לדברי הפנים מאירות הנ"ל, דכיון דדרכן של נשים מעולם לכסות ראש הרה לזנונים, וכיון שכן דרכן (תנאסורה) [תו אסורה] מדאורייתא כמו שביארנו,
And there is no distinction between women who have sex out of wedlock and widows and divorcées at all, and we force her to cover her hair since her revealing her hair in public violates a Torah prohibition, which is not the case for betrothed women, whose practice it is to appear in public with their hair exposed, and thus, they have no need to cover it.	ואין חילוק ביני הזונות לבין נשואות ואלמנות וגרושות כלל וכלל, וכופין אותה לכסות ראשה מפני שגילוי שער שלה אסור מדאורייתא, משא"כ ארוסות דדרכן לילך בגילוי הראש אין צריכין לכסות.

R. Babad's disagreement with the *Panim Meirot* is based on sociology. He argues that since women who have children out of wedlock generally cover their hair, then doing so is a halakhic requirement, and even if a given woman would rather not, she must. This even has the force of a Torah law, even though, in theory, if mothers who had children out of wedlock practiced differently, and did not cover their hair, then it would not even be a rabbinic obligation to do so.

With that, the *Sefer Yehoshua* can return to the case at hand:

> According to this, since we have already clarified that according to the Rishonim, betrothed women may appear in public with exposed hair, the fact that this woman covered her hair is not evidence that she has been betrothed. For what kind of proof can this be for betrothal, since even if she were betrothed, she would not need to cover her hair, so what she did is just an act with no significance and has no ramifications.

> ולפ"ז כיון שכבר ביארנו דדעת הראשונים דהארוסות יצאת בראש פרוע, אין מזה שכיסתה את ראשה שום ראיה להיות מתקדשת, [ד]מאי ראיה הוא זה לקידושין כיון דאפילו נתקדשה א"צ כיסה ראשה, ועשיות דבר בעלמא הוא ואינו כלום,

Knowing that there is still room for argument, R. Babad takes note of what he imagines the opposition will say and responds to this as well:

> Now, do not suggest that since we only do a betrothal ceremony together with the *chuppah*, consequently betrothal on its own is an unusual event, and in matters that are uncommon the concept of custom is not relevant, as the Rama says in *Choshen Mishpat* [331:1] – for this is not the case. Since the custom of Jewish women for centuries was that virgin women who were betrothed would not cover their hair before the *chuppah*, if so, even in our society, in which we do not perform independent betrothal ceremonies, nevertheless, if one were to betroth independent of a marriage ceremony, the ancient practice [of betrothed women leaving their hair uncovered] remains in effect, since no opposite practice has arisen to conflict with the ancient custom. And this needs no proof.

> ואין לומר כיון דלדידן דאינו מקדשין כי אם בחופה, וא"כ קידושין כי הני מלתא דלא שכיחא, ובדבר שאינו מצויה לא שייך בו מנהג כמ"ש הרמ"א בחוה"מ סי' (ל"ז) [של"א סעיף א'], זה אינו, כיון שמנהגן של ישראל שנהגו כדורות הראשונים בקידושין שקודם החופה היו שלא לכסות ראשן של בתולות ארוסות, א"כ ניהו דאין מקדשין, מ"מ אי איתרע באחד שקידש המנהג הראשון קיים, כיון שלא נשתנו בפועל נגד המנהג של הראשונים, ואין צריך ראיה,

Here, R. Babad has added something new: In the absence of any social practice to determine norms, halakha reverts to previous generations and what was considered proper then. Perhaps his implicit assumption is that this forms a kind of baseline, which can be utilized as precedent, and likely would be the starting point if ever Jewish practice returned to independent betrothals. Thus, even if a woman were to be betrothed and not immediately married, standard practice as established by precedent would be that she need not cover her hair.

He continues briefly with some further pieces of evidence:

I have further proofs of this from the Bible, [specifically] from Rebekah and Tamar. In a commentary called *Zera Avraham*, [the author] brings there, in *Parashat Chayei*, from a midrash called א״ז, that that with which Rebekah covered herself was a *hynuma*, and it appears that until he [Isaac] approached, her hair was uncovered since she was [only] betrothed. But I have already expounded on this matter too much, and this is not the place for it. And the wise person will understand why here I prefer only to mention this point in passing.[26]	ועוד יש לי ראיות מן המקרא מרבקה ותמר, והביא בפירוש הנקרא זרע אברהם שם בפרשת חיי במדרש בשם א״ז דהאי דכיסתה רבקה היא הינומא, ונראה דעד ביאתו היה ראשה מגולה כי ארוסה היתה, והרחבתי בזה הדיבור ואין כאן מקומינו, והמשכיל יבין לאשר כאן אהבתי את הקיצור.

Though "modesty" is an ironic concept in Tamar's case, since she was seducing her father-in-law dressed like a harlot, perhaps the argument is more about how she was, in her own mind at least, performing a levirate marriage, if not technically – he did not know who she was – then at least conceptually. In the case of Rebekah, the *Sefer Yehoshua* spells out the point: she was only betrothed before she met Isaac, so she did not cover her hair. But, once she saw Isaac, and he was going to take her to

---

26. I do not know the midrash to which he refers, nor do I know what book he means by *Zera Avraham* and which midrash is implied by the acronym *aleph zayin*. While this article was in galleys, the ever thoughtful Gershon Klapper suggested that the reference to "Zera Avraham" was to the *Zera Avraham* commentary by Abraham Helin of Głogów to the Midrash Rabbah, noticing that in the 1725 first edition הינומא is also misspelled נהומא. However, Genesis Rabbah (*Chayei Sarah*, 60) notes that Rebekah and Tamar both wore veils, and both had twins, implying that their "modesty" gave them this merit:

"The servant said 'that is my master' and she took the veil and covered herself" (Gen. 24:65) – Two women covered themselves with a veil and gave birth to twins: Rebekah and Tamar. Rebekah – "and she took the veil and covered herself." Tamar – "and she covered herself with a veil" (Gen. 38:14).	ויאמר העבד הוא אדני ותקח הצעיף ותתכס שתים הן שנתכסו בצעיף וילדו תאומים, רבקה ותמר, רבקה ותקח הצעיף ותתכס, תמר ותכס בצעיף (שם /בראשית/ לח יד).

his mother's tent, this was the beginning of their marriage, so she covered her hair.

Having made this point, he returns to summarize the halakha as he sees it, which is in stark contrast with the position of the *Panim Meirot*, with which he polemicizes:

Thus we arrive at the rule, that a betrothed woman need not cover her hair, but promiscuous single women, hear the word of God, should cover their hair, since that has been the practice till now. And a promiscuous woman who is unsatisfied with this matter, it is right to force her; since [covering hair] has been the practice, her revealing her hair is a violation of a Torah prohibition as we explained.	זכינו לדין דארוסה אינה צריכה לכסות שער ראשה, והזונות שמעו נא דבר ה' לכסות ראשן כיון שנהגו כבר בכך, והזונה אשר לא תשבע אל הדבר הזה מהראוי לכפותה כיון שנהגו בכך הוי גילוי שערות גבה איסור דאורייתא כמו שביארנו.

Having come to the opposite conclusion as the *Panim Meirot* regarding a woman who becomes pregnant out of wedlock, the *Sefer Yehoshua* pushes the argument further:

In any case, I don't understand why the *Panim Meirot* wrote that [the rule about non-virgins covering their hair] was for their own good. Maybe it was enacted for the good of all Jewish women. For uncovered hair [at the wedding] is a sign of a virgin, who gets a ketubah of two hundred [*zuz*]. But if all women who had premarital sex would appear in public with their hair uncovered, [then even the virgins] would lose their [larger] ketubot, since their husbands would claim: "I married you when you were no longer a virgin." The orphans would also make this error [claiming that their fathers married these women when they were no longer virgins, even if they were]. And appearing in *hynuma* with hair uncovered would not be a proof of virginity, if non-virgins aren't forced to cover their hair. And the Tosafot in b. Gittin (17b, s.v. "*zenut*") and at the	ובלא"ה לא ידעתי מה שכתב הפנים מאירות דהוא לטובתה נתקן, דלמא לטובת תקנות בנות ישראל תיקנו, דהא האי דראשה פרוע הוא סימן לבתולה וכתובתה מאתים, ואי כל הבעולות הזונות ילכו ג"כ בפרוע, הרי יאבדו כתובתן, דיאמרו בעליהן בעולה נשאתיך, וכן היתומים יטעו כך, והינומא וראשה פרוע אין ראיה נגד בעולות אם לא יכופו אותן לכסות ראשן, והתוס' בגיטין [י"ז ע"ב ד"ה זנות] וברי״ש כתובות [ב' ע"א ד"ה שאם] כתבו דזנות שכיח,

beginning of b. Ketubot (2a, s.v. *"she-im"*) wrote that promiscuity is rampant.

> Moreover, [the reverse would also be the case:] promiscuous women will be able to collect a ketubah payment of two hundred [*zuz*] utilizing the witnesses who saw her appear in *hynuma* [with her hair uncovered], from the orphans or other people with liens, which is against halakha. Therefore, it is my humble opinion that she should be forced to cover her hair, whether this really is a Torah law or whether it is just a [rabbinic] enactment, without concern [that maybe she is not obligated to].
>
> ועוד תוכלו הזונות גם כן להוציא כתובה מאתים בעידי הינומא מיתומים וממלקוחות שלא כדין, לכן נלע"ד לכופה לכסות ראשה אם מדאורייתא ואם מן התקנה בלי פקפוק.

With that, R. Babad completes his argument against the position of the *Panim Meirot*, which, he claims, is not only misguided, but destructive to the practice of *ketubot* for virgins, who are counting on the higher payout.

The *Sefer Yehoshua* ends this section of the responsum with a general statement:

> In the end, this virgin (Roiza) may appear with her hair uncovered like all the other virgins, and there is no smidgeon of prohibition here and nothing about which to complain, whereas promiscuous women must cover their heads. And may God guide me down the path of truth and may no one trip on a stumbling block [because of what I have written].
>
> סוף כל סוף, דהבתולה תגלה ראשה כמו כל הבתולות, ואין בזה שום נדנוד ופקפוק בעזה"י, והזונות כסו יכסו את ראשן. וה' ינחני בדרך האמת ולא יבא ע"י שום מכשול.

The *Sefer Yehoshua*'s main point in this section of the responsum is to argue that betrothed women need not cover their hair; while non-virgins – even if they have never been married – do need to cover their hair. Insofar as halakha is concerned, the former is an academic question, since it is still the case that no one betroths without immediately marrying, and that the latter is certainly not the contemporary practice in any community at all.

Nevertheless, for our purposes, the theory behind the *Sefer Yehoshua*'s decisions is critical, for he is the first to state, explicitly and unequivocally, what I have argued is the clear meaning of the Ashkenazi poskim such as R. Tam and Ra'aviah, as well as the Ra'avad, Maharam Al-Ashkar and others who take these positions.

In short, according to the *Sefer Yehoshua*, these poskim all believe that there is no such thing as an objective definition of *erva* for hair (or possibly anything else other than genitalia). Instead, the halakha is that Jewish women must appear modestly dressed in public. For millennia, this also meant covering hair, or braiding hair, and it applied to married women, though in some societies even single women.

That which we inherited, the distinction between virgins and non-virgins, may be intuitive or not, and may reflect ancient practice or not, but its power comes from the fact that it reflects the social norms of the day. Thus, he argues, if somehow these norms would switch, and only virgins would cover their hair, that would be the halakha – even the Torah law. There is no way to know for sure what R. Babad would say in a society where no women, even very modestly dressed women, cover their hair, and that covered hair only demonstrates that someone is an Orthodox Jew – not that they are modest. Would there be any requirement for any woman to cover her hair? I would venture to say not, since otherwise, the halakha has become entirely circular. (Women do it because it is the halakha and it is the halakha because women do it.)

It is this reading of the Ashkenazi poskim, Ra'avad and Maharam Al-Ashkar, that has led some contemporary authorities to argue that covering hair is no longer a requirement in our society, as we will see in the final chapter.

Excursus Five: The Differences of Modesty for Married and Unmarried Women

As we transition away from the words of the Codes and Acharonim in the previous two chapters to the positions of modern authorities, it is worth elaborating on a view that has disappeared from normative Jewish law in the last century but which helps explain some of the classical practices within the contemporary Jewish community. This note elaborates on Rashi's approach that distinguishes between married and single people for the rules of modesty. It argues that there is Talmudic precedent to recognize a difference between married and single people vis-à-vis matters of sexuality. This view permitted greater erotic activity between people who are single and who were thinking of becoming married – particularly to each other – than is permitted to people who were already married. It is the purpose of this excursus to elaborate on this view.

Rashi, in his commentary on the Talmudic phrase *shok be-ishah erva* ("the calf of a woman is immodest") (Berachot 24a), writes: שוק - באשת איש ("calf: of a married woman"), which is unneeded in the flow of the Talmudic discussion and is only written to make a normative Jewish law point: the rule does not apply to unmarried women. Rashi limits the prohibition of showing her calf to a married woman; the calf of single women can be shown. Similarly, R. Shmuel ben Uri Shraga Phoebus in his classical commentary on the *Shulchan Arukh*, *Beit Shmuel*, when discussing the prohibition of hearing singing voices (*kol be-ishah erva*) in *EH* 21:4, states אבל קול פנויה או קול אשתו מותר, "the voice of a single woman or the voice of one's wife is permitted" (see also *Pri Megadim*, *Mishbetzot Zahav OC* 75:2, and summary of other positions in *Yabia Omer OC* 1:6). Like Rashi, he rules that the singing voice of a married woman is prohibited to all others except her husband, but the singing voice of a single woman is permissible to all. And, of course, the universal Jewish legal practice distinguishes between married women and single women regarding hair, where no substantial contemporary Jewish community directs that single women cover their hair.

In this view there are three categories regarding eroticism and the duty to cover, not two. One category is things that are so sexually charged that nobody should reveal them outside the confines of marital sexuality – one's private parts and those parts of the body connected to the reproductive process. The second area is what we would call secondary areas – hair, voice and leg. These areas are not part of the woman's body (quite literally that is so in two of these areas, and the third one is not on the torso) and are areas that should be covered by a woman who is married precisely because they are parts of one's body or activities that are sufficiently erotic that men look at them and ponder matters of sexuality, but yet are not so erotic that single women may not reveal them. The third category comprises those parts of a woman, such as her speaking voice, or toes or hands or nose or eyes, which are simply not sexually charged at all and which everyone may reveal, married or single.

This school of thought, which has essentially disappeared from modern Jewish law with regard to modesty, has its origins in these words of Rashi and is worthy of understanding for three reasons. First, it explains the practice of close to a millennium regarding hair covering and single women. The custom of single women uncovering their hair can be explained in a variety of ways, as noted throughout this book, but one of them is that single women are entitled to reveal more than married women.

Second, it helps explain a formulation in the *Shulchan Arukh* nicely. In *Even HaEzer* 21:3 it states:

It is permissible to gaze at an unmarried woman to determine if she is fine in order to marry her, whether she is a virgin or has already been intimate. Moreover it is proper to do so; however, one may not look at her in a promiscuous way, and about this it is said: "I made a covenant with my eyes, and how can I look upon a virgin?"[27]	מותר להסתכל בפנויה לבדקה אם היא יפה שישאנה בין שהיא בתולה או בעולה ולא עוד אלא שראוי לעשות כן אבל לא יסתכל בה דרך זנות ועל זה נאמר ברית כרתי לעיני ומה אתבונן על בתולה:

The *Shulchan Arukh* recognizes that people who are not yet married engage in a sort of courtship that has an undertone of sexuality in which people examine whether this is a person whom they are interested in being married to and will be sexually compatible with. In this view, men, in the process of dating, are allowed to look at a woman's legs and ask, "Are those legs appealing to me?" (Whether the word *shok* here means calf or thigh is but a footnote to this issue, but the notion according to Rashi that an unmarried woman reveals more than a married woman makes some sense.) Rashi's view also helps explain why the *Shulchan Arukh* in EH 21:3 expands the Maimonidean formulation (found in *Hilkhot Issurei Biah* 21:3) which only permits a man to look at a woman's face (which Jewish law permits all to reveal) while pondering marriage. Exactly because Rashi permits single women to reveal more than married women, Rabbi Karo deletes the word "face" when he cites this rule in his code.

Finally, this view helps explain why Rabbi Moshe Feinstein's incorporation of the view regarding singing (*Iggerot Moshe OC* 1:26), but limiting this to females prior to puberty, is unduly limiting as a matter of halakha.[28] Rabbi Feinstein's approach seems inconsistent with the basic model of

---

27. Job 31:1
28. Putting aside for this conversation the question of whether a niddah is an *erva*, as that is a vast dispute among the poskim generally: see *Tzitz Eliezer* 6:40:8:8 for a discussion of the issue and the many who rule that a niddah is not an *erva* for these rules.

Rashi: when it comes to matters like those discussed in *EH* 21 (hair, voice, and legs), the word *penuya* (single woman) includes a single woman who is a niddah precisely because such a woman is one who one can marry. Certainly, that is our practice regarding all the other issues discussed in *EH* 21 and the *Beit Shmuel* notes the same for hair, where it is clear that a *betulah* who may uncover is certainly a niddah. More significantly, in this school of thought, there is a recognition of the fact that an obligation to cover recognizes that single women can reveal more of themselves than married women precisely because they are *seeking* to get married and thus a certain amount of lesser sexuality is permissible. That's why מותר להסתכל בפנויה, לבדקה אם היא יפה שישאנה must logically refer to a woman regardless of her niddah status.

Indeed, Rabbi Feinstein builds on this general observation elsewhere and offers a different division that is also important. He argues that there are certain body parts that need not be objectively covered, but are prohibited as they will typically cause improper sexual thoughts. While Rabbi Feinstein does not directly derive from this that revealing these parts will be less problematic for single women than married ones, this middle category can be applied in such a way.[29]

Despite the fact that this view has not been elaborated upon in many of the sources we have examined in the previous chapters, it is a category that explains much of the practices discussed in those sources and will help frame the discussions we will see in the final chapters.

Conclusion

The cases discussed in this chapter, both the case of partial uncovering and hair covering by betrothed women, provide intellectual insight into the obligation of married women and hair covering. Both the case of partial covering and the case of partial marriage provide a variety of

---

29. One can argue that sexual thoughts are more problematic when the subject is a married woman than when the subject is single. (This, for example, is the position of Rabbeinu Yonah (*Iggeret HaTeshuva* 19:20) cited in *Beit Yosef* (*EH* 21) and can be seen as well in *Semak* 30 and *Iggerot Moshe EH* 1:69 and *EH* 1:102.) See also Rabbi Binyamin Zilber in *Torat HaHistaklut*, Chapter 6, and see Rabbi Menashe Klein, *Mishneh Halakhot* 7:235, who rejects any expansive reading of this area of Jewish law. (It is worth adding that a close comparison of the manner in which this area of Jewish law is quoted by Rambam and *Shulchan Arukh* cited above might be reflective of this dispute.)

possible approaches to the duty to cover hair and the general construct of modesty. The basic approach of Maharam Al-Ashkar and the Sefer Yehoshua adopts the clear view that all of modesty and hair covering is societally determined, whereas other views cited in this chapter adopt views that are grounded in objective notions of the obligation both to cover and to be modest. These authorities have set the table for the view that no covering at all is permitted when such covering is unconnected to modest conduct.

CHAPTER 8

Uncovered Hair and Modern Jewish Law: The Objective School Dominates, but Some Modern Authorities Endorse the Subjective Approach

CHAPTER 8 COLLECTS AND SUMMARIZES THE VIEW OF many authorities of the last generations who endorse the subjective approach, while exploring and explaining their view. After noting that the dominant view in contemporary Jewish law endorses a standard that does not bend to subjective societal norms, this collection of authorities provides an additional layer of textual understanding of the Jewish law of modesty.

The Dominant Contemporary View: Hair Covering in Some Form Is Always Mandatory in Public for Married Women

Since the early 1900s (and perhaps even before) it has been the deep and wide consensus of mainstream Jewish law authorities that the obligation for married women to cover their hair is biblical and objective, at least in public. This is the prevalent view of Ashkenazic and Sephardic poskim, whether they live in Israel or in the Diaspora.

This consensus is well demonstrated by simply turning to the *Mishnah Berura* and the *Arukh HaShulchan*. These works were seen as the leading Jewish law authorities of the late 19th and early 20th centuries, and each was compiling his legal code at a time when Orthodox Jewish women generally ceased covering their hair.[1] Both discuss the problem of married

---

1. This is the reality that the *Mishnah Berura*, *Arukh HaShulchan*, *Ben Ish Chai*, and many of the other commentaries mentioned in this chapter are responding to.

women who come to synagogue with their hair uncovered, and while they reached different conclusions on the question of prayer in such cases, their analyses are quite germane to our discussion.

As discussed in Chapter 6, *Shulchan Arukh* rules that a man may not recite the Shema while standing in view of a woman's hair which she is accustomed to covering. He may, however, recite the Shema in front of the hair of a single woman when it is normal for her to uncover her hair. Faced with the reality that many married women no longer cover their hair, these two Jewish law giants discuss the obvious problem that emerges: how can a man recite Shema in the presence of these women?

In this context, Rabbi Epstein in the *Arukh HaShulchan* laments[2] that for many years married women have been ignoring the halakhic requirement to cover their hair. He decries the fact that in his own day this shameful state of affairs has become endemic. Despite this change in social norms (for the worse, in his view), Rabbi Epstein rules that men may now pray and recite Shema in front of a married woman's uncovered hair, since seeing such hair is no longer erotic. To support this contention, Rabbi Epstein cites the 13th-century authority Mordechai ben Hillel HaKohen (known as the Mordechai) who quotes Rabbi Eliezer ben Yoel HaLevi (known as the Ra'aviah): The Mordechai rules that an unmarried woman's hair is not considered a form of *erva* which would normally prevent men from being able to recite the Shema. This is because men are so accustomed to seeing it that it does not lead to improper thoughts, and the common custom is for unmarried women to uncover their hair.[3] The *Arukh HaShulchan* extends this logic to the hair of married women as well. Because men are long-accustomed to seeing uncovered hair of

---

Rabbi Yaakov Brecher, in his *Katuv Yosher Divrei Emet* p. 87, writing in this period, attests to the fact that women were not covering their hair in France, Germany, Italy, Austria, Bukovina, half of Galicia, many other European countries, and America.

2. See:

ועתה בואו ונצווח על פרצות דורינו בעוונותינו הרבים שזה שנים רבות שנפרצו בנות ישראל בעון זה והולכות בגילוי הראש וכל מה שצעקו על זה הוא לא לעזר ולא להועיל ועתה פשתה המספחת שהנשואות הולכות בשערותן כמו הבתולות אוי ולנו שעלתה בימינו כך מיהו עכ"פ לדינא נראה שמותר לנו להתפלל ולברך נגד ראשיהן המגולות כיון שעתה רובן הולכות כך והוה כמקומות המגולים בגופה וכמ"ש המרדכי בשם רא בי"ה בסס"ג וז"ל כל הדברים שהזכרנו לערוה דוקא בדבר שאין רגילות להגלות אבל בתולה הרגילה בגילוי שיער לא חיישינן דליכא הרהור עכ"ל וכיון שאצלינו גם הנשואות כן ממילא דליכא הרהור]והרי"ף והרמב"ם השמיטו לגמרי דין שיער וקול משום דס"ל דלאו לק"ש איתמר עב"י[:

3. Mordechai on Berachot, end of the third chapter, quoted above in Chapter 5.

even married women, there is no fear of improper thoughts upon seeing such sights during prayer. Thus, a married woman's hair is not considered nakedness, and prayers may be said while in sight of it. However, Rabbi Epstein holds that uncovering remains a sin.

The exact opposite approach is taken by the *Mishnah Berura*. Indeed, quoting his words might help highlight his approach. He states:

And you should further know that even if this woman and her friends in that place have a practice of going out with their hair [literally "head"] uncovered in public in the way of those who are immodest, it is still forbidden [to pray in their presence] no different than the case of uncovered calf [thigh]⁴ which is forbidden under all circumstances. As we have explained in note 2 above, since this woman is required to cover her hair by operation of Jewish law (and this involves a Torah prohibition, because the verse says "And he shall uncover the woman's head," which implies that her hair was covered initially), and also all Jewish women who observe Torah law have been careful about this from the time of our ancestors a long time ago until the present day, uncovered hair is considered a nakedness and it is forbidden to pray in its presence. The *Shulchan Arukh* does not mean to imply [otherwise] by mentioning single women who are permitted to go with their heads uncovered no matter what or [that even married women] can have some exposed hair outside their covering, since whether this is permissible or not all depends on the custom of the place. If the	ודע עוד דאפילו אם דרך אשה זו וחברותיה באותו מקום לילך בגילוי הראש בשוק כדרך הפרוצות אסור וכמו לענין גילוי שוקה דאסור בכל גווני וכנ"ל בסק"ב כיון שצריכות לכסות השערות מצד הדין [ויש בזה איסור תורה מדכתיב ופרע את ראש האשה מכלל שהיא מכוסה] וגם כל בנות ישראל המחזיקות בדת משה נזהרות מזה מימות אבותינו מעולם ועד עתה בכלל ערוה היא ואסור לקרות כנגדן ולא בא למעט רק בתולות שמותרות לילך בראש פרוע או כגון שער היוצא מחוץ לצמתן שזה תלוי במנהג המקומות שאם מנהג בנות ישראל בזה המקום ליזהר שלא לצאת אפילו מעט מן המעט חוץ לקישוריה ממילא בכלל ערוה היא ואסור לקרות כנגדן וא"ל מותר דכיון שרגילין בהן ליכא הרהורא וכדלקמיה

---

4. The Talmud defines the *shok* as an *erva* in b. Berachot 24a. The commentaries debate whether the *shok* refers to the thigh or the calf. I have translated *shok* as thigh here in accordance with the position of the *Mishnah Berura* himself in 75:2 following the opinion of the *Pri Megadim Orach Chayyim* 75:1. See, however, *Bach Orach Chayyim* 75 s.v. *vi-khen*, who defines it as calf. The *Chazon Ish Orach Chayyim*

custom in this place is that all Jewish women are careful not to reveal even the tiniest part of their hair, then, when revealed, it is considered as a form of nakedness and it is forbidden to pray in its presence. Do not say that such is permitted since once one is used to it exposed it does not generate erotic thoughts as I explain later on.[5]

Whatever the merits of this dispute – and most Jewish law authorities side with the *Arukh HaShulchan* on this narrow dispute[6] – what is clear is that nearly all post–1850 Jewish law decisors rule that married women are required to cover their hair in public. One is hard-pressed to find a leading Jewish law authority who disagrees with the views of these two great authorities of Jewish law.

In the last generation, the list of Jewish law authorities who rule that married women must cover their hair in public includes almost a *who's who* of normative Jewish law as well as almost every other Jewish law authority of any important renown in the last century.[7] Included on this list:

1. Rabbi Moshe Feinstein[8]
2. Rabbi Ovadia Yosef[9]
3. Rabbi Shlomo Zalman Auerbach[10]
4. Rabbi Eliezer Yehuda Waldenberg[11]
5. Rabbi Yitzchak Weiss[12]
6. Rabbi Yechiel Yaakov Weinberg[13]

16:8 leaves the debate unresolved. Some contemporary authorities have accepted the strict view. See, for example, Rabbi Shmuel Wosner in *Shevet HaLevi* 1:1. See my comments on pages 195 and 393 as well as many other places in the book.

5. *Mishnah Berura* 75:10. The final reference is to 75:13.
6. See, for example, *Yabia Omer Orach Chayyim* 6:13, *Iggerot Moshe Orach Chayyim* 1:39 and 1:42.
7. For a fuller list, see *Otzar HaPoskim, Even HaEzer* 21:4.
8. *Iggerot Moshe, Even HaEzer* 1:53, 57
9. See, e.g., *Yechaveh Daat* 5:62; see also *Yabia Omer, Even HaEzer* 3:21 and 4:3.
10. In *Aleihu Lo Yibol* (*OC* 59) and as cited in *Halichot Shlomo* 2:17, and *Ohr LeTzion* 2.
11. *Tzitz Eliezer* 6:48 and 7:48.
12. *Minchat Yitzchak* 6:106.
13. *Seridei Eish* 3:30.

Indeed, the modern classical work on Jewish family law, *Otzar HaPoskim*, does not cite any Jewish law authorities who disagree with this view.[14] Nevertheless, they are out there, and their existence is a driving force behind this book as a whole and this chapter in particular.

There are, in my view, a plethora of Rishonim, codifiers, and Acharonim who advance rationales that permit married women to uncover their hair in a society where such is not immodest; in fact, these authorities and their views were discussed at length in the previous chapters. However, these authorities were dealing with theory and were thus merely advancing rationales that could explain such behavior, rather than discussing the contemporary reality of uncovering.

Their theoretical construct, which was made clear repeatedly in previous chapters, is that the obligation for married women to cover their hair derives from custom alone. Yet, this position has not been cited (and was, one could argue, ignored) by most Jewish law authorities in the last two hundred years.

I believe this is unfortunate and perhaps even misguided. A careful analysis of the primary sources supports exactly such a view, and this is why the majority of this work has been dedicated to constructing an argument from the primary sources of halakha. Due to the importance of these primary sources, each was divided into sections and elucidated. We also explored the positions of several major Acharonim, such as Maharam Al-Ashkar and *Shevut Yaakov*, who propounded the position that the obligation for married women to cover their hair is driven by custom and not by objective, unchanging standards.

In the remainder of this chapter, we cite many modern authorities who came to similar views. While their interpretations are significant, this group alone cannot challenge a century's worth of leading poskim who rule to the contrary. Nevertheless, the fact that some modern authorities have reached similar conclusions as those we presented above, whether for the same reasons as we did or not, does lend a measure of support to the practical acceptance of our argument.

We will try to frame the positions of what we might call these counter consensus authorities, but we will not elucidate them in detail (in some cases, barely at all). Rather, we will collect their positions with minimal comment and thus leave it for the reader to complete his or her picture of

---

14. So too, popular works of Jewish law almost never cite any view that hair covering is not mandatory.

the modern halakhic landscape, bearing in mind that these voices, even if they are in the minority, are a part of it.

There is, however, one major authority on a par with the *Mishnah Berura* and *Arukh HaShulchan* who did accept the lenient position. He wrote this not in his main works of halakha, but in a work aimed at the laity. This insight is found in a recently discovered comment of the *Ben Ish Chai*, one of the most important halakhic authorities for many Sephardim and members of *Edot HaMizrach*. The next sections will frame this position.

Ben Ish Chai: The Important Authority Who Permits Married Women Not to Cover Their Hair When Modest Women Do Not

The spread of colonialism into the Sephardic lands and the introduction of Western dress that accompanied it forced 19th- and 20th-century Sephardic poskim to address issues which had heretofore been theoretical. This encompasses a variety of women's issues, including the obligation of married women to cover their hair.[15]

Primary among them was Rabbi Yosef Chayyim of Baghdad (1835–1909), known by the name of one of his works, the *Ben Ish Chai*. Rabbi Chayyim was known throughout the Middle East, East Asia, and Europe as one of the leading halakhists and kabbalists in the world. Born in 1835 into a leading rabbinic family and marrying into another, he was recognized as a leading scholar at a very young age. For a sense of the stature of the *Ben Ish Chai*, see Rabbi Mordechai Eliyahu in his Introduction to *Kitzur Shulchan Arukh* (an edition containing his emendations for Sephardic practice) noting that the *Ben Ish Chai* is the last great authority of Jewish law for Sephardim (*posek acharon*) and should be followed.

Chayyim was a prolific author. He wrote over one hundred works covering the entire gamut of Jewish rabbinic thought. Among the changes to women's daily life he addressed were abortion, increased education, and hair covering, rendering a "lenient" judgment on each.[16] Furthermore,

---

15. See, for example, Yaron Harel, *Syrian Jewry in Transition 1840–1880*, Littman Library of Jewish Civilization, 2014.
16. For his view of abortion, see *Responsa Rav Pealim* (1: EH4) and *Responsa Tzitz Eliezer* (13:102). For his attitude toward women's education, see Ilan H. Fuchs, "'Sephardic' Halakhah? The Attitude of Sephardic Decisors to Women's Torah Study: A Test Case," in Leib Moscovitz, ed., *The Manchester Conference Volume* [=*Jewish Law Association Studies* 20] (The Jewish Law Association, 2010), 43–74. Nonetheless, on most matters of ritual, he tended to be stringent.

he became a significant authority on matters of halakha for the Sephardic community generally.

Ben Ish Chai's treatment of women's hair covering can be found in his work *Sefer Kanun-al-Nissa* (קאנון אל נסא), first published in 1906. What distinguishes this work from all the others previously cited is that it was written for the masses and in the Judeo-Arabic vernacular. In this work, the Ben Ish Chai makes it clear that the obligation for women to cover their hair in public is sociologically dependent. While the general tenor of the work is one which advocates for modesty and covering consistent with the prevailing practice of turn-of-the-century Baghdad,[17] the discussion of sociological changes to the prevailing practice accepted by Jew and gentile alike make clear that as a matter of law, absent licentiousness, societal norms dictate. *Tzniut* thus becomes a matter of propriety and orderliness. What follows is a line-by-line translation of the original Judeo-Arabic. The new translation reads:

| Look at the women of Europe whose custom is not to hide themselves from strangers. Nonetheless their clothes are orderly; they do not reveal their bodies except only their faces, necks, palms, and heads. It is true that their hair is uncovered and this custom of theirs is not possible according to our laws. But, they have one justification. They say, "Yet still, this custom (of having their hair uncovered) was accepted by all their women – both Jewish and gentile – to go with their hair uncovered like the revealing of their faces and hands. It does not cause sexual thoughts in men when they see it with their eyes." These are their words which they answer for this custom and we do not have an answer to push away this answer of theirs. | ושופו נסוואן אהל אירופא. סלוכהום מא יתכבון מן אל גרבא. ומע האדה חוואסהום מרתבא. מא יביין מן גסמהום. גיר פקט וגהום וחלקהום. וכפופהום וראסהום. וצחיח מכשוף שערהום. ומוגב דייאנתנא לם יגוז הל מסלך להום. לאכן אכו פרד עצר ענדהום. יקולון מא זאל האדה מסלך גמיע נסוואן בלאדהום. במלתהום וכארג מלתהום. סאר שוף שערהום. מתל שוף וגהום ואידיהום. מא בקאלו שעשעה ענד אל רייאגיל. בשוף עינהום. האדא כלאמהום. אלדי יגאוובון עלא האדה מסלכהום. ומא ענדנא גוואב נגרח להאדא גוואבהום. |

---

17. See for example the next few paragraphs in the same chapter cited below praising those who remain covered from head to heel even in the extreme heat of the Baghdadi summer, as well as those who veil their faces.

Until recently, this position was not widely known and copies of the original *Kanun* were difficult to find.[18] The most widely circulated Hebrew translation, compiled by Rabbi Ben Tzion Mutzafi and published in 1950 by Machon Ben Ish Chai, has an edited/censored version of the paragraph above. Significantly, he removes the final sentence approving of the rationale set forth by European women for uncovering their hair which makes it clear that the rationale was more than just a *limmud zekhut*.[19]

The ambiguities in the mistranslation caused various translators and interpreters to struggle with the Hebrew "*lo nityashev*." On the one hand, "this custom" must mean the custom to go with hair uncovered as this is the custom under discussion. Yet, it makes little sense to say that the custom to go with hair uncovered was not accepted by the general population. That would run contrary to the argument ostensibly put forth by European women in their own defense. Hence, the ambiguity. The Arabic portion reads: *Ma Zal hada*.... The Arabic *ma* plays a role similar to the Hebrew *lo* which may have caused Mutzafi to translate it as *lo nityashev*. Nonetheless, the expression *ma zal* literally means, "has not ceased," or colloquially, "yet, still." Translated correctly, the paragraph makes sense.

An English translation (presumably based on the aforementioned Hebrew version) of the *Kanun* appeared a few years ago. It diverges from the original to a greater degree than R. Mutzafi's version and actually amends the text to transform the Ben Ish Chai's lenient position into a rather forceful denunciation of the practice.

> One should not think that this law [to dress modestly] is only binding in Islamic countries, where custom dictates that women must

---

18. The material on the Ben Ish Chai was aided by the thoughtful work of Jacob Sasson, entitled "The Ben Ish Hai and Women's Hair Covering: An Interesting Case of Censorship" which can be found at http://text.rcarabbis.org/the-ben-ish-hai-and-women%E2%80%99s-hair-covering-an-interesting-case-of-censorship-by-jacob-sasson/ as well as many conversations with the author, who graciously gave me of his time. This material is derivative of his, and the translations of Judeo-Arabic are his, and I am grateful.

19. This work is entitled *Sefer Chukei HaNashim* and it reads:

והביטו הנשים על אנשי אירופה, מנהגם לא להסתר מפני זרים, ובכל זאת מלבושיהם מסודרים, לא מתגלה מגופם, רק פניהם וצוארם, כפות ידיהם וראשם. ואמת נכון מגולה שערם, ולפי הדין שלנו אסור הדבר, אבל יש להם איזה התנצלות, כי אומרים לא נתיישב המנהג הזה אצל כל נשותיהם, מבנות אומתם וחוץ לאומתם, נעשה גילוי השער, כמו גילוי פניהם וכפות ידיהם, ואינו גורם הרהור אצל האנשים, במבט עיניהם

Otzar HaMizrach 1979 (page 55) available at http://rcarabbis.org/pdf/Sasson_Ben_Ish_Hai_Hebrew.pdf

not be seen by strangers. Even in Europe, where it is acceptable for women to speak to strangers, Jewish women, nevertheless, dress in accordance with the above-mentioned guidelines. And although it is true that many of their women do not cover their hair, which is strictly prohibited according to Torah law, they claim in their defense that uncovered hair is not considered any more immodest than the hands or the feet, since it does not cause Jewish men in Europe to think unclean thoughts. Thus, we see that even those who are lenient about covering the hair agree in principle that a woman must dress modestly, and that other parts of her body must remain covered.[20]

Indeed, a phrase by phrase translation makes it abundantly clear that *Ben Ish Chai* is providing a justification for women to not cover their hair when other modest women do not. He states:

Look at the women of Europe	ושופו נסוואן אהל אירופא.
whose custom is not to hide themselves from strangers.	סלוכהום מא יתכבון מן אל גרבא.
Nonetheless their clothes are orderly; they do not reveal their bodies except only their faces, necks, palms, and heads.	ומע האדה חוואסהום מרתבא. מא יביין מן גסמהום. גיר פקט וגהום וחלקהום. וכפופהום וראסהום.
It is true that their hair is uncovered and this custom of theirs is not possible according to our laws. But, they have one justification.	וצחיח מכשוף שערהום. ומוגב דייאנתנא לם יגוז הל מסלך להום. לאכן אכו פרד עצר ענדהום.
They say "Yet still, this custom (of having their hair *uncovered*) was accepted by all their women – both Jewish and gentile – to go with their hair uncovered like the revealing of their faces and hands.	יקולון מא זאל האדה מסלך גמיע נסוואן בלאדהום. במלתהום וכארג מלתהום. סאר שוף שערהום. מתל שוף וגהום ואידיהום.
It does not cause sexual thoughts in men when they see it with their eyes."	מא בקאלו שעשעה ענד אל רייאגיל. בשוף עינהום.
These are their words which they answer for this custom and we do not have an answer to respond to this answer of theirs. [Omitted from Hebrew]	האדא כלאמהום. אלדי יגאוובון עלא האדה מסלכהום. ומא ענדנא גוואב נגרח להאדא גוואבהום.

---

20. Rabbi Yosef Chaim, *Laws for Women*, translated into English by Moshe Schapiro, edited by S.D. Kaplan, Yeshoua Salem [sic], Salem Books, 5771, p. 96.

Thus, we see that Ben Ish Chai accepted in practice that in a society where women regularly uncovered their hair, such as Europe in his time, it would be permitted to do so. However, it should be noted that his audience was a community where the norm was to be extremely strict about issues of modesty, including hair covering, and thus his ruling was not meant to be practically implemented by the audience to whom it was directed.

Framing Those Who Are Lenient in Practice

Many of the Acharonim who contend that hair covering is subject to communal custom emerge from analysis of the comments of Rashi to Ketubot. To understand their views, we must briefly review Rashi.

As cited above, Rashi explains how the derasha from Numbers works according to the baraita as follows.

A warning –	– אזהרה
a. From the fact that we do this to sully her looks, a tit for tat since she did the same in order to improve her looks for her lover, we can deduce that doing so [for any purpose] is forbidden.	א. מדעבדינן לה הכי לנוולה מדה כנגד מדה כמו שעשתה להתנאות על בועלה מכלל דאסור
b. Alternatively, since the verse states "and he shall expose," one can deduce that up until that point [her hair] was not exposed. One learns from this that it was not the way of Israelite women to go out with their hair exposed – this is the main point.	ב. א״נ מדכתיב ופרע מכלל דההוא שעתא לאו פרועה הות שמע מינה אין דרך בנות ישראל לצאת פרועות ראש וכן עיקר.

Rashi offers two interpretations of how this derasha functions. The first assumes that the humiliating punishment of the woman is intended to be measure for measure by mimicking some forbidden behavior on her part. Her hair is made unattractive because she had beautified herself to seduce her lover. The second explanation argues that the derasha focuses not on why the kohen is uncovering her hair, but rather on the simple fact that he is exposing her. The derasha derives the norm from the exception – if the kohen uncovering the woman's hair is noteworthy, that must be because it is an aberration. Thus, we can conclude that in general Jewish women did cover their hair. Whether that is because this was obligatory, or merely because that was the custom, is the subject of dispute, as we will see.

WHY THE NEED FOR THE TWO EXPLANATIONS?

Many Acharonim were bothered by Rashi's need to present his *first* argument, considering that the second is accepted as primary. Rabbi Pinchas Horowitz (1731–1805, Frankfurt) writes as follows in his commentary to b. Ketubot 72a in his *Sefer Haflaah*:

It seems that in [Rashi's] first formulation, the implication that at that time she was not *parua*, does not make [hair covering] biblical; even though this custom was thus, and the custom was written in the verse, it is not biblical...	נראה דבלשון ראשון ס"ל דמהא דמשמע דההיא שעתא לאו פרוע הוא אין זה נקרא דאורייתא דאע"ג דמנהג הוא כן וכתיב המנהג בקרא אינו דאורייתא...
Furthermore, perhaps it is different in the Temple courtyard, for even on the Temple Mount there was a need to act with added awe, as it says in the Mishnah, "a person should not enter the Temple Mount etc." Even in a synagogue, it is brought in *Shulchan Arukh* (*Orach Chayyim* 91:3) that one should not enter with an uncovered head, even men. [If so,] how could we derive this for other places? According to the first explanation, it makes sense, as the punishment indicates that she sinned originally by uncovering her hair.	ותו דילמא בעזרה שאני דהא אפי' בהר הבית היו צריכין להתנהג באימה יתירה כדאי' במשנה לא יכנס אדם להר הבית וכו', והרי אפי' בבית הכנסת איתא בשו"ע או"ח סי' [צא סע' ג] דלא יכנס בראש מגולה אפי' באנשים ומנ"ל במקום אחר, ולפי' הראשון א"ש דמוכח מהעונש שעשתה עבירה בתחלה בגילוי ראשה.

Rabbi Horowitz assumes that there must have been some inherent weakness in Rashi's second (and accepted) interpretation, which drove Rashi to at least offer an alternative. Rabbi Horowitz offers two reasons regarding why Rashi was not fully convinced by his second explanation:

First, Rabbi Horowitz understands that according to the second explanation of Rashi, the fact that the Torah records the custom of married women to cover their hair grants that custom biblical status. However, Rabbi Horowitz suggests that Rashi entertained the possibility that a custom, even when recorded in the Torah, does not reach the level of law. Assuming this was the case, it would be possible that uncovering hair is not biblically forbidden. Thus, one would need another reason to explain why the Torah included the uncovering of the sotah's hair as part of her punishment process. To explain this, Rashi posits that the adulteress had beautified herself to attract her lover and needed to be punished for that act. Thus, the Torah has the priest make her hair less attractive.

Second, Rabbi Horowitz suggests that Rashi was not convinced one could conclude from the fact that the priest uncovered the sotah's hair in the *Temple* that this indicated that women were *always* required to cover their hair. One could have understood that the obligation for married women to cover their hair was unique to the Temple. If this was the case, again, the verse about the priest uncovering the head of the sotah could not be used to generate a biblical obligation for married women to cover their hair, thus requiring Rashi to offer an explanation that focused on the punishment aspect of the kohen's actions.

This latter argument was rejected by several later Acharonim. R. David b. Isaac Bonan, in his *Dei Hashev* (Livorno 1846), *Even HaEzer* 4, as well as Rabbi Yehuda Herzl Henkin[21] reject the second suggestion of Rabbi Horowitz. They note that the purpose of the sotah process is to humiliate the adulteress. However, they argue, the humiliation is only caused by uncovering a part of the body that is normally private. If the obligation to cover hair was only in the Temple, but outside the Temple women regularly uncovered their hair, this act of uncovering would not cause shame. It would be the modern equivalent of a woman who only covers her hair in synagogue, but wears her hair uncovered at all other times, accidentally being seen with her hair uncovered in synagogue. Such a situation, even if abnormal for her, is unlikely to generate embarrassment. Consequently, Rabbis Bonan and Henkin argue that Rabbi Horowitz's construction is untenable as it would not explain why the uncovering of the hair was part of the humiliation of the sotah.

Even without this rejection, however, the first position of Rashi within this analysis is not relevant for legal purposes, as Rashi rejects it. The above was only needed to explain why Rashi was less than convinced of his final explanation. However, despite his hesitations, Rashi did accept the latter explanation. According to Rabbi Horowitz, based on Rashi's second and preferred interpretation, there would indeed be a biblical obligation for a married woman to cover her hair.[22]

---

21. See "*Shi'ur Kisui Rosh Shel Nashim*," note 31 on page 288.
22. The simplest understanding of *Haflaah* is that he is explaining why Rashi was not fully convinced by his second and preferred explanation but would still accept that for halakhic purposes the second explanation is primary. However, Rabbi Yosef

NETZIV

Rabbi Naftali Tzvi Yehuda Berlin (Netziv) grants the first explanation in Rashi more halakhic weight. In his *Emek HaNetziv* commentary to the *Sifre* (*Nasso* 11) he writes:

> Derived, etc: from the fact that we disgrace her in this manner commensurate to her act of making herself attractive to her lover [by uncovering her head] we can infer that it is forbidden. Alternatively, since Scripture states, "And he shall uncover," we can infer that at that time her head was not uncovered; we thus deduce that it is not the practice of the daughters of Israel to go out with their heads uncovered: this is the main explanation – so writes Rashi, b. Ketubot 72a. These [two explanations] are dependent on the dispute between Ra'avad and Rosh, Moed Katan 3:3. According to Ra'avad, the uncovering of the head of a mourner is a biblical obligation: since it states with regard to the sons of Aaron, "Do not let your hair go wild [and do not tear your garments] in order that you not die," we can infer that any other who does not uncover their head is subject to death at the hands of the divine – this corresponds to the second explanation. Rosh disagrees and maintains that the verse is necessary to teach the selfsame law: that it is forbidden for kohanim to uncover their heads in mourning, but all others are authorized to do so.²³

> לימד. מדעבדינן הכי כדי לנוולה מדה כנגד מדה, כמו שעשתה להתנאות על בועלה מכלל דאסור, א״נ מדכתיב ופרע מכלל דבההיא שעתא לאו פריעה הוית, ש״מ אין דרך ב״י לצאת פרועות ראש, וכן עיקר, רש״י כתובות ד׳ ע״ב א׳. ותלוי במחלוקת ראב״ד ורא״ש במ״ק פ״ג סי׳ ג׳. דהראב״ד ז״ל סובר דפריעת ראש באבל מה״ת, מתכתיב בבני אהרן ראשיכם אל תפרעו ולא תמותו, מכלל דאחר שלא פרע חייב מיתה בידי שמים מה״ת, והיינו כפי׳ הב׳. והרא״ש ז״ל חולק וכו׳ דאיצטריך לגופי׳ דהם אסורים לפרוע, אבל אחר רשות.

Messas (*Collected Letters* 1884) understood that Rabbi Horowitz was accepting Rashi's first answer as primary. Rabbi Moshe Feinstein (*Iggerot Moshe Even HaEzer* 1:57) rules that we must be stringent for the first explanation and treat it as a *safek deorayta*, a doubtful case of a biblical law. Thus, under normal circumstances he will take the stringencies that accompany a prohibition.

23. On the line in the Sifre "though there is no explicit proof to the matter…," the Netziv comments, "that it should be a legal obligation, but rather *dat Yehudit*, as the Mishnah in Ketubot (7:6) states, 'One who goes out with uncovered head.'"

According to Netziv, the dispute with regard to hair covering is a manifestation of a fundamental dispute between Rosh and Ra'avad. Ra'avad maintains that in general, when the Torah mandates that a specific act be performed in a particular place or time ("He shall uncover her head;" "do not let your hair grow wild"), one is *forbidden* to perform that act in any other context. Since the Torah commanded Aaron and his sons to cut their hair even though they were in mourning, every other person is biblically forbidden to do so. Rosh, however, maintains that when the Torah mandates that a specific act be performed in a particular place or time, there is no attendant biblical prohibition to perform the same act outside the parameters which the Torah outlined. Thus, even though the Torah commanded Aaron and his sons to cut their hair during their period of mourning, everyone else is biblically permitted to do so; only Aaron and his sons are required.

What is most important is that Netziv has opened the possibility that the first position in Rashi, while not accepted by Rashi himself, may be correct according to other Rishonim. Thus, according to Netziv, a perspective based on the Rosh in combination with an understanding of the Gemara similar to Rashi's first interpretation would generate a legal position that there is no biblical obligation for married women to cover their hair. [24]

RABBI YERUCHAM FISHEL PERLOW

A student of Netziv, Rabbi Yerucham Fishel Perlow had an even more radical reading, arguing that it is the *second* interpretation offered by Rashi that relegates hair covering to the realm of custom rather than law. In other words, it would be the *accepted legal position* of Rashi that married women need only cover their hair due to custom.

---

24. The rationale of the Netziv can also be found in R. Moshe Zev HaCohen, *Tiferet LeMoshe* 2:10. He maintains that the dispute among the Rishonim as to whether the requirement of a ketubah is explicitly found in the Torah or merely a biblical custom appears with regard to hair covering. In his view, there is a dispute among the Rishonim – when the Torah records an ancient practice (whether the dowry of virgins [*mohar habetulot*] or hair covering), does it have the status of custom or law? And he posits that whoever holds that there is no biblical obligation of ketubah would likewise maintain that there is no biblical obligation for women to cover their hair. A similar view can also be found in *Yeshuot Yaakov, Even HaEzer* 21; he maintains that the practice of uncovering the hair described in Numbers 5:18 is a biblical custom and not a biblical law. Perhaps this is the rationale of the second view presented by Rashi, m. Ketubot 72a, as we will see below.

UNCOVERED HAIR AND MODERN JEWISH LAW 391

Rabbi Perlow (Commentary to *Sefer HaMitzvot* of Rabbi Saadiah Gaon, *Aseh* 96) first suggests that according to all opinions, the obligation for a married woman to cover her hair is of biblical origin. The dispute, he suggests, is simply whether it is formally counted as a mitzvah, as the technical rules for what is counted in the 613 mitzvot is the subject of much debate among the Rishonim.

However, he then moves to an argument that assumes the issue at hand is indeed the question of the existence of and extent of the obligation. He understands the first interpretation of Rashi as follows:

However, it seems that the essence of this issue requires investigation. Where does it imply that there is a prohibition in this? It makes sense according to the first interpretation of Rashi, "that one could say." For the explanation of this issue is that since [uncovering her hair] is done to her to make her disgusting, measure for measure, as she did to make herself beautiful for her adulterer, it implies [that in general, having her hair uncovered] is forbidden. For there can be no punishment without warning, and since the punishment is explicit in the verse, it is as if the warning were written explicitly in the Torah, as Rambam explains (*Shoresh* 14 in *Sefer HaMitzvot*), see there. At any rate, since we see that the Torah punished her for it, we can conclude that it was forbidden to do this.	איברא דבעיקר הדבר צ"ע לכאורה מהיכא משמע להו שיש איסור בדבר. ובשלמא לפירוש הראשון של רש"י אפשר לומר. דביאור הדבר הוא דכיון דעבדינן לה הכי לנוולה מדה כנגד מדה כמו שעשתה להתנאות על בועלה מכלל דאסור. דאין עונש בלא אזהרה. וכיון שהעונש מפורש בקרא הרי זה כאילו האזהרה מפורשת בקרא. וכמו שביאר הרמב"ם ז"ל (בסה"מ שורש י"ד) עיי"ש. וע"כ"פ מיהת כיון דחזינן שענש הכתוב עלה ש"מ דאסור לעשות כן

Rabbi Perlow understands that the fact that the Torah would punish her by having her hair uncovered implies that under any other circumstance she would be obligated to cover her hair. However, this is only according to Rashi's *rejected first opinion*. According to the second explanation, which Rashi accepts, there would be only a custom, not an obligation, for a married woman to cover her hair.

However, according to Rashi's second explanation, which he indicated to be the main explanation, there is a great difficulty: Just because [not going with their heads uncovered] was the practice	אבל לפי' שני של רש"י שכתב עליו שהוא העיקר קשה טובא. וכי משום שכן נהגו בנות ישראל נימא דאית בה איסור דאורייתא. ודילמא אין

> of the daughters of Israel, must we say that it has the status of a biblical prohibition? Perhaps it only has the status of a custom that the daughters of Israel adopted of their own accord. And even though this custom is mentioned in the Torah, it nevertheless does not generate a biblical prohibition, since a husband's ownership rights to the dowry assets [*nichsei melog*] of his wife is only a rabbinic decree, as mentioned in several places, even though it is mentioned in the Torah... Thus, even though the custom is mentioned in the verse, nevertheless, it only has the status of a mere custom.
>
> בה אלא תורת מנהג שנהגו בו בנות ישראל מדעתן. ואף על פי שנזכר מנהג זה בתורה. מכל מקום לא משום זה יש בו איסור דאורייתא שהרי בעל בנכסי מלוג של אשתו תקנתא דרבנן. כמבואר בכמה דוכתי אף על פי שנזכר בקרא. כדדרשינן (סו"פ השולח מ"ז ע"ב) מדכתיב ולביתך מלמד שאדם מביא ביכורי אשתו וקורא... הרי דאע"ג שנזכר המנהג בקרא. מכל מקום אין לו אלא תורת מנהג בעלמא

According to this analysis, Rashi's *accepted opinion* would be that a married woman covering her hair only has the *status of a custom*, albeit one that was prevalent in the biblical period.[25] However, while Rabbi Perlow notes that this reading is tenable in the Sifre, he thinks it is against the simplest understanding of the Talmud which does seem to assume an obligation for married women to cover their hair. To explain how it could be biblical, even without an explicit source, he propounds the following argument:

> If so, from where is it derived that uncovering hair is a prohibition, as from the verse we only have evidence that this was the custom of Jewish women? This requires investigation. In truth, according to the language of the *Sifre* (*Nasso*, section *HaIsha – limed al benot yisrael she-hein mechasot*): "Alternatively: this teaches that the daughters of Israel cover their heads. And although there is no explicit proof to the matter, there is an indication: 'And
>
> וא"כ מנ"ל איסורא בפריעת ראש. כיון שאין לנו ראיה מקרא אלא שכך הי' מנהג בנות ישראל. וצ"ע בזה. ובאמת דלפי לשון הספרי (נשא פיסקא האשה לימד על בנות ישראל שהן מכסותי"א) ופרע את ראש ראשיהן. ואף על פי שאין ראיה לדבר זכר לדבר. ותקח תמר אפר על ראשה עיין שם. משמע שאין

---

25. It is worth noting that Rabbi Moshe Feinstein (*Iggerot Moshe, Even HaEzer* 1:57) also understood the first explanation of Rashi as implying there was a prohibition. However, unlike Rabbi Perlow, while he maintains that the first explanation of Rashi expresses a prohibition, he believes that the second delineates a negative corollary of a positive biblical obligation. While both are biblical, the latter is not prohibited in the face of a monetary loss greater than twenty percent of one's wealth.

Tamar placed ashes (*epher*) upon her head,'" see there. This implies that there is not a biblical prohibition, and it only learned from the verse that this was the custom.

However, in the Talmud it is clear that a biblical prohibition was derived from this verse, as I brought above. Perhaps one might answer that we do not derive a biblical prohibition from the verse itself, but because the verse teaches us that such was the custom of the daughters of Israel, we conclude that this is a matter of promiscuity and leads to sexual immorality; accordingly, such conduct would itself be biblically forbidden as it falls into the category of "Do not place a stumbling block before the blind." Based on this, there would be no room at all for the question of Rashbatz of blessed memory, even without that which we explained above, for we have no intrinsic prohibition. Rather it is included in the prohibition of "before the blind." If so, there is no room to count it as its own commandment, for the prohibition of "before the blind" was already counted by Rambam and the other enumerators of mitzvot.

בה איסור דאורייתא. ולא למד מקרא אלא שכן נהגו.

אבל בתלמודין מבואר דאיסורא דאורייתא יליף מהך קרא. וכמו שהבאתי לעיל. ואולי אפשר לומר דלא מהך קרא גופי׳ יליף איסורא. אלא דכיון דשמעינן מקרא דדרך בנות ישראל בכך. ש״מ דדבר פריצות הוא ומביא לידי גילוי עריות. וא״כ ממילא יש בו איסור דאורייתא. דהו״ל בכלל לאו דלפני עור לא תתן מכשול. ועפ״ז שוב ממילא אין מקום כלל לקושית הרשב״ץ ז״ל גם זולת מה שביארנו לעיל. משום דכיון דאין לנו בזה איסור מצד עצמו כלל. אלא שזה הוא בכלל לאו דלפני עור. א״כ אין מקום למנותה מצוה בפ״ע. שהרי לאו דלפני עור כבר מנו הרמב״ם וכל שאר מוני המצות:

Rabbi Perlow accepts the possibility that for the Sifre there is no biblical obligation for a married woman to cover her hair. Conversely, for the Talmud he does not. He accepts the possibility that there is no *intrinsic* prohibition. He argues, therefore, that it is promiscuous for a married woman to leave her hair uncovered because it will cause men who see her to sin, thus violating *lifnei iver,* which is rabbinically understood to forbid people from causing others to sin.

While Rabbi Perlow does not argue that it is permitted for a married woman to leave her hair uncovered, he does open the logical possibility that in a society where men are not sexually enticed by a woman's uncovered hair, it would be permitted for a woman to uncover her hair.

This argument, one that agrees with the second position of Rashi, also appears in the Novellae of R. Dov Beresh Meisels (Mahardam, 1798–1870, Cracow) to Rambam's *Sefer HaMitzvot* (*Aseh* 175) who states:

> Regarding that which [Rambam] did not count a woman's going out with uncovered head, which is biblically prohibited, as the Talmud in b. Ketubot stated: "Going out with an uncovered head is a biblical prohibition, as it is written, 'And he shall uncover her head' (Num. 5:18), and the school of R. Yishmael taught that this is a warning to the daughters of Israel that they should not go out with uncovered head" – we must answer that he is of the same view as the second explanation presented by Rashi, that from the verse "And he shall uncover…" we infer that at that time her head was not uncovered, and we thus deduce that it is not the practice of the daughters of Israel to go out with their heads uncovered. And it is this explanation that Rashi indicated to be the main one. *According to this explanation, it is not a full-fledged prohibition, but rather a practice of the daughters of Israel that is ascribed Torah status, and for that reason [Rambam] did not count it in his enumeration of the commandments.*

> ומה דלא חשבו פריעת הראש באשה דאסרה התורה, כמו שאמרו שם בפרק המדיר ראשה פרוע דאורייתא היא דכתיב ופרע את ראש האשה, ותנא דבי ר' ישמעאל אזהרה לבנות ישראל שלא תצאנה בפרוע ראש, צ"ל דס"ל בפירוש הב' שכתב רש"י ז"ל מדכתיב ופרע מכלל דההוא שעתא לאו פרועה הות, ש"מ אין דרך בנות ישראל לצאת פרועות ראש. ועל פירוש הזה כתב רש"י, וכן עיקר. ולפי פירוש הזה לאו איסור גמור הוא, אלא מנהג בנות ישראל מה"ת, ומש"ה לא חישב ליה במנין המצות.

Per Rabbi Meisels' understanding, Rambam (and Rashi) rules that uncovering one's entire head does not constitute a biblical violation. The *Kiryat Sefer*, which collects all of the biblical laws Rambam codifies, also does not include any halakha about hair covering. R. Henkin writes, "[T]his makes sense according to the view of Rambam, that hair covering is only a rabbinic obligation, and the verse is merely an allusion." (See his *Shi'ur Kisui Rosh Shel Nashim.*)[26]

YASHIV MOSHE

Rabbi Moshe Turetsky (*Responsa Yashiv Moshe, EH* 3), a modern Israeli authority, takes this line of argumentation one step further. He was asked

---

26. See note 31 on page 288.

whether a married woman may have her hair uncovered if only non-Jewish men will see her. In his response, he makes the following set of arguments, which are essentially an embrace of the position of Ra'aviah as explained above in Chapter 6, namely that the *ervot* described in b. Berachot are to be defined in context. Rabbi Turestsky's view aligns with the argument made by Rabbi Perlow (following the second position of Rashi):

1. The *ervot* described in b. Berachot are contextually defined, due to the effect they will have on men. Thus, they are in truth manifestations of the prohibition of *lifnei iver*, placing a stumbling block before those men.
2. This prohibition will only apply when the men who will see the woman's hair, or other parts of her body enumerated in b. Berachot, will have improper thoughts.
3. If men are desensitized such that they will not have such thoughts, there is no prohibition on the woman to have those body parts uncovered.
4. Non-Jewish men are presumed to be exposed to so much that they are not affected by the sight of uncovered hair. (He also has a discussion about Torah scholars who are in full control of their passions.)
5. He notes that the above argument could be true even if non-Jews are forbidden by Jewish law to have sexual thoughts, though that issue is subject to dispute.

Rabbi Turetsky outlines two possible rationales for the obligation of a married woman to cover her hair, neither of which assumes an objective obligation unique to hair.

| If the prohibition on women exposing [hair] to a Jewish man is due to the man's prohibition, in that she may cause him to stumble in the prohibition on looking [at forbidden sexual matters] as explained in the laws of marriage, *Even HaEzer* 21:1, which is a violation of *lifnei iver*, as the man will come to violate the biblical prohibition of "You shall guard yourself from every evil thing" (Deut. 23:10) – one should not engage in improper thoughts during the day which would lead to impurity at night | אם מה שאסורה לאשה להתגלות לפני יהודי הוא משיום איסור האשי שהיא מכשילה אותו באיסורי הסתכלות המבוארים באבן העזר הל' אישות סימן כ"א סעיף א', דהיינו איסור לפני עיור, שהאיש יעבור על איסור תורה של ונשמרת מכל דבר רע, שלא יהרהר ביום ויבוא לידי טומאה בלילה (עבודה זרה דף כ'). או משום איסור |

> (Avodah Zarah 20b)? Or, alternatively, if it is due to a woman's prohibition, in that she has an obligation to be modest in the presence of others, and her prohibition against behaving in a promiscuous manner is similar to that which the *Shulchan Arukh* wrote in the subsequent paragraph (ibid., 21:2) ["The daughters of Israel should not go out in the marketplace with their heads uncovered, no matter if they are unmarried or married"]?
>
> האשה שיש חיוב עליה להיות צנועה בפני בני אדם, ואיסור זה שעליה מלמהיות פרוצה הוי כעין דברי השו"ע שם סעיף ב.

Since he rules that these two prohibitions do not apply in a place where there are only gentiles, Rabbi Turetsky concludes that it is permissible for a woman to uncover her hair in such a place. In his view, there is no independent prohibition for a woman to go with her hair uncovered; it only falls under the rubric of other prohibitions (e.g., not to put a stumbling block before the blind).

While Rabbi Turetsky does not expand on it, what emerges from his argument is that in a culture where all men, Jewish or not, are accustomed to seeing women with uncovered hair, the prohibition would not apply. He entertains this possibility in a short comment:

> From this it emerges that a handbreadth [of skin] on a woman is not considered promiscuous in front of a non-Jew. For just as he is accustomed to hair and voice, the same is true here. And nowadays, with regard to Jews in our great iniquity, there is room to be a bit lenient.
>
> וממילא אין טפח עור של אשה הגדר פריצות לפני גוי וכמו שרגיל בשערות ובקול כמו כן כאן. ביהודים בזמן הזה בעוה"ר מצינו גם כן מקום להקל קצת.

A similar argument, though not explicitly applied to hair, is presented by R. Yom Tov Lipman Heller, in his *Divrei Chamudot* commentary on the Rosh, where he writes that according to Rosh (Berachot 3:37):

> ...it is logical to conclude that [the laws in] every place should be dependent on local practice as a consequence of the above rationale, yet parts of a woman's body that are not normally covered are not considered *erva*, for men are not aroused by looking at them, as later regarding voice and hair...
>
> ומסתבר דכל מקום ומקום לפי מנהגו דמידי הוא טעמא אלא דדברים שרגילה שלא לכסותם לא מקרי ערוה משום דלא אתי בהו לידי וכו' כיון דרגיל בהו וכדלקמן גבי קול ושער:

R. Heller's view is quite straightforward: Wherever the custom of modest religious women is to uncover a particular part of their body (such as forearms, and certainly hair), according to Rosh, there is no prohibition to do so.[27] In fact, in Rosh's view there is a dispute among the Talmudic passages in b. Ketubot 72 and b. Berachot 24.[28]

---

27. R. Aaron Samuel Kaidanover, commenting on this in his *Tiferet Shmuel* on the Rosh Berachot 3:37, writes: "meaning, he comes to exclude that which women normally uncover, such as the face and neck and hands, but it seems simple to me that the practice of women to regularly uncover their forearms and have their garments open nearly to their breasts is an evil practice; to them I apply the term a no-good place: an exposed handbreadth of a woman is considered *erva*."

28. Only in the *Shulchan Arukh* of R. Shlomo Chelma (Shlomo Ashkenazi ben Moshe Rappaport, author of the *Mirkevet HaMishneh* commentary on Rambam), entitled *Shulchan Tamid Even HaEzer* 115:3–4, do we find a code of law which rules that uncovering all of one's hair is considered a violation of *dat Moshe*. He writes that there are three types of behavior included in the category of *dat Moshe*:

1. Causing one's husband to violate a prohibition.
2. Performing a prohibited act whose punishment is death [at the hands of heaven], where one's children die even though the husband has violated nothing.
3. Performing a prohibited activity that is promiscuous and raises suspicion of infidelity.

In his view, in a time when uncovered hair is not an indicator of promiscuity approaching infidelity, then it is not categorized as *dat Moshe*. Based on this, we can explain the view of Rosh and the *Tur*. Rosh writes (Ketubot 7:9) that a woman's uncovered hair raises suspicion of infidelity; it is possible that Rosh maintains that in a time and place where such is an act of promiscuity leading to infidelity, such conduct is biblically prohibited. However, the *Tur*, who writes the law in a general manner, in an ordinary place, where there is no attendant suspicion of infidelity (in a place or time when such is not promiscuous behavior), writes that everything is dependent on the category of *dat Yehudit*. (According to this approach, Rosh might be of the same view as the *Yereim* [*mitzvah* 392], that the prohibition is in fact to distance oneself from forbidden sexual relationships.) One could also suggest that only in a time and place that uncovered hair would indicate impudence and a suspicion of infidelity would it be forbidden (even were one to argue that it is a biblical prohibition). A related idea is found in Rambam with regard to the law that it is prohibited to enter the Temple precincts with one's hair uncovered. Rambam (*Bi'at Mikdash* 1:17) rules:

> Similarly, it is prohibited for anyone, whether kohen or ordinary Israelite, to enter the entire Temple, from the beginning of the outer courtyard and inward, after having consumed wine or while drunk or with one's head uncovered in a disgraceful manner or with torn clothes – even though the latter is not included in the biblical admonition, for it is not befitting of the honor and reverence due to the great, holy site to enter in a disgraceful manner. However, a person who

RABBI SHIMON SIDON

Rabbi Shimon Sidon of Kunitz (1815–1891), a student of *Chatam Sofer*, offers a brief defense of the practice of many women to not cover their hair (*Shevet Shimon, Chiddushei Sugyot*, pp. 56–7).[29] He argues that the obligation is for women to cover that which is normally covered by married women. Thus, in a place where women cover most of their hair but allow some to come out of their head coverings, that hair is not problematic. Possibly, he suggests, the same is true when the norm becomes that no women cover their hair. To explain the Talmudic evidence, he suggests that married women covering their hair was a custom accepted by women upon themselves which made leaving hair uncovered a degrading act.[30] However, this is not a formal obligation, and thus is subject to changing norms.

THE EXPLICIT ARGUMENTS

With the exception of *Yashiv Moshe*, who raises it as a possibility, none of the poskim cited above explicitly writes that the law would change in modern times. Nonetheless, several modern authorities, aware that in today's reality most women do not cover their hair, fully accepted the notion that the law can and should change as social norms evolve.[31]

RABBI ISAAC HUREWITZ

R. Isaac S. Hurewitz, in *Yad HaLevi*, his commentary to Rambam's *Sefer HaMitzvot* (Positive Commandment 175), rules:

However, the rabbis of old, giants of their time, who were not accustomed to seeing the daughters of Israel go about with their heads uncovered, with only wigs on their heads, they railed loudly against this, and	ואמנם רבנן קשישאי גאוני עולם בזמנם שלא הסכינו לראות בנות ישראל יוצאות וראשן פרועה בפאה נכרית על ראשן הרעישו עליהן עולם

---

grew out his hair such that it is smooth and no longer disgraceful is permitted to enter the outer courtyard.

29. Thanks to Dr. Marc Shapiro for this reference.

30. He compares this to the *chumra de-Rabbi Zeira*, Rabbi Zeira's codification of the custom accepted by women to treat all potential menstrual blood with the stringencies of *zivah* blood, requiring seven bloodless days, rather than seven days total, to become pure from niddah impurity.

31. Indeed, scattered throughout this book are many other modern Jewish law authorities who adopt views that also would permit married women to not cover their hair in a society where such is not customary among modest women.

were concerned about the promiscuity and despoiling of their souls much more than any physical harm which might come from wearing wigs made of human hair, and rightly so: since women did not conduct themselves this way generally, it was indeed a matter of promiscuity and a violation of *dat*, as we have discussed. But through their fierce opposition to promiscuity, they have distorted for us – intentionally or unintentionally – the simple understanding of the teachings of the sages (b. Shabbat 64, b. Nazir 28, and the beginning of the second chapter of Ketubot), to the point that even an intelligent person cannot sort this out; see ibid. The truth is that these matters of law, prohibited and permitted, are not based on the Talmud or the early decisors, but on the public conduct of women in a given place and time. I have written all this not to rule as a matter of practical halakha, but to find an *ex post facto* justification for the practice of the daughters of Israel.

I have expanded upon this more than is called for, yet it nevertheless seems to me that hair covering ought not to be included in the enumeration of the *mitzvot*, even though the Talmud stated that it is a biblical obligation. Once we have concluded that it is dependent on place and time, then in a place where the practice of women is to go with their heads uncovered, there is no obligation nor interdiction, either biblical or rabbinic. Perhaps it is for this reason that the Tashbetz himself did not include it in his enumeration of the *mitzvot*. Notwithstanding, there ought not to be even a wisp of a question raised from barriers (*chatzitzin*) or hair covering or the many other instances in which the Talmud states that something is biblical.

ומלואה, וחששו על הפריצות מקלקול נשמתן יותר מסכנת גופם הנשקפת להן מהפאה נכרית ובצדק ובמשפט עשו זאת. כי אחרי שלא היו דרכן בכך היה באמת פריצות ועבירת דת כאמור, אלא שבשנאתם לפריצות עקמו עלינו – אם במתכון או שלא במתכון – את פשטות דברי רז״ל (שבת ס״ד נזיר כ״ח ורפ״ב דכתובות) עד שמי שיש לו מוח בקדקדו לא יסבול זאת, עיין בדבריהם. והאמת שענין דברים אלו האסורין והמותרין, אין בש״ס ופוסקים ראשונים יסוד, אלא במנהג הליכות הנשים במקום ובזמן ההוא, כתבתי כל זה לא להלכה למעשה רק ללמד זכות על בנות ישראל.

הנה הארכתי יותר מהצורך לעניינו ועכ״פ נראה כי אין מקום להכניס פריעת ראש במנין המצות אם כי בגמרא אמרו דאורייתא הוא, אחרי שתלוי במקום ובזמן, ובמקום שדרך הנשים לילך בפרועת ראש, אין בו לא מצוה ולא מניעה לא מדאורייתא ולא מדרבנן, ואולי מזה הטעם לא הכניס הרשב״ץ עצמו במנין מצותיו, ובלא״ה אין כאן ריח קושיא מחציצין פריעת ראש וכיוצא באלו הרבה שאמרו בש״ס דאורייתא הוא, אם כי כן הוא האמת, אבל כ״ז שאין מקרא בתורה בלשון מצוה או אזהרה מורה ע״ז לא

> This may be correct, but so long as there is no passage in the Torah expressly stating an obligation or admonition on this matter, it is not to be included among the *mitzvot*, because the only commandments to be enumerated among the 613 are those where the actual wording of the Torah denotes a positive action or a prohibition.
>
> יחשבו בענין המצות, כי אין לנו במנין התרי״ג אלא לשון התורה עשה או ל״ת.

Among the arguments he propounds is that presented above by Rabbi Perlow within the second reason of Rashi.

RABBI EFRAIM ZALMAN SLUTZKI

Likewise, R. Efraim Zalman Slutzki, *Responsa Etz Efraim* (*OC*, responsum starting on p. 12 12b (22)),[32] writes:

> Accordingly, the difficulty facing all the commentators has been solved ... Now that in our multitude of transgressions, Jewish women have breached this fence and go with their heads uncovered, the situation is analogous to what the *Bach* wrote with regard to towns where the women go barefoot, and their legs are always exposed.
>
> ולפ״ז הותר כל אשר עמדו המפרשים בזה... ואחרי אשר פרצו בעה״ר נשי ישראל ללכת פרועת ראש והר״ז דרכם לגלות גם השער הרי זה כמו שכתב הב״ח בעיירה שהולכין יחף שלעולם רגלי׳ מגולין.

RABBI CHAIM HIRSCHENSON

Rabbi Chaim Hirschenson presents a unique series of arguments to defend the practice.[33] His first approach is premised on the idea that there can be decrees from the time of the giving of Torah (that is, the time of Moshe) that do not rise to biblical law. R. Hirschenson notes that the Redid HaZahav (*Bereishit* 29:22), in a discussion involving *takkanot* (decrees), assumes precisely this. Using this paradigm of rabbinic decrees with biblical mandates that remain merely rabbinic, Rabbi Hirschenson applies this same construct to custom. Based on this, in a world where it is customary that most women do not cover their hair, it is permitted for married women to uncover their hair. As a corollary to this argument, R.

---

32. I would like to thank Dr. Marc Shapiro for calling this source to my attention.
33. *Chiddushei HaRav Chaim Hirschenson, Nasso* 69. I would like to thank Dr. Marc Shapiro for pointing out this source and position.

Hirschenson seems to understand Rashi's first explanation as assuming the obligation for married women to cover their hair was derived from custom. As such, it was merely the breach of custom that made it humiliating for the sotah to have her hair uncovered.

In the end, R. Hirschenson moves away from the above analysis in favor of one mentioned in Chapter 1, namely, that the term of *periat ha-rosh* refers to wild hair rather than uncovered hair. Accordingly, there would be no obligation for a woman to cover her hair. She must simply keep it neat. Regardless of which approach seems sounder or more reasoned, one thing is clear. R. Hirschenson concludes that the practice of women who do not cover their hair can be defended as a matter of halakha.[34]

RABBI YOSEF MESSAS

The modern authority who most extensively defends the practice was Rabbi Yosef Messas, and therefore we will present his responsum in full. It is critical to frame his argument within the positions we have outlined above. Rabbi Messas accepts the lenient interpretations of Rashi offered by both the Neztiv and Rabbi Perlow (though he does not cite either), arguing that according to *both the first and second explanations* of Rashi, there is only a custom, rather than an obligation, for a married woman to cover her hair. He additionally draws on the comments of Rashi on the Torah and the responsum of Maharam Al-Ashkar, which we have discussed above in Chapter 7. Following Rabbi Messas, we will present the position of Rabbi Moshe Malka who essentially accepts the position of Rabbi Messas. This piece is from the Responsa of Rabbi Yosef Messas (as printed in *Otzar HaMikhtavim* III:1884) on the "Topic of the Requirement for Women to Cover Their Hair.")[35]

---

34. It is not entirely clear whether he thinks even keeping the hair neat is subject to changes in custom, or if at this point he has abandoned his understanding that the issue at hand is custom. What drives him to this conclusion is a desire to reject the claim put forth by Torah Temimah (*Nasso* 5:18, n. 95–96) that the question of whether the problem is for women to have their hair wild or uncovered is a dispute between Rabbi Yishmael and the sages. Rabbi Hirschenson offers his arguments to negate this view. It is worth noting that in order to develop his argument, he suggests several textual emendations, without which his claims are much more difficult. See also note 67 on page 76 for the unique way Rabbi Hirschenson understands the b. Berachot 24a source.

35. This translation and many of the notes on this translation were done by Rabbi

2. Inquiry: His illuminating letter reached me, but due to my being extraordinarily busy I was not able to answer until now. I saw that his halakhic inquiry was a *sheilat hakham hanoga'at le'atzmo*,[36] and it is as follows: This year he married a woman, who covered her head, from the region of Oujda (Morocco) and now he has found a place to work in Casablanca (Morocco). He sends for his wife to join him there, and she is willing to come, but on condition that she be allowed by him to have her hair uncovered according to the custom of that place and time.[37] The honorable sir did not want to agree to this, but after many letters passing back and forth between them and feeling the physical discomfort of enduring a prolonged separation, he eventually accepted her condition to come to Casablanca with her head uncovered. His parents, however, prevented him from going through with this, telling him that she should not uncover her head in any way. His wife, however, would not relent, being single-minded in her desire to uncover her hair. And now he is left standing between

(2) מכתבו הבהיר הגיעני, ולרוב הטרדות לא יכולתי להשיב עד כה. ראיתי שאלתו שאלת חכם הנוגעת לעצמו, והיא, זה כשנה נשא אשה בראשה מכוסה, ממחוז וג׳דא, ועתה מוצא מקום עבודה בקאזא בלאנקא, ושלח אחר אשתו שתבא אצלו, ותאבא לבא, ואך בראש מגולה כמנהג המקום והזמן, וכבודו לא רצה, ואחר כמה חליפות מכתבים שעברו ביניהם וצערא דגופא שסבל, קבל תנאה לבא בראש מגולה, ואך הוריו מעכבים על ידו בזה שלא תגלה ראשה בשום אופן, והיא באחת ולא תשוב, רק לגלות, והוא עומד בין הבנים ואינו יודע איזה דרך ילך, אם ישמע לקול הוריו או לאשתו, ובעי מר מנאי לחוות דעתי להמציא לו צד היתר בענין זה ולהראותו להוריו, ולהשקיט המיית לבבם הסוער ולשפות שלום בין כל המשפחה.

Yehuda B. Ilan and I am grateful to him for allowing me to use his translation in this book. Added to his excellent translation and notes are paragraph numbers to allow the reader to move more easily from the Hebrew to the English in such a complex text and occasional other small comments, as well as a few other changes from his original translation.

It is worth adding that Rabbi Messas writes something similar in a responsum as well (*Mayyim Chayyim* 2:110):

> Know, my child, that the prohibition for women to uncover their hair is extremely well founded! For the custom practiced by all women of ancient times was to cover their hair, and one who did not do so was considered to be promiscuous... Thus, nowadays when women worldwide have abandoned the ancient custom and reverted to the simple practice of not covering their hair, it in no way indicates a deficiency in their modesty or promiscuity, God forbid...

36. A halakhic question about which a Torah scholar feels that he cannot be entirely objective in settling the matter for himself being that it is too personal in nature.
37. In mid-twentieth century Morocco.

them, not knowing which path to take; whether to listen to the voice of his parents or that of his wife. So now the honorable sage would like me to state my opinion, and to find for him a halakhic basis on which to be lenient in this matter so that he can present what I say to his parents in order to silence the raging emotion of their hearts and to effect peace among the entire family.

3. *Responsum*: Know, my child, that the prohibition of married women uncovering their hair used to be quite strong among us here [in Meknes].³⁸ And so it was in all the cities of the west before the arrival of the French. But only a short time after their arrival, Jewish women broke with societal norms in this matter which caused a great scandal among the rabbis, the Sages, and intelligent God-fearing people, but gradually the uproar began to quiet and the dissenting voices ceased. This was because no manner of rebuke was effective with them, neither when gentle nor when raining down fire, for as the ancients said, "There is nothing so stubborn as a woman." And now all of the women go out with their heads uncovered and their hair unbraided, except for the older women who do cover their heads, although not entirely, leaving a portion of their hair uncovered around their face. And when I went, with the help of Heaven, to render holy service in the praised city of Tlemcen (Algeria) when I was about thirty years of age,³⁹ I saw something which was ubiquitous in the entire region among all the women there, even the elderly, that all of them had their

(3) **תשובה**. דע בני, כי אסור גלוי הראש לנשואות היה חמור אצלנו פה מחזק,' וכן בכל ערי המערב טרם בוא הצרפתים, ואך אחרי בואם במעט זמן, פרצו בנות ישראל גדר בזה, וקמה שערוריה גדולה בעיר מהרבנים והחכמים ונבוני עם יראי אלהים, ואך מעט מעט קם השאון לדממה, ויחדלו הקולות, כי לא הועילה שום תוכחת, לא בנחת, ולא באש מתלקחת, כי אין חזק כאשה אמרו הקדמונים, ועתה כל הנשים יוצאות בריש גלי פרועי שער, זולת הזקנות הן שמכסות את ראשן, ולא כולה, רק מניחין חלק גלוי מצד פנים. ואני בלכתי בס"ד לשרת בקדש בעי"ת תלמסאן זה כשלושים שנה, ראיתי הדבר פשוט שם ובכל המחוז אצל כל הנשים, גם הזקנות, שכלם פרועי ראש, עם כמה מיני תגלחות משונות, כאשר נמשך הדבר גם פה בכל ערי המערב.

---

38. The Arabic term for Morocco.
39. Rabbi Messas went to Tlemcen, Algeria, in 1924 at the age of 31.

hair down, uncovered, and wore haircuts in various styles, just as the women do now in all of the cities of *Al-Maghreb* [North Africa].

4. And so, at that time, I set my heart to finding a halakhic justification for their actions since trying to revive the previous practice of covering the hair was simply not a viable option, for this continues to develop along with everything else in the world that changes with the progression of time. When I undertook to search in the words of the halakhists who were before me, I found only one restrictive interpretation and one ban piled upon another. So I said, "I will obtain my knowledge from afar"[40] and draw directly from the source – the Mishnah, Gemara, and their commentaries which were before me. Perhaps a "door of hope" can be found for them, I thought, through which they can enter. For in truth it is difficult for women and their husbands to transgress commandments which are contingent upon a set period of time, and in this matter more than any other since her uncovered hair is obvious and apparent to all.[41] And thanks be to God, we found many doors through which one might enter into such a practice, with halakhic permission and not through violating a prohibition, and they are as follows:

5. Behold! The strong foundation upon which all of the halakhists base their arguments when dealing with the subject of women covering their heads in public – who have built their "sanctuary" upon

(4) ובכן נתתי לבי ללמד עליהם זכות, כי אי אפשר להעלות על לב להחזיר הדבר מאז, כי הדבר הולך ומתפתח עם התפתחות הזמן בכל דבר, ובגשתי לחפש בדברי הפוסקי' אשר לפני, מצאתי רק חומרא על חומרא ואסור על אסור, ובכן אמרתי אשא דעי למרחוק לשאוב מן המקור, משנה וגמרא ונושאי כליהם הנמצאים לפני, אולי נמצא להם פתח תקוה להכנס בו, כי באמת קשה לנשים ולבעליהן לעבור על מצות עשה שהזמן גרמא בעניין זה יותר מכל דבר, בהיות הדבר הזה גלוי לעין כל, והודות לאל כי מצאנו הרבה פתחים למקום ליכנס בו בהיתר ולא באיסור, והם:

(5) הנה. יסוד מוסד לכל הפוסקים, אשר בנו עליו כמו רמים מקדשם, הוא מה שדרש ר' ישמעאל, ופרע את ראש האשה, אזהרה לבנות

---

40. Cf. Job 36:3.
41. In other words, in the mind of Rabbi Messas, there must have been a good reason for religious Jewish couples' apparent flouting of a halakhic requirement. Therefore, he sought a firm legal basis for their actions.

it "like the heights" – is the exposition of Rabbi Yishmael: "'And the kohen shall uncover the hair of the woman.'[42] This verse is a warning to Jewish women[43] that they should not go out with their heads uncovered," as it is written in tractate Ketubot at the end of 72a. And Rashi z"l comments, *"A warning* – From what we do to her for the sake of humiliating her, treating her measure for measure. In other words, just as she uncovered her hair and let it down privately for the pleasure of her paramour, so also it is done to humiliate her in public. And this implies that it is forbidden. Another interpretation of the verse where it says 'the kohen uncovers' is that it implies that at that moment her hair was not uncovered. Thus, we learn from it that it is not the practice of Jewish women to go out in public with their heads uncovered – and this is the main interpretation."

6. The difference that exists between these two interpretations is that according to the first it is implied that the reason that they uncover her hair is in order to humiliate her, and to do to her just as she did for her paramour, pleasuring him with her uncovered head. It further implies beyond all doubt that it is forbidden for us to uncover her hair in order to humiliate her without due cause, but in order that she should receive punishment measure for measure, the Torah permitted us to engage in this prohibition in order to shame her. However, she herself is under no prohibition whatsoever not to uncover her head, since if she wanted to humiliate herself, she may do so at any time she so

ישראל שלא יצאו בפרוע ראש, כמ"ש במס' כתובות דף ע"ב סוף ע"א, ופרש"י ז"ל, וז"ל, אזהרה, מדעבדינן לה הכי לנוולה מדה כנגד מדה כמו שעשתה להתנאות על בועלה, מכלל דאסור, אי נמי, מדכתיב ופרע, מכלל דההיא שעתה לאו פרוע הוה, שמע מינה אין דרך בנות ישראל לצאת פרועות ראש, וכן עיקר, עכ"ל.

(6) וההבדל שיש בין ב' הפירושים הוא עפ"י א' משמע, שהטעם שמגלין שערה, כדי לנוולה בגלוי, כמו שעשתה היא לבועלה להתנאות לפניו בראש מגולה, משמע שאנן הוא שאסור לן לגלות שערה ברבים כדי לנוולה על חנם, ואך כדי לעשות לה מדה כנגד מדה התירה לנו התורה אסור זה כדי לנוולה, אמנם היא אין לה שום אסור בגלוי ראשה, שאם רצתה לנוול עצמה, תנוול לכל עת שתרצה, ובכל מקום שתרצה בבית ובשדה. ואך מפי ב', ופרע, מכלל דעד

---

42. I.e., the *sotah*, the woman accused of adultery (cf. Numbers 5:11–31).
43. *Bnot yisrael* (בנות ישראל) – translated as "Jewish women" throughout.

desires and in any place she would like, whether in the house or in the open field. But the second interpretation implies that until the point when the kohen uncovered her hair it was not that way. And what is the reason that it gives for this? It states that her hair was not uncovered because "it is not the practice of Jewish women to go out with their hair uncovered." This implies that it is even forbidden for her to uncover her own hair. And it is for this purpose, so the line of reasoning goes, that the verse comes to warn her that she should not deviate in any way from the practice of Jewish women in this regard.

השתא לאו פרוע הוה, ומה טעם? משום דאין דרך בנות ישראל לצאת פרועות ראש, משמע שאסור לה גם עצמה לגלות שערה, שלכך בא הכתוב להזהירה שלא תשנה מדרך בנות ישראל בשום אופן.

7. So you see explicitly that according to the first explanation she does not have a prohibition at all since the only concern is that of shame, and if she wants to shame herself she may halakhically do so. According to the second explanation there is likewise not a prohibition from the standpoint of the act of uncovering the hair itself, but only from the standpoint of the custom of Jewish women who were accustomed to cover their heads because covering the hair was considered in their time to be a matter of feminine modesty. A woman at that time who uncovered her hair in public was considered to be someone who broke with societal norms of modesty and it is for this reason that the Torah warned every Jewish woman not to overturn the custom of Jewish women in this regard.

(7) הרי לך מפורש, דלפי א', אין לה בזה אסור כלל, שאין בזה רק משום נוול, ואם תרצה לנוול עצמה, תנוול, ולפי' ב ג"כ אין האסור מצד עצם הדבר של גלוי שער, רק מצד מנהג בנות ישראל שנהגו לכסות ראשן, משום שחשבו בזמנם שיש בזה צניעות לאשה, והמגלה שערה נחשבת פורצת גדר הצניעות, ולזה הזהירה תורה לכל בת ישראל שלא תעשה היפך מנהג בנות ישראל בזה.

8. Therefore, now that all Jewish women[44] agree and are of the opinion that covering the head does not represent a matter of

(8) וא"כ עתה שכל בנות ישראל הסכימה דעתן שאין להן בכיסוי הראש שום צניעות וכ"ש שאין להן בגלוי הראש שום נוול, ואדרבה גלוי שערן הוא הודן והדרן ויופיין ותפארתן ובגלוי שערה מתגאה האשה לפני בעלה

---

44. Or most Jewish women, which counts as "all" under the principle of *rubo kekulo* ("the majority is counted as the entirety").

modesty – and all the more so that going out with an uncovered head does not represent any sort of shame, but rather the revealing of their hair is their glory, their splendor, their prettiness, their beauty, and nowadays a woman confidently and unabashedly uncovers her head in front of either her husband or her paramour – this being the case, the prohibition has been uprooted from its very base and it has now become permissible.

9. In addition, we find that the implicit reasoning of the first explanation in Rashi z"l is explicitly attributed to the holy Tanna, Rabbi Akiva (may his merit protect us. Amen.) on b. Bava Kamma 90a in the Mishnah, where it states: "It once happened that someone uncovered the head of a woman in the marketplace. The woman brought her complaint for this before Rabbi Akiva and he ruled that the man was obligated to pay her damages in the amount of 400 *zuz* [on account of his having shamed her in the open marketplace, since at that time the uncovering of a woman's head was considered to them to have been a shameful thing]. The man said to Rabbi Akiva, 'Give me some time.' And he gave the man some time. It happened that while the woman was standing in the opening to her courtyard, he broke a vial containing expensive perfume in front of her, to which she responded by uncovering her head, dripping the oily perfume from her hand, and placing her hand on her head. The man appointed witnesses against her and came before Rabbi Akiva, saying, 'To such a woman I am supposed to give 400 *zuz*?' Rabbi Akiva said to him, 'Your argument means nothing, for the one

ובועלה, א"כ נעקור האסור מעיקרו ונעשה היתר.

(9) ומה גם עוד דסברת פי' א' שכתב רש"י ז"ל, מצאנוה מפורשת להתה"ק ר' עקיבא זיע"א, במס' ב"ק דף צ' ע"א במשנה, וז"ל ה מעשה באחד שפרע ראש האשה בשוק, באת לפני ר' עקיבא וחייבו ליתן לה ד' מאות זוז, [ועל שנוולה בשוק כפי זמנם שגלוי הראש היה נחשב לנוול] א"ל, רבי, תן לי שמן, ונתן לו זמן, שמרה עומדת על פתח חצרה, ושבר את הכד בפניה ובו כאסר שמן, גלתה את ראשה והיתה מטפחת ומנחת ידה על ראשה, העמיד עליה עדים ובא לפני ר' עקיבא, א"ל לזו אני נותן ד' מאות זוז? א"ל לא אמרת כלום, שהחובל בעצמו אע"פ שאינו רשאי פטור, אחרים שחבלו בו חייבים. עכ"ל.

who harms himself – even though it is not proper to do so – is exempt, but if others harm him in the very same way they are culpable.'"

10. We need to understand what the meaning of "exempt" is here in the Mishnah, i.e., from what is the person exempt? In this case the assessment of monetary damages is irrelevant since to whom would a person pay damages? To himself? The obvious reference is to lashes by the court, since where do we find that one who harms himself is liable to lashes? I also saw that the Tosafot [Bava Kama] 91b, beginning with *ha-chovel...*," were confused over this and then settled the apparent contradiction[45] with a very strained line of reasoning that surrounds the meaning of "exempt" in this context, which is that "exempt" here does not indicate being exempt from an obligation – which is its normal usage – but rather that a person did not properly preserve his body (see there).

11. In my humble opinion, it appears to me that Rabbi Akiva did not adopt the meaning that was employed by the Tosafot in their explanation, but only borrowed metaphorically from the law of "the one who harms," which contains an aspect that it is halakhically prohibited for one to harm himself. But in our case, there is no actual harm,[46] just general embarrassment, and according to all opinions it is completely acceptable for someone to embarrass himself, but others who embarrass him are liable. This is explicit on b. Bava Kamma 91 (see there), and so it is stated in the comments

(10) וצריכים לדעת, מה פי' פטור דקתני, מאיזה דבר פטור, מתשלומין לא שייך, דלמי ישלם, האם לעצמו? ממלקות פשיטא, דהיכן מצינו שהחובל בעצמו חייב מלקות, ושו"ר להתוס' דף צ"א ע"ב ד"ה החובל וכו', שנתעוורו בזה, ויישבו בדוחק, דפי' פטור הכא, היינו שאין בזה צד חיוב רק שאינו חס על גופו, יעוי"ש.

(11) ולדעתי המעט נר' כי רע"ק לא נקט האי לישנא דהחובל וכו' רק בלשון השאלה מדין חובל שיש בו צד איסור לחבול בעצמו, אבל בנידו"ד אין כאן חבלה רק ביש בעלמא, ולכ"ע רשאי אדם לבייש את עצמו, אבל אחרים שביישוהו חייבים, וכמו שמפורש שם דף צ"א, יעוי"ש, וכן איתא בהגהות מא"י שבגליון הרי"ף בתלמוד החדש דפוס מינכאן, שכתבו על דברי רע"ק הנ"ל, וז"ל,

---

45. I.e., that a person is liable to receive lashes, yet is at the same time said to be exempt from them.
46. I.e., physical harm.

of the *Alfas Yashan* (printed in the *Gilyon HaRif* included in the New Talmud edition from Munich), in which they wrote on the statements of Rabbi Akiva mentioned above as follows, "The one who harms (52) – who embarrassed herself." Indeed, this is in exact accord with our explanation.

12. Even according to the naiveté of one particular scholar who wrote me to the effect that, in his opinion, the text is not referring to mere embarrassment but to actual harm, I responded to him that such a position is incredibly naive, whether from the standpoint of common sense or whether from the standpoint of interpreting the Talmudic statement there at the bottom of 91a where it says, "And surely the Mishnah is referring to embarrassment" (see there). But even according to his naive view, we find there in a baraita that according to Rabbi Akiva it is permissible for a person even to harm himself. There are also explicit statements there of several Tannaim who also hold that it is permissible for a person to harm himself. It was also obvious to the scholars of the Mishnah and baraita, such as in tractate Shevuot 27a (see there). And as for the meaning of the word "permissible," it is obvious to every intelligent person that there is no indication of prohibited activity inherent in this term. So you see that according to the opinion of Rabbi Akiva in the Mishnah, the opinions of several Tannaim that are found elsewhere, and the first explanation in Rashi z"l there is not any prohibition for a woman to uncover her head since if she desires to shame herself she may halakhically do so. And all the more so according to the truth that there is nothing in this act other

החובל, נ"ב, שביישה את עצמה, עכ"ל, הרי כדברינו ממש.

(12) ואף לדעת פתיית חכם אחד, שכתב לי זה כמה, שדבר זה נקרא לדעתו חובל, השבתיו, דזו פתיות גסה לחשוב כן, הן מצד השכל הישר, הן מצד דבפי' אתמר שם בש"ס דף צ"א סוף ע"א, וז"ל, והא מתניתין בבושת היא וכו' יעוי"ש. ואף לפי פתיותו, מצינו שם תנא דברייתא אליבא דרע"ק דס"ל רשאי אדם לחבול בעצמו, וכן מפורש עוד התם דאיכא תנאי דס"ל רשאי אדם לחבול בעצמו וכן מפרש למארי מתני' ובברייתא דמס' שבועות דף כ"ז ע"א, יעוי"ש. ופי' רשאי פשוט לכל מבין שאין בדבר שום איסור, הרי לך שלדעת רע"ק דמתני' ולדעת כמה תנאי כפי' א' של רש"י ז"ל, שאין שום איסור לאשה לגלות ראשה, שאם רצתה לנוול עצמה תנוול, וכ"ש כפי האמת שאין בזה אלא צד ביוש, ולפי' רשאי אדם לבייש את עצמו וכמש"ל.

than an aspect of personal embarrassment, and as we already learned, it is completely permissible for a person to embarrass himself.

13. We further find that the Tannaim are not of the opinion that "a prohibition may be established through a negative inference." In tractate Shevuot (35a), for example, the Mishnah states there, "May God not strike you, or May God bless you, or May it be well with you. Rabbi Meir holds them liable on account of such things, but the sages exempt them." The commentary of Rashi z"l explains that the person saying these things in the Mishnah meant implicitly "May God not strike you – if you testify on my behalf, but if you do not give testimony on my behalf, then may God strike you." And Rabbi Meir holds that such implied curses incur liability since he is of the opinion that a prohibition may be established through implication – see there. But the sages exempt such implicative statements from liability since they do not hold that a prohibition may be established through implication. If this is so, then also here in our case we may say that they do not hold like Rabbi Yishmael that the phrase "and the kohen shall uncover" indicates an actual prohibition because we do not say that a prohibition may be established from mere implication.

(13) ועוד מצינו תנאי דס״ל, דלא דאמרינן מכלל הן אתה שומע לאו, כמ״ש במס׳ שבועות דף ל״ה ע״א במשנה, אל יכך ויברכך וייטיב לך ר״מ מחייב וחכמים פוטרים, ופרש״י ז״ל ר״מ מחייב מכלל לאו אתה שומע הן, אל יככה אם תעידוני, ואם לא תעידוני יכך, ע״ש. ורבנן פוטרים דאין אומרים מכלל לאו וכו׳, וא״כ הכא נמי בנד״ד נימא דלא ס״ל כר׳ ישמעאל, ופרע אזהרה ללאו, דאין אומרים מכלל הן, וכו׳.

14. Even better than all of this is the actual meaning of Rabbi Yishmael's words. They do not mean what we superficially understand them to mean, leaving them to stand only on one foot – that it refers to uncovering the head only – but his words stand on two feet, as it were, which are two shameful actions: uncovering the hair

(14) ועוד דעדיפא מכל זה, כי פי׳ דברי ר׳ ישמעל, אינו כמו שאנו מבינים בשטחיות דבריו שעומדים על רגל אחד דהיינו גילוי הראש לחוד, אלא דבריו עומדים על ב׳ רגליים, דהיינו ב׳ רעותות. גלוי שכר וסתירת שער מקליעתו וקשריו, אבל

and loosening it from its braids and ties. But the mere uncovering of the hair by itself is not a part of the warning to Jewish women at all. This conclusion is forced by the plain meaning of the Mishnah in Sotah (7a) where it says, "And the kohen takes hold of her garments... until he reveals her heart. Then he loosens her hair." The commentary of Rashi z"l states, "This means that he unties her hair from its braid, and it will be discussed later in the Gemara." The discussion is on page 8a where it says, "Our rabbis taught in a baraita, 'And the kohen shall uncover the head of the woman.' From this passage I can only learn about the uncovering of her head. From where do we learn that her body is uncovered [i.e., 'her heart,' as mentioned in the Mishnah]? Therefore, the verse includes the seeming superfluous word 'the woman' [i.e., which implies that her body is also uncovered ('her heart'), as was accepted by the scholars of the Mishnah]. If so, then what does it mean that he 'uncovers her head' except to teach that the kohen loosens her hair." That is, he dishevels her braided locks, undoing it and spreading it on her neck and shoulders. Doing this is considered ugly[47] even in our present time. That is, if a woman who has long hair were to loosen it from its braids and place it here and there, tangled and snarled, it would be seen as ugly. The idea that the word 'uncover' means to loosen hair from its braids is exactly what the *Magen Avraham* (Rabbi Avraham Gombiner) writes in *Orach Chayyim* (75:2), in exposition of what Rabbi Yosef Karo writes in *Even HaEzer*, "The daughters of Israel do not go out with their heads

גלוי שער לחוד אינו באזהרה כלל, ופי' זה מוכרח ממשנה בסוטה דף ז'. וז"ל ה, והכהן אוחז בבגדיה וכו' עד שמגלה את לבה, וסותר את שערה, ופירש רש"י ז"ל, סותר את שערה מקליעתו ולקמן יליף לה, עכ"ל. והילפותא היא בדף ח' ע"א, וז"ל, תנו רבנן ופרע את ראש האשה, אין לי אלא ראשה גופא [ולבה דקתני במתני'] מנין? ת"ל האשה [משמע גופה דהיינו לבה כמו שקבלו מארי מתני'] וא"כ מה ת"ל ופרע את ראש האשה? אלא מלמד שהכהן סותר שערה דהיינו הורס קווצותיה הקלועים ומתירן ופושטן על צווארה וכתפותיה, וזה נפל אף בזה"ז לאשה בעלת שער ארוך לסתור אותו מקליעותו ולהניחו פרוש אנה ואנה מעורבב ומדובלל, וכ"כ המג"א בא"ח סי' ע"ה סק"ב דמ"ש מרן באה"ע לא תלכנה בנות ישראל פרועות ראש, היינו שסותרות קליעת שערן והולכות בשוק עכ"ל ע"ש.

---

47. The text here is emended from נפל to נוול.

'uncovered,' that is, with the braids of their hair undone and walking around in the open marketplace" (see there).

15. "It has been shown you"[48] that the meaning of "and the kohen shall uncover the head of the woman" is that he both uncovers her hair and loosens it. This was what Rabbi Yishmael stated as a warning to Jewish women when he said that they should not go out "with uncovered heads," that is, with their hair uncovered, loosened from its braids, being tangled and snarled. But if, however, she merely uncovers it and wears it either braided or combed and styled – so that there is no appearance of ugliness or unkemptness – then we are not concerned about it. And all of this was applicable even in the times of the Mishnah and Gemara.

16. A certain scholar once wrote me a proposed proof to forbid women from uncovering their hair. His argument was brought from the account of Kimchit who merited to have seven of her sons serve as kohen gadol in her lifetime because, as she states there, the rafters of her house "never saw the braids of her hair." From this statement, this scholar maintained, it can be implied that (a) it is a severe prohibition for a woman to uncover her hair even within her own house and (b) that a woman should be cautioned that there is a great reward for doing so, even in this world. I responded to him that he must have heard the story this way from an old woman telling fables instead of seeing it as it is actually recorded in its source, which is in b. Yoma 47a. It says, "Our rabbis taught

(15) הראת לדעת דפי' ופרע ראש האשה, היינו שמגלהו וסותרו, ועל זה אמר ר' ישמעאל אזהרה לבנות ישראל שלא יצאו פרועות ראש, דהיינו שערן מגלה וסתור מקליעתו ומדובלל, אבל אם רק מגלה וקלוע או סרוק ומתוקן שאין לה בו שום נוול לית לן בה, וכל זה הוא אפי' לפי זמניהם.

(16) וחכם אחד כתב לי ראיה לאסור, ממעשה דקמחית שזכתה לז' בנים ששימשו בכהונה גדולה בחייה בשביל שלא ראו קורות ביתה קליעת שערה, דמשמע מזה שהוא אסור גדול, והנזהרת בו יש לה שכר גדול אפי' בעוה"ז, והשבתיו, כי ודאי שמע המעשה מאשה זקנה המספרת מעשיות, ולא ראה המעשה במקורו, שהוא ביומא דף מ"ז ע"א וז"ל ת"ר ז' בנים היו לקמחית וכלם שמשו בכהונה גדולה, אמרו לה חכמים מה עשית שזכית לכך, אמרה להם מימי לא ראו קורות ביתי קלעי שערי, אמרו לה הרבה עשו כן ולא הועילו, עכ"ל.

---

48. *hor'eta le-daat* (הראת לדעת), cf. Deuteronomy 4:35.

in a baraita – Kimchit had seven sons and all of them served as kohen gadol. The sages said to her, 'What have you done that you have merited to such things?' She said to them, 'Never in all of my days have the rafters of my house seen the braids of my hair.' They said to her, 'Many have done likewise and it was not useful to them.'" So you see that the sages rejected her words as being nothing more than chattering of an old woman, for they knew that there was no prohibition involved, but only a custom that was practiced among Jewish women.

17. The conclusion to this entire line of reasoning is that the entire matter of women covering their heads is specifically a custom which was considered in previous times to be a part of feminine modesty. Those who acted in opposition to the custom were viewed as being lewd and immodest. However, now that women have come to the consensus that having uncovered hair is neither ugly, unkempt, or lewd, *chalilah*, and that covering the head is no longer connected with modesty – only decoration[49] – time has passed this commandment which is dependent on a specific period of time. Therefore, there is no longer any prohibition.

18. And if you say, "So because they flouted a prohibition, the prohibition becomes uprooted from its place?!" I say that this does not present a difficulty. First of all, the uprooting of an actual prohibition is

הרי לך שחכמים דחו דבריה שאינם אלא שיחת אשה זקנה, כי הם ידעו שאין בזה אסור רק מנהג שנהגו בנות ישראל.

(17) המורם מכל זה, שדבר זה של כסוי הראש בנשים אינו אלא מצד המנהג דוקא, שחשבוהו בזמן הקודם לצניעות, והעושה הפך המנהג, היתה נחשבת לפרוצה, אולם עתה שהנשים עלו בהסכמה, שאין להם בזה שום נוול ושום פריצות חלילה, ואין בכסוי הראש שום צניעות, רק צביעות, ועברה על מצוה שהזמן גרמא, א״כ אזדא ליה אסורא.

(18) וא״ת וכי מפני שנהגו היתר בדבר אסור, נעקר האסור ממקומו? זו אינה קושיא חדא! שאין זה אסור, אלא מנהג שבטל טעמו, שאף

---

49. *tzeviut* (צביעות), a play on the word *tzeniut*. Note – I chose to render the word here as "decoration" in relation to its less-common meaning of "coloring" or "painting." The reason for this choice is due it being used as a fairly obvious antonymic pun on the word for "modesty" (צניעות). My colleague at Emory, Rabbi Dr. Don Seeman, proposes that "He means to call it hypocrisy dressed up as piety" idiomatically. That is possible.

not under discussion, but only a custom – the reason for which no longer applies. However, even an actual prohibition can be abolished once the reason for it no longer exists or is applicable. Take, for example, the prohibition on drinking liquids that have been left uncovered. Even though it is listed as "a dangerous matter more severe than a prohibition," and although it was a prohibition prescribed by the Sanhedrin (as the Tosafot write in b. Beitzah 6a, beginning with *Vehaedna*...[50]), nevertheless now that snakes are no longer common among us it has become permissible to drink such liquids (as Maran writes in *Yoreh Deah* 115:1 – see there), and all the more so in our case which is based on a custom of women, the reason of which no longer applies.

19. We further find the following statement by the eminent teacher and scholar, Rabbi Moshe Al-Ashkar z"l, in his responsa (#35): "An inquiry from a friend as to whether or not we need to be concerned about these women who are accustomed to reveal some of their hair from underneath their hairnets in order to beautify themselves. Since there are those whom we have heard teach that to do so is completely prohibited on the basis of the Talmudic statement 'the hair of a woman is nakedness.' Answer: There is no place for concern regarding such hair at all since they are accustomed to regularly leave it uncovered, even while reciting the Shema. And the statement in the Talmud that 'the hair of a woman is nakedness' does not relate to any hair except that which is normally covered by women, similar to the span of a *tefach*, etc. etc.'" – see

---

50. The text had a misprint which we corrected.

אסור שבטל טעמו לגמרי בטל אסורו, שהרי גלוי משקים, אף שהוא מילתא דסכנתא דחמירא מאיסורא והוא דבר שנאסר במנין, כמ"ש בתוס' ביצה דף ו' ד"ה והאי דינא וכו', ע"ש, עכ"ז עכשיו שאין נחשים מצויים בינינו, מותר, כמ"ש מרן ביו"ד סי' קט"ז ס"א, יעוי"ש, וקו"ח לנד"ר שיסודו הוא מנהג נשים שבטל טעמו.

(19) ועוד מצינו להגאון מוהר"ם אלאשקר ז"ל בתשובותיו סי' ל"ה, וז"ל, שאלת הידיד אם יש לחוש לאלו הנשים שנהגו לגלות שערן מחוץ לצמתן להתנאות בו, לפי מה ששמענו מי שהורה להם אסור גמור, ובפי' אמר שער באשה ערוה. תשובה, אין בית מיחוש לאותו שער כלל, כיון שנהגו לגלות, ואפי' לק"ש, והיא דשער באשה ערוה לא מיידי אלא בשער שדרך האשה לכסותו, דומיא דטפח וכו' וכו', ע"ש מה שהאריך, והוסיף עוד משם ראבי"ה ז"ל, שכל אלו שהזכירו לערוה דוקא בדבר שאין רגילות לגלות. אבל בתולה הרגילה בגלוי השער

UNCOVERED HAIR AND MODERN JEWISH LAW   415

his explanation in detail there. And he also adds in the name of the Ra'aviah z"l that everything which is mentioned in that passage as being "nakedness" is specifically referring to something which women are not accustomed to leave uncovered, but we are not concerned at all about unmarried women who regularly leave their hair uncovered (see there). He further adds there that even if they come from a place where the custom is to cover such hair, it is permitted for them to uncover it in a place where the custom is to leave it uncovered (see there).

20. And we add to this another point which is obvious even to the student[51] that nowadays, since all women reveal all the hair of their heads, the hair of married women has returned to a state similar to that of unmarried women for they are all appropriately accustomed to uncovering it. And so, for the same reason that we are no longer concerned about unmarried women not covering their hair in public, i.e., that due to them regularly leaving it uncovered, the fact that it is visible is no longer considered lewd. It is also the case, by the same logic that, since nowadays married women regularly leave their hair uncovered, there should not be any consideration that it is lewdness, *chalilah*. So too regarding the idea that 'hair of a woman is erotic' [Brachot 24]. It is for this reason that the hair of an unmarried women does not generate erotic thoughts by seeing it, so too, with married women nowadays who do not cover their hair, there is no eroticism when one is used to this. Every man "will see [the truth of this statement] from

לא חיישינן יעוי"ש, והוסיף עוד שם, שאפילו הבאים ממקום שרגילים לכסות אותו שער מותר להם לגלותו במקום שנהגו לגלותו, ע"ש. לא חיישינן יעוי"ש, והוסיף עוד שם, שאפילו הבאים ממקום שרגילים לכסות אותו שער מותר להם לגלותו במקום שנהגו לגלותו, ע"ש.

(20) ואנן נוסיף עוד דבר המובן מאליו לכל עם תלמיד, שהאידנא שכל הנשים מגלות שער כל ראשן, חזר שער הנשואות כשער הבתולות שכלן מתאימות רגילות לגלותו, כי מדי הוא טעמא בבתולות, משום דרגילות לגלותו לא מקרי בגלויין פריצות, הוה"ד והוא הטעם האידנא בנשואות הרגילות לגלותו, דלא הוי בזה שום פריצות חלילה, וכן לענין מ"ש שער באשה ערוה [ברכות כ"ד], מדי הוא טעמא בבתולות משום שאין הרהור ברגיל לראות, הוה"ד בנשואות הרגילות האידנא, אין הרהור ברגיל, וכל אדם מבשרו יחזה, שרואה אלפי נשים עוברות לפניו יום ויום בראש מגולה, ואינו שם לבו להן, והמהרהר, לא מחמת שער גלוי מהרהר. זהו ידידי הנר' לקוצ"ד ברור בכל זה,

---

51. Cf. 1 Chronicles 25:8.

his own flesh"[52] for thousands of women pass before him each and every day with uncovered heads and he does not even pay attention to them, and those that do pay attention and have licentious thoughts are not doing so because of uncovered hair. This is it, my friend, and everything that I have said is clear and apparent even to my limited ability.[53] There is much more that could be explained in detail regarding this matter, but the time is not currently available for me to do so. Also, there is no need to be so lengthy since now the eyes of your parents will see and rejoice. And "there shall be peace within your walls and prosperity within your palaces."[54] Amen.

ועוד יש הרבה מה להאריך בזה, ואין הפנאי מסכים, ומה גם שאין עוד צורך, באורך, ומעתה עיני הוריך יראו וישמחו, ויהי שלום בחילך, שלוה בארמנותיך, אמן

RABBI MOSHE MALKA

Rabbi Moshe Malka, who was the chief rabbi of Petach Tikva, accepted the position of Rabbi Messas in a series of letters written to Dr. Marc Shapiro. The first piece is from *Responsa Veheshiv Moshe* #34:

The Question:

To the great Rabbi Melech Shapiro shlit"a in the United States, greetings and many blessings.

לכבוד הרב הג' כמוה"ר מלך שפירא שליט"א ארה"ב, שלום ורו"ב!

You have asked me to explain to you the issue of women's hair covering, since our great master, teacher, Rabbi Yosef Messas, ruled in his book *Mayim Chayyim* 2:110, that in our days, since all women in the world appear in public with their hair uncovered, the prohibition is no longer extant. His honor wishes to know if this should be relied upon and how people practice in Morocco.

שאלני להודיעך בעניין גלוי ראש של נשים, שהרה"ג מוהרדר"מ פסק בספרו מים חיים, חלק ב' סי' קי', שבז[ומן] הז[ה] שכל נשי העולם חזרו לגלות את ראשן פקע איסוריה, וכת"ר מבקש לדעת אם כדאי לסמוך על זה, ואיך נוהגים במרוקו?

---

52. Cf. Job 19:26.
53. Cf. Rambam, *Mishneh Torah, Hilkhot Me'ilah* 8:8.
54. Cf. Psalms 122:7

The answer:

> Answer: You should know that I also had difficulty with the Gaon's (i.e., R. Yosef Messas's) comment. Since the matter is set out in the Gemara, in the seventh chapter of Ketubot (72a): "Going out with her hair undone violates a Torah law!" The Rif, the Rambam, and the Rosh all quote this, so how can the Gaon call it a custom?!
>
> But after I looked carefully at the words of our Master (=R. Joseph Karo) in [the *Shulchan Arukh*] *Orach Chayyim* 75:2, I saw that the Gaon was correct, for this is what it says: "It is forbidden to recite [the Shema] in the presence of [a woman exposing] the hair that a woman generally covers." It seems from his phrasing that only hair that a woman generally covers is part of the category of "a woman's hair is *erva*." But hair that she usually exposes is not considered *erva*.
>
> And this is what the *Kaf HaChayyim* wrote there, #15:2, in the name of the *Ben Ish Chai*, that it is permitted to recite [Shema] in the presence of women from European cities, whose way it is to always appear in public with their hair undone, since it is the way of all these women, see there for details. And these are his words:
>
> The *Ben Ish Chai*, "*Parashat Bo*," #12, wrote as follows:
>
>> It is forbidden to recite [the Shema] or pray or say blessings in the presence of a woman [exposing] her hair, which she generally covers, etc., but in the presence of virgins, whose practice it is to appear in public with their hair out, and [the hair of] women in some countries, who generally let some hair stick out

תשובה: דע לך שגם אני נתקשיתי בדברי הגאון ז"ל, כי דבר זה הוא גמרא ערוכה בפרק המדיר עה' "ראשה פרוע דאורי[יתא] היא." הביאה הרי"ף, הרמב"ם והרא"ש, ואיך הגאון ז"ל קורא לה מנהג?

אך אחר העיון בדברי מרן באו"ח סי' עה' ס"ב, ראיתי שצדק הגאון וז"ל: "שער של אשה שדרכה לכסותו, אסור לקרות כנגדו." משמע מדבריו ז"ל שרק שער שדרכה לכסותו הוא שיש בו משום שער באשה ערוה ואסור לקרות כנגדו, אבל שער שדרכה לגלותו אין בו משום ערוה.

וכ"כ הכה"ח שם ס"ק טו"ב בשם הבן איש חי, שהנשים של ערי אירופא שדרכן תמיד לילך פרועי ראש מותר לקרות כנגדן כיון שכל הנשים דרכן בכך, יעו"ש, וז"ל,

הבא"ח בפרשת בא אות יב, וזל"ה:

"שער של אשה שדרכה לכסותו ערוה הוא ואסור לקרות ולהתפלל ולברך כנגדו וכו' אבל בתולות שדרכן לילך פרועות ראש, וכן שערות של נשים שרגילים לצאת חוץ לצמתן בקצת ארצות מותר

from under the covering, it is permitted to recite [the Shema] in their presence, since it is their practice and [men] are used to them. Similarly, women whose practice it is to braid their hair and let it fall behind them [without covering it], since this is their practice, it is permitted to recite [the Shema] in their presence. And in my small book, *Mekabtziel*, I noted that since European women always appear in public with their hair uncovered, it is permitted to recite [the Shema] in their presence, since all women [in their societies] appear this way.

From here you learn that only the hair of a woman that is [generally] covered can be called *erva*, and in a society in which it is generally covered, but if it is exposed in a society in which women expose it, this is not called *erva*.

And the reason appears to be that whenever hair that is generally covered is exposed, it can lead to erotic thoughts, but this is not the case when it is always revealed, and men are used to seeing it all the time; then it doesn't lead to erotic thoughts. This parallels [the law about] virgins, where there is no prohibition to reveal the hair, since it is always revealed, and for this reason, in European cities, where women appear in public with their hair uncovered as a matter of course, this does not count as [exposing] *erva*.

The R. Moses Al-Ashkar said even more than this – his words are quoted in the *Kaf HaChayyim* #8 – that even those women who come from countries where women generally cover their hair [who move to countries where women do not] are per-

לקרות כנגדן כיון שדרכן בכך ורגילין בהם, וכן נשים שדרכן לעשות שער ראשן קליעות משתלשלות מאחוריהן, כיון שדרכן בכך מותר לקרות כנגדן. ובסה"ק מקבציאל, העליתי שהנשים בערי אירופא שדרכן לילך תמיד פרועי ראש מותר לקרות כנגדן, כיון שכל הנשים דרכן בכך." עכ"ל.

מכאן אתה למד, שאין השער באשה נקרא ערוה אלא אם הוא מכוסה, ובמקום שדרכן לכסותו אבל אם הוא מגולה במקום שדרכן לגלותו אינו נקרא ערוה,

והטעם נראה דכל שהשער מכוסה ונתגלה מביא לידי הרהור, לא כן אם הוא במקום שהוא תמיד מגולה שבני אדם רגילים לראותו תמיד, אי' מביא לידי הרהור, דומיא דבתולות שאין איסור בגלויי כיון שהוא תמיד מגולה, ומשום כך בערי אירופא שהנשים יוצאות תמיד פרועי ראש אין בזה משום ערוה.

וגדולה מזו כתב הר"מ אלשקר ז"ל, הב"ד הכה"ח אות ח', שאפי[ולו] אותן נשים הבאות מארצות שדרכן לכסות למקום שדרכן לגלות, מותרי' הן לגלות אם אינן

mitted to stop covering their hair, assuming they do not wish to return [to their native countries]. See there for further discussion.

With this in mind, the words of the Gaon our master stand firm, for the matter is all dependent on practice. Thus, anywhere in which all the women in a given city appear in public with their hair exposed, there is no concern about erotic thoughts. And it would appear that this is what modern [religious] women, who appear in markets and on the street with their hair uncovered, are relying on, and no one tries to stop them, since it can be argued that they have a reasonable view to rely upon.

For this reason, we need to suggest that when the Gemara says "uncovering hair is a Torah violation," this refers to undoing braided hair; in other words, making her hair free-flowing and brushing it back behind themselves, like lewd women do. This is what the Gemara calls "a Torah violation." But not a simple hairstyle, that is braided or coiffed and sits above their heads – this would give someone no cause to come to lewd thoughts.

And this is how Rashi explained the verse "and [the priest] shall undo the woman's hair" – "he undoes the braids on her head" (Num. 5:18). And this is also explicit in the words of the *Ben Ish Chai* referenced above, who wrote:

> And so too, women whose practice is to braid their hair and let the braids fall behind them, since this is their normal way of appearance, it is permitted to recite [the Shema] in their presence."

We see from this that if their hair is braided, this does not count as *erva*.

רוצות לחזור, יעו"ש.

מעתה קמו ועמדו דברי הגאון מהר"מ זלה"ה שהדבר תלוי במנהג וכל שאנשי העיר כולן נהגו לגלות אין בזה משום הרהור, וכנראה שעל זה סמכו הנשים בימינו אלה שהן הולכות בגלוי ראש בשווקים וברחובות ואין מוחה בידן, הואיל וי"ל על מה שיסמוכו.

משום כך אנו צריכים לומר דמ"ש הגמרא פריעת ראש דאוריתא היינו פריעת הראש מקליעת השער והיי' הסותרות שערותיהן וסורקות אותן מאחורי' כדרך אותן הפרוצות, לזה קראה הגמרא איסור דאוריתא, אבל לא שערות סתם והן קלועות ומסודרות על ראש שאין בזה שום פליאה למיתי לידי הרהור.

וכך פירש רש"י על הפסוק ופרע את ראש האשה, סותר את קליעת ראשה (במדבר ה"יח), וכן מוכח מדברי הבא"ח הנ"ל שכתב:

> "וכן הנשים שדרכן לעשות שער ראשן קליעות משתלשלות לאחוריהם. כיון שדרכן בכך מותר לקרות כנגדן."

הרי שאם השערות קלועות אין בהן משום ערוה.

In our community in the Diaspora (=Casablanca), it was well known that all women would appear in public with their hair uncovered, except for Chareidi women who would wear a wig or a head scarf. Nevertheless, it was understood even by those authorities who took a strict position that [non-Chareidi] women were unwilling to pay attention to them and cover their hair, and for this reason, there was no one who tried to stop them practicing this way, since "it is better to sin unwittingly, etc." See the laws of Yom Kippur (*Shulchan Arukh*, OC 608:2).

אצלנו בחו"ל היה הדבר גלוי ומפורסם, שכל הנשים היו הולכות בגלוי ראש, פרט לחרדיות שהיו חובשות פאה נכרית או מטפחת, ומ"מ אפילו אלו המחמירים היו יודעים שאין הנשים מוכנות לשמוע להם לכסות ראשן, ומשום כך לא היה מי שימחה ע"ז, משום מוטב שיהיו שוגגות וכו' עיי' הלכות יוה"כ.

If only the matter would remain at revealing hair and not spread to other covered places that would be considered *erva* according to everybody. But contemporary women have already allowed themselves to walk in the streets and marketplaces with bare thighs and arms – and in places where there is mixed swimming how much more so [is this a problem]! But we cannot establish the yoke of religion (i.e., we cannot stop this practice by force) until the righteous redeemer comes, may it be speedily in our days.

והלואי שיהיה הדבר נשאר בגלוי שערות ולא יתפשט גם למקומות מכוסים שבדברי הכל יש בהם משום ערוה, וכבר הרשו לעצמן נשי הזמן להתהלך ברחובות ובשווקים חשופות שוקיים וזרועות, ובמקומות שחיה מעורבות על אחת כמה וכמה, ואין בידנו להקים את עול הדת עד בוא גואל צדק במב"י א.

This is what I have to answer in response to your questions, and nothing more.

זה מה שנ"ל לענות על שאלתך ותו ל[א] מ[ידי]

I sign with the blessing of Torah: A small one among the tribes of Judah, Moshe Malka.

החותם בברכת התורה: הצב"י משה מלכה

Rabbi Malka returns to this discussion in Responsum 35.

Petach Tikva, 15th of Iyyar, 5751 (April 29, 1991)

פתח תקוה טו"ב אייר תשנ"א

To the great Rabbi Melech Shapiro shlit"a in the United States,

למעלת הרה"ג כמוה"ר מלך שפירא שליט"א ארה"ב

UNCOVERED HAIR AND MODERN JEWISH LAW

Dear Rabbi! I received all your letters, and I apologize that I have not had time to answer them because of my communal and personal responsibilities, and it has had to wait till now, and I request your forgiveness.

With regard to a woman's hair covering, that his honor sees what seems to be a contradiction in the words of my first letter that I sent him, and he asks me for an explanation.

Dear Rabbi! I do not understand how you have come to see a contradiction when what I wrote explicitly is: "Nevertheless, it was understood even by those authorities who took a strict position that [non-Chareidi] women were unwilling to pay attention to them, etc." And it is known of course, to his honor, that not every lenient interpretation is accepted by every sage.

For instance, the great sage of our generation, Rav Ovadia shlit"a, opposes wigs, and correctly, since women choose expensive and beautiful wigs, and this is often worse (=more attractive) than their natural hair! But even so, Chareidi women wear wigs with easy spirits and no one [in that community] is concerned. I say this to point out that in all matters there are those who are strict and those who are lenient.

I explained first the words of R. Yosef Messas z"l, and I brought proofs from other poskim, that in a place where women's practice is to appear in public with hair uncovered, there is no prohibition, but that not everyone agrees with this.

רב יקר! קבלתי את כל מכתביך, והנני מצטער שלא הייתי יכול לענות עליהם בזמן מחמת עול הצבור והיחיד המוטל עלי, ואחר עד עתה ועמו הסליחה.

בעניין כסוי ראש האשה שכב' ראה כאילו ישנה סתירה בדברי המכתב הראשון ששלחתי לו, והוא דורש ממני הסבר.

רב יקר! אינני יודע איך הגעת לידי סתירה כזו, כאשר אני כותב במפורש: "ומ"מ אפילו המחמירים היו יודעים כי אין הנשים שומעות וכו'" והנה כידוע לכת"ר שלא כל קולא מתקבלת אצל החכמים כולם.

הלא תראה, הגאון מופת הדור הרב עובד' שליט"א מתנגד לפאה נכרית, ובצדק, כי הנשים בוחרות להן פאה חשובה ומהודרת, וזה גרוע לפעמים משער טבעי, ובכל זאת חרדות הולכות בפאה נכרית בשופי לית דחש, להודיע שבכל דבר ישנם מחמירים וישנם מקילים,

אני הסברתי תחילה את דברי הר"י משאש ז"ל והבאתי סמוכים מדברי שאר הפוסקים, שבמקום שהנשים נוהגות ללכת בראש מגולה אין שם איסור, אך לא כולם מודים לזה,

And there are those who are strict and say that if the Gemara says that exposing hair is a Torah prohibition, the simple meaning of the words is their intent, and we should not listen to anyone who tries to explain them differently.	וישנם המחמירים ואומרים אם הגמרא אומרת פריעת ראש דאורייתא, פשוטם כמשמעם ואין לשמוע לכל מי שמפרש אותם אחרת,
Now certainly, people who think this way believe it is forbidden for women to appear in public with their hair uncovered, but then why don't these people stop [the women] from doing so? It was to answer this question that I wrote that they know the women will not listen to them, and this is why they did not try to stop them, since "it is better, etc."	אלא ודאי סוברים שאסור לאשה ללכת בראש גלוי, ואיך למה לא היו מוחים בידם? על זה כתבתי שהם היו יודעים שאין הנשים שומעות להם ולכן לא מחו בידם כי מוטב וכו׳.
Nevertheless, I was happy to see what R. HaLevi[55] wrote in his book *Sefer HaMitzvot*, and he can be considered an authority that supports what I wrote. Continue in strength and blessing! (=thank you).	ועכ״פ שמחתי לראות את מה שכתב הרב הלוי, בספרו ״ספר המצות,״ והוא תנא דמסייע למה שכתבתי חזק וברוך.

Thus, both Rabbis Messas and Malka accept the societally based understanding of the prohibition, and thus rule as a matter of practical law that married women in modern society, where the norm is not to cover their hair, are permitted to go with their hair uncovered.

RABBI YAAKOV BRECHER

A 19th–20th century scholar, Rabbi Yaakov Brecher, attests to the fact that married women in many countries around the world no longer covered their hair. In a brief piece (*Katuv Yosher Divrei Emet* pp. 86–87), he presents a radically different understanding of the prohibition. He argues that it was simply a custom of married women intended to distinguish them from single women. He even compares it to a wedding ring.[56] In an

---

55. This refers to the *Yad HaLevi* which was discussed above.
56. While at first glance this approach is appealing, it does not withstand a close textual review. First, as we explained above in Chapters 2–4, the classical Talmudic texts do not clearly distinguish between married and single women. Second, this explanation is simply unstated as a reason (and if it were the reason, it should cause an *arusah* to cover her hair). Third, it defies the modesty-driven explanation found in so many Rishonim.

era where married women covered their hair, leaving it uncovered would be like a married woman walking around without her ring, presumably to hide her marital status, thereby inviting promiscuity. However, when the custom changes, he argues, there is no prohibition whatsoever.[57]

Excursus Six: Details of Hair Covering: Starting When, With What, Where, and How Much

This work has been devoted to developing the argument that the obligation for married women to cover their hair is based on social convention, and therefore does not apply in an era where most married women do not cover their hair. If this contention is correct, the material in this excursus is essentially not needed, since the "correct" answers to all of these questions are that women must only cover their hair when, with what, where, and how much as modest women do in their society.

This excursus discusses four topics.

- When must a woman start covering her hair?
- How much hair should be covered?
- Hair covering in non-public locations
- Hair covering with a wig, rather than a hat or a snood

A. COVERING HAIR OF A BRIDE AT THE WEDDING

As explained many times in this book, normative Jewish law ruled that single women need not cover their hair. Furthermore, this has been the common practice in the Jewish community (other than Yemen[58]) for many centuries. When a woman becomes obligated to cover her hair (assuming such an obligation) – specifically, whether a bride must cover her hair on her wedding day, is in dispute.[59] The *Mishnah Berura* (*OC* 75:11) rules that a woman must cover her hair as soon as she becomes an *arusah*, after the first stage of marriage, even before *sheva berachot* are

---

57. His position was challenged vociferously by Rabbi Chaim M. Roller (1868–1946) in *Responsa Be'er Chaim Mordechai* 3:52. Thanks to Rabbi Jonathan Ziring for these references.
58. For more on Yemen and a few other Sephardic places, see Ilan Fuchs, "Hair Covering for Single Women: A New Reading of Mizraḥi Halakhic Rulings" *Nashim: A Journal of Jewish Women's Studies & Gender Issues*, No. 23:35–59 (Spring–Fall 2012) and Rabbi Yitzchak Ratzabi, *Shulchan Arukh Hamekutzar*, Chapter 202 (on single women covering their hair in Yemen).
59. Before any intimacy takes place.

recited and before she is fully married. This position follows the view of Rabbi Akiva Eger (Comments on *Shulchan Arukh OC* 75), who cites the Mahari HaLevi. As Rabbi Moshe Sternbuch (*Responsa Teshuvot VeHanhagot* 5:334) notes, this would essentially obligate a bride to come to the wedding with her hair covered, even before she is married.

While there are a variety of opinions on what constitutes each stage of marriage (see *Shulchan Arukh EH* 55:1), it would be impractical for a bride to cover her hair in the middle of a wedding ceremony. The practical reality is reflected in Rabbi Sternbuch's position.[60]

Other poskim, however, believe it is the consummation of marriage that creates the obligation for a woman to cover her hair. However, this position further divides. Some rule that after *yichud*, where *in theory* the couple could consummate their marriage, as they are left secluded for the time needed to consummate the marriage, a woman must cover her hair, though the couple has not in fact been intimate. Furthermore, according to some, yichud constitutes nissuin.[61] However, Rabbi Sternbuch notes that since realistically the couple is not intimate during yichud, there is room to argue that this yichud does not constitute real nissuin. Other poskim contend that the obligation for a married woman to cover her hair begins after the actual consummation of the marriage, when she becomes "sotah eligible." This is the position of *Chatam Sofer* and was accepted by Rabbi Moshe Feinstein in an unpublished responsum.[62]

Still other poskim provide alternative grounds to permit this conduct. Rabbi Yehuda Henkin in *Responsa Bnei Banim* 3:23 argues that even if this newly married woman would be obligated to cover her hair, the wedding hall is not considered a public place for these purposes. Rabbi Wosner in *Shevet HaLevi* 8:259 suggests that while a bride may be obligated to cover her hair, her veil covers much of her hair and is sufficient as a *kalta/hynuma* (see Excursus Three above). Rabbi Shlomo Zalman Auerbach is quoted in *Ishei Yisrael* Ch. 55 n. 77 as preferring a bride cover her hair but argues that *bediavad* one need not enforce this where it will cause tension.[63]

---

60. Mahari HaLevi himself (*Responsa Mahari HaLevi* 9) argues that a woman must cover her hair during the period of *erusin*, but the obligation is waived on the day of the wedding when it is clear that she is a bride.
61. See, for example, *Shevut Yaakov* 103.
62. See *Responsa Chatam Sofer YD* 195 and the unpublished responsum available here: https://tinyurl.com/y472p748.
63. For further details on this issue, see R. Dovid Emanuel Feinberg, "When

B. HOW MUCH HAIR SHOULD BE COVERED?

The arguments in this book about the custom of covering and *dat Yehudit* explain some of the various positions among those poskim who contend that married women must, in accordance with *dat Moshe*, cover their hair in some form. While these poskim hold that *dat Moshe* does not change, they argue for allowing women to cover less than all of their hair when such conduct is modest in their time and place.

Some argue that a woman must, or at least should, cover all her hair, based on the Zohar (see *Responsa Chatam Sofer OC 36*). The *Mishnah Berura* (*OC* 75:14) endorses this conclusion by combining the Zohar and the story of Kimchit. The *Chazon Ish* is cited as saying that a woman must cover all hair as a matter of law, and that even the hair that sticks out of the head covering must be covered due to custom (see Rabbi Moshe Sternbuch's discussion in *Responsa Teshuvot VeHahanhagot* 2:692). However, Rashba, in the context of the *keriat Shema* discussions, writes that hair that sticks out of a woman's hair covering is not considered *erva*, as that is normally uncovered and therefore does not distract men. This accords with our interpretation of Rashba (that he did not understand this to be a biblical prohibition) in Chapter 5.

As we have discussed earlier, Maharam Al-Ashkar (Responsum 35) argues that where it is the norm for women to leave some of their hair uncovered, a woman is permitted to do so. While we took the position that this indicated a subjective understanding of the law, as developed by Rabbi Yosef Messas in this chapter, other poskim have argued that this was not the intention of Maharam Al-Ashkar. Rather, they argue that the basic obligation for women to cover some of their hair is non-negotiable, although how much must be covered may be societally dependent. This, for example, is the position of R. David Y. Zilberstein (1820–1884) in *Shevilei David OC* 75:2, although he does not explain the minimum amount that women must cover. Several poskim argue that a woman may leave a *tefach* (handbreadth, between 3.15 to 4.0 inches) of hair uncovered. This measure is the smallest size prohibited, based on b. Berachot regarding *erva*. Consequently, Rabbi Shlomo Tabak (*Responsa Teshurot Shai* 1:51) argues that one must cover the entire head but allows a total of

---

is a Kallah Required to Cover Her Hair," *Journal of Halacha and Contemporary Society* LXVIII, p. 102 and R. Yehoshua Van Dyke, "Kisui Rosh HaKallah Beseudat Hanissuin," *Techumin* 36 and many other sources cited therein. See also *Migdal Chananel* by Chananel Shlossberg (2018), *Even HaEzer* 55.

a tefach to be exposed. This is how he understands the kalta – that only a tefach of hair will be visible through the holes.

Rabbi Moshe Feinstein (*Responsa Iggerot Moshe OC* 1:58), on the other hand, argues slightly differently. He contends that the biblical obligation is for a woman to cover her head, not hair. The rest of the hair must be covered by dint of *dat Yehudit*. However, as evidenced by the fact that unmarried women need not cover their hair, then hair is not truly erva; so less than a tefach cannot be considered problematic, as even by erva the minimum size for many of the prohibited areas is only a tefach. In a society in which there is no applicable *dat Yehudit*, Rabbi Feinstein would permit a considerable amount of non-head hair to be uncovered, and this is endorsed by Rabbi Mordechai Willig (*Am Mordechai* Berachot, p. 69). The logic of this position is that there is no *dat Yehudit* present, and once the *dat Moshe* is fulfilled, no more hair needs to be covered. Rabbi Yehuda Henkin (*Responsa Bnei Banim* 3:21) argues that Rabbi Feinstein's intent is a square tefach. However, Rabbi Tzvi Hirsch Meisels (*Responsa Mikadshei Hashem* 1:97) argues that what needs to be covered is a tefach by any width. While Rabbi Henkin prefers accepting this position, or even being more stringent, he admits that there is room to argue that one need only cover the majority of the head based on the principle of *rubo kekulo*, that the majority is like the entirety. However, he does indeed note that there is photographic evidence that many wives of rabbis from two and three generations ago covered their head but left out more than a tefach of hair, which may imply the acceptance of an even more lenient standard.

Some rabbis have been quoted (but not in writing) as saying that some form of covering the hair is non-negotiable, but anything beyond that is societally dependent and therefore no longer relevant. Similarly, some have been quoted as saying that a woman need only wear something that indicates that she is married, such as a headband (this is similar to Rabbi Brecher's comparison to a wedding ring).[64] Again, these positions have

---

64. Explaining these two views logically, rather than precedentially, is simple. If there is a Torah obligation not grounded in modesty rules but in something else, it can have only four basic parameters: (1) All; (2) All but a handbreadth; (3) Most; (4) A nominal amount. The parameters are explained as follows: All that is needed is something to dishevel or uncover. Since this rule is a Torah-mandated commemoration of the sotah ritual, all that is needed is enough that when it is revealed, one can say "now that is uncovered" and it should not matter whether that is 25% or 52% of the woman's hair. The position that a wedding ring is sufficient is grounded in a completely different understanding of the mitzvah unrelated to the

not been recorded in writing and have not been adopted by any major posek to the best of my knowledge, though it has become a common practice in some communities.

C. HAIR COVERING NOT IN A PUBLIC PLACE

A third relevant issue concerns where a woman must cover her hair if other men will see her. (We are not referring here to those who suggest following the stringency of the Zohar to cover hair even when no men are around, similar to Kimchit.) The Gemara in Ketubot 72a–b clearly distinguishes between public places, semi-public places, and private places, and seemingly only demands even partial covering in places that are as public as a *chatzer* (courtyard) or more. Based on the fact that the Gemara only discusses partial coverings in a chatzer, some poskim have contended that, in a woman's own home, she need not cover her hair even if others are present. This seems to follow the position of both Rashi and Tosafot in b. Ketubot 72b who understand that even in a chatzer women did not cover their hair. Moreover, they make no distinction between cases where men are present and where they are not.

However, others have argued that the location distinctions are only relevant due to the probability that men will see the woman's hair. However, in a case where men will surely see her hair, she must cover it. This, for example, is the position of Rabbi Henkin, (*Responsa Bnei Banim* 3:24) on the basis of a comment by Ritva (b. Ketubot 72b). Rabbi Henkin therefore rejects a suggestion by his interlocutor that no such obligation should exist within the home. In an earlier responsum (3:21), he even argues that the position of Maharam Al-Ashkar to uncover some of the hair was only in the home, which implies quite a strict standard even in private, and even more so in public! This accords more closely with the position of *Bach* (*EH* 115), who rejected the possibility that women could walk in a chatzer without at least a partial covering.

Rabbi Yosef Tzvi Rimon notes that these two positions may depend

---

Sotah ritual, but to the idea that the Torah mandates that married women identify themselves as such, as explained in some sources above. For more on this view, see https://www.deracheha.org/head-covering-2-rationale-and-meaning/ (accessed Sept. 12, 2023) which notes that one explanation for why women cover their hair is to show marital status, writing: "*A sign of Marriage.* The Mishnah teaches that a Jewish bride's hair left loose in the public procession to her wedding was a sure sign that she had not been married before."

on how one deals with the seemingly contradictory comment of Ritva. As Rabbi Rimon writes:

> The Ritva mentions the reason behind this leniency: "... since nobody sees." Later in his comments, however, he cites the Yerushalmi's definition of a chatzer: "an alley that does not have many people intruding through it is considered a 'chatzer.'" This definition suggests that people do, in fact, look into the chatzer, only not "many people." Accordingly, we should perhaps reread the Ritva's earlier phrase as "since not many people see."[65]

The core of this idea, that seeing the hair of a married woman is not universally forbidden but rather depends on location, assumes that hair is not intrinsically erotic or immodest. Otherwise, such distinctions would make little sense.

It is worth noting that the idea that a woman need never cover her hair in her home no matter who is around is widely considered the view of Rabbi Ovadia Yosef and is recorded as such by Rabbi Yehuda Naki, the secretary of Rabbi Ovadia Yosef, in the name of Rabbi Yosef. In *Shut Maayan Omer* Rabbi Naki records that when he asked Rabbi Yosef whether a woman must cover her hair in her home, he answered that she does not. Even after clarifying that he was asking about cases when men were present other than the woman's husband, Rabbi Yosef maintained his position. In the footnotes, Rabbi Naki notes that this is the simplest understanding of *Beit Yosef* as derived from Rashi.[66]

---

65. See Rabbi Yosef Tzvi Rimon, "Woman's Hair-covering in a Chatzer" at https://www.etzion.org.il/en/womans-hair-covering-chatzer, note 2. In note 3, he discusses the nature of the prohibition as to how it affects this discussion.

66. Rabbi Yehuda Naki, *Shut Maayan Omer* Volume 11, *EH* 15. Rabbi Naki notes, however, that while Rabbi Yosef was comfortable expressing his lenient position, he refused to elaborate on the rationale. Rabbi Naki speculates that Rabbi Yosef felt that ideally a woman should be strict to cover her hair at home even without men present out of deference to the position of the *Chatam Sofer* based on the story of Kimchit. Nevertheless, Rabbi Yosef did not want to spell this out, as from a halakhic perspective there was no real reason to be strict in this way, and "even a Torah scholar and fearer of God should not refrain from marrying such a woman if she fears God, is careful about *mitzvot*, and has good character traits." Thus, Rabbi Yosef simply stated his lenient position clearly and succinctly to leave room for committed Jews to follow either position. While, like Rabbi Naki, one can only speculate as to the exact policy concerns of Rabbi Yosef, it seems certain that from

D. THE SHEITEL – COVERING THE HAIR WITH A WIG

One of the most interesting developments of Jewish law in the area of hair covering is the trend – now many centuries old – of women covering their hair with a wig, rather than with a hat. As the normative practice of secular people changed and modest secular women ceased covering their hair generally, the sheitel (wig) developed in many segments of Orthodox Jewish society as the perfect social and religious compromise: It allowed one to remain in conformity with the basic requirements of Jewish law (that one's hair be covered), while simultaneously recognizing

---

a legal perspective Rabbi Yosef felt that there was no reason for a woman to cover her hair at home, even if men other than her husband were present.

The question of whether a woman should cover her hair while on a Zoom call or while being photographed is driven by this issue. Unlike the question of hair covering in the home, which is amply discussed in a variety of sources going back to the Talmud and is repeatedly discussed in each of the many eras since then, the question of how to view general modesty standards in a photographic setting is without direct precedent. Classical Jewish law prohibits men and women from engaging in revealing of body parts which are thought of as erotic or sexual or immodest. The Talmudic rabbis always understood this to cover a wider variety of body parts for women than men, reflecting their (and our) general understanding of human sexuality and eroticism. No one has ever questioned whether this covers erotic photographs or movies, technologies that are more than a century old. The reason is obvious: erotic behavior is prohibited as a matter of Jewish law in any and every manner outside the marital context. But, hair has always been understood to be different from other body parts in that it is not truly erotic at all. Indeed, as many have noted, one can find countless pictures of wives of Torah scholars who happily posed for pictures in their backyards or homes with their hair uncovered, and yet otherwise completely modestly dressed. This is exactly because hair was not identical to other body parts; based on that, women wear sheitels and unmarried women do not cover their hair, neither of which would be acceptable if hair was truly erotic. I see little difference between posing for a picture in one's backyard and appearing on Zoom. Hair then is uniquely situated because there remains a fundamental dispute about whether exposed hair is erotic at all. Those who think hair is covered because it is erotic rule that appearing on Zoom with hair uncovered is prohibited. Those who think hair is covered and thus has become erotic also think that hair needs to be covered in a Zoom call. Those who think married women need to cover their hair for other reasons (*sotah, chok* or other approaches), and allow women to appear with their hair uncovered routinely in such situations even around men who are not part of their family, rule that exposed hair is not immodest and may be exposed when Jewish law permits it to be (unless it is for reasons external to halakha and immodest in the specific time and place), and then permit a woman in her home to expose her hair. Whether a woman should cover her hair on a Zoom call or photograph is dependent on whether she covers her hair in the home when people visit.

that uncovered hair was no longer strictly a sign of immodest conduct. Women who desire to obey Jewish law while socially fitting into Western society found wearing a hat or a scarf to be a burden. Hence, the sheitel became the perfect compromise because it promotes conformity with both Jewish law and Western culture.[67]

Whether this compromise was acceptable according to halakha has been a dispute for many centuries. The Mishnah (Shabbat 6:5) states that a woman may wear a wig into a place where carrying is prohibited on Shabbat.[68] Writing in the middle of the 16th century, the famous commentator on the Rif, the *Shiltei HaGibborim* (64 29:1(1)) notes that this Mishnah implicitly permits a married woman to go out in public covering her hair with a wig and nothing else. Others promptly disagreed, the most prominent being *Beer Sheva* (no. 18, published first in 1614) who quotes R. Ezekiel Katzenellenbogen as polemically insisting that this approach was wrong: rather, he maintains that the various "in passing" discussions of wigs found in any pre-modern source must only be discussing wearing a wig under a hat. Of course, he posits that a married woman may not cover her hair with only a wig.

Rabbi Moshe Isserless (Rama), in his commentary on the *Tur* and again in his glosses on the *Shulchan Arukh* itself,[69] adopts the view that wigs as a head covering are permitted and this is endorsed by many prominent commentaries on the *Shulchan Arukh* including *Levush*, *Magen Avraham*, *Pri Megadim*, *Gra*, and *Shulchan Arukh HaRav*.[70] One is hard-pressed to find a prominent authority, other than the *Chatam Sofer*, who flatly rejects the view permitting head covering with a wig in modern times in the Ashkenazi community.[71] *Mishnah Berura* (75:15) summarizes

---

67. I made a similar point in a different context in a popular article "The Case for the Sheitel," *The Forward*, March 14, 2011 at https://forward.com/sisterhood/136137/the-case-for-the-sheitel/.
68. Shabbat 64b in the Talmud. The discussion is, on its face, unrelated to the rules of modest conduct and only discussing the rules of carrying on Shabbat.
69. *Darkhei Moshe*, Orach Chaim 303:6 and *Shulchan Arukh* 75:2.
70. See *Ein Mishpat* Nazir 28b (number 50) for one of the few times where the author of this reference work shares his view of Jewish law, which permitted married women to wear a wig and rejects the view of the *Beer Sheva*.
71. Indeed, even the *Kaf HaChayyim* adopts this view; see *Kaf HaChayyim* 75:19. But see R. Yaakov Emden in *She'eilat Yaavetz* 1:9 and *Chatam Sofer* (notes on *Magen Avraham* 75:5) who do reject this view. For a very comprehensive review of the literature, see *Otzar HaPoskim* on Even HaEzer 21:2 (24:5–8).

the debate while leaving one with the impression that it is acceptable to wear just a wig.[72]

However, this matter was re-opened in the middle of the twentieth century by Rabbi Ovadia Yosef[73] who argues at length in many different forums that covering one's head exclusively with a wig is without a shadow of a doubt forbidden. He essentially advances three arguments, two grounded in Jewish law and one a subjective assessment of the sociology. First, he argues that wigs cause the same sexual thoughts as regular hair and thus cannot be permitted. Second, even if hair no longer causes any sexual thoughts, women who wear wigs look like they are sinning and thus this conduct is prohibited. Finally, he seems to posit that wig wearing is the first step of generally abandoning observance of the mitzvah. His formulation is harsh and complex and deeply critical of those who do not agree. He notes:

> The correct view is that like most, and nearly all, recent authorities (mentioned above) who prohibit a wig. It is a vast mitzvah to publicly share that wig wearing is prohibited, in particular to Sephardim who had always conducted themselves this way and in times past. Only now have they started to learn from those who ruled liberally for themselves without the consent of the Sages, since these women learn the perversion and not the solution. It is a mitzvah to tell them that this is a serious breach in the rules of modest conduct of proper Jewish women as is noted by great Rabbi Avraham Teomim in his work *Chesed le'Avraham* who states that one must object and protest Jewish women who go out with a wig. (Even more so, one must warn the editors of the Orthodox Jewish papers who have made wigs totally permissible against sharing the location of wig sellers who lead the

> והעיקר כדברי רוב ככל האחרונים הנ"ל לאסור בזה, ומצוה רבה לפרסם האיסור ברבים, ובפרט לספרדיות שנהגו לאסור מימות עולם ומשנים קדמוניות, ורק כעת התחילו ללמוד מאלו המורות היתר לעצמן שלא ברצון חכמים, דילפי הני נשי מקלקלתא ולא מתקנתא, ומצוה להודיען שזוהי פירצה חמורה בגדר הצניעות של בנות ישראל הכשרות, וכמ"ש הגאון מהר"א תאומים בעל חסד לאברהם: שצריך למחות ולמנוע בנות ישראל לצאת בפאה נכרית. (ומה מאד יש להזהיר את עורכי העתונות הדתיים שנעשה להם כהיתר לפרסם המקומות שמוכרים: פאה נכרית, ומכשילים בזה את

---

72. Interestingly, *Arukh HaShulchan* is simply silent on this issue, although you could read his comments *OC* 303:20 as permitting wigs and thus upon a close examination of *OC* 75 conclude that this is what he actually says here as well.
73. *Yabia Omer*, 5: *EH* 5.

public astray.) Every woman who accepts on herself this matter [not to wear a wig] and to go out only with a hat or a snood that covers all her head, she should be blessed with all the blessings in the Torah, bountiful sustenance and learned children and blessed to see children accomplished in Torah and love of heaven, leaders of the Jewish community.

הרבים). וכל אשה המקבלת עליה לשמור לעשות ככל דברי רבותינו הפוסקים שאסרו הדבר בכל תוקף, ולצאת אך ורק בכובע או מטפחת המכסה את כל ראשה, תתברך בכל הברכות שבתורה, ובמזוני רויחי ובבני סמיכי, ותזכה לראות זרע קודש בנים גדולים בתורה ויראת ה׳ טהורה, מורי הוראות בישראל.

Many contemporary Sephardic authorities have followed his view and aver that wearing a wig alone is not an acceptable practice in the Sephardic community or anywhere.[74]

Those who rule leniently point directly to the responsum of Rabbi Moshe Feinstein, *Iggerot Moshe, EH* 2:12, who permitted wig wearing with two simple observations. First, he observes that Jewish law mandates that married women cover their hair and a wig is a covering. Second, there is no real prohibition of looking like one's hair is not covered since the average person (in our community) knows that women cover their hair with wigs all the time.[75] Indeed, Rabbi Feinstein is clear that even if the husband objects to his wife's practice of wig wearing and wants her to wear a hat, she can ignore his objections and continue to wear a wig.[76]

---

74. This was not the consensus of Sephardic poskim historically (See *Yaskil Avdi* 7:16, for example) although there is no doubt that Rabbi Yosef's deep opposition to married women wearing wigs as a form of head covering has changed the Sephardic consensus. For a view of more than one hundred authorities on the question of wig wearing, see https://tinyurl.com/ycyu9na5. There is little doubt that wigs are less common in Israel than America for a set of social reasons outside the parameters of this book.

75. Rabbi Feinstein's famous comparison is to a man shaving with an electric shaver, which he avers is not prohibited as people might think one shaves with a razor.

76. I think that there is some truth to the sociological observation of Rabbi Yaakov Hoffman that:

"The *yeshivish* preference for wigs might have to do with the fact that in recent history, many Orthodox women did not cover their hair at all. In such a societal reality, *sheitels* became associated with those pious women who covered their hair at all times, as opposed to others who donned hats only for religious functions. Thus, the *sheitel* came to be thought of as the mark of a scrupulously observant woman."

https://www.torahmusings.com/2019/01/reconsidering-the-sheitel/

From the tone of Rabbi Feinstein's writings, it seems reasonable that he does not think that wearing a wig is a step in the wrong direction, but a step in the right direction. He states:

Thus as a matter of Jewish law, you, my questioner, cannot stop your wife – the eminent *rebbetzin* – from wearing a wig. Even if you wish to be strict, you cannot push your stricture on her since this is just her Jewish law matter; since she is conducting herself completely properly, as [wigs as head coverings are permitted in] the view of most poskim and which logic inclines one to follow, you cannot be strict to her on this matter, even if she does not wear anything on top of the wig.	ולכן לדינא אין כתר"ה יכול למחות ביד אשתו הרבנית החשובה מללבש פאה נכרית, שאף אם כתר"ה רוצה להחמיר אינו יכול להטיל חומרותיו עליה שזהו רק דין שלה, וכיון שהיא עושה כדין שהוא כרוב הפוסקים ושגם נראה כמותם, אינו יכול להחמיר עליה אף אם לא תכסה כלל הפאה נכרית,

Thus, Rabbi Feinstein completely validates wigs and Rabbi Yosef totally invalidates them.

A compromise view is taken in many letters of Rabbi Menachem Mendel Schneerson, the Rebbe from Lubavitch, who thought that it was much better for a woman to wear a wig than a hat, since when one wears a hat or even a snood, natural hair of the woman will protrude and that is a violation of Jewish law. He states simply that the essential obligation is that "the purpose and intent of a *sheitel* is for all the hair to be covered."[77] In the words of one recent commentator:

> The Rebbe's opposition to wearing kerchiefs was due to the likelihood that some hair would be exposed – even temporarily – and thus lead a woman to transgress a "major prohibition" as explained in *Shulchan Arukh, Orach Chaim* 75 (*Igros Kodesh*, vol. XIX, p. 428).[78]

The Satmar community, and a few other smaller Chasidic communities, continue to adhere to the position of the *Chatam Sofer* that a wig alone is not sufficient.[79] This community follows the practice of wearing both a wig and a hat on top of a wig.[80]

---

77. Menachem Mendel Schneerson, *Igros Kodesh*, vol. VIII, p. 217.
78. See Esther Vilenkin, "Only Sheitels Cover Every Strand Of Hair" at *Jewish Press*, January 17, 2019 at https://www.jewishpress.com/indepth/opinions/only-sheitels-cover-every-strand-of-hair/2019/01/17/.
79. This is based on the view of the *Chatam Sofer* and its endorsement by Divrei Chaim *YD* 59. Divrei Chaim is clear that what he favors is wigs plus a hat.
80. See the fine article by my colleague, Rabbi Dr. Gidon Rothstein, "Chatam

Socially, what we are left with is a few different head covering practices in the Orthodox community. The Sephardic community is insistent that wigs are prohibited and only hats, snoods or other such covers are permitted. The mainstream Ashkenazic community is of the view that either wigs or hats are fine and acceptable. The Chabad community endorses wigs only as the ideal and the rest of the Chasidic community endorses a wig with a hat on top of it. What one can say for sure is that the practice of wearing a wig as a head covering is well established in the Orthodox Jewish world and is unlikely to go away.

CONCLUSION TO THIS EXCURSUS

For those who reject the central thesis of this book (or who choose to be strict, even if they believe the thesis of the book to be correct), the above four discussions will require more extensive investigation. However, we include them here for completeness, although as noted, if our central contention is correct, these issues are rendered moot since all is dependent on the custom of modest Jewish women.

Conclusion

As noted at the outset of this chapter, the main halakhic arguments in this book were made in the earlier chapters where the primary sources from the Talmud, Rishonim, and main codes of Jewish law were analyzed in great detail. In this chapter, we have attempted to outline and explain the minority of modern voices that reach similar conclusions to those developed earlier in this book – that in a society where the majority of married women do not cover their hair, there is no halakhic obligation to do so. While our position may not be the dominant one in modern discourse, as we have shown, it emerges from many Acharonim, and was embraced even by several modern authorities who were cognizant of the changed reality in which many if not most married women no longer covered their hair.

Sofer on Women's Hair Covering" at https://www.torahmusings.com/2019/06/chatam-sofer-on-womens-hair-covering/.

CHAPTER 9

Conclusions: Jewish Law and Modesty: Hair as a Test Case

CHAPTER 9 CONCLUDES THIS BOOK AND HAS FOUR short sections. The first section is a summary of the arguments in this book, and it is followed by a more detailed chapter-by-chapter recitation of the arguments found in this work. The next part of this section discusses some methodological issues in Jewish law, focusing on the relationship between Talmudic reasoning and modern Jewish law. The final part of this conclusion focuses on some sociological observations about modern Jewish life that help explain, perhaps, the tension between the approach most modern Jewish law authorities have taken and the dominant view in the law codes and Rishonim.

Conclusions to books that are very textual are never simple in that they must both summarize what the book concludes and argue why this book and its conclusion are important generally. This conclusion aims to accomplish that dual mission.

A Summary of the Arguments in This Book

This book can be easily summarized: It contains an elaborate and highly textual argument about whether Jewish law mandates that married women cover their hair – or parts thereof – no matter what the social norm around them dictates. It concludes that there is a significant school of thought that validates the fully subjective approach to all issues of modesty, including hair covering. Support for this fully subjective approach is present in the Talmud (as discussed in Chapter 2) and the Geonim (Chapter 3). It can also be found in the post-Talmudic Jewish law authorities, be they

Ashkenazi or Sephardi (Chapter 5). Support extends to many members of the Tosafist school, as well as the *Tur* and *Shulchan Arukh* (Chapter 6). It is further seen in many post-*Shulchan Arukh* works that discuss brides covering and partially covering their hair (Chapter 7).

Significantly, this subjective approach is commonly articulated and adopted by many great authorities throughout the ages until the modern era. Nevertheless, as this book concedes at the beginning of Chapter 8, virtually all the noteworthy Jewish law authorities of the last 150 years have ignored this common pre-modern view and ruled directly that married women must cover at least some part of their head as a matter of biblical (Torah) law, no matter what the sociology around them is and no matter how other women dress. With but a few and rare exceptions, it is hard to find any prominent Jewish law authority post-emancipation who endorses the view that married women do not have to cover their hair when other modest women in the general society do not. The only important Jewish law authority to the contrary seems to be the Ben Ish Chai (and only in passing in a work written in Judeo-Arabic). This is true even as large numbers of generally observant Jewish women ceased covering their hair due to the pressures of modern life.

A Concluding Methodological Note

If the argument to permit married women to uncover their hair, or that all of the rules of modesty generally, were based on the reputational authority of those modern decisors of Jewish law cited in the last chapter, I would have to concede that – based on these authorities alone – the arguments found in this book would carry little weight. However, normative halakha is – according to most – decided primarily on the basis of analysis of the Talmud, the Rishonim, and the central codes of Jewish law such as the *Tur* and *Shulchan Arukh* and not based on the Jewish law authorities of the few most recent centuries. It is in that spirit that this book is written: Most Jewish law authorities of great renown over the last millennium were in the school of thought that labeled modesty – including even hair – purely subject to the cultural norms of the society one inhabits, and not anything else.

Rabbi Moshe Feinstein's responsum repeatedly justifies reaching conclusions of Jewish law contrary to that deemed normative by contemporary authorities when challenged for issuing a lenient ruling against the modern consensus. He writes:

And that which my dear correspondent wrote asking how we are permitted to rely in practice on such innovative insights as those I have presented, particularly when such a view contradicts the position of some latter-day authorities, I say: Has there already been an end or boundary set for Torah study, God forbid, that we should only rule according to what is found in existing works, but when questions arise that have not been posed in our traditional works we will not decisively resolve them even when we are able?! Certainly, in my humble opinion, it is forbidden to say this, as certainly Torah study will continue to flourish now in our time; therefore, everyone who is able must rule decisively on each halakhic question posed to him, to the best of his ability, with diligent investigation in the Talmudic sources and the works of halakhic decisors, with a clear understanding and valid proof, even if it is a new application of the halakha which has not been discussed in our Jewish law works. And even for a halakha which has been discussed in our Jewish law works, the one issuing a ruling must certainly understand the issue, too, and reach a conclusion in his own mind before issuing a ruling, and not rule solely based on a ruling that can be found on the topic in other halakhic works, as that is considered as one who decides points of law merely from reading law books, about which it is said, "Those who merely recite the Mishnah bring destruction upon the world, for they decide points of law from their recitation of the texts" (b. Sotah 22a; see Rashi ad loc.). And even if one's decisions sometimes go against those of eminent latter-day rabbinic authorities, so what? We are certainly permitted to disagree with latter-day authorities (Acharonim), and sometimes even with medieval authorities (Rishonim) when one has valid proofs, correct reasoning in particular – on matters like this, our Sages stated, "A judge has but only what his eyes see [before him]" (as explained in b. Bava Batra 131a; see Rashbam ad loc.) – so long as one does not contradict the undisputed opinion of the *Shulchan Arukh* and its commentaries which have been widely accepted in our community; on these types of matters it has been said, "[our predecessors] left room [for us] to distinguish ourselves" [See b. Chullin 7a].[1]

---

1. *Iggerot Moshe Yoreh Deah* 1:101, towards the end. I alluded to the importance of this framing for my approach to this topic in my earlier article in *Tradition*, n. 98, and I elaborate on this now. Much of this material is explained in even greater detail in a work I co-authored with Shlomo Pill, entitled *Setting the Table: An Introduction*

Particularly in a case such as this one, where so many pre-modern authorities are of the subjective view, there is no reason to hesitate to voice a view that runs directly contrary to the dominant contemporary view.

Indeed, many great rabbinic scholars severely criticized and rejected the general approach that post-Talmudic modern precedent, whether in codes, restatements, or responsa, could or should establish binding norms of halakha; the more modern the code, the less binding it is.[2] Rulings based on modern post-Talmudic codes and precedents are never really binding in any classical sense because the structure of Jewish law does not allow such modern codes to bind.[3] Thus, Rabbi Judah Loew (1526–1609) argued that relying on modern post-Talmudic precedents is mistaken because such texts "were merely authored for practical instruction, and not to learn the law from,"[4] meaning that post-Talmudic accounts of the halakha are useful handbooks of practical instruction for the times and places in which they were written, but they cannot be regarded as the law itself: They are merely timely applications of timeless rules. "It is more appropriate," Rabbi Loew continues, "to rule based directly on the Talmud, for while there is room to fear that in doing so one may… rule incorrectly… nevertheless, a wise man has only what his own mind understands from the Talmud," and he may thus rely on his own judgment.[5] It is for this reason that significant segments of this book focus on the Talmud and the early (more binding) authorities.

Indeed, a basic theme of this book in Chapters 4, 5, and 6 is that, in reality, the seemingly determinate rulings found in various post-Talmudic works were no more clear-cut than the meandering discourses of the Talmud itself, and therefore offered little real advantage to rabbinic scholars seeking knowledge of correct halakhic norms in regard to issues related to hair covering.[6] Chapters 6 and 7 show that – even as the modern

---

to the Jurisprudence of Rabbi Yechiel Mikhel Epstein's Arukh haShulchan (Academic Studies Press, 2021).

2. For a comprehensive explanation of why halakhic rulings should not merely follow existing precedents, whether in the codes or other rabbinic materials, see Rabbi Tzvi Hirsch Chayes, *Darkhei HaHoraah* 11 in *Kol Sifrei Maharitz Chayes* (1958), Vol. 1: 249–250.
3. See, e.g., Rabbi Chayyim ben Betzalel, *Viku'ach Mayim Chayyim*, sec. 1, 94.
4. Rabbi Judah Loew, *Netivot Olam*, Netiv HaTorah, ch. 15.
5. Ibid. See also Rabbi Judah Loew, *Derekh Chayyim* 6:7.
6. See Rabbi Solomon Luria, *Yam Shel Shlomo*, Introduction to Bava Kamma

recitation of Jewish law cites the classical codes as objectively requiring covering – actually that is not correct and the subjective view is well represented. Because of this, halakhic decision makers may as well engage directly with the Talmud and Rishonic works – the true repository of Jewish law – and rule in accordance with their respective understandings of the primary sources.

Since relying on secondary works also requires substantial interpretation and analysis as abstract rules are applied to specific cases, it is better that such legal reasoning engage the normative halakha itself through independent Talmudic and Rishonic analysis rather than rely on secondary sources several steps removed from the ultimate source of halakhic authority.[7] Moreover, many scholars opposed ruling from late post-Talmudic precedent because they thought that such reliance on such secondary sources was bound to lead rabbinic decisors to reach incorrect results in practice. Rabbi Joel Sirkes (1561–1640), for instance, argued that "those who [mechanistically] issue rulings based on the [precedential authority] of the *Shulchan Arukh* are ruling not in accordance with the halakha, for they do not know the roots of the halakha from which these specific rules emerge."[8] The heart of this book is the argument that the earlier the sources one examines, the more clear the subjective approach is.

More recently, two important 20th-century halakhic authorities firmly rejected the possibility that rabbinic scholars can be bound by any precedent, and instead affirmed that each must rule in accordance with his own independent judgment of the issue.[9] Rabbi Moshe Feinstein (1895–1986), the preeminent halakhic authority in the United States during the latter half of the 20th century, wrote that the scholars of later generations are permitted, and indeed required, to resolve halakhic questions in accordance with their own considered understanding of the relevant sources, even if their rulings conflict with the opinions of earlier

---

(arguing that every time one attempts to author an account of the halakha, "there is an even greater need for clarifications, and clarifications upon clarifications. For it is impossible that the initial clarification of the law would be free of all doubts and nuances such that there would be no need for further elaboration.")

7. See, e.g., Rabbi Solomon Luria, *Yam Shel Shlomo*, Introduction to *Bava Kamma*.
8. *She'elot uTshuvot HaBach HaYeshanot* (*Yeshanot*), no. 80.
9. See generally Jeffrey Woolf, "The Parameters of Precedent in Pesak Halakhah," *Tradition* 27:41–48 (1993).

authorities, and even if they themselves might be objectively less qualified and learned than scholars of earlier generations.[10] Rabbi Hayyim David HaLevi (1924–1998), Chief Rabbi of Tel Aviv, put this view even more stridently. Speaking about contemporary halakhic decisors, he wrote, "No precedent binds him, even a ruling of a court composed of scholars greater than he, and even of his own teachers."[11]

Based on this approach, I have written this work – arguing that most of the great Jewish law authorities of the last 150 years have been hesitant to rigorously reexamine the precedent in this area and have incorrectly reasoned the rules – and the correctness of this work rests on the classical sources analyzed.

A Concluding Sociological Observation

As shown in the initial seven chapters of this book, in every epoch of Judaism until modern times, important voices of mainstream Jewish law endorsed the subjective theoretical construct with regard to hair covering and modesty in general. Indeed, Ashkenazi Jewish law authorities unhesitantly permitted single women to uncover their hair when that become the normal practice about 1,000 years ago and Sephardic authorities soon concurred. But here, notwithstanding the clear path of authorities of Jewish law – that others could have seen just as easily as I did – post-emancipation Jewish law authorities were virtually silent about this lenient school of thought in their discussion of these issues once it became clear that modest women actually did not cover their hair.

Nor was it because this uncovering was sociologically foreign to them and they did not see what was happening. The rabbinic discussion about the sociology of married women not covering their hair abounds. Such discussions took place in such diverse areas as synagogue life, grounds for divorce, the permissibility to marry a woman who does not plan to cover her hair, and many other areas as well. But yet virtually no one sought to justify the underlying practice (the goal of this book). And yet, as this book shows, with diligence a small number of decisors did so; and furthermore, anyone who faithfully examines the literature with an

---

10. See Introduction to *Iggerot Moshe, Orach Chayyim*, vol. 1. See also *Iggerot Moshe, Yoreh Deah* 2:88 as well as the above, quite famous, quote from Rabbi Feinstein on page 436.
11. *Aseh Lecha Rav* 2:61 (1989).

open mind and intellectual honesty would see that such a path is available. Furthermore, as the preface notes, we have a common rabbinic practice to seek to justify such common customs – and yet it was not followed in this case.

Why?

I suspect that there are no fewer than five important answers to that question and this conclusion will share them. Indeed, a close review of the opening chapter and other important places in this work hints at this.

First, conservative approaches to matters of sexuality and modesty became core values within Orthodoxy and many authorities of Jewish law saw social value in what has become known as the "hair wars" of the late 20th century. Like the *mechitzah* (separation between men and women in prayer) which became a litmus test of the Orthodox community 65 years ago, hair covering became a way for people to identify with the Orthodox community. The heart of this argument was that *sheitel* (wig) – like *tzitzit* or kippah – served as a social and cultural barrier to sexual improprieties. Furthermore, it allowed head covering to serve as an aspect of religious identification for women. This is even more so true, given – as Chapter 1 shows – the normalcy of hair as a sexual feature of many societies (including rabbinic ones).

Second, the development of the refined and human hair wig (sheitel) as a cultural norm within the Orthodox community reduced the religious pressure by women who just needed a practical way to function in the secular community economically while covering their hair. Similarly, the expansion of multi-cultural dress norms has allowed many more women to wear a hat to work, something that was much less acceptable within the American business community in years past. The creation of a Jewish state in Israel, where "Jewish dress" was part of the cultural revival of traditional Judaism, further reduced this pressure: in modern Israel, dressing Jewish is normal. This approach highlighted a different reality – the acknowledgment that hair was less sexual than other previously erotic body parts, since no modest person covers immodest parts with reproductions of immodest parts. This change also validated the sheitel and hat in our cultural norms.

Third, the distinction between married women and single women has grown in social importance within our "family centered" Orthodox community and this moniker has become a convenient social distinction (like *tallit* for men) between those who are married and those who are single. Hair covering has become the Jewish wedding ring, so to speak. This also very much resonates with the rabbinic sense (found in Chapters 4 and 6) that there are important distinctions about modest conduct between married people and single people, of which only hair covering remains, but others were present in the classical sources. This approach also validates hair covering as a unique marital practice or custom with all of the cultural significance it causes.

Fourth, the community within the Orthodox universe that commonly did not cover their hair was, for many years, less interested in the type of detailed textual discussion of the sources that is needed to validate a practice. Particularly since Rabbi Joseph B. Soloveitchik's wife simply did not cover her hair (and she was not unique in this regard 75 years ago), no more justification than this was needed in some communities.[12] It is no surprise to this writer that such a mimetic tradition is hard to maintain in modern times and current reality.[13] Furthermore, the general weakness (both religious and communal) of parts of the more modern Orthodox community is religiously apparent, and this is creating a sense that the basic modern Orthodox approach here of having married women not cover their hair was a religious mistake, whatever the sources permit,

---

12. Dr. Tonya Lewit Solovetchik. Indeed, the fact that the Rav's wife did not cover her hair was repeatedly noted to me countless times by many in the first decades of my writing and thinking on this topic. Reflecting this influence, the Hebrew manuscript version of this work (which is still intentionally unpublished, but was written many years ago as a translation of the *Tradition* article of mine published in 2009 on this topic) bore the following dedication:

> This article is dedicated to the memory of HaRav Yosef Dov HaLevi Soloveitchik, זצ"ל, and his beloved Rebbetzin Tonya Soloveitchik, ז"ל. Together they built Torah structures and practices in America and we are all deeply indebted to them to this day. (Regarding the view of R. Soloveitchik on this topic, cf. R. Hershel Schachter, *Nefesh HaRav* (Reishit Jerusalem: 1994), 55; R. Dov Frimer, "Grounds for Divorce," [full cite is in the Introduction, p. xxv; and R. Hershel Schachter, "*Mi-Peninei ha-Rav*," 267–68 (Beth Midrash of Flatbush, 2001), all purporting to be in the name of the Rav).

In 2010, Rabbi Norman Lamm directly told this writer that the citation found in the *Mi-Peninei ha-Rav* was what Rabbi Soloveitchik told him was the practical rule of Jewish law that he should follow and repeat to others. It is no secret that Rabbi Lamm told this to countless people.

13. For more on this issue, see Haym Solovietchik, "Rupture and Reconstruction: The Transformation of Contemporary Orthodoxy," *Tradition*, Vol. 28, No. 4 (Summer 1994), which can be found at https://traditiononline.org/rupture-and-reconstruction-the-transformation-of-contemporary-orthodoxy/.

since it did not lead to heightened Jewish identity, but instead was part of what produced a weaker, less robust, and less dedicated community.

Finally, Orthodox Judaism finds value in uniformity on many levels and created strong social pressure to identify as part of the community of the faithful. This gave rise to greater uniformity in dress as a way of crafting greater unity. The sheitel or hat became a trademark sign of being an Orthodox Jew,[14] and this has deep social virtues beyond any question of the formal technical requirements of Jewish law. Indeed, as Chapter 1 notes, both the academic and cultural literature are already full of references to the fact that Jewish women cover their hair with hair and the issues that this creates.

All of these factors created a sense that a profound and abiding reexamination of the sources to seek to justify this practice was not helpful to the Orthodox Jewish community (as I have been reminded many times, by countless Orthodox Jews!).

But yet, notwithstanding this, I have undertaken to do so for three reasons, each with their own values, both intellectual and religious.

First, the critical concept that the texts speak volumes about the Jewish tradition. The truths of the text have a life of their own within the Jewish tradition, and this is of value independent of the expediency of the conclusions they reach in any given society. This idea strikes me as a central one of the Jewish tradition and the proper place of Jewish law in Orthodox Jewish life. Traditional Orthodox Judaism is grounded in the text and not the community, and this work continues that tradition. Whatever the public policy of any given community is, Jewish law texts should speak on their own terms. There is deep religious value to faithfully determining what the Talmud, Commentaries, and Codes intend, and that value is in and of itself profoundly important. This reason alone for me is enough to explain the significance of the study I have undertaken.

Second, there are still many parts of the community of Orthodox Jews – both in Israel and in America – where married women do not cover their hair; explaining the Jewish law justification for their conduct is a religious imperative that resonates with me (as the introductory material notes). Communities have a sacred mission to explain and justify their

---

14. See for example, the fine video posted by the "Jew in the City" blogger at https://jewinthecity.com/2019/01/why-do-orthodox-jewish-women-wear-wigs-if-they-look-better-than-hair/ which seeks to explain such conduct to those who are not Orthodox.

conduct. This work is a fulfilment of that religious idea. Furthermore, demonstrating that the subjective school of modesty has widely acknowledged roots within the Talmud, Codes, and Commentaries serves important goals beyond the question of hair covering and addresses many difficulties endemic to men and women in modern Western society. To some extent, this book argues that any conduct that is without sexual overtones – not just hair covering – is permitted between genders in the Jewish Tradition.

Third, times change; the needs of communities evolve; and one can never be completely certain when approaches that no longer resonate as valid public policy will return to being a wise policy. Arguing that hair covering is an immutable obligation of Jewish law – like Sabbath beginning on Friday night, or circumcision being needed on the eighth day for boys, so that if we are denied these rites we will be inauthentic to our roots – is not an argument that strikes me as truthful. It reduces the flexibility of halakha to continue to function in diverse cultural norms.

So, the conclusion of this book is clear. Important views of Jewish law, found in the Talmud, medieval commentaries (Rishonim), and the classical codes of Jewish law including the *Shulchan Arukh* and many of its commentaries, provide ample justification for the uncovering of hair by women in a society in which such conduct is widely seen as normal and modest. Indeed, this provides ample justification for the subjective approach to all matters of modesty as a matter of Jewish law.

AFTERWORD

A Concluding Letter [to My Daughters] About This Book

THE EPILOGUE IS MORE PERSONAL AND LESS SCHOLARLY and is written as a letter to my daughters, both of whom are living in Israel now. It is designed to address questions of practice that go beyond the technical matters addressed in this book.

Where the Law Ends and Moral Guidance Begins

Dear beloved daughters,

I promised your mother that once I completed this book on modesty and hair covering I would write you a letter that explains some issues not found in the body of the book, but found in the life we live. The theme of this letter is why I have never encouraged you to dress fully secularly, even as I think it is not a violation of the technical halakhic rules of modesty.

If you read the book, you will see that I have stuck to my basic view of Jewish law that there is not much in the laws of modesty that is objectively *assur* according to mainstream and normative sources. I do not think that married women have to cover their hair when modest women generally do not. I do not think that modest women need to cover their elbows when modest women do not. I do not think that modest women need to cover their legs when modest women do not. Furthermore, I think that the same social construct of modesty applies to men and women: people need to dress in a modest way as determined by the time and place they live in.

This book is an elaborate argument that nearly all of the rules related to *tzniut* that you both were taught in day school and yeshiva are wrong, and

I trace it in the Gemara, Rishonim and *Shulchan Arukh*. I am convinced that my view is correct.

I think that halakha requires that women dress as modest people in their society dress. Nothing more and nothing less. There are very few immutable halakhic rules of modesty beyond that idea.

Seems simple and easy.

But yet, as you know quite well, this has never been my view in practice, but only in theory. Almost always when asked, I favor less bold and more conservative answers to these questions from the many people who ask (frequently to their surprise, I sense). I am more adventurous in theory than in practice in this area. Seems pretty schizophrenic for someone who has written ten articles and now one book against the contemporary Orthodox concept of *tzniut* to be actually, as one of you said to me, "a closet frummy."

So, I write this letter to explain my practical view, independent of the sources. The truth in this short letter is not halakhic in the classical sense and it does not belong as anything other than an appendix to a work of halakha. In this letter, I make six points, each deeply important to me. I hope you appreciate them.

First, I started my work on hair covering more than 30 years ago to defend the practices of our Modern Orthodox community of many generations in which married women did not cover their hair and yet were otherwise *frum*. Simply put, that was the Orthodox norm for many generations – now close to 200 years – and it is worthy of a detailed halakhic defense. It was the normative practice in Lithuania a century ago and America 50 years ago. No one should think that they come from an Orthodox community that had community-wide sinful practices and we have a long tradition of writing *lemudai zekhut* for wide communal practices. Our holy community deserves a defense of its apparently non-halakhic practices no different than the many other such defenses published in other Orthodox communities. I was happy to do that; indeed, over time, I have grown more than convinced that my view is correct.[1]

---

1. Although not explicitly part of this work, in past discussions of these issues I have been less certain that my view was really correct – since it was contrary to so many contemporary poskim. In the course of writing this book, the hard read into so many Rishonim has persuaded me that the subjective view is not only the dominant view in the Rishonim and the view of *Shulchan Arukh* and Rama, but also well founded in the Talmudic sources.

Second, and perhaps most importantly, I think modesty in dress by women's choice aids the cause of progressive intellectual women. The same is true for men: modesty in dress aids the cause of progressive intellectual men. I – and thus you – come from a long line of progressive, intellectual, accomplished Orthodox women. Your mother is a renowned lawyer and my sister a professor of radiology at Yale Medical School. My mother is a prominent scientist and professor at NYU from an era when women scientists were exceedingly rare. My grandmother was a lawyer by training, in an era when that was even rarer. We want that same level of opportunity for you. On the whole, I am a huge supporter of the feminist revolution of the last century: from the right of women to vote and be elected, to study everything both secular and religious, to learn all there is to master, and to accomplish and be paid equally and fairly – all of that is positive, virtuous and compatible with the halakhic tradition. Indeed, the core tenets of the historical feminist ideology in America – autonomy of body, independence of thought, personal agency, the right to be treated as a full person with political equality – are also all part of (or at least compatible with) the Judaism I know and love. However, the sexual revolution of the last 50 years has, in my view, not been a step in a positive direction and has undermined many feminist goals. It has instead produced objectification, sexualization, and, ultimately, degradation. Orthodox Judaism has spurned that aspect of feminism for good reason, and it has not served women well generally.

Related to that, and of importance to me practically, as sexual modesty started to collapse in America and the West (Israel, too!) in the late 1960s with the onset of the sexual revolution, Modern Orthodoxy began to drift. This deprived the Modern Orthodox community of one of the pillars to validate its conduct on matters of modesty: If there were no detailed halakhic standards then all that a Torah-authentic Jew can do is look to secular standards. If the secular community is so adrift that it has no real standards to prevent sexual looseness, then the modern Orthodox community is also lost.[2] That is what has happened here: the standard 1950s answer to questions of how to dress in our community was, "Dress like modest secular people dress themselves and that is fine as a matter of halakha." I think this approach is correct – **but it leaves us rudderless**

---

2. For example, I am perfectly happy to concede that the Torah's model of what constitutes men's and women's clothing is societal: but what should one do if a society has no concept of men's or women's clothes, but prefers sexualized cross-dressing?

if there is no critical mass of modest secular people to imitate. If you define modesty in a non-circular way – modest people are people who are committed to confining sexuality to marriage – then halakha can easily say, "Look at the community that seeks to confine sexuality to marriage and dress that way." Sadly enough, that community hardly exists in our modern American world, leaving us with little secular anchoring to validate our conduct; maybe in some parts of the United States the fundamentalist Christian community fits this bill.[3] This has always driven me to practically – but not theoretically – endorse a much more modest lifestyle than halakha thinks is theoretically possible.[4]

Third, I have grown more sociologically comfortable with the Orthodox "uniform" (in the sense of modes of dress that allow us to identify each other as Orthodox) and think it has valuable and important sociological advantages for both men and women to dress "Orthodox." I tell men that they should do their best to wear a kippah nearly always; but when you press me, I do not think it is a halakhic requirement – just a really good idea. I think that garb that identifies people with the Orthodox community is valuable and important. If you take my book to its halakhic conclusion, you see no uniform: rather, people dress by secular standards. Even as I think that halakha does not require a uniform, I think it is wiser to have some uniform rather than none. I think dressing completely secularly is a bad social idea and it is sometimes part of the process of leaving the community on many levels. (Yes, I agree that there are a lot of problems with uniforms also: They can be stifling, over-conforming and create superficial and nasty attitudes. They frequently make people want to scream. And not only for women: actually I'm also thinking of the black-and-white dress code which narrowly limits a man's wardrobe in many Orthodox communities. In truth, I find it ideologically disturbing. Care must be taken to allow both the individual to flower and the community to grow for both men and women.)

---

3. See for example, "Trends in Premarital Sex in the United States, 1954–2003" in the Public Health Rep. 2007 Jan–Feb; 122(1): 73–78 which starts its conclusion section with the statement "Almost all Americans have sex before marrying."

4. Judy Heicklen noted to me that my logic here is somewhat flawed. Really, I am not endorsing much more modest dress than halakha allows; rather I am endorsing exactly what I believe theoretically – that we should dress as modest people in our society dress. However, our society is not a modest one in general, so it is hard to find that benchmark. But if we could find that benchmark (the segment that lives as if it was the 1950s or the fundamentalist Christians) then I would endorse that benchmark.

Fourth, in an era of sexual permissiveness, our interactions with the secular community will need to be different from what they were in the era before that "great awakening." Modern Orthodoxy truly needs to live by the model implied by the gemara in Megillah 9b that the "best of secular culture needs to live in Orthodox Judaism." The honest truth is that the promiscuity in much of our secular society is not something any of us really wants in our Torah community; it is far from the best of anything. There is so much that is good and valuable in secular culture – from science to math to medicine, with important insights from poetry and literature, as well as social justice and law – but I cannot admire that aspect of the culture I live in. How to build a worldly, vibrant, open to women, Modern Orthodox community does elude me at some level, but I have always thought that it involves three basic ideas: (1) vibrant Torah education for all; (2) vibrant secular education for all; (3) a public square desexualized as much as possible. The final idea is not accomplished by the modern western mode of dress for men or women, independent of exact halakhic concerns.

Fifth, the centrality of Israel in Jewish life is changing our models of modesty. In fact, Israel is a more insularly Jewish society, with little interest in evaluating the validity of ideas based on the gentile community both within it and around it. As the focus of the Orthodox community shifts to Israel and America becomes a satellite community to Israeli Orthodoxy, our standards of proper dress within the Orthodox community will, I fear, no longer reflect the needs of American Orthodoxy, but will be driven by the Israeli Orthodox community of many different flavors and varieties, which finds (for obvious social reasons) little interest in dressing by the cultural norms of the Islamic community around it. Whether it is Bnei Brak or Efrat – or many other communities in Israel – a sense of modesty and proper dress will come more from Israel, and less from the modest non-Jewish community in America. I am not sure this is exactly wise, but I sense that it is inevitable. The Diaspora will, of course, continue to exist for Orthodox Judaism; but it will be a suburb of Israel, rather than its own town.

Sixth, there is the reality around me, which I see clearly now. We live, both in Israel and in America, in a robustly sexually adventurous secular society where public intellectuals – women[5] as well as men who write

---

5. The saddest part of modern America might well be this issue: liberty has turned into hedonism. I am thinking here of the trend common in America for even

newspaper columns and are widely seen as public intellectuals – can share the variety of sexual adventures they have had. The general coarseness of society – two of our last four presidents are adulterers and much of our secular society hardly thinks of "cheating" as bad – has left me leery of building an Orthodox community dependent on our secular society in these areas. We Modern Orthodox are struggling to build an ideal society based on a variety of issues (I like that), and the religious ideal includes subjective standards of modesty as a matter of halakha. But it simply will not work, I fear, in a secular society that identifies women as sexual objects, glorifies sexual variety as an ideal, subjects people to social pressure to be sexual, and mocks communities of loyal monogamous families as antiquated or worse – castigates those who refuse to participate in the festivities. In that society, the legend of Icarus gnaws at me: I do not want to soar so high to a halakhic ideal that can work in theory, but does not work in fact.

So, here is the Jewish law reality as I see it:

As a matter of halakhic theory, I think that women need only dress as modest people in their society dress. Nothing more and nothing less is needed as a matter of halakha and the subjective school is correct.[6]

But, in reality, this approach to halakha does not work in America in the current decade – even as it works in theory. Thus, in practice, I counsel a much more conservative approach to modes of dress and I think dressing in a fully secular manner is a mistake in practice.

With love,
Dad

---

women to 'buy into' this model of life. Consider for example the *New York Times* columnist Pamela Druckerman.

6. I would add three more considerations that are of importance in the model of being liberal on this issue. First, hair covering creates a false (in the sense of not mandated by halakha) Orthodox boundary issue such that people who should be embraced by the Orthodox community sometimes find themselves and their rabbis outside of it because of this one issue. I fear this will improperly diminish Orthodox Judaism for the next generation. Second, there are still plenty of Orthodox women who do not cover their hair and it is wrong to call them sinners, when a better read of important sources validates this conduct. Third, there is still a substantial subset of people who struggle with Orthodoxy and for whom this is a very sensitive issue, touching as it does on matters of gender and identity. Even people who do not agree with me on this issue would not want to lock the door against those who want to return.

P.S. Of course, this epilogue gives rise to the question of why address this issue if I really do not think it should apply in practice in our modern American society? But the answer is also clear to me, as I explain in the conclusion. Halakha has both a timeless and a timely component. The purpose of this book is to clarify that timeless aspect; whereas the purpose of this epilogue is to share my view of the timely. The timely changes and the timeless endures.

About the Author

Rabbi Michael J. Broyde is a Professor of Law at Emory University School of Law, and the Berman Projects Director of its Center for the Study of Law and Religion. He was a Senior Global Scholar for the United States Fulbright Scholars Program at Hebrew University, he was a visiting professor at Stanford University School of Law, and has visited at many other law schools. He teaches Advanced Jewish Law at Columbia University School of Law and is a Professor in the Tam Institute of Jewish Studies at Emory University. He has held a variety of rabbinic positions in the past, from rabbi of the Young Israel Congregation in Atlanta to Director of the Beth Din of America, as well as Rosh Kollel of the Atlanta Torah Mitzion Kollel. He can be reached at mbroyde@emory.edu.

Index

A

Abaye 45, 59–60, 62–63, 96, 118, 157, 190, 227–228, 234
Abba Shaul 15, 17, 56, 92, 158, 165
Albeck, Chanoch 273
Aptowitzer, R. Avigdor (Victor) 164–166
Arukh HaShulchan (R. Yechiel Michel Epstein) 255, 377–378, 380, 382, 431, 438
arusah 44, 306, 310, 329, 343, 422–423
Asher ben Yechiel (Rosh) 173, 188, 238
Auerbach, R. Shlomo Zalman (*Ishei Yisrael*) 380, 424

B

Ba'er Heiteiv (R. Judah ben Simon Ashkenazi of Tykocin) 249–250, 254
Bach (R. Joel Sirkes) xxvi, 102, 164–167, 240, 247–250, 254–255, 257, 265, 282, 289, 323, 327–328, 330, 332–333, 335, 350, 379–380, 400, 424, 427, 439
bat tzid'a 300
Be'er Sheva 233
Behag (*Halakhot Gedolot*) 92–95, 97, 123, 159, 166–167, 169, 200–201, 212–213, 363
Beit Hillel 3–5, 36–38, 41, 43, 249–250
Beit Shammai 3–5, 7–8, 10, 36–38, 41, 43
Beit Shmuel (R. Shmuel ben Uri Shraga Phoebus) 2, 232–233, 248, 250, 253–255, 265, 282, 284, 288–289, 352, 367, 373, 375
Beit Yosef (Karo, R. Yosef) 89, 233, 243, 291–292, 322, 363, 375, 428
Ben Ish Chai (R. Yosef Chayyim of Baghdad) 377, 382–386, 417, 419, 436
Berlin, R. Naftali Tzvi Yehuda (Netziv) 389
Betzalel Ashkenazi (*Shita Mekubetzet*) 102, 264–265, 353–355, 365
Bigman, R. David 162
Birkat Eliyahu (R. Baruch Rakover) 281–282
Biur HaGra 281
Bonan, R. David b. Isaac (*Dei Hashev*) 388
braided hair 34, 261–264, 338, 357, 363, 419
Brecher, R. Yaakov (*Katuv Yoshar Divrei Emet*) 378, 422
Bromberger, Christian xxxvii, xxxix

C

capillatus 58, 60, 128–129, 153
Chatam Sofer 398, 424–425, 428, 430, 433
Chavot Yair 323–324, 326–331, 333, 343
Chayes, R. Tzvi Hirsch 438
Chazon Ish 379, 425
Chelkat Mechokek 248, 250, 252–255, 265, 280, 282, 289, 360, 367
Chiddushei HaRashba 211
Conforte, David (*Kore HaDorot*) 135

D

Dagul Mervava (R. Ezekiel Landau) 250–253, 265, 267
Darkhei Moshe (R. Moshe Isserless (Rama)) 430
David ben Levi of Narbonne (*Sefer HaMikhtam*) 182

455

Dei Hashev (R. David b. Isaac Bonan) 388
Dembitzer, R. Chaim N. (Cracow) 163
Dikdukei Soferim HaShalem 59
Divrei Chaim 433
Divrei Chamudot (R. Yom Tov Lipman Heller) 396
Dublitzky, R. David 164

E

Eger, R. Akiva 424
Ein Mishpat 430
Eisenstadt, R. Abraham Tzvi Hirsch (*Pitchei Teshuva*) 254–255, 345
Eisenstadt, R. Meir ben Isaac (Maharam Ash) 344
Emden, R. Jacob (Yaavetz) 266–272, 276, 279–282, 290, 430
Emek HaNetziv (R. Naftali Tzvi Yehuda Berlin (Netziv)) 389
Encyclopedia Talmudit 287
Epstein, R. Yechiel Michel (*Arukh HaShulchan*) 255, 377–378, 380, 382, 431, 438
Ettinger, R. Mordechai Ze'ev (*Magen Gibborim*) 262–266

F

Falk-Katz, R. Joshua (*Perisha*) 247–249, 255, 257, 282, 289, 335
Farber, R. Zev xxviii, 272
Feinstein, R. Moshe (*Iggerot Moshe*) xli, 110, 131, 133, 286–287, 374–375, 380, 389, 392, 424, 426, 432, 436–437, 439–440
Fränkel-Te'omim, R. Baruch 280, 286

G

Gigi, R. Baruch 162
Ginat Veradim (R. Avraham b. Mordechai HaLevi of Cairo) 284, 286
Gombiner, R. Avraham (*Magen Avraham*) 256–267, 269, 272, 279–280, 282, 290, 336–338, 346–347, 353, 355–358, 363–364, 411, 430

H

Hagahot HaAsheri (R. Israel of Krems) 190
Hagahot Maimoniyot (R. Meir ben Yekutiel HaKohen) 89, 199–201, 228, 321, 360, 362
Henkin, R. Yehuda (*Responsa Bnei Banim*) xxxiv, 102, 286, 291, 424, 426–427
Hertz, R. Hillel ben Naphtali Hertz 249
Hirschenson, R. Chaim 76, 400
Hoffman, R. Yaakov 432
Horowitz, R. Pinchas (*Sefer Haflaah*) 387
Hurewitz, R. Isaac S. (*Yad HaLevi*) 398, 422
hynuma 237, 248, 268–270, 272–282, 290, 307–308, 313, 338, 346, 353–354, 358, 366, 369–371, 424

I

idolatry 5–7, 81
Iggeret HaTeshuva 375
Iggerot Moshe (R. Moshe Feinstein) xli, 110, 286–287, 374–375, 380, 389, 392, 426, 432, 437, 440
immodest behavior 1, 17, 35–36, 53, 55, 91, 147, 219–220, 235, 289
Imrei Baruch (R. Baruch Fränkel-Te'omim) 280–281
infidelity 2, 9, 30, 44, 125, 143, 171, 189, 193, 213, 286–287, 397
Ishei Yisrael (R. Shlomo Zalman Auerbach) 424

J

"Jew in the City" (blog) 443
jewelry 23–24, 73–74, 93, 166–167, 176–177, 187, 193, 300
Johnson, Sara Raup 33

K

Kaf HaChayyim 417–418, 430
Kagan, R. Yisrael (*Mishnah Berura*) 377, 379–380, 382, 423, 425, 430
Kaidanover, R. Aaron Samuel 397
Kallah Rabbati 80, 176
Kaminsky, Menucha xxxv

INDEX

Kanarfoel, R. Ephraim 156
kerchief xxxviii, 59, 105–108, 122, 128, 136–137, 141, 233, 239, 242, 245, 280, 288, 329–330, 433
Kimchit 85–87, 412–413, 425, 427–428
Kiryat Sefer 394
Kitzur Piskei HaRosh 191, 196
Klein, R. Menashe (*Mishneh Halakhot*) 375
Kol Bo 139–140
Kuntres HaRe'ayot 120

L

Landau, R. Ezekiel (*Responsa Noda BeYehuda; Dagul Mervava*) 2, 250–253, 265, 267
Lechem Shamayim (Yaavetz) 267–268, 271
Levush Malchut (R. Mordechai Yoffe) 244
lewd thoughts 68, 94, 198, 201, 246, 419
Lifschitz, R. Israel (*Tiferet Yisrael*) 278
Lytton, Tim xxxii

M

Machatzit HaShekel (R. Samuel ben Natan HaLevi Loew Kelin) 256–257, 259, 261
Magen Avraham (R. Avraham Gombiner) 256–267, 269, 272, 279–280, 282, 290, 336–338, 346–347, 353, 355–358, 363–364, 411, 430
Magen Gibborim (R. Mordechai Ze'ev Ettinger) 262–266
Maharam Al-Ashkar 111, 183, 212, 288, 293–294, 296–297, 299–301, 306, 312, 361, 372, 376, 381, 401, 425, 427
Maharam Schiff (R. Meir ben Jacob HaKohen Schiff) 280–281
Malbim (R. Meïr Leibush Michel Weiser) 25–26, 28
Meisels, R. Tzvi Hirsch (*Responsa Mikadshei Hashem*) 426
Messas, R. Yosef 388, 401, 416–417, 421, 425
Meyer, Mindy xxxvi

Midrash Aggadah 80, 176
Midrash Lekach Tov 10
Midrash Tannaim 4–5, 10
Migdal Chananel (R. Chananel Shlossberg) 425
Minchat Ani (R. Yosef David Sinzheim) 232–233
Minchat Yitzchak 380
Mishnah Berura (R. Yisrael Meir Kagan) 377, 379–380, 382, 423, 425, 430
Mishneh Halakhot (R. Menashe Klein) 375
Mishneh Torah (Rambam) 45, 106, 109–110, 121, 136–137, 139, 184, 200, 238, 282, 350, 416
Mor u-Ketzia (Yaavetz) 266–267, 270
Mordechai ben Hillel (*The Mordechai*) 199, 378
Musaf He-Arukh (R. Benjamin Musafia) 277
Musafia, R. Benjamin 277
Mutzafi, R. Ben Tzion 384

N

Nachalat Tzvi (R. Tzvi Katz) 249–250
Nekudot HaKessef (R. Shabbetai ben Meir Hakohen (Shach)) 350
Netivot Olam (R. Judah Loew (Maharal)) 438
New York Post xxxv
niddah 107, 121, 127, 176, 350–352, 374–375, 398
nissuin 251, 255, 274, 306–307, 312, 328–329, 342–343, 352, 424–425
norms-
  biblical 344
  cultural xxxi, xlii, 149, 237, 436, 441, 444, 449
  halakhic 438
  Jewish 313
  social 52, 54, 56, 63, 131, 140, 147, 161, 206, 219, 283, 372, 378, 398
Novick, Laurie xl
Numbers Rabbah 10, 85, 87

O

Ohel Moed (R. Samuel b. Meshulem Yerundi) 154, 204–205
Or Zarua (R. Isaac of Vienna) 73, 186, 188, 206, 224
Orchot Chayyim (R. Aharon ben Jacob HaKohen) 136–137, 140, 154, 183, 299
Ornstein, R. Jacob Meshullam (*Yeshuot Yaakov*) 390
Otzar HaGeonim 275–276
Otzar HaMikhtavim 401
Otzar HaPoskim 380–381, 430

P

Panim Meirot (R. Meir ben Isaac Eisenstadt) 255, 344–349, 353, 356–357, 367, 370–371
Pappos ben Yehuda 8, 38, 41–42
penuya 241, 247–248, 250, 265–266, 281, 289, 375
Perisha (R. Joshua Falk-Katz) 247–249, 255, 257, 282, 289, 335
Piskei Riaz (R. Isaiah (ben Elijah) di Trani the Younger) 119, 235
Pitchei Teshuva (R. Abraham Tzvi Hirsch Eisenstadt) 254–255, 345
Pri Megadim (R. Joseph ben Meir) 254, 259–262, 373, 379, 430

R

R. Ada bar Ahava 220–221, 340
R. Adda bar Achuha 49
R. Aharon ben Jacob HaKohen (*Orchot Chayyim*) 135–137, 140, 154, 183, 299
R. Assi 59, 96, 118, 190
R. Avin HaLevi 165
R. Avraham b. Mordechai HaLevi of Cairo (*Ginat Veradim*) 284, 286
R. Avraham ben David of Posquières (Ra'avad) 177, 179, 183, 210–213, 296–299, 322–323, 372, 389–390
R. Avraham ben Natan Even HaYarchi (Ra'avan) 164, 175
R. Babad 349–352, 354–355, 357, 359, 361–362, 364–368, 371–372
R. Chananel 73, 94, 122, 168–169, 184, 186–188, 200–201, 274–275, 277, 279, 425
R. Chanina of Sura 46
R. Chayyim ben Betzalel 438
R. Chisda 53, 70, 74–75, 78–79, 93, 118, 157, 159, 178–179, 187, 190, 194–196, 211, 295, 298, 322
R. Chiya bar R. Shlomo of Barcelona (*Sefer HaShulchan*) 212–213
R. David b. Isaac Bonan (*Dei Hashev*) 388
R. Duran 145–147
R. Elazar 39, 48, 78, 81–82, 159, 162, 186, 198–199
R. Elazar of Worms (*Sefer HaRokeach*) 162
R. Eliezer ben Yoel HaLevi (Ra'aviah) 94, 162–170, 200–201, 240, 292, 298–299, 308–309, 317, 321–322, 339, 372, 378, 395, 415
R. Elijah ben Shlomo (Vilna Gaon) 28, 281
R. Hai Gaon (*Shaarei Teshuva*) 98–99, 174–175, 199–200, 203–204, 275, 295–296, 308
R. Huna 72–73, 178–180, 228
R. Isaac of Corbeil (*Sefer Amudei Golah, Sefer Mitzvot Katan, Katsar, Semak*) 138, 183–184, 199, 315
R. Isaac of Vienna 186
R. Isaac Tyrnau (*Sefer Minhagim*) 315
R. Isaiah (ben Elijah) di Trani the Younger (Riaz) 117, 119–120, 235
R. Isaiah (ben Mali) di Trani the Elder (*Tosefot Rid*) xxvi, xxxvii–xxxviii, 4, 16, 33, 59, 64, 77–78, 80–81, 104, 114, 117–119, 137, 140, 153, 220–221, 263, 271, 273–277, 288, 293, 312, 314–316, 338–340, 360, 380, 423–424, 427, 436, 440, 444
R. Israel of Krems 190
R. Jacob ben Meir of Ramerupt (R. Tam) xxvii, 22, 27–28, 51, 76, 103, 132–133, 139–140, 154–155, 159–163, 167, 170–171, 177, 182–183, 185–186, 198–201, 204–205, 224, 235, 299,

330, 342, 369, 372, 393, 397–398, 424–425, 428, 430, 433–434
R. Joseph ben Meir Teomim (*Pri Megadim*) 254, 259–262, 373, 379, 430
R. Judah ben Simon Ashkenazi of Tykocin (*Ba'er Heiteiv*) 249–250, 254
R. Judah Loew 438
R. Kahana 59–60, 62–63, 71, 85, 96, 118, 186, 190
R. Mari xxxix, 73, 157, 186
R. Meir 8–10, 12, 16, 38, 41–44, 47, 110, 125, 127–133, 144, 154, 170–172, 251–252, 255, 259, 281, 286–287, 316, 344–349, 353, 356–357, 367, 370–371, 410
R. Meir ben Shimon HaMeili (*Sefer HaMeorot*) 180
R. Meir ben Yekutiel HaKohen 200
R. Meir of Rothenberg 156
R. Menachem HaMeiri 127
R. Menachem Rekanati (*Ta'amei HaMitzvot*) 154, 196–199
R. Mesharshia 38, 40
R. Meshullam ben Moshe of Béziers (*Sefer HaHashlama*) 132, 177–182
R. Moses ibn Al-Ashkar (Maharam Al-Ashkar) 293
R. Moshe ben Yitzhak Yehuda-Lima (*Chelkat Mechokek*) 248
R. Moshe ibn Chaviv (Maharam Chaviv) 320
R. Moshe Isserless (Rama) xliii, 52, 212, 237–238, 243–244, 246, 273, 276–277, 289, 368, 430, 446
R. Moshe Malka 401, 416, 420
R. Moshe of Coucy (*Sefer Mitzvot*) 120, 125, 142, 184
R. Moshe of Evreux (Ram) 156
R. Moshe Zev HaCohen 390
R. Nachman 64–66, 68, 72, 78, 81, 83, 125, 132, 180, 211
R. Nachman bar Yitzchak 72
R. Nechuniah 69, 72
R. Nissim ben Reuven (Ran) 144

R. Ovadiah of Bartenura 279
R. Pappa 45, 73, 83, 97, 186, 274, 276–277, 279, 302
R. Peretz 138, 184, 186
R. Samuel b. Meshulem Yerundi 204
R. Sheshet 73–76, 93–94, 159, 177–179, 187, 193–194, 295, 308, 311–312, 317, 321, 362
R. Sheyla 37
R. Shimon bar Tzemach Duran 145
R. Shimon Sidon (*Shevet Shimon, Chiddushei Sugyot*) 398
R. Shlomo Chelma 397
R. Shmuel bar Nachmani 78, 83
R. Shmuel ben Uri Shraga Phoebus (*Beit Shmuel*) 2, 232–233, 248, 250, 253–255, 265, 282, 284, 288–289, 352, 367, 373, 375
R. Tam (R. Jacob ben Meir of Ramerupt) xxvii, 22, 27–28, 51, 76, 103, 132–133, 139–140, 154–155, 159–163, 167, 170–171, 177, 182–183, 185–186, 198–201, 204–205, 224, 235, 299, 330, 342, 369, 372, 393, 397–398, 424–425, 428, 430, 433–434
R. Tarfon 15, 17, 54–55, 92–93, 130, 158, 165, 202
R. Tuvia 139, 154, 198–199
R. Ukva 54
R. Vidal of Tolosa 110, 231
R. Yaakov bar Iddi 81, 83
R. Yehuda B. Ilan 402
R. Yehuda ben Nathan (Rivan) 102
R. Yehuda HaNasi 5–7
R. Yehuda Naki (*Shut Maayan Omer*) 428
R. Yehuda of Diskarta 45
R. Yerucham ben Meshullam (*Sefer Meisharim*) 141
R. Yerucham Fishel Perlow 390
R. Yishmael 5–7, 22, 24–27, 58, 61, 117, 121–122, 128, 189, 197, 210, 234–235, 394, 401, 405, 410, 412
R. Yitzchak Alfasi (Rif) 95
R. Yitzchak bar Nachman 81

R. Yitzchak ben Abba Mari (*Sefer HaIttur*) 157
R. Yitzchak Weiss 380
R. Yochanan 23–25, 39, 43–44, 52, 57–63, 79–80, 95–96, 118, 125–126, 144, 157–158, 186, 190–191, 210, 213, 218, 220, 233–235, 250–251, 268, 274, 276, 279
R. Yochanan ben Beroka 23–25
R. Yochanan ben Nuri 43–44, 125–126, 144, 210, 213
R. Yom Tov ben Avraham of Seville (Ritva) 80, 213–215, 217, 219–221, 232–233, 235, 427–428
R. Yonah Gerundi 203
R. Yonah Landsofer (*Responsa Me'il Tzedakah*) 288
R. Yosef Chaim 385
R. Yosef Chayyim of Baghdad (*Ben Ish Chai*) 377, 382–386, 417, 419, 436
R. Yosef ibn Migash (Ri Migash) 276
R. Yossi the Galilean 18
R. Zeira 59–60, 62–63, 95, 118, 120, 398
Ra'avan (R. Avraham ben Natan Even HaYarchi) 164, 175
Ra'aviah (R. Eliezer ben Yoel HaLevi) 94, 162–170, 200–201, 240, 292, 298–299, 308–309, 317, 321–322, 339, 372, 378, 395, 415
Ra'avad (R. Avraham ben David of Posquières) 177, 179, 183, 210–213, 296–299, 322–323, 372, 389–390
Rabbah 10, 52–54, 56, 85, 87, 369
rabbinic prohibition 110–111, 231–233, 284, 287
Rakover, R. Baruch (*Birkat Eliyahu*) 281–282
Rambam (Maimonides) xxxviii, xliii, 45, 59, 102, 105–106, 108–113, 115, 120–125, 130–132, 137–140, 142, 183–184, 186, 200, 203, 218, 227, 230–233, 235, 238–240, 256, 268–271, 278, 282, 284, 288–292, 296, 308, 319, 329–330, 335–338, 355, 375, 391, 393–394, 397–398, 416–417

Ramban (Nachmanides) 110, 125–127, 144–145, 210
Ran (R. Nissim ben Reuven) 52, 79, 110, 144–145, 170, 233
Rash (R. Samson of Sens) xliv, 43–44, 47, 59, 72–73, 76, 79, 89, 102, 129–131, 150–154, 158, 171–173, 175, 183, 206–212, 217–218, 223, 227, 229, 233, 235, 239, 242–243, 257, 259–260, 262–264, 276, 278–281, 283, 285, 288, 290, 296–299, 309–311, 313–314, 322, 330, 334, 336–337, 353–356, 358, 365, 372–375, 386–395, 400–401, 405, 407, 409–411, 419, 425, 427–428, 437
Rashba (R. Shlomo ben Adret) 183, 206–212, 235, 242–243, 298–299, 313, 322, 330, 353–355, 365, 393, 425, 437
Rashi xliv, 43–44, 47, 59, 72–73, 76, 79, 89, 102, 129–131, 150–154, 171–173, 175, 217–218, 223, 227, 229, 233, 235, 239, 257, 259–260, 262–264, 276, 278–281, 283, 285, 288, 290, 296–297, 309–311, 314, 334, 336–337, 356, 358, 372–375, 386–395, 400–401, 405, 407, 409–411, 419, 427–428, 437
Rava 38, 40, 43–45, 71
Redid HaZahav 400
Reischer, R. Jacob ben Joseph (*Shevut Yaakov*) 59, 254, 263–264, 283, 333–335, 337–344, 358, 381, 424
Responsa Be'er Chaim Mordechai (R. Chaim M. Roller) 423
Responsa Bnei Banim (R. Yehuda Henkin) 286, 291, 424, 426–427
Responsa Etz Efraim (R. Efraim Zalman Slutzki) 400
Responsa Mahari HaLevi (R. Isaac HaLevi Segal) 306, 424
Responsa Me'il Tzedakah (R. Yonah Landsofer) 288
Responsa Mikadshei Hashem (R. Tzvi Hirsch Meisels) 426
Responsa Noda BeYehuda (R. Ezekiel Landau) 2

INDEX

Responsa Rav Pealim (Ben Ish Chai) 2, 382
Responsa Sefer Yehoshua (R. Yehoshua Heschel Babad) 349–351, 353, 355–358, 360–361, 363, 365–372, 376
Responsa Teshuvot VeHanhagot (R. Moshe Sternbuch) 424
Responsa Tzemach Tzedek (R. Menachem Mendel Schneerson) 283–284
Responsa VaYashev Moshe 231
Responsa Yabia Omer (R. Ovadia Yosef) 3, 288, 373, 380, 431
Responsa Yashiv Moshe (R. Moshe Turetsky) 394, 398
Ri Migash (R. Yosef ibn Migash) 276–277
Riaz (R. Isaiah (ben Elijah) di Trani the Younger) 117, 119–120, 235
Rif (R. Yitzchak Alfasi) xliii, 59, 79, 89, 91, 95–98, 113, 125, 130, 144–145, 170, 177–183, 189, 203, 233, 296–297, 409, 417, 430
Rimon, R. Yosef Tzvi 427–428
Ritva (R. Yom Tov ben Avraham of Seville) 80, 213–215, 217, 219–221, 232–233, 235, 427–428
Rivan (R. Yehuda ben Nathan) 102–104
Roller, R. Chaim M. (*Responsa Be'er Chaim Mordechai*) 423
Rosanes, R. Judah 230
Rosh (R. Asher ben Yechiel) 59, 89, 162, 170, 173–174, 188–189, 191–196, 205, 233, 235, 238, 252–253, 266, 286–288, 298, 308, 311, 317, 321, 339, 360, 362, 388–390, 394, 396–397, 417, 425
Rosh Pinah (R. Shmarya Shmeril Brandris) 252–253, 266
Rothstein, R. Gidon 433
rumor 35, 43–44

S

Sash, Esther Adina xxxv
Schiff, R. Meir ben Jacob HaKohen 281
Schneerson, R. Menachem Mendel (*Igros Kodesh*) 433
Schneerson, R. Menachem Mendel (*Responsa Tzemach Tzedek*) 283–284
seclusion 227–228, 230–231, 286, 288
Sedei Chemed 89, 110, 287
Seeman, Don xxviii, 413
Sefer Al HaKol 155
Sefer Chasidim 160–162
Sefer HaAgudah (R. Alexander Suslin HaKohen) 201–202
Sefer HaEshkol (R. Avraham ben Issac Av Beit Din) 99, 174–175
Sefer Haflaah (R. Pinchas Horowitz) 387
Sefer HaHashlama (R. Meshullan ben Moshe of Béziers) 132, 177–182
Sefer HaIttur (R. Yitzchak ben Abba Mari) 157–158
Sefer HaManhig (Ra'avan) 175, 177
Sefer HaMeorot (R. Meir ben Shimon HaMeili) 180
Sefer HaMikhtam (R. David ben Levi of Narbonne) 182
Sefer HaNaim 350
Sefer HaRokeach (R. Elazar of Worms) 162
Sefer HaShulchan (R. Chiya bar R. Shlomo of Barcelona) 212–213
Sefer HaVatik (R. Babad) 350
Sefer HaYereim (R. Elazar of Metz) 159, 199–202
Sefer HaZechut (Ramban) 126
Sefer Kanun-al-Nissa (Ben Ish Chai) 383
Sefer Meisharim (R. Yerucham ben Meshullam) 141, 143
Sefer Minhagim (R. Isaac Tyrnau) 315
Sefer Mitzvot (R. Moshe of Coucy) 120, 183–184
Segal, R. David HaLevi 248
Semak 183–184, 199, 204, 315, 375
Seridei Eish 64, 380
sexuality xxxiii, xxxv–xxxviii, 5, 42, 71, 284, 372–375, 429, 441, 448
Shaarei Teshuva (R. Hai Gaon) 98–99, 174–175, 199–200, 203–204, 275, 295–296, 308
shaven head xxxvii
sheitel (wig) xxxiv–xxxvi, xxxviii, xl–xli,

243, 246, 398–399, 420–421, 423, 429–434, 441, 443
Shema 69–77, 93–94, 97–100, 109, 111, 123, 131–133, 139–140, 143–144, 151, 154–156, 159–160, 163, 168, 170, 175, 178–179, 181–182, 185–188, 193–196, 198–205, 211–213, 240–241, 243, 245–246, 294–299, 301, 306–309, 317–318, 320–322, 346, 360–363, 378, 414, 417–418, 420, 425
Shevet HaLevi (R. Shmuel Wozner) 110, 380, 424
Shevet Shimon 398
Shevilei David (R. David Y. Zilberstein) 425
Shevut Yaakov (R. Jacob ben Joseph Reischer) 254, 263–264, 283, 333–335, 337–344, 358, 381, 424
Shimon 56, 86–87, 145, 180, 341–342, 398
Shita Mekubetzet (R. Betzalel Ashkenazi) 102, 264–265, 353–355, 365
Shlossberg, R. Chananel (Migdal Chananel) 425
Shmuel 2, 52–56, 59, 61–62, 64–71, 74–75, 77–79, 83, 91–94, 96, 102, 110, 117–119, 127, 158–159, 169, 174, 178, 186–188, 190–191, 194, 196, 208, 210–211, 217, 219, 225, 232–235, 248, 250, 253–255, 265, 273, 282, 284, 288–289, 295, 302, 352, 367, 373, 375, 380, 397
shok 74, 76, 195, 373–374, 379
Shulchan Arukh xliii–xliv, 2, 52, 212, 233, 237–238, 242–244, 246–249, 256, 260, 262, 264–268, 270, 272, 280–282, 289–292, 321, 327–329, 332, 334–337, 339, 345–346, 350, 355, 360, 366–367, 373–375, 378–379, 382, 387, 396–397, 417, 420, 423–424, 430, 433, 436–437, 439, 444, 446
Shulchan Tamid 397
Shut Maayan Omer (R. Yehuda Naki) 428
Sifra 19
Sifre Numbers 20, 91

singing voice 112, 131–132, 159, 198, 200, 205, 373
Sinzheim, R. Yosef David (Minchat Ani) 232–233
Sirkes, R. Joel (Bach) xxvi, 102, 164–167, 240, 247–250, 254–255, 257, 265, 282, 289, 323, 327–328, 330, 332–333, 335, 350, 379–380, 400, 424, 427, 439
Slutzki, Efraim Zalman 400
Sokoloff, Michael 277
Soloveichik, R. Aaron 153
Soloveitchik, R. Joseph B. 442
Song of Songs 76, 91, 97, 160–161, 309
Surchav bar Pappa 274, 276–277, 279
Susanna 32
suspicion of infidelity 189, 193, 286–287, 397

T

Ta'amei HaMitzvot (R. Menachem Rekanati) 154, 196–199
Tabak, R. Shlomo (Responsa Teshurot Shai) 425
tanura 274, 276–277
Tashbetz 146, 175, 399
Taz 248, 289, 306
Terumat HaDeshen (R. Yisrael Isserlein), 105, 221–222, 224–226, 230, 232–233, 235
Tiferet Shmuel (R. Aaron Samuel Kaidanover) 397
Tiferet Yisrael (R. Israel Lifschitz) 278
Toledot Adam ve-Chava (R. Yerucham) 143
Torah Temimah 401
Torat HaHistaklut (R. Binyamin Zilber) 375
Tosafot HaRosh (R. Asher ben Yechiel), 170, 173–174, 194–195
Tosafot Yom Tov (R. Yom Tov Lipmann Heller) 279
Tosefot Rid (R. Isaiah (ben Mali) di Trani the Elder) xxvi, xxxvii–xxxviii, 4, 16, 33, 59, 64, 77–78, 80–81, 104, 114, 117–119, 137, 140, 153, 220–221, 263, 271, 273–277, 288,

293, 312, 314–316, 338–340, 360, 380, 423–424, 427, 436, 440, 444
Tur xxxix, xliii, 24, 89, 192, 217, 233, 235, 237–242, 244, 246–248, 265–268, 270, 272, 279–281, 284, 289–291, 318–321, 327–329, 335, 337, 360–362, 394–397, 430, 436
Tzedah LaDerekh (R. Menachem b. Aaron b. Zerah) 205–206
Tzitz Eliezer 4, 374, 380, 382
tzniut xxxi, xxxiv, 140, 232, 291, 383, 445–446

V

Van Dyke, R. Yehoshua 425

W

Waldenberg, R. Eliezer Yehuda 380
weaving 9, 15, 39, 52–54, 92, 97, 105, 138, 157, 165, 184, 190, 205, 218
wedding canopy 114
wedding day 256, 278, 336, 339, 344, 355, 423
wedding litter 273
wedding song 33, 273–274
Weinberg, R. Yechiel Yaakov 64, 380
Weiser, R. Meïr Leibush Michel (Malbim) 25–26, 28

wig xxxiv–xxxvi, xxxviii, xl–xli, 243, 246, 398–399, 420–421, 423, 429–434, 441, 443
Willig, R. Mordechai (*Am Mordechai*) xxv–xxvi, xxviii, 230–231, 287, 426

Y

Yaavetz (R. Jacob Emden) 266–272, 276, 279–282, 290, 430
Yad HaLevi (R. Isaac S. Hurewitz) 398, 422
Yalkut Shimoni 87, 342
Yalta 65, 68, 132, 180, 211
Yaskil Avdi 432
Yeshuot Yaakov (R. Jacob Meshullam Ornstein) 390
yichud 286, 424
Yisrael Isserlein (*Terumat HaDeshen*) 221
Yoffe, R. Mordechai 244
Yosef, R. Ovadia (*Yabia Omer*) 3, 288, 380, 428, 431

Z

Zilberstein, R. David Y. (*Shevilei David*) 425
Ziring, R. Jonathan xxviii, 423
Zohar 133, 135, 196–197, 301, 425, 427

www.ingramcontent.com/pod-product-compliance
Lightning Source LLC
Chambersburg PA
CBHW070159240426

43671CB00007B/489